Mental Health and Criminal Justice

CRIMINAL JUSTICE SERIES

Mental Health and Criminal Justice

Anne F. Segal, J.D., Ph.D.

L. Thomas Winfree, Jr., Ph.D.

Stan Friedman, Ph.D.

Printed in the United States of America.

2 3 4 5 6 7 8 9 0

ISBN 978-1-4548-7745-5

Library of Congress Cataloging-in-Publication Data

Names: Segal, Anne F., author. | Winfree, L. Thomas, Jr., 1946- author. |
    Friedman, Stan (Clinical psychologist), author.
Title: Mental health and criminal justice / Anne F. Segal, J.D., Ph.D., L.
    Thomas Winfree, Jr., Ph.D., Stan Friedman, Ph.D.
Description: New York : Wolters Kluwer, [2019]
Identifiers: LCCN 2018027367 | ISBN 9781454877455 (pbk.)
Subjects: LCSH: Mentally ill offenders--United States. | Mentally ill
    offenders—Legal status, laws, etc.—United States. | Mental health
    laws—United States. | Forensic psychiatry—United States. | Criminal
    justice, Administration of—United States.
Classification: LCC HV6133 .S385 2019 | DDC 364.3/80973—dc23
LC record available at https://lccn.loc.gov/2018027367

About Wolters Kluwer Legal & Regulatory U.S.

Wolters Kluwer Legal & Regulatory U.S. delivers expert content and solutions in the areas of law, corporate compliance, health compliance, reimbursement, and legal education. Its practical solutions help customers successfully navigate the demands of a changing environment to drive their daily activities, enhance decision quality and inspire confident outcomes.

Serving customers worldwide, its legal and regulatory portfolio includes products under the Aspen Publishers, CCH Incorporated, Kluwer Law International, ftwilliam.com and MediRegs names. They are regarded as exceptional and trusted resources for general legal and practice-specific knowledge, compliance and risk management, dynamic workflow solutions, and expert commentary.

Summary of Contents

Contents

CHAPTER 2
A Brief History of Mental Illness 47

PART II
Providing Justice, Providing Mental Healthcare *139*

CHAPTER 5
First Responders and Street Encounters *141*

CHAPTER 6
Involuntary and Voluntary Commitments *173*

CHAPTER 7
Legal Competency and the Criminal Trial 201

CHAPTER 8
Mentally Ill Defendants: Defenses, Pleas, and Verdicts 225

CHAPTER 9

Correctional Treatment of the Mentally Ill *259*

CHAPTER 12

Justice for the Mentally Ill: Human Rights and At-Risk Groups 373

About the Authors

Anne Fisher Segal is an attorney and retired judge. She received a Bachelor of Science (journalism and political science) from the University of Arizona; a law degree from University of San Diego School of Law; and a doctor of philosophy (educational leadership and management) from New Mexico State University. During her legal career, she worked as a public defender in California and as a prosecutor in Illinois. She was an adjunct instructor at Doña Ana Community College (Las Cruces), New Mexico State University (Las Cruces), University of Arizona (Tucson), and Arizona State University (Phoenix). Internationally, she also taught courses in Cuidad Juarez, Mexico and the Interuniversity Centre of Dubrovnik (Croatia). Segal was elected for two terms as Doña Ana Magistrate Judge in Las Cruces, New Mexico. In 2007, Segal was elected as a Justice of the Peace in Tucson, Arizona and served for six years. She co-authored *Law and Mental Health Professionals: New Mexico* with Peggy Kaczmarek and Elaine S. LeVine (American Psychological Association, 2006), and developed curricula for numerous courses.

L. Thomas Winfree, Jr. is a disabled veteran, having served in the U.S. Army during the Vietnam War era. He received a Bachelor of Arts (sociology) from the University of Richmond; a master of science (sociology) from Virginia Commonwealth University; and a doctor of philosophy (sociology) from the University of Montana. In his teaching career, he held academic positions, up to and including the rank of professor (tenured), at the University of New Mexico, Texas A&M University-Commerce, Louisiana State University (Baton Rouge), New Mexico State University (Las Cruces), and Arizona State University (Phoenix). He also taught at the Catholic University of Leuven (Belgium), Tübingen University (Germany), Kiel University of Applied Sciences (Germany), and the Interuniversity Centre of Dubrovnik (Croatia). Winfree is co-author or co-editor of nine books in numerous editions and over 100 refereed journal articles and book chapters. His most recent books include *Introduction to Criminal Justice: The Essentials* (Wolters Kluwer, 2015), co-authored with G. Larry Mays and Leanne F. Alarid; and *Essentials of Criminological Theory* (Waveland Press, 2017), co-authored with Howard Abadinsky. While he is retired from teaching, he continues to write textbooks and research articles, the latter focusing mainly on law-related issues of the young, including drug use and abuse and gang behavior, and criminological theory.

Stan Friedman, now retired, received a Ph.D. in Clinical Psychology from the University of Louisville, after completing a clinical internship at Galesburg (IL) State Research Hospital. He has been licensed as a Clinical Psychologist in California, Wisconsin, and Florida, and was a member of the American Psychological Association and the American Association of Correctional Psychologists. His work experience includes: Psychology Assistant at the U.S. Army Medical Research Lab., Ft. Knox, Kentucky; Research Psychologist, Louisville Child Guidance Clinic; Research Psychologist, Louisville Child Psychiatry Research Center; Lecturer in Clinical Psychology at Knox College, Galesburg, Illinois; Chief Clinical Psychologist, Kern County, California Department of Mental Health; Clinical Psychology Consultant, Department of Human Services, Pierce County, Wisconsin; Clinical Psychology Consultant, Lutheran Social Services, Hudson, Wisconsin; Chief Clinical Psychologist, Wisconsin Department of Corrections, Bureau of Clinical Services; Clinical Psychologist, Florida Center for Cognitive Therapy; Clinical Psychology Consultant for the Florida Department of Vocational Rehabilitation. He has published in the areas of developmental learning, child sexual abuse, and treatment of sex offenders. His publications include *Outpatient Treatment of Child Molesters* (Professional Resource Exchange, 1991). Friedman has presented many workshops about child sexual abuse and was a co-founder of the Eau Claire (Wisconsin) Family Incest Treatment Program, which was awarded a federal grant and was designated by the University of Wisconsin (Madison) Law School as the model incest treatment program for the State of Wisconsin.

Acknowledgments

All book authors owe debts that are rarely repaid, except by, as in this case, an acknowledgment. In this regard, we wish to thank our developmental editor, Elizabeth Kenney. Thank you, Betsy, for standing by us and providing such good support and useful insights into this process. Thank you, as well, to David Herzig, Associate Publisher with Wolters Kluwer, who saw something worthwhile in our initial ramblings about this topic, and to Renee Cote for copy editing and Kaesmene Banks for coordinating production.

We wish to acknowledge the input of our reviewers: Deborah A. Eckberg, Metropolitan State University; William Fisher, University of Massachusetts-Lowell; Diana Grant, Sonoma State University; Kathy Latz, Sam Houston State University; Cara Rabe-Hemp, Illinois State University; Christina Tartaro, Stockton University; Mark Winton, University of Central Florida; and Kento Yasuhara, University of New Haven.

Finally, we thank several individuals, whose efforts, great and small, contributed to the completion of this book. First, we thank Eileen Winfree, who has read more criminal justice-related books in draft form than she wishes to recount. Her insights and imaginings have helped them, and this book, to be better finished products. Similarly, we acknowledge the assistance rendered by Jane Mathers, Julie Bogen, J. Bradley Segal, and Molly Callahan. The following individuals read and commented upon various chapters in the book: Dana Peterson, Associate Professor in the School of Criminal Justice, State University of New York at Albany; Rick Ruddell, Law Foundation of Saskatchewan Professor, Chair in Police Studies in the Department of Justice Studies, University of Regina; and G. Larry Mays, Regents Professor Emeritus, Department of Criminal Justice, New Mexico State University. Thank you. We appreciate all your insights into the various topics included in this book, including suggestions for improving the delivery of said material. All errors, however, remain the work of the authors.

Anne Fisher Segal, Tucson, Arizona
Tom Winfree, Los Lunas, New Mexico
Stan Friedman, Los Lunas, New Mexico

Introduction

LEARNING OBJECTIVES

After reading this Introduction, you should be able to:

▶ Express the purpose of this book, using metaphors and concrete examples.
▶ Understand how the terms systemic interface and entropy relate to the issues confronting any mentally ill person that interacts simultaneously with both the mental health and criminal justice problems.
▶ Appreciate the structure of this book and all its fundamental parts.
▶ Understand the general thinking and rationale behind inclusion of the various topics in the 12 chapters.
▶ Link the various special features of the text to the goals outlined in each chapter's Learning Objectives.

PROLOGUE

The following vignette is based on an ancient parable from the Indian subcontinent that illustrates one of this book's primary messages: Humans tend to project their partial experiences as the whole truth.

Four visually impaired friends, walking in single file, approach a giant beast, not knowing exactly what stands before them. "We must determine what animal this is. We can hear it breathing, and it sounds quite fierce," says Bill, the unofficial leader of the group. He continues: "The noises it makes sound vaguely like a trumpet, but then it makes those snorting noises as well. John," he says to the man at the head of the line, "approach the beast and use your sense of touch to discover what it is."

John approaches the beast and grasps an object that flits past his face, only to have it curl first around his arm and then around entire his body, literally caressing him in its embrace. "Oh," says John, "it is a snake. But it doesn't crush me, as it is gently touching me as I touch it."

"Mary," intones Bill, "it's your turn. What is this beast?"

Mary cautiously approaches the gently thrumming noise ahead of her. She reaches out her hand and it is immediately slapped by something large and leathery. "Why if I didn't know better," Mary says, "I would say it is a manta ray. This feels like one of its flukes." She drops the leathery object and asks a sighted friend: "Take me to the beast's tail. A manta ray has a long, slender tail and is very strong. But don't let my hand touch the tail's end, because the manta has a sharp barb there." And, of course, Mary is right. The beast's tail is long, strong, and quite leathery, just like its "fluke." "It's a walking manta ray," she exclaims.

It was now Joshua's turn. Walking forward, his cane touches the animals leg. He leans toward the object and grasps it. "This is a tree, not an animal at all. That odd noise must be the wind blowing through its leaves and that large object you encountered, Mary, must have been a huge leaf," he further speculates.

"Bill, it's your turn," observes Joshua. "This beast cannot be all these things. Please settle the matter. Tell us what it is."

Bill walks slowly forward, like his peers using his cane to find his way. He walks into the side of the beast, immediately recoiling. "My stick went under it," he exclaims. "And I felt like I walked into a wall. Whatever it is, I agree that its skin feels like leather, as you have all observed. I think it is the beast's side. But what it is, I cannot tell. And you, my friends, haven't helped me much."

The four friends walk away, each arguing with the other about what they had just experienced. They agreed that it was indeed a mystery, but each steadfastly maintained the correctness of his or her own impressions and interpretation.

Our apologies to the Indian philosopher who first told this parable of the blind men and the elephant. Tom Winfree's father, who lost his vision at the age of 50, first told his son a version of this parable to explain how different people, looking at the same object or event, can come away with his or her own ideas about it. It was the experiences, biases, and insights of witnesses, he explained, that shaped how each one "saw" the same thing viewed by all. The story stuck.

In the present context, the elephant is the convergence or overlay of what are known as the criminal justice and mental health systems. The American criminal justice system includes police, courts, and correctional agencies operating at the local, state, and federal levels, all of which work to protect the nation from wrongdoers, punish those guilty of criminal offenses, serve the public, and maintain social order. The nation's mental healthcare system is structured around public and private agencies, organizations and institutions that employ a wide range of healthcare providers. From its doctors, clinicians, and nurses to other no less important basic-service providers, this system treats those afflicted with various types of mental infirmities, diseases, and defects, ones we will explore in detail in the coming chapters. These systems come together when an offender or victim (or in some cases both) is mentally ill. The mentally ill person in question could also be a witness or otherwise involved tangentially in the criminal event.

Personnel from various parts of each system look at the same set of circumstances and often have quite different insights into what it is that confronts them. They might be a law enforcement officer, a fire fighter, a social worker, a judge, or a correctional worker; they could be a doctor, a nurse, or some other kind of mental health worker; or they might be a citizen on the street. They are all seeing the same thing—a mentally ill person involved as a possible offender, or as a victim of or witness to a crime, but each actor sees and interprets the events employing the intersection of his or her own vocational, educational, and experiential perspectives.

Introduction Overview

The purpose of this book is to present, in a logical fashion, insights into how society evolved to this place and suggest ways to remedy the dilemma of the "blind" persons. We are not suggesting that the various personnel in the healthcare and criminal justice systems are truly blind to the problems of the mentally ill as victims, perpetrators, or witnesses. Rather, they may not know all the subtle and not-so-subtle elements that create the impasses and conflicts that can arise when a mentally ill person enters the nexus of justice and healthcare. This unawareness has the potential to cause such situations to spiral downward into ever worsening legal, medical, social, and psychological states.

In this Introduction, we present four topics intended to assist the reader in becoming an informed consumer of this book's content. First, we look at a set of orienting ideas that should help the reader understand exactly what we are doing throughout the book. We refer to this as Framing the Issues. As an example, check out this Introduction's Framing the Issues.

The second topic is Chapter Structure. In this section of the Introduction, we specify the common elements or themes employed across all subsequent chapters of the book.

Third, we review each of the book's topical areas. We divide the nexus of criminal justice and mental health into 12 chapters.

The fourth and final topic reviews the books Special Features, which exist in two types: boxed inserts and a glossary. The boxes are intended to assist the reader in understanding each chapter's content. The glossary is a detailed dictionary of key terms that are bolded throughout the text and included in a Key Terms section at the end of each chapter.

This Introduction, then, serves as an introduction to the pedagogical or instructional approach we have taken to the central themes that converge in this book. We are preparing the reader for the journey that lies ahead. We enjoyed being first on that journey; we hope that you enjoy being next.

FRAMING THE ISSUES

Framing the Issues sections consist of a set of central themes, ideas, or concepts related to a chapter's content. We turn next to one such set of concerns that should help readers understand why we included this kind of information in each chapter.

Two ideas emerge as underlying much of what is described in this book. The first can be described as **systemic interface**, by which we mean the interconnectivity between two or more public-serving entities, or, in this case, between the criminal justice system and the mental healthcare system. We describe it as systemic as such interconnectivity requires input across the entire spectrum of activities within a given entity and potentially impacts the whole entity and not just its parts; moreover, this text's two systems must focus their attention on a person suffering from a mental illness or disorder who is also a crime victim, a criminal offender, or a witness to an offense. Each system has important contributions to make, but it is when those various contributions are connected in meaningful ways that this merger works best.

For example, researchers in the United Kingdom examined the interface between the courts and mental health workers. This is a classic mental health–justice interface situation, one that assists the courts in addressing questions about mental health commitment orders (Chapter 6), legal competency (Chapter 7), defenses, pleas, and verdicts (Chapter 8), or even the execution of the mentally ill (Chapter 9). Summarizing the responses of over 2,000 court workers, the researchers reported three key challenges to information transfer: "(1) delays in report production, (2) perceived inadequacies in the report content, and (3) report funding" (Hean, Warr, and Staddon, 2009: 170). Similar findings characterize studies of mental health–criminal justice interface in the United States (Hollen, Ortiz, and Schacht, 2015; Johnson, 2010; Taxman, Wurzburg, and Habert, 2016).

Solutions to interface problems, such as shared medical health services data within a jail environment, have shown promise, despite legal barriers to its implementation, including patient privacy and records' confidentiality and security (Hollen et al., 2015). However, unless all partners in such an endeavor work in equal measure to facilitate, in a timely fashion, the smooth interagency transfer of clients and information from one partner to the other, then interface is a nice idea, but not a reality.

Possible origins of breakdowns in systemic interface deserve our attention, if only briefly at this point in the book. As related in Chapter 1, healthcare and criminal justice are huge "industries" in the United States, employing hundreds of thousands of personnel and providing services to tens if not hundreds of millions of people annually, including clients who overlap with one another. The sheer size of each system is an impediment to systemic interface. Mental healthcare facilities and those organizations associated with the administration of justice in the United States are tied to federal, state, and local governments, which makes coordinated efforts, especially information sharing on a national level, difficult if not, given current technologies, impossible. Moreover, both systems exist as private and public entities, including not just for-profit mental healthcare services, but also for-profit criminal justice services, such as private jails and prisons. Managing costs and providing for interface with the public sector can be a problem in the for-profit world.

The world of business offers insight into why these two systems can be characterized as lacking sufficient systemic interface. We refer to the idea of **entropy**, which is defined as a measure of disorder or randomness in a closed system. Business borrowed the idea from physics. Entropy, according to the Second Law of Thermodynamics, can never decrease in a closed system (Lieb and Yngvason, 1999). In the business world, then, the presence of entropy tells us that in **closed systems**, represented by highly bureaucratic organizations, energy (i.e., resources and personnel) is distributed evenly but is less able to do work, leading to inefficiency and eventually disorder and even chaos, that is, a tendency toward entropy. Organic organizations, characterized as **open systems**, welcome innovation and creativity; they also evidence a tendency toward the free exchange of ideas and information, along with organizational resources, which promotes organizational survival and efficiency (Jing, 2012; Schneider and Somers, 2006). In layperson's terms, then, the actions of large, closed systems tend to become, over time, disordered, dysfunctional, and even chaotic as they attempt to achieve their goals. Open systems, on the other hand, can respond to changing demands on services and create new methods to support systemic interface.

These ideas, while somewhat abstract, make a modicum of sense in the exploration of systemic interface between what are the largely bureaucratic organizations currently providing mental healthcare and criminal justice services. As you read about the forms and types of problems that emerge when a mentally ill person encounters the criminal justice system, we suggest that you reflect on the idea of systemic interface and entropy. We also suggest that you pay particular attention to situations in which the absence of interface creates problems, such as entropy, that would otherwise not exist or at least not exist at the same level in the presence of collaborative systemic interface.

CHAPTER STRUCTURE

Each chapter begins, as did this Introduction, with Learning Objectives. These are generalized goals for the content of the ensuing chapter. Their purpose is to sensitize the reader to the chapter's central themes.

Next the reader encounters a section entitled Prologue, which is represented as a vignette, a sort of brief story based on the authors' insights, observations, education, lifetime experiences, and, yes, probably our biases as well. The vignette's purpose is to stimulate the reader to think about exactly what it is that makes the chapter's content important to an overall understanding of what happens when the mentally ill encounter both the criminal justice system and the mental health system. They are often provocative in nature, but always, we think, interesting reads. We recommend that you read the vignette twice: Once at the beginning of each chapter and then again after you have examined its content. The importance of the vignette to each chapter will become clear by following this simple prescription.

As described in the previous section, Framing the Issues will provide the conceptual tools needed by the reader to appreciate the finer details of each chapter's implications for justice and mental health. A typical Framing the Issues consists of ideas, events, movements, or developments related to either criminal justice or mental health or both systems that had a major impact on their convergence to address the problems of mentally ill offenders, victims of crime, and witnesses to crime. In this Introduction, for example, the Framing the Issues elaborates on systemic interface.

Next, each chapter consists of five to six topical areas, indicated by their status as major headings in both the Chapter Outline and the body of the text. They elaborate on the chapter's basic theme. Deciding on exactly what to include was no easy task. We suspect that some readers will think that we left out important topics. And, we probably did. But, overall, we believe that the specific topics included reveal central insights into the issues, controversies, and solutions associated with this overlay of criminal justice and mental healthcare services.

We conclude each chapter with an Epilogue, which generally consist of two types: (1) an actual criminal/civil case (sometimes, however, employing pseudonyms to protect the identities of the parties involved) and its implications for the information covered in the chapter; or (2) a fact-driven, case- or example-based discussion intended to coalesce the information covered in the chapter.

The Summary provides a review, in a bulleted format, of the chapter's major points. These bulleted items do not capture the entire content of a chapter, but rather seek to draw attention to those points that drive its central themes. After the Summary, we include Chapter Review Questions, which are not only fact-based questions related to the chapter's content, but also analytical questions that will require the reader to apply the chapter's content. In the Instructor's Manual, we also provide additional Critical Thinking Questions that you can use for further discussions, research, or for greater application and analysis of the topics discussed throughout the chapter.

THEMATIC ORGANIZATION

This book, representing a merger of two rather large systems in American society, necessarily takes an idea-driven approach to the convergence or overlay of those systems. Rather than employ a format that represents the central tenets of one or more of the academic disciplines that are engaged when a mentally ill person encounters the criminal justice system, we use a broader perspective organized into three thematic topics: Tools for Understanding; Providing Justice, Providing Mental Healthcare; and Special Issues.

The book, then, contains the following 12 chapters:

▶ Part I—Tools for Understanding—This thematic area includes the specific "tools" required to examine the remaining topics from an informed perspective.
  ○ Chapter 1 (Mental Health and Criminal Justice)—This chapter provides an overview of both the mental health and criminal justice systems. The reader may have knowledge of one or both systems; however, their convergence generally represents a new set of concerns and issues, ones that rest on an understanding of the key parts of each system.
  ○ Chapter 2 (A Brief History of Mental Illness)—Any society is the product of its history. This generalization is true of the current topic areas as well. Hence, we provide a brief historical overview of how various cultural and geopolitical entities, including our nation, have responded through time to the mentally ill. Included in this chapter is a review of critical changes in public policy and practice that resulted in the criminalization of the mentally ill.
  ○ Chapter 3 (The Brain and the Mind)—This chapter is intended to give you a baseline reference to understand how the brain and mind act as one entity. We also provide an understanding of the brain, how it functions and how it guides our behavior as human and social beings.

o Chapter 4 (Etiology of Mental Illness)—Etiology means the study of causes. In this chapter we provide biological, medical, psychiatric, psychological, and sociological information that is central to an understanding of the origins of mental disorders and societal reactions to them. Again, given a broad reading audience, we provide this information in as low a level of scientific abstraction as possible, with no preconceived knowledge base. We discuss it in as straightforward a manner as possible, especially given the central nature of causes and correlates to an understanding of this book's central tenets.

▶ Part II—Providing Justice, Providing Mental Healthcare—This book is about more than the operation of criminal justice agencies as they interact with the mentally ill in their communities. The focus is on providing justice for everyone concerned, from the general citizenry to the mentally ill persons involved, no matter the nature of their involvement. Hence, each chapter in this thematic area examines the services and actions of both the criminal justice and mental healthcare systems.

o Chapter 5 (First Responders and Street Encounters)—Police encounters with the mentally ill are important and treated in some detail. However, many mentally ill persons, whether as victims, perpetrators, or witnesses to crimes, first come to the attention of one or both systems literally on the nation's streets. This chapter includes a discussion of "best practices" for such encounters and questions of legal liability and risk management that emerge because of them.

o Chapter 6 (Involuntary and Voluntary Commitments)—In this chapter, we explore when or if an individual should be committed to a mental health facility. In this instance, we look at various state laws and consider if a person is a danger to himself or a danger to others when determining if the court has the authority to detain a person against his will in a mental health facility. As you will learn, the proceedings are heavily reviewed by the court.

o Chapter 7 (Legal Competency and the Criminal Trial)—If a person who is accused of a crime does not have the mental ability to understand the criminal proceedings and/or is unable to effectively communicate with his attorney, the accused may be incompetent and the prosecution is suspended. This chapter examines the constitutional, procedural, evaluative, and ethical considerations associated with determining a defendant's competency to stand trial.

o Chapter 8 (Mentally Ill Defendants: Defenses, Pleas, and Verdicts)—This chapter explores the use and relevance of defenses of insanity, temporary insanity, and diminished capacity. This chapter examines the legal theories that defense attorneys present during a trial to exonerate their client by proving there was no specific intent to harm, but the criminal act was triggered by mental disabilities.

o Chapter 9 (Correctional Treatment of the Mentally Ill)—The mentally ill persons who are found guilty of criminal offenses typically end up in jail or prison, a topic that is addressed in considerable detail in this chapter. However, correctional treatment is about more than institutional corrections; hence, this chapter also looks at community-based programming, including sentencing alternatives, probation, and parole.

▸ Part III—Special Issues—As complete as the preceding topic area may seem, some special aspects of engagement between the mentally ill and both systems merit special attention. The three sets of issues included in this topical area may not represent all the unique and specialized needs that should be addressed, but they represent a starting point for any such discussion.

○ Chapter 10 (Juveniles and Mental Illness: Special Considerations)—Juveniles, those children typically aged 10 to 17, are given special consideration in this chapter. The issues central to the justice received by juveniles is explored in four "strands": juvenile justice system; adolescents and the mental health system; specific needs and child protection services; and children, mental health, and education.

○ Chapter 11 (Mental Health Issues in the Community)—This chapter looks at types of behavior that can have a mental health component, including hoarding, homelessness, and stalking and other harassing behaviors. In it, we also consider typical legal responses to such conduct, including protective orders. In the context of directing personal, non-criminal behavior, you will also learn about guardianships and when there is a need for a power of attorney.

○ Chapter 12 (Justice for the Mentally Ill: Human Rights and At-Risk Groups)— This chapter first explores mental healthcare as a human right and then examines the intersection of mental healthcare and criminal justice for four at-risk populations: the elderly; military veterans; gay, lesbian, bisexual, transgender and queer communities; and racial and ethnic minorities. There is nothing about membership in any of these groups that necessarily causes mental illness; rather, owing to their heightened vulnerabilities in contemporary society, we focus on the differential responses of both the criminal justice and mental health systems toward members of these groups who happen to evidence mental illness. We selected these four groups in the hope that they will engage the reader to think more deeply about the range of possible systemic interface problems that one could encounter when the justice system meets the mental healthcare system.

SPECIAL FEATURES

This book has four different types of boxes. Each expands on or amplifies an idea reviewed in the chapter. The first such box is entitled What Would You Do? First, we offer a scenario taken from real life. The reader is then asked a series of question concerning possible responses to the concerns, issues, and ideas represented in the scenario, the central question being, what would you do?

Thinking About the Issues is the second type of box, which follows the discussion of an important set of issues. These boxes contain a statement that refers to the issues and ask the reader a series of questions. The intent is to start the reader questioning why we do what we do when encountering a mentally ill person in a situation that involves the legal system.

Law and Mental Health is the third type of box. Each chapter contains one such box, in which we describe and elaborate on a legal response to a major issue, problem, or concern that involves this nexus of criminal justice and mental health. The issue may be a litigated case or more general code or law.

In several chapters, we also provide a series of general boxes intended to expand on or amplify an idea presented in the text. Their presence varies through the book, but they include case studies or examples of various aspects of the intersection of the criminal justice and healthcare systems.

We also provide a detailed Glossary of the terms that are bolded in the text and listed at the end of each chapter in a section entitled Key Terms. The Glossary includes a definition of each term, as well as identifying the specific chapter in which it is first described.

EPILOGUE

This epilogue is derived from accounts by Abadi (2017); Crime Sider Staff (2017); Luo (2007); Mark (2017); Martinez and Melzer (2017); and Montgomery, Oppel, Jr., and Delreal (2017).

On a pleasant fall day in late 2017, churchgoers inside the First Baptist Church of Sutherland Springs, Texas, gathered in their sanctuary, giving praise in song for their blessings. Over their own voices, however, the worshippers began to hear the distinctive sounds of gunfire and, indeed, bullets began pouring through the sides of the church.

Within minutes Devin Patrick Kelley had killed 26 parishioners and injured another 20. His victims ranged in age from 18 months to 77 years of age. Kelley, upon exiting the church, was shot at and, after a vehicle chase through the countryside, brought to ground by two members of the local community. As police closed in, Kelley took the way out of his situation employed by many previous spree shooters: He shot himself in the head with his own handgun.

Police investigators speculated that, given the presence of his former wife's family as members of the church and his familiarity with the community—he had recently attended a social function in the area—Kelley's actions were linked to a family feud. Investigators could establish no clear motive, especially for the circumstances of the mass shooting itself.

Investigators did find that 26-year old Kelley had a running feud with his most recent ex-wife's Texas-based family, especially her mother, who was a member of the First Baptist Church of Sutherland Springs. To reinforce this view, authorities revealed that Kelley had recently sent her threatening e-mail messages.

Law enforcement officials also discovered that Kelley had a history of violence directed at an ex-wife and her son, his stepchild. For over a year, he repeatedly struck, choked, and kicked his then-wife. Kelley once hit his stepson so hard he fractured the child's skull, causing a severe hematoma. At the time, Kelley was a member of the U.S. Air Force stationed in Holloman Air Force Base (AFB) in Alamogordo, NM. After an alleged assault in 2012, he was convicted at general court martial—the most serious such legal remedy available to the Air Force—of two assault charges (domestic violence), and confined for a year. At the end of his incarceration, the Air Force gave Kelley a bad conduct discharge, which generally follows a conviction on charges that are like civilian misdemeanors.

But investigators found more information that suggested a major failure of interface between mental health services, the U.S. military, and federal law enforcement. Specifically, in June 2012, prior to the conclusion of his court martial, Kelley was sent to a behavioral health facility in southern New Mexico for evaluation. Kelley escaped from this facility and made his way to nearby El Paso, Texas, where local police apprehended him at a bus station. Witnesses noted that Kelley was acting as if he "suffered from mental disorders" and was a danger to himself or others. Police were also informed, according to the police report, that Kelley had smuggled firearms onto Holloman Air Force Base and had made threats against his commanding officer. Kelley was apprehended by El Paso police without incident and returned to the custody of police in New Mexico, who returned him to the behavioral health facility. Later, back at Holloman AFB, Kelley pleaded guilty to domestic abuse charges, was convicted, and ordered confined, prior to his bad conduct discharge.

Kelley's conviction should have triggered an Air Force report to federal authorities through the Department of Defense, concerning Kelley's conviction on domestic violence. This event alone should have resulted in his inclusion in a federal data bank, disqualifying him from gun purchases. The statute in question, 18 U.S.C. §922(g)(9), which is entitled "Restrictions on the Possession of Firearms by Individuals Convicted of a Misdemeanor Crime of Domestic Violence," was enacted in 1996. Despite this prohibition, over a period of four years, Kelley was able to purchase four firearms in Texas, including the murder rifle and suicide handgun. He also passed a background check to serve as an unarmed guard for a security company, but was denied a concealed-carry permit by Texas.

Was Kelley unique in this regard? The Air Force later admitted that there were dozens of other cases like Kelley's, individuals whose conviction records would disqualify them from purchasing weapons, but whose conviction records were not forwarded to the Bureau of Alcohol, Tobacco, and Firearms (ATF). The Secretary of the Air Force directed the Air Force Inspector General's office to conduct a complete review of the case and further promised to review Air Force policies to prevent this failure of interface in the future.

Moreover, it is not just a military problem. In 2007, gunman Seung-Hui Cho, who killed 32 people and injured another 17 in two separate attacks at Virginia Tech, had previously been ordered by a court into mental health treatment. However, Cho's court order was never forwarded to ATF, as federal law requires when a person has been adjudicated "mentally incapacitated" or "involuntarily committed" (18 U.S.C. §922(d)(4) & (g)(4)). Cho, too, committed suicide after his killing spree.

Perhaps you have thought of another question: Should not Kelley's institutionalization for mental illness, no matter how brief, also have disqualified him from purchasing firearms? The answer is complex, but it is generally no, not unless the threat is immediate and ongoing, although you will read more about mental illness and firearms later in this book.

This epilogue places no blame, except on the shooter. Rather, it highlights the problems that often emerge after the fact, when, on cold reflection, society examines a horrific event such as this church shooting and tries to make sense of it. As with many such incidents, and we review others in this text, there are rarely easy answers. And that is the crux of why the content of this book is important to so many in the fields of mental health, community health, social work, medicine, law, and criminal justice.

SUMMARY

- A group of people can "view" an object (or a situation) and come away with very different ideas of what they just observed.
- The overlay or intersection of the criminal justice system and the mental healthcare system provide the central focus of this book, along with any issues that emerge because of this situation.
- The individual that stands at the center of attention in this text is the mentally ill individual who may be a crime victim, a crime perpetrator, or the witness to a crime.
- One theme found throughout this text is the question of systemic interface, that is, to what extent do the two systems in question coordinate their actions when responding to a perceived need?
- Entropy, an idea taken from business and science, suggests that highly bureaucratic organizations, through their actions intended to distribute resources evenly, tend to be inefficient and prone to disorder or worse, while organic organizations, open to innovation and creativity, promote the organization's survival and efficiency.
- Each chapter in this book consists of the following elements: Chapter Outline, Learning Objectives, Prologue, and Framing the Issues, followed by the substantive material that addresses the chapter's topic. At the end of each chapter, there is an Epilogue, followed by a Summary, Chapter Review Questions, and Key Terms, Cases, and Legislation cited in the chapter.
- The book is divided into three parts. Part I consists of four chapters that provide the reader with the Tools for Understanding, which are essential for the complete comprehension of the remaining chapters. Part II, Providing Justice, Providing Mental Healthcare, consists of five chapters that look at how mentally ill persons work their way through the justice system. The final part, Special Issues, examines three topics: (1) mentally ill juveniles as special "clients" of the justice system, (2) mental health issues in the community, and (3) mental healthcare as a human right, reviewing how four

distinct at-risk subpopulations have, to a greater or lesser extent, been denied access to this human right.
- Each chapter also includes at least three types of boxes.
- Key Terms are provided at the end of each chapter and defined in the Glossary.
- The epilogue provides insights into what can go wrong when systemic interface fails.

CHAPTER REVIEW QUESTIONS

1. What is meant by the phrase systemic interface? How does the term entropy relate to the presence of problems with systemic interface?
2. In what ways does the parable of the four blind persons and the elephant represent systemic interface issues involving the criminal justice and healthcare systems?
3. Which of the 12 topical areas do you anticipate will provide the greatest problems of systemic interface? Explain your thinking. [NOTE: We suggest you write your answer to this question down and consult it again after reading the entire book.]
4. Reflecting on the totality of Devin Patrick Kelley's story, note the specific failures of the system to protect the public. Can you think of any ways to remedy this situation or ones like it?

KEY TERMS

Closed systems

Entropy

Open systems

Systemic interface

REFERENCES

Abadi, M. (November 7, 2017). "The Texas church shooter has a disturbing history of domestic violence, including charges of animal cruelty and fracturing his infant stepson's skull." *Business Insider*. Retrieved at http://www.businessinsider.com/devin-patrick-kelley-texas-church-shooter-arrested-harassment-animal-cruelty-2017-11 on 3 January 2017.

Crime Sider Staff (November 6, 2017). "Texas church shooting: How was Devin Patrick Kelley discharged from the Air Force?" *CBS News*. Retrieved at https://www.cbsnews.com/news/texas-church-shooting-how-was-devin-patrick-kelley-discharged-from-the-air-force/ on 3 January 2018.

Hean, S., J. Warr, and S. Staddon (2009). "Challenges at the interface of working between mental health services and the criminal justice system." *Medicine, Science and the Law* 49: 170-8.

Hollen, V., G. Ortiz, and L. Schacht (2015). *Behavioral Health and Criminal Justice Systems: Identifying New Opportunities for Information Exchange.* Falls Church, VA: NASMHPD.

Jing, D. (2012). "The study of business growth process management entropy model." *Physics Procedia* 24: 2105-110.

Johnson, W.W. (2010). "Rethinking the interface between mental illness, criminal justice and academia." *Justice Quarterly* 28: 15-22.

Lieb, E.H., and J. Yngvason (1999). "The physics and mathematics of the second law of thermodynamics." *Physics Reports* 310: 1-96.

Luo, M. (April 20, 2007). "Cho's mental illness should have blocked gun sale." *The New York Times*. Retrieved at http://www.nytimes.com/2007/04/20/us/20cnd-guns.html on 3 January 2018.

Mark, M. (November 7, 2017). "The Texas gunman escaped from a mental health facility after assaulting his wife and infant stepson." *Business Insider*. Retrieved at http://www.businessinsider.com/devin-patrick-kelley-texas-shooter-escaped-mental-health-facility-2017-11 on 3 January 2018.

Martinez, P., and L. Melzer (November 7, 2017). "Texas church shooting victims: Pregnant mother, children among lives lost." *CBS News*. Retrieved at https://www.cbsnews.com/news/texas-shooting-massacre-victims-sutherland-springs-first-baptist-church/ on 3 January 2018.

Montgomery, D., R.A. Oppel, Jr., and J.A. Delreal (November 6, 2017). "Air Force error allowed Texas gunman to buy weapons." *The New York Times*. Retrieved at https://www.nytimes.com/2017/11/06/us/texas-shooting-church.html on 3 January 2018.

Schneider, M., and M. Somers (2006). "Organizations as complex adaptive systems: Implications of Complexity Theory for leadership research." *The Leadership Quarterly* 17: 351-65.

Taxman, F.S., S. Wurzburg, and K. Habert (2016). "Process measures at the interface between the justice system and behavioral health: Advancing practice and outcomes." New York: Justice Center: The Council of State Governments.

LEGISLATION

18 U.S.C. §922 (Chapter 44—Firearms) (1968, as amended)

Part I

Tools for Understanding

Tools for understanding the area under study are an essential part of any academic endeavor. To this end, the first part of this text provides, in four chapters, a set of shared tools needed to understand the interface between the criminal justice system and the mental health system. Chapter 1 explores in detail the two systems, and provides a brief overview of how people come into contact with the mental health system through their criminal justice experiences. Chapter 2 grounds the discussion in the history of mental illness, examining how the conditions we understand today as constituting an illness were less charitably received in the past. The third "tools" chapter, Chapter 3, examines the duality of the mind and the brain: how the brain and the mind represent something unique in each individual, as well as how they contribute to our understanding mental illness. Finally, Chapter 4 examines in layperson's terms the causes of mental illness as we understand them today. Some illnesses derive from injuries or disease, while others are due to unintended or self-inflicted biochemical imbalances; most of these causal forces are understood in medical or psychiatric terms. Some causes are more psychological or even sociological in origin. What we learn in this chapter is that while we have learned much about mental illness since the start of the 20th century, much remains to be uncovered.

Mental Health and Criminal Justice

LEARNING OBJECTIVES

After reading this chapter, you should be able to:

▶ Understand the nature and extent of the nation's mental health system and its criminal justice system

▶ Describe the U.S. mental healthcare system, including the roles played by the states and federal government, and the public-private sector divide in service delivery.

▶ Describe the nation's criminal justice system, including its legal elements and major component parts.

▶ Explain the central issues generated by contacts between the justice system and mentally ill individuals who are accused of crimes, who are the victims of crimes, and who witness crimes.

PROLOGUE

This prologue is based on an actual police-citizen encounter described to one of the book's co-authors by the attending officer. As this encounter did not become part of an official record, but was handled informally by the officer, some information has been altered to protect the identities of both the officer and the citizen.

It's 03:30 hours. Officer Herman Garcia has been on duty since 18:00 hours the previous day. He's closing in on shift change and looking forward to his bed.

The previous day was the hottest of the year, as the Valley of the Sun hit 100 degrees for the first time. As Officer Garcia approaches an intersection in the downtown area of his beat, he notices a stooped-over person walking resolutely in an easterly direction, following the roadside curb. Given the hour and apparent difficulty in walking revealed by the individual's rolling gait and occasional stumble, Garcia turns on his unit's high beams, activates its light bar, and hits the siren once.

A crinkled but smiling face turns back to the unit. It is evidently an elderly man, wrapped in a bathrobe and wearing bedroom slippers, although the footwear is nearly shredded and his bloody toes exposed. He stops and collapses to the curb, as Officer Garcia pulls his unit to the side of the road, providing a protective barrier between the street and the obviously struggling pedestrian. Before exiting his unit, Garcia pulls a bottle of water out of a six-pack on the passenger's seat. This is the Valley of the Sun after all, even at night.

"Are you OK, sir?" asks Officer Garcia.

"Wouldn't turn down a drink of water," replies the civilian.

Handing him the unopened bottle of water, Officer Garcia continues: "Are you lost, sir? It's pretty late and these streets can be dangerous at night."

"Oh no, officer, I'm not lost," says the walker indignantly, handing back the bottle of water. "But could you open this please? My hands don't work like they used to."

Opening the bottle and returning it, Officer Garcia asks: "Where are you headed? Where did you come from?" At this point, Officer Garcia does not think the man is intoxicated or poses a threat to others. But there is something just not right about this encounter. Garcia has had hundreds of other strange encounters in his five-year career with the P.D., but none quite like this one.

Obviously confused, the walker responds: "Now just ask one question at a time, and I will try to answer each one. I live in Peoria," he says, indicating a town about 25 road miles to the west. "But," he continues, "I am heading home to Indianapolis. Should be there tomorrow."

Officer Garcia helps the elderly man into the back of his unit. "What do I do with him now," he wonders aloud.

"What do I do now?" We suspect that many first responders have asked this question when dealing with a person whose mental state was in question. For instance, encounters between law enforcement officers and disoriented senior citizens are far more commonplace today than even a decade ago, especially as the Baby Boomer generation ages. Demographers who study these trends tell us that in the future such encounters will become even more frequent, a problem we address in this book's final chapter. Awareness of the symptoms and behaviors associated with dementia, a progressive type of mental disease that takes many forms, is becoming essential for serving officers. In fact, awareness of a wide range of mental illnesses is proving to be crucial for all first responders, from police officers to fire personnel to average citizens. For example, a police officer, arriving at the scene of a car accident, may initially find it difficult to tell the difference between someone who is a devious criminal, a drug-involved person, a victim of a medical problem, or, as in this case, a probable Alzheimer's disease victim.

Education, training, and experience can make all the difference in a police-citizen encounter. If Officer Garcia had, upon exiting his vehicle, been approached in a threatening manner by an evidently mentally disoriented person, his response would likely have been different. If the "walker" had been a mentally challenged minor with obvious signs of physical abuse, even more alarm bells should have sounded. Recognizing which specific situation represents what kind of issue, and knowing how to respond appropriately, can be the difference between good law enforcement and a quickly deteriorating and even life-threatening police-citizen encounter.

Chapter Overview

Two major systems support this book's core. For its part, the mental healthcare system serves society's mentally ill persons, while the criminal justice system addresses concerns of general safety and security, serving as a bulwark against crime and criminals. As described in this chapter's first major section, we address the implications of the rule of law and due process for the convergence of these two systems, which can occur when a mentally ill person has contact with the criminal justice system.

In the second major section, we examine the nation's mental healthcare delivery system as a subset of its far larger healthcare system. An understanding of the overall U.S. healthcare picture allows us to contextualize what is happening with mental healthcare. This section details the roles played by the federal and state government, along with the public and private divide in service delivery.

In the third section, we provide a brief overview of the American criminal justice system. Laws, especially criminal laws, are central to this system's operation. Moreover, this section reviews the various agencies that make up the component parts of the administration of justice, including law enforcement, the judiciary, and the correctional system.

The fourth section explores the events that can take place when an individual is taken into custody by law enforcement agents and subjected to further processing. As we examine the critical steps that take a suspect from arrest to initial court appearance, there is a special focus on situations in which a mentally ill person may be disadvantaged. What occurs at these early junctures in justice processing can serve as a roadmap to—and a portent of—what lies ahead in this book.

The epilogue is a composite of several cases. In its totality, this vignette suggests that once a mentally ill person becomes involved with the criminal justice process, there are several critical decision-making points at which timely intervention can serve both criminal and social justice. That is, society is often afforded more than one opportunity to do what is not only correct according to the laws of the land, but what is morally right as well. This composite case also serves as a warning about what can go irreversibly wrong when no one exercises the level of oversight such situations often require.

FRAMING THE ISSUES

Two largely decentralized, nationwide systems frame this chapter's content. First, we explore the U.S. mental healthcare system. The World Health Organization (2004) defines **mental health** as "a state of well-being in which the individual realizes his or her own abilities, can cope with the normal stresses of life, can work productively and fruitfully, and is able to make a contribution to his or her community." When a person does not enjoy good mental health, the discussion often turns to questions about a possible mental defect, disease, or disorder. Consider the following definition of **mental illness**, one offered by the National Alliance on Mental Illness (NAMI, n.d.): "A mental illness is a condition that affects a person's thinking, feeling or mood. Such conditions may affect someone's ability to relate to others and function each day. Each person will have different experiences, even people with the same diagnosis . . ." The **mental healthcare system**, then, is an agency-based, loosely arrayed service-delivery approach to mental health and mental illness, organized at the federal, state, and local levels, consisting of public and private ventures that care for millions of persons in need.

Second, we provide an overview of the nation's **criminal justice system**, a generic term used to describe the operational aspects of the nation's response to criminal law violations. The criminal justice system consists of several interrelated agencies, each with its own criminal law-related policies, practices, and procedures, all intended to provide for the community's safety and security. The various subsystems or component parts of that overall system seek to control crime and punish those who engage in it.

In the present context, each of these entities—the mental healthcare system and the criminal justice system—must follow the dictates of **due process**, giving the greatest possible protection to people who have some form of mental illness, disease, debilitation, or disability. This emphasis on due process, which translates into respecting all legal rights owed an individual, irrespective of his or her legal status, is also a hallmark of the **Rule of Law**. Both legal doctrines are centrally important to anyone, including a mentally ill person, who has an encounter with one or more component parts of the criminal justice system (see Box 1.1).

Throughout this book, we refer to many different mental health issues. The example of dementia in the prologue alerts us to the complex nature of all mental health issues. Moreover, it is not just the mentally ill suspect who should be afforded all relevant legal protections, but also mentally ill victims and witnesses as well. Consequently, an in-depth understanding of the nature and extent of the nation's mental healthcare delivery system is essential when looking at what happens when justice and mental health issues intersect.

AMERICAN MENTAL HEALTHCARE SYSTEM

On average, the United States spends more than $3 trillion a year on healthcare, which is roughly $9,000 per person (U.S. Department of Health and Human Services [DHHS], 2017). A recent study by the Commonwealth Fund found that among 13 high-income nations around the world, the United States spends the most on healthcare, whether measured as a per capita ($9,086) expenditure or as a percentage (17.1%) of the nation's gross national product (Squires and Anderson, 2015: 2). Our nation spends 50 percent more of its economy on healthcare than any comparably wealthy nation. Yet, America receives a poor return for its investment in terms of health outcomes, as the Commonwealth Fund ranks the United States quite low among its peers in this category. While the Commonwealth Fund study contains several reasons for these disparities (e.g., greater utilization of expensive technology and higher prices), the fact remains that general healthcare in the United States is very costly.

BOX 1.1

Rule of Law

A concern for the Rule of Law's presence and influence on governments dates to antiquity. As Cicero noted in defense of Aulus Cluentius Habitus Minor, the latter accused of poisoning his father: "We are servants of the law so that we can be free." This statement is taken to mean that liberty and obedience are two sides of the same coin: Together they ensure the people's freedom by requiring that everyone's actions be predictable. Ancient texts, including Leviticus 19:15 and the somewhat more recent English *Magna Carte* (1215), include references to the idea that everyone is equal before the law and no one is above it, not even the monarch.

In contemporary times, the Rule of Law is generally taken to include the following four universal principles:

1. **Accountability**—This term refers to the idea that the government and the private sector are both governed by and held answerable to the law.

2. **Just Laws**—A nation's laws must be clear, publicized, stable, and fair; they must protect fundamental rights, which include the rights of citizens to safety and security in their lives and property, as well as core human rights.

3. **Open Government**—This idea captures a central theme in the Rule of Law: The processes by which laws are enacted, administered, and enforced must be accessible, fair, and efficient.

4. **Accessible and Impartial Dispute Resolution**—This statement reflects, at its core, the Rule of Law's emphasis on an independent judiciary: Competent, independent, and ethical representatives—persons who represent their constituencies and possess adequate and unfettered resources—must deliver justice in a timely fashion.

Whatever the specific manifestation of the Rule of Law, the bottom line is this: Everyone is equally accountable to publicly disclosed legal codes and processes. The converse is also taken as equally important: No one is above the law.

Sources: Cicero (1967); Katz (2005); World Justice Project (n.d.).

Mental healthcare services are a fraction of the nation's overall healthcare expenditures. In 2010, the United States spent $113 billion on mental health and substance abuse treatment, which was less than 6 percent of that year's total spending on healthcare (Mark, Levit, et al., 2011). This level of spending is on par with the world's "developing nations," such as Romania, South Africa, or Chile, and not its wealthiest, industrialized nations, although Australia and France report similar percentages (World Health Organization, 2003). When compared to other nations, the pattern reflected in mental healthcare expenditures appears to be the same as reported for overall healthcare in the United States.

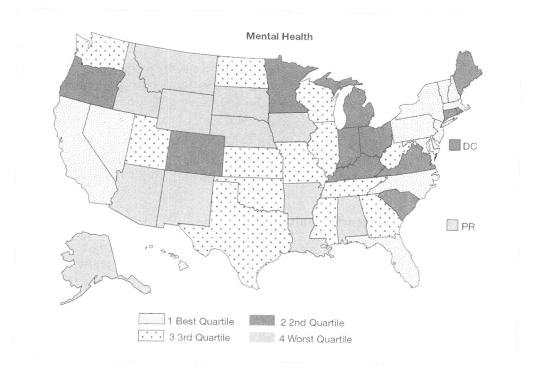

Mental Health

1 Best Quartile   2 2nd Quartile
3 3rd Quartile   4 Worst Quartile

FIGURE 1.1 Mental Health in the United States: A National Assessment

Source: U.S. Department of Health and Human Services (2012).

As represented in Figure 1.1, access to mental healthcare varies widely across the United States. In this figure, the states and territories are placed into quartiles, based on the percentage of that unit's population that may not have adequate access to service providers. To put this figure in perspective, the top or first quartile represents the best served states/territories in the nation, while those in the bottom fourth quartile are the worst served. The quantitative differences in services between the top and bottom quartiles are considerable. For example, in the fourth quartile, the worst rates of service states or territories include the Virgin Islands (97%), Wyoming (75%), Puerto Rico (70%), and Idaho (69%), while in the first quartile, Delaware (0%), New Jersey (1%), and New Hampshire (4%) had the best service rates (DHHS, 2012: Chapter 8). Where you live matters when it comes to access to mental healthcare in the United States.

In addition to disparities in access to mental healthcare services, the nation's capacity to deal with the mentally ill has declined in recent years. During the 1960s and 1970s, there was a shift from placing the mentally ill in psychiatric hospitals to the use of community-based mental health facilities. The net result was a loss of bedspaces for the mentally ill. But this trend did not end in the 1970s. According to the American Hospital Association (2012), between 1995 and 2010, the nation saw about 200 mental hospitals close; community hospitals also lost another 1,000 psychiatric units, meaning only one in four community hospitals had such a unit in 2010. Moreover, 55 percent of all counties have no practicing psychiatrists, psychologists, or social workers. At the same time, emergency room admissions for mental health issues rose by 20 percent between 2006 and 2009 (DHHS, 2017). When it comes to mental healthcare services, the United States is experiencing a shortage of both personnel and institutional resources that some claim constitutes a national crisis (American Hospital Association, 2012; Mark et al., 2011; Squires and Anderson, 2015; Sundararaman, 2009).

The remainder of this section covers two main topics. First, we examine federal and state laws and policies on mental healthcare, which determine the extent to which governments at all levels can and do respond to the needs of the mentally ill. Second, we review the mental healthcare services provided by the public and private sectors.

Policies and Laws on Mental Healthcare

Mental healthcare is, for the most part, delivered at the local level. However, federal and state laws, policies, and practices often determine how well those delivery systems function. Knowing this information is essential to our overall understanding of the nation's mental healthcare system's ability to meet existing and future demands.

Federal Actions. The federal government plays a central role in four health-related areas (Mental Health America, n.d.). First, the federal government regulates systems and providers. Legislation at this level takes a great deal of time to go from idea to law to action, but it can profoundly impact how services are delivered and to whom. Congress also provides rules clarifying the implementation of various acts, including the 1973 Rehabilitation Act, the 1990 Americans with Disabilities Act (ADA), the 2008 Mental Health Parity and Addiction Equity Act, and the 2010 Patient Protection and Affordable Care Act (ACA). Various federal agencies also issue guidance in response to questions about compliance.

Second, the federal government is often the major guarantor of legal protections for the mentally ill across many different settings, ranging from the workplace to schools to treatment facilities. The federal government sets privacy standards, prohibits abuse, and fights discrimination based on, among other things, a person's mental health.

Consider, too, that while the U.S. Congress legislates on behalf of these protections, sometimes litigation must occur to see them realized. For example, in Olmstead v. L.C. (1999), the U.S. Supreme Court ruled that unjustified segregation of persons with mental disabilities constitutes unlawful discrimination as defined by ADA. The Rehabilitation Act and ADA protections also extend to prison inmates, including those with physical and mental disorders. By ruling unanimously in favor of Tony Goodman's claim of discrimination in *United States v. Georgia*, the Court also validated Congress's role in mandating services for disabled state prison inmates under Title II of the ADA.

Third, the federal government is also a major contributor to the funding of mental healthcare services, largely through Medicare and the Veterans Administration (VA), the latter being a topic to which we return in Chapter 12. Under current laws, the federal government matches state Medicaid and CHIP (Children's Health Insurance Program) spending; the amount varies from 50 percent to 70 percent, depending on state law. The **Community Mental Health Services Block Grant (MHBG)** program provides funds to all 50 states, the District of Columbia, Puerto Rico, the U.S. Virgin Islands, and six Pacific Ocean jurisdictions, enhancing their provision of community mental health services. The MHBG program specifically targets adults with serious mental illnesses and children with serious emotional disturbances by assisting the states and other U.S. geopolitical entities in building out their services to this client base. Medicaid is the largest single provider of funds for mental healthcare services in the United States. Jail and prison offenders can qualify for funds from Medicaid, Medicare, and the VA, although this statement is tempered by the willingness of states to match funds in the case of Medicaid.

Finally, research into the cause and treatment of mental diseases and disorders, as well as information dissemination, is the fourth area of federal engagement. For example, the National Institutes of Health operates the **National Institute of Mental Health (NIMH)** as one of its 27 institutes and centers. NIMH has four goals: (1) define the mechanisms of complex behavior, including mental disorders; (2) chart mental illness trajectories to determine when, where, and how to intervene; (3) strive for prevention and cure; and (4) strengthen the public health impact of NIMH-supported research (NIMH, n.d.). Congress created the Substance Abuse and Mental Health Services Administration (SAMHSA) in 1992 with the express purpose of making substance use and mental disorder information, service, and research more accessible. SAMHSA is an agency within the U.S. Department of Health and Human Services, which also plays a critical role in monitoring healthcare services.

State Actions. The states play similar roles in state-level regulations, legal protections, services funding, and research into causes and treatments. A review of state-level activities in these four areas yields two generalizations. First, the range and scope of services they can provide or research projects in which they can engage are limited by their far smaller state budgets. Second, given their size relative to the federal government, states can often field different and more creative responses to mental health and drug treatment modalities far faster than is the case for the federal government.

Consider the following observations about the state role in mental healthcare:

- State agencies created to deal with the mentally ill, like their federal counterparts, must abide by all relevant state and federal laws. The case of *United States v. Georgia* (2006) stands as a cautionary example to those state governments that would ignore federal requirements.
- Personnel at state-funded universities and colleges often participate in mental health research. However, as revealed in *Wyatt v. Stickney* (1971), sometimes those same resources can also be used to challenge questionable mental healthcare practices. In this case, the faculty at the University of Alabama sued Alabama for failing to provide adequate services for mentally ill persons institutionalized in a state-run facility.

▶ Even though states receive funding for mental healthcare services through Medicaid and the MHBG program, each one is free to design its own mental healthcare system. However, the states must follow federal funding guidelines, federal law, and appellate court decisions impacting the mentally ill, including prison inmates.

The flexibility and creativity used by some states to provide mental healthcare services can lead to innovative delivery systems that may be adopted by other states or the federal government.

Providing Mental Healthcare

The provision of mental health services across the nation is a patchwork of public and private agencies. Distinctions between for-profit and not-for profit entities add a second layer to our look at mental healthcare. Public-service facilities fall into the not-for-profit category. Private services, however, can be either for-profit or non-profit entities. The primary distinction is ownership: Public facilities are operated by the federal, state, or local governments, while private facilities are essentially owned and operated by an individual, a group of individuals, or an incorporated entity. These distinctions hold true whether we are talking about psychiatric hospitals, clinics, or outpatient services.

The Substance Abuse and Mental Health Services Administration regularly surveys all U.S. mental health facilities. The 2016 SAMHSA survey (2017) provides a comprehensive look at the nation's mental health services. What follows is a review of three aspects of this survey: (1) forms of public services, (2) forms of private services, and (3) the number of clients served by both sets of services.

Public Services. In 2016, 2,295 public agencies or departments served the nation's mentally ill residents. State mental health agencies (SMHA) supervised four-fifths of 465 departments, operating them as community mental health programs, outpatient mental health facilities, and psychiatric hospitals; the remainder were residential treatment programs for adults or some other designation. Other departments of state government managed another 465 facilities, mainly as outpatient mental health, or community mental health facilities; psychiatric hospitals, adult residential treatment centers, or some similar designation accounted for the remaining one-third. Regional or district authorities operated 875 facilities, four-fifths of which were either outpatient mental health or community mental health centers, the rest being mainly general hospitals. The VA operated 460 facilities. VA medical centers accounted for 9 in 10 VA-operated facilities for the mentally ill, most of the rest being community mental health centers; however, the VA also operated two psychiatric hospitals and six general hospitals. In sum, the public services model, apart from the VA, provided mental healthcare services primarily through non-residential community-based centers.

Private Services. Private non-profits operated 7,709 mental health facilities in 2016. Two-thirds of these operations were outpatient mental health facilities or community mental health centers; most of the rest were general hospitals, residential treatment centers for adults, and residential treatment centers for children. Barely one in 20 were multi-setting health centers, such as non-hospital residential plus outpatient or day treatment or partial hospitalization, and psychiatric hospitals. Five states had more than 300 such private non-profit institutions, including California, Florida, New York, Ohio, and Pennsylvania. At the other extreme, 20 or fewer private non-profits operated in six states, including Delaware, Hawaii, Idaho, Nevada, North Dakota, and South Carolina.

Private for-profit entities ran 2,168 facilities across the nation. The most common form—accounting for half of the operations—was an outpatient mental health provider or a community health center. The rest were residential facilities, including psychiatric hospitals, general hospitals, residential treatment centers for adults or children, and partial hospitalization or day treatment facilities. Six states had more than 100 such for-profit institutions, including Arizona, California, Florida, Idaho, North Carolina, and Wisconsin; collectively, they accounted for over one-third of all for-profit mental health facilities.

Clients Served. The SAMHSA survey provides a snapshot of where mental patients received treatment. On April 29, 2016, the nation's 12,172 mental health facilities served over 4.3 million clients, including inpatients, residential patients, and outpatients. Public sector psychiatric hospitals accommodated nearly 70,000 patients, while private sectors ones added another 121,000; however, general hospitals were nearly as busy as both types of psychiatric hospitals, treating over 187,000 mental patients. All other types of residential treatment centers housed another 132,000 adults and children. Veterans facilities added 400,000 patients, just under 10 percent of all such patients in the survey. By far the largest number of mentally ill persons—over 3.2 million people—received treatment in either community mental health centers or outpatient mental health facilities. The rest, some 170,00 individuals, were patients in either partial hospitalization/day treatment facilities or multi-setting mental health facilities.

America's mental healthcare system consists mainly of community-based services, where most of its clients receive services. That client base is huge, numbering in the millions. As importantly, facilities used to confine even temporarily those persons whose behavior is a threat to themselves or others are becoming increasingly scarce. Long-term residential facilities for the mentally ill are even harder to find. Nationwide, mental healthcare expenditures are a fraction of those allocated to general health issues. Keep these generalizations in mind as we explore the next major topic, the criminal justice system.

AMERICAN CRIMINAL JUSTICE SYSTEM

To understand better the intersection of mental health and criminal justice on the mentally ill, we provide an overview of the key elements of the American system of justice: criminal laws, law enforcement, courts, and corrections. In this review, we locate several key points where mental health can impact justice system processing.

Criminal Laws

American criminal laws share at least two legal elements. First, the **Equal Protection Clause** of the 14th Amendment to the U.S. Constitution guarantees that everyone be treated the same. Given that standard, laws written to prohibit, restrict, direct, or punish conduct must be clear and inform the alleged offender. Second, every state law must give due process notice that a specific prohibited action or behavior is a violation of the law. Moreover, state and federal **statutes** must specify the punishments associated with a conviction for each crime.

We find three basic types of criminal laws in force today. At the lowest level of importance are "laws" enacted by local communities, called **ordinances**, that spell out the standard of care people must exercise in their interactions with others. Many ordinances are the same throughout the country. Regardless of whether one lives in Los Angeles, California, or Atlanta, Georgia, all licensed vehicles must have the same type of car headlights and taillights when driving on public roads. Some ordinances, such as those spelling out the appropriate use of public parks, are unique to communities that use such laws to control the homeless.

Moving up in importance, we encounter laws intended to define and punish offenses called misdemeanors. **Misdemeanors** are crimes of low seriousness and are accorded a monetary fine up to a fixed amount, perhaps as much as $5,000, or no more than a year of imprisonment in jail, or both. Such acts have different classifications (Class A, B, C, or D; Class 1, 2, 3, or 4), depending on how threatening they are to the peace and tranquility of the community. A Class A (or Class 1) misdemeanor has been deemed the most threatening of the "minor offenses" covered under most state and federal misdemeanor statutes, including, for example, assault resulting in bodily harm or possession of a controlled substance. A Class D (or Class 4) misdemeanor is viewed as the least serious of the minor offenses. Examples of the latter include the theft of an item of little value. Imprisonment is rarely used for the lower two forms of misdemeanors (Class C or Class D), while the fines associated with each class increase significantly as one goes from Class D to Class A.

A **felony** is the most serious form of crime. Here, too, there is considerable variation. A system like that used for misdemeanors ranks the seriousness of felonies. A Class A/Class 1 felony is the most heinous form of crime circumscribed by the law. In a worst-case scenario, offenders found guilty of a Class A felony such as first-degree murder are sentenced to death or life in prison without the possibility of release from prison. A large monetary fine, perhaps a $100,000 or more, may be tied to a conviction for this class of felony. At the other extreme, a person convicted of a Class D/Class 4 felony such as battery, theft of property worth $1,000 or more, or stalking may result in a prison sentence of as little as three years and a $10,000 fine.

System Components

The term jurisdiction underlies any review of the various component parts of the nation's criminal justice system. **Jurisdiction** means the power to make legal decisions and judgments about the administration of justice in a geographical area. In practice, juris-diction is a complex issue. The federal government has jurisdiction over a rather limited range of crimes. Most crimes are the domain of state and local governments. Thus, one of the most seminal questions to be asked in a criminal matter is, who has jurisdiction? Jurisdiction determines which law enforcement agency investigates the offense, which public prosecutor's office takes charge of the prosecution, which court hears the case, and which correctional component takes control of the defendant in the event of a conviction.

Law Enforcement. Law enforcement refers to government-authorized social control agents. The stated goals of most law enforcement agencies include, but are not limited to, the following (Grant and Terry, 2008: 136):

- ▸ The prevention of crime
- ▸ The protection of life
- ▸ The upholding and enforcement of laws
- ▸ The combating of public fear of crime
- ▸ The promotion of community safety
- ▸ The control of motorized and other traffic
- ▸ The encouragement of respect for the law
- ▸ And the protection of civil rights and liberties of individuals

These goals are common to **general service law enforcement agencies**, a term which encompasses nearly all local law enforcement (Walker and Katz, 2007: 3).

There are nearly 18,000 state, county, and local law enforcement agencies in the United States (Reaves, 2011: 2). They employ over one million individuals, of which roughly 75 percent are sworn full-time employees (Reaves 2011: 2). Most sworn officers work for local police, followed by sheriff's offices and state police. Most general service law enforce-ment agencies at the local level are small, employing fewer than 25 officers. Mega-agencies, those employing more than 1,000 officers, number fewer than 50 across the nation, or 0.4 percent of all such agencies, but employ one in five sworn officers.

The federal government's law enforcement agencies have national reach, but are far smaller in size and deal with a far more restricted range of legal matters than is the case for either state or local policing agencies. Most but not all federal law enforcement agencies are organized under two federal bureaucracies: the U.S. Department of Justice and the U.S. Department of Homeland Security (Winfree, Mays, and Alarid, 2017: 115-25). The Justice Department essentially supervises the Federal Bureau of Investigation, the Drug Enforcement Administration, the U.S. Marshals Service, and the Bureau of Alcohol, Tobacco, Firearms and Explosives; it employs around 23,000 full-time law enforcement personnel. Homeland Security consists of U.S. Customs and Border Protection, U.S. Coast Guard, U.S. Immigration and Customs Enforcement, and the Secret Service. Homeland Security employs around 50,000 full-time law enforcement officers.

Courts. A court is a tribunal presided over by a judge or several judges; we some-times use the term judiciary to refer to such tribunals. Any discussion of the judiciary must address the question of jurisdiction. We may describe court structure as a pyramid with courts of limited jurisdiction at its base. Judges at this level, federal or local, are commonly called magistrates, while others serve as municipal court judges. **Courts of limited jurisdiction** hear charges that include but are not limited to most driving offenses, minor thefts, domestic violence altercations if there is no or little physical harm, and cases of public intoxication, public urination, trespass, and littering. The maximum punishment in these courts is typically a fine or no more than one year in the local jail. However, local and federal magistrates also conduct preliminary hearings for more serious crimes. These courts frequently hear cases involving mentally ill persons who, while not harmful or dangerous, may constitute a public nuisance.

Courts of general jurisdiction constitute the next higher layer of criminal courts. States have different names for these courts: Superior Court, District Court, County Court, Commonwealth Court, or Supreme Court. For example, in New York state, the Supreme Court is a court of general jurisdiction, while the state's highest court is the Court of Appeals. The judges assigned to courts of general jurisdiction hear felony charges, including but not limited to murder, rape, armed robbery, and possession of large quantities of illegal drugs. Trials at this level can be either bench trials (i.e., judge only trials) or jury trials (i.e. trials by one's peers). In most cases, the trial court judge imposes the sentence. These courts also hear cases on appeal from courts of limited jurisdiction; however, the cases are heard in their entirety, as a *trial de novo*.

If a person is found guilty, but subsequently argues that (1) the trial judge made mistakes in accepting certain types of evidence, (2) the defendant was mentally incompetent despite a judge's findings, or (3) the defense attorney was not competent, then the defendant may request a hearing on the verdict at the **appellate court** level. In a typical intermediate appellate court review, one operating between the court of general jurisdiction and the highest court, three judges hear arguments presented by specially trained appellate attorneys. Appellate courts do not accept testimony, but only listen to and review legal arguments to decide if the lower court correctly applied the state law to the facts. If the case was heard in federal court, the U.S. Court of Appeals for the appropriate Federal Circuit will hear the arguments. The United States is divided into 12 such regional circuits. For example, the Ninth Circuit reviews cases for Arizona, California, Oregon, Idaho, Montana, Alaska, and Hawaii.

All states and the United States have a final court of review, commonly known as the **supreme court**, established to review appellate court decisions. Supreme court judges decide whether to accept jurisdiction regarding the review of a verdict; they must determine if the alleged violation meets constitutional standards. If there is a legal conflict between states, then the case is appealed from state or federal courts to the U.S. Supreme Court.

Corrections. Any review of the correctional process must consider (1) where the services are rendered and (2) who has jurisdiction. The first criterion reflects the differences between institutional corrections, generically called prisons and jails, and community-based corrections, the most common varieties being probation and parole. The second criterion is tied to previous distinctions between state or local jurisdictions and federal jurisdictions. We include an appreciation for both sets of criteria in this brief overview of corrections.

The first kind of institutional corrections facility is the **local jail**, which operates at the city or county level and commonly serves as both pre- and post-conviction detention facilities. The nation's nearly 3,300 local jails hold almost three-quarters of a million inmates on any given day (Minton and Zeng, 2016: 1). If the legal issue involves federal jurisdiction, then the accused person may find him- or herself housed in a local jail or a U.S. Bureau of Prisons facility. These latter facilities also house persons subject to confinement for post-conviction appeals or punishment for federal misdemeanors. Jails generally have few resources designed to aid mentally ill detainees, a topic to which we return in Chapter 9.

If a person pleads to or is convicted of a misdemeanor with a sentence of one year or less, then he or she is typically sent to a local jail, the same place where those accused of crimes but not convicted are housed. [NOTE: The maximum length of misdemeanor sentences can vary from state to state, with some expressing it as less than a year.] About 40 percent of a jail's inmates on a given day are serving a sentence, while most of the rest are awaiting trial, sentencing, or an appeal (Minton and Zeng, 2016). If a person pleads guilty to or is found guilty of a felony and sentenced to a year or more, then the defendant is transferred to prison.

There are exceptions to this last statement. First, federal misdemeanants may serve their sentences in a federal Metropolitan Detention Center or Metropolitan Correctional Center. For example, Metropolitan Correctional Center, Chicago holds male and female prisoners at all security levels prior to and during court proceedings for the Northern District of Illinois; it also houses inmates serving misdemeanor or other brief sentences. Second, a few states, owing to prison crowding, place limits on the absolute number of prison inmates by policy, practice, or court order. In these states, including California and Texas, low-threat offenders may be jailed under a contract between the sentencing authority and the public or private entity operating the facility (Couzens and Bigelow, 2017; Vander Werff, 2016). Third, some states provide for jail sentences of more than one year for certain misdemeanors. For example, in Massachusetts certain misdemeanor sex offenses can result in a jail sentence of two and a half years (Massachusetts Sentencing Commission, 2015).

Prisons constitute the second form of institutional corrections. Every state operates at least one prison and large states have a dozen or more, although the actual names used to describe them vary to include penitentiaries and correctional institution. Consequently, there are over 1,700 state prisons and more than 100 federal facilities spread across the United States and its territories (Stephan, 2008). On a given day, the nation's prisons house more than 1.5 million inmates (Carson and Anderson, 2016: 1).

There are two primary forms of community-based corrections. Both forms employ **conditional release**, which in this case simply means that the convicted offender is at liberty, meaning free to reside in the community, so long as he or she follows a set of general instructions or conditions. **General conditions** of release usually require that releasees avoid certain kinds of people or places and engage in lawful conduct. Additional instructions, called **special conditions**, may include abstaining from alcohol, attending certain kinds of treatment or therapy, and making restitution (i.e., repayment) for harms committed during the commission of the offense of which the releasees were convicted.

The first form of community-based programming serves those individuals convicted of a felony and sent to prison. Most prison inmates are released back into the community under the conditions of **parole**. Some inmates serve the entire sentence, but this is a rarity. When paroled, inmates may be reintegrated at a residential facility called a halfway house, including ones operated by the states and federal government, or released directly into the community. In either case, they become part of a parole officer's caseload. Parolees must also follow all general and special conditions of release. Should a parolee be found in violation of one or more of these conditions, and it is a serious violation, he or she could be returned to prison to serve out the remainder of the original sentence, plus any additional sentence (e.g., a new felony conviction). Parole is a function of the executive branch of government, be it the office of the state governor or the President of the United States.

Some convicted felons are sentenced to **probation**, which functions as the second and largest form of community-based corrections. In most jurisdictions, the sentencing court maintains jurisdiction over its probationers. Probationers are, like parolees, subject to community supervision, this time by a probation officer, although 34 states use a combined probation/parole officer (Mays and Winfree, 2014: 80). At the federal level, the U.S. Probation and Pretrial Services (USPPS) provides supervision for its probationers, along with those federal prisoners who are released prior to the completion of their entire sentences, as the federal government abandoned parole in the early 1990s. USPPS also supervises federal defendants released prior to trial. Finally, the release conditions for probationers are nearly identical to those imposed on parolees. Probationers found in violation of their release conditions may be brought before a judge and the original prison sentence reinstated, resulting in removal to a state facility or, in the case of federal releasees, a federal one.

The number of persons on parole and probation is staggering. In 2015, there were an estimated 4.65 million probationers, parolees, and others on some form of post-prison supervision. This figure represents about one in every 53 adult citizens of the United States (Bureau of Justice Statistics, 2016).

Criminal law, police, courts, and corrections form the American criminal justice system. These component parts are intended to work together, forming a process through which defendants, victims, and witnesses to crimes must navigate in search of justice (see Box 1.2).

CRIMINAL JUSTICE MEETS MENTAL HEALTH

When members of the public discuss mentally ill offenders, we suspect that there is a tendency to focus on notorious offenders, including serial murderers, sexual predators, or child molesters. We further suspect that few people would be bothered by the prospect of sending psychologically damaged criminals like David Berkowitz ("The Son of Sam"),

BOX 1.2

Thinking About the Issues

Given the review of the criminal justice system as a frame of reference, how would you answer each of the following questions?

1. Complete this statement and offer your rationale for what you claim: The biggest concern that could emerge when one of the criminal justice system's component parts confronts a mentally challenged person is _____.

2. At what point in the criminal justice process, from initial contact with a mentally challenged person to that person's sentencing, do you think system personnel would best benefit from a book such as this one? Why do you feel this way?

Charles Manson (murder-cult guru), or Brian Mitchell (the rapist and the child abductor of Elizabeth Smart) to prison for very long sentences or possibly even executing them. Rarely do such discussions involve the intertwining of mental health disorders and everyday misdemeanor offenses, such as trespass, loitering, petty theft, or public intoxication.

In practice, however, the latter type of mentally ill criminal suspects far outnumbers the former, and several stages in the criminal justice system process may severely disadvantage them. First, the crimes of the mentally ill often include substance abuse–related offenses, loitering, trespassing, and other non-violent minor offenses, which, as Class A or B misdemeanors, are subject to jail time. Second, once individuals are arrested, the mentally ill are often sent to jail rather than diverted to treatment. A report by the Treatment Advocacy Center captures the significance of this practice:

> One of the sad things is you'll see people who commit a minor offense, say trespassing. They're in jail but not stable enough to arraign [be advised of the court proceedings]. So, you're holding them until they're sane enough to enter a plea. And if they don't get treatment, they can't get sane enough to enter a plea (Torrey et al., 2010: 8).

The deinstitutionalization of the mentally ill, which began in the 1960s, essentially emptied the nation's mental hospitals in a decade or less, freeing them from the prolonged confinement in mental asylums (Pollack, 2013). Society then redirected them, like people in revolving doors, to be spun into jails or prisons and back on the streets (Baillargeon, Binswanger, et al., 2009). The depredations suffered by individuals enmeshed in this overlap of criminal justice and mental health is due to the former's propensity to impose criminal consequences for nearly all legal transgressions. A second factor is tied to the decision about what is criminal conduct versus behavior linked to mental illness. Such decision making is commonly within the discretion of the law enforcement officer, community worker, or other community-based social worker who first encounters the mentally ill person. To place this problem in its proper perspective, we suggest that you revisit the analogy offered in the book's Preface prior to exploring the rest of the chapter.

Mentally Ill Offenders: Preliminary Concerns

The decision to arrest and incarcerate a person may also depend on whether the conduct occurs in a small town or a metropolitan center. If a man is yelling and cursing on a corner in New York City (population 8.4 million), it is likely that pedestrians and police officers alike will simply skirt him and walk on; almost assuredly this will be the response if he does not seem a danger to himself or others, but is simply a nuisance. If the same thing happened in a town of 1,500 residents, the "offender" may get locked up, especially if he is a stranger to the village's only part-time police officer. Despite his obvious mental illness, the arrest may be deemed necessary to maintain the peace of the small community, but it would not enough to warrant the paperwork in a big (and criminally active) city. We suggest that neither totally ignoring a mentally ill individual, nor locking that person up is an appropriate response to his illness.

Moving a suspect through the criminal justice system may appear straightforward (Figure 1.2), although it is often a question of lurching forward awkwardly one step at a time, while time in between the steps seems to stand still. In the case of mentally ill persons, the concern is that their problems may not be noticed or addressed early enough in the process.

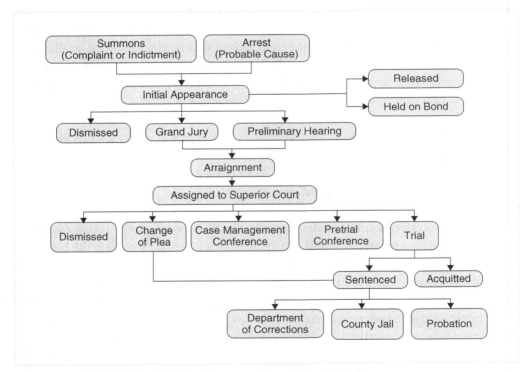

FIGURE 1.2 **The Criminal Justice Process: From Entry to Exit**

As this book explores in detail, law enforcement officers, emergency medical and fire-fighting personnel, social workers, and public health workers, among others, should possess an operational contingency plan that enables an encounter to remain lawful and safe for all parties, regardless of any mental issues afflicting the alleged offender. While the same Rule of Law and due process rules apply to all criminal investigations (see Box 1.1), if the person detained or questioned is impaired by illness, medications, or illegal drugs, then additional legal protections may be required. Even the questioning of witnesses or victims who show indicators of mental illness or impairment may require a heightened level of officer sensitivity to ensure their statements and observations are given respect and value.

We turn next to the basic criminal procedures that confront the accused person, perhaps suffering from a mental disease or defect, between arrest and prior to trial. Before moving to this section, however, consider the legal elements found in a "typical" police-citizen encounter, as summarized in Box 1.3. These complex procedures can challenge anyone subject to them, let alone a mentally ill defendant.

From Arrest to Initial Court Appearance

We turn next to a review of the criminal procedures that can occur between arrest and initial court appearance (see Figure 1.1). If they have a clear understanding of what is permissible in such situations, law enforcement officers, and any accompanying

BOX 1.3

Law and Mental Health: Legal Elements of a "Typical" Police-Citizen Encounter

Understanding the escalation of legalities that occurs during the first encounter between a criminal suspect and law enforcement can be challenging. For example, a threshold of lawful contact applies whether asking about the welfare of a child or the reasons for a street beggar being at a specific location. Retrospective reflection as to what should have occurred versus what did occur is the mainstay of judicial review.

As we explore the criminal justice system's complexities, you may feel that the requirements for compliance with legal procedures, due process, and local laws seem to defy common sense, logic, or fairness. Every person is presumed innocent until proven guilty or pleads guilty, called the **presumption of innocence**. This caveat should be the guiding consideration for every first encounter. The U.S. Supreme Court, in *Terry v. Ohio*, acknowledged that law enforcers, as well as anyone acting under the **color of law**, including social workers and mental health workers, must occasionally approach and question individuals if there is a reasonable basis to do so. A missing taillight or a broken windshield can reasonably trigger a lawful inquiry. However, a patrolman cannot stop a vehicle because the car is blue or the driver is unknown to the officer. To place these ideas in their proper context, we suggest you consider the chapter's prologue, which represented a police officer's lawful actions in response to a situation with an apparently disoriented citizen, alone and vulnerable.

Other appellate cases are important to initial police-citizen contacts, including *Rodriguez v. United States*, which prohibits prolonged detentions while conducting a dog-search for drugs in a vehicle; *Arizona v. Johnson*, which provides stop and frisk is lawful if the officer has reason to believe the suspect has a weapon; and *Utah v. Streif*, in which a prolonged detention is permissible when the suspect is reported to have an outstanding arrest warrant. By **settled law** and practice, there must be **articulated circumstances** to justify the detention of any person.

If the encounter has a reasonable, fair, or rational basis, then matters can escalate if the law enforcement officer has probable cause to arrest. Probable cause to arrest, no matter the charge, is based on the **totality of the circumstances**, which means the officer has reason to believe a crime was committed and the arrestee likely committed that crime. The arrest itself is not evidence that the person committed a crime, only that there were facts and factors supporting the officer's actions. Such necessary factors can include eyewitness observations and interviews, physical evidence such as fingerprints and deoxynucleic acid (DNA) tests, statements by the accused that indicate knowledge of the crime, or other documented events leading up to the crime. Again, even if a person is arrested, no matter the perceived or documented mental state, the presumption of innocence remains in force.

Sources: Arizona v. Johnson (2009); *Rodriguez v. United States* (2015); *Utah v. Streif* (2016); *Terry v. Ohio* (1968).

---

social workers or mental health workers, can adjust their responses in the event there are indicators of mental illness. This section is not a complete review of all criminal procedures employed in police-citizen encounters; rather, the ones included represent a sampling of such procedures that should communicate a sense of their complex nature.

Book and Release. **Book and release** is the process by which a defendant is detained, arrested on probable cause, and cited for a criminal offense, but subsequently released back into the community. The accused may be taken to jail and photographed and fingerprinted. The suspect is typically not detained in jail if the offense is non-violent, the accused is a first-time offender, the offense is an ordinance violation or a minor misdemeanor, or the accused has a mental illness and can be released to a family member or guardian. Instead, he or she is given a date and time to appear in court. Should the accused not appear in court, an arrest warrant generally is issued. This process can become even more complicated should the accused suffer from mental disabilities, as keeping track of court dates and related events, such as meeting with one's defense counsel, can prove challenging.

Book and Detain. In **book and detain**, the officer has reasonable suspicion to detain and probable cause to arrest the accused for a criminal offense. The offense may have occurred in the arresting officer's presence or probable cause may be based on an extensive criminal investigation. A magistrate could approve an arrest warrant. The accused is subsequently arrested and advised of the nature of the criminal charges. If law enforcement or prosecutorial investigators wish to question the accused about a possible crime, then a *Miranda* **warning** against self-incrimination must be administered. The accused is taken to jail and processed into the facility, and photographed and fingerprinted. Bond (see Release from Custodial Detention below) is set with a pre-approved schedule that relates to the most serious offense charged and is usually reviewed within 48 hours by a magistrate judge.

Custodial Arraignment. Sometimes defendants are not released from custody. If that is the case, they must be brought before a judge within a specified time, again usually within 48 hours. Some inmates have physical or mental health issues that make transfer to court a difficult proposition. In such cases, they may be taken to a special room at the jail and the proceedings video-transmitted to the courthouse. Under the terms of a **custodial arraignment**, a judge advises the accused concerning constitutional rights. It is not uncommon during this proceeding for mental health issues to emerge. At this arraignment, the court may appoint an attorney to represent the defendant if he or she does not have private counsel.

Release from Custodial Detention. One way for a defendant to leave custodial detention is through bail. Bail is a guarantee, given as a pledge, that the accused will appear in court at all proceedings, as well as a means to ensure the community's public safety (Sheppard, 2012). **Bail** cannot be set to punish the accused nor can it presume guilt. There is no constitutional right to bail, although the Eighth Amendment to the U.S. Constitution prohibits "excessive bail." Some crimes are considered so heinous or threatening to public safety that no bail amount is set or an amount is set at a level believed beyond the accused's ability to pay. Detainees at a high flight risk may also be denied bail. In most states, judges periodically review bond settings and conditions. Bail, usually through a monetary pledge called a **bond**, is posted with the court and the accused exits jail.

The defendant may be a first-time offender or have no record of failing to appear for court appearance, and the accusation may not be a violent crime. In these situations, the defendant may be released on a "promise to appear," or **release on recognizance (ROR)** or **own recognizance (OR)**. Failure to appear at the appointed time, however, will generally result in the issuance of an arrest warrant; subsequent extensions of ROR are unlikely.

No matter the specific release mechanism, the accused generally has behavioral restrictions imposed as a condition of release, like those levied on probationers and parolees. These conditions generally include remaining law abiding, not contacting any witnesses or victims involved in the criminal accusation, and remaining employed or in school. If the accused violates any condition of release, the bond can be revoked, at which time the defendant may be ordered to remain in custody until the criminal case is concluded.

Mentally ill offenders may be kept in jail if there are drug dependency issues; they may need time to detoxify or to get their medications stabilized prior to release. Moreover, even a minimal amount of bond may pose an insurmountable barrier for many mentally ill defendants, particularly those who are homeless and street-bound.

Non-Custodial Arraignment. In a non-custodial arraignment, the accused is either summoned to court or receives a Notice to Appear (NTA) through a mailed or hand-delivered summons, citation, or criminal complaint. The person receiving an NTA is presumed to be trustworthy and typically no bond is required. He or she receives the same information that is given to all accused persons about the right to an attorney, the right to trial, and the right to remain silent throughout the proceedings. The defendant receives prior notice of all proceedings and is given a specific court date.

Grand Jury Deliberations or Preliminary Hearing. Under the Fifth Amendment to the U.S. Constitution, all criminal accusations or complaints must be screened to confirm that the law enforcement agency has passed a threshold of probability. In states where it is used, a **grand jury** will consider evidence presented by the prosecution. The grand jury may issue a **true bill**, which confirms the prosecutorial decision, and send an **indictment** to the trial court, which is like an arrest warrant.

An equivalent procedure is known as a **preliminary hearing** or **probable cause hearing**. In this case, threshold information is presented to a magistrate who decides if the prosecution has met the baseline of proof of probable cause for the arrest of the defendant. In both instances, the judge or grand jury members hear sworn testimony by the investigating officer that formed the basis of the opinion. In the preliminary hearing, however, the defendant and his or her attorney is present and the witnesses may be cross examined by counsel.

Post-Arraignment Modifications. After the preliminary hearing and arraignment, the defendant is once again advised of his or her constitutional rights by the court of general jurisdiction. The presiding judge may take a "second look" at the conditions of bail and either reduce the bond or modify bond conditions.

This section has followed the accused from arrest to preliminary court appearances. We have noted several junctures in this process where concerns for the accused's mental state can play a role in determining the quality of justice received. Decisions made at any of these junctures can shape what follows for any defendant. As the epilogue suggests, the mentally ill may be at high risk of falling through the cracks in the criminal justice process.

EPILOGUE

What follows is the case of the United States v. John Doe. It is a composite of several cases involving mentally challenged defendants. Some parts of the case have been fictionalized, all with the intent of protecting the identities of the parties concerned.

John Doe's mom was drunk when she arrived at the hospital in the final stages of labor. Her blood alcohol was .21, almost three times the legal limit for DWI. Her car was later found embedded in the hospital's parking lot fence, but no one could prove she drove the car, so she was not charged with DUI. Shortly after delivering her baby, she left "to party a little more," abandoning her newborn. Parental rights were terminated immediately, and John was adopted by Sarah and Sam.

The medical records indicated that John had all the symptoms and behaviors associated with fetal alcohol spectrum disorders: At birth, he had small eye openings, a smooth philtrum (the area between the nose and mouth), a thin upper lip, and a small head. As he developed, he demonstrated poor coordination, short height, low intelligence, and neurodevelopmental disorders. Sarah and Sam knew their baby had special needs when they added him to their growing family of five children; they gave him unconditional love and stability.

As John grew up, Sarah and Sam enrolled him in special education programs, academic stimulation, and numerous training programs. Life, however, presented John with many challenges beyond those associated with his disabilities. When he was 16 years old, John was arrested for possession of a loaded weapon, after friends convinced him to hold it while they robbed a convenience store. He was sent to a juvenile detention facility for two years, where he was abused by the staff and his fellow inmates.

At 19, John was arrested as a "meth courier" for a mid-level supplier he met at the juvenile detention center. This time he was sentenced as an adult to state prison. During intake, prison staff determined that John could benefit from training to work as a support person in healthcare, food service, or construction industries. He chose food services.

The pattern of abuse that began in the juvenile detention center continued in the state prison. While John did not complain about the beatings and sexual assaults, he spent considerable time in the prison's infirmary, recovering from injuries. John's good behavior earned him an early release.

On his 25th birthday, John received the maximum 10-year prison sentence for attempting to drive a car containing 75 pounds of heroin through a U.S. Border Patrol checkpoint. As the specific felony charge was drug trafficking/distribution (21 U.S.C. Chapter 13, §843), John was arraigned before a Federal Magistrate and tried in the U.S. District Court, District of Arizona—Tucson. At trial, John, who claimed the car belong to a friend named Adam, also stated that he did not know Adam's last name. John further claimed that he did not know there were bad things hidden behind the car's door panels. Adam told John that the car contained prescription drugs that were cheaper in Mexico, and they would be given away free to poor people in Tucson.

The Presentencing Report (PSR) noted some but not all of John's mental challenges; moreover, there were no official statements of the abuse he had suffered during previous state-level incarcerations attached to the PSR. The U.S. Pretrial Services officer responsible for John's PSR, which was one of several dozen due that same day, indicated the defendant did not appear to be a suitable candidate for probation or any other available diversion programs. She recommended a ten-year prison sentence for John. At sentencing, the federal District Court judge, following the PSR recommendations, noted John's previous state-level conviction for a drug charge and his apparent inability to avoid crimes of this nature as contributing factors.

John was transferred to the control of the U.S. Bureau of Prisons (BOP). Due to the severity of John's developmental issues, the intake team that processed him into the medium-security facility determined that he was not eligible for, nor would he benefit from, any of the available programs. Given his work and training experiences, John was assigned to work in the food service division at the Federal Correctional Institution, Tucson.

During an incident in the dining hall, John suffered a traumatic brain injury. The BOP transferred him to the Federal Medical Facility, Rochester, Minnesota. While he received treatment at the facility, it is doubtful that he will ever be returned to any BOP facility's general population.

As John worked his way through the justice system, from arrest to incarceration, many people made decisions about what would happen to him. As we ask in Box 1.4, what would you have done differently?

BOX 1.4

What Would You Do?

There were other options available to the state and federal courts that heard John's cases. Consider that the U.S. Bureau of Prisons has pegged the annual cost of incarcerating a medium-security prisoner at $28,364, while the annual cost for the Federal Medical Facility is $60,667. California puts the average annual cost of incarcerating an inmate in its prison system at $71,000. In Utah, the cost of a six-person residential group home is approximately $80,000 per year for 24-hour staffing, rent, food, and utilities, which breaks down to less than $15,000 per year per client. While current costs of each alternative in every state may not be identical to these figures, it is highly likely that the differentials among these four options have not changed.

Decisions were made in John Doe's case that resulted in a series of negative outcomes. Identify these decisions and decision makers. What would you have done differently had you been involved at any level in John's case? Would a residential group home have been the best alternative for John? Suppose John's crime had taken place in your home town, and it was a state and not a federal offense. What would you have liked to see happen and why?

Sources: Bureau of Prisons (2017); Jardine (2011); Legislative Analyst's Office (2017).

SUMMARY

- Separating criminal law violations from displays of mental illness can represent a challenge for first responders at all levels, from police to community mental health professionals to the average citizen.
- The criminal justice and the mental healthcare systems are intertwined with the overarching purpose of guaranteeing due process and equal protection to all people facing criminal charges, regardless of their mental health.
- The American healthcare system is a massive, decentralized trillion-dollar business, while mental healthcare is a far smaller subsystem in which the nation invests far less resources.
- The movement away from large institutional responses to mental illness in the 1960s meant that hundreds of thousands of mentally ill persons moved onto the nation's streets, which was followed by a massive decline in available bedspaces for temporary or long-term confinement of the mentally ill and a similar decline in the number of associated mental healthcare professionals.
- The federal government's role in mental healthcare is largely found in four areas: regulations, legal protections, services funding, and research into causes and treatments.
- An analysis of state mental health services across these same four areas reveals two generalizations: states have fewer resources to allocate to regulations, legal protections, services funding, and research into causes and treatments, but, given their smaller size, they can often respond and change more quickly than the federal government.
- The provision of mental health services for the millions of mentally ill persons across the nation is a patchwork of public and private agencies, and most such services are offered in the community-based facilities, rather than in an institutional or hospital setting.
- American laws must be written and be very specific in detailing what conduct is illegal or unlawful, and must also meet constitutional requirements and offer equal protection to all people affected by the law.
- The federal, state, and local governments have separate policing agencies, courts, and correctional systems, each with its own jurisdictional authority.
- Those who are arrested for criminal offenses and have mental illness are often caught in "revolving door" justice, as they move from jail to the streets and back again.
- The complexities of the pre-trial procedures often place mentally ill defendants at a severe disadvantage when it comes to participating fully in their own defense.

CHAPTER REVIEW QUESTIONS

1. Define the following terms and indicate how each is important to the interface between the administration of criminal justice and services to the mentally ill: mental healthcare system, criminal justice system, due process, and the Rule of Law.

2. What single piece of information about the issues found within the nation's general healthcare system or its mental health subsystem most concerns you and why?
3. Describe the actions of both the federal government and the states concerning the policies and laws that impact services for the mentally ill.
4. How would you characterize the services provided by the public and private sectors for the mentally ill across the nation?
5. What is the purpose of criminal laws? What does the term jurisdiction mean in their context?
6. Explain what is meant by the term law enforcement. Explain the role played by jurisdiction in the determination of who does what to whom.
7. Explain what is meant by the term judiciary. Explain the role played by jurisdiction in the determination of who does what to whom.
8. Corrections consists of institutional and community-based elements. Describe each element, including the differences encountered by variations in jurisdiction.
9. Trace the important steps/decisions between arrest and the initial court appearance of any criminal defendant, identifying, where appropriate, pitfalls for the mentally ill.
10. What do you see as the single most important "lesson" contained in *United States v. John Doe*? Explain your answer, grounding it in the information contained in this chapter. You might want to consider any issues related to jurisdictional interface as you frame your answer.

KEY TERMS

Appellate court
Articulated circumstances
Bail
Bond
Book and detain
Book and release
Color of law
Community Mental Health Services Block Grant (MHBG)
Conditional release
Courts of general jurisdiction
Courts of limited jurisdiction
Criminal justice system
Custodial arraignment
Due process
Equal Protection Clause
Felony
General conditions

General service law enforcement agencies
Grand jury
Indictment
Jurisdiction
Local jail
Magistrates
Mental health
Mental illness
Mental healthcare system
Miranda warning
Misdemeanors
Municipal court judges
National Institute of Mental Health (NIMH)
Non-custodial arraignment
Ordinances
Own recognizance (OR)
Parole
Preliminary hearing

Presumption of innocence
Probable cause hearing
Probation
Release on recognizance (ROR)
Rule of Law
Settled law

Special conditions
Statutes
Supreme Court
Totality of the circumstances
Trial *de novo*
True bill

REFERENCES

Baillargeon, J., I.A. Binswanger, J.V. Penn, B.A. Williams, and O.J. Murray (2009). "Psychiatric Disorders and Repeat Incarcerations: The Revolving Prison Door." *The American Journal of Psychiatry* 166: 103-109.

Bureau of Justice Statistics (2017). "BJS Finds Inmates Have Higher Rates of Serious Psychological Distress than the U.S. General Population." Washington, DC: U.S. Department of Justice.

Carson, E.A., and E. Anderson (2016). *Prisoners in 2015*. Washington, DC: Bureau of Justice Statistics.

Cicero (1967). *De Oratore*. Edited by H.H. Warmington. Cambridge, MA: Harvard University Press. Oxford University Press.

Couzens, J.R., and T.A. Bigelow (2017). *Felony Sentencing After Realignment*. Sacramento, CA: State of California. Retrieved at http://www.courts.ca.gov/partners/documents/felony_sentencing.pdf on 20 January 2018.

Grant, H.B., and K.J. Terry (2008). *Law Enforcement in the 21st Century*. Boston: Allyn-Bacon.

Katz, S. (2005). *Oxford International Encyclopedia of Legal History*. Oxford, UK: Oxford University Press.

Legislative Analyst's Office (March 2017). "How much does it cost to incarcerate an inmate?" *The California Legislature's Nonpartisan Fiscal and Policy Advisor*. Sacramento, CA: Legislative Analyst's Office. Retrieved at http://www.lao.ca.gov/PolicyAreas/CJ/6_cj_inmatecost on 4 February 2018.

Mark, T.L., K.R. Levit, R. Vandivort-Warren, J.A. Buck, and R.M. Coffey (2011). "Changes in US spending on mental health and substance abuse treatment, 1986-2005, and implications for policy." *Health Affairs* 30: 284-92.

Massachusetts Sentencing Commission (2015). *Felony and Misdemeanor Master Crime List*. Boston, MA: Massachusetts Sentencing Commission.

Mays, G.L., and L.T. Winfree, Jr. (2014). *Essentials of Corrections*. 5th ed. Malden, MA: Wiley Blackwell.

Mental Health America (n.d.). "Federal and state role in mental health." Alexandria, VA: Mental Health America. Retrieved at http://www.mentalhealthamerica.net/issues/federal-and-state-role-mental-health on 12 January 2018.

Minton, T.D., and Z. Zeng (2016). *Jail Inmates in 2015*. Washington, DC: Bureau of Justice Statistics.

National Alliance on Mental Health (n.d.). "Mental health conditions." Retrieved at https://www.nami.org/Learn-More/Mental-Health-Conditions on 8 February 2018.

National Institute of Mental Health (n.d.). "The National Institute of Mental Health strategic plan." Rockville, MD: NIMH. Retrieved at https://www.nimh.nih.gov/about/strategic-planning-reports/index.shtml on 12 January 2018.

Pollack, H. (July 12, 2013). "What Happened to U.S. Mental Health Care After Deinstitutionalization?" *Washington Post*. Retrieved at https://www.washingtonpost.com/news/wonk/wp/2013/06/12/what-happened-to-u-s-mental-health-care-after-deinstitutionalization/?utm_term=.ecd143bafd11 on 14 July 2017.

Reaves, B.A. (2011). "Census of state and local law enforcement agencies, 2008." Washington, DC: U.S. Bureau of Justice Statistics.

Sheppard, S.M. (2012). *Bouvier Law Dictionary*. New York: Wolters Kluwer Law & Business.

Squires, D., and C. Anderson (October 8, 2015). "U.S. Health care from a global perspective: Spending, use of services, prices, and health in 13 countries." Washington, DC: Commonwealth Fund.

Substance Abuse and Mental Health Services Administration (2017). *National Mental Health Services Survey (N-NHSS): 2016 Data on Mental Health Treatment Facilities*. Rockville, MD: Substance Abuse and Mental Health Services Administration.

Sundararaman, R. (2009). "The U.S. mental health delivery system infrastructure: A primer." Washington, DC: Congressional Research Service.

Torrey, E.F., A.D. Kennard, D. Eslinger, R. Lamb, and J. Pavle (2010). *More Mentally Ill Persons Are in Jails and Prisons than Hospitals: A Survey of the States. Treatment Advocacy Center*. Arlington, VA: Treatment Advocacy Center. Retrieved at http://www.treatmentadvocacycenter.org/storage/documents/final_jails_v_hospitals_study.pdf on 1 July 2017.

U.S. Bureau of Prisons (2017). "Federal Prison System—Per Capita Costs—FY 2015." Washington, DC: U.S. Department of Justice.

U.S. Department of Health and Human Services (2012). *National Healthcare Quality Report 2011*. Washington, DC: U.S. Department of Health and Human Services.

U.S. Department of Health and Human Services (2017). *2016 National Healthcare Quality and Disparities Report*. Washington, DC: U.S. Department of Health and Human Services.

Vander Werff, J. (February 26, 2016). "Texas state jails typically house lower-level classifications of prisoners." *Cove Herald*. Retrieved at http://kdhnews.com/copperas_cove_herald/opinion/crime_trends/texas-state-jails-typically-house-lower-level-classifications-of-criminals/article_d3e3acaa-db83-11e5-b61d-a76d8e71015c.html on 11 January 2018.

Walker, S., and C.M. Katz (2007). *The Police in America: An Introduction*. 6th ed. Boston: McGraw-Hill.

Winfree, Jr., L.T., G.L. Mays, and L.F. Alarid (2015). *Introduction to Criminal Justice: The Essentials.* New York: Wolters Kluwer.

World Health Organization (2003). *Mental Health Financing.* Geneva: World Health Organization.

World Health Organization (2004). *Promoting mental health: concepts, emerging evidence, practice (Summary Report).* Geneva: World Health Organization.

World Justice Project (n.d.). "The Four Universal Principles." Washington, DC: World Justice Project. Retrieved at https://worldjusticeproject.org/about-us/overview/what-rule-law on 11 January 2018.

CASES

Arizona v. Johnson, 555 U.S. 323 (2009)
Olmstead v. L.C., 527 U.S. 581 (1999)
Rodriguez v. United States, 135 S. Ct. 1609 (2015)
Terry v. Ohio, 392 U.S. 1 (1968)
United States v. Georgia, 546 U.S. 151 (2006)
Utah v. Streif, 136 S. Ct. 2056 (2016)
Wyatt v. Stickney, 325 F. Supp. 761 (M.D. Ala. 1971)

LEGISLATION

Americans with Disabilities Act of 1990 (42 U.S.C. §1210)

Mental Health Parity and Addiction Equity Act, Public Law 110-343, 122 Stat. 3765 (October 3, 2008)

Patient Protection and Affordable Care Act, Public Law 111-148, 124 Stat. 119 (March 23, 2010)

Rehabilitation Act of 1973, as amended (29 U.S.C. §792).

Drug Abuse Prevention and Control—Offenses and Penalties (21 U.S.C. Chapter 13, §843)

CHAPTER 2

A Brief History of Mental Illness

CHAPTER OUTLINE

LEARNING OBJECTIVES

After reading this chapter, you should be able to:

- Appreciate how the various societies in ancient times viewed and treated those whose behavior we would today recognize as mental illness.
- Understand the long and sometimes tortuous path taken by communities to define and treat those persons whose conduct was viewed as deriving from a mental condition.
- Describe repetitive themes found in communities worldwide about those afflicted with mental illness or diseases.
- Make sense of the treatment of the mentally ill in the United States, from colonial practices to the 1960s deinstitutionalization movement.

PROLOGUE

The often told story of Joan of Arc is gleaned from many sources, chiefly DeVries (1999) and Lucie-Smith (1976).

In the early 1400s, a young French peasant girl hears voices. Angels, she claims, have visited her, including the Archangel Michael. They tell her to don the clothes and even the armor of a warrior, acts themselves that are forbidden for a woman of her time by the laws of man and God and punishable by death. After many false starts and not a few questions as to her state of mind, she leads the French Army to victory after victory against the hated English.

A series of military setbacks results in her capture by the Burgundians, allies of the English. Turned over to the English in exchange for a monetary reward, the maiden is tried by the Bishop of Rouen, another ally of the English King Henry VI, for heresy, cross-dressing, and other crimes. Before her trial, she attempts to escape several times, including a bold jump from a 70-foot tower. Witnesses claim she thought she could fly, which was seen by some as proof that she was in league with the devil. In prison, she continues to wear men's clothing, a guard against being raped by her captors, say her supporters, or further proof of her guilt, say her detractors.

The trial was filled with controversy. At one point, the defendant was taken to the place of execution in the Old Market of Rouen and told that she would be executed immediately if she did not abjure, that is, if she did not renounce her claims of holy visitations and the wearing of men's clothing. Faced with a horrific death, she agreed to abjure. However, she subsequently recanted this repudiation prior to signing the formal document of abjuration. Indeed, under Roman Catholic law, it was this recanting of her abjuration (called relapsing in canon law) that allowed the judges to sentence her to death. Two days later she was taken back to the place of execution and burned at the stake. After her death, the English executioners twice more burnt her body to prevent her cremains from becoming religious relics; they tossed the ashes into the Seine.

Was Joan of Arc, to use the terminology of the 15th century, mad, suffering from a mental malady little understood at the time? Was she in league with the devil, since her rag-tag army overcame superior military forces only with her at its head? Was she a victim of political infighting among the French or simply viewed as a military threat to the English claims in France? Was she a saint, carrying out the will of God, who was supporting the French over the English?

Messenger of God. Minion of the devil. Political pawn. Lunatic. These are but a few of the terms that have been used to describe Joan of Arc and many others who have exhibited similar conduct. As we will reveal more clearly in later chapters, modern psychiatry reduces many mental illnesses to biological sources, while psychology and sociology attribute them to other causes. However, societal responses to mental illness throughout human existence continue to frame our current attitudes. And it is with these earlier discourses on mental illness that our quest begins.

Chapter Overview

This chapter is framed by several important ideas. The first is that over the millennia, humankind has evolved several ways to view and respond to what we call mental illness today. In this regard, the first section explores two gross categorizations, called taxonomies, used by societies in earlier times to look at what we now call mental illness: One taxonomy considered mental illness to be a matter of determining if those afflicted were simply odd or bad; the other taxonomy looked at whether the mentally ill were blessed or damned. While we may not find these terms in today's scientific or legal literature—and, indeed some people may be offended by their use—they were commonly employed through much of human recorded history. As such, these taxonomies are essential for a complete understanding of the different fates faced by the mentally ill through time.

The historical analysis of madness begins with how ancient peoples dealt with the mentally ill. Characterizations range from what might even be considered enlightened and embracing of the mentally ill to downright horrific and inhuman treatment.

The second section reviews madness in European history, from medieval times to the Renaissance to the Age of Reason, which is important as it helped to shape colonial America's responses to mental illness. An important development in this time frame is the insane asylum, which was the locus of mental illness treatment well into the 20th century.

American policies and practices toward the mad and insane, as the mentally ill were characterized at the time, largely followed European practices into the 19th century. As we see in the third section, what were intended to be more humanistic and moralistic ideas about mental illness eventually led to a reliance on the psychiatric hospital, which was a modern incarnation of the Age of Reason's insane asylum. The nation's mental health professionals also experimented with dubious therapeutic treatments, many of which left the afflicted worse off after treatment than before. However, perhaps the most important development discussed in this section is the deinstitutionalization movement and subsequent criminalization of the mentally ill.

This chapter's epilogue looks at a unique series of events in American history, the Salem witchcraft trials. The trials and the events that led up to them amplify how circumstances that may or may not be related to mental illness can overwhelm a community and lead to responses that threaten and, in fact, cost human life.

FRAMING THE ISSUES

As we examine social responses to mental illness through time, we must be cognizant of the fact that there are several different ways of viewing those exhibiting symptoms of what we understand today to be mental illness, each of which implies different things about those responding to the mentally ill and those suffering from it. These are not precise medical or legal terms. Rather, they summarize in gross categorizations—what social scientists call **taxonomies** (Zetterberg, 1966)—which in this case refers to clusters of ideas that themselves are not necessarily mutually exclusive, but serve to pigeonhole the historical record on societal responses to mental illness.

One distinction often used when reviewing historical assessments of persons suspected of being mentally ill centers on whether they are simply odd or truly bad, a kind of secular taxonomical assessment of their threat level. Again, we acknowledge that these terms hold no legal or scientific significance today, but they continue to find their way into contemporary public discourse about the mentally ill, especially when the mentally ill engage in behavior that is beyond our understanding. Both types of nonconforming people are often characterized as creative, opinionated, outspoken, or inappropriate, and nearly as often these fringe characteristics are not only tolerated but celebrated. Celebrity status, wealth, and the socio-political tenor of the times no doubt played a role in the fact that certain people are defined as odd rather than bad. Indeed, as American anthropologist George Marcus (1995) has observed, what would be viewed as mental illness in a poor person is considered eccentricity in a person of great wealth.

Anthropology provides an interesting example of this form of odd person, one who might today be considered mentally ill. The "Contraries" of the Plains Indians of North America were a tolerated and even accepted group of eccentrics. First categorized as having a unique social role late in the 1890s by American anthropologist George Grinnell (Plant, 1994; see Steward, 1931), Contraries were individuals within the Lakota and Santee tribes who spoke and acted exactly the reverse of what was expected in each situation and context. If they said "no," they meant "yes"; if they said "come," they meant "go." Reverse warriors, a kind of Contrary, charged when called upon to retreat and retreated when ordered to charge. Considered a kind of tribal clown, Contraries were not only accepted, but also celebrated for their contributions to the tribe. Their behavior, taken out of its cultural context and reported objectively, could be considered as symptomatic of a mental disease or defect. Within that cultural context, a rather different interpretation is given.

So, who could be considered bad? These would be equally eccentric people, but whose mental illness threatens or harms others. Often, like the odd, the bad are complicated, multi-faceted individuals, combining both brilliance of thought and deed with other far less desirable characteristics that make them repugnant, especially to their contemporaries. In some cases, their "reputation," like Rome's Caligula or London's Jack the Ripper, follows them down through the ages.

Badness generally involves activities classified as crimes. Society may condemn the deed and classify it as expressing more than a little madness. This is often the case if there is no suspect, where the attribute of madness is given to the unknown perpetrator owing to the horrific nature of the acts, as in the saying: "Only a crazy person could have done that!" Killing people without justification or defense is clearly a crime; killing them and then desecrating their bodies moves the deed into a whole different behavioral category. Consider by way of example the case of the "Mad Butcher of Kingsbury Lane," also known as "The Cleveland Torso Murderer." Between September 23, 1935 and August 16, 1938, at least 12 and perhaps as many as 15 persons were murdered by an unknown subject, mostly in the Cleveland, Ohio, area. The Mad Butcher brutalized the recorded victims by post-mortem dismemberment and burning of the bodies. As with Jack the Ripper in 1880s London, officials believed that the Cleveland Torso Murderer had experience as a butcher, doctor, or a professional with similar skills. Unlike Jack, he murdered men and women; like Jack, he was never caught or identified. By definition and deed, serial offenders would fall into this category.

Religious elements are at the core of the second set of terms, both of which derive from the more neutral idea of **spirit possession**: the blessed and the damned. This perspective can be traced back to Plato, who distinguished between good and bad madness (Plato, 1925). Indeed, throughout the recorded history of religion, those persons exhibiting signs of mental illness were generally placed in one of these two categories. However, as the case of Joan of Arc clearly demonstrates, the same person may be accorded both statuses, just by different constituencies. For the English, Joan was clearly in league with the devil; for the supporters of the Dauphin's claim to the French throne, she was blessed by God. There is even a term for this form of mental illness: **divine madness**. Moreover, it is found in many diverse religions, including Christianity, Buddhism, Sufism, Hinduism, and Shamanism (McDaniel, 1989). Divine madness is viewed as an expression of godly love or religious ecstasy (Aymard, 2014).

Examples of divine madness abound in a wide range of religious literature. Early Christians embraced the notion of madness, and they consider the "stigma" of being called crazy for their beliefs a positive state (Macdonald, 2013). Saints, too, often exhibited behavior that if observed today might result in a diagnosis of mental illness. For example, St. Catherine of Siena (b.1347-d.1380) said that Christ visited her and gave her a wedding ring made from his foreskin. St. Theresa of Avila (b.1515-d.1582) claimed that the Devil interrupted her prayer sessions with visions of hell. Marabouts, or holy men, of West African Sufism also engaged in pre-Islamic activities such as telling the future and the use of amulets, which were considered outside Sunni Islamic beliefs and practices. Mad Marabout saints were accorded special status. Sunni Islam prohibits such a status, as it does not recognize divine madness as a form of spirit possession (Chouiten, 2015). Hinduism and Buddhism both have long celebrated religious ecstasy that bordered on madness, conduct which was viewed by both religions as divine enlightenment (Ardussi and Epstein, 1978; Kinsley, 1974).

The damned present an altogether different perspective on divine madness, as it is often referred to as **demonic possession**. Again, Joan of Arc stands as an example of a person seen by her enemies as in the control of the devil. Another classic example, reviewed at the end of in this chapter, is the so-called Salem witch trials of the late 17th century. As with divine madness, the theme of the damned is found throughout the world's religions. The degree of **free will**, that is, whether the person possessed sought out this relationship with a demonic spirit, varies; indeed, demonic possession is often viewed as unwitting and not the responsibility of the person in whom the demon resides. And, interestingly, while most religions fail to provide a prescription for ridding the victim of divine possession, nearly all describe a means of ridding the victim of demonic possession, mostly through an **exorcism**, which is a highly ritualized spiritual ceremony intended to rid a person of demonic possession.

Throughout this chapter, the terms "madness" and "insanity" are widely used, sometimes interchangeably. As used here, they refer to primitive, non-scientific descriptions of what today we call mental illness. Madness, as a common term, is rarely used today, except colloquially, as in "you must be mad to jump into a freezing lake on New Year's Day!," or, as described in Box 2.1, when we look at people who commit unfathomable acts and wonder if they are insane or, even more informally, crazy. Insanity evolved to become a legal and not a medical or scientific term (see Chapter 7). But for most of the historical record on mental illness, certainly prior to the 20th century, madness and insanity were the preferred terms.

MENTAL ILLNESS IN ANCIENT TIMES

If the actions of a mentally challenged person, whatever the immediate cause of that condition, confuses us in the 21st century, imagine for a moment that you are living hundreds, if not thousands, of years in the past. What would you have made of a loved one—or even a stranger—who insisted on walking around spouting nonsensical statements, tearing at his or her clothing, or engaging in other socially unacceptable if not outright bizarre

BOX 2.1

Thinking About the Issues

Consider each of the following situations concerning the fate of those defined as mentally challenged by some element of contemporary society.

1. In 1978, more than 900 U.S. men, women, and children who followed charismatic leader Jim Jones of the People's Temple to Jonestown, Guyana, voluntarily drank cyanide-laced lemonade and died. Was their religious fanaticism, which included poisoning their children as a form of "revolutionary suicide," a type of mental illness? What do you know about the willingness of people to murder friends and family as an expression of their own spiritual beliefs? Is there a counter-argument to such beliefs?
2. Almost daily, we find news articles about suicide bombers who willingly kill unknown bystanders and themselves to perpetuate political and religious dogma. If you could negotiate with any person who felt that spiritual messages were guiding him into violent conduct, what counter-message would you try to deliver?

behavior? Moving the clock back several thousand years might help bring the question in perspective.

Linking Evil Spirits and Madness

While we can only imagine the form a community-level response might have taken to any given act millennia ago, we do have some anthropological and archeological evidence, as well as some written documentation, as to how communities in the distant past responded to mental illness in their midst. Dichotomies such as the odd and the bad, the damned and the blessed, for example, represent historical explanations of madness found in various cultures around the world. These descriptions of mental illness and what happens to those who manifest its symptoms are more than mere stories. Throughout much of human history, bodies of men, including law courts, looked to religious works for guidance in how to treat persons so afflicted, especially those persons with such symptoms who committed crimes.

Three related ideas held by early humans about mental illness are important, especially as they portend contemporary views on the subject. First, if a mad person is possessed by an evil spirit, then it is only logical that a way be made for that spirit to exit its host. Scientists suspect that this was the thinking behind **trephination**, an 8,000-year-old practice that involved drilling holes in a victim's head, which allowed evil spirits trapped within to escape. This claim derives from modern studies of ancient skulls that show evidence of trephination and cave art that describes the technique (Faria, 2015; Froeschner,

1992; Restak, 2000). Trephination continued after the Neolithic era, as there is more modern evidence of its use. For example, "medical" equipment was developed in the 17th century to facilitate the drilling process. And, as described later in this chapter, lobotomies are a modern manifestation of this practice. Thus, a procedure that started out as a way to expiate the devil or other evil spirit morphed over the millennia into a modern "cure" for mental diseases and disorders.

Second, some religions portray mental illness, indeed all illnesses, as a trial or test of one's beliefs (Islam and Campbell, 2014; Scull, 2015a, b). Supernatural powers were at work (Cockerham, 2016). For example, there are references in both the Old and New Testaments to the driving out of evil spirits, including by King David (1 Samuel 16:23) and Jesus (Matthew, 17:14-40). Notions that mental illness is the work of evil spirits, demons, and devils can also be found in the 21st century. Many contemporary Muslims blame the influence of jinns, or evil spirits, even though the Qur'an does not specifically mention their ties to mental illness (Islam and Campbell, 2014; Khalifa and Hardie, 2005). Some fundamentalist Christian groups also view mental illness, and indeed all illness, as a matter of faith, often resulting in the stigmatization of the mentally ill (Almanzar, 2017; Scrutton, 2015).

Finally, for thousands of years, humankind practiced shunning and banishment to remove not only the mentally ill from their midst, but also others suffering from equally incurable diseases, such as leprosy. Throughout much of recorded history, the mentally ill were not just objects of pity or ridicule, but, given their involvement with evil, were actively pushed out of the community, relegated to wander the countryside, surviving as best they could (Scull, 2015a). Such ancient views on mental illness were not limited to Western societies, as evidenced in Box 2.2. Moreover, as we discuss later in this chapter, in the wake of the mid-20th-century removal of the mentally ill from psychiatric hospitals and other mental asylums—described in this chapter as the deinstitutionalization movement—hundreds of thousands of mentally ill persons moved to the streets in a modern form of banishment (Eisenberg and Guttmacher, 2010).

Madness in Classical Antiquity

Classic Greek and Roman accounts describe charms, spells, and purification rites used to resolve mental illness. The work of Greek physician Hippocrates (b.460-d.377 B.C.E.) is particularly instructive in this regard. He was one of the first of the ancient philosophers to describe and identify cures for mental illness. He wrote that mental impairment should be resolved by internal resolution through calm intervention. His teachings are akin to today's understanding of some aspects of psychological impairment. Although the times prohibited any dissection of human anatomy or physiology, Hippocrates wrote that no demons or gods caused mental disorders. Hippocrates recognized that the brain was the

BOX 2.2

Ancient Chinese Views on Madness

Observations about the impact of mental illness on families were not limited to European culture. The following passage is taken from an ancient Chinese medical text supposedly written by Huang Ti (2674 B.C.E.), the third legendary emperor. While historians now believe that the actual text was written later, possibly during the seventh century B.C.E., its import is not less significant:

> The person suffering from excited insanity initially feels sad, eating and sleeping less; he then becomes grandiose, feeling that he is very smart and noble, talking and scolding day and night, singing, behaving strangely, seeing strange things, hearing strange voices, believing that he can see the devil or gods.

The social stigma against mental disorders was as strong in China as in any country where family honor and reliance on the power of marriage to create business alliances was prevalent, conditions also found later in medieval Europe. In ancient China, the mentally ill were reported to be concealed by families for fear community members would believe the affliction of mental illness could beget "bad fate." In time, this led to the perception that mental illness was contagious, which was also an idea that emerged in Europe as it faced plagues of all sorts.

Source: Phillips (1998).

central organ of intellectual activity and that mental disorders were due to brain pathology. He understood and emphasized the importance of heredity and predisposition to mental disorders and wrote that injuries to the head could also cause sensory and motor disorders.

Hippocrates classified all mental disorders into three general categories—mania, melancholia, and phrenitis; he detailed clinical descriptions of the specific disorders by relying on clinical observations. Hippocrates believed in treating people with techniques not rooted in religion or superstition, but that considered the individual and his or her mental disorders. The man we call the father of medicine (Leff and Leff, 1956) advanced the idea that the resolution of mental illness could be achieved by changing the patient's environment or occupation and by employing medications. He prescribed exercise, tranquility, and, in some cases, as was popular then, bloodletting to establish **humoral balance**; he warned against attempting spiritual exorcisms as lacking in medical merit (Brown and Menninger, 1940). Hippocrates' legacy extended far beyond Greece in the fifth century B.C.E., as is made clear in Box 2.3.

BOX 2.3

The Legacy of Ancient Greece

The years between the civilizations of ancient Greece and modern America saw raw, indifferent, and frequently inhuman treatment and care of those who were perceived by their societies as "mad." Hippocrates' somewhat perceptive and humane approach to mental illness contrasts with other methodologies known to be used from ancient times through the Middle Ages. Other techniques to "cure" the mentally ill included a return to trepanning to allow the spirits to escape (without anesthetics) or placing a patient's head into an oven, causing him to sweat profusely and thereby evaporate delusional thoughts. Balance of the humors, the notion that illness was attributed to an excess or deficiency of one or more of the four humors (i.e., blood, yellow bile, black bile, and phlegm) was a recurrent theme in the work of Hippocrates, an idea that would continue well into the 18th and even 19th centuries.

It should be noted, however, that Hippocrates and his followers also popularized the notion of **hysteria** as a specialized form of feminine mental illness. Throughout ancient and even into modern history, medical practitioners subjected women to what can only be viewed as a form of discrimination that was in some cases deadly, and nearly always painful. Specifically, Hippocrates held that the cause of women's mental illness was due to a "wandering womb," or as expressed by Plato:

> the same is the case with the so-called womb or matrix of women; the animal within them is desirous of procreating children, and when remaining unfruitful long beyond its proper time, gets discontented and angry, and wandering in every direction through the body, closes up the passages of the breath, and, by obstructing respiration, drives them to extremity, causing all varieties of disease.

The cure was to require patients (women, of course) to inhale noxious odors to chase the uterus back into place. Sometimes, the uterus was removed, as well as other vital feminine organs, to resolve these feminine nomadic tendencies.

Sources: Cornford (1997 [1935]); Tasca, Rapetti, et al. (2012).

EUROPEAN HISTORY AND MENTAL ILLNESS

The fall of Rome signaled the beginning of a period in European history known colloquially as the Dark Ages, but more correctly as the Middle Ages, which itself consisted the Early Middle Ages (c. 400–c. 1000), the High Middle Ages (c. 1000–c. 1300), and the Late Middle Ages (c. 1301–c. 1500). Throughout these historical periods, responses to the mentally ill underwent many changes, mostly influenced by Christian values and the Roman Catholic church. By the late medieval period, however, catastrophic events transpiring in Europe, including a series of bubonic plagues, threatened the region's social fabric. While the Protestant Reformation, the discovery of the Americas, and the Renaissance were still on the historical horizon, increasing urbanization and the end of serfdom were also changing life in Europe.

Madness in Medieval Europe

As religious beliefs strengthened their hold over medieval society, religious doctrine also pointed to the use of miraculous cures for madness. In these times, the ability to resolve insanity focused on the use of relics and saints to heal the victims, stopping their visions, voices, and incantations. The tombs of saints like St. Margaret of Antioch (b.289-d.304 C.E.) and St. Dymphna of Geel (c. seventh century), each of whom was beheaded, were popular places of prayer for those families seeking relief from mental distress for their loved ones (Scull, 2015a).

In medieval Europe, families had to either provide for the upkeep of their loved ones who had some form of mental dysfunction or abandon them to the pity and care of the community. By the late medieval period, in the 1400s and 1500s, those mentally ill persons deemed relatively harmless—the odd—lived within their community, probably in similar fashion to the many mentally challenged members of the current homeless population in the United States. Contemporary accounts indicate that most forms of madness were not a cause for concern or a cause for an accusation of criminal conduct. Basically, those who were mad were possessed by demons and visions through no fault of their own. The families of mentally ill persons viewed their loved ones' conditions as religious deficiencies, and the clergy acted as "physicians of the soul" (Houston, 2004).

The Renaissance and the Contagion Model

The European Renaissance (1300-1700 C.E.) brought a surge of art, music, literature, and architectural development that remains unequaled in any era. Europe was still in the late medieval period when it began, but cultural shifts and views on a broad range of social ills began to develop quickly during the first two centuries. With this rise in cultural awareness, however, there was also demand for the invisibility of those who were "different." The decline in the need to identify and isolate people with leprosy led to the increase of identifying and isolating those with mental illness (Hinshaw, 2007; Scrambler, 2009).

Towns and villages, if not entire kingdoms, were thought susceptible to "an outbreak of the madness," much like the Black Plague and other contagious diseases that had recently decimated Europe, if the community was exposed to insanity. Thus, there were two responses to the perceived threat: (1) turn out into the countryside those who were considered mad to fend for themselves, or (2) lock them up in mental hospitals that were essentially warehouses. The thinking behind these responses was that as there was no known cure for those who were insane, be they harmful or harmless, it was best to silence them in secure institutions or get rid of them entirely by what was essentially banishment (Foucault, 1962; Kemp, 1985; Scull, 1977). Of course, as Box 2.4 suggests, when a king is involved, the process becomes a bit more difficult.

The Age of Reason and the Asylum

Tolerance for itinerate wanderers and beggars slackened with the rise of capitalism and the Industrial Revolution, starting in the late 18th century (Foucault, 2006). Only hard work should be rewarded; non-productive persons, including the mentally ill, were a drain on society. Moreover, as families and small communities fragmented with the increasing number of men, women, and children working in industrial factories, acceptance of village fools waned. Family units became less able to provide care for the insane.

In response, **workhouses** were established to "teach the able bodied 'proper' work habits through order and discipline" (Scull, 1977: 217). The insane who could perform tasks, no matter how limited, were assigned to workhouses to earn pennies from exploitive managers and operators. Contemporary reports described scenes of the insane being chained in the cellar, fastened to a table or tied to a post, left half-naked and half-starved. It was noted at the time that jail was not a good place to confine the mentally ill due to safety concerns for the other inmates (Scull, 1977: 220).

Coterminous with the Industrial Revolution and the rise of capitalism, the **Age of Reason** also endorsed the belief that the mentally ill must not be allowed to roam free, but rather should be confined with other of society's undesirables (Foucault, 2006; see Paine, 1794). The result was the start of **The Great Confinement**, as the insane were locked away in ever greater numbers in **asylums**, often with the aged, criminals, prostitutes, and beggars. Madness was regarded as another type of social immorality and the mad were regarded as no more than unwieldy, unworldly, and untrainable animals (Foucault, 2006: 9). Lacking the capacity for reason, they were also believed to be immune to pain, meaning that life in the asylum often represented a descent into hell on earth.

London's Bethlehem Royal Hospital was the most famous institution to emerge in England during this era of proscribed isolation and institutionalization. This institution began as a 13th-century priory that operated a hospital during the reign of Henry III. At the start of the 15th century, English Charity Commissioners, a sort of watchdog group, first noted the presence of **lunatics** at the facility (Andrews et al., 1997). In 1634, the hospital moved from its medieval period into its early "modern" era of administration as a mental facility. By this time, the Royal Hospital had devolved into a specialized facility for the housing of those characterized as "lunatics."

The hospital's name, especially the corruption of it as **Bedlam**, became synonymous with madness, irrationality, and chaos. This idea is graphically represented in a series of paintings called "A Rake's Progress" produced between 1732 and 1733 (Sadowsky, 1999). These works by English artist Willam Hogarth (b.1697-d.1764) depicted how communities

BOX 2.4

Law and Mental Health When the King Goes Mad: The Case of Henry VI of England

Early Anglo-Norman laws, deriving from the eleventh- and twelfth-century law texts, described excessive anger as a form of madness. At the time, there were two sources of such madness, the deadly sin of wrath and the somewhat more familiar demonic possession. The nobility (a step below the royals) who exhibited madness often had its origins attributed to wrath and excessive anger. Kings, however, exhibited righteous anger against those who would challenge their authority, while rebels exhibited blameworthy anger and madness. Thus, in its early legal manifestations in English law, madness had a decidedly political and hierarchical bent to it.

The case of Henry VI of England (b.1421–d.1471) posed an interesting and serious challenge to these views. Henry was King of England from 1422 to 1461, removed from the throne only to return from 1470 to 1471. He was a catalyst for the infamous English civil war called the War of the Roses. Henry was a mentally fragile child and a not much better adult; moreover, his maternal grandfather, France's King Charles VI, also called Charles the Mad, displayed similarly aberrant behavior. In the summer of 1453, upon learning of the loss of the English protectorate of Bordeaux in France, Henry had a mental breakdown so severe that he barely communicated with anyone for over a year. Centuries later, psychologists much later suggested that he suffered from schizophrenia, as Henry experienced profound hallucinations. He refused to wash or change his clothing. He was given sundry potions and laxatives; he was subjected to bloodletting and his head shaved and purged to rid his brain of its black bile and restore the balance of the humors. Nothing seemed to work.

While other kings, including Charles VI, had manifested signs of mental illness, Henry's condition was so debilitating that he was judged unfit to rule, replaced in March 1454 by Richard of York. In January 1455, Henry recovered his senses and resumed his role as King of England. Civil War broke out in 1460, and Henry was deposed in 1461, after which he suffered another breakdown. Captured by his enemies in 1465, he was imprisoned in the Tower of London, released again and restored to the crown briefly in 1470, and then re-imprisoned in 1471. He died in the Tower on 21 May 1471, a death officially attributed to melancholia and his deteriorating mental condition. More likely, he was killed by his enemies.

Evidently, mental illness manifested by royalty is acceptable only to a point and less likely to be condoned when there is an attempt to replace one royal family with another or when the threat to the kingdom was so great as to be impossible to ignore. After all, legal scholars have observed that late medieval ecclesiastical or **canon law** and **civil law** recognized a continuum from sanity to insanity, and that short of being a raving madman (i.e., a **furiosus**), one's location on that continuum was not easily or readily discerned. At least once, and perhaps motivated by political pressures, Henry's position on that continuum was easily and expediently identified.

Sources: Green (1993); McGrath (2010); Rushton (2010); Turner (2013).

isolated and treated those with mental illness: a religious zealot is chained to a straw pallet; a delusional musician wears five manacles; and townswomen paid the asylum keepers to watch the mentally ill urinate on the institution's walls. Patients were generally chained to walls or tables and left naked (Mercier, 1900: 1853).

It was not just an isolated set of conditions at Bedlam. At the County Lunatic Asylum in Lancaster, England, muzzles, chains, metal girdles, handcuffs, manacles, and leg-locks were used to contain mentally ill patients, as early as 1809. Established as a refuge for the most vulnerable of men and women, it became a warehouse for the forgotten. At York Asylum, investigators found evidence of physical and sexual abuse. Common practices included keeping 200 patients in spaces designed for 50, forcing people into dark and unventilated rooms, not providing adequate or any clothing, and intermingling violent patients with harmless ones. A contemporary account described the asylum: "[F]our hidden cells only eight feet square and inches deep in excrement were discovered to have housed thirteen elderly women. Further, up to seven females and six male occupants were assigned to each bedchamber with multiple occupation of most beds" (Digby, 1983: 225). One female inmate reported that she had been chained for 36 years due to mental illness. It was generally perceived that the mentally ill, although confined for years and subjected to neglect and abuse rather than meaningful treatment, were usually harmless. They did not pose a threat to anyone and seemed consent "to drift along, lost in the fog of their dementia" (Karp, 1984: 7).

MENTAL ILLNESS IN AMERICA

By the late 18th century in Europe, a more compassionate regimen and attitude toward the treatment of the mentally ill emerged. Physicians at the Bedlam began to distinguish between "'maniacs' whose outrageous behavior called for authority, chiding and threatening"—i.e., punishment and incarceration—and "'melancholics' who needed music and other activities that was once enjoyed" (Shimmon, 2011: 6; see Andrews, 1990). The idea was to encourage the mentally ill to engage in self-discipline and self-control with what was described as a philosophy of "moral restraint." While kindness, exercise, and structure replaced chains and manacles, the humanistic care of this epoch devolved in the face of a lack of supervision and the imposition of oppressive regimes. The goal of internalized change led to the introduction of solitary cells, padded rooms, and even surgical interventions, all of which were viewed at the time as "humane" responses to mental illness. This was the epoch of "modern" treatment for the insane in which the American response began.

From Moral Treatment to the Insane Asylum

At nearly the same time Bedlam was evolving and the asylum model was gaining followers in Europe, events were also occurring in what would become the United States that would shape that nation's response to the mentally ill well into the 20th century. The first American state mental hospital for lunatics was opened in Williamsburg before the American Revolution, using public funds from the Colony of Virginia to care for the insane (Deutsch, 1949: 230). Dr. Benjamin Rush (b.1746-d.1813) later opened the Friends Asylum in Pennsylvania, an institution dedicated to providing humane moral treatment for the mentally ill. Within 30 years, the Society of Friends, also known as the Quakers, established 30 such asylums for moral treatment.

Quaker reformer Samuel Tuke (b.1784-d.1857) advocated **moral treatment** and kindness for the mentally ill, arguing that if patients are treated civilly, they will behave civilly. In the late 1800s, a reform movement, sparked by American activist Dorothea Dix (b.1802-d.1887), led to an even more humane treatment regimen for mentally ill persons. Dix recognized the need to separate mental care from physical medical treatment. Eventually, following her strong leadership, 32 states built **insane asylums** to provide separate treatment and care for the mentally ill.

Despite efforts of the Friends and those reformers influenced by Dix's views on insanity, treatment slid into neglect and abuse. Most American communities combined private and public care systems for those needing physical medical care with those needing treatment for severe symptoms of mental illness. Private and public hospitals set aside separate wards for the mentally ill who were too violent or disruptive to remain at home. Private hospitals depended on the money paid by wealthy families to care for their own mentally ill dependents as support for their overall mission of caring for the physically ill (D'Antonio, n.d.). Eventually, however, economic considerations triggered a downturn in care. Local governments became overwhelmed with the costs of sustaining the elderly in the asylums as senility was incorporated into care and treatment of a psychiatric problem. The promise of soothing interventions for cure became unobtainable, as patients with dementia did not respond to any form of contemporary treatment, thereby diluting the quality of care received by everyone. The U.S. mental health system began a downward spiral to similar circumstances seen during the Industrial Revolution.

"Modern" Responses to Mental Illness

Early in the 20th century, partly because of its failures, psychiatry was perceived by many in society and medicine to be an inexact science (Alexander and Selesnick, 1966). There is a long history to this generalization. The *Journal of Mental Science* (Anon, 1900: 781) pointed to the "apparent inefficacy of medicine in the cure of insanity," and further observed that "though medical science has made great advances during the 19th century, our knowledge of the mental functions of the brain is still comparatively obscure."

The ebb and flow of attitudes toward the mentally ill slowly changed. As will become evident in future chapters, this evolution continues, as the asylums were dismantled and the harmless mentally ill again wander in the streets and in the community. Those who are disturbed or disturbing are again restrained, not in hospitals and asylums but in prisons and jails. As Foucault (2006) maintained, institutional psychiatry has been used to smother social nuisances. Those persons whose behavior has been defined as "disturbing" have themselves been labeled "disturbed," worthy of being certified and shut away, out of sight and out of mind. Recognition of this evil was one of the heartfelt impulses behind the introduction of the policy of "community care." As we shall see in future chapters, however, saying that care is available in the community and providing that care are two different things entirely.

From the mid-19th century onward, the new psychiatric professionals have claimed that lunacy falls within the medical domain; and the mentally ill have undergone a long succession of **therapeutic interventions**. Throughout the 20th century, medical studies in microbiology, oncology, and infectious diseases generated tremendous improvements, if not outright cures, for a wide range of diseases and disorders; however, psychiatric treatments did not keep pace. Critics of today's therapies might say that things have not changed much in hundreds of years.

Although those treating mental illness in the late 19th and early 20th centuries employed bloodletting, head warming, inhalation of noxious odors, and trepanation, the inventiveness of their cruelty continues to amaze. The following is a list of only a few of the documented therapeutic interventions used, none of which cured mental illness, even if they change the symptomology (Berrios, 1997; Darnton, 1968; Faria, 2015; Gralnick, 1946; Read, 1940; Rudorfer, Henry, and Sackeim, 2003):

1. *Lobotomies* — This procedure involves cutting into the skull of an afflicted person, generally while the patient is awake, employing a drill-like device or a sharp-bladed instrument, exposing brain matter. As we discussed earlier in this chapter, the practice of **trepanning** or trephination had been employed since Neolithic times in Europe and in the Americas. By the mid-1930s, this procedure had evolved into the **lobotomy**, also called a **leucotomy**; the most common surgical method, the **transorbital lobotomy**, employed an icepick-like device that was thrust through the top of each eye socket and effectively destroyed the area of the brain in the frontal lobes responsible for emotionality; it is still performed in highly limited cases today. The originator of the modern lobotomy procedure, Egas Moniz (b.1874-d.1955) shared the 1949 Nobel Prize for Physiology or Medicine, specifically for his role in developing the leucotomy. The procedure is rarely used today, except as a response to violent forms of epilepsy.

2. *Mesmerism* — The Swabian physician Franz Mesmer (b.1734-d.1815) argued that mental illness was caused by the gravitational pull of the moon. Episodic bouts of depression and schizophrenia rose and fell with the movement of the ocean tides and bodily fluid, all powered by the full moon's gravitational pull. He initially argued that magnets could redistribute mental equilibrium, but later employed a form of individual and group hypnosis as a treatment modality. Physicians discontinued using **Mesmerism** in the 1850s; however, there remains today a strong belief in the power of magnets to heal a wide variety of physical ailments.

3. *Convulsive Therapies* — In 1927, Austrian-American physician and neuropsychiatrist Manfred Sakel (b.1900-d.1957) first injected schizophrenics with enough insulin to induce a coma, which he claimed then cured schizophrenia. **Insulin-coma therapy** was largely unproven and 2 percent of his patients died. By the 1970s, it had largely fallen out of favor with the medical establishment. Other drugs and practices followed. Hungarian psychiatrist and neuropathologist Ladislas Joseph Meduna (b.1896-d.1964) began using a drug known as metrazol to cause seizures in the early 1930s; he felt that there may be an absence of certain chemicals in the schizophrenic brain. Memory loss, fractured bones, and only short-term positive results caused **metrazol therapy** to be abandoned by the late 1930s in favor of more easily managed **electroconvulsive therapy** (ECT or "electro-shock" therapy), whose use as a treatment modality in the United States declined the early 1980s. It is still employed for a narrow range of behaviors, although seizure therapy remains controversial.

Looking back from our vantage point, these methods may seem to border on the barbaric. Yet, as Box 2.5 reveals, some were used well into the 20th century, often with unintended consequences for the patient of such therapeutic interventions.

Deinstitutionalization and Criminalization of the Mentally Ill

The U.S. mental health industry was in crisis as the mid-point of the 20th century approached. At its peak, there were more than 500,000 patients in state mental hospitals in the 1950s (Canales, 2012). This emphasis on "asylum-style" facilities declined beginning in the 1960s and continuing until the early 1970s, as new psychotropic drugs and burgeoning numbers of community-based mental health centers enabled states to close hundreds of public mental hospitals across the nation. This policy shift constituted a movement described as the **deinstitutionalization of the mentally ill** (Eisenberg and Guttmacher, 2010; Szasz, 2007; Torrey, 2010). The deinstitutionalization movement is part of the history of our nation's response to mental illness. As importantly, it was the primary vehicle by which the mentally ill became vulnerable to the predations of the street, and, not coincidentally, vulnerable to negative interactions with the nation's first responders.

During the "transfer of services" from state asylums to the small community programs, the funding funnels became an invisible way to re-allocate the funds historically used for mental health treatment to other state purposes. The re-allocation of funds from inpatient mental hospital programs to outpatient community centers became a politically convenient way to trim budgets and reduce the number of state mental health employees (Grob, 1992). This elimination of centralized residential treatment hospitals caused a marked increase in the severely mentally ill among the homeless (Honberg, Kimball, et al., 2011). This shift in responsibility for the care of mentally ill individuals who are socially disruptive, or violent, or not capable of caring for themselves or being cared for by familial

BOX 2.5

What Would You Do?

Rose Marie Kennedy, the eldest daughter of Rose and Joseph Kennedy, was by all accounts a wonderful child, attractive and docile. She was deprived of oxygen at her difficult birth, which may have caused her to be developmentally challenged. As she matured, but certainly by her late teens and early 20s, however, she began to be assertive and rebellious, unlike, apparently, her siblings, but especially her high-achieving brothers, Joe Jr., Jack, Bobby, and Teddy. She also lacked their academic prowess or physical achievements. Her family thought perhaps she suffered from a developmental disorder, epilepsy, or some undiagnosed mental illness. Prone to mood swings, Rosemary, as she was known, became a source of great concern to her father, who worried that she might bring eventual embarrassment to her politically and socially powerful family.

Hearing about a new procedure intended to calm such mood swings and occasional violent outbursts in young women, Joe Kennedy authorized a lobotomy on the 23-year old Rosemary. By all contemporary accounts Rosemary was not mentally ill; nonetheless, the procedure was performed in late 1941. Critics suggest that the surgery was botched as Rosemary's mental capacity was reduced to that of a 2-year old, and she could not walk, or talk coherently, or control her bodily functions. Rosemary was institutionalized in a series of facilities over the next decade and eventually resided in an institute in Wisconsin, where she lived out her days, dying of natural causes in 2005.

Rosemary Kennedy's story is not a clearly criminal justice–related case. However, it does highlight the issues behind a practice that was seen as preventive, one that could take an at-risk person from a path toward illegal or, in her case, immoral behavior. Would you have acted differently, given the "facts" in this case? Considering the Kennedys' wealth and position, do you assess their response as appropriate, especially given the times in which they lived? It is easy to look back in history, especially knowing what we know today about lobotomies, but what other options existed for the Kennedy family, other than to follow the best medical advice available at the time? As we have seen, mental illness lives large in books and other media representations, but in people's lives, mental illness is often hidden away, relegating the afflicted to life in an attic loft or a basement dungeon.

Sources: Ellis and Abrams (2009); Kessler (1996).

support systems inevitably led to contact with law enforcement (Stroman, 2003). In truth, community-based treatment programs were unable to meet the needs created by the deinstitutionalization movement.

To recap, by the mid-1960s, the number of institutionalized mental patients had fallen from its peak of 560,000 in the 1950s. After the deinstitutionalization movement began in earnest, it fell even more, to 130,000 patients in 1980. By 2000, the number of state psychiatric hospital beds per 100,000 people was 22, down from 339 in 1955 (Fuller, Sinclair, et al., 2016; Torrey, Kennard, et al., 2010). Perhaps the most damning claim is made by Borum (2000: 333; see also Borum and Rand, 1999): "In 1955, [0].3 percent of the U.S. population was mentally ill and residing in a mental institution; whereas in 1999, [0].3 percent of the national population is mentally ill and is in the criminal justice system." The nation's jails and prisons had, by the 1980s, become a modern-day asylum, a characterization that remains relevant today (Torrey et al., 2010).

At roughly the same time that the deinstitutionalization of the mentally ill gained momentum, a debate raged in the criminal justice community. This 1970s debate consisted of two parts, the first of which centered around the following question: Are the nation's jails and prisons, asked the critics, achieving any significant behavioral change goals? Researchers questioned whether the wide array of treatment programs instituted after World War II were achieving their stated goals. By the late 1960s and early 1970s, the consensus view was that few extant studies showed positive results. Robert Martinson (1974) characterized this failure as the "nothing works" perspective. As Martinson (1974: 25) noted: "With few and isolated exceptions, the rehabilitative efforts that have been reported so far have had no appreciable effect on recidivism. Studies that have been done since our survey was completed do not present any major grounds for altering that original conclusion." While the research to which Martinson referred did not show that all rehabilitative programs failed, "nothing works" became the correctional catchword of the 1970s (Sarre, 2001).

The second part of the debate focuses on what to do for and with all criminals. At literally the same moment in time as Martinson's report surfaced, a new orientation on justice was emerging. Known as **just deserts**, this perspective—defined in large part by the work of Norval Morris (1974), David Fogel (1975), and Andrew von Hirsch (1976)—suggested that offenders "earned" the punishments that society dealt them, and that anything short of the maximum allowable sanction under the law constituted as great an injustice as the original crime. After all, offenders have free will and choose to violate the criminal law. As consequence, they are deserving of the punishment accorded them. As Fogel (1975: 192) wrote: "The justice perspective demands accountability from all processors, even the 'pure of heart.' *Properly understood, the justice perspective is not so much concerned with administration of justice as it is with the justice of administration*" (emphasis in the original).

The deinstitutionalization of the mentally ill began in almost exactly the same time frame as the "nothing works" and just deserts perspectives gained traction. These changes in police practices and mental health philosophy resulted in the cycling of millions of inmates a year through the nation's ill-equipped jails and prisons, hundreds of thousands of whom suffered from symptoms of mental illness before, during, or after the commission of their crimes. The essence of this overlay of shifts in public policies was captured by Marc Abramson (1974) in the term **criminalization of the mentally ill**. Abramson observed that mentally ill defendants underwent a transition from being mentally ill patients to being mentally ill criminals. First responders, often the police, can initiate this process of criminalization, and it is these interactions that set in motion the forces described in subsequent chapters, including the nation's law enforcement, courts, and correctional systems.

EPILOGUE

A series of events in the Massachusetts Bay Colony in the late 17th century have intrigued sociologists, medical researchers, legal scholars, historians, religious writers, and others for hundreds of years. While on the surface, the witchcraft trials appear to be about the dark arts, witches, and devilry, they cannot be understood completely without considering their medical, psychological, social, political, and economic contexts. The descriptions and analyses that follow derive in large part from Carlson (1999); Demos (1970); Erickson (1966); Hoffer (1997); Kocić (2010); Linder (n.d.); Matossian (1982); and Sidky (1997).

A dark moment in early American history, law, and mental health occurred between February 1692 and May 1693, during what became known as the "Salem witch trials." The events of that period were set in motion when several young playmates in the town of Salem, Massachusetts developed strange and unexplainable behaviors, including diving under furniture, contorting in pain, and developing high fevers. After a medical exam failed to reveal any cause for their behavior, belief that the children's symptoms were due to witchcraft was widely accepted. The community turned its attention to an enslaved woman, Tituba, who had been ordered to bake a rye cake with the urine of a victim and then feed the cake to the dog, which she did, in order to discover the identity of the victim's afflictor. After Tituba confessed to having seen the devil, the witch hunt began, culminating in the arrest, conviction, and four-month imprisonment of Sarah Goode and her 4-year old child, Dorcas. After she watched her mother be hanged as a witch, Dorcas reportedly went insane.

All total, 25 individuals died as a direct result of the incidents in Salem. Nineteen people were executed, all by hanging, including 14 women. One individual, Giles Corey, was pressed to death, refusing to the end to admit he was in league with witches and the devil. Another four, including two infant children—one of whom was born in jail—died during the incarceration phase of the trial or immediately after the verdict but before execution.

As was the case with Joan of Arc, many arguments have emerged to explain the occurrences in Salem, other than the presence of witches in the community. Two explanations center on biochemistry, a topic explored in Chapter 4. In the first, it is suggested that the girls involved in the trial were poisoned by rye bread infested with fungus *Claviceps purpurea*, a natural substance used in the production of LSD, although there is disagreement as to the presence of all the symptoms of ergot poisoning. Another biological explanation suggests that a bird-borne illness, a form of encephalitis, caused a wave of sleeping-sickness, which included hallucinations.

Sociologists and psychologists offer a different perspective on the Salem witch trials. Some social psychologists note that the primary witnesses against the so-called witches were nearly all teenage girls. Perhaps, it has been suggested, their actions were born of jealousy, spite, and self-aggrandizing behavior. The "victims" of witchcraft psychologically projected such feelings onto the matron class, from whom the defendants were largely drawn. Sociology-based gender studies lay the blame on gender inequality in colonial America in general and Puritan Massachusetts in particular. The defendants were largely past childbearing age and no longer caregivers, but more likely to be care receivers; moreover, these women did not fit the classic ideal of Puritan women. Consequently, such women were expendable.

One of the most enduring sociological explanations centers on the downward spiral of the Puritan influence in the Massachusetts Bay Colony. The Puritan fathers of the Colony saw the scurrilous and highly suspect claims of witchcraft as offering a chance to show clearly the need to return to the basic tenets of the faith, and so consolidate power and support.

As an interesting legal footnote to this case, appeals of the convictions began almost immediately after the executions. It was not only about rehabilitating the reputations of the deceased; rather, the living—those found guilty of witchcraft but not executed—could have been subject to further prosecution and, in the minds of some, persecution for the alleged acts. Twenty-nine persons had been convicted of witchcraft. After years of litigation, the Massachusetts General Court passed a bill in 1711 reversing 22 of those convictions in the names of those for whom the appeal had been mounted. Those persons or the next of kin of those executed split £578, 12 shillings.

SUMMARY

- ▶ Persecution often occurred in ancient times against people who were perceived as "different" due to lifestyle or religious beliefs.
- ▶ Religious zeal and religious perceptions (or misperceptions) often resulted in persecution of people thought to be different or too independent of the social mores and standards of their times.
- ▶ In ancient Greece and Rome, there was a recognition that mental illness was a disease, but the cures were either unknown or inconsistent.
- ▶ At various times in human history, people with mental illnesses and disabilities lived on the streets, sustained by the villages and communities as "village idiots" and tolerated as part of the community's responsibilities.
- ▶ The widespread incarceration of the mentally ill began during the Age of Reason, justified by the belief that the mentally ill, lacking reason, knew no better and felt no pain at their imprisonment.
- ▶ Despite early dependence on the wealthy to sustain the hospitals for all forms of illness, eventually the mentally ill were separated and segregated and ultimately ignored and profoundly neglected.

▶ Early American history saw the establishment of hospitals that eventually became virtual warehouses for the mentally ill.

▶ Looking back, many of the so-called medical procedures used to combat mental disorders in the 20th century seem not just anachronistic even when they were used, but so potentially dangerous to the patient as to question why they would even be considered in the first place.

▶ Because of the deinstitutionalization movement, hundreds of thousands of mentally ill persons left mental hospitals and other asylums, often to reside on the nation's streets, a trend that continues today.

▶ Coterminous with the deinstitutionalization movement was the criminalization of the mentally ill, whereby thousands of mentally ill persons regularly moved in and out of the nation's jails and prisons.

▶ The Salem witchcraft trials, which saw 19 people executed, were an example of religious, economic, and political motivations at work in the 17th century; the actions of the accused however, may require an understanding of biology, biochemistry, psychology, and sociology.

CHAPTER REVIEW QUESTIONS

1. This chapter began with an examination of two dichotomies, the odd-bad and the blessed-damned. What do you think about these four ways to describe mentally ill individuals? Are they simply ideas that worked hundreds or even thousands of years ago, or are they viable ways to think about human conduct in the 21st century? Explain your answer.

2. In the past, some religious values have been portrayed as central to the intolerance shown mentally ill people. In what ways is this portrayal true of contemporary life? How is it a false portrayal today?

3. Do you think traditional religious practices in our contemporary world, including Hari Krishnas, Hassidic Jews, Islamic fundamentalists, Christian fundamentalists, and the Amish, affect contemporary community perceptions as a people who are different, even described as "crazy"? Do their religious practices affect the community?

4. The mental asylum took hundreds of years to take shape, but only a couple of decades to virtually vanish from the mental healthcare landscape. In your opinion, was this a good thing or a bad thing? Why do you feel this way? Should society consider re-inventing the mental asylum? [NOTE: You may want to revisit this question as you progress through the book.]

5. Most communities have people living on the streets without visible support, and many of these individuals have mental illness or substance abuse diagnoses. How do you think that the public views such people? How do you feel about their

presence in your community? What do you see as an appropriate community response to them?

6. Review the story of Rosemary Kennedy. What do you think was the primary motivation of Joe Kennedy as he allowed his daughter to undergo a lobotomy? Do you think that there are equivalent cases today? What are they?

7. Historically, treatment of mental illness has ranged from brain dissection to lobotomies to electroshock treatments. These treatments usually followed a request by the family and not the mentally ill patient. Do you believe that a person who is diagnosed with mental illness should be required to receive involuntary treatment, or should treatment only occur if the patient desires it?

8. The criminalization of the mentally ill occurred along with at least two other large-scale social movements. What were they? How did they contribute to the transformation of mentally ill patients into mentally ill criminals?

9. This chapter began and ended with stories that were 400 to 600 years old. How are they as relevant in the 21st century as they were in the 15th and 17th centuries? How do you see them as irrelevant in the 21st century?

10. Throughout this chapter, political motivations have found their way into the treatment of mentally ill persons. How do you think these views were justified by those who held them? Could this happen today? Explain your answers.

KEY TERMS

Age of Reason
Asylums
Bedlam
Canon law
Civil law
Criminalization of the mentally ill
Deinstitutionalization of the mentally ill
Demonic possession
Divine madness
Exorcism
Electroconvulsive therapy
Free will
Furiosus
Great Confinement, The
Humoral balance

Hysteria
Insane asylums
Just deserts
Insulin-coma therapy
Leucotomy
Lunatics
Mesmerism
Metrazol therapy
Moral treatment
Spirit possession
Taxonomies
Transorbital lobotomy
Trepanning/Trephination
Therapeutic interventions
Workhouses

REFERENCES

Abramson, M.F. (1972). "The criminalization of mentally disordered behavior: Possible side effect of a new mental health law." *Hospital and Community Psychiatry* 23: 101-5.

Alexander, F.G., and S.T. Selesnick (1966). *The History of Psychiatry: An Evaluation of Psychiatric Thought and Practice from Prehistoric Times to the Present*. New York City: Harper and Row, Publishers.

Almanzar, S. (2017). "Christianity and mental illness: Evil or sickness." *Ecronicon: Open Access: EC Psychology and Psychiatry*. London: Ecronicon, Ltd. Retrieved at https://www.ecronicon.com/ecpp/pdf/ECPP-04-00135.pdf on 15 January 2017.

Andrews, J. (1990). "A respectable mad-doctor? D. Richard Hale, F.R.S. (1670-1728)." *Notes and Records of the Royal Society of London* 44: 169-204.

Andrews, J., A. Briggs, R. Porter, P. Tucker, and K. Waddington (1997). *The History of Bethlem*. New York: Routledge.

Anon (1900). "Occasional Notes: British Medical Association: The section of psychology at the annual meetings." *Journal of Mental Science* XLVI: 780-1.

Ardussi, J., and L. Epstein (1978). "The saintly madman in Tibet." Pp. 327-338 in James F. Fisher (ed.), *Himalayan Anthropology: The Indo-Tibetan Interface*. Paris: Mouton & Co.

Aymard, O. (2014). *When a Goddess Dies: Worshipping Ma Anandamayi After Her Death*. New York: Oxford University Press.

Berrios, G.E. (1997). "The origins of psychosurgery: Shaw, Burckhardt and Moniz." *History of Psychiatry* 8(29): 61-81.

Belcher, J.R. (1988). "Are jails replacing the mental health system for the homeless mentally ill?" *Community Mental Health Journal* 24: 185-95.

Borum, R. (2000). "Improving high risk encounters between people with mental illness and the police." *Journal of the American Academy of Psychiatry and the Law* 28: 332-7.

Borum, R., and M. Rand (2000). "Mental Health Diagnostic and Treatment Services in Florida's Jails." *Journal of Correctional Health Care* 7: 189-207.

Borzecki M., and J.S. Wormith (1985). "The criminalization of psychiatrically ill people: A review with a Canadian perspective." *Psychiatric Journal of the University of Ottawa* 10: 241-7.

Brown, J.F.; with K.A. Menninger (col) (1940). *The Psychodynamics of Abnormal Behavior*. New York, NY: McGraw-Hill Book Company.

Canales, C. (2012). "Prisons: The new mental health system." *Connecticut Law Review* 44: 1725.

Carlson, L.W. (1999). *A Fever in Salem: A New Interpretation of the New England Witch Trials*. Chicago: Ivan R. Dee.

Chouiten, L. (2015). *Isabelle Eberhardt and North Africa: A Carnivalesque Mirage*. Lanham, MD: Lexington Books.

Cockerham, W.C. (2016). *Sociology of Mental Disorder*. 10th ed. New York: Taylor and Francis Group.

Cornford, F.M. (1997) [1935]. *Plato's Cosmology: The Timaeus of Plato, Translated with a Running Commentary*. Indianapolis: Hackett Publishing Company, Inc.

Darnton, R. (1968). *Mesmerism and the End of the Enlightenment in France*. Cambridge, MA: Harvard University Press.

D'Antonio, P. (n.d.). "History of psychiatric hospitals." Retrieved at https://www.nursing.upenn.edu/nhhc/nurses-institutions-caring/history-of-psychiatric-hospitals/ on 12 June 2017.

Demos, J. (1970). "Underlying theme in witchcraft of seventeenth-century New England." *The American Historical Review* 75: 1311-1326.

DeVries, K. (1999). *Joan of Arc: A Military Leader*. Stroud, Gloucestershire: Sutton Publishing.

Digby, A. (1983). "Changes in the Asylum: The Case of York, 1777-1815." *The Economic History Review, New Series* 36: 218-239.

Eisenberg, L., and L. Guttmacher (2010). "Were we all asleep at the switch? A personal reminiscence of psychiatry from 1940 to 2010." *Acta Psychiatrica Scandanavica* 122: 89-102.

Ellis, A., and M. Abrams (2009). *Personality Theories: Critical Perspectives*. Thousand Oaks, CA: Sage Publications, Inc.

Erickson, K.T. (1966). *Wayward Puritans: A Study in the Sociology of Deviance*. New York: Allyn and Bacon.

Faria, M.A. (2015). "Neolithic trepanation decoded—A unifying hypothesis: Has the mystery as to why primitive surgeons performed cranial surgery been solved?" *Surgical Neurology International* 6: 72.

Fogel, D. (1975). *We Are Living Proof: The Justice Model for Corrections*. Cincinnati, OH: Anderson.

Foucault, M. (2006). *History of Madness*. New York: Routledge.

Froeschner, E.H. (1992). "Two examples of ancient skull surgery." *Journal of Neurosurgery* 76: 550-2.

Fuller, D.A., E. Sinclair, J. Geller, C. Quanbeck, and J. Snook (2016). *Going, going, gone: Trends and consequences of eliminating state psychiatric beds, 2016*. Arlington, VA: Treatment Advocacy Center.

Gralnick, A. (1946). "A three-year study of electroshock therapy: Report of 276 cases; Comparative value of insulin-coma therapy." *The American Journal of Psychiatry* 102(5): 583-593.

Green, V. (1993). *The Madness of Kings: Personal Trauma and the Fate of Nations*. Mt. Pleasant, SC: The History Press.

Grob, G.N. (1992). "Mental health policy in America: Myths and realities." *Health Affairs* 11: 7-22.

Hinshaw, S.P. (2007). *The Mark of Shame: Stigma of Mental Illness and an Agenda for Change*. New York: Oxford University Press.

Hoffer, P.C. (1997). *The Salem Witchcraft Trials*. Lawrence, KS: University of Kansas Press.

Honberg, R., A. Kimball, S. Diehl, L. Usher, and M. Fitzpatrick (2011). "State mental health cuts: The continuing crisis." Arlington, VA: National Alliance on Mental Illness.

Houston, R.A. (2004). "Clergy and the case of the insane in Eighteenth-Century Britain." *Church History* 73: 114-138.

Islam, F., and R.A. Campbell (2014). "'Satan has afflicted me!' Jinn-possession and mental illness in the Qur'an." *Journal of Religion and Health* 53: 220-43.

Karp, D. (1984). "Madness, mania, and melancholy: The artist as observer." *Philadelphia Museum of Art Bulletin* 80: 1-24.

Kessler, R. (1996). *The Sins of the Father: Joseph P. Kennedy and the Dynasty He Founded.* New York: Grand Central Publishing.

Khalifa, N., and T. Hardie (2005). "Possession and jinn." *Journal of the Royal Society of Medicine* 98: 351-53.

Kinsley, D. (1974). "'Through the looking glass': Divine madness in the Hindu religious tradition." *History of Religions* 13: 270-305.

Kocić, A. (2010). "Salem witchcraft trials: The perception of women in history, literature and culture." *Facta Universitatis: Linguistics and Literature* 8(1): 1-7.

Leff, S., and V. Leff (1956). *From Witchcraft to World Health*, London and Southampton: Camelot Press Ltd.

Lamb, H.R.L., and L.E. Weinberger (2005). "The shift of psychiatric inpatient care from hospitals to jails and prisons." *Journal of the American Academy of Psychiatry and the Law* 33: 529-34.

Linder, D. (n.d.). "The Witchcraft Trials in Salem: A Commentary." Retrieved at http://law2.umkc.edu/faculty/projects/ftrials/salem/SAL_ACCT.HTM on 6 June 2017.

Lucie-Smith, E. (1976). *Joan of Arc*. Bristol: Allen Lane.

Marcus, G. (1995). "On eccentricity." Pp. 43-58 in Debbora Battaglia (ed.), *Rhetorics of Self-Making*. Berkeley, CA: University of California Press.

McDaniel, J. (1989), *The Madness of the Saints: Ecstatic Religion in Bengal*, Chicago: University of Chicago Press.

McGrath, K. (2010). "Royal madness and the law: The role of anger in representations of royal authority in Eleventh- and Twelfth-Century Anglo-Norman texts." Pp. 123-145 in Wendy J. Turner (ed.), *Madness in Medieval Law and Custom*. Leiden, The Netherlands: Brill NV.

Macdonald, D. (2013). "Classical Greek poetry and the acts of the Apostles: Imitations of Euripides' Bacchae." Pp. 463-496 in Stanley E. Porter and Andrew W. Pitts (eds.), *Christian Origins and Greco-Roman Culture: Social and Literary Contexts for the New Testament*. Boston: BRILL Academic.

Martinson, R. (1974). "What works? Questions and answers about prison reform." *Public Interest* 35: 22-54.

Matossian, M. (July-August 1982). "Ergotism and the Salem witchcraft affair." *American Scientist* 70(4): 355-57.

Mercier, C. (1900). "Lunacy and Its Treatment." *British Medical Journal* 2: 1852-54.

Morris, N. (1974). *The Future of Imprisonment*. Chicago: University of Chicago Press.

Phillips, M.R. "The transformation of China's mental health services." *The China Journal* 39 (Jan. 1998): 1-36.

Plant, J. (1994). *Heyoka. Die Contraries und Clowns der Plainsindianer*. Wyk auf Foehr: Verlag fur Amerikanistik, Deutschland.

Plato (1925). *Plato in Twelve Volumes*, Vol. 9 translated by Harold N. Fowler. Cambridge, MA, Harvard University Press; London, William Heinemann Ltd.

Read, C.F. (1940). "Consequences of metrazol shock therapy." *American Journal of Psychiatry* 97: 667-76.

Restak, R. (2000). *Mysteries of the Mind*. Washington, DC: National Geographic Society.

Rudorfer, M.V., M.E. Henry, and H.A. Sackeim (2003). "Electroconvulsive therapy." Pp. 1865-1901 in A. Tasman, J. Kay, and J.A. Lieberman (eds.), *Psychiatry*, 2nd ed. Chichester: John Wiley & Sons Ltd.

Rushton, C.J. (2010). "The King's stupor: Dealing with royal paralysis in late medieval England." Pp. 147-175 in Wendy J. Turner (ed.), *Madness in Medieval Law and Custom*. Leiden, The Netherlands: Brill NV.

Sadowsky, J.H. (1999). *Imperial Bedlam: Institutions of Madness in Colonial Southwest Nigeria*. Berkeley, CA: University of California Press.

Sarre, R. (2001). "Beyond 'What Works': A 25-Year jubilee retrospective of Robert Martinson's famous article." *The Australian and New Zealand Journal of Criminology* 34: 38-46.

Scrutton, A.P. (2015). "Is depression a sin or a disease: A critique of moralizing and medicalizing models of mental illness." *Journal of Disability and Religion* 19: 285-311.

Scull, A.T. (1977). "Madness and segregative control: The rise of the insane asylum." *Social Problems* 24(3): 337-351.

Scull, A.T. (2015). *Madness in Civilization: A Cultural History of Insanity, from the Bible to Freud, from the Madhouse to Modern Medicine*. Princeton, NJ: Princeton University Press.

Scull, A.T. (April 22, 2015). "Madness and meaning: Depictions of insanity through history." *The Paris Review*. Retrieved at https://www.theparisreview.org/blog/2015/04/22/madness-and-meaning/ on 9 June 2017.

Scrambler, G. (2009). "Health-related stigma." *Sociology of Mental Health* 31(3): 441-455.

Sidky, H. (1997). *Witchcraft, Lycanthropy, Drugs and Disease: An Anthropological Study of European Witch Hunts*. New York: Peter Lang.

Steward, J.H. (1931). "The ceremonial buffoon of the American Indian." *Papers of the Michigan Academy of Sciences, Arts, and Letters* 14: 187-202. Chicago: University of Chicago Press.

Stroman, D. (2003). *The Disability Rights Movement: From Deinstitutionalization to Self-Determination*. Washington, DC: University Press of America.

Szasz, T. (2007). *Coercion as Cure: A Critical History of Psychiatry*. New York: Routledge.

Tasca, C., M. Rapetti, M.G. Carta, and B. Fadda (2012). "Women and hysteria in the history of mental health." *Clinical Practice and Epidemiology in Mental Health* 8: 110-119.

Torrey, E.F. (2010). "Documenting the failure of deinstitutionalization." *Psychiatry* 73: 122-4.

Torrey, E.F., A.D. Kennard, D. Eslinger, R. Lamb, and J. Pavle (2010). "More mentally Ill persons are in jails and prisons than hospitals: A survey of the states." Arlington, VA: Treatment Advocacy Center. Retrieved at http://www.treatmentadvocacycenter.org/storage/documents/final_jails_v_hospitals_study.pdf on 20 June 2017.

Turner, W.J. (2013). *Care and Custody of the Mentally Ill, Incompetent, and Disabled in Medieval England*. Turnhout, Belgium: Brepols.

von Hirsch, A. (1976). *Doing Justice*. New York: Hill & Wang.

Zetterberg, H.L. (1966). *On Theory and Verification in Sociology*. Totowa, NJ: Bedminster Press.

CHAPTER 3

The Brain and the Mind

CHAPTER OUTLINE

LEARNING OBJECTIVES

After reading this chapter, you should be able to:

▶ Clarify the extent to which the mind is a separate entity from the organ of the brain.
▶ Understand how the brain and mind function separately.
▶ Comprehend how the health of the brain is evident in the health of the mind.
▶ Describe when and how a healthy mind can be evaluated or even detected.
▶ Explain what is considered the baseline of health for the brain.

PROLOGUE

The following is based on real-life events. As these are not public figures and their situations remain private, the names have been changed to protect their identities.

Chad grew up in a wealthy and stable home in the Midwest. His father was a senior manager for a large corporation, while his mother, a licensed psychologist, stayed home with Chad and his older sister. Young Chad was described as brilliant. His IQ scores revealed a superior intellect. He was successful in school and athletics. He attended Harvard College, graduating with a social economics degree just as the Vietnam War was beginning. A pacifist, Chad volunteered for the Peace Corps.

Despite Chad's Peace Corps service—Selective Service rules allowing for alternative service were several years in the future—he was drafted by the Army and sent to Vietnam. His commitment to pacifism led him to a position as a chaplain's assistant. Chad found himself in combat at the start of the January 1968 Tet Offensive. In the first days of the offensive, his unit's chaplain was killed and Chad, never religious, was required to give last rites to body parts of dead soldiers. Later, trekking through the jungles after the military sprayed them with Agent Orange, a toxic defoliant, Chad scraped the powdery residue from his face and hands.

Returning from Vietnam, Chad was unable to pursue his childhood ambition of becoming an attorney as he now avoided all confrontations. He had frequent flashbacks and nightmares about his experiences, but at the time Vietnam veterans were subjected to scorn for trying to impose democracy on another nation by force of arms. Chad found it was easier to just smile, nod, and skim over his year in Vietnam and talk instead about his work building wells in Africa while serving as a Peace Corps volunteer. He was admitted to Stanford Graduate School of Education and decided to become an elementary school teacher. While in graduate school, Chad met and married Diane. Within three years of their marriage, they had two children. After ten years, they divorced. Diane blamed combat-related PTSD, post-traumatic stress disorder, a medical condition recognized since the 1950s but which had only recently come to the forefront as an explanation for the dissolution of social relations affecting Vietnam war veterans. No one talked about Agent Orange at the time.

When Chad met Britney, he had been divorced for six years. His quiet and thoughtful demeanor was attractive to Britney, a vivacious, outgoing, and lively person. At the time, he had become an elementary school principal in a small Midwestern town as he enjoyed helping teachers more than classroom teaching. Britney worked at an alternative school for troubled teens and relied on Chad's steady analysis of her students' problems to reach solutions. Chad relied on Britney's sense of community and connections to help him feel part of the people with whom he worked. They were married within a year of meeting. Chad was 45 and Britney was 33.

Throughout the first decade of their marriage, Britney marveled at the acuity of Chad's thinking. He accepted people who were different and the same as he was. Although he came from a privileged background, his tastes and needs in material goods were simple. He liked jazz and loved old disc-format record players. He insisted that his children be with him at least half of the week and for vacations. He spoke to his mother every Sunday night. He was kind. He listened to people complain about co-workers and guided them to amicable resolutions. He was a master of mediation and problem solving.

As Chad turned 55, Britney noticed that he had trouble recalling words and was slow to remember recent events. His quiet demeanor became quieter. This brilliant and witty man slowly disintegrated into confusion. When he was frostbitten shoveling snow because he forgot to come in the house and did not notice the deepening cold, Britney took him to a neurologist. The neurological evaluation showed that although he once tested with superior cognition, his knowledge, comprehension, and intellectual skills were in decline.

By age 60, Chad resided at the local Veterans Administration Community Living Center. He would smile as Britney entered the room but did not know who she was. He did not know her name or why she was there. He babbled nonsense sounds. He could still feed and "toilet" himself, but was incapable of getting dressed and undressed without assistance. Externally, Chad looked the same. His smile was bright and cheerful. He stood tall and swung his arms easily as he walked. Taking a walk outside one day, Britney was ecstatic when Chad said, "I'm cold." It was the first coherent sentence he had spoken in weeks and was a correct response to his personal condition: It was cold. Chad continues to live and decline in his room at the veterans center, and now appears to have no coherent thoughts and is unable to speak.

Chad's case exemplifies the progression of a mind from healthy to diseased. Many possible reasons for his progression into mental illness exist: organic or biochemical roots, physical or social-environmental origins, early Alzheimer's disease due to genetic causes, dementia, and still other unknown causes. It is unknown whether Chad's later mental decline was brought on by his highly emotional wartime experiences, related to his repeated exposure to a chemical substance with known neurotoxicity, a reflection of genetic factors, or even some combination of these forces (Boyle, Decoufle, et al., 1987; Veterans Administration, 2016; see also Yaffe, Vittinghoff, et al., 2010). But was Chad's **mind** the reason for his cognitive loss or was it damage to his **brain**? The answer to this question is not easily discerned, as we shall see in the remainder of this chapter.

Chapter Overview

This chapter provides another set of tools to aid your examination of the interface between mental healthcare and the criminal justice system. In this chapter, we explore the complexity of the mind and brain as a healthy, living organ. We describe the brain as a kind of book, as well as the difficulties encountered trying to "read" it. First, we will consider how historically the mind was thought to be a separate entity from the brain. Now, through modern philosophical and physiological studies, neuroscientists and psychiatrists have learned that the mind and the brain work as one. Although they have separate functions, activity of the mind is associated with specific parts of the brain (Smart, 2017).

The second section explores the structure of the mind and how it is controlled. We examine the distinctions between the unconscious, preconscious, and conscious functioning of the mind, using psychoanalyst Sigmund Freud's iceberg metaphor. The third section shifts to the study of the brain as an organ and the various parts of it that regulate how we behave, voluntarily and involuntarily. This section reviews reflective and instinctual behavior, personality, and cognitive reasoning. Moving to the fourth section, recent developments in brain mapping provide a means of tying together our understanding of the biology of the brain and its emotive elements. We also consider what happens when the brain dies before the body.

The epilogue is an opportunity to learn about what can happen when a brain suffers serious and repetitive insults. Such injuries, often experienced in a contact sport such as football, can lead to a progressive disorder of the brain called chronic traumatic encephalopathy (CTE).

FRAMING THE ISSUES

In the 17th century, French philosopher, scientist, and mathematician René Descartes (b.1596-d.1650) proposed that the mind was separate from the body (see Descartes, 1641). He saw the mind as related to human organs, but also very different and separate from the body or brain. Over the past four centuries, philosophical and medical understandings about the linkages between the mind and brain evolved, including the idea of **functionalism**, which holds that the mind is "a function of the brain and [the] product of its physical activity" (Hansotia, 2003: 331; see Sperry, 1982; Swartz and Begley, 2002).

The consensus within the scientific community is that the brain and mind are distinct entities within one organ: The brain is a complex physical entity and the mind exists within the organ (Stanford, 2000). The brain, like all human organs, can suffer impairment or functional loss when there is an illness, disease, or injury. For example, consider traumatic brain injuries, encephalitis (inflammation of the brain from a virus or bacteria), or hydrocephalus (a birth defect that causes spinal fluid to accumulate in the brain). In Huntington's disease, a single genetic mutation results in dramatic personality changes, dementia, and early death. As the mind deteriorates with the progress of the disease, cognition is lost, along with memory and language function, perception, and emotional control. However, the brain continues to function as an organ, automatically, like the liver or lungs, directing the body to breathe, eliminate, digest food, and even sneeze. As we will read, ultimately a vegetative state emerges as parallel progressive atrophy of the brain as an organ occurs due to evident increased levels of plaque or damage, and a shrinking of the brain ensues, until ultimately there is bodily death (Hansotia, 2003: 331).

The mind also is the functional component of a human being that enables awareness of existence, as in Descartes' (1637) famous dictum, "*Cogito ergo sum*" ("I think, therefore I am"). It is the filter and recipient of human experiences that processes consciousness, thought, memories, experiences, reflections, and responses. Words that describe mental senses, such as reasoning, judgment, understanding, and synthesis, symbolize the processing of the information that flows throughout a person's brains cells. These nerve cells, connected by chemical gaps called **synapses**, move the information into a central cortex, where it is then simultaneously redistributed into a reaction, and then to the mind's storage facilities to become a long-term or short-term memory. The brain also administers information to inform and direct experience, knowledge, and observations.

We can use a book metaphor to represent the human mind; this metaphor can help us visualize the concept of how a human brain and mind interconnect, interrelate, and interact:

> To see how we can consider the separation of the information from the actual nervous system [to the brain and mind] itself, think of a book. The book's mass, its temperature, and other physical dimensions can now be considered as roughly akin to the brain. Then think about the informational content (i.e., the story the book tells or claims it makes). In the computational theory, that is akin to the mind. The mind, then, is the information **instantiated** in and processed by the nervous system (Henriques, 2011a; see also Henriques, 2011b).

On the outside, all books look pretty much the same—as essentially do all brains. It is the contents of the book that makes the difference. The stories in books are commonly organized in a sequential pattern with a discernable beginning, middle, and ending. Some books are organized differently and the patterns of story differ. Some have better editors than others. Imagine, though, if a book's pages were simply tossed into the air, scattering the pages of contents, and then re-bound into a set volume. This may occur with some forms of mental disease. To expand on this metaphor, while the book cover and jacket may be the same, the organization and ability to retrieve information may be disjointed or incomprehensible. Does that lack of organization in thought or inability to

BOX 3.1

Thinking About the Issues

Consider following issues:

1. Does that lack of organization in thought (i.e., a jumbled table of contents) or inability to locate information (i.e., a bad job of indexing the book) make a person less human or useful?

2. Is it critical for people to understand and appreciate the differences in the table of contents of people and recognize that we can use different approaches to evaluate whether conduct may be healthy or destructive?

3. How are these concerns related to mental health or mental illness, or is the issue in the "eye of the beholder"?

locate information make a person less human or useful? It is critical for people to understand the differences in people's "table of contents" and recognize that there are different approaches to evaluating whether conduct may be healthy or destructive.

The book metaphor is useful. However, as suggested in Box 3.1, it may have its limits. At the end of the day, a key question remains unanswered: How do we know if a mind is healthy?

UNDERSTANDING THE MIND

Over a hundred years ago, Austrian neurologist Sigmund Freud (b.1856-d.1939) was one of the first scholars of the brain to theorize that the brain and mind were biologically the same but divided by levels of consciousness (or the functionality of the brain/mind) and unconsciousness (also known as the reactive, submerged, and invisible functionality of the brain/mind). Freud claimed that consciousness was only a small portion of mental processes and that awareness of mental activity was not the only evidence of brain activity. His recognition that the brain is an active storage facility for unconscious as well as conscious thought was validated by later scientific findings of the interdependence and co-existence of the mind and brain. Freud successfully argued that the mind and brain were not, as was believed during this historical period, separate physical entities like lungs and kidneys. Until late in the 19th century, prior to Freud's research, the brain was treated as an organ, while the mind was thought to exist in an invisible halo-like cloud. He maintained that people are not categorically different in terms of good and evil; they just think and act according to their respective personalities.

Following Freud's theories, personal conduct emerges as one of the essential bonds between the mind and the brain. Subjective awareness, along with subconscious reactions and assessments, trigger the mind/brain connections to reveal individual traits and outgoing behavior. Our everyday evaluations of ourselves and others, even today, often reflect Freud's theories of standardized behavioral traits that he developed a century ago. He recognized that humans demonstrate rational and irrational neurotic traits, repressive and evident states, and healthy and unhealthy personas, but human behaviors are bundled into predictable integrated interactive traits that exist within the mind and, therefore, the brain. The collective characteristics of the average or normative patterns of responsive behavior in humans are fortunately indicia of a "typical" mind.

As a pioneer in exploring the linkages between the mind and the brain, Freud was also one of the first to theorize that humans will also demonstrate physical symptoms or erratic behavior in order to mask or to camouflage mental conflicts or disorders. Basing his revolutionary theories on the existence of standardized human psychological behaviors, he contended that there was also a correlation between mental and brain dysfunction, rather than spiritual problems. His ideas about the rationality and interweave of the brain with the mind were wild and revolutionary.

Freud (1900, 1905) developed a topographical model that illustrated the mind's structures and functions, using an iceberg to illustrate the three levels of the mind (see Figure 3.1). Although Freud initially expounded his theories more than 100 years ago, the modern use of MRI imaging re-confirms that his topographical analogy between the mind and the brain remains relevant. On the surface, or visible to nearly all people, are our immediate thoughts, the **conscious mind**: I am cold, I am hungry, I am anxious. When electrodes are connected for human study, certain parts of the brain, cerebral sections, light up in response to the activation of our immediate thoughts. Demonstrating brain/mind connectivity, the correlative emotive paths emerge even if a person does not actually experience an awareness of being cold, hungry, or anxious.

The alternative or second state, suggested Freud, is the **preconscious mind**, which remains readily accessible to the conscious mind as immediate memories are retrieved from it (Freud, 1913). Humans collect thoughts, tell stories, and share knowledge based on what they store in their minds; the brain later sorts through this information, effectively organizing the mind. It is in this second mental state or organizational system that each person's experiences and recollections are stored. The third level is the unconscious, which we will explore later, is the primitive, hidden self. Again, although all brains are organically the same, the ability to remember matters, integrate the materials, and expound or respond to what the second level of what the brain collects and keeps depends on each person's mental health, acuity, training, and genetic predisposition. The complexity of the connections between brain power, intellect, and memories depends on a variety of factors and issues, including environmental changes, age, and social exposure. It is relatively easy now to see how an illness could jumble, confuse, or

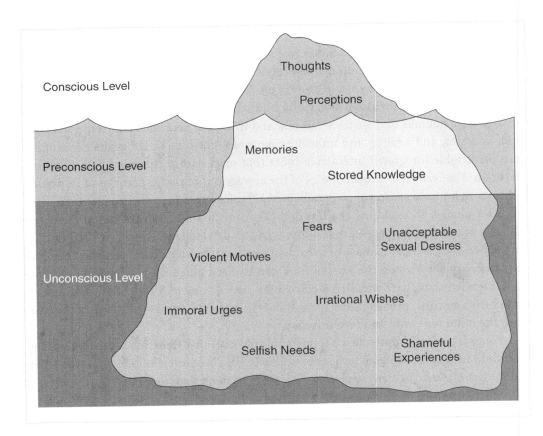

FIGURE 3.1 **Freud's Iceberg Map of the Mind**

interfere with a person's ability to retrieve and use information from this second level of the mind.

These various states of consciousness will challenge mental health providers and first responders to engage in immediate assessments to determine what, if anything, can or should be done to provide care to a person struggling with cognition or issues of mental acuity. This is the focus of much of this chapter: By knowing ways a healthy mind/brain operates, there is a comparative platform to assess when there may be an illness, disorder, or disease—mental or physical—affecting the conscious and immediate brain functions of a person.

To truly understand all of Freud's theories, the third level of his philosophical research—the passion of his life's work—should be known as well. These thoughts are described as the hidden, bottom-of-the-iceberg base of mentality and was the crux of his psychological and psychiatric analyses. This is the **unconscious mind**. It is at the lowest level of mental or cognitive thought, according to Freud's theory, where the true cause of most of human beings' predictable and unpredictable behavior is found, a theory embraced by modern psychologists today. Again, referring again to the iceberg analogy (Figure 3.1), the unconscious mind is the part that is invisible to others, and especially to one's self. The unconscious mind is a repository or the book shelf for the storage or accumulation of rapid, impulsive behavior and uncontrollable thoughts. It is argued now that when the unconscious mind controls the conscious mind, there is a resulting lack of control over impulsive or irrational, or even destructive behavior. This lack of control over the unconscious mind may be evidence of mental illness. The lack of control in the unconscious mind could cause a mild, easy-going person to become enraged or harmful.

UNDERSTANDING AND MEASURING BRAIN FUNCTION

Now that we understand that the complexity of the mind is meshed into the organic function of the brain, we delve deeper into the processing of mental function. In this section, we expound on Freud's theories of the mind's conscious awareness and mental unconsciousness to address several basic sets of skills and procedures to understand the human **psyche**. This is the base biological activity of humans that emerges with instinctual behaviors. The overlay, the psyche, encompasses the psychological mind and brain functions such as **ego**, inner person, subconscious, intellect, and human motive force (Hasselmann and Schmolke, 1993; see also Axmann, 2015).

Reflexive Behaviors

First, we will learn about baseline and primitive awareness, the reflexive or **instinctual** behaviors. This framework for neuro-information is the control guide for nature's instinctual actions, such as pleasure and pain. Being angry, smiling, or feeling scared are non-verbal actions of the subjective component of the reflexive actions known as "qualia." No matter where a person is born, what language he speaks, or the depth, strength, or complexity of his intellectual capacity, a healthy mind responds to immediate contact with fire by the reflexive mental command to withdraw. Such actions are the purview of instinctive behavior, as it is quite literally automatic behavior, done without cognitive thought.

Once we understand that as with all biological creatures we have automatic responses, then we will delve later in this chapter into learning how we are individually different through our **personality**. Personality shapes individual conduct. While most humans will shed tears in response to an emotional situation, how and why a person cries varies according to the individual's psychological personality. The measurement and clinical assessment of personality behaviors evolved during the last century and are widely used as indicators of why people act the way they do. In this context, we explore **psychometric tests** that measure certain aspects of one's personality and intelligence or **cognition**. While heavily criticized by scientists, psychometric tests are widely used in our educational, business, military defense, and criminal justice communities.

Today, modern tools of medicine easily capture our internal bodily functions. Through x-rays, miniaturized cameras, and ultrasound imaging, doctors see human heart chambers, the process of the intestines, and even the embryonic development of the unborn. These biological activities are performed by our bodies without conscious directives or mental engagement. We don't "tell" our intestines to digest our dinner. Nevertheless, medical personnel and first responders must engage in external observations and tests to immediately determine what, if any, reflexive connectivity exists in a physically or mentally disabled person. For example, a stroke victim (i.e., a person who suffered from a loss of oxygen supply in the brain due to a blood clot) can present external behaviors that are mistaken for intoxication or drug impairment. Through knowing what behaviors are reflexive, versus unconscious conduct that is masked by a substance, appropriate intervention can occur.

Reflexive movements, such as eye blinking, moving the tongue when chewing, optic responses to a pinpoint of light to one eye, or even responses to certain tastes assist in a reflexive evaluation. While the evaluation of such external indicators is only intended to illustrate the simplicity of assessment tests, compared to the gravity of the harm, for the depth of information sought, specific medical training is required to respond appropriately. Obviously, a woman who drives her car onto a sidewalk crowded with people will need an emergency assessment: What caused the incident? If she fails field sobriety tests (e.g., inability to walk a straight line or hold up one foot up while counting to ten), this may suggest intoxication. But it could also mean other forces are at work as well. Is it a case of a cranial blood clot and stroke or four glasses of wine?

Appropriate reflexive responses to stimuli are critical indicators of healthy brain activity. Field sobriety tests provide one example. However, it is not just the peace officer who pulls over a suspected drunk driver and asks for a demonstration of the driver's reflexes or examines pupilar responses to light for whom such tests prove to be vital. The family or loved ones reporting erratic behavior may notice that Grandpa or Grandma is a "little off," but not know why. Having knowledge of appropriate reflexive behavior saves lives. Recognizing behaviors that are non-responsive or inappropriately responsive also provides critical information to medical personnel, responders, and 911 operators that avoids complexity of damages, expensive and unnecessary surgeries, or erroneous neglect of a critical problem.

While there are obviously physical and psychological reasons for behaviors, what if the cause for changes in a healthy brain is due to environmental conditions? Think about the situations described in Box 3.2.

BOX 3.2

Law and Mental Health: Brain Death and Living

Consider the legal decision of the judges in the matter of *Fonseca v. Kaiser Permanente Med. Ctr. Roseville*, a 2016 reported appellate court ruling. Although the concept of brain death is accepted by the majority of physicians, lawyers, and ethicists, controversies over the determination of when the brain as an organ is dead persists. In the *Fonseca* decision, the Kaiser hospital determined that a 2-year old child suffered irreversible cessation of all functions of his entire brain and therefore was brain dead. The child had been brought to the emergency room following a severe asthma attack. Within a short period of time, he lapsed into a coma following cardiac arrest, but continued to breathe through a ventilator, assisted by medical intervention. Under California law, essentially the cessation of brain and brain stem function is the equivalent of death and therefore, by the operation of law, the child was no longer alive. According to hospital policy, the physician signed a death certificate for the child and then sought to terminate the life support. The child's mother filed a court order to prohibit physicians from ordering the end of the child's medical interventions. She legally objected to the hospital's decision, arguing that its definition of "death" was a violation of her due process rights and in violation of other constitutional principles.

In a hearing prior to the appellate court decision, the medical director testified that the child's brain was not telling his organs how to function. This meant there had to be continuous artificial substitution of brain activity to regulate blood pressure, hormone levels, demand for nutrition, and even to meet the need for bodily warmth. The body and brain did not have the ability to detect and combat infections, react to stimulus, or recognize cognitive needs. At most, the child had some reflex movement, but it was not certain he could breathe on his own.

In denying the request to continue life support, the court found that the California statute incorporated accepted national medical standards that acknowledged that if there is an end to all functions of the entire brain, then there is no longer life, and death occurs. The decision of the doctors was under the **color of law** or the application of statutory standards to factual circumstances. The court further found that no parent has the right to demand healthcare be administered to a person who is not alive in the eyes of the state law and that the hospital correctly determined that the patient was dead. The hospital's medical determination was through the independent testing of three different doctors, and its policies permitted the family to have any other examinations they felt were necessary. While the mother's maternal instincts and moral position were understandable, the judges found that her request for relief was not fundamentally or legally sound.

People might not see a distinction between someone who is brain dead and an apneic patient in a coma: Both feel warm to the touch, both have an audible heartbeat, and both appear to be in a deep slumber—few would guess that the law does not ascribe equal meaning of death in both scenarios. In the *Fonseca* case, the California court ruled that the hospital had the authority to declare the child died. Law enforcement officers may be challenged to describe death both according to its legal meaning and compared to medical usage.

A brain-dead person may not be dead, according to some doctors. Consider the still-evolving case of Jahi McMath, involving a teenage girl who, following surgery in 2013, when she was 13 years old, suffered unpredicted complications, massive blood loss, and consequent cardiac arrest and loss of cognitive function. Without dispute, McMath met the formal criteria for brain death in 2013. However, her mother refused to terminate care and, in medical twist, widely respected neurologist Alan Shewman submitted court documents attesting that "Jahi McMath [did] not currently fulfill the accepted medical standards for brain death" (*Winkfield v. Benioff Children's Hospital Oakland*, p. 3). As of 2018, she remains alive, even though her brain is not functioning. The conflicts as to when a person is dead or alive raises complex emotional and legal issues that are not readily resolved or addressed. Think about a few questions that can emerge with an issue of brain death:

1. In the future, do you think that there will be ways to correct brain death or change its status? Do you think that the definition of death may change as more discoveries are made about organ rejuvenation or transplants?

2. If a law enforcement officer is investigating a homicide, what information may be necessary to determine if there is brain death? Can he make that decision? What process do you think must be followed if a death occurs outside of a hospital?

3. When there is a medical decision to terminate life support, do you think hospitals' ethical policies address whether there is a homicide or the killing of one human being by another? Do you think this is why the hospital in *Fonseca* actually issued a death certificate for the patient before the termination of life support was ordered?

Sources: Fonseca v. Kaiser Permanente Med. Ctr. Roseville (2016);
May (2018); Segal (2018); Winkfield v. Benioff Children's Hospital Oakland (2017).

DEFINING AND MEASURING PERSONALITIES

Many human characteristics are instinctual, reflexive, or automatic. The brain is wired to direct traffic without interaction from the mind or thinking. Here, as we have described, there is no need for cognitive thought or mental reasoning. For the most part, this is the same for all people. When there is not automatic functionality, then there are observable misfires or miscues. This changes with the emergence of individual personality. The essence of the different ways to describe and depict human behaviors, interactions, and responses with other humans is categorized as differences in personalities. Easily the most complex, yet understandable, explanation of human behavior, personality refers to individual differences in patterns of thinking, feeling, and characteristics that are bundled into descriptive social behaviors. For example, we may say a person has an easy-going personality, meaning that the individual is pleasant and interactions with her are predictable. But the term also reflects the nature, disposition, temperament, or even the psyche (mentality) of people. We know that pets, wild creatures, and even inanimate objects seem to have personalities. Our focus, however, is on personalities associated with human beings.

Categorically, personality has three baseline classifications: positive, neutral, and negative. However, there are 638 different personality descriptors within the categories, of which 234 traits (37%) are positive, including caring, calm, brilliant, and fair; 112 traits (18%) are neutral, including ambitious, mellow, and impressionable; and 292 traits (46%) are negative, ranging from boisterous, abrupt, or gloomy (Ideonomy, 2017).

Experience in recognizing the categorical differences in personalities is important as to when and how to objectively gauge an encounter with a stranger. Recognizing patterns of common or similar behaviors may help a first responder appreciate why and when different personalities occur and how to best respond to them. As we continue to delve more deeply into mental illnesses and disease, it is critical to have a baseline appreciation of common mind and brain activity.

Some traits that emerge with first impressions is whether a person is outgoing and social or tends to be quiet and observant. According to psychologists, personality is wired through brain chemistry as being either **introverted** or **extroverted**. Although whether a person is an introvert or an extrovert is not a cookie cutter outline, introverts are known to be quieter and more energized when alone, while extroverts prefer verbalization and gain energy from being with groups of people. Extroverts exhibit characteristics of charm, charisma, and persuasion, while introverts exhibit their creativity when they are able to work alone and are commonly described as thoughtful and better listeners. Clearly, there is a huge spectrum of behaviors that links extroversion and introversion personality traits. It may depend on work, environment, or even developmental experiences as to whether a person is categorically or responsively introverted or extroverted. Being an introvert does not mean a person always behaves like a monk, and being an extrovert is no guarantee to social precedency.

Physiologically, in an early study of the correlation between the brain as an organ and the conductivity of the mind, psychologist Randy Buckner (b.1970-) discovered that introverts tend to have a larger, thicker portion of grey matter in the prefrontal cortex—a region of the mind associated with abstract thought and decision making — while extroverts have less grey matter in this region of the brain. This may account for the introverts' mental (and therefore physical) ability to withdraw and think before acting or reacting and the extroverts' tendency to take risks without processing every aspect or consequence and "live in the moment."

BOX 3.3

Historical Perspective on Identifying Personality Categories

To develop deeper understanding of the evolution of the study of personality, consider how early social scientists developed the concept of categorizing personalities. In the earliest known study of human behavior, Greek physician Hippocrates (b.460-d.370 B.C.E.) applied ancient Mesopotamian medical concepts of bodily fluids and opined that human moods, emotions, and behavior also flowed directly within the same balance of the four fluids or *humors*: yellow bile, black bile, phlegm, and blood. Later, the Greek psychologist Galen (b.130-d.210 C.E.) deduced that humans had four temperaments: the *sanguine*, an enthusiastic, social person; the *choleric*, a short-tempered, irritable person; the *melancholic*, an analytic, wise person; and *phlegmatic*, a relaxed, peaceful person. Around the turn of the first millennia, the Persian philosopher Avicenna (b.980-d.1037) observed that "emotional aspects, mental capacity, moral attitudes, self-awareness, movements, and dreams" were all within the construct of personality. For nearly 700 years, the dissection of four temperaments directed the analysis of personality types. However, by the end of the 18th century, philosopher Immanuel Kant questioned the correlation of bodily fluids to the mental behaviors.

By the start of the 20th century, psychiatrists began to systematize personality types, tying the basic concept of what is **normative behavior** (e.g., what personality traits make a good or even happy person) and non-normative behavior (e.g., what makes a criminal or mentally disturbed individual). Then Carl Gustav Jung (b.1875-d.1961) first administered tests to distinguish and describe personality types. Jung, a Swiss-trained psychiatrist, known as the founder of analytical psychology, studied word associations in his patients and discovered he could categorize people's symbolic behaviors through patterns and thereby identify behavioral complexes. The complexes or "symbols" of conscious behaviors generate predictable patterns that then defined personality types. His research recognized that similar behavioral traits exist, regardless of the person's culture, economics, or religious beliefs.

Sources: Jung (1921); Kant (1785); Lutz (2002).

As both personality types have advantages and disadvantages, one could ask whether an extrovert is an extrovert for life and likewise with introverts. These questions have existed throughout the history of research into the human personality (see Box 3.3). It appears that people float between the two. Hungarian psychologist Mihaly Csikszentmihalyi (b.1934-) noted that his most artistic patients often drifted between introversion and extroversion: "[They're] usually one or the other," he wrote, "either preferring to be in the thick of crowds or sitting on the sidelines and observing the passing show."

Clinical Assessment of Personality Types

Jung's personality typing system eventually evolved into the **Meyers-Briggs Type Indicator (MBTI)**. The MBTI is based directly on Jung's theories of mental function that "we all have specific preferences in the way we construe our experiences and these preferences underlie our interests, needs, values and motivation" and direct today's categorization of personality types (Kaplan and Saccuzzo, 2009: 449).

What personality type are you? The MBTI is one of the most definitive and often used psychometric tests of personality type. It must be administered by a professional clinician and should be used only if a professional opinion of personality is needed. It consists of 93 questions and takes about 15 minutes. While quick, self-administered versions allow people to superficially learn about themselves, it takes a trained professional to interpret what the results imply.

Below are the 16 different clusters of types, with the associated Meyers-Briggs descriptors (Meyers-Briggs Foundation, 2017; NERIS Analytics, 2017):

A.   Analyst Category

Logician — Innovative, inventors with an unquenchable thirst for knowledge

Architect — Imaginative strategic thinkers with a plan for everything

Commander — Bold, imaginative and strong-willed leaders, always finding a way or making one

Debater — Smart and curious thinkers who cannot resist an intellectual challenge

B.   Diplomats Category

Advocate — Quiet and mystical, yet very inspiring and tireless idealists

Mediator — Poetic, kind and altruistic people, always eager to help a good cause

Protagonist — Charismatic and inspiring leaders, able to mesmerize their listeners

Campaigner — Enthusiastic, creative and social free spirits who can always find a reason to smile

C.   Sentinels

Logistician — Practical and fair-minded individuals whose reliability cannot be doubted

Defender — Very dedicated and warm protectors, always ready to defend their loved ones

Executive — Excellent administrators, unsurpassed at managing things or people

Consul — Extraordinary caring, social and popular people; always eager to help

D.   Explorer

Virtuoso — Bold and practical experimenters, masters of all kinds of tools

Adventurer — Flexible and charming artists, ready to explore and experience something new

Entrepreneur — Smart and energetic and very perceptive people who truly enjoy living on the edge

Entertainer — Spontaneous, energetic, and enthusiastic people; life is never boring around them

Tests like the MBTI provide a concrete depiction of who you are and why you do things the way you do. While the descriptions are generally positive, the extreme ends of these personality descriptors can stretch into a disordered or distorted personality.

There are countless personality tests and assessments available through the internet. Entering "personality test" in a search engine will yield dozens of free ones, and we offer no endorsement of any specific test. The various personality assessments rely on how honestly the questions are answered. Sometimes there are inconsistencies between self-assessment and perceptions. Everyone has biases, blind spots, and sensitivities. Consequently, many of the questions that ask for a resolution of common life situations result in a depiction of how a person *would* react rather how he or she *should* react.

One of the best known, but time-consuming, psychological tests is the **Minnesota Multiphasic Personality Inventory (MMPI)**. It is one of the most commonly administered psychometric tests, following IQ and school-based standardized testing. Originally designed in 1939 as an adult measure of psychopathology and personality structure, the MMPI-2 evolved into a 567-item evaluative questionnaire, although there is a 370-item version as well.

The MMPI is important as it is used on both ends of the criminal justice spectrum. Law enforcement agencies frequently administer it to recruits to "screen out" unsuitable candidates. The MMPI-2-RF assesses behaviors such as depression, psychopathy, paranoia, anxiety, bizarre thinking, antisocial practices, and paranoia. Equally important, a version of the MMPI-2 is often administered to prison inmates as a way of determining suitability for rehabilitation and intra-institutional programs, including possible threat-level classifications (Grover, 2011).

A major criticism of the MMPI is that non-whites tend to score higher for unfavorable behaviors and that the results may not be an accurate indicator of non-white overt or subvert personality factors (McCreary and Padilla, 1977). Moreover, the same differences are noted in non-institutionalized populations (Castro et al., 2008). No good explanation is known for the statistically significant differences, but it is suggested that there is inherent racial bias embedded within the test. Other tests, including the Thematic Apperception Test (Morgan, 2002) and the Rorschach Ink-Blot Test (Dana, 2002), were developed to overcome both the racial and cultural influences in intelligence testing and to eliminate the influence of verbal intelligence. However, the MMPI and the MBTI remain among the most popular tests, largely owing to their ease of administration and large data bases confirming their reliability and validity.

Cognitive Functions

While personality assessments are helpful to understand and navigate working with other people, another critical assessment is the determination of the intellectual ability of a person. Wild animals, pets, and most biological creatures seem to demonstrate innate personality, but intelligence or **cognitive reasoning** is demonstrably different in people. Another aspect of healthy brain and mind activity is clear evidence of the ability to engage in cognitive reasoning. **Cognition** is the accumulation of information, intelligence, and cybernetic knowledge that informs the mind to process experiences and then translate the experiences into language and intellectual action. Essentially, cognitive reasoning and responses is the combination of the mind's ability to process reflexive knowledge and various personality behaviors through intelligent or intellectual reasoning. Assessments for cognition include observations of attention span, memory, reasoning, and other brain activities that evidence complex mental processes. If a person is mentally diseased or disabled, then although he or she may evidence quick reflexes and a charming personality, evidence of impaired cognition or the inability to process information can guide the first responder into deeper or more thorough assessments.

Essentially, the mind's cognitive distribution is the translation of the flow of information through the conscious nervous system. For example, if you were asked to throw a baby out of a window, your mental cognitive process would resist the behavior. Your experience, intellect, and mental wiring would inform you that this action is flawed or immoral. However, if your intellectual processing also enables you to rationalize that there is a fire and your action will enable the baby to survive, then your cognitive reasoning will process the information differently. The judgment and decision making is performed in a split second.

In the past, testing for intelligence—that is, evidence of cognitive abilities—emerged and culminated in what was described as IQ (intelligent quotient) tests. While the intelligence test provided a directional compass to predict some aspects of intellectual abilities, academic success, and acumen, such tests are incapable of measuring talent, artistry, social adeptness, or even normalcy. IQ tests, as tests for cognitive reasoning, are somewhat biased psychometric exams that look at intelligence through word analysis and spatial reasoning. They compare the test taker to others who are the same age and, frequently, in the same school grade. One controversy that emerged with IQ tests is that they dissuaded talented people from trying to compete in academic pursuits if their IQ was lower than that of their peers. The IQ tests also failed to address cultural, linguistic, or intellectual influences.

As with personality inventories and reflex assessments, there are online tests for scaling cognition, similar to but broader-based than the IQ test. Those using the tests should be aware that the quizzes may be a source of data collection for commercial purposes or just give a thumb-nail review. In any circumstances, self-administered tests are as objective as the person taking them. Such tests, while based on the evaluation of intellectual development, critical thinking, and abstract analysis, nevertheless still generally fail to provide clear and unimpeachable answers to questions concerning intelligence. Such tests determine whether a person can make reliable decisions, use reasoning to solve problems, and react appropriately to new or complex circumstances, questions, and people. Once again, we do not endorse online tests; rather, we suggest that they be approached as a means of understanding how such tests function and what they reveal. The purpose of knowing about cognitive tests is to familiarize community providers with alternatives when engaging in assessments for mental health or mental illness.

THE FUTURE: UNDERSTANDING AND MEASURING BRAIN FUNCTION

Psychologists and neuroscientists are joining forces to map the brain and mind (Boccia, Piccard, and Guariglia, 2015). With developing technology, it is likely that in the future physical exams, written tests, and even verbal cognitive assessments will become obsolete. The use of **functional magnetic resonance imaging (fMRI)** is a sophisticated technique to study the interactions and interrelationship between the mind and brain through imagery and known response to stimuli (Belliveau, Kwong, et al., 1992). It is reasonable that brain imaging will evolve into giving practitioners the ability to simply "read" mental cognition in a map of the brain rather than test for it. Today MRI bioneurological studies link psychological studies and correlate the relationship between the two forms of research. Since 1993, the investigation into mental and brain scans with MRIs has increased at least 200 percent (Berman, Jonides, and Nee, 2006). Using neuro-imaging studies that route brain/mind responses to specific mental stimuli, researchers and scientists may soon pinpoint all biological sources in the brain for positive and negative effects of associated behaviors and conduct. Genetic studies will expand this roadmap of the brain, along with providing greater insights into the mind, brain, and body relationships.

Although studies are limited, results imply there is specific activation of specific brain areas when a person is stimulated with certain kinds of relevant information. Patterns of self-regulation of behavior, problem solving skills, and adaptive behavior are revealed through repetitive brain scans during mental stimulus. For example, a recent study (Kragel, Knodt, et al., 2016) revealed that emotional states are revealed as "flickering images" across the surface of the human brain. In this study, 32 people were scanned and exposed to identical stimuli that underlie 7 emotional responses. The subjects thereafter completed a written questionnaire to validate their responses to the study. An algorithm then disclosed a correlation of networks of mapped brain activity that uniformly linked observable physical activity to the mental and emotional responses associated with contentment, amusement, surprise, fear, anger, sadness, and neutrality. The written responses to the emotional queries correlated to the MRI brain study's disclosure of various areas of the brain.

The use of technology to predict the likelihood of disease is inevitable, but is not yet in use. Computer models that can translate the massive amounts of brain scan data and information on DNA samples are no longer simply in the realm of imagination. The analysis of all of the variables that contribute to mental illness, including childhood trauma, homelessness, or even sleep patterns, to be assimilated into computer analysis for individualized outcomes is foreseeable. When this happens, it will easier to implement integrated medical and mental health treatment practices before damage and disease occur (Lu, 2016).

Using diagnostic imaging, brain mapping, and anticipated reactive responses with patient neutrality, psychiatrists and scientists will also soon diagnose physiological, biological, and mental disease through brain scanning. Research suggests that neuro-imaging will then match patients to effective treatments and ease symptoms. Care and relief will be quickly provided, and patient treatment will be assimilated by information acquired from biomarkers such as DNA, hormone levels, and brain imaging. Current treatment dictates that people with the same diagnosis for a disorder are given the same medical care. Through brain imaging, however, researchers can foresee through fMRI scans how different brains respond to the reward of individualized medical treatments. Examining patterns of brain connectivity will help scientists recognize if people with social disorders have an immediate positive or negative response to non-medical therapy by instantaneous comparisons of their brain images before and after a treatment session.

Medical studies are beginning to catalogue brain maps associated with mental recognition of objects and emotions through advanced MRI in a venture called the Human Connectome Project (HCP). For example, now there is discernable activity in the right lateral cortex when human subjects are shown images of the human body, as opposed to objects. The HCP data will then also help identify when neurological pathologies emerge, such as with a brain-damaged infant or adult. A recent report from researchers associated with the HCP revealed a great deal about the outermost layer of the brain, the cerebral cortex (Glasser, Coalson, et al., 2016). There are over 180 unique areas of the brain that "were robustly and statistically significant from their neighbors" (Glasser et al., 2016: 180). The researchers noted that these areas and location in the brain vary in size from person to person, are in the same place, and appear to be associated with human cognition, mental disease, and learning disabilities.

As a society, we have conquered the seas and understand outer space. One of the last frontiers for human mastery is understanding and, maybe, even regenerating our individual brains. Will the day come when our intellectual abilities, personalities, and functions be downloaded into a computer, adjusted, and then fed back into us like an intravenous transfusion? We all appreciate the strength, balance, and complexity of the brain as an organ and the mind as a force within the brain. What happens, though, if the brain dies? Who decides when death occurs if the mind continues to direct the body to digest and breathe? Think about the legal scenario described in Box 3.4.

SUSTAINING A HEALTHY BRAIN (AND A HEALTHY MIND)

While various objective tests and critical self-reflection can assess brain and mental acuity and function, it is equally important to sustain healthy mental function and encourage it through professional and personal efforts. The history of human evolution shows a definitive link between our physical health and psychological well-being (Boccia et al., 2015). Mind and body practices, such as yoga and meditation, illustrate other forms of physiological mechanisms that can control behavior, yet we don't know why ancient forms of mind and body exercises work. We also can't predict when a healthy brain will fail (Zeidan, Emerson, et al., 2015).

BOX 3.4

What Would You Do?

In the future, person-to-person tests are likely to be replaced by personal analysis performed by genetic scrutiny and brain mapping. At a genomics institute at the Rady Children's Hospital and the University of California, San Diego, blood is used to sequence the genome of newborns who have unexplained illnesses at birth. By using genetic testing and analysis, doctors are able to prescribe treatment medications tailored to resolve some symptoms that were otherwise untreatable in infants. It is reasonably foreseeable that mapping the DNA of babies will be as standard as ordering a blood test. Infants often carry the answer to their illnesses in their genetic patterns.

In other studies, scientists found that there are genetic links between personality traits and psychiatric diseases through using the **genome** (the DNA code). Genetic associations to certain aspects of character are emerging from characteristic genetic variants. According to the analysis of 60,000 samples, correlations are emerging between specific genetic features, personality traits, and psychiatric disorders. While intelligence is known to be a combination of inherited DNA, genetic features, and life experiences such as having good teachers when growing up, isolating genetic markers particularly linked to personality traits has not yet been accomplished. There are theories that technology, using DNA mapping and genetic associations, will be able to engineer the perfect baby. By using editing techniques, called CRISPR-Cas-9, researchers claim the ability to engineer the genetic make-up of pigs and cattle by sliding in beneficial genes and removing bad ones. Theoretically, this process could apply to humans as well.

1. What if a future test disclosed that your infant daughter had low intellectual functioning? Alternatively, what if the future test disclosed that she had a personality trait that you didn't like? For example, she had diplomatic tendencies, such as being quiet and mystical, while you wanted someone like yourself — a Myers-Briggs Explorer who is a bold and practical experimenter. Do you think that environmental and cultural changes can affect personality development?

2. You are extremely close to your father. The sun rises when he does. The two of you think, act, and even look alike. He asks you to go with him to get the results of an Alzheimer's screening exam. You know that his prognosis will likely be your prognosis. What do you do?

Sources: Nield (2016); Park (2017); Regalado (2015).

Ancient Greeks philosophized that a sound body equated to a sound mind. Although there is an ominous prediction of "future shock" that theorizes humans have experienced too much change in too short a period of evolution, the argument remains that people take responsibility for the well-being of their community. Consider the inventions humans have developed over the past two centuries and their staggering impact on human life: the steam engine (1804); the telephone (1876); harnessed electricity with power plants (1882); the production-line automobile (1902); the television (1927); the jet plane (1943); the personal-use computer (1967); the cell phone (1973); and the internet (1983). The accelerated changes in communication, energy, and transportation reshaped human dynamics. These modern inventions have also reshaped our bodies, our minds, and our lives. Remember that many changes occurred within a few years compared to the gradual changes that occurred in several million years.

The unified theory of psychology and physiology of brain and mind is not definitive nor complete in its research. In the exploration of people and of criminal justice, the connectivity of the mind is singular. If you and another person both picture a rose and then each describe what you visualized, each description will be different, but it is unlikely that either of you will describe a footstool. The responses illustrate how each mind is different, but also how each person's brain is accurate, imaginative, and responsive.

No one yet knows what people need to be brain healthy. There are many lists of things that people need to do to keep their minds and their bodies healthy, but few of those lists have been subjected to lengthy scientific scrutiny, and most are considered common-sense dicta. For example, Bergland's (2007) "athlete's way" dictates engaging in daily physicality, encouraging intellectual curiosity, fostering creativity, creating and maintaining social bonds, establishing a spiritual connectedness, and maintaining a balanced caloric intake, and it embraces the idea that simplicity in one's life results in a healthy brain. In this section, we have reflected on all that we do know about when the brain and the mind are healthy, but when physical or mental illness occurs, there are overt signs of illness and often indirect obtuse signs of disease. To prepare for this transition to the unhealthy mind, we turn next to the final story in this chapter.

EPILOGUE

The following sources provided much of this epilogue's content: Almasy and Kounang, 2017; Armstrong, 2017; Bieler, 2017; Candiotti and Ferrigno, 2015; Candiotti, Dolan, and Sanchez, 2015; Diamond, 2017; Kounang, 2017; Lehman, 2017; Mez, Daneshver, and Kiernan, et al., 2017; Watson, 2017.

Aaron Hernandez had it all in May 2013: At 23 years old, he was a tight end for the New England Patriots football team, catching a touchdown pass in the 2012 Super Bowl; he was a superb team player at the University of Florida; he negotiated a seven-year $40 million extension contract with the Patriots and was a rising National Football League (NFL) superstar; he donated $50,000 to the Patriots' charity; he was the proud father of a baby girl; he received the Inspiration to Youth Award by Pop Warner, the country's best-known youth football organization. He was the picture of good mental and physical health. On June 26, 2013, Hernandez was arrested for the murder of a friend; shortly afterward, he was linked to a double homicide and numerous other violent episodes.

Hernandez's freefall into violence, personal destruction, and ultimate suicide was possibly linked to a type of brain injury called **chronic traumatic encephalopathy (CTE)**. Hernandez was found to suffer from this physiobiological condition associated with repeated blows to the head, during the 2017 forensic autopsy of his brain. An outstanding child athlete in Bristol, Connecticut, Hernandez was singled out as the "golden boy," participating in football, basketball, and track.

Aaron Hernandez was convicted of the murder of Odin Lloyd. During the inquiry into Lloyd's death, investigators discovered that six years earlier, in April 2007, officers in Florida interviewed Hernandez, then a college freshman, in connection with the shooting of two men in Gainesville. That year he also he got into a fight with a restaurant manager, rupturing the victim's eardrum. During college, he was also suspended for drug use. In 2012, two men killed in a Boston drive-by shooting were tied to a confrontation with Hernandez, who became enraged when one of the victims spilled a drink on him. In February 2013, Alexander Bradley was shot in the face and left for dead, following a remark Bradley made to Hernandez about the drive-by shooting.

On April 15, 2015, a Massachusetts jury found Hernandez guilty of murdering Lloyd with "extreme atrocity or cruelty." Hernandez was then tried in April 2017 for the 2012 drive-by shooting. He was found not guilty on April 14, 2017. Five days later, Hernandez hanged himself in his jail cell.

By his death during the pendency of an appeal of his conviction in the Lloyd murder case, Hernandez's suicide invoked a complicated Massachusetts law, whereby he was then legally acquitted of the murder of Lloyd. In an interesting legal twist, the acquittal may trigger Hernandez's right to back pay from the Patriots, paving the way to financial security for his daughter and fiancée. His financial acumen was noted in his suicide letter advising his heirs that "you are rich."

Brilliant? Violent? Athletic leader? Loser?

The cause of this 27-year old football star's stark descent into senseless violence so troubled his family that they donated his brain for CTE research at the Boston University Center for Traumatic Encephalopathy. Neuropathologist Ann McKee, the program's director, reported it was the first case in which they found a significant degree of damage in a person of Hernandez's age. Hernandez's degree of damage was more common in someone at least 20 years older.

CTE can cause changes in the brain months, years, or decades after the last brain trauma or end of active athletic involvement. The evidence of CTE in Hernandez was significant and traumatic. The pathology researchers knew that with repeated blows to the head, the resulting brain injuries often lead to aggressive behavior, depression, dementia, and suicide. Hernandez went from All-America college athlete to the NFL in 2010, and five years later a jury found him guilty of a brutal murder. McKee concluded that Hernandez had chronic traumatic encephalopathy, Stage 3 on a 4-stage scale (Stage 4 being the most severe). Stage 3 is commonly associated with cognitive and memory loss, as well as behavioral changes and impaired judgment.

Neuroscientists also believe that repeated trauma to the head results in a buildup of the abnormal protein tau in the brain. The Boston University forensic investigators found that Hernandez had early brain atrophy and large perforations in the septum pellucidum, a central membrane to the brain. The changes in the brain, indeed, revealed tau protein deposits and neurofibrillary tangles that were consistent with brain degeneration and are attributable to behaviors such as memory loss, confusion, impaired judgment, impulse-control conflicts, aggression, depression, and progressive dementia. Basically, tau protein deposits and neurofibrillary tangles in the brain interrupt mental transmissions that results in brain damage. The neurodegenerative disease also has Alzheimer's-type symptoms, including memory loss, confusion, aggression, and rage. Currently, CTE can only be diagnosed after death. CTE is believed to be caused by repeated head trauma and not just from concussions, and it is suspected that experiencing repeated trauma events, often occurring during tackles and collisions with the ground, damages the brain. These injuries have been given a special designation: "subconcussive hits." There is no treatment or cure for this degenerative disease.

A 2017 study by Jesse Mez and associates examined the donated brains of U.S. football players. CTE was neuropathologically diagnosed in 177 players across all levels of play (87%), including 110 of 111 former NFL players. Among the players, the median age at death was 66 years; they played an average of 15 years of football. However, the study also included the brains of 3 high school players and 48 who played in college. CTE was found across the highest level of play, with the high school players having mild pathology and most of the college players having a moderate form of CTE. Semiprofessional and professional (86%) had severe indications of CTE. The leading cause of death for those with mild CTE was suicide. The cause of death for athletes with severe CTE was listed as dementia-related or Parkinson's-related.

Mez and associates also conducted interviews with those close to the deceased donors, who reported behavioral and/or mood disturbances and cogitative impairments including impulsivity, depression, apathy, and anxiety. Those close to the deceased players described them expressing hopelessness, and displaying explosivity, verbal violence, physical violence, and suicidal ideation, as well as experiencing loss of memory, executive function, attention, language, and visuospatial systems. Dementia was common in severe cases.

In Hernandez's case, tests disclosed the presence of a metabolic gene variant that is associated with a higher risk for Alzheimer's and other neurodegenerative diseases. In 2017, the National Football league agreed to a $1 billion settlement with the families and players for football-related head injuries. In February, 2018 the Estate of Aaron Hernandez filed a separate concussion-related claim against the NFL and the New England Patriots for not disclosing the likelihood of CTE, but the NFL contends that Hernandez's personal tragedies do not arise only from football injuries. Hernandez's litigation faces additional legal challenges as it may be dismissed being inherently part of the class action settlement. As this chapter's content indicates, the brain and mind are the central source of functionality for humans. The importance of the health of both is clear, while, at the same time, the reasons for the loss of mental health are not yet understood.

SUMMARY

▸ Early personality philosophers believed the mind was distinct from the brain and operated as a separate, independent, and superior bodily entity.

▸ Contemporary studies indicate that the brain and mind are within one organ but the brain, as an organ, has distinct and different functions than the mind.

▸ The mind enables the processing and expression of thoughts, experiences, ideas, and information regardless of the language, culture, environment, and economic status of the individual. The functional operations of a mind are similar for all human beings.

▸ Basic human responses are observable through quick assessments of brain/mind reflexive connectivity and automatic reactions. Responses such as eye blinks, tongue movements, pupil reactions, or even reactions to certain tastes and smells are simple measures of basic brain activity. These are instinctual and reflexive responses.

▸ Human engagement is established through personality or interactive social characteristics. A personality reflects one's nature, disposition, temperament, or even psychological responses. There are as many as 638 persona descriptors.

▸ Through the objective testing of the Myers-Briggs Type Indicator, distinct categories of personalities emerge: Analyst, Diplomat, Sentinel, Explorer. The test can be used to help a person develop a greater understanding of personal strengths.

▸ Given the advancement of mental mapping through technological brain imaging and scans, as well as genetic testing, scientists will correlate mental responses to observable brain activity to develop personal profiles.

▸ Humans benefits from various activities to sustain a healthy mind, such as engaging in physical activities, sustaining gradual and not sudden lifestyle changes, fostering intellectual curiosity with creativity, and following healthy eating practices.

CHAPTER REVIEW QUESTIONS

1. Do studies show that every person is unique and different and therefore no one can be bundled into a "type"?
2. What is the meaning of brain death?

3. If people are acting in an ordinary manner, should there be any reason to engage in any behavior, cognitive, or personality tests?
4. Sigmund Freud's ideas and philosophical approach to the human psyche were revolutionary in his time. What was his "iceberg" theory?
5. Explain the process of an MRI scan.
6. Explain how a fMRI works to complete a diagnosis.
7. Why does being able to distinguish between signs of mental illness and physical illness matter to a first responder?
8. What does the MMPI stand for and accomplish?
9. Describe the Greek philosophy regarding the diagnosis and treatment of mental illness with respect to humors or fluids.
10. How would bundling people into certain types help first responders and street clinicians develop better communication or relationship skills?

KEY TERMS

Brain
Cognitive reasoning
Cognition
Color of law
Conscious mind
Ego
Extroverted
Functional magnetic resonance imaging (fMRI)
Functionalism
Instantiated
Instinctual

Introverted
Mind
Minnesota Multiphasic Personality Inventory (MMPI)
Normative behavior
Personality
Preconscious mind
Psyche
Psychometric tests
Synapses
Unconscious mind

REFERENCES

Axmann, G. (2015). "What Is Psyche?" Gordon-Practice Blog. Retrieved at http://www.gordonpraxis.de/mindpsyche/ on 6 July 2017.

Bergland, C. (2007). *The Athlete's Way.* New York: St. Martin's Griffin.

Belliveau, J.W., K.K. Kwong, D.N. Kennedy, J.R. Baker, C.E. Stern, R. Benson, D.A. Chesler, R.M. Weisskoff, M.S. Cohen, R.B.H. Tootell, P.T. Fox, T.J. Brady, and B.R. Rosen (1992). "Magnetic Resonance Imaging Mapping of Brain Function Human Visual Cortex." *Investigative Radiology* 27: S59-S65.

Berman, M.G., J. Jonides, and D.E. Nee (2006). "Studying mind and brain with fMRI." *Social Cognitive and Affective Neuroscience* 1(2): 158-161.

Boccia, M., L. Piccardi, and P. Guariglia (2015). "The Meditative Mind: A Comprehensive Meta-Analysis of MRI Studies." *BioMed Research International*. Retrieved at https://www.hindawi.com/journals/bmri/2015/419808/ on 24 July 2017.

Boyle, C., P. Decoufle, R.J. Delaney, F. DeStefano, M.L. Flock, M.I. Hunter, M.R. Joesoef, J.M. Karon, M.L. Kirk, P.M. Layde, D.L. McGee, L.A. Moyer, D.A. Pollock. P. Rhoes, M.J. Scally, R.M. Worth. (1987). *Postservice Mortality Among Vietnam Veterans*. Atlanta: Centers for Disease Control. 143 pp. CEH 86-0076.

Castro, Y., K.H. Gordon, J.S. Brown, J.C. Anestis, and T.E. Joiner, Jr. (2008). "Examination of Racial Differences on the MMPI-2 Clinical and Restructured Clinical Scales in an Outpatient Sample." *Assessment* 15: 277-86.

Dana, R.H. (ed.) (2000). *Handbook of Cross-Cultural and Multicultural Personality Assessment*. Mahwah, NJ: Lawrence Erlbaum Associates, Inc.

Descartes, R. (1960) [1637]. *Discourse on Method and Meditations*. Translated by Laurence J. Lafleur. New York: The Liberal Arts Press.

Descartes, R. (1996) [1641]. "Meditation VI," in *Meditations on the First Philosophy*. Translated by J. Cottingham. Cambridge: Cambridge University Press.

Freud, S. (1913). *Interpretation of Dreams*. English Edition. New York: MacMillan.

Freud, S. (2013) [1905]. *Jokes and Their Relation to the Unconscious*. Translated by A.A. Brill. Redditch: Read Books Ltd.

Glasser, M.F., T.S. Coalson, E.C. Robinson, C.D. Hacker, J. Harwell, E. Yacoub, K. Ugurbil, Jesper Andersson, C.F. Beckmann, M. Jenkinson, S.M. Smith, and D.C. Van Essen (2016). "A Multi-Model Parcellation of Human Cerebral Cortex." Nature 536(7616): 171-78.

Grover, B.L. (2011). "The Utility of MMPI-2 Scores with a Correctional Population and Convicted Sex Offenders." *Scientific Research* 2(6): 638-42.

Hansotia, P. (2003). "A Neurologist Looks at Mind and Brain: 'The Enchanted Loom.'" *Clinical Medicine & Research* 1(4): 327-332.

Hasselmann, V., and F. Schmolke (1993). *Welten der Seele (Worlds of the Soul)*. Berlin: Goldman.

Henriques, G. (2011a). "What is the mind?" Psychology Today Blog. Retrieved at https://www.psychologytoday.com/blog/theory-knowledge/201112/what-is-the-mind on 6 July 2017.

Henriques, G. (2011b). *A New Unified Theory of Psychology*. New York: Spring.

Ideonomy (2017). List of personality traits. Retrieved at http://ideonomy.mit.edu/essays/traits.html on 9 July 2017.

Jung, C.G. (1971) [1921]. Psychological Types. London: Routledge.

Kant, E. (1974) [1785]. *Anthropology from a Pragmatic Point of View*. Translated by Mary J. Gregor. The Hague: Martinus Nijhoff.

Kragel, P.A., A.R. Knodt, A.R. Hariri, and K.S. LaBar (2016). "Decoding Spontaneous Emotional States in the Human Brain." *PLoSBiol*14(9): e2000106. doi:10.1371/journal.pbio.2000106.

Kaplan, R.M., and D.P. Saccuzzo (2009). *Psychological Testing: Principle, Applications, and Issues*. Belmont, CA: Wadsworth.

Lutz, P.L. (2002). *The Rise of Experimental Biology: An Illustrated History*. Totowa, NJ: Humana Press.

May, P. (2018) "Expert: Jahi McMath is alive, getting better." Retrieved at https://www.mercurynews.com/2017/07/24/expert-videos-show-jahi-mcmath-is-alive-getting-better/ on 22 February 2018.

McCreary, C., and E. Padilla (1977). "MMPI differences among Black, Mexican-American, and White Male Offenders." *Journal of Clinical Psychology* 33(1): 171-2.

Morgan, W.G. (2002). "Origin and history of the earliest thematic apperception test." *Journal of Personality Assessment* 79(3): 422-445.

Myers-Briggs Foundation (2017). "Objectives and Mission." Retrieved at http://www.myersbriggs.org/my-mbti-personality-type/mbti-basics/home.htm?bhcp=1 on 17 July 2017.

NERIS Analytics Ltd (2017). *16 Personalities*. London: NERIS Analytics Limited. Retrieved at https://www.16personalities.com/ on 19 July 2017.

Nield, D. (2016). "Scientists have found genetic links between personality traits and psychiatric diseases." *Science Alert*. Retrieved at https://www.sciencealert.com/scientists-find-genetic-links-between-personality-traits-and-psychiatric-diseases on 7 March 2018.

Nisbett, R. (2009). *Intelligence and How to Get It: Why Schools and Culture Count*. New York: W.W. Norton and Company.

Park, A. (2017). "Genetic Testing Is Providing New Hope for Babies Born with Mysterious Ailments." *Time Magazine*. Retrieved at http://time.com/4951200/genetic-testing-providing-hope-babies-ailments/ on 7 March 2018.

Regalado, A. (2015). "Engineering the perfect baby." MIT Technology Review. Retrieved at https://www.technologyreview.com/s/535661/engineering-the-perfect-baby/ on 7 March 2018.

Segal, J.B. (2018). "The ethics of organ donation: First, do no harm?" Senior Honors Thesis (unpublished). Cambridge, MA: Harvard Medical School.

Smart, J.J.C. (2017). "The Mind/Brain Identity Theory." *The Stanford Encyclopedia of Philosophy,* spring ed. Retrieved at https://plato.stanford.edu/entries/mind-identity/#toc on 22 February 2018.

Sperry, R.W. (1982). "Commentary: Mind-brain interaction: mentalism, yes; dualism, no." *Neuroscience* 5: 195-206.

Swartz, J.M., and S. Begley (eds.) (2002). *The Mind and the Brain. Neuroplasticity and the Power of Mental Force*. New York: Barnes and Noble.

Veteran's Administration (2016). "VA Research on Post-Traumatic Stress Disorder (PTSD)." Washington, DC: Department of Veterans Affairs. Retrieved at https://www.research.va.gov/pubs/docs/va_factsheets/ptsd.pdf on 24 July 2017.

Wolf, R.C., and Koenigs, M. (2015). "Brain imaging research on violence and aggression: Pitfalls and possibilities for criminal justice." *Science in the Courtroom* 1. Retrieved at http://koenigslab.psychiatry.wisc.edu/pdfs/wolf_koenigs_ScienceInCourt.pdf on 28 July 2017.

Yaffe, K., E. Vittinghoff, K. Lindquist, D. Barnes, K.E. Covingsky, T. Neyland, M. Kluse, and C. Marmar (2010). "Post-traumatic stress disorder and risk of dementia among U.S. veterans." *Archives of General Psychiatry* 67: 608-614.

Zeidan, F., N.M. Emerson, S.R. Farris, J.N. Ray, Y. Jung, J.G. McHaffie, and R.C. Coghill (2015). "Mindfulness meditation-based pain relief employs different neural mechanisms than placebo and sham mindfulness meditation-induced analgesia." *The Journal of Neuroscience* 35: 15307-15325.

CASES

Fonseca v. Kaiser Permanente Med. Ctr. Roseville, 222 F. Supp. 3d 850 (2016)

Skinner v. Oklahoma, 316 U.S. 525 (1942)

Winkfield v. UCSF Benioff Children's Hospital Oakland, Rosen et al. Unreported civil action retrieved at https://www.scribd.com/document/305588638/Winkfield-v-Rosen-FAC on 6 March 2018.

LEGISLATION

California Uniform Determination of Death Act (CUDDA), Cal. Health & Safety Code §7180 *et seq.*

Etiology of Mental Illness

LEARNING OBJECTIVES

After reading this chapter, you should be able to:

▶ Appreciate the complex nature of the causal questions that are at the heart of our search to better understand mental illness.

▶ Provide a more complete response to the question, What is mental illness?

▶ Discuss the breadth of theoretical arguments drawn from biology, biochemistry, psychology, sociology, and other academic disciplines about the cause of mental illness.

▶ Comprehend the significance of the term comorbidity for a fuller understanding of mental illness in contemporary society.

▶ Understand the idea of psychopathy and its implications for both mental health and criminal justice.

PROLOGUE

NOTE: We consulted the following sources in the preparation of this prologue: CBS News (2017); Fields (2015); Fink (2017); Frederick (2016); Marso (2017); Phillips (2017); The Telegraph (2017); Thomas (2017).

Two men died in 2017 whose deaths merit our attention. They lived worlds apart. One was a convicted criminal serving a 53-year sentence for attempted murder and aggravated battery in a Kansas prison. The other was a wealthy gambler/investor, living the high life in Nevada. Both would die, one quickly, by his own hand, and the other far more slowly and far more painfully, under what can be charitably described as highly controversial circumstances. Each, at the end of life, exhibited behavior described by others using terms like bizarre, horrific, and unfathomable. In both cases, mental health questions emerged shortly after each one's death. Consider each case in turn.

On October 1, 2017, Stephen Paddock broke out two windows in his corner suite on the 32nd floor of the Mandalay Bay hotel. He surveyed the scene below and about 400 meters away, where thousands of people watched an ongoing concert. Selecting a rifle equipped with a "bump stock" that allowed it to fire like a fully automatic weapon, he began shooting and continued doing so until at some point he decided to take his own life. In the event's aftermath, 58 people had died and over 500 were wounded.

In the aftershock of the worst mass shooting in the nation's history to that date, pundits and experts alike struggled to come up with a reason or reasons for Paddock's actions. He had gambling problems, said some, compounded by ongoing legal troubles. Others pointed to a family history of mental illness. Still others found prescriptions in his name for antidepressants. Perhaps, it has even been suggested, Paddock's involvement in domestic violence is a part of his pathology. Finally, in the search for biological answers, tissue samples taken from Paddock's brain were sent to Stanford Medical Center for analysis. A similar brain study was undertaken in the 1960s of Charles Whitman's brain, Whitman being the sniper in the University of Texas's tower who killed 13 people in 1966. Whitman's brain was found to contain a pecan-sized tumor, although it was not definitively shown to be the cause of his rampage. Neuroscientist R. Douglas Fields, author of *Why We Snap*, suggests that the brains of individuals engaged in terrorism or mass shootings rarely have actual brain abnormalities, but their actions can be triggered by psychiatric problems. The search for answers in Paddock's case continues.

The second case had a far clearer resolution, but no fewer questions emerged. According to witnesses, Marques Davis felt that something was eating his brain. Over an eight-month period, he went from a reasonably healthy prison inmate to someone who drank his own urine and repetitively moved items on the floor of his cell, stacking and unstacking and restacking toilet paper, books, a water pitcher, and cup. Davis's bizarre behavior was even captured on a surveillance camera in his isolation cell in the Hutchinson (Kansas) Correctional Facility.

Twenty-seven-year old Marques Davis died on April 13, 2017, days after being filmed acting in a very disoriented fashion. The prison facility conducted an MRI of his brain, which revealed a widespread fungal infection. A CT scan later would reveal that the upper part of Davis's brain was forced downward into the lower part. Davis's complaints of back pains and numbness in his right leg, along with the feeling that something was wrong with his head, apparently went unheeded by the prison's medical and administrative staff. The case has moved to the litigation stage and many questions remain unanswered.

Two cases, one a dead suspect in a mass shooting and the other a dead incarcerated felon. In the first case, the forces behind the mass shooting are far more elusive and difficult to determine, if they can ever be fully understood. In the other situation, the prisoner's bizarre behavior appears to have had organic origins, a virulent bacterial infection of the brain. The search for a definitive cause in the mass shooting case includes inquiries into the state of the suspect's brain.

Society, including law enforcement, correctional officials, medical professionals specializing in the behavior of criminals, and the general populace, feels the need to understand why harmful behavior of this nature occurs in the first place. Normal people, they might observe, simply do not act this way.

Chapter Overview

This chapter's goal is daunting: In a single chapter, we condense and relate, using largely layperson terms, a wide range of theories on the causes and effects of mental disorders. To make this task more manageable, we selected a series of topics and issues that reflect the convergence of the mental health and criminal justice systems described in Chapter 1.

The driving idea in this chapter is etiology or the causes of events. Hence, the first task is to describe in sufficient detail what that term means and its relevance for the current topic. This is no mean task, as any discussion of etiology must deal with several complicated ideas, such as identifying an event's origins and distinguishing them from the ensuing events or effects. We contend that such ideas are essential to a full appreciation of theory's role in guiding the policies and practices of both the mental health and criminal justice systems.

We turn next to a second set of important topics: the goals of theories and definitions of mental illness. Some people think the goal of theory is to confuse, but nothing could be further from the truth. Mental illness theory attempts to make sense out of what seems to be incomprehensible behavior. With the goal of clarifying and informing us about mental illnesses' causes, theory describes the object of study, provides an understanding of it, predicts its occurrence, and ultimately seeks to control it—all reasonable goals, considering our emphasis on the ties between mental health and criminal justice. Not surprisingly, then, we offer several definitions of mental illness, which may reveal as much about those persons employing them, whoever they are, as they do about the behavior being observed and categorized.

The chapter continues with a necessarily brief review of four sets of causal forces drawn from the academic disciplines of biology, biochemistry, psychology, and sociology. What becomes clear after this review is that no one set of forces alone can entirely explain why a given mentally ill person acts as he or she does. This realization is called "multi-causal modeling," meaning that it is often the case that a more complete understanding of the connections between mental health and criminal justice lies in an overlay of all four disciplines.

This chapter, like those before and after it, ends with an epilogue. In this case, we examine in detail the special case of the psychopath. Perhaps no other form of "mental illness" concerns the public and the criminal justice system in the same way as crimes committed by a psychopath. Yet, as this section of the chapter makes clear, this is a rare, if fear-provoking form of mental disease, which does not always manifest in criminal ways.

We offer a final caveat prior to framing the issues. This is not a comprehensive review of all mental health or mental illness theories. The material covered in this chapter is not written from a medical or even a predominantly psychological perspective. Rather, its intent is to make the reader familiar with the terminology, concerns, and issues associated with contemporary efforts to understand mental disorders and their impact on the administration of justice.

FRAMING THE ISSUES

This chapter's title includes the term **etiology**, which means the study of origins or causes of diseases or other conditions, suggesting that such a search is the domain of medicine.

However, the range of disciplines that provide insights into mental illness is far broader than this restricted use of the term suggests, extending beyond medicine into law, psychology, sociology, and criminology. Before, we can look in any meaningful way at the etiology of mental illness, we must first consider what it is we seek versus what it is we may find.

Cause is a special term in both logic and science, whether we are talking about physical science, behavioral science, or social science. A **cause** is something that produces an outcome or effect, hence the term "cause-and-effect." For a causal relationship to exist, three conditions must be present. First, the alleged or putative cause must precede the outcome in time. This requirement is sometimes called the time-order-sequence requirement. The amount of time, whether it is a second, minutes, days, weeks, months, or even years, is irrelevant.

Second, scientists look for a statistical relationship, or a measurable degree of association, between a putative or assumed cause and its effect. If two things exhibit an association with one another, then as one of them experiences a change, there is also a change in the other. A positive association means that as one increases, there is a similar increase in the other, while a negative association means that as the values of one increases, the other experiences a decrease. We describe relationship as very strong to non-existent or somewhere in between. According to this requirement, a suspected cause that fails to exhibit a measurable relationship with an outcome cannot be its cause. However, the presence of a relationship alone does not mean that the two entities are causally connected. That is, correlation does not equal causation. For example, what if we observe a statistical correlation between armed robberies and organic food sales: As sales of organic food increase, the number of armed robbery cases increases. In this case, no one is suggesting that organic food sales cause armed robberies. Rather, it is simply a random statistical association. That is, for purely non-causal and inexplicable reasons, the two things vary together: As one increases, so does the other.

The third requirement is the demonstration of any absence of spurious interpretations. A spurious interpretation is said to exist when the relationship between two entities is thought to be causal, because it meets the first two requirements, when, in fact, that relationship is due to the interaction of both entities with a third force, which in fact causes the first two. For example, someone notices that the number of fire engines at a fire is directly correlated with the amount of property loss suffered, as in the more fire engines at the scene, the greater the damage. From this observation, he makes the following causal statement: Fire engines cause property loss. In fact, it is the size of the fire that necessitates more fire engines and determines the property loss. To demonstrate the absence of spuriousness, researchers typically introduce as many methodological or statistical controls as possible into their studies to eliminate, to the extent possible, the influence of any possibly misleading factors. If a researcher claims that current mental condition Y results from an alleged preceding cause X, then he or she must eliminate as many competing explanations as possible. As the example of a traumatic brain injury in the next section demonstrates, sometimes this goal is easier to describe than achieve. This task is one that most researchers leave in the hands of data analysts called statisticians.

THE ROLE OF THEORY

The role of theory in knowledge-building efforts is important to understand. Scientific disciplines of all ilk share an abiding interest in the theories that not only guide their inquiries and applications, but also help to make sense of real-world occurrences. A **theory** is a highly organized statement based on systematic observations concerning the phenomenon or class of phenomena under study. Mental illness is a broad class of phenomena, as we shall see in the next major section. And many theoretical explanations exist for their manifestation in humans.

Theories are constructed from two or more mental representations of a thing, object, or idea called **concepts**. In Chapter 1, we offered the following definition of mental illness that is endorsed by the National Alliance on Mental Illness (2017): "A mental illness is a condition that affects a person's thinking, feeling or mood. Such conditions may affect someone's ability to relate to others and function each day. Each person will have different experiences, even people with the same diagnosis." Statements about mental illness link other factors or forces identified as its cause. Before we can examine any alleged relationships between concepts, each one must be transformed by the operationalization process into at least one variable. Operationalization refers to a series of mental steps taken by a researcher to transform an abstract concept into an empirically measurable **variable**. Researchers must be able to provide valid and reliable indicators of the concepts whose presence or absence can be determined using one or more of the five human senses.

Consider the following example. A person has been recently diagnosed with a mental illness; he suffered a major traumatic brain injury (TBI) during a car accident six months ago. His family members describe a radical change in personality over the past few months such that the previously calm and loving son has become frustrated and quick to anger, even acting out in a violent fashion toward loved ones and strangers alike. In this case, the concept of mental illness has been defined in measurable terms; moreover, the concept of a TBI has also been operationalized into something that can be identified and measured, in this case by a series of neurological tests. The physician can identify no other possible "causes" for the radical change in personality that is impacting the patient's ability to function and interact with others, although it is always possible that such preexisting causal forces may have gone unnoticed. At the end of the day, these two concepts, a TBI, as a specific set of observations made by the neurologist, and a specific type of mental disorder, manifesting (and measured) as fast developing frustration and violent outbursts, are causally linked and measurable in the patient.

Whether that doctor can convince others of the correctness of this causal analysis, perhaps in a legal hearing, represents a different set of issues entirely, and one to which we return in later chapters. At this point, it is sufficient to observe that the physician or other mental health clinician, the latter being a highly trained professional capable of diagnosing and treating mental illness, can point to a well-established body of scientific research about the significance of TBIs for a range of mental disorders.

The Goals of Theories

Theories should accomplish several goals. First, as in the hypothetical case of the TBI and mental illness, theories describe the phenomenon or class of phenomena under study. Hence, **description** is the first goal of theories: *What* is it that we are studying? In this case, we expect theories of mental illness to describe the phenomenon's nature and extent. For the purposes of this discussion, let us again employ the definition of mental illness from Chapter 1: "A mental illness is a condition that affects a person's thinking, feeling or mood. Such conditions may affect someone's ability to relate to others and function each day. Each person will have different experiences, even people with the same diagnosis." In short hand, then, a mental illness is a mood-altering condition that causes a person to experience difficulties when relating to others or functioning in everyday life. While this definition is still a bit broad, it gives us a starting point as to what it is we are studying and seeking to understand.

Mental illnesses can be defined in much detail, as in current edition of the American Psychiatric Association's (APA) *Diagnostic and Statistical Manual (DSM-5)*. This work classifies and categorizes a wide range of mental illness. It is also important to note that past and present editions of the *Diagnostic and Statistical Manual* included statements to the effect that it is an atheoretical work, unconnected to any specific theory about mental illness, but instead provides definitions, diagnoses, and treatments of mental disorder without reference to a given theoretical framework. In fact, the *Diagnostic and Statistical Manual* is generally viewed as a taxonomical scheme, rather than a theoretical work (Lane, 2013; Nemeroff, Weinberger, et al., 2013). A taxonomical scheme is a method of classifying things or concepts into distinct groups, as well as the basis upon which decisions are made to place things or concepts into those groups. All sciences have, at their core, one or more taxonomical schemes.

Historically, the absence of theory was necessitated by the wide range of theoretical perspectives found in psychology and psychiatry (Ahn and Kim, 2008). Moreover, while *DSM-5* definitions are in widespread use, the work is not without its critics. For instance, the National Institute of Mental Health (NIMH) views the compendium as unscientific and subjective, lacking a sufficient biological emphasis as to the origins of mental disorders (Jabr, 2013; Lane, 2013).

Once the phenomenon under study has been defined, the second goal is to seek a cause that will yield a more complete **understanding**. This goal represents another central question for theory: *Why* does the problem exist? This question, often expressed in summary fashion as understanding, is perhaps the most challenging one for theorists and practitioners alike. If we claim that we understand why something occurs, then we are stating that we know all the related causal factors and when they result in the outcome.

Where we look for answers to the why question is circumscribed by the concepts and variables that a given theory includes in its causal mix. In the case of mental illness, however, discerning a single cause is nearly impossible. Moreover, using a single disciplinary orientation—that is, only seeking answers that originate in a single academic discipline, for example, only in biology—may also be shortsighted. Human behavior as complex as mental illness rarely has a single distal (distant) or even proximal (immediate) cause. Hence, in the search for a more complete explanation of the phenomenon under study, we may provide support for treatment responses (see goal four below). In the present instance, the search often crosses disciplinary boundaries and approaches mentally ill persons on multiple levels, including biology, biochemistry, psychology, psychiatry, and sociology.

Third, theories allow for prediction. This goal represents a third question: *When* is the behavior likely to occur? That is, at what point will the causal forces produce the problematic conduct? Prediction is the specification of when and under what circumstances something, including mental illness, is likely to occur. Only the most profoundly disturbed person continuously exhibits mental illness symptoms. Mental health professionals often link their predictions about when a form of mental illness is likely to manifest itself to the patient's use of illicit drugs. It is also possible that environmental factors, such as the stress associated with finding food and shelter, influence a severe break with reality, rationality, and sanity, the latter term being a legal one, topics examined in Chapters 7 and 8.

Fourth, robust and mature theories allow us to **control** the phenomenon or class of phenomena under study. Specifically, control of an outcome refers to the modification or alteration of the alleged cause, followed by a concomitant change in the effect. The control of mental illness is viewed largely but not exclusively as the purview of mental health professionals, therapists, clinical psychologists, and medical doctors. They look at the diagnosis at hand, review their training and theoretical foundations, and devise an appropriate therapy or treatment. For instance, some mental health treatments are behavioral. Others depend on the timely ingestion of psychotropic drugs, medicines intended to control that part of the mind associated with the disease symptomology. And controlling the symptoms of the disease may be the only treatment goal, especially if the cause cannot be addressed by available treatments. It may also be that socio-environmental factors are at work, meaning the mentally ill person may require resettlement in a more stable living situation, one which allows the therapies drawn from biogenic and psychogenic explanations to respond more completely to the causal factors identified in the diagnosis. Remember this claim when you read about the causes of mental illness later in this chapter, not to mention the actions of the correctional system in Chapter 9. The locus of the treatment can prove as crucial to controlling or eliminating the undesired conduct as the therapeutic measure itself.

Research and Etiology

Theorists, researchers, practitioners, and others who test the implications of theories use information, called data by insiders, that is collected by a variety of means. Some types of data are considered more significant when it comes to providing insights into theoretical arguments, especially for those theories that suggest causal sequencing. For example, the gold standard for research is the controlled experiment. In its most basic form, subjects are randomly assigned to either experimental group, which receives the alleged cause of something called a treatment, or a control group, which receives a placebo whose effects are assumed to be negligible. Its most reliable and valid form is the double-blind experiment, whereby neither the subjects nor the researchers know who is in which group. Some experiments are conducted in laboratories, which provides a control for all or nearly all competing explanations—recall spurious interpretation. An alternative is the clinical or field trial/experiment, which takes place in the real world, but it is assumed that control and experimental groups receive the same or similar environmental influences.

Time is also an important factor to consider, and we call research that includes several data collections at different points in time longitudinal studies. The foremost type is the panel study, which employs multiple measures of the same group or groups of individuals—and they could be experimental or control subjects—over an extended period. For example, scientists wishing to study a drug intended to reduce hyperactivity typically employ two groups. One group gets the actual drug and the other receives a placebo. Researchers then follow up every couple of months with various tests for a fixed period. They subsequently compare the behavioral results to determine if those experienced by the experimental group are different from and more desired than the results experienced by the control group.

A cohort study explores the identical group or groups over time, but does not provide individual subject information for each interval. For example, assume the object of study is the mental health issues reported by persons in a specific and geographically distinct location born in 1990. We could gather measures of the mental states for all persons living in that location with that birth year every five years. We would only know aggregate changes for the cohort at the various points in times and not, as in the panel study, individual changes over time.

The final type of longitudinal research is a trend study. This method looks at what is happening to similar groups through time, but does not look at the same individuals or even the same groups. Rather, the members of the groups selected at each interval share characteristics with previously examined groups. For example, we might be interested in a type of mental health drug prescribed for 15- to 18-year old males in 1988, 1998, 2008, and 2018.

Selecting subjects is a problem as well, but one resolved in several ways by researchers. The group of subjects about which we wish to know more is called a population. One method is to collect information from everyone in the population, which is called a census. For example, we might be interested in the prevalence of mental illness in the nation's jails, which could be determined by sampling every jail inmate incarcerated on a given day. Failing to complete a census, we might use a random sample which, using this example, would be to select a representative group or cluster of jails across the nation and then sample everyone in the selected jails. The sample is said to represent the population under study, in this case the nation's jail inmates. While prone to errors, called sampling errors, the random sample employs a faster and cheaper method of data collection than the census, which is evident by the fact that the federal government conducts the census at ten-year intervals, but the U.S. Bureau of the Census randomly samples representative clusters of the nation in the interim.

Less representative data are also gathered by researchers, but they can provide important insights. For example, some researchers use the case study method, an in-depth examination of individuals or events that reveals important findings about the object of study. For instance, at the end of this chapter, we look at psychopathy. Much of what we know about this phenomenon comes from individual case studies of people diagnosed with the disorder. Finally, some researchers resort to the use of availability samples. Also called convenience sampling, the researcher collects data from members of the population who are readily available, for example, a survey conducted on Facebook™ or a similar platform. Unlike censuses and random samples, the findings are generally viewed as far less reliable and less valid when using availability samples and case studies.

Many of the insights about mental illness and criminal justice come from research employing one or more of these designs and methods. It is incumbent upon the consumer, in this case you, to separate the wheat from the chaff when considering the researchers' claims. This brief review of research and data collection methods should help inform that decision.

DEFINING MENTAL ILLNESS

Clearly, then, any attempt to understand the etiology of a phenomenon begins with defining the thing under study. Earlier in this chapter, we repeated the NAMI definition of mental illness. That definition is like the one endorsed by the APA (n.d.): "Mental illnesses are health conditions involving changes in thinking, emotion or behavior (or a combination of these). Mental illnesses are associated with distress and/or problems functioning in social, work or family activities." Consider, too, that in Chapter 2 we used the definitions of a given historical period to define mental illnesses, ranging from madness to devil possession to insanity.

The *DSM-5*, discussed earlier in this chapter, provides practitioners with diagnostic descriptions and defines a mental illness as

> a syndrome characterized by clinically significant disturbance in an individual's cognition, emotion regulation, or behavior that reflects a dysfunction in the psychological, biological, or developmental processes underlying mental functioning. Mental disorders are usually associated with significant distress or disability in social, occupational, or other important activities. An expectable or culturally approved response to a common stressor or loss, such as the death of a loved one, is not a mental disorder. Socially deviant behavior (e.g., political, religious, or sexual) and conflicts that are primarily between the individual and society are not mental disorders unless the deviance or conflict results from a dysfunction in the individual, as described above (APA, 2013: 5).

Three parts of this definition bear further review. First, the *DSM-5* organizes most syndromes or patterns of mental illness into "disorders." This nearly 1,000-page document includes 541 diagnoses. The most commonly diagnosed mental illnesses around the world are depressive disorders, which impact 300 million people; bipolar and related disorders, diagnosed in 60 million people; neurocognitive disorders or dementia, with 48 million victims; and schizophrenia spectrum and other psychotic disorders, which impact around 21 million individuals (World Health Organization, 2017). These disorders, along with **Attention-Deficit/Hyperactivity Disorder (ADHD)**, Conduct Disorders, Personality Disorders, Post-traumatic Stress Disorder (PTSD), and Substance-Related and Addictive Disorders, are central to any understanding of how mental health impacts the administration of justice and vice versa. As there are some 541 such syndromes and disorders, we cannot review all of them in this section of the chapter or in the book in its entirety. When we examine a specific disorder, we will describe it and its significance for the operation of the criminal justice system.

Second, the syndrome must cause significant **distress**, which is taken to mean a painful associated symptom, or **disability**, which is taken to mean an impairment in one or more important areas of functioning. For example, **schizophrenia** victims often report unpleasant delusions, hallucinations, and disorganized speech or behavior. Persons with dementia are typically unable to manage their personal affairs and often wander from home, creating problems for their families, criminal justice agencies, and the community at large (Sun, Gao, et al., 2017; White and Montgomery, 2014).

Third, it is important to note that this definition also includes behaviors that are *not* included under the umbrella of mental disorder. For example, a highly emotional and depressed individual undergoing bereavement at the loss of a loved one is not generally viewed as mentally ill. Also, engagement in socially deviant behavior, conduct outside the boundaries of generally accepted conduct, is not, by itself, a symptom of mental illness; rather, deviant behavior becomes mental illness when it can be linked to significant distress or disability.

The diagnoses used for specific mental illnesses provide insights into why those afflicted disproportionately end up in the criminal justice system. While the NAMI, the APA, and the *DSM-5* definitions are important, they are not the only definitions used in this text. Researchers studying mental illness in the various component parts of the criminal justice system employ additional definitions. For example, Chapters 7 and 8 examine the legal distinctions between sanity and insanity, neither of which are found in the psychological literature. Moreover, the nation's correctional system uses definitions of mental illness derived primarily from the NIMH.

What this section amplifies is the idea that the available definitional lenses can cause confusion. Some professionals in the mental health field see the NAMI or APA definition as overly simplistic, while others see the *DSM-5*'s definition and accompanying disorders and diagnoses as far too detailed, too atheoretical, and too driven by behavioral symptoms. Perhaps it is not unexpected that the psychiatric and psychology communities question the validity and reliability of the *DSM-5*, a debate that originated with the *DSM-I* (Blashfield, Keeley, et al., 2014). Not surprisingly, then, a patient's specific diagnosis or diagnoses could vary from one mental health clinician to the next. While this may be the case if the clinician views the information in the *DSM-5* as a suggested diagnosis and not an absolute one, the central issue concerning a patient's mental health is rarely in debate: This person is ill and a clinical response is appropriate (Ahn and Kim, 2008; Blashfield et al., 2014; Nemeroff et al., 2013).

Clearly, not all mental health clinicians follow a single etiological theory about the origins of a given mental illness, as they do not adopt wholesale the taxonomical scheme represented by the *DSM-5* or its predecessors. As Ahn and Kim (2008: 6) note when speculating about why mental health clinicians tend to be theory-based reasoners: "Categorization based on theories rather than surface features is considered to be more scientifically fruitful; that is, it provides framework for explanation, prediction, and general scientific understanding." As is the case in most sciences, when it comes to the dependent variable in the mental health literature, there is some consensus about what constitutes the *basic* definition of mental illness, but less concordance about its specific forms and causes. Hence, it is also not surprising there are multiple answers to the central question of this chapter: What causes mental illness?

In the next section, we begin our review of four sets of alleged causes of mental illness. A word of caution, however, is appropriate. Identifying the necessary and sufficient cause of any specific mental illness, one in whose presence mental illness is inevitable, is a proven difficult task. Exact causal forces are difficult to isolate, especially when a person presents with symptoms of multiple issues. This is a condition called **comorbidity**, which is taken to mean the presence of one or more additional disorders, diseases, or otherwise diagnosable conditions in addition to a primary disease or disorder diagnosis.

Consequently, some mental health professionals use slightly different terminology when looking at the origins of mental illness. That is, many prefer to employ the **4-Ps factor model** made up of three risk factors and one protective factor (Racine, Riddell, et al., 2016). The first "P" is a **predisposing risk factor**, meaning a factor or identifiable element that increases a person's susceptibility to a specific mental disorder. This is not a cause, per se, but rather a factor that, when present, is more likely to result in that disorder than in its absence.

Second, the presence of a **precipitating risk factor**, or an event or other force present in a person's immediate physical environment, increases the likelihood of a specific mental disorder. Precipitating factors include major stressors, any acculturative stressors experienced when living or working in a new socio-cultural environment, or catastrophic events. Mental illness follows the presence of a precipitating risk factor, which, of course, is one of the conditions required for causation. However, a precipitating factor alone may not result in a psychotic episode. That is, a precipitating factor alone may not always result in a psychotic episode and, therefore, cannot be classified as a cause.

Third, a **perpetuating risk factor** is an important idea for first responders and others to grasp, as its presence continues the specific mental disorder and inhibits the patient's recovery, perhaps even causing a further decline. Drug use, as we shall see, can constitute such a perpetuating factor, which is an idea contained in the concept of comorbidity. Perpetuating risk factors can also include bullying, abusive relationships, social withdrawal and isolation, insomnia, and certain personal characteristics, including poor coping skills and low self-esteem.

Finally, the presence of one or more **protective factors** is just as important as the influence of risk factors. The former refers to those personal or environmental influences that assist victims of mental illness in dealing with their sickness. Successful and ongoing treatment for a substance abuse problem is a possible protective factor. Moreover, general influences such as good interpersonal relationships with family, friends, and acquaintances; high self-esteem and coping skills; and even average or above average intelligence can prevent an occurrence or reoccurrence of mental illness.

Guided by these distinctions, we turn to the first cluster of factors that many mental health professionals view as causally linked to mental illness. Where it is appropriate, we will identify those elements that are viewed as risk or protective factors, rather than causal ones.

BIOLOGICAL CAUSES

A cause is said to be biological in origin, or biogenic, if it is produced or brought about by a living organism. In the case of mental illness, researchers and clinicians look at the individual's biology—searching for the presence of any genetic, brain structure, or biochemical abnormalities—for the source of the problem.

Genetic Disorders

Genetics is not a new science. **Genetics**, as the study of heritability, began in earnest in 1900, following Gregor Johann Mendel's (b.1822-d.1884) studies of plant species' inherited traits. Two key terms provide the key to understanding the science of genetics: chromosomes and genes. **Chromosomes** are high-density genetic storage devices. They carry the hereditary characteristics that reside in all the body's cell nuclei. An ordinary body cell contains 23 pairs of chromosomes, each with thousands of genes. Males have an X and a Y chromosome in each cell; females have two X chromosomes. **Genes**, made of **deoxyribonucleic acid (DNA)**, are chromosome segments that do the work of transmitting inheritable characteristics from one generation to the next. In humans, the sum of all genes is called the human genome, which is essentially molecular-level "written" instructions for building a specific human being.

Genetic links to human behavior began early in the 20th century, and as unscientific as they may sound today, held sway nearly to mid-century. Modern ideas about genetics and mental illness are based on the best science of today, but, then, so were the ones described in Box 4.1. The case of the Buck women is important because science and mental health issues combined to deprive them of their reproductive rights, which sounds odd to us in the early 21st century. But the case remains instructive, nonetheless.

Five mental disorders appear to have genetic ties (NIMH, n.d.). Research recently located variations in four chromosomal sites that show strong ties to autism, ADHD, bipolar disorder, major depression, and schizophrenia (Smoller, Ripke, et al., 2013). Essentially,

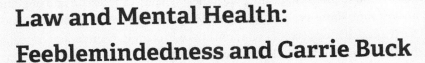

BOX 4.1

Law and Mental Health: Feeblemindedness and Carrie Buck

In the early 20th century, the term feebleminded was a medical diagnosis largely supported by the studies of Henry Goddard. The feebleminded were diagnosed by a low IQ, typically of 70 or lower, and exhibited a propensity for immoral conduct. Goddard did not work in a philosophical, medical, or legal vacuum. By the start of the 20th century, there was a growing human eugenics movement around the world, including in the United States. **Human eugenics** is the practice of altering the hereditary qualities of people by selectively breeding in certain desirable characteristics and breeding out unwanted ones. Not surprisingly, Goddard became an early proponent of sterilization and other eugenic practices. In 1907, Indiana was the first U.S. state to enact a law authorizing the forced sterilization of certain types of individuals, primarily criminals and people deemed to be mental defectives. By 1930, 30 states had enacted such laws, including in 1924 the Commonwealth of Virginia.

As a test of the Virginia law, the superintendent of the Virginia State Colony for Epileptics and Feebleminded filed a petition to have Carrie Buck, an 18-year old Caucasian woman, sterilized in 1924; Buck, the superintendent maintained, was a genetic threat to society. Carrie's mother was determined to have the mental age of a 5-year old and was engaged in immoral behavior (i.e., prostitution). Both mother and daughter were classified as feebleminded and promiscuous. Carrie herself gave birth to an illegitimate child, although it was later determined that she had been raped by a member of her "adoptive" family.

After a sterilization order was issued for Carrie, an appeal, which reached the U.S. Supreme Court in 1927, claimed that her due process rights as an adult had been violated, along with the Equal Protection Clause of the 14th Amendment. In *Buck v. Bell* (1927), the Court rejected these arguments, ruling 8-1 that it was in the Commonwealth's interests to sterilize this threat to society. The decision, authored by Associate Justice Oliver Wendell Holmes, one of America's most distinguished jurists, argued that the public's interests outweighed the interests of the individual in terms of bodily integrity. Holmes specifically argued the following:

> We have seen more than once that the public welfare may call upon the best citizens for their lives. It would be strange if it could not call upon those who already sap the strength of the State for these lesser sacrifices, often not felt to be such by those concerned, to prevent our being swamped with incompetence. It is better for all the world, if instead of waiting to execute degenerate offspring for crime, or to let them starve for their imbecility, society can prevent those who are manifestly unfit from continuing their kind. The principle that sustains compulsory vaccination is broad enough to cover cutting the Fallopian tubes.

He also penned one of the most famous quotations relative to mental illness in American legal history: "Three generations of imbeciles are enough." Even though we live more than three-quarters of a century past the times that supported such a statement and recognize its inherent faults, we must acknowledge that Justice Holmes's sentiments, and ones like it, supported programs that sterilized the mentally ill well into the 1970s.

The 20th-century idea of the feebleminded may not sound important to those of us living in the 21st century. And, indeed, the concept was long ago abandoned by the mental health-care system. However, this case is important if only as a warning. Goddard, applying the best "science" of his day, supported use of the term feeblemindedness as a diagnosis for both general mental defectives and criminals. Conditions we define today as mental diseases or disorders could, in the future, be viewed as equally out of step with reality and unsupportable by both science and medical ethics.

Five additional legal postscripts provide even more context to this case. First, *Buck* upheld Virginia's law and, by extension, all the other state statutes on forced sterilization of the medically incompetent. Second, while challenged and blunted by *Skinner v. Oklahoma* (1942) so that its use generally was placed in legal limbo, forced sterilization remained the law in many states until the early 1960s. Indeed, it is still legal in Virginia to sterilize an individual against his or her will if there is a compelling state interest. Third, during the post–World War II Nuremburg Trials, Nazi doctors explicitly and unsuccessfully cited *Buck* as supporting their own practices. Fourth, it has been suggested that an examination of Carrie Buck in the 1980s revealed a person of normal intellect. Finally, *Buck* has never been formally repudiated by any court of law.

Sources: Bruinius (2007); Buck v. Bell (1927); Gordon (2003); Lombardo (2008); Skinner v. Oklahoma (1942).

two of the sets of chromosomes regulate the flow of calcium into cells, so there is a biochemical component as well. The researchers examined data taken from over 60,000 patients, roughly half of whom had the various disorders and half who were controls. Smoller and associates (2013) examined all five disorders as if they were the same disease; the findings indicated that this was not the case. Previous research had shown that genetic overlap was linked to pairs of disorders, such as schizophrenia and bipolar disorder, but the researchers (Smoller et al., 2013) found that autism, ADHD, bipolar disorder, major depression, and schizophrenia were linked to these four sites. As the researchers note, this work moves psychiatry beyond descriptive syndromes and into the realm of a disease-linked method of classifying mental disorders.

Autism, ADHD, bipolar disorder, major depression, and schizophrenia have also proven problematic for criminal justice agencies, largely based on associated troublesome behaviors, some of which have already been discussed and others of which will reappear in later chapters. For example, **autism spectrum disorder,** which can be reliably diagnosed during the first two years of life, range from mild to severe, but tend to manifest as one of two main types: restrictive/repetitive behaviors (e.g., repeating certain behaviors or exhibiting unusual behaviors such as hitting oneself or banging one's head against an unyielding barrier) and social communication/interaction behaviors (e.g., making little or inconsistent eye contact and responding in an unusual way when others show anger, distress, or affection). Persons with ADHD, whose symptoms can appear as early as 3 to 6 years of age but must be diagnosed prior to age 12, tend to be inattentive, fail to follow through on instructions, and are easily distracted; moreover, they tend to be impulsive and constantly on the go. **Bipolar disorder** is a complicated cluster of mental diseases, existing in several forms, all of which have radical shifts in mood, ranging from having "up" or energized periods (i.e., manic episodes) to having "down" or hopeless periods (depressive episodes). The key differences are the length of time in which the person is "up" or "down," although the "down" or depressed state tends to dominate the person's life. Depressive symptoms can include being easily tearful; feelings of worthlessness or guilt; loss of energy; and trouble thinking, making decisions, or concentrating; manic symptoms can include behaving impulsively or in risky ways; being overly happy, excitable, or irritable; and being restless or agitated and easily distracted. **Psychotic depression**, which can occur at any time in the life cycle, is said to exist when an individual has severe depression plus some form of psychosis, including delusions or hallucinations. Sufferers generally express a "theme," such as being poor, guilty of something, or suffering a physical illness. Finally, signs of **schizophrenia**, whose onset generally occurs between 16 and 30, fall into three categories: positive symptoms (e.g., losing touch with reality through hallucinations, which include hearing or seeing things that others cannot hear or see; delusions or disturbing false beliefs; unusual ways of thinking; and unusual body movements); negative symptoms (e.g., reduced expression of emotions or "flat affect," reduced feelings of pleasure, difficulty starting and continuing activities, and increased periods of non-communicativeness); and cognitive symptoms (e.g., subtle to severe changes in memory or other aspects of thinking, which can include inability to process information necessary to make decisions, poor mental focus, and the inability to use information after learning it).

The power of genetics as a source of insights into mental health is the science at its core. The medical and scientific communities continue to explore the human genome and its connection to a broad range of illnesses, including mental health issues. As brain researcher Steven E. Hyman (2000; 455) has observed: "Genetics should yield new therapies aimed not just at symptoms but also at pathogenic processes, thus permitting the targeting of specific therapies to individual patients."

Progressive Mental Disorders

The group of biogenic diseases termed progressive mental disorders are organic brain disorders that develop over time and decrease mental functioning. Organic mental disorders differ from mental illnesses in that the root cause is a medical or physical disease, rather than a psychiatric illness. Progressive changes in the brain's structure can be quick or slow, depending on various environmental, biological, and social factors. The DSM-5 refers to these diseases as **neurocognitive disorders**. Included in this category are various forms of dementia, such as **Alzheimer's disease (AD)** and other age-related disorders, which manifest as a gradual decrease in the ability to think and remember, and **amnestic disorder**, which includes mild to major loss of memory loss. Amnesiacs can pose problems for criminal justice. However, among progressive mental disorder sufferers, it is AD victims who, given their high numbers, pose perhaps the greater criminal justice challenge, an idea to which we return in Chapter 12.

The mechanisms causing dementia have so far eluded scientists, although there are several "leading candidates." For example, autopsies of persons with AD suggest answers may lie in the presence of abundant deposits of the protein fragment beta-amyloid (plaques) and twisted strands of the protein tau (tangles). Other brain changes are also noted in those with other forms of dementia. Age, family history, and heredity may be keys factors in developing AD. With respect to heredity, certain genes have been associated with AD (Alzheimer's Association, n.d.): An identified protein gene is perhaps the most potent risk gene, one which increases the likelihood of the disease but does not guarantee it; other proteins are thought to be deterministic genes, ones which cause "familial Alzheimer's disease." How these genes work is also not understood. Thus, while AD has a strong genetic component, we elected to include it here since it differs from the other genetic disorders.

Chapter 1 described an interaction between a police officer and a man who likely had AD. Any person who suffers the external symptoms associated with one of the many progressive mental disorders not only poses challenges for police-citizen interactions, but also, as many become "lost" by wandering away from caregivers, hundreds of person-hours can be spent in the search for them (Sun et al., 2017; White and Montgomery, 2014). Persons with progressive mental disorders also are often the victims of abuse by caregivers and others (Burgess and Phillips, 2006; Flannery, 2003). How, then, can AD victims be held accountable for any law-violating actions they may take when out of the control of a caregiver since they may not have the ability to formulate the intent to commit a crime? When reading about legal competency in Chapter 7, remember the AD victim.

Traumatic Brain Injury

According to the *DSM-5*, a **traumatic brain injury (TBI)**, which can range from mild to major, is a neurocognitive disorder like dementia and amnestic disorder. TBIs are a major health problem and a leading cause of epilepsy (Bruns and Hauser, 2003). A TBI typically follows a head impact or rapid movement or displacement of the brain within the skull, plus one of the following conditions: (1) loss of consciousness; (2) post-traumatic amnesia; (3) disorientation and confusion; or (4) other neurological signs, which include neuro-imaging of an injury, seizures, reductions in one's visual field, or a weakening of one side of the body (hemiparesis). Primary causes include transport-related accidents, sports injuries, and falls, although a not insignificant number are suffered by crime victims (Bruns and Hauser, 2003: 7). Because of the high use-rate of improvised explosive devices by enemy forces in various theaters of war, the United States is seeing larger numbers of military-service TBIs today than 30 years ago (Bell, Vo, et al., 2009; McKee and Robinson, 2014); given its significance, we return to this topic in Chapter 12.

Consistent with other *DSM-5* diagnoses, TBIs evidence themselves in their impact on distress and disability, ranging from mild to major; moreover, there may be changes of varying degree in the victim's personality and emotionality as well. In addition, medical researchers have observed that following a TBI, victims can exhibit symptoms indistinguishable from schizophrenia when they have a family history of schizophrenia (Malaspina, Goetz, et al., 2001).

This chapter contains a hypothetical example of a TBI and subsequent changes in the victim's personality. In Chapter 3's epilogue, we present a real-world case involving Aaron Hernandez's descent in crime. Indeed, having three or more TBIs is associated with greater violence in offenses when contrasted with persons having fewer or no TBIs (Williams, Cordan, et al., 2010). Moreover, criminal defendants apparently suffer TBIs at a rate higher than a matched control group (Turkstra, Jones, and Toler, 2003). Finally, a random sample study of Ontario (Canada) prison inmates found that over 50 percent of the males and nearly 40 percent of the females reported previous TBIs, rates far higher than in the general population (Colantonio, Hwan, et al., 2014). What we know to date suggests that TBIs are a very real concern for the nation's criminal justice system from first encounter to corrections treatments.

BIOCHEMICAL CAUSES

The human brain and, indeed, the entire human body, could be described as a chemistry experiment in search of **stasis**, or a state of equilibrium or balance capable of sustaining a healthy individual, including a healthy brain. Biochemical compounds are the stuff that keep humans in balance. The right amounts and people are fine; if some are out of balance, then the consequences for the individual can range from symptoms of mental illness to death.

Biochemistry in a Nutshell

Next, we consider what occurs when we ingest biochemical compounds, such as licit and illicit drugs, into our biological system. While we learned that targeted psychotropic drugs can benefit the mentally ill, the introduction of drugs that are not prescribed can alter the human biology. A **biochemical compound** is a term that refers to these essential elements of life. A compound is a substance made up of two or more molecules, a molecule being the smallest physical unit of an element or a compound and itself consisting of two or more atoms. For example, carbon dioxide, the product of respiration in living entities including humans, is a compound consisting of one carbon atom and two oxygen atoms. A biochemical compound, then, contains carbon, which is the basic element found in all living things (e.g., humans are a carbon-based life form). All biochemical compounds also contain hydrogen and oxygen, but may also be constructed from nitrogen, sulfur, and phosphorous.

Biochemical compounds exist in four forms. Carbon, oxygen, and hydrogen combine to form **carbohydrates** such as sugars, starches, and cellulose. **Lipids** are constructed from fatty acids. They cannot be dissolved in water, but do become soluble in organic solvents. The fat our bodies store, as well as oils and waxes, are examples of lipids. **Proteins**, such as hormones and enzymes, are far more complex than carbohydrates, and contain carbon, oxygen, hydrogen, nitrogen, and sulfur. They consist of clusters of amino acids grouped in what are called chains. It is protein imbalances that are often linked to mental illness. Finally, **nucleic acids** are the most complex form of biochemical compounds; they include the same elements as proteins, but tend to have phosphorous rather than sulfur. Examples include deoxyribonucleic acid (DNA) and ribonucleic acid (RNA), the molecules that determine who we are.

Humans can, by their actions or inactions, influence stasis. For example, researchers trace the decline in omega-3 fatty acids from fish to an increasing incidence of major depression (Rao, Asha et al., 2008). Beside the imbalances that can occur within humans, many compounds can be replicated outside the body and introduced artificially into it, often with negative results. Some chemicals, what we call drugs, increase or decrease the presence of naturally occurring proteins. For example, the loss of some proteins, including neurotransmitters such as serotonin, dopamine, and noradrenaline, is associated with depression and can cause symptoms of mental illness (Jensen, Decker, and Anderson, 2006; Rao et al., 2008). Of course, sometimes the host defines the imbalances created by both the natural substances (e.g., the endorphins that surge through a person's body after a stress-producing situation) and compounds from other molecules outside the human body (e.g., morphine, which is chemically the same as the naturally occurring endorphins) as a pleasurable experience. Clearly, then problems can arise from the ingestion of drugs, which are themselves chemical compounds capable of upsetting the stasis existing for all the body's naturally occurring biochemicals necessary for maintaining what we have come to define as "a normal life."

Neurotoxins and Behavior

Biochemicals have the potential to influence human behavior, including shaping personality and mental cognitive functioning. Nowhere is that clearer than with neurotoxins. **Neurotoxin** is a term that refers to any chemical that destroys nerve tissue, creating a condition of neurotoxicity. Neurotoxins are generally viewed as external or exogenous substances that are introduced into, in this case, the human body with obvious negative results. However, some chemicals, such as dopamine, are endogenous or internal to human cell structure, and capable of destroying nerve tissues (Seo, Patrick, and Kennealy, 2008).

Human societies have been slow to remove neurotoxins from our immediate environment, even though they have long known of their harmful properties. Consider, for example, the effects of lead on children, whether that lead comes from lead-based paint in furniture or other household fixtures or through eroded water pipes (Lidsky, 2003). The result is often the same: permanent damage to the developing brains of children. Ethyl alcohol has long been recognized as a "poison," but only in the past several decades has its impact on the developing fetus been shown through studies of **fetal alcohol spectrum disorders (FASD)** (Jones 1973; Kingdon, Cardoso, and McGrath, 2015; Riley, Clarren, et al., 2011). Children should not be exposed to lead; pregnant women should avoid drinking alcoholic beverages.

The scientific community is somewhat ambivalent about the ties between other neurotoxins and human behavior. For example, practitioners of **biocriminology**, a cross-over subdiscipline in criminology, have long suspected the influence of neurotoxins in the immediate physical environments of persons who later became criminals (Monaghan, 2009; Winfree and Abadinsky, 2017: 46-49). It might be heavy metals, including lead and antimony, in the childhood environment that "causes" them to become adult criminals. Also, we know that dopamine imbalance is linked to aggression and comorbidity. As Adriane Raine (2013: 52) notes, "genetic and biological factors interact with social factors in predisposing someone to later antisocial and violent behavior." Proof positive of neuro-logical agents' influence on human behavior has proven elusive.

Drug Abuse and Comorbidity

Drug use and abuse are important concepts for our understanding for several reasons. Before considering these points, however, we should define drug use and abuse. **Drug use** refers to experimentation or low use patterns of illicit drugs or diverted legal drugs, while **drug abuse** implies that the chemicals, whether they are legal drugs or illegal ones, are being consumed on a far more regular basis or their consumption has morphed into compulsive use (APA, 2007). The *DSM-5* includes substance-related and addictive disorders as a diagnosis. To be diagnosed as suffering from a substance-related addiction, the individual must have a "craving or strong desire or urge to use a substance," along with several other criteria (APA, May 17, 2013: 16). Specifically, the *DSM-5* includes ten additional criteria, ranging from taking the drug of choice in larger amounts and for longer than intended to recurrent use of the drug of choice in hazardous situations; subsequently, if two to three of the criteria are met, the person has a mild substance use disorder, four to five is moderate, and six to seven is severe (APA, 2013).

While any addictive disorder impacts a person's ability to function in society, the like-lihood of criminal justice engagement increases substantially when substance use and dependence are comorbid with another mental illness diagnosis and criminal conduct. In fact, the odds of a police encounter are directly related to violent behavior in combination with the non-medical use of a controlled substance (Borum, Swanson, et al., 1994). Indeed, sufferers from co-occurring or comorbid mental and substance abuse issues are found throughout the criminal justice system in greater numbers than in the general population (Peters, Wexler, and Lurigio, 2015). We should not overlook the fact that drug abuse itself, a diagnosable *DSM-5* condition, is a problem for the criminal justice system, as 80 percent of offenders abuse drugs, nearly 50 percent of jail and prison inmates are clinically addicted, and 60 percent of arrestees test positive for a controlled substance at the time of their arrest (National Council on Alcoholism and Drug Dependence (NCADD), n.d.). Alcohol, even more than illegal drugs, is closely associated with violent crime, being a factor in 40 percent of all violent crime (NCADD, n.d.). The interaction of mental illness, drugs, and violence is complicated, as revealed by a recent systematic review of the literature on schizophrenia. The results of this meta-analysis suggest that while there is an association between schizophrenia and violence, substance abuse increases the strength of that association; moreover, the increased risk associated with comorbidity is nearly identical to that observed for drug abuse alone (Fazel et al., 2009). Drug abuse alone and in concert with other mental illnesses is a large problem for many persons caught up in the criminal justice system.

PSYCHOLOGICAL CAUSES

This section's theories originate largely with psychological forces, rather than genetic or organic causes. The distinctions between psychology and psychiatry, then, are important, as they help us understand how treatment staff employing a psychological perspective can look at a mentally ill person and see one set of issues at work, while a psychiatrist might provide an entirely different diagnosis. Psychiatry is a medical subdiscipline dedicated to the study and treatment of brain diseases. For instance, most doctors, during their training, go through a rotation in a hospital's psychiatric unit. In other words, to be a psychiatrist means the practitioner is a physician first and then receives additional training in the medicine of the mind or the study and treatment of mental illness or abnormal behavior from a medical point of view. Some psychiatrists base their psychotherapies on Freudian ideas about mental illness, which suggests the uncovering of unconscious origins of behavior, but most look for causes or risk factors within a person's biology or biochemistry.

Psychology, on the other hand, is the study of the human mind and its functions. Practitioners of psychology have advanced degrees, generally a Ph.D. in general psychology, clinical psychology, or forensic psychology or a DPsy (Doctorate of Psychology), and must pass a specific state licensure to practice their craft. Another distinction, found in many states, is that while psychiatrists can prescribe psychotropic drugs, this is generally not allowed for psychologists, although in some states psychologists may take state-level exams in this area and receive such privileges. In the absence of prescribing privileges, if a psychologist wishes to prescribe a drug, a physician, psychiatrist or otherwise, must see the patient as well.

Again, some psychologists look to Freudian or Jungian psychology for insights into mind-based mental illnesses versus explanations based solely on biological or medical causes. Other treatment professionals, however, use a variety of therapies, ranging from psychotherapies to the learning and establishing of new behavioral patterns, the latter of which is achieved through a wide range of specific "talk" therapies. Cognitive and behavioral therapies focus on the ways we think and the ways we act, recognizing that it is possible to change—what the therapists call "reconditioning." The goal is to overcome specific problem thoughts and actions. In sum, psychologists' strengths include the practice of mental health counseling and interventional behavior modification therapy, while psychiatrists tend to focus on mental health issues as biochemical imbalances or having biological origins, resolving the problems with medications and even surgical procedures.

Consider, for example, the condition of paranoia, which is commonly viewed as an unfounded fear or suspicion that something untoward is about to happen. Paranoia is a symptom of several *DSM-5* disorders, including paranoid personality disorder (PPD), which has no known biological or genetic component. PPD is often confused with schizophrenia, the latter of which can be comorbid with PPD or separate from it. While there is no recognized cure for PPD, both medication, which requires medical license to dispense and is generally the province of the psychiatrist, and psychotherapy, which can be practiced by both psychiatrists and psychologists, can reduce the symptoms. When combined with schizophrenia, the victims, who suffer from auditory hallucinations, anger, aggression, and suicidal ideation, are treated with the same drug-therapy regimen as those suffering from PPD. Besides schizophrenia and PPD, paranoia occurs through other diagnosable illnesses, including dementia, Parkinson's disease, and stroke, to name a few. Consequently, first responders can misunderstand the causes for the problem conduct.

We have previously written about the problems experienced by persons suffering from schizophrenia at various junctures in criminal justice processing, from first contact to corrections. Persons with PPD are suspicious of others, particularly their motivations, and expect to be maltreated. As victims of crimes, they are unlikely to trust or confide in others, including investigators and prosecutors. As suspected offenders, particularly given some of their behavioral issues, they likewise rarely cooperate with police, investigators, or even their own attorneys. As prison inmates, women with PPD, but only those who had not previously been incarcerated, experienced increased odds of adjustment difficulties (Mahmood, Tripodi, et al., 2012). In sum, researchers suggest that PPD is a prime clinical risk factor for unpredictable, sometimes violent, behavior (Johnson, Cohen, et al., 2000; Nestor, 2002).

SOCIOLOGICAL CAUSES

Sociologists look at a wide array of forces and factors in a person's social environment that may, through the operation of the 4-Ps or through causal actions, cause or exacerbate existing mental illnesses. To this point in the chapter, the focus has been largely if not exclusively on individual characteristics. This section shifts the focus to two primary areas: social circumstances and environmental factors (World Health Organization, 2012). With respect to the former, engagement with family members and extended friendships can address issues related to loneliness, bereavement, neglect, and family conflict. Additional problematic social circumstances include exposure to violence and abuse, low income and poverty, difficulties and even failure in educational spheres, and work-related stress and unemployment. At the environmental level, social forces such as poor access to basic services; injustice and discrimination; social, gender, and sexual orientation inequalities; and exposure to war and natural disasters can trigger mental health issues (see Box 4.2).

Other sociological theories offer unique insights into mental illness, especially as it is perceived by mentally ill persons and others that encounter them. For example, the labeling theory perspective suggests that the reactions of others to a mental patient can and do have a profound impact on how that person sees him- or herself, including that person's

---

BOX 4.2

Social Forces and Mental Disorders

Adverse social factors can be linked to, among other mental health problems, major depressive disorders and post-traumatic stress disorder (PTSD), both of which are *DSM-5* diagnosable illnesses. These two forms, owing to their widespread occurrence and importance for criminal justice, merit additional attention.

There is a range of depressive disorders included in the *DSM-5*. Also, importantly, a physician can rule out medical reasons for depression, leading to the mental disorder's probable cause being sociologically linked to adverse mental health determinants. A diagnosis of PTSD is only possible if there is an identifiable pre-occurring etiological event, a traumatic stressor. Such stressors include direct or indirect threats or actions against a person's life and well-being or the life and well-being of others close to the individual. Also, similar direct or indirect threats to the person's physical integrity, such as a physical assault or rape, again including persons close to the patient, are traumatic stressors.

PTSD victims suffer dramatic mood shifts and disruptive behavioral symptoms, including angry, impulsive, reckless, or self-destructive behavior patterns. Psychologists employ a wide range of therapies or treatment modalities to reduce symptoms, as well as, where they can or in concert with a physician, correct the problematic conduct with psychotropic drugs.

Both military- and civilian-acquired PTSD show linkages to involvement with the criminal justice system and violent crime. Not only are PTSD victims overrepresented in the criminal justice system as perpetrators of violence and other crimes, but they are also likely to be overrepresented among the victims of such acts. Researchers studying a random sample of jailed females describe a pathway to crime circumscribed by the triangulation of serious mental illness (e.g., severe depression), PTSD stemming from personal victimizations, and substance abuse. A longitudinal study of incarcerated youth revealed the same linkages between PTSD, trauma, and comorbid psychiatric disorders.

Sources: Abram, Teplin, et al. (2013); ACA (2013); Ardino (2012); Donley, Habib, et al. (2013); Lynch, DeHart, et al. (2012).

ability to fit into the community. The label of mentally ill person, or some less charitable and more pejorative term for such a person, when used consistently and repeatedly can have the effect of becoming a self-fulfilling prophecy (Merton, 1957): The labeled become the person they are defined as being. Edwin Lemert (1951) described this adoption of the "deviant label" as **secondary deviation**, whereas primary deviation reflects a far deeper social and psychological commitment to the role of, in this case, a mentally ill person. In sum, labeling theory, as applied to mental illness, reveals that how people see the mentally ill and how the mentally ill see themselves critically impacts adaptations to social life, including discrimination against them, loss of socio-economic status, estimates of their own self-worth, and increased symptoms (Markowitz, 2013; Scheff, 1974).

Sociology has much to add to the diagnosis and treatment of the mentally ill. The consideration of sociological variables also provides insights into the impact of mental illness on criminal justice processing and the impact of criminal justice processing on the mentally ill. Indeed, criminologists, who study the causes of crime and the origins of criminal behavior from largely a sociological or social psychological perspective, acknowledge the potential for studying diagnoses of mental illness alongside traditional criminological theories; one enhances the insights provided by the other (Vogel and Messner, 2011).

Now that you have explored multiple ways of viewing mental illness, defining it, and even responding to it, we recommend that you consider the exercise found in Box 4.3. What might be useful in this regard is if you write down your answers to the various questions, and, then, after finishing the book, revisit them. Would any of your answers be different after 12 chapters rather than after only 4?

BOX 4.3

What Would You Do?

A close relative, a son or daughter, brother or sister, nephew or niece, has started to act in rather bizarre ways, far outside that person's normal range of conduct. You have talked with others in the family and agree that something is wrong and that to allow the situation to continue without an appropriate response would be a mistake. There is no history of mental illness in the family. Your relative had a normal childhood and never manifested any symptoms of mental illness until family members started noticing that things were just not right.

Just prior to your talk with the family, you read the first four chapters of this book. How would you respond to your extended family? Where would you suggest that the family start the search for understanding and, perhaps, control of your relative's problematic conduct? Which content area would you select as your starting point and why? What if you discover, for example, that drugs are not involved and that's where you started? What's next? What set of explanations makes the most sense to you and why?

EPILOGUE

The case of the psychopath represents a unique blending of mental state and criminal act. Consider the cases of Arthur Shawcross and Tommy Lynn Sells and each one's respective crimes:

▶ Arthur Shawcross (b.1945-d.2008) — Later known as the "Genesee River Killer," Shawcross began killing in the early 1970s. He was sentenced to 25 years in 1972 for the murder of two children in Watertown, New York, but only served 12 years before being paroled, despite the prison psychiatrist's warning that Shawcross was a "schizoid psychopath." Between March 1988, less than a year after being paroled, and December 1989, Shawcross killed at least 12 women near the Genesee River in Rochester, New York. He was apprehended after being spotted by a police surveillance team as he urinated near the body of one of his victims. At trial, which included graphic descriptions of mutilation and cannibalism, a prosecution psychiatrist maintained that Shawcross suffered from antisocial personality disorder, which we know also as psychopathy. His own psychiatrist described Shawcross as the victim of child abuse, PTSD, multiple personality disorder, and brain damage, despite military records that showed he had average intelligence. Found guilty and sentenced to life in prison, Shawcross died in New York's Sullivan Correctional Facility of a cardiac arrest.

▶ Tommy Lynn Sells (b.1964-d.2014) — Sells was a transient killer, crisscrossing the nation, who killed his first victim at 16, and eventually, after two short prison stays, increased that total to at least 22 people. Unfortunately for Sells, one of his last victims was killed in Texas, a state that frequently imposes the death penalty. Diagnosed in prison with a personality disorder with antisocial, borderline, and schizoid features, he also suffered from a chronic drug abuse problem, bipolar disorder, a major depressive disorder, and psychosis. None of these conditions, however, would save Sells from his date with the executioner. Prior to his death, he claimed to have killed at least 70 people, largely stemming from an uncontrollable hatred for others and the fact that he enjoyed seeing people die. In one inexplicable act, Sells confessed to killing a person whose mother had been convicted of his death; she was later acquitted. The State of Texas executed Sells by lethal injection in 2014, three decades after his killing spree began.

These two criminals share the label of psychopath. We often hear a common refrain with respect to crimes such as theirs, which goes: "He must be a crazy psychopath. Look at the way the victim was treated." At trial, however, the problem is that since most serial-offending psychopaths also cover up their crimes, this act alone shows intent and, consequently, that they are not legally insane. For example, one of the most memorable killers in recent times is Ed Gein (b.1906-d.1984), the model for the main characters in the movies *Psycho, Texas Chainsaw Murder, Silence of the Lambs*, and, of course, *Ed Gein*. Upon his capture in 1957, Gein was found to be incompetent to stand trial for murdering two women, not to mention exhuming other corpses from local graveyards. Eleven years later, the court found him competent for trial, where he was adjudged insane at the time of the crimes but guilty. Remanded by the court to a Wisconsin mental health facility in 1968, Gein died of complications due to cancer in 1984. If this case and the verdict confuses you, then keep reading, as we return to the topic of competency and sanity in Chapters 7 and 8. The issue at hand, however, is the unique diagnosis of psychopathy and, Gein, who may have been a psychopath—a psychological condition—was found by a court to be insane—a legal status.

The "diagnosis" of psychopathy has confounded psychologists, psychiatrists, judges, police officers, prosecutors, and correctional personnel for over 100 years. French physician Phillipe Pinel (b.1745-d.1826) referred to a condition whereby patients engaged in episodic violence, impulsive acts, and even self-harm as "insanity without delirium." British physician J.C. Pritchard (b.1786-d.1848) coined the term moral insanity 30 years later. Finally, the German psychiatrist J.L.A. Koch (b.1841-d.1908) used the term psychopathic inferiority to describe persons who suffered from emotional and moral aberrations owing to congenital conditions. However, it was the American physician Hervey Cleckley (b.1903-d.1984) who formalized the modern use of the term psychopath to describe a person who is psychiatrically normal but engages in self-destructive behavior, as opposed to dangerous behavior that threatened others. Indeed, Cleckley (1941) felt that although prisons may contain many psychopaths, we are far more likely to encounter them in everyday business and politics.

Cleckley was instrumental in the creation of the diagnostic criteria for antisocial personality reaction/disturbance, which was included in the *DSM-I* (APA, 1952). The *DSM-5* (APA, 2013) employs the term **antisocial personality disorder (APD)**, although many practitioners describe this disorder as **psychopathy** (Hare, 1996a). As stated in the *DSM-5*, "the essential features of a personality disorder are impairments in personality (self and interpersonal) functioning and the presence of pathological personality traits" (APA, 2012). The *DSM-5*'s detailed diagnostic criteria are beyond the scope of this text. However, some of the central characteristics of APD include ego-centrism (i.e., self-esteem derived from personal gain, power, or pleasure); self-direction (i.e., goal setting based on personal gratification); impairments in empathy or intimacy; antagonism characterized by manipulativeness, deceitfulness, callousness, and hostility; and impulsivity and risk taking (APA, 2012). Diagnostically and behaviorally, then, we understand what to look for in psychopaths. Note, too, that violent or criminal conduct is not necessarily a diagnostic trait.

Over the past 40 years, no one has done more to move psychopathy into the criminal justice mainstream than Canadian psychologist Robert Hare. In the 1970s, Hare, retaining the work of Cleckley, devised a method to determine whether a person was a psychopath using a checklist, which came to be known as the Hare **Psychopathy Checklist-Revised (PCL-R)** (Hare 1996a, 1996b, 1998). The PCL-R consists of a 20-item rating scale. Each item was scored 0 (does not apply to the subject), 1 (a reasonably good match to the subject), or 2 (a full match to the subject). Potential scores on the PCL-R ranged from 0 to 40. Noncriminals averaged scores around 5, criminal offenders averaged around 22; Hare

(2007) viewed a score of 30 to be the threshold for psychopathy. Hare (1998) believed the items clustered around four facets, including (1) manipulative interpersonal style, (2) deficits in affective resonance, (3) a social deviant lifestyle, and (4) antisocial behavior. The PCL-R also includes two items measuring marital and sexual relationships, but these items are not used by all trained clinicians administering the checklist. The diagnosis of psychopathy relies on a series of two interview sessions, which together can last from two to six hours, covering the subject's work history, education, marital and family status, and criminal background. As lying is second nature to many convicted offenders, but especially psychopaths for whom evasiveness and prevarication are part of who they are, much of the information must be cross-checked by a review of his or her criminal and personal history.

While in general use across the globe, several concerns remain concerning the PCL-R's value. First, the scores used to determine psychopathy are not the same in different nations. For example, in German-speaking nations (i.e., Germany, Austria, and Switzerland), researchers found that the threshold for psychopathy was 25 versus 30 in North America (Mokros, Hollerbach, et al., 2013). Second, when diagnosis is completed, treatment is difficult, as the utility of available treatment modalities used to prevent, alter, or even reduce psychopathy in adults have yet to be confirmed (Da Silva, Rijo, and Salekin, 2012), while similar treatments for juveniles have shown promise (Kiehl and Hoffman, 2011). Third, gender is problematic for PCL-R proponents, as identification of the female psychopath has proven difficult (McCuish, Corrado, et al., 2014). Finally, even the method to diagnose psychopathy is debated, as researchers and clinicians use at least two other methods besides various forms of the PCL-R, including the *DSM-5*'s Antisocial Personality Disorder subscale, the **Childhood Psychopathy Scale**. As we reflect on the actions of Shawcross and Sells, we are left with the observations of cynics about the value of the concept of psychopathy who believe it to be a tautology: Psychopaths are people who engage in psychopathic (i.e., extremely crazy) actions (Winfree and Abadinsky, 2017: 73).

Finally, **sociopathy** is a related term. It is used to describe psychopathic behavior that has sociological origins (e.g., an individual who is poorly socialized into appropriate ways of interacting with others) or to differentiate between persons with antisocial personality disorder (APD) who do appear to have a conscience (sociopaths) and those who have no conscience (psychopaths) (cf. Lykken, 2006; Winfree and Abadinsky, 2017: 69-73). A third use of the term suggests that psychopaths as criminals are cool and collected offenders, while sociopaths as criminals tend to be agitated and volatile (Bonn, 2014). Whichever position is closer to the truth, and at present we do not know which is, consider the questions posed in Box 4.4 as to how we should respond to a person diagnosed either as a psychopath or a person with APD.

The net result of the case studies cited at the outset of this chapter, and other related case studies, and reviews of both APD and psychopathy studies is that psychopathy is inevitably linked with violent behavior. However, a recent prison-based study of both the PCL-R and the psychopathic personality inventory or PPI (Lilienfeld and Andrews, 1996) suggests that violent behavior is not necessarily the hallmark of psychopaths (Camp,

BOX 4.4

Thinking About the Issues

The suggestion that some people may be psychopaths and that tests for psychopathy or APD are predictive of certain kinds of unwanted behavior brings into play several policy questions. How would you respond to each of the following?

1. Should all criminal suspects, upon entry to the justice system, be subjected to brain scans and psychometric screening for antisocial personality disorder, what some call psychopathy? Do you agree with argument that these tests are not invasive and no different from DNA tests required in some jurisdictions or fingerprinting?

2. In the event that offenders test "positive" for APD and are convicted in a court of law, what should be done with them?

3. If we developed a medical treatment plan for convicted offenders, should they be subjected to it, even against their will?

Skeem, et al., 2013). The authors, in fact, warn against making broad generalizations about the ties between psychopathy and violence (Camp et al., 2013), suggesting that, after more than 70 years of study, we are only beginning to understand the significance of psychopathy for the intersection of criminal justice and mental health.

SUMMARY

▸ Etiology is the study of the causes of diseases or other conditions; however, some mental health professionals prefer to talk about risk and protective factors.

▸ A theory is a highly organized statement based on systematic observations concerning the phenomenon or phenomena under study; theories seek to describe, understand, predict, and control the objects of study.

▸ Researchers employ many methods to collect data; however, the most valid and reliable ones for exploring causal relationships come from experiments.

▸ Mental illness has many definitions, some of which provide general insights into the phenomenon, and others of which include very specific diagnostic and statistical information as well.

▸ Comorbidity is a crucial idea when it comes to understanding how the mentally ill encounter personnel of the criminal justice system, especially negative contacts.

▸ The science of genetics shows that genetics may be causally linked to many forms of mental illness.

▸ Biochemistry lies at the heart of much mental illness, especially medical issues associated with imbalances in various bodily systems.

▸ Psychology holds many insights into mental illness and provides unique avenues for treatment of a range of mental illnesses, especially those that do not appear to have their origins in medical problems.

▸ Sociological forces may not cause specific mental illness, but they can be the source of risk factors for some forms of mental problems, especially depression and PTSD.

▸ Psychopathy represents a unique and largely misunderstood form of mental disease, about which there are many myths as opposed to realities.

KEY TERMS

Alzheimer's disease (AD)
Amnestic disorder
Antisocial personality disorder (APD)
Attention Deficit/Hyperactivity Disorder (ADHD)
Autism spectrum disorder
Biocriminology
Bipolar disorder
Carbohydrates
Cause
Childhood psychopathy scale
Chromosomes
Comorbidity
Concept
Control
Deoxyribonucleic acid (DNA)
Description
Disability
Distress
Drug abuse
Drug use
Etiology
Federal Gun Control Act of 1968
Fetal alcohol spectrum disorders (FASD)

4-Ps factor model
Generalizability
Genetics
Lipids
Nucleic acids
Neurocognitive disorders
Neurotoxin
Placebo
Perpetuating risk factor
Precipitating risk factor
Predisposing risk factor
Proteins
Protective risk factor
Psychopathy
Psychopathy Checklist-Revised (PCL-R)
Psychotic depression
Random sample
Schizophrenia
Sociopathy
Stasis
Theory
Traumatic brain injury (TBI)
Understanding
Variable

CHAPTER REVIEW QUESTIONS

1. Define theory. What are the three characteristics of a causal relationship? List and discuss the goals of theory. In your discussion, employ examples tied to mental illness.
2. What is considered the "gold standard" of research? What are its elemental parts?
3. How does the idea of time influence research? Name and discuss the three types of research that accommodate the movement of time.
4. What is a sample? What is a census? How do these two methods of collecting information differ from one another?
5. What is a case study? What is an availability sample? How do samples influence a study's generalizability? [NOTE: It would be a good idea to define generalizability.]
6. What is the definition of mental illness that is associated with the *DSM-5*? What three parts of this definition can help its users understand what is and is not included?
7. Provide a review of the biological causes contained in this chapter. Which one do you feel provides the best explanation for the broadest range of mental illnesses? Explain your answer.
8. How do biochemicals influence behaviors? How do biochemical compounds, including neurotoxins, influence behavior? Provide a review of the biochemical causes contained in this chapter. Which one do you feel provides the best explanation for the broadest range of mental illnesses? Explain your answer.
9. Provide a review of the psychological and psychiatric causes of mental illness contained in this chapter. Which one do you feel provides the best explanation for the broadest range of mental illnesses? Explain your answer.
10. Who is the psychopath? What do you see as the true meaning of this term? Do you think the emphasis given to psychopaths by both the mental health and criminal justice communities is justified? Explain your answer.

REFERENCES

Abram, K.M., L.A. Teplin, D.C. King, S.L. Longworth, K.M. Emanuel, E.G. Romero, G.M. McClelland, M.K. Dulcan, J.J. Washburn, L.J. Welty, and N.D. Olson (2013). "PTSD, trauma, and comorbid psychiatric disorders in detained youth." Juvenile Justice Bulletin. Retrieved at https://www.ojjdp.gov/pubs/239603.pdf on 4 December 2017.

Ahn, W., and N.S. Kim (2008). "Causal theories of mental disorder concepts." *Psychological Science Agenda*. American Psychological Association. Retrieved at http://www.apa.org/science/about/psa/2008/06/ahn.aspx on 24 November 2017.

American Psychiatric Association (1952). *Diagnostic and Statistical Manual of Mental Disorders*. Washington DC: American Psychiatric Association.

American Psychiatric Association (2007). *Practice Guidelines for the Treatment of Patients with Substance Use Disorders*. Arlington, VA: American Psychiatric Association.

American Psychiatric Association (2012). "*DSM-IV* and *DSM-5* criteria for the personality disorders." Arlington, VA: American Psychiatric Association. Retrieved at http://www.psi.uba.ar/academica/carrerasdegrado/psicologia/sitios_catedras/practicas_profesionales/820_clinica_tr_personalidad_psicosis/material/dsm.pdf on 28 July 2017.

American Psychiatric Association (2013). *Diagnostic and Statistical Manual of Mental Disorders*. 5th ed. Arlington, VA: American Psychiatric Association.

American Psychiatric Association (May 17, 2013). "Highlights of changes from DSM-IV to DSM-5." Arlington, VA: American Psychiatric Association.

American Psychiatric Association (n.d.). "What is mental illness." Retrieved at https://www.psychiatry.org/patients-families/what-is-mental-illness on 28 November 2017.

Ardino, V. (2012). "Offending behaviour: The role of trauma and PTSD." *European Journal of Psychotraumatology*. Retrieved at https://www.ncbi.nlm.nih.gov/pmc/articles/PMC3402156/ on 4 December 2017.

Bell, R.S., A.H. Vo, C.J. Neal, J. Tigno, R. Roberts, C. Mossop, J.R. Dunne, and R.A. Armonda (2009). "Military traumatic brain and spinal column injury: a 5-year study of the impact blast and other military grade weaponry on the central nervous system." *Journal of Trauma and Acute Care Surgery* 66(4 Supplement): S104-11.

Blashfield, R.K., J.W. Keeley, E.H. Flanagan, and S.R. Miles (2014). "The cycle of classification: DSM-I through DSM-5." *Annual Review of Clinical Psychology* 10: 25-51.

Bonn, S.A. (January 22, 2014). "How to tell a sociopath from a psychopath." *Psychology Today*. Retrieved at https://www.psychologytoday.com/blog/wicked-deeds/201401/how-tell-sociopath-psychopath on 30 November 2017.

Borum, R., J. Swanson, M. Swartz, and V. Hiday (1997). "Substance abuse, violent behavior, and police encounters among persons with severe mental disorders." *Journal of Contemporary Criminal Justice* 13: 236-50.

Bruinius, H. (2007). *Better for All the World: The Secret History of Forced Sterilization and America's Quest for Racial Purity*. New York: Vintage Books.

Bruns, J., and W.A. Hauser (2003). "The epidemiology of traumatic brain injury: A review. *Epilepsia* 44: 2-10.

Burgess, A.W., and S.L. Phillips (2006). "Sexual abuse, trauma, and dementia in the elderly: A retrospective study of 284 cases." *Victims and Offenders* 1: 193-204.

Camp, J.P., J.L. Skeem, K. Barchard, S.O. Lilienfeld, and N.G. Poythress (2013). "Psychopathic predators? Getting specific about the relation between psychopathy and violence." *Journal of Consulting and Clinical Psychology* 82: 467-80.

CBS News (October 30, 2017). "Doctors prepare to examine Las Vegas shooter Stephen Paddock's brain." *CBS News*. Retrieved at https://www.cbsnews.com/news/stephen-paddock-doctors-examine-brain-las-vegas-shooting/ on 23 February 2018.

Cleckley, H. (1941). *The Mask of Sanity: An Attempt to Reinterpret the So-Called Psychopathic Personality*. St. Louis, MO: Mosby.

Colantonio, A., H. Kim, S. Allen, M. Asbridge, J. Petgrave, and S. Brochu (2014). "Traumatic brain injury and early life experiences among men and women in a prison population." *Journal of Correctional Health Care* 20: 271-79.

Da Silva, D.R., D. Rijo, and R.T. Salekin (2012). "Child and adolescent psychopathy: A state-of-the-art reflection on the construct and etiological theories." *Journal of Criminal Justice* 40: 269-77.

Donley, S., L. Habib, T. Jovanovic, A. Kamkwalala, M. Evces, G. Egan, B. Bradley, and K.J. Ressler. (2012). "Civilian PTSD symptoms and risk for involvement in the criminal justice system." *Journal of the American Academy of Psychiatry and the Law* 40: 522-9.

Fazel, S., G. Gulati, L. Linsell, J.R. Geddes, and M. Grann (2009). "Schizophrenia and violence: Systematic review and meta-analysis." *PLOS-Medicine* 6(8): e1000120. Retrieved at http://journals.plos.org/plosmedicine/article?id=10.1371/journal.pmed.1000120 on 27 November 2017.

Fields, R.D. (2015). *Why We Snap: Understanding the Rage Circuit in Your Brain*. New York: Dutton.

Fink, S. (October 26, 2017). "Las Vegas gunman's brain will be scrutinized for clues to the killings." *The New York Times*. Retrieved at https://www.nytimes.com/2017/10/26/us/las-vegas-shooting-stephen-paddock-brain.html on 23 February 2018.

Flannery R.B. (2003). "Domestic violence and elderly dementia sufferers." *American Journal of Alzheimer's Disease and Other Dementias* 18: 21-3.

Frederick, E. (July 30, 2016). "Experts still disagree on the role of Tower shooter's brain tumor." *The Daily Texan*. Retrieved at http://www.dailytexanonline.com/2016/07/30/experts-still-disagree-on-role-of-tower-shooters-brain-tumor on 23 February 2018.

Gao, Y., A.L. Glenn, R.A. Schug, Y. Yang, and A. Raine (2009). "The Neurobiology of Psychopathology: A Neurodevelopmental Perspective." *Canadian Journal of Psychiatry* 54(12): 813-823.

Giffords Law Center (n.d.). "Mental health reporting." Retrieved at http://lawcenter.giffords.org/gun-laws/policy-areas/background-checks/mental-health-reporting/ on 28 November 2017.

Glenn, A.L., and A. Raine (2014). *Psychopathy: An Introduction to Biological Findings and Their Implications*. New York: New York University Press.

Gordon, L. (2003). *The Moral Property of Women: A History of Birth Control Policies in America*. Urbana: University of Illinois Press.

Hare. R.D. (1996a). "Psychopathy and antisocial personality disorder: A case of diagnostic confusion." *Psychiatric Times* 13: 39-40.

Hare, R.D. (1996b). "Psychopathy as a risk marker for violence: Development and validation of a screening version of Revised Psychopathic Checklist." Pp. 81-98 in *Violence and Mental Disorder: Developments of Risk Assessment*, J. Monahan and H.J. Steadman (eds.). Chicago, IL: University of Chicago Press.

Hare, R.D. (1998). "The PCL-R: Some issues concerning its misuse." *Legal and Criminological Psychology* 3: 99-119.

Hare, R.D. (1998). "Psychopathy, affect, and behaviour." Pp. 105-139 in *Psychopathy: Theory, Research and Implications for Society*, D. Cooke, A. Forth, and R. Hare (eds.). Dordrecht: Kluwer.

Hare, R.D. (2007). *Hare Psychopathic Checklist-Revised (PCL-R): Technical Manual*, 2nd ed. Toronto, Ontario, Canada: Multi-Health Systems.

Hyman, Steve E. (2000). "The genetics of mental illness: Implications for practice." Bulletin of the World Health Organization 78: 455-63.

Jabr, F. (2013). "The DSM-5 ignores biology of mental illness." *Scientific American*. Retrieved at https://www.scientificamerican.com/article/new-dsm5-ignores-biology-mental-illness/ on 23 November 2017.

Jensen, L.W., L. Decker, and M.M. Anderson (2006). "Depression and health promotion lifestyles of persons with mental illness." *Issues in Mental Health and Nursing* 27: 617-34.

Johnson, J.G., P. Cohen, E. Smailes, S. Kasen, J.M. Oldham, A.E. Skodol, and J.S. Brooks (2000). "Adolescent personality disorders associated with violent and criminal behavior during adolescence and early adulthood." *American Journal of Psychiatry* 157: 1406-12.

Jones, K. (1973). "Pattern of Malformation in Offspring of Chronic Alcoholic Mothers." *The Lancet* 301(7815): 1267-271.

Kingdon, D., C. Cardoso, and J.J. McGrath (2015). "Research review: Executive function deficits in Fetal Alcohol Spectrum Disorders and Attention-Deficit/Hyperactivity Disorder—A meta-analysis." *Journal of Child Psychology and Psychiatry* 57: 116-131.

Lane, C. (2013). "The NIMH withdraws support for DSM-5." *Psychology Today*. Retrieved at https://www.psychologytoday.com/blog/side-effects/201305/the-nimh-withdraws-support-dsm on 20 November 2017.

Levine, A. (November 11, 2017). "Massing shooting and mental illness: Almost everything you've been told is wrong." *Newsweek.com*. Retrieved at http://www.newsweek.com/mass-shootings-mental-illness-been-told-wrong-708892 on 28 November 2017.

Lidsky, T.I. (2003). "Lead neurotoxicity in children: Basic mechanisms and clinical correlates." *Brain* 126: 5-19.

Lilienfeld, S.O., and B.P. Andrews (1996). "Development and preliminary validation of a self-report measure of psychopathic personality trains in noncriminal populations." *Journal of Personality Assessment* 66: 488-524.

Lykken, D.T. (2006). "Psychopathic personality: The scope of the problem." Pp. 3-13 in *Handbook of Psychopathy*, C.J. Patrick (ed.). New York: Guilford Press.

Lynch, S.M., D.D. DeHart, J. Belknap, and B.L. Green (2012). *Women's Pathways to Jail: The Role and Intersection of Serious Mental Illness and Trauma*. Washington, DC: Bureau of Justice Assistance. Retrieved at https://www.bja.gov/publications/women_pathways_to_jail.pdf on 4 December 2017.

Kiehl, K.A., and M.B. Hoffman (2011). "The criminal psychopath: History, neuroscience, treatment, and economics." *Jurimetrics* 51: 355-97.

Mahmood, S.T., S.J. Tripodi, M.G. Vaughn, K.A. Bender, and R.D. Schwartz (2012). "Effects of personality disorder and impulsivity on emotional adaptations in prison among women offenders." *Psychiatric Quarterly* 83: 467-80.

Malaspina, D., R.R. Goetz, J.H. Friedman, K.A. Kaufmann, S.V. Faraone, M. Tsuang, C.R. Cloninger, J.I. Nurnburger, and M.C. Blehar (2001). "Traumatic brain injury and schizophrenia in members of schizophrenia and bipolar disorder pedigrees." *American Journal of Psychiatry* 158: 440-46.

Markowitz, F.E. (2013). "Labeling theory and mental illness." Chapter 3 in *Advances in Criminological Theory*, D.P. Farrington and J. Murray (eds.). New Brunswick, NJ: Transactions.

Marso, A. (October 17, 2017). "Fungus destroyed inmate's brain while Kansas prison contractor did nothing, suit says." *The Kansas City Star*. Retrieved at http://www.kansascity.com/news/business/health-care/article179322916.html on 23 February 2018.

McCuish, E.C., R. Corrado, P. Lussier, and S.D. Hart (2014). "Psychopathic traits and offending trajectories from early adolescence to adulthood." *Journal of Criminal Justice* 42: 66-76.

McKee, A.C., and M.E. Robinson (2014). "Military-related traumatic brain injury and neurodegeneration." *Alzheimer's and Dementia* 10: S242-S253.

Metzl, J.M., and K.T. MacLeish (2015). "Mental illness, mass shootings, and the politics of American firearms." *American Journal of Public Health* 105: 240-49.

Mokros, A., P. Hollerbach, K. Vohs, J. Nitschke, R. Eher, and E. Habermeyer (2013). "Normative data for the psychopathy check-list revised in German-speaking countries." *Criminal Justice and Behavior* 40: 397-412.

Monaghan, P. (April 17, 2009). "Biocriminology." *Chronicle of Higher Education*. 55/33: B4.

National Alliance on Mental Illness (2017). "Mental Health Conditions." Retrieved at https://www.nami.org/Learn-More/Mental-Health-Conditions on 13 July 2017.

National Council on Alcoholism and Drug Dependence (n.d.). "Alcohol, drugs and crime." New York: National Council on Alcoholism and Drug Dependence, Inc. Retrieved at https://www.ncadd.org/about-addiction/alcohol-drugs-and-crime on 4 December 2017.

National Institute of Mental Health (n.d.). "Genetics and mental disorders: Report of the National Institute of Mental Health's genetic workgroup." Washington, DC: NIMH.

Nestor, P.G. (2002). "Mental disorders and violence: Personality dimensions and clinical features." *American Journal of Psychiatry* 159: 1973-8.

Nemeroff, C.B., D. Weinberger, M. Rutter, H.L. MacMillan, R.A. Bryant, S. Wessely, D.J. Stein, C.M. Pariante, F. Seemüller, M. Berk, G.S. Malhi, M. Preisig, M. Blume, and P. Lysaker (2013). "DSM-5: A collection of psychiatrist views on the changes, controversies, and future directions." *BMC Medicine* 11: 202. Retrieved at https://bmcmedicine.biomedcentral.com/track/pdf/10.1186/1741-7015-11-202?site=bmcmedicine.biomedcentral.com on 23 November 2017.

Phillips, K. (2017). "'Something is eating my brain,' an inmate said. A lawsuit claims he was left to die." *The Washington Post*. Retrieved at https://www.washingtonpost.com/news/post-nation/wp/2017/10/27/something-is-eating-my-brain-an-inmate-said-a-lawsuit-says-he-was-left-to-die/?utm_term=.3e03cf203ccf on 23 February 2018.

Peters, R.G., H.K. Wexler, and A.J. Lurigio (2015). "Co-occurring substance use and mental disorders in the criminal justice system: A new frontier for clinical practice and research." *Psychiatric Rehabilitation Journal* 38: 1-6.

Raine, A. (1993). *The Psychopathology of Crime: Criminal Behavior as a Clinical Disorder*. San Diego: Academic Press.

Raine, A. (2013). *The Anatomy of Violence: The Biological Roots of Crime*. New York: Random House.

Rao, T.S.S., M.R. Asha, B.N. Ramesh, and K.S.J. Rao (2008). "Understanding nutrition, depression and mental illness." *Indian Journal of Psychiatry* 50: 77-82.

Riley, E.P., S. Clarren, J. Weinberg, and E. Jonsson (2011). *Fetal Alcohol Spectrum Disorder: Management and Policy Perspectives of FASD*. New York: Wiley-Blackwell.

Scheff, T.J. (1974). "The labeling theory of mental illness." *American Sociological Review* 39: 444-52.

Seo, D., C.J. Patrick, and P.J. Kennealy (2008). "Role of serotonin and dopamine system interaction in the neurobiology of impulsive aggression and its comorbidity with other clinical disorders." *Aggression and Violent Behavior* 13: 383-95.

Smoller, J.W., S. Ripke, et al. (2013). "Identification of risk loci with shared effects on five major psychiatric disorders: A genome-wide analysis." *Lancet* 381(9875): 1371-9.

Sun, F., X. Gao, H. Brown, and L.T. Winfree, Jr. (2017). "Police officer competence in handling Alzheimer's cases: The roles of AD knowledge, beliefs, and exposure." *Dementia*. First published January 13, 2017. https://doi.org/10.1177/1471301216688605.

The Telegraph (October 29, 2017). "Brain of Las Vegas gunman Stephen Paddock to undergo forensic examination." The Telegraph. Retrieved at http://www.telegraph.co.uk/news/2017/10/29/brain-las-vegas-gunman-stephen-paddock-undergo-forensic-examination/ on 23 February 2018.

Thomas, P. (October 7, 2017). "Investigators believe Las Vegas gunman had severe undiagnosed mental illness: Sources." *ABC News*. Retrieved at http://abcnews.go.com/US/investigators-las-vegas-gunman-severe-undiagnosed-mental-illness/story?id=50346433 on 23 February 2017.

Turkstra, L., D. Jones, and Hon. L. Toler (2003). "Brain injury and violent crime." *Brain Injury* 17: 39-47.

Vogel, M., and S.F. Messner (2011). "Social correlates of delinquency for youth in need of mental health services: Examining the scope and conditions of criminological theories." *Justice Quarterly* 29: 546-72.

White, E.B., and P. Montgomery (2014). "Dementia, walking outdoors and getting lost: Incidence, risk factors and consequences from dementia-related police missing-person reports." *Age and Mental Health* 19: 224-30.

Williams, W.H., G. Cordan, A.J. Mewse, J. Tonks, and C.N. Burgess (2010). "Self-reported traumatic brain injury in male young offenders: A risk factor for re-offending, poor mental health and violence?" *Neuropsychological Rehabilitation* 20: 801-12.

Winfree, Jr., L.T., and H. Abadinsky (2017). *Essentials of Criminological Theory.* 4th ed. Long Grove, IL: Waveland Press.

CASES

Buck v. Bell, 274 U.S. 200 (1927)

Roe v. Wade, 410 U.S. 113 (1973)

Skinner v. Oklahoma, 316 U.S. 525 (1942)

LEGISLATION

Arkansas Code §5-73-103

California Welfare and Institutions Code §§8100-8108

D.C. Code title 11 §1448

Federal Gun Control Act of 1968; 18 U.S.C. §922

Iowa Code §724.15

Mississippi Statutes Revised §45-9-101

Title 27 C.F.R. §478.11

Part II

Providing Justice, Providing Mental Healthcare

Two systems, criminal justice and mental healthcare, often interact when a person with a mental illness, disease, or defect is viewed as a threat to public order, even when that threat is minor or poorly understood. Sometimes, however, the threat is clear and may involve both the mentally ill person and others in the community. This part of the text examines the ways that people move through the justice system, owing to those perceived or real threats. Chapter 5 introduces the idea of the first responder, or the person who first encounters the mentally ill person because of public or private behavior that causes concern in others. This chapter describes several "best practices" for such encounters and examines two major concerns for first responders: legal liability and risk management. Chapter 6 examines two important situations that often confront mentally ill persons: voluntary or involuntary commitment to a secure mental health facility. Such decisions are closely watched by the courts and other legal authorities, and this chapter explores these processes and decisions using a four-state comparison, examining provisions for their application in New York, North Carolina, Oregon, and Arizona. Chapter 7 centers on the important question of competency, examining the key issues surrounding the constitutional, procedural, evaluative, and ethical considerations that determine a defendant's ability to stand trial. The fate of the mentally ill at trial is covered in Chapter 8. This chapter explores the use and relevance of defenses of insanity, temporary insanity, and diminished capacity. The final chapter in this part, Chapter 9, examines what happens to the mentally ill in the event they are held in one of the nation's many institutions of confinement. But corrections is about more than prisons and jails, as it details other forms of community-based alternatives to incarceration. Importantly, this chapter details many treatments available to those placed in confinement or given alternative sanctions.

First Responders and Street Encounters

LEARNING OBJECTIVES

After reading this chapter, you should be able to:

▶ **Understand** how deinstitutionalization, along with other changes in public **policy**, resulted in the "criminalization of the mentally ill."

▶ **Distinguish** between various street solutions employed by first responders, including law enforcement, fire, and emergency personnel, as well as other public employees.

▶ **Explain** the "best practices" employed by communities seeking humane treatment of the mentally ill who run afoul of law enforcement officials.

▶ **Understand** the legal liability and risk management issues associated with official responses to mentally ill citizens by public employees.

▶ **Describe** how the police use of force, especially deadly force, is an omnipresent concern for police and citizens alike.

PROLOGUE

This prologue is based on a composite of several incidents observed by the authors over the years.

City 911 dispatch alerted patrol units near the intersection of Main Street and Broad Avenue of a possible public disturbance call. Two individuals, indicated the dispatcher, were engaged in "threatening behavior."

Officer Johnson, a ten-year veteran of the force, headed for the intersection. This was not his first visit to this location. He had responded to other calls here from a woman when she felt that her brother was acting crazy. However, in each previous case, Officer Johnson's arrival had de-escalated the situation and the sister had refused to press charges, despite obvious wounds to her face.

As he drove into the intersection, Johnson saw that it was indeed the very familiar brother and sister gesturing wildly and shouting obscenities. Officer Johnson activated the camera on his bullet-proof vest and requested backup. As he approached, Johnson observed the brother turn quickly away from his sister to face him, then put his right hand behind his back. Johnson later testified he thought he heard the brother say, "Stop trying to control me with your superpowers. I can neutralize you."

Within seconds, the assailant—as Johnson saw him—swung his right hand forward while his face twisted into a fearsome snarl. He coiled his body like a tight spring and his right arm came forward, revealing a shiny object in his hand, followed by a soft clicking sound. Johnson testified that he thought it was a knife. In a recent training session, Johnson had learned that a knife in the hands of an assailant within ten feet was as deadly as a gun.

Johnson, a natural left-hander, reached for his stun gun, which he wore on the right side of his utility belt. Unfortunately, in an instinctual action, he reached with his dominant left hand, which was the side on which he wore his service automatic, a 9 mm Glock. Johnson then fired his gun, fatally wounding 29-year old Jimmie Baker. Later, medical and law enforcement records revealed that Jimmie had a history of mental health commitments. In his hand was a folding comb, but it was shaped like a switch-blade knife.

Officer Johnson held his gun over Jimmie's body, listening to the sister scream. "What did you do? He is all the family I had. You will pay for this!" Johnson radioed dispatch, asking, "Where is my backup?" The entire interaction was shown in the body camera video playback at the coroner's inquest.

As a matter of police policy, Officer Johnson will be suspended from active service while there is an internal investigation. His body camera will help the administrative review of his conduct and re-create the scene to determine if his lethal actions were ones of self-defense and were undertaken as a form of justifiable homicide. The systematic review may find his decision was in accordance with police policy for personal protection, but could require retraining and internal corrections, such as wearing his stun gun on his dominate left hand side. If, however, the administrative review finds that Officer Johnson did not act rationally in light of the circumstances, but deliberately and intentionally engaged in gunfire, his case could be referred for criminal prosecution and he would face criminal murder charges.

Regardless of what police administrative decisions are made, the victim's sister will likely file a civil wrongful death lawsuit against Officer Johnson and the city police department. Civil liability may be found if a judge or jury determines the death occurred due to carelessness or negligent behavior. If so, the city pays for defending Johnson against the lawsuit and would also pay for the compensatory losses to the sister, as Johnson was an employee at the time.

Chapter Overview

The opening composite illustrates how quickly an encounter between a mentally ill citizen and police can move from threatening to deadly. The police and other first responders have the power to de-escalate or exacerbate a street encounter, which in this context refers to any public or private contact between first responders and mentally ill individuals. The good news is that very few end up being resolved in a criminal prosecution. The bad news is that it does happen and the costs to those involved, including victims, alleged perpetrators, and first responders, can be immense and long-lasting.

This chapter looks at those persons whose public behavior warrants a response, whether it be the formal induction into the machinations of the criminal justice system or some less formalized action. This is the province of the first responder, who may be a police officer, a school official, a social worker, an EMT, or an average citizen. Whether the troubled or troublesome person in question is left alone, guided to an alternative setting, transported for mental health evaluation, or is ultimately arrested, the material in this chapter describes how first responders try to defuse, de-escalate, or defend persons and property during an unpredictable encounter with a person suffering from mental illness or a psychiatric episode. The goal is that the course of last resort becomes the never-to-use resort: the use of deadly force. Instead, trained professionals should have a battery of alternative solutions from which to choose. In such circumstances, training will always achieve a better result than instinct.

We begin our look at street encounters by exploring the influence of two movements on the American mental health industry: deinstitutionalization and the confluence of the "nothing works" and just deserts perspectives on offenders. We examine how these changes in social, political, and legal practices arguably led to the criminalization of the mentally ill.

Next, we turn to street solutions to encounters such as that described in the prologue. The emphasis in this second section of the chapter is on traditional responses, including so-called wellness checks, which can be both physical and verbal in nature.

The third topic is a review of "best practices," those recent approaches to handling potentially volatile public encounters with mentally ill persons. We first define the parameters of such encounters. Next, we give a detailed review of the critical incident team approach, along with several other ways to proactively handle situations involving first responders and the mentally ill that could easily degenerate into harmful or even deadly situations involving first responders and the mentally ill.

Legal liability and risk management are natural "down-stream" concerns deriving from almost any police-citizen encounter. As this section of the chapter suggests, it is best to train for and against such encounters than to wait and deal with them in real time.

The prologue described a violent confrontation between a law enforcement official and a mentally ill person. The fifth section of this chapter examines a critical concept known as **police assisted suicide**. In fact, very few mentally ill people are violent. Knowing the triggers that can shift the situation from a friendly wellness check to a deadly confrontation can prove indispensable for the first responder.

The epilogue provides several examples of what can go horribly wrong in a police-citizen incident. The question of police liability is central to this chapter, and the epilogue explores the question of liability and the subsequent issue of compensation or the financial settlement of litigious use-of-deadly-force incidents.

FRAMING THE ISSUES

As described in Chapter 2, Marc Abramson (1972) coined the term criminalization of the mentally ill. Abramson observed that mentally ill defendants underwent a transition from being insane to being a criminal simply because their behavior did not conform to societal norms and expectations and there are no interim resources. This characterization is all too familiar as a consequence of the inadequate number of mental health treatment facilities, the loss of subsidized housing, and the increase in substance and alcohol abuse. The opportunity to intervene and be aware of alternatives in the course of an encounter requires patience, experience, and a framework of "go to" options. First responders, often the police, can initiate this process of criminalization or avoid it. It is these interactions that are the subject matter of this chapter.

Scholars point to five sets of factors as contributing to the modern transition of mentally ill people who were committed indefinitely to insane asylums to mentally ill people who are now being imprisoned or jailed with underlying mental illnesses for long periods of time (Belcher, 1988; Borzecki and Wormith, 1985; Lamb and Weinberger, 2005). First, as described above, deinstitutionalization flooded the community with hundreds of thousands of individuals with moderate to severe mental disorders. The idea was that such people could be treated in community-based treatment centers, but the bed spaces and availability of such facilities were not up to the task, nor have they grown to meet the current needs.

Second, the civil commitment process became far more stringent beginning in the late 1960s and early 1970s. Like the goal of deinstitutionalization, changes to the civil commitment process were intended to impact mentally ill citizens in positive ways, curbing past abuses. The net result was that such commitments were used far less often and were of far shorter duration. As Lamb and Weinberger observed, the more dangerous mentally ill patients continued to be institutionalized, while the far more numerous, less dangerous ones were left largely untreated in the community.

The third factor, limited access to treatment resources in the community, has several important consequences for mentally ill offenders. In the main, the resources, including adequate case management, are simply not available or severely limited in capacity. What resources are available may be the wrong kinds, for example, **outpatient services**, where the clients come to the provider, rather than **outreach services**, where the providers find the clients in the field. Moreover, accepting agencies may see mentally ill arrestees, defendants, or convicted offenders as resistant to treatment, or they may not have arrangements to maintain adequate security and custody over the individual.

Fourth, the police role is often poorly defined and poorly articulated with mental health providers. Simply linking with the mental health community can be an exhausting and time-consuming process for police officers. Moreover, while the mental health community may refuse to take a disruptive mentally ill arrestee, criminal justice is, in the words of Borzecki and Wormith, the system "that can't say no." Similarly, the police may simply arrest and jail a mentally disturbed person simply because there is no other viable option available.

Finally, the public had become, in concert with the evolution of just deserts, far less tolerant of all offenders, including those with mental illness. Moreover, providing "special treatment" for one group of offenders, perhaps at the expense of other equally "meritorious" groups, may offend those persons that adhere to equal justice before the law.

Taken together, these forces—sometimes in concert with each other and often independently—helped to create what we know today as the criminalization of the mentally ill. Those interested in turning around this development are faced with the unenviable task of reversing these forces, which have deep roots in both the nation's fiscal and social policies.

STREET SOLUTIONS

Typically, mentally ill persons are arrested for minor offenses, such as disorderly conduct, public intoxication, or trespassing, and these offenses are often more symptomatic of mental illness than criminality (Cooper, McLearen, and Zapf, 2004). Obviously, there are many factors for first responders, medics, and treatment personnel to consider in determining the disposition of any person who is having a public mental health-related incident. If there is law enforcement present, the officers may have to decide between taking actions such as arrest, involuntary hospitalization, or informational disposition (e.g., conflict resolution or mediation), or taking no action (Godfredson, Ogloff, et al., 2010). The mental health specialists in Box 5.1 had different choices when handling a mental health situation. Consider the process that they used.

Street Encounters

While every encounter is different, having a mental checklist of options or reasonable alternatives based on a presented scenario may be as effective as an arrest and could avoid worse, more violent outcomes. Take, for example, the case of police-citizen interactions when the citizen is clearly (or not so clearly) impaired by mental illness. The evidence suggests that training in the best methods for working with persons who appear to have a mental illness or disorder can increase an officer's confidence in his or her ability to deal with similar situations (Watson, Morabito, et al., 2008). The goal should be de-escalation of the situation, and **verbal de-escalation** is the key. While most individuals with mental illness are not dangerous, a special set of skills is required to have a mutually successful end to any street encounter (Dufrense, 2011; Gur, 2010). A variety of professional responsibilities and responses exist when an individual is being socially or domestically disruptive. The police can serve as gatekeepers for community resources, and it is often within a law enforcement officer's discretion to determine if a mentally ill person will receive psychiatric services or jail.

Encountering the Homeless

They sleep on sidewalks, use libraries and bus stations for bathing, and rely on 24-hour fast-food restaurants for respite from the weather. Many walk the streets, communicate with the unseen, and live in abandoned buildings, shelters, and under bridges. It is

BOX 5.1

What Would You Do?

A man in his 20s walks into a county mental health clinic, agitated and wearing a large hunting knife in a sheath on his belt. The office receptionist calmly informs the young man, who seems confused and upset, that the doctor will be right out to meet with him. The receptionist then phones the therapist, telling him that there is an unscheduled, "walk-in" client in the waiting room who seems agitated and is carrying a large hunting knife. When the therapist comes into the waiting room, he says to the young man, "You don't have to worry. We're not going to let anybody take your knife. We'll just leave it with the receptionist for safekeeping." The young man seems confused, because he never actually raised any issue of concern about someone stealing his knife. However, apparently comforted by the calmness expressed by the receptionist and the therapist, he complies, and the knife is left with the receptionist. The young man is escorted back to the therapist's office, where he describes how medical books that he has written have been stolen and published by others using their names. The man is obviously delusional and is possibly dangerous to others. The therapist listens patiently and non-confrontationally to the young man and informs him that there is a doctor at an adjacent clinic who "specializes" in such situations of plagiarism and can clear up this problem. The therapist subsequently "escorts" the young man to the nearby "clinic," which is, in fact, the psychiatric ward of the adjacent county hospital.

Note that the "solution" to the situation is presented in a non-hesitant, confident manner, specifically avoiding putting the young man in the position of having to "decide" whether to comply with the surrender of his knife. The "solution" is presented as a non-issue and the young man accompanies the therapist to his office and, subsequently, to the inpatient psychiatric ward. Here the situation was confined in a setting where the concern about "immediate danger to self or others" was resolved without triggering further escalation with a show of force or confrontation. Frequently, first responders will need to be creative and develop appropriate responses to fit unique situations. The immediate task, when there is a real potential for violence, is to de-escalate the situation. Do you agree with the solution? What would you have done differently? What is the basis of your answer?

Sources: Professional encounter experienced by one of this book's co-authors; Kerr, Morabito, and Watson (2010).

reported that homelessness shelters are so populated by mentally ill wanderers that they have the appearance of psychiatric wards (Treatment Advocacy Center, 2016).

It is a mistake to ignore the factor of homelessness in connection with mental illness, drug and alcohol abuse, and street encounters. Not all homeless people have mental illness and not all the mentally ill are homeless. Nonetheless, problematic encounters between the homeless and community members are increasing, as is the intolerance expressed toward the homeless living on residential sidewalks. In Honolulu, a study found that 74 percent of the law violators who were believed to have a mental disorder were also homeless. In major cities from San Francisco to Miami, homeless people with severe mental illness are a common part of the urban landscape. The trend is emerging in smaller cities as well. For example, in Roanoke, Virginia, population approximately 950,000 residents, the homeless population increased 363 percent between 1987 and 2007, and 70 percent had received or were receiving mental health treatment (Hammack and Adams, December 15, 2007). San Diego, California, reported outbreaks of Hepatitis C in 2017 involving more than 400 people who had contact with human feces on the sidewalks. The health of the homeless and the public at large is threatened by the lack of consistent access to bathrooms and hand washing (McPhate, September 8, 2017).

According to a recent U.S. Housing and Urban Development survey (2015) based on a one-night count of people sleeping on the streets, there are an estimated 564,700 homeless, of which 436,921 were adults. Of this number, 104,083, or 24 percent, were identified as severely mentally ill (Substance Abuse and Mental Health Services Administration [SAMHSA], 2016). Given the difficulty of counting a homeless population, the National Coalition for the Homeless (2009) estimated the total homeless population to be 1.3 million; a conservative estimate would be that 25 percent are mentally ill. This translates to 325,000 seriously mentally ill homeless people (SAMHSA, 2016). Whichever estimate is more correct, it is clear that there are at least 100,000 and possibly over 300,000 homeless people suffering from serious mental illness.

While law enforcement officers often find themselves functioning as both police and psychiatric social workers, they have the added responsibility of recognizing and responding appropriately to mentally ill persons who live without a stable home shelter. The ready availability of bystanders' video cameras and body cameras makes every action fully reviewable in occasional regrettable retrospect. Police officers generally will not arrest the mentally ill who are homeless for minor offenses, but the cost for personnel and police resources for alternative consequences makes community treatment in lieu of incarceration difficult to undertake (Kerr, 2010). As we will see in a later chapter, the courts' attempt to keep the flood of adjudicating the mentally ill homeless population in perspective with mental health courts as well as mobile mediation and resolution processes, but the issues are not abating.

Welfare Checks: "Howya doin'? Whatcha doin'?"

The transition from long-term commitments in psychiatric facilities to treatments in community outpatient facilities created a gap that is visible to the community at large. Today, one of the foremost issues in community dialogues is what law enforcement should do to resolve problems presented by mentally ill people, in a way that is perceived by the public to be fair, consistent, and constitutional while also assuring overall safety to the officers, the mentally ill person, and bystanders. In common practice, a police officer should not simply approach a person and initiate a criminal inquiry based on a "hunch" (*Terry v. Ohio*, 1968). There must be *reasonable suspicion* to detain and frisk a person.

Street encounters can create conflict for a first responder when the person is approached for what is known as a **welfare check** (Batterton, 2011). In this instance, while there is no evidence of criminal conduct or activity, the officer may have a duty to inquire as to the well-being of a person. The question of the safety of a person must be balanced against the right to be left alone. While there is an affirmative obligation to inquire into the wellness of a man slumped against a wall in subzero temperatures or a woman walking hurriedly alone at night, the same question could trigger a civil rights violation or be an invasion of privacy if it's a balmy summer day or 2:30 in the afternoon. The situation is more complex if the person being questioned is dressed in a loin cloth and wearing a crown or is standing on a street corner shouting to an imaginary friend, while people are standing in line to attend a symphony concert. First responders and community providers must weigh whose right to be left alone prevails.

Consider, too, what happens if questioning a person about his well-being escalates into a confrontation. If the officer had no lawful purpose to detain or question a person, other than that he is sleeping in a park during the day, then the discovery of controlled substances in his pocket is likely to result in an ultimate court ruling of improperly seized evidence. What if questioning a person about his well-being escalates into gunfire or use of a Taser? Was the purpose of the confrontation lawful?

Although non-invasive physical pat-downs are considered proactive policing, a recent study found that "stop and frisk" police contact with young men increased their reluctance to cooperate with police in general and generated increased anxiety and trauma for them. In addition to the possibility of impacting the mental health of the detainees, decreasing trust and confidence in the law, the study suggested that the involuntary contact with police also increased the subjects' involvement in crime, as well as undermined any willingness to cooperate with police in resolving criminal activity (Geller, Fagen, et al., 2014).

More than this, over the course of a year, there are dozens if not hundreds of media accounts about violent confrontations between law enforcement officers and mentally ill or developmentally disabled persons (Cooper et al., 2004). Researchers report that persons with mental illness are four times more likely to be fatally shot by police than citizens without mental illness; alternatively, although police line-of-duty deaths are rare, when they do occur, the law enforcement person is five times more likely to be killed by a mentally ill assailant (Mulvey and White, 2013). Although it is clearly established that jails are serving as mental institutions, what is now being acknowledged is that police are the first responders to the mentally ill (Madhani, 2016).

The officers may perceive the disturbance to be an out-of-control dangerous situation when it is not. Lacking the de-escalation skills necessary for working with mentally ill people, officers may use force to quickly resolve the situation, which can result in injuries to the officer and the person having the breakdown (Watson et al., 2008). The cases cited in Box 5.2 suggest why such actions may not be in the best interests of the officer, the jurisdictional authority employing the officer, or the community.

BOX 5.2

Law and Mental Health: Legal Impetus for Changing Police Policies and Practices

In *City of Canton, Ohio v. Harris* (1989), the U.S. Supreme Court notified law enforcement agencies that training is required for law professionals when they engage with a mentally distraught person. In this case, Geraldine Harris was arrested and brought to a police station following resistance during a traffic stop. While being transported by the officers, Ms. Harris became incoherent and had noticeable physical and emotional distress. She was released to her family who then took her to a hospital by ambulance.

In a subsequent civil lawsuit against the Canton police department by Ms. Harris, the U.S. Supreme Court demanded that law enforcement personnel have demonstrable training to determine if a person detained by police needs any form of medical attention. The Court found that the City of Canton had a policy of vesting complete authority with the police supervisor as to when medical treatment, mental or physical, was to be administered to a person in police custody. Therefore, if there was evidence of inadequate training of a law enforcement officer to recognize when medical intervention was needed, a jury could find civil liability for "deliberate indifference" to the condition of the incarcerated.

In *Walker v. City of New York* (1992), the U.S. Supreme Court established a framework to guide law enforcement agencies as to what training is needed for mental health encounters. The Court noted three conditions that should be present: "(1) [the] policymaker knows 'to a moral certainty' that its employees will confront a given situation; (2) either [the] situation presents employees with [a] difficult choice that will be made less so by training or supervision, or there is a record of employees mishandling [the] situation; and (3) [a] wrong choice by employees will frequently cause [the] deprivation of constitutional rights" (*Walker*, at 293, 297-298). When all three conditions are met, the policymaker should have known that inadequate training or supervision was "so likely to result in the violation of constitutional rights, that the policymakers of the city can reasonably be said to have been deliberately indifferent to the need" (Walker, at 298).

Sources: Achtenberg (n.d.); *City of Canton, Ohio v. Harris* (1989); *Walker v. City of New York* (1992); Watson et al. (2008).

BEST PRACTICES

Knowing that it is certain that first responders, police officers, and community treatment personnel will interact with people in a mental crisis, employers should require that all law enforcement personnel be trained to make appropriate choices, or they may face the possibility of a constitutional violation and civil liability lawsuit for an employee's poor reactive decision. When first responders have the requisite training, education, and experience to work effectively with mentally ill persons, the courts are more like to exonerate law enforcement personnel from criminal, as well as civil, liability when there is a death or serious injury resulting from an encounter with a mentally ill person.

Police-Citizen Encounters: Defining the Parameters

Officer encounters with people with mental illness can often take much more time than other calls for service, can require officers to have special training and skills, and may increase the officers' professional stress depending on the availability of community mental health resources (Cooper et al., 2004). For example, officers in Honolulu, Hawaii reported that they spent an average of 145 minutes transporting a person to a hospital for an emergency evaluation, while an arrest took 64 minutes and informal dispositions were resolved in 23 minutes. In Lincoln, Nebraska, the police department handled 1,500 "mental health-based" investigations in 2002 and found that officers spent more time on those encounters than on investigations for traffic accident injuries, burglaries, or felony assaults (Reuland, Schwarzfeld, and Draper, 2009). Such cases can generate extra work, or as one officer noted: "It is too much of a hassle to get someone involuntarily committed," noting that his comments were specific to a given hospital and the presence of insurance (Cooper et al., 2004: 9).

Law enforcement officers often have repeated contact with the same individuals who have unresolved mental health needs, and officers are commonly called to address the same person committing the same type of minor or nuisance offenses (Reuland et al., 2009). The American Bar Association standards state that misdemeanants who are mentally ill should be diverted into a mental health system, but in reality they are often arrested. Although police have discretion, the conflict between handling mentally ill from a legal perspective versus a medical model generates external accountability demands and organizational constraints that do not favor "catch and release" into the community. Some commentators note that as police are aware of the stringent criteria for civil commitment, they regard arrest as a more reliable method of securing involuntary detention, treatment, and/or safety and health for the individual (Cooper et al., 2004).

Mental health intervention training positively alters officers' views of mentally ill persons (Compton, Esterberg, et al., 2006). Furthermore, the absence of a collaboration between law enforcement and mental health systems was a driving force in the criminalization of the mentally ill (Teller, Munetz, et al., 2006). Unfortunately, as the Police

Executive Research Forum reported, new recruits received an average of 8 hours of mental health crisis intervention training compared to 58 hours on firearm training. As early as 1980, progressive law enforcement agencies collaborated with mental health advocates to design specific and specialized training programs for U.S. law enforcement departments.

Crisis Intervention Teams (CITs)

Mental health intervention training can alter the way officers view mental illness (Goode, April 25, 2016). For example, in 1988, the shooting of a mentally ill person by a Memphis, Tennessee police officer led to the formation of a highly innovative training program for mentally ill people in crisis. Known as a **Crisis Intervention Team** (CIT), the program evolved into a partnership with the Alliance for the Mentally Ill, the University of Memphis, and other local health providers. Now part of the community policing initiative, the program brings together law enforcement personnel, mental health professionals, consumers, and advocates for the common goal of improving, understanding, and creating safety standards and comprehensive services to mentally ill people, as well as to the community and families (Cochran, Deane, Borum, 2000). The key goal in the training is to improve officer safety and the safety of the mentally ill person, minimize the use of force, and facilitate referral to treatment in lieu of incarceration when appropriate (Compton, Bakeman, et al., 2014).

In the three years before implementing the CIT program, the rate of injuries to Nashville officers responding to mental disturbance calls was one in 28,000 contacts. In the three years following the CIT implementation, the rate decreased to one in 143,000 events. Furthermore, with CIT intervention training, the rates of referral and transport to mental health emergency services, as opposed to transportation to a jail, increased by 42 percent (Reuland et al., 2009). A three-city analysis comparing responders who participated in a mobile crisis team, co-responder program, or a CIT training program found that officers were more likely to transport an individual to a mental health treatment program and resolve incidents informally and without arrest than officers in communities without any interventional program. Of those individuals who were diverted to mental health program, 31 percent received emergency room services and 35.6 percent received hospital services. For the people taken to or treated at a hospital, 81.6 percent received medication, 57.5 percent received counseling, while none of them received jail or incarceration (Reuland et al., 2009).

CIT training includes 40 hours of verbal de-escalation, scenario-based training and offers officers the opportunity to interact with people who have gone through a mental health crisis. The officers self-select to participate in the program. Upon completion of the training, officers receive certification that recognizes them as specialized, first-line responders for all calls involving people in crisis (Compton et al., 2006).

Ideally, every city and town would incorporate the standards and training for CIT into their police services. Forty-five states have crisis intervention training, as well as the District of Columbia, and while many counties have multiple programs, rural areas remain underserved. The cost for training, as well as knowing if an officer has the personal temperament to handle mental health de-escalation, remains a balancing factor against all law enforcement personnel receiving crisis interventional training.

CIT Training Scenario. In the CIT training scenario, an actor performs the role of a mentally ill person. There is no actual threat or provocation that might imply the need for force. However, the actors are instructed not to cooperate with the officer until there is demonstrated sincere empathy with the non-threatening/non-violent mentally ill "customer." The customer is in crisis and has a special need, but, more importantly, also has the need to have an authentic assurance of safety and security within the crisis. The officer addresses the delusions of the mentally ill person by dialoguing, answering questions, and generally conversing until there is de-escalation.

While CIT training scenarios are modeled after real-life situations, not all training scenarios are identical to one another. The training provides many levels of different interactions, each gradually increasing in complexity, to enable the trainees to learn incrementally how to accept different roles within police tactical behaviors through the employment of humane intervention. The following situation is not an uncommon scene, but to the person responding, every encounter is unique and remarkable.

BOX 5.3

Suicidal Ideation and a Test for Calm Intervention

There is a popular pedestrian and traffic bridge in the middle of the city. It links the business side of the town, with its hotels and the tony residential side, with its trendy restaurants. The bridge has only four lanes and the stop signs on each end are surrounded by seasonal landscaping. It also perches well above a high-speed, multi-lane freeway. If a person jumped off, he would not only kill himself, but would also likely cause disastrous collisions below. Recently, during a rainy night, a man wearing a furry bomber's hat, thick cloth coat, and no shoes leaned against the cement railing with his arms outstretched, pin-wheeling back and forth. Someone observed him and called for emergency services. On a side street, three police cars quickly convened and began to strategize.

One of the officers, Dave, in plain clothes, but trained in CIT, sauntered up, whistling, his hands in his pockets. His training had taught him to recognize suicidal ideation. This is a mental expression of stress or depression in a person that produces suicidal thoughts that can be temporary or fleeting. Greater pressure or increased tension on a person contemplating suicide can trigger increased thoughts of self-harm. Persistent feelings of sadness or loss of interest can also bring on thoughts of suicide, but not necessarily plans to implement it. Alternatively, excessive use of psychoactive drugs can also lead to physical, social, or emotional harm that mimics suicidal behaviors, but does not necessarily mean that they are imminent. Dave knew he had to act carefully, deliberately, and predictably to avoid the catastrophic result of the subject jumping, or worse, falling while trying to get away from him. Dave had to de-escalate.

Dave spoke from the other side of the street. "Hey, buddy. How are you? Are you thinking about suicide?" The floppy-hatted man stared at him uncomprehendingly. There are steps the trained professional relies on when approaching someone having suicidal ideation to interrupt the death wish and get the person treatment or help. By asking about suicide directly, the professional helps ground the conversation and assures the subject there is no judgment in the question. As he listened to the man's answer, Dave was able to ascertain that his subject was likely inebriated but was also aware of Dave's presence. He leaned forward toward Dave, another good sign. Dave saw a button pinned to his jacket — a peace sign. Dave smiled and said, "You know I agree that we have too much violence in the world," making the effort to slowly connect to the confused world of a man considering ending his life. Slowly, Dave went through the mental health training exercises he had learned to engage the man and to disengage him from suicidal thoughts. It took about an hour, but when the moment was right, and Dave was certain, Dave extended his arm for a distant handshake and the man stepped forward, accepted the grasp, and sagged into him.

Source: Personal observations of one of the book's co-authors; Be the One to Save a Life (n.d.).

Under the CIT protocol, when the police emergency dispatchers are notified of a mental illness incident, the call is assigned to a crisis intervention team (Cochran, Dean, and Borum, 2000). The lead team officer assesses the situation at the scene, considers the degree of risk, and intervenes if necessary to ensure the safety of all, and then determines an appropriate disposition. It may be through de-escalation (i.e., no arrest), negotiation, (i.e., voluntarily go to treatment facility), or engaging in a verbal crisis intervention (i.e., talk it through with the family or caretakers). Alternatively, the officer can bring a treatment provider to assist the person in crisis, provide a referral to treatment, or transport the mentally ill person to the psychiatric emergency department.

In the training, officers are exposed to lectures, presentations, and de-escalation experiences that focus on specific mental health diagnoses, such as schizophrenia (Compton et al., 2006). The training gives officers knowledge and techniques that are essential to identify signs and symptoms of mental illnesses, as well as making appropriate dispositions when confronted with conflicts. Because a first responder, street provider, or law enforcement officer receives special information, formal and informal rules emerge that are applicable to the unique situation. CIT training helps guide the shift in dispositions decisions when there is not a mandate to arrest, but there may be an option for treatment or voluntary compliance with a medication schedule (Compton et al., 2014).

Modifications to the CIT program have also proven successful in practice. In San Antonio, Texas, a jurisdiction that has had a full-time CIT unit for nine years, officers may respond to a mental health call wearing plain clothes and driving an unmarked car. This avoids psychological reactions to the uniform and permits the officers to decrease volatility. In Portland, Oregon, plans were reviewed to require all officers to be trained in the CIT approach, based on the belief that all responders should be prepared to be effective. More recently, CIT programs have emphasized the importance of having the "right officers" receive mental health calls, as "some officers are not well suited to be CIT officers" (Watson et al., 2008: 11). Watson stressed that the CIT model is more than just training; rather, collaboration is critical to its success, where each stakeholder brings his or her own training and understanding of the problem to the immediate situation. The first piece of a CIT program is to have the trained personnel in the field. "The other piece is for emergency communicators to have the training and information to identify calls and send the right officers from the beginning" (Blumberg, December 29, 2015). As of 2016, about 2,700 of the nation's 18,000 police departments—about 1 in 6—offer the crisis intervention training, according the National Alliance on Mental Illness (2016); however, as we suggest in Box 5.4, some in the public may disagree about its use.

Alternative Approaches

The need for specialized training in responses to mentally ill persons in their communities has led to a wide variety of alternative approaches. What follows is a brief overview of some of the strategies and approaches employed across the nation.

Simulations and Situational Training. Other jurisdictions train law enforcement officers to learn how to respond to tense situations through a common practice to study the "gone-wrong" aspects of a video of police shooting. Consider, for example, the case

---

BOX 5.4

Thinking About the Issues

Some people feel that the CIT approach is too soft and not reflective of law enforcement's commitment to apply laws and retain control of the scene. Nevertheless, as the statistics clearly show, all law enforcement personnel will have some contact with the mentally ill on the streets. Having a strategic framework can help achieve resolution without violence.

1. What do you see as the primary strengths of the CIT approach to police resolution of street encounters with the mentally ill?
2. What do you see as the primary weaknesses of such an approach?
3. Could you see this approach working in your community? If yes, why? If not, why not?

of a bat-wielding college student in the throes of a mental health crisis. Trainees witness the officers mistakenly shoot the young man's middle-aged neighbor during the confrontation. By reviewing videos, conversations, and reports, the officers learn to familiarize themselves with like scenarios and discuss less violent alternatives and non-confrontational options (Madhani, October 2, 2016).

The Maryland chapter of the National Alliance on Mental Illness employs simulated examples of schizophrenic psychotic episodes using videos and voices to help train campus security officers. Throughout the training sessions, the law enforcement professionals were exposed to "constant voices" informing them, "You're worthless. We hate you." A TV weatherman talked directly to them, again in a simulated imagery, illustrating how the mentally ill may hear things differently and see and process disturbing messages in an innocuous medium. The experience mimics a schizophrenic psychotic episode to help the college law enforcement personnel recognize and appropriately respond to mental illnesses in people 16 to 24 years old. Some college students experience their first mental psychotic episode while away from home and are terrified, confused, and do not know where to turn for help.

Some of the training programs also use "Mindstorm," a psychosis simulator (Tabar, October 1, 2007). This computer-based replication program gives users a few minutes of insight into the mind of a person who is hallucinating. The experiential process occurs during an intensive training program in which the officers go into the community to try to accomplish certain tasks, all the while listening to voices through headphones (Bishop, August 19, 2013).

In Portland, Oregon, prodded by a 2012 study, the Portland Police Bureau developed a program for how police should interact with people with mental illness. Consider an actual scenario the Portland police addressed: A man was observed in a secluded part of a deserted beach with a sword. At 2:30 a.m., after spending hours trying to engage the man, asking him to put down the sword, the officers decided to withdraw. The man ran off and the officers let him go. The result is controversial: What if the man hurt someone? He did not. What if they shot him? They did not. The man had not committed a crime, the confrontation was police-instigated, and nothing happened (Goode, April 25, 2016).

Co-Responding/Team Approach. Other jurisdictions are exploring different forms of training to heighten sensitivity to emergency mental health encounters with public street providers (Steadman et al., 2000). In Knoxville, Tennessee, law enforcement uses a mobile crisis unit to service a five-county area. The unit responds to calls and handles telephone calls and referrals from the local jail, which does not have a mental health program (Steadman, Williams, et al., 2000).

Some jurisdictions use a mental health and law enforcement partnership for on-the-scene consultations and assistance for individuals in need of mental treatment, known as the "co-responder" model. For example, police in Birmingham, Alabama, deploy a teamwork approach. **Community service officers (CSOs)** provide crisis interventions and follow-up assistance. The CSOs are civilian police employees with professional training in social work or related fields. They do not carry weapons, nor do they have the authority to arrest, but are required to complete a six-week classroom and field training program that is offered through the police academy. The CSOs provide social service calls and transportation, present shelter options, and respond to other requests. In 1997, they answered 2,189 calls, mostly pertaining to mental health interventions (Steadman et al., 2000). In Overland Park, Kansas, the 250-member police force hired a single responder to assist officers. In 2016, the responder assisted in 129 calls, averted 40 arrests, and saved over $61,000 in jail expenses (Madhani, October 2, 2016).

Communities can make officers aware of who within a neighborhood has disabilities and who provides services for that individual (Godfredson, Ogloff, et al., 2010). In small towns, one strategy is for law enforcement officers to stand by while a known caretaker works to help his or her disabled client. Even if a person is screaming, swearing, or causing a disturbance, the police stand by and allow the professional the time to talk down the agitated mentally ill patient (Steadman et al., 2000). By having officers, first responders, and street social workers intimately know the community members or work with mental health providers, the trained law enforcement professionals recognize when their help is needed or when a mental health service provider is more effective to avoid incarceration and even more mental decline (Godfredson et al., 2010).

In another approach, the Dayton (Ohio) Police Department formed a Citizen Police Academy to orient civilian volunteers to the point of view of police when addressing issues of mental health problems. The civilians could also aid police officers in tempering aggressive solutions. This collaborative program involves police officers shadowing mental health professionals during their work with mentally ill persons (Dayton Police Department, n.d.).

De-escalation Training. Although there may be an inclination by law enforcement to intervene immediately, aggressive police action may not be the most effective response. If there is no immediate danger to the mentally ill person himself or an immediate danger to others, taking the time to make an assessment may prove to be the best strategy (Dufresne, 2003). By listening to what the person is saying in an unrushed manner, responding not only with words, but also with body language and tone, the first responder will be in a better position to establish a calm presence rather than a confrontational one (Dufrense, 2011; Tartakovsky, 2013). De-escalating the situation may prove the wiser tactic. **Tactical repositioning** is one such de-escalation technique. In many cases, officers can move to another location that lessens the level of danger. An example is an incident involving an individual with a knife. By increasing the distance from the individual, officers greatly reduce the risk to their safety and can explore additional options before resorting to a use of force, notwithstanding the need to control the threat to others. Many of these steps—speaking calmly, positioning oneself in a non-threatening manner, and establishing rapport through the acknowledgment of what the person is feeling—are easily transferred from crisis intervention training for persons affected by mental illness to de-escalation encounters with people in general. While these tactics are recommended steps, officers must continually reassess each situation with the understanding that force may be necessary if de-escalation techniques are not effective.

One concern with de-escalation is that it can place officers in unnecessary danger. By overemphasizing the importance of de-escalation, officers might hesitate to use physical force when appropriate, thereby potentially resulting in an increase in line-of-duty deaths and injuries. Consequently, it should be stressed that de-escalation is not appropriate in every situation, and officers are not required to use these techniques in every instance. If the individual poses a threat of injury or death to the officer or another, the officer must be permitted to use the level of force necessary to reasonably resolve the situation.

The most important action in a crisis is for every professional person involved to remain in control of him- or herself. This is known as "rational detachment" (Dufresne, 2003: 1). To detach rationally, every responder must have a plan and a team approach, be positive, and recognize his or her personal limits and then, when the situation is defused, have the professional insight to debrief and select those aspects of the encounter that were positively and appropriately handled to be used again and again (Dufresne, 2003). Box 5.5 describes what happens when the responder does not have a positive plan.

BOX 5.5

When Things Go Wrong, They Go Terribly Wrong

Consider the situation faced by the Vidal family. At 18 years old, 135-pound Keith Vidal was in high school, an average adolescent who liked basketball, played the drums, and enjoyed going to the beach. But he also began to act erratically about this time, though not dangerously. His mother said her son was having a bad day and did not seem connected to reality, but he was not violent. His stepfather called 911 for someone to help take the youth for a mental health evaluation. The stepfather also said the teen had a screwdriver and was threatening his mother. The responding officer starting shooting within minutes of arriving at the scene. In a chilling body-camera depiction, the police officer broke down the door to the family room and begin firing, killing the boy as his mother screamed, "No, no, no!"

Bryon Vassey, the Southport, South Carolina, police detective whose shots killed Keith Vidal, was indicted for manslaughter. Although Vassey was ultimately acquitted two years later, his last words to the teenager — "We don't have time for this" — were the basis of the prosecution that derailed his career and life. The trial took 14 days and resulted in a million-dollar civil settlement. Vassey's confusion and misunderstanding of the concerns of the family resulted in the unnecessary death of a teen-ager and ruined the detective's career.

Source: Lucas (2016).

RISK MANAGEMENT

Responsibility for first-responder actions and mentally ill suspects, as suggested by the case described in Box 5.5 and throughout this chapter, tends to involve the police, as they are the primary first responders who can legally employ deadly force. Sometimes first responders may perceive that the disturbance is an out-of-control dangerous situation when in fact it is not. Consider the situation in which the police fatally wounded an unarmed man after his sister called for help when the man was having a mental health crisis, or the video of a 17-year old who was gunned down holding a small pocket knife, and then compare these two scenes to another situation in which the parents of an adult son called for help as he was destroying their home. In the latter case, the first responder, with the assistance of a mental health assistant, talked the young man out of the family bathroom and into taking his medications. Although all three scenes paint highly volatile situations, the police reliance on an intervention by a mental health professional in the latter one avoided bad press, legal liability, and the guilt of killing an innocent person (Madhani, 2016).

Contemporary Concerns

Lacking the de-escalation skills necessary for working with people with mental illness, professional, highly trained law enforcement specialists often use force to try to quickly resolve minor criminal conflicts, such public urination, disorderly conduct, or trespassing. The effort to unilaterally control a criminal contact may only escalate the situation to violence that often results in injuries to the person having a mental breakdown and, sometimes, to the law enforcement personnel (Watson et al., 2008). In a 2010 decision, *Bryan v. MacPherson* (630 F.3d at 829), the U.S. Court of Appeals for the Ninth Circuit poignantly stated:

> A mentally ill individual is in need of a doctor, not a jail cell, and in the usual case — where such an individual is neither a threat to himself nor to anyone else — the government's interest in deploying force to detain him is not as substantial as its interest in deploying that force to apprehend a dangerous criminal. Moreover, the purpose of detaining a mentally ill individual is not to punish him, but to help him. The government has an important interest in providing assistance to a person in need of psychiatric care; thus, the use of force that may be justified by that interest necessarily differs both in degree and in kind from the use of force that would be justified against a person who has committed a crime or who poses a threat to the community.

The following two cases are also illustrative of civil rights challenges involving mentally ill suspects with whom the police engaged during a street encounter:

▶ In *United States v. City of Portland*, a federal investigation that arose from a civil rights challenge, the Department of Justice detailed its discoveries of 700 incident reports over an 18-month period. The investigative inquiry of the Portland police looked for and found a pattern or practice of unconstitutional use of force against persons with actual or perceived mental illness (Perez and Marshal, 2012). What that investigation revealed was a pattern of physical abuse, repeated discharging of non-lethal weapons, such as stun guns, and possible violations of citizens' Fourth Amendment rights.

▶ *Champion v. Outlook Nashville, Inc.,* dealt with the circumstances leading to the death of a 32-year old autistic person who was, due to his mental illness, unresponsive and unable to speak. Although advised Champion was mentally ill, the officer repeatedly asked for his name after his caretaker called for assistance due to Champion's escalating agitation in a public area. Champion was hitting and biting himself and, although he was advised to stop, he continued to approach the officer. He was then sprayed in the face with a pepper discharge. After he was laid on the ground, handcuffed, and his ankles were hobbled with restraints, the officer continued to spray a chemical agent in the face of this handcuffed and hobbled autistic man. He vomited several times before dying.

Given these and other legal efforts to resolve an issue with a person who is suffering from a mental deficiency, it is also useful to know what other types of training officers are provided. In the face of lawsuits and community condemnation, law enforcement officers are trained to be more proactive and patient with a person who commits a minor offense while evidently in an altered state of mental health. While officers must clearly keep safety as their priority, the need to balance safety with all possible solutions is also critical. Caretakers, friends, or family members often call for police assistance specifically because they do not want their mentally ill loved one to die. Kind words and easy, quiet banter may slowly defuse a situation, while shooting the individual will certainly end the dilemma, but the civil lawsuit and officer investigation that will certainly result will take a lot more time and money.

Organizational Responses

Any law enforcement agency can attempt to limit its fiscal liability through training that demonstrates that agency's commitment to professional development. Then, if there is a physical injury or death, liability is blunted by evidence of the effort to use training and knowledge. The following risk management guidelines are useful in this regard (Reiter, n.d.):

1. Conduct an assessment of what training officers receive from the academy, in-service training, or specialized program offerings and delve further into areas that may contain elements of this training that may not be titled specifically on the subject;

2. Ensure that training includes realistic scenario segments involving elements of diffusing tactics (actions of containment, coordination, or use of resources and command; communication strategies and elongation of the time of the

encounter) for encounters with this special population. (This refers to people who have permanent or organic mental loss, severe emotional impairment, short-term or long-term cognitive disabilities, or physical impairments that may affect mental health.)

3. Create a partnership with local mental health professionals to develop a program that incorporates the essential elements of the newest, expanded police training for these critical tasks;

4. Ensure that written guidelines (manual, orders, and/or procedures) are up to date and include the essential elements of handling by field officers of this special population with emphasis on diffusing field tactics; and

5. Develop a reporting format that captures data on field encounters involving this special population. This is very important should an agency have a fatal or serious injury encounter involving a member of the mentally disabled or special population. This type of documentation shows that officers normally handle these types of incidents successfully without injury.

As police consultant Lou Reiter (n.d.; emphasis added) further notes:

Unfortunately, not all encounters with *emotionally* disturbed, mentally ill persons will end peacefully with the consumer being given the professional treatment necessary for his/her special needs. But most of the time, they will. The tactical approach of the officers can assist in bringing these critical tasks to a successful conclusion. *In those rare instances when they don't, these steps may enhance the liability protection of law enforcement agents, employees, agency and community.*

LETHAL FORCE AND STREET ENCOUNTERS WITH THE MENTALLY ILL

This chapter opened with a vignette concerning the use of deadly force. Deadly violence goes both ways. The Federal Bureau of Investigation reported that nationally 1,114 officers were assaulted by a person with mental illness in 2007 (Kerr et al., 2010). In 2015, there were 462 officers killed throughout the country, of which 124 incidents appeared to involve people suffering from a mental illness; moreover, 45 of the incidents involved police summoned to help a person in need of medical treatment or intervention (*The Washington Post*, 2015). While severely mentally ill people account for only 3 to 5 percent of all violent crimes, other behaviors may be harbingers of physical aggression. Through specialized training, such as that described earlier in this chapter, officers can gain necessary insight to prevent an outburst of frustration or rage and the ensuing violence (Arkowitz and Lilienfeld, 2011).

Most people today are familiar with the phrase suicide by police (also known as suicide by cop). This term, which first appeared in the 1980s but did not gain popular usage until the early 21st century, is used to describe an situation in which "a suicidal individual intentionally engages in life-threatening behavior towards law enforcement officers or civilians to specifically provoke officers to shoot the suicidal individual in self-defense or to protect civilians" (Hutson, Anglin, et al., 1998: 665; see also Van Zandt, 1993). One study of 843 police shootings estimated that 50 percent were deaths by provoking the police into a lethal and fatal response. (Parent, 2004). A more "conservative" estimate of 707 North American police shootings puts the number at 36 percent (Mohandie, Meloy, and Collins, 2009). Whatever the actual prevalence rate among police shootings, suicide by police response is generally recognized as an actual medical diagnosis and not simply a cultural designation, although the preferred medical term is **law enforcement-forced-assisted suicide** (Hutson et al., 1998).

Police use of deadly force, however, is not simply a shoot–don't shoot situation. Deadly force is one of several elements of the police use of force, which itself is defined as "the amount of effort required by police to compel compliance by an unwilling subject" (International Association of Chiefs of Police [IACP], 2001: 66). In support of this definition, the IACP, as one of the premier policing organizations in the world, recognizes a "street continuum" of force, which includes (2001: 66-7):

▶ Physical force (the use of fists, feet, hands, etc.);
▶ Chemical force (the discharge of MACE, CAPSTUN, OC, CS, and CN devices);
▶ Electronic force (the discharge of TASER, Stun Gun, or other electronic weapons);
▶ Impact force (the use of a baton, other impact weapon);
▶ Firearm (lethal) force (the discharge of any kind of firearm).

However, the National Institute of Justice's Police Use of Force (2012), described next, seems to fit best the kind of responses described in this chapter:

1. *Physical Presence* — Merely by being at the scene, one or more officers may be able to control a situation before it gets out of hand.
2. *Verbal Commands* — Using the spoken word, officers may be able to get suspects to comply with their words (commands such as "place your hands on the trunk of the car" or "lay on the ground, face down").
3. *Physical Restraints* — This can involve holding or striking a suspect with the hands, the application of holds applied to pressure points, or the use of handcuffs.
4. *Less-Lethal Force* — In this category are the use of the baton, pepper spray or other chemical agents, beanbag rounds fired from shotguns, and conductive energy devices.
5. *Lethal Force* — Normally, this will result from the use of some type of firearm.

After the initial response, other decisions must be made by the officer as first responder. The exercise of discretionary actions, including whether to arrest a person or instigate commitment procedures, may be influenced by the "public-ness" of the behavior, whether the offender is a known neighborhood charge, the degree to which the person becomes a greater behavior problem during the encounter, and whether the officer believes there is an element of violence and dangerousness (Cooper et al., 2004). A person who is mentally ill does not just "snap" — there is a general progression of behaviors toward violence. A skilled law enforcement officer can recognize and control escalation rather than engage in it. Law enforcement officials have repeatedly stated that interactions with people who have mental illness are the most unpredictable calls for service to which officers must respond quickly, as there may or may not be an element of danger by or to people with mental illness. The circumstances are often unpredictable. (Kerr et al., 2010). Public service providers, parents, teachers, friends, and law enforcement in the community may recognize behavioral warning signs, but it is challenging to get help for someone who doesn't believe he needs help (Rueve, 2008).

A major difficulty in working with the mentally ill who benefit from pharmaceuticals and medications is that after they are prescribed medications, they begin to get better, becoming more socially engaged and less demonstrative of mental illness. At this point, they think, "Hey, I'm fine, I don't need my medicine." They stop taking it and crash or spiral out of control again (Olfson, King, and Schoebaum, 2015). In addition, as described in Box 5.6, when mental illness and drug abuse are coterminous, the situation can spiral into violence.

If a law enforcement officer, social worker, or community service provider is engaging in an investigative inquiry about erratic or downward spiraling behavior, warning signs may justify a mental health intervention. Common signs and symptoms include withdrawal or loss of interest in others; an unusual drop in functions at school or with social activities; problems with concentration, memory, or logical thought; increased sensitivity; apathy; and vague expressions of being disconnected to one's surroundings (Parekh, 2015).

Police administrators and community members share concerns about training, policy, and lawfulness when force is used, as well as the review for accountability of officers who engage in force during encounters with the mentally ill (Kerr et al., 2010). In situations where the violence is instigated by the mentally ill person, the behavior can trigger the stages of involuntary commitment for civil proceedings, as outlined in Chapter 6. In this instance, if the offender is subdued by force or resignation, then the officer may opt for the paperwork for an involuntary commitment to an inpatient mental health treatment facility rather than take the offender to jail (Cooper et al., 2004).

EPILOGUE

The Christopher Dorner "manhunt" took place in Orange, Los Angeles, and Riverside Counties in California. The two innocent victims in the case were shot by Los Angeles Police Department officers. The Eric Garner case took place in Staten Island, New York. The descriptions that follow are based on several sources: Balko (2014); Huffington Post (2016); and Winton (2017).

In 2013, two women were mistakenly shot and killed as they delivered newspapers during the manhunt for Christopher Dorner, a former police officer who had killed and

BOX 5.6

Synthetic Mental Illness: Drug Abuse and Violence

As we are aware, severe mental illness such as schizophrenia, bipolar disorder, or psychotic depression can accompany unpredictable aggression. Researchers suggest, however, that rather than thinking people with severe mental illness are being generally dangerous, an accompanying factor may augur violent behavior: drug abuse. A recent study evaluated 35,000 people with respect to mental health, history of violence, and use of substances. The researchers found while having a mental illness did not predict violence, having a mental illness and a substance abuse problem increased the likelihood of a risk of violence. Of those with severe mental illness, law enforcement or service provider agencies reported that 2 percent were violent episodes. However, of those with major depression *and* substance abuse issues, 7 percent had a reported history of violence. Of those with schizophrenia, 5 percent reported violent behavior within two years, but when a person with schizophrenia also had substance abuse issues, 13 percent reported violent behavior within two years.

Persons suffering from drug or alcohol dependency had ten times the risk of violence of those individuals who only had mental illness. Almost a third of the severely mentally ill patients with substance abuse problems engaged in one or more violent acts in the year after leaving a treatment facility. With people who suffer from delusions, hallucinations, and disorganized thinking *and* are abusing substances or drugs, the first responder or community service provider obviously should exercise greater caution and circumspection as there is a greater likelihood of violence and aggressive confrontation. A violence risk assessment study led researchers to suggest that proper treatment of mental illness through appropriate psychotropic medications accompanied by the withdrawal from inappropriate illicit drugs with adherence to treatment could lessen the chances that persons with severe mental illness will behave violently.

Sources: Arkowitz and Lilienfeld (2011); Elbogen and Johnson (2009).

wounded people in a rampage against law enforcement personnel and their families. Officers fired over 100 bullets into their truck, costing the city $4.2 million in a civil lawsuit, or $42,000 a bullet. On September 11, 2015, New York City settled a wrongful death claim with the family of Eric Garner for $5.9 million after he died from a chokehold by a NYPD police officer. Garner was selling untaxed cigarettes. As of May 9, 2017, the Los Angeles Police department paid nearly $81 million in legal settlements during one fiscal year. Over a five-year period, the largest American cities paid over $1 billion for police civil liability or compensation for physical harm caused during the course of a police encounter with a civilian, likely suspected of engaging in criminal behavior.

If a person is charged with a criminal offense, even a police officer, the case is prosecuted by the government as a violation of the law. If a person is sued for financial compensation for a loss, this is referred to as a tort and is the basis of a civil lawsuit. A civil lawsuit may arise when a person is injured or killed and the victim or his family believe the wrongful injury or death was due to the negligent, careless, or reckless conduct of another person. Even if the shooter is a police officer and she kills a person in the course of her police work, a civil lawsuit for the value of the loss of life can be justifiably filed against the police officer.

The first question to be considered is whether there is liability. Liability means, in this example, that the officer's conduct in shooting a person was a breach of the duty to protect the victim of the shooting from harm. Liability for the action is imposed if the officer could have avoided the injury by using reasonable or practical alternatives. Through investigations, known as "discovery," accomplished through interviews, sworn statements, incident reconstruction, and a comparison of the state's laws to the facts, the attorneys for the city who represent the police officer will recommend whether there should be an admission or a denial of liability.

If there is an admission of liability or that the death or injury could have been reasonably avoided, then there will be a recommendation for financial settlement to compensate the injured person or his family in the event of death. The family is referred to as "the estate of John Smith [the name of the deceased person]." The attorneys for the parties will determine the value of the damages or the loss, even if the officer feels strongly that she did nothing wrong and that she followed the recommendations of best practices for conduct. The attorneys may feel that sympathy, antagonism toward police, or the circumstances of the victim are too volatile for public consideration. In some cases, there will be a formal admission of liability and then a settlement conference or trial to establish how much financial loss should be awarded. If, however, there is a decision that the harmful incident was purely an accident or was instigated by the person who is claiming compensation, then there can be a trial. A jury or a judge will decide if there is liability and then, if liability is found, compensable financial damages for the person initiating the lawsuit will be assessed. In all cases in which there is a civil lawsuit, it is very expensive, time-consuming, and draining for all involved.

SUMMARY

▶ First responders have street encounters with the mentally ill and often face a legal conflict as to whether there can be lawful contact without any evidence of reasonable suspicion to believe criminal activity occurred.

▶ Encounters to ascertain the well-being of a person who appears to be mentally ill could be constitutionally challenged if there are not articulated circumstances to believe a mentally ill person is in danger or at risk of harming another person.

▶ Despite the possibility that a person may be a danger to him- or herself, a person cannot be detained by police unless there is evidence of extreme danger to another person. Being disruptive is not a sufficient basis for an involuntary commitment.

- ▸ Training and knowledge of how to intervene to resolve a mental crisis are required of law enforcement personnel if there is a custodial encounter with a mentally ill person.
- ▸ There are innovative programs, known as Crisis Intervention Teams (CITs), which are designed to train officers to appropriately respond and react to a mentally ill or limited person to help avoid any escalation of emotions or show of police force.
- ▸ Many communities also pair law enforcement officers and trained community workers to resolve mental illness crisis situations and avoid incarceration or violent encounters.

CHAPTER REVIEW QUESTIONS

1. Discuss the five sets of forces that led to the criminalization of the mentally ill.
2. Who are the homeless? Why do they pose a problem for communities? How does adding mental illness to the mix complicate matters for the police?
3. What are some tactical interventions to keep a mentally ill person's fears, hysteria, or spiraling behavior from escalating?
4. What is CIT? How does it work? Why is the training effective?
5. In consideration of the community problems created by severely mentally ill homeless persons, what arguments can be marshalled in favor of society considering the resurrection of large-scale mental institutions? What are the counter-arguments?
6. Given that medication and treatment can control mental illness, should people be compelled to remain in a residential facility if they won't take medication?
7. Which of the different methods of de-escalation that were presented do you think would work if you were faced with a man wanting to jump off a bridge? Would you trust these methods?
8. Violent encounters between first responders, especially law enforcement officers, and mentally ill persons can escalate quickly into life-threatening situations for both parties. How does the use-of-force continuum help officers respond to these situations?
9. Define law enforcement-forced-assisted suicide. Explain how training/policy devices such as the street continuum of force can reduce such incidents.
10. Discuss the legal liability issues that can confront first responders when they encounter a mentally ill person. What do you see as the best practices for minimizing litigation in such situations?

KEY TERMS

Crisis intervention team (CIT)
Community service officers (CSOs)
De-escalation training
law enforcement-forced-assisted suicide
Outpatient services

Outreach services
Suicide by police
Tactical repositioning
Use-of-force continuum
Welfare check

REFERENCES

Achtenberg, D. (n.d.). "Petition to decision: Papers of the Supreme Court Justices on Civil Rights Cases: City of Canton v. Harris, 489 U.S. 378 (1989)." Retrieved at http://www1.law.umkc.edu/justicepapers/CantonDocs/CantonMainPage.htm on 27 October 2017.

Arkowitz, H., and S.O. Lilienfeld (2011). "Deranged and Dangerous: When Do the Emotionally Disturbed Resort to Violence?" *Scientific American*. Retrieved at https://www.scientificamerican.com/article/deranged-and-dangerous/ on 28 October 2017.

Abramson, M.F. (1972). "The criminalization of mentally disordered behavior: Possible side effect of a new mental health law." *Hospital and Community Psychiatry* 23: 101-5.

Batterton, B. (July 2011). "Welfare checks, suicide and the fourth amendment." Legal and Liability Risk Management Institute. Retrieved at http://www.llrmi.com/articles/legal_update/2011_11th_roberts.shtml on 23 October 2017.

Be the One to Save a Life (n.d.). Retrieved at http://www.bethe1to.com on 23 February 2018.

Balko, R. (October 1, 2014). "U.S. cities pay out millions to settle police lawsuits." *The Washington Post*. Retrieved at https://www.washingtonpost.com/news/the-watch/wp/2014/10/01/u-s-cities-pay-out-millions-to-settle-police-lawsuits/?utm_term=.321157db47e7 on 23 February 2018.

Belcher, J.R. (1988). "Are jails replacing the mental health system for the homeless mentally ill?" *Community Mental Health Journal* 24: 185-95.

Bishop, T. (August 19, 2013). "Campus Police Get Mental Illness Training." *The Baltimore Sun*. Retrieved at http://www.baltimoresun.com/news/maryland/education/blog/bs-md-safe-campus-20130819-story.html on 4 October 2017.

Blumberg, N. (December 29, 2015). "Mental health crisis training for cops faces funding gaps, lack of buy-in," *Chicago Tonight, WTTW broadcasting*. Retrieved at http://chicagotonight.wttw.com/2015/12/29/mental-health-crisis-training-cops-faces-funding-gaps-lack-buy-in on 28 October 2017.

Borum, R. (2000). "Improving high risk encounters between people with mental illness and the police." *Journal of the American Academy of Psychiatry and the Law 28*: 332-7.

Borum, R., and M. Rand (2000). "Mental Health Diagnostic and Treatment Services in Florida's Jails." *Journal of Correctional Health Care* 7: 189-207.

Borzecki, M., and J.S. Wormith (1985). "The criminalization of psychiatrically ill people: A review with a Canadian perspective." *Psychiatric Journal of the University of Ottawa* 10: 241-7.

Canales, C. (2012). "Prisons: The new mental health system." *Connecticut Law Review* 44: 1725.

Cochran, S., M.W. Deane, and R. Borum (2000). "Improving Police Response to Mentally Ill People." *Psychiatric Services* 51: 1315-16.

Compton, M., R. Bakeman, B. Broussard, D. Hankerson-Dyson, L. Husbands, S. Krishan, T. Stewart-Hutto, B. D'Orio, J. Oliva, N. Thompson, and A. Watson (2014). "The police-based crisis intervention team (CIT) Model: II. Effects on level of force, resolution, referral and arrest." *Psychiatric Services* 65: 523-9.

Compton, M., M. Esterberg, R. McGee, R. Kotwicki, and J. Oliva (2006). "Crisis intervention team training: changes in knowledge, attitudes and stigma related to schizophrenia." *Psychiatric Services* 57: 1199-202.

Cooper, V., A. McLearen, and P. Zapf (2004). "Dispositional decisions with the mentally ill: Police perceptions and characteristics." *Police Quarterly* 7: 295-310.

Cordner, G. (2006) "People with Mental Illness." Center for Problem-Oriented Policing. Washington, DC: U.S. Department of Justice.

Dayton Police Department (n.d.). "Citizens Police Academy." Retrieved at http://www.daytonohio.gov/607/Citizens-Police-Academy on 22 October 2017.

Department of Housing and Urban Renewal (2015). *HUD 2015 Continuum of Care, Homeless Assistance Programs, Homeless Populations and Subpopulations.* Washington, DC: U.S. Department of Housing and Urban Renewal.

Dufresne, J. (2003). "De-escalation tips." *Law and Order Magazine.* Retrieved at https://www.crisisprevention.com/Blog/June-2011/De-escalation-Tips on 16 October 2017.

Eisenberg, L., and L. Guttmacher (2010). "Were we all asleep at the switch? A personal reminiscence of psychiatry from 1940 to 2010." *Acta Psychiatrica Scandanavica* 122: 89-102.

Elbogen, E., and S.C. Johnson (2009). "The intricate link between violence and mental disorder. Results from the National Epidemiologic Survey on Alcohol and Related Conditions." *Archives of General Psychiatry* 66: 152-161.

Friedersdorf, C. (May 15, 2015). "Think Twice Before Calling the Cops on the Mentally Ill." *The Atlantic.* Retrieved at https://www.theatlantic.com/politics/archive/2015/05/dangers-of-calling-the-cops-on-the-mentally-ill/393341/ on 28 September 2017.

Fuller, D.A., E. Sinclair, J. Geller, C. Quanbeck, and J. Snook (2016). *Going, going, gone: Trends and consequences of eliminating state psychiatric beds, 2016.* Arlington, VA: Treatment Advocacy Center.

Geller, A., J. Fagan, T. Tyler, and B.G. Link (2014). "Aggressive policing and the mental health of young urban men." *American Journal of Public Health* 104: 2321-7.

Godfredson, J.W., J.R.P. Ogloff, S.D.M. Thomas, and S. Leubbers (2010). "Police discretion and encounters with people experiencing mental illness: The significant factors." *Criminal Justice and Behavior* 37: 1392-405.

Goode, E. (April 25, 2016). "For Police, a Playbook for Conflicts Involving Mental Illness." *The New York Times*, Health Section. Retrieved at https://www.nytimes.com/2016/04/26/health/police-mental-illness-crisis-intervention.html on 20 October 2017.

Grob, G.N. (1992). "Mental health policy in America: Myths and realities." *Health Affairs* 11: 7-22.

Gur, O. (2010). "Persons with mental illness in the criminal justice system: Police Interventions to prevent violence and criminalization." *Journal of Police Crisis Negotiations* 10: 220-40.

Hammack, L., and Adams, M. (December 15, 2007). "Roanoke turns its focus on homeless." *Roanoke Times*. Retrieved at http://www.roanoke.com/webmin/news/roanoke-turns-its-focus-on-homeless/article_0449a5e8-f769-50cb-ba4f-cebbf4db6c49.html on 9 November 2017.

Honberg, R., A. Kimball, S. Diehl, L. Usher, and M. Fitzpatrick (2011). "State mental health cuts: The continuing crisis." Arlington, VA: National Alliance on Mental Illness.

Huffington Post (September 11, 2016). "Largest legal settlements against police." Huffpost. Retrieved at https://www.huffingtonpost.com/moneytips/largest-legal-settlements_b_8122202.html on 22 February 2018.

Hutson, H.R., D. Anglin, J. Yarbrough, L. Hardaway, M. Russell, J. Strote, M. Canter, and B. Blum (1998). "Suicide by cop." *Annals of Emergency Medicine* 32: 665-9.

International Association of Chiefs of Police (2001). *Police Use of Force in America*. Washington, DC: IACP.

Kerr, A., M. Morabiot, and A. Watson (2010). "Police Encounters, Mental Illness and Injury: An Exploratory Investigation." *Journal of Police Crisis Negotiation* 10: 116-32.

Lamb, H.R.L., and L.E. Weinberger (2005). "The shift of psychiatric inpatient care from hospitals to jails and prisons." *Journal of the American Academy of Psychiatry and the Law* 33: 529-34.

Lucas, L. (September 28, 2016). "Changing the way police respond to mental illness," CNN video depiction of shooting. Retrieved at http://www.cnn.com/2015/07/06/health/police-mental-health-training/index.html on 21 October 2017.

Madhani, A. (October 2, 2016). "Police departments struggle to get cops mental health training." *USA Today*. Retrieved at https://www.usatoday.com/story/news/nation/2016/10/02/police-departments-struggle-cops-mental-health-training/91297538/ on 28 October 2017.

McPhate, M. (September 8, 2017). "California today: A deadly outbreak stalks San Diego." *The New York Times*. Retrieved at https://www.nytimes.com/2017/09/08/us/california-today-a-deadly-outbreak-stalks-san-diego.html on 23 October 2017.

Mohandie, K.J., R. Meloy, and P.I. Collins (2009). "Suicide by cop among officer-involved shooting cases." *Journal of Forensic Sciences* 54: 456-62.

Martinson, R. (1974). "What works? Questions and answers about prison reform." *Public Interest* 35: 22-54.

Maryland Chapter of the National Alliance on Mental Illness. Retrieved at http://www.namimd.org/ on 28 October 2017.

Morris, N. (1974). *The Future of Imprisonment*. Chicago: University of Chicago Press.

National Alliance on Mental Illness (2016). "Law enforcement and mental illness." Retrieved at https://www.nami.org/Get-Involved/Law-Enforcement-and-Mental-Health on 29 October 2017.

National Institute of Justice (2012). "Police use of force." Retrieved at https://www.nij. gov/topics/law-enforcement/officer-safety/use-of-force/Pages/continuum.aspx on 5 November 2017.

Olfson, M., M. King, and M. Schoenbaum (2015). "Benzodiazepine use in the United States." *JAMA Psychiatry* 72(2): 136-42.

Parekh, R., M.D. (September 2015). "Warning signs of mental illness." *American Psychiatric Association*. Retrieved at https://www.psychiatry.org/patients-families/ warning-signs-of-mental-illness on 12 October 2017.

Parent, R. 2004. *Aspects of Police Use of Deadly Force in North America — The Phenomenon of Victim-Precipitated Homicide*. Unpublished Ph.D. dissertation. Burnaby, British Columbia: Simon Fraser University.

Perez, T.E., and A. Marshall (2012). "Investigation of the Portland Police Bureau." Retrieved at https://www.justice.gov/sites/default/files/crt/legacy/2012/09/17/ppb_ findings_9-12-12.pdf on 27 October 2017.

Perry, N. (2017). "The 10 risks police agencies face (and how to avoid them)." PoliceOne. com Retrieved at https://www.policeone.com/Officer-Safety/articles/445523006-The-10-risks-police-agencies-face-and-how-to-avoid-them/ on 28 October, 2017.

Reiter, L. (n.d.). "Reasonable training and policing direction on handling of the mentally ill and emotionally disturbed persons? PoliceLink: The Nation's Law Enforcement Community. Retrieved at http://policelink.monster.com/training/articles/2095-reasonable-training-and-policy-direction-on-handling-of-the-mentally-ill-and-emotionally-disturbed-persons- on 7 November 2017.

Reuland, M., M. Schwarzfeld, and L. Draper (2009). "Law enforcement responses to people with mental illness: A guide to research-informed policy and practice." New York: Council of State Governments Justice Center.

Sarre, R. (2001). "Beyond 'What Works': A 25-Year jubilee retrospective of Robert Martinson's famous article." *The Australian and New Zealand Journal of Criminology* 34: 38-46.

Steadman, H., M. Williams, R. Borum, and J. Morrissey (2000). "Comparing outcomes of major models of police responses to mental health emergencies." *Psychiatric Service* 51: 645-9.

Substance Abuse and Mental Health Services Administration (2016). 2015 Mental Health National Outcome Measures: SAMHSA Uniform Reporting System.

Szasz, T. (2007). *Coercion as Cure: A Critical History of Psychiatry*. New York: Routledge.

Stroman, D. (2003). *The Disability Rights Movement: From Deinstitutionalization to Self-Determination*. Washington, DC: University Press of America.

Tabar, P. (October 1, 2007). "Mindstorm: Simulating psychosis." Behavioral Healthcare Executive. Retrieved at https://www.behavioral.net/article/mindstorm-simulating-psychosis on 6 November 1017.

EPILOGUE Tartakovsky, M. (2015). "9 Things Not to Say with Someone with Mental Illness." *World of Psychology*. Retrieved at https://psychcentral.com/blog/

archives/2013/04/29/9-things-not-to-say-to-someone-with-mental-illness/ on 15 October 2017.

Teller J., M. Munetz, K. Gil, and C. Ritter (2006). "Crisis intervention team training for police officers responding to mental disturbance calls." Psychiatric Services 57: 232-7.

Torrey, E.F. (2010). "Documenting the failure of deinstitutionalization." *Psychiatry* 73: 122-4.

Treatment Advocacy Center (2016). "Serious mental illness and homelessness." Arlington, VA: Treatment Advocacy Center.

Van Zandt, C.R. (1993). "Suicide by cop." *Police Chief* 60: 24-24.

Watson, A., M.S. Morabito, J. Draine, and V. Ottati (2008). "Improving police response to persons with mental illness: A Multi-level conceptualization of CIT." *International Journal of Law and Psychiatry* 31: 359-68.

Winton, R. (May 9, 2017). "LAPD settlements soar as officials close the books on high-profile lawsuits against police officers." *The Los Angeles Times*. Retrieved at http://www.latimes.com/local/lanow/la-me-ln-lapd-litgation-costs-20170509-story.html on 22 February 2018.

CASES

Bryan v. MacPherson, 630 F.3d 805, 829 (9th Cir. 2010)

Champion v. Outlook Nashville, Inc., 380 F. 3d 893 (6th Cir. 2004)

City of Canton v. Harris, 489 U.S. 378 (1989)

Roberts v. Spielman, 2011 U.S. App. LEXIS 11995 (11th Cir. 2011)

Terry v. Ohio, 391 U.S. 1 (1968)

Walker v. City of New York, 974 F.2d 293 (2d Cir. 1992); 1992 U.S. App. LEXIS 21261 (2d Cir. 1992)

United States v. City of Portland, Docket Number 3:13-CV022650SI0 (D. Or. 2012)

CHAPTER 6

Involuntary and Voluntary Commitments

CHAPTER OUTLINE

LEARNING OBJECTIVES

After reading this chapter, you should be able to:

▶ Know the difference between voluntary and involuntary commitments.
▶ Recognize a danger to self, contrasted with a danger to others.
▶ Understand the component parts of a voluntary commitment compared to an involuntary commitment.
▶ Appreciate the differences in state approaches to the topics of voluntary and involuntary commitments.
▶ Understand why the topic of voluntary and involuntary commitments is important to criminal justice agencies, agents, and the public at large.

PROLOGUE

This vignette represents a composite of several cases noted by one of the book's co-authors. The names of participants, along with some facts in the case, have been altered to protect their identities.

On February 4, 2014, Jillian W., a 45-year old Caucasian female, was observed walking naked down a main street of small northern Minnesota town. She had on shoes and a cap, which she set at a jaunty angle on her recently shaved head. After a passing motorist stopped and wrapped a blanket around her, Jillian explained to him that aliens had replaced her body, and she had just returned to Earth. She was wearing the latest Angoinoeoing fashion. The motorist recognized Jillian as the wife of a prominent attorney from a neighboring community. It was well known to residents of the nearby small towns that Jillian's teenage daughter, Sammy, had died a few months ago, in a distracted driver accident involving both Sammy and Lars, her son, the latter escaping the accident without injury.

Jillian alternatively spoke gibberish and clear sentences. She said that she was planning to kill her son to protect the Earth from disintegrating. The motorist put Jillian in his car and drove her to the emergency room, where she was later transferred to the hospital's mental ward. Jillian refused voluntary commitment for mental health treatment, claiming that the mother ship was coming back for her, and she needed to have her hair done. Her husband, Adolf, then signed a petition requesting that she be held for observation and mental health treatment as an involuntary patient.

Next, consider the following scenario: On July 4, 2012, Larry R. arrived by medical transport at the West Hills Mental Health Hospital. Larry explained to the woman at the hospital's information desk that he wished to commit himself to the care of the facility.

Earlier that day, he had felt his usually relaxed personality fade away and morph into one of irritation and resentment. Larry fell into what he described as "stress-related despair," and began to daydream about using a gun to end his life. Instead of acting upon this fantasy, he called the local sheriff's office.

Upon arriving at Larry's home, Deputy Askew asked Larry if he was OK and whether he wanted anyone notified. Larry asked Deputy Askew to call his wife, Laurel, who had volunteered for a holiday shift at a local foodbank. As soon as Laurel returned home, she thanked Deputy Askew and drove Larry to the local emergency room. After a brief assessment, the admitting doctors realized that they could do little for him, so Larry was subsequently transported to the West Hills Mental Health Hospital for psychiatric observation. Larry, with his wife's help, underwent a voluntary commitment because he felt that he was likely a danger to himself.

To this point, we have stressed the responsibilities of first responders toward the mentally ill during a crime-related encounter. In this chapter, we shift the focus from the street to the judicial civil process. Through supervised judicial proceedings, a person can be temporarily detained in a closed or locked mental health facility. The detainment can occur even if a person has not committed a criminal act. In some circumstances, as we will learn, a person who is accused of a crime can be detained in a mental hospital as a condition of bail and in lieu of jail.

This process is known as a **civil commitment proceeding**. Following the filing of a court petition, a judge hears evidence about the civil petition and determines, based on a review of the record, if a person should be detained. Following the receipt of the petition, a review of substantiating evidence and a finding that it is in the best interest of the mentally ill person to be committed or to remain, a judge will issue an order of commitment, and the mentally ill person is then held in a closed or locked facility and is not free to leave. The commitment process has strict review and release standards.

In this chapter, we will address the following issues:

1. The legal or statutory restrictions that can affect when or if a person is voluntarily or involuntarily committed to a mental health treatment facility.
2. The process that is followed for voluntary admission and discharge from a mental health treatment facility.
3. The process that is followed when or if a person is involuntarily committed to a mental health treatment facility.

We will ground this discussion in the civil commitment law and processes of four states: Arizona, New York, North Carolina, and Oregon, as these states have typical commitment proceedings. A complete examination of all such laws and processes is beyond this book's scope. However, an abbreviated review suffices to expose the breadth of ideas about civil commitments. Before turning to these topics, we examine voluntary and involuntary commitments.

Chapter Overview

This chapters turns on two key terms: voluntary commitments and involuntary commitments, discussed in the first section. The place of commitment is typically a hospital, although it is conceivable a jurisdiction might use a state-run forensic facility for the criminally insane as the locus for the commitment, including any assessments or treatments.

A central concern when it comes to commitment order is the danger posed by the individual to himself or others. There are certain behavioral elements that both legal authorities and behavioral specialists look for in a person either seeking a voluntary commitment or for whom an involuntary commitment order is sought. The second section of the chapter concludes with a four-state analysis of legal definitions surrounding such commitments, as well as a brief analysis of those laws.

The next two sections of the chapter provide a detailed examination first of involuntary commitments and then of voluntary commitments. The review of involuntary commitments includes an analysis of the state statutes for the four states mentioned above, along with what happens at petition filings and hearings. The involuntary commitment section concludes with a brief look at common practices regarding the length of stay.

Voluntary commitments, owing to their very nature, are quite different from involuntary ones. This section provides a review of statutes for the selected state jurisdictions, for the commitment process, as well as the procedures to obtain a discharge from an involuntary commitment.

The epilogue then reviews the key elements of this chapter through a case of civil commitment. This epilogue is instructive in many regards as it illustrates how a civil commitment can be used in the context of a criminal prosecution and enable the defendant to get mental treatment while waiting for the criminal case to be resolved.

FRAMING THE ISSUES

Voluntary commitment occurs when a person willingly consents to go into a mental hospital, psychiatric ward, or other facility or institution for psychiatric assessment and treatment (LeFrancois, 2014). For this to happen, a person must have enough insight to understand that help or intervention is needed before he becomes a danger to himself or to others. This voluntary commitment initially enables an individual to agree to treatment in a mental health facility. Despite this self-initiative act, the commitment process is reviewed and evaluated within the judicial process. Even if a person voluntarily commits himself for treatment, a medical officer or court authority will review the petition and circumstances of the commitment to make certain no coercive tactics were used.

Criteria for voluntary commitment generally involve the following conditions (LeFrancois, 2014): (1) the person is or was diagnosed as having a mental disorder; (2) the person is considered suitable for voluntary commitment or has the potential to benefit from treatment; (3) the person understands the nature and implications of the request for voluntary commitment; and (4) the person is willing to sign a voluntary admission form or consent verbally to admission. The patient must also demonstrate by actions, intent, words, or threats that she is a danger to herself or a threat to others (we will address the meaning of these triggering events in more detail in a later section). After admission, the person seeking inpatient treatment can request discharge. Details about subsequent release, even if it is simply the passage of a specified amount of time, are included in the commitment process. No person can be admitted either voluntarily or involuntarily into a facility without a specific date for review and/or release.

Treatment specialists often face a professional dilemma when it comes to voluntary commitments. That is, if a person has enough insight to know that she is a danger to herself or could hurt someone else, is that person mentally ill? In other words, individuals so self-aware, self-compassionate, or cognitive of their personal mental state may not need institutional mental health intervention and treatment (Duval and Wicklund, 1972; Goleman, 1995; Self, Rude, and Kirkpatrick, 2007; Van Dam, Sheppard, et al., 2011). When this occurs, especially when there are limited resources for residential treatment, some providers will encourage a patient to seek intensive, outpatient, community-based mental health services to enable the patient to continue to function in society, thereby enabling another, more acutely ill person to have access to care.

Involuntary commitment applies to a judicially mandated edict for a person to undergo interventional skilled residential mental health treatment. A court order to commit an individual, without personal consent, to a closed and locked mental health facility triggers very specific constitutional requirements that the commitment process adhere to due process standards and equal protection procedures. There must be clear and convincing evidence that (1) the person has a form of mental illness and (2) due to or because of the mental illness, is engaging in behavior that poses a danger to self or, by conduct or expression, a danger to others (Hickey, 2014). A commitment may also be mandated if a person is **gravely disabled**. People are considered gravely disabled when they are unable to care for themselves or meet their basic needs. Some states also have commitment proceedings for individuals who have a psychiatric history and are on a "deteriorating course," or are being cared for by a family member and face loss of that care (Hickey, 2014, see also *Harvard Law Review*, 1974, 2008).

As previously noted, in both types of proceedings, there is the requirement for evidence of danger to self and danger to others. Consider the questions contained in Box 6.1, and then we will turn to a thorough review of the important elements necessary to justify the civil commitment.

BOX 6.1

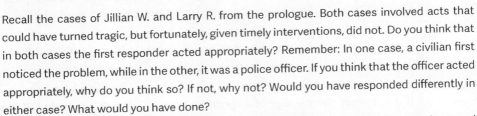

What Would You Do?

Recall the cases of Jillian W. and Larry R. from the prologue. Both cases involved acts that could have turned tragic, but fortunately, given timely interventions, did not. Do you think that in both cases the first responder acted appropriately? Remember: In one case, a civilian first noticed the problem, while in the other, it was a police officer. If you think that the officer acted appropriately, why do you think so? If not, why not? Would you have responded differently in either case? What would you have done?

What if while you were driving Jillian to a mental hospital, her husband stopped you and said he wanted to take her home and not have her be committed. He said she's just a little strange, but he needs her to care for his sick mother. What if he argued that you were just over-reacting, but as you watched, Jillian seemed to be terrified of her husband? Are you familiar with the procedures in your area for mental health commitments?

DANGER TO SELF AND OTHERS

The standard to determine when a person is thought to be a danger to self or a danger to others differs throughout the United States. A central theme in the **danger to self** is that unless the state takes immediate formal action, there is the potential for individuals to immediately cause physical injury to themselves. In the case of **danger to others**, there is a similar, but variant, starting definition: Unless the state takes immediate formal action, there is the potential for an individual to cause physical injury to another person or other persons or property. For example, every state has a statute mandating commitment when a person expresses suicidal ideation or attempts suicide (Melton et al., 2007). However, there often is not a sharp, definitive mandate for the timing of a legal test (Wexler, 2013). If a person is homeless, coatless, and without food and shelter on a cold night, is he conclusively a danger to himself? Each situation is considered separately when a court or a committing agency decides whether a person should be placed in a community treatment program, committed to a secure mental health facility, or just left alone. Similarly, those "in the trenches," first responders such as law enforcement personnel, social workers, fire fighters, and community volunteers, must make an initial assessment: Do they provide minimal resources, such as a blanket and food, and then leave, or take the person into custody, or request help from other professionals?

Behavioral Elements: A Starting Point

At the first formal inquiry about an individual's potential as a danger to self, many factors are considered by the first responders. The decision to intervene in another person's life, especially if the person doing the intervening is a police officer or fire fighter and not a psychiatric social worker, can be fraught with indecision and second-guessing.

The following list of characteristics offers a starting point to determine if a person may constitute a danger to self (El-Mallakh, Roberts, and El-Mallakh, 2014; see also Ward, 2014):

1. Current suicidal thoughts or prior suicide attempts or current or constant knowledge of others who have attempted or committed suicide
2. Diagnosis or documentation of a mental illness(es) (especially depression)
3. Intoxication or ongoing substance use
4. No current support structure at home or in the community
5. Current or history of high anxiety episodes
6. Recent break-up with loved one
7. Recent loss of loved one due to death
8. Recent loss of job or schooling
9. Debilitating physical illness.

Generally, the presence of one such marker is not enough to trigger an intervention, although suicidal ideation may result in a more thorough investigation. However, if several markers are present, then an investigator might ask for more details in order to evaluate cognitive functioning.

The risk factors to consider when an individual is suspected of being a danger to others are largely based on verbal cues and first-hand observations. As with the concern for danger to self, it may be best to observe the person of concern and determine if an immediate intervention is necessary. In this regard, the following list of characteristics may prove useful in deciphering the current threat level to others:

1. Does the person have signs of intoxication or ongoing substance abuse?
2. Is the person living on the street or without an evident or current support structure at home or in the community?
3. When talking to the person during the encounter, is there a current or recent history of episodes that disclose an inability to cope with high anxiety and is there evidence by words and actions of high anxiety?
4. Does the person express or refer to unresolved emotional responses to a recent break-up with a loved one, and express any form of hostility, animosity, anger, or revenge for perceived (or misperceived) conduct?
5. Is there expression of grief or overwhelming emotional reactions due to the recent loss of loved one due to death?
6. Has there been a recent loss of job or schooling that appears to be blamed on a third person, an incident, or an independent triggering event?
7. In running a background check, is there any history, record, or indicia of violent behavior that involves hurting animals, insects, birds, or other non-domesticated creatures? [Note: Harm to such creatures is commonly criminal.]
8. Is there evidence of the individual being paranoid or having paranoia? This mental condition is typically associated with delusions of persecution,

unwarranted jealousy, or exaggerated self-importance/grandeur, which are commonly expressed and elaborated into a well-structured and organized system of thought.

9. In conversing with a person who may be demonstrating all or many of the above behaviors, is there any admission or indication of a fascination with and playing with fire or dangerous objects, such as fireworks or mechanical devices? Is there any admission or indication of anti-social behaviors (very few friends), being a victim of abuse at home or at school, or not taking responsibility for oneself?

As an individual gains experience dealing with such risk factors, making this assessment becomes easier and more objective (see Box 6.2). It is critical that first responders engage in objective analysis, as "gut instinct" could sidetrack an appropriate course of conduct due to personal biases and inaccurate evaluations. The criteria need to be based on a concern for community well-being, as well as the health and welfare of the person being questioned. If all or most of the points are met, but there is still some uncertainty as to the appropriateness of pursuing an involuntary commitment to a mental hospital, it may be necessary to ask a court or a psychological professional to make a final determination.

BOX 6.2

Law and Mental Health: Tortious Liability

First responder evaluations of a person demonstrating any mental health risk factors often give rise to issues of **tortious liability**. Every such responder must weigh factors of liability (i.e., civil responsibility), which means that if there is a duty to provide care, intervention, protection, or services and the person responsible or charged with the duty fails to act, or "breaches" the duty, then there can be financial responsibility for the resulting harm. What happens if the police officer ignores a person sitting on the edge of a building and then the person commits suicide? Is there municipal responsibility? What if the officer removes the person and then she goes someplace else and shoots herself? How much intervention is necessary? What if the department chief announces that due to spending cuts, there is no money for involuntary placements?

The responsibilities of the state, county, city, or town to provide services to the mentally ill constitute but one layer of legal concern. First responders, as governmental employees, also need to know and act according to their employing department's policies and general practices that come into play when interacting with citizens who may have mental health issues. Making the correct decisions, under a given set of circumstances, not only can benefit the citizen, but also shield the community, the department, and the officers involved from legal liability.

While the two sets of assessment factors aid in determining whether the individual in question is a danger to self or a danger to others, the commitment process also generates an immediate, but summary, review in both categories that prompt a commitment. For example, having an interest in playing with fire can be a danger to oneself as well as a danger to others. Remember, too, that the factors are as applicable to the commitment of a 9-year old as a 90-year old.

The primary factor to consider during a street encounter with a person demonstrating personally dangerous conduct is whether that behavior, if carried further, could result in major problems for her family, friends, or the community (Wexler, 2013). Hence, many states also require a finding, evidence of, or grounds of dangerousness before a commitment petition is filed. The individual must be in an immediate danger zone, danger being the threat of actual or reasonably likely physical harm to self. If it is known that more than one attempted suicide was attempted or disclosed, or if overt acts or threats of violence are coupled with clear indicia of mental instability, then a civil commitment may be necessary (Gordon, 2016). For example, if a person starts cutting herself with a razor blade and there is evidence of scars from other self-destructive behaviors, the conduct is classified as dangerous, even though there were no verbal or witnessed threats of harm. By considering threat to self and others collectively as "dangerousness," the commitment process weaves together the different standards for institutional commitment into one course of action. By reviewing the definitions of the two standards used by our four example states (i.e., Arizona, North Carolina, New York, and Oregon), we gain insight into the decision to detain a person in a treatment facility.

State Legal Definitions

Arizona. In Arizona, first responders should be aware that a commitment for *danger to self* may occur under the following circumstances:

▸ There is "[b]ehavior that, as a result of a mental disorder, constitutes a danger of inflicting serious physical harm upon oneself, including attempted suicide or the serious threat thereof, if the threat is such that, when considered in the light of its context and in light of the individual's previous acts, it is substantially supportive of an expectation that the threat will be carried out" (Ariz. Rev. Stat. §36-501).

▸ This process does not include circumstances in which the individual has an organic condition known as a **grave disability**, such as Down syndrome, intellectual disability, or brain injury.

▸ The judgment of a person who has a mental disorder is so impaired that the person is unable to understand the need for treatment and, as a result of the mentally disordered behavior, can reasonably be expected, on the basis of competent medical opinion, to result in serious physical harm (Ariz. Rev. Stat. §36-501).

A commitment based on *danger to others* occurs if there is an independent medical assessment based on objective criteria. The following questions about the assessment must be asked and answered:

- Can interventional care only be rendered by a medical doctor?
- Can the admitting facility rely on previous medical records?
- Does there need to be a hearing?
- Is there is a special review proceeding or precedent for commitment?

North Carolina. In North Carolina, the following standard for *danger to self* is employed:

> The individual has acted in such a way as to show: That s/he would be unable, without care, supervision, and the continued assistance of others not otherwise available, to exercise self-control, judgment, and discretion in the conduct of his daily responsibilities and social relations, or to satisfy his need for nourishment, personal or medical care, shelter, or self-protection and safety (N.C. Gen. Stat. §122-C3).

In deciding if there should be a commitment, there must be a reasonable probability that unless adequate treatment is given a person will suffer serious physical debilitation, that a person is suicidal, or that a person has engaged in self-mutilation. If there is behavior that is grossly irrational and the individual is unable to control it, or the behavior is grossly inappropriate to the situation, or there is other evidence of severely impaired insight and judgment, then an initial inference is taken to exist that the individual is unable to care for himself (N.C. Gen. Stat. §122-C3). The following behaviors are taken as indicators of this requirement being met:

- The individual has attempted suicide or threatened suicide and that there is a reasonable probability of suicide unless adequate treatment is given pursuant to this chapter (N.C. Gen. Stat. §122-C3).
- The individual has mutilated himself or attempted to mutilate himself and that there is a reasonable probability of serious self-mutilation unless adequate treatment is given pursuant to this chapter (N.C. Gen. Stat. §122-C3).

By contrast, if there is a concern in a street encounter that there should be an involuntary commitment due to *danger to others*, that decision will be based on the following:

1. Is there, within the relevant past, information that the individual inflicted or attempted to inflict or threatened to inflict serious bodily harm on another?
2. Has the person demonstrating danger acted in such a way as to create a substantial risk of serious bodily harm to another, or has the person engaged in extreme destruction of property?
3. Is there is a reasonable probability that this conduct will be repeated?

North Carolina's law enforcement officers and mobile mental health care workers should be aware that previous episodes of dangerousness to others may be considered when determining reasonable probability of future dangerous conduct.

New York. In New York, there is evidence of danger to self when manifested by threats of or attempts at suicide or serious bodily self-harm or other self-directed conduct (N.Y. Mental Hyg. Law §9.4). There is an allegation of danger to others when manifested by homicidal or other violent behavior, which places others in reasonable fear of serious physical harm (N.Y. Mental Hyg. Law §9.4).

Oregon. Oregon places dangerous to self or others as a subset of "mentally ill person,"

A commitment process can be implemented if:

a. a person is unable to provide for basic personal needs that are necessary to avoid serious physical harm in the near future, and is not receiving such care as is necessary to avoid such harm (Or. Rev. Stat. §426.005);

b. an individual [has] a chronic mental illness and, within the previous three years, has twice been placed in a hospital or approved inpatient facility by the authority or the Department of Human Services (Or. Rev. Stat. §426.005).

c. [an individual is] exhibiting symptoms or behavior substantially similar to those that preceded and led to one or more of the hospitalizations or inpatient placements;

d. Who unless treated, the patient will continue, to a reasonable medical probability, to physically or mentally deteriorate (Or. Rev. Stat. §426.005).

Analysis. Notice the differences and similarities between the commitment for being a danger to self or to others in each of these localities. Oregon law presents a clear example of the terms' similarities since both terms are applicable to a "person with mental illness." By stating that the commitment process "[i]ncludes a person who is unable to provide for basic personal needs that are necessary to avoid serious physical harm in the near future," it is indicated that the standard for commitment applies both to danger to self and danger to others. After all, "serious physical harm" is not explicitly inherent within the terms. This is generally true in many jurisdictions.

Considering the United States as a whole, suicide is mentioned in every state as a *danger to self*, but is often omitted as "danger to others." As for *danger to others*, most of the states mention a serious or substantial risk of harm to others, apart from Oregon and Arizona. Oregon merely states, "serious harm *in the near future*." Arizona's statute provides, "result(s) in serious physical harm." States also may be vague about the nature of the harm, whether it is by past conduct or future possibility. This tension creates a difficult challenge for first providers to assess accurately or predictably what is best for the person who may need mental health interventions.

All states, including your own if it is not one of the four reviewed here, have slightly different standards and considerations (see Box 6.3). These legal considerations help law enforcement personnel or community health care providers make objective decisions about proceeding with a civil commitment. This observation is especially true when there is only a perceived possible harm and no actual harm to any person.

BOX 6.3

Thinking About the Issues

Complete a statutory search for your state and try to determine what types of situations may require the initiation of a mental health proceeding if a person is a danger to self or a danger to others. Consider the following in that search:

1. Are there any differences with regard to danger to self and danger to others (or property)?
2. Prepare a checklist of different behaviors that fit into each category.
3. Why are such checklists needed?
4. Find actual cases that involved violations of official policies or practices, as such situations can serve as important lessons going forward.

INVOLUNTARY COMMITMENT

If a person is found to be acting in a fashion that could be construed to be danger to self or others and that person is unwilling to seek treatment, then a different process comes into play. Recall Jillian W. from the prologue. A person suspected of being a danger to self or others, also called the **respondent** or the person against whom the action is taken, could face involuntary commitment to a secure treatment facility. When deciding whether a respondent should be involuntarily committed, it is important to balance the forced result of a judicial intervention against the fact that the individual has not committed a criminal act. There may be a single, initial event that can be described as either a danger to self or a danger to others, or as both. However, the four states considered in this text all have different legal procedures by which a person is temporarily committed into an institution.

As a general observation, the involuntary commitment process has five typical steps:

1. An interested party files the petition against the mentally ill person.
2. A contested hearing is held before a judge. The respondent has the right to be present and the right to have an attorney present.
3. Evidence is presented by witnesses to describe or verify what dangerous conduct occurred. The witness can be a family member or a police officer. The court can also accept police reports in lieu of actual testimony if no party objects to its use.
4. An expert witness, a psychiatrist or licensed clinical psychologist, testifies as to whether there exists a dangerous or deteriorating mental condition. This testimony is based on objective tests (see Chapter 2).
5. If the involuntary commitment is approved, the attorneys will present arguments regarding the length of the stay, then the judge will determine the length of stay, up to six months, or earlier with another review.

Before discussing these five steps, we provide an examination of the relevant state statutes.

State Statutes

Arizona. Ariz. Rev. Stat. §36-540 (A) — For in patient:

> If the court finds by *clear and convincing evidence* that the proposed patient, as a result of mental disorder, is a danger to self, is a danger to others, is persistently or acutely disabled or is gravely disabled and in need of treatment, and is either *unwilling or unable* to accept voluntary treatment, then an involuntary treatment and commitment order is entered.

North Carolina. N.C. Gen. Stat. §§122C-268(j), 122C-3(11), 122C-267(h), 122C-263(d)(1), 122C-271(a) — For inpatient: Danger to self/others/property. Explicitly includes reasonable probability of suffering serious physical debilitation from the inability to, without assistance, either exercise self-control, judgment, and discretion in conduct and social relations; *or* satisfy need for nourishment, personal or medical care, shelter, or self-protection and safety.

New York. N.Y. Mental Hyg. Law §§9.31(c), 9.01, 9.60(C) — If a person is being hospitalized for inpatient treatment of care for a claim of "danger to self/others" and treatment in a hospital is essential to welfare, then an involuntary commitment occurs when the patient is unable to understand need for care and treatment.

Oregon. Or. Rev. Stat. §426 — In Oregon, a county circuit court makes a commitment order to the Oregon Health Department when it determines that such a commitment is in the best interests of the respondent (Or. Rev. Stat. §426.060). Moreover, if a respondent fails to abide by the conditions of treatment in a lower-security facility, appropriate changes in security level may be ordered (Or. Rev. Stat. §426.275). Oregon law also enables a person to be committed for outpatient care, rather than be hospitalized, if it is in the patient's best interests (Or. Rev. Stat. §426.127).

Analysis. Again, all four states have somewhat different procedures, and there is little standardization concerning the location of patient treatment. North Carolina and New York have specific requirements that differentiate between putting a person into an inpatient care facility versus requiring clinical care. On the plus side, courts have an easier time in determining whether an individual requires inpatient or outpatient treatment or whether she requires any treatment at all. On the negative side, specific standards strictly structure the inpatient commitment process, which often results in fewer and shorter commitments than outpatient orders (American Psychiatric Association, 1999). In addition to this, only the most dangerous individuals are usually hospitalized, which is due to such stringent standards. The less dangerous persons are released and may be undertreated or even untreated (American Psychiatric Association, 1999). The case described in Box 6.4 is instructive in this regard.

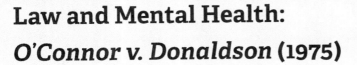

BOX 6.4

Law and Mental Health:
O'Connor v. Donaldson (1975)

In 1956, 48-year old Kenneth Donaldson was civilly committed to a mental institution with a diagnosis of paranoid schizophrenia. At the time, he was visiting his parents in Florida. Kenneth was transferred to Florida State Hospital under a commitment order and held for more than 14 years. During his involuntary commitment, Kenneth petitioned for release several times, claiming that he was denied his right to counsel at his commitment hearing, that he was not a danger to himself or others, and that he was not mentally ill. Kenneth also argued that he was provided proper mental health treatment by the hospital and, as a result, was entitled to be released as no longer being in danger. In 1963, "a reputable Minnesota half-way home" (Helping Hands) for mentally ill persons offered to assume responsibility for Kenneth. In addition, a college friend asked the state release Kenneth to his care. All three requests were ignored, and litigation ensued.

On June 26, 1975, the U.S. Supreme Court ruled that Kenneth be released, and it further directed that every state adopt standards incorporating three requirements for an involuntary commitment. First, a finding of a mental illness by itself could not justify confining persons against their will. Second, the Court ruled that state hospital officials were liable to pay personal injury damages if, by their actions, they denied patients their constitutional rights. Third, the Supreme Court decision created a national standard for involuntary commitments by requiring each state to adopt processes with definitive time limits for commitment, review of commitment orders, and judicial intervention and investigation into all involuntary commitment orders for non-criminal mental health treatment. The Court stressed the importance of protecting mentally ill individuals' rights by encouraging separate state review of similar cases.

Donaldson guarantees that people who demonstrate mental illness symptoms be made aware that no individual can be committed to a facility solely for mental illness. Furthermore, Donaldson restricted the definition of dangerousness as it applies to an involuntary commitment, holding that a person with a mental illness is not always a danger to himself or others. In other words, dangerousness is not determined merely based on demonstrating or being diagnosed with a mental illness. Rather, there must be specified, documented behaviors, conduct, and actions that sustain the allegations. Also, regardless of the diagnosis, there must be a framework to review the commitment period.

Source: JRank.Org (n.d.); *O'Connor v. Donaldson* (1975).

Filing the Petition

Arizona. In Arizona (Ariz. Rev. Stat. §36-533), a petition for court-ordered treatment must allege that the patient needs a period of treatment because the patient, owing to a mental disorder, is a danger to herself or to others, has a persistent or **acute disability**, or a grave disability. The treatment alternatives must be appropriate or available, and the court must find that the patient is unwilling to accept or incapable of accepting treatment voluntarily. The petition must be accompanied by the affidavits of two physicians participating in the evaluation and by the affidavit of the applicant for the evaluation if the latter exists. The physicians' affidavits are required to describe in detail the behaviors that indicate that, due to a mental disorder, the person (1) is a danger to self or to others; (2) has an acute disability or a grave disability; and (3) needs full-time commitment, based on the physicians' observations and study of patient information.

Those individuals responding to a mentally ill person's acute episode may have to weigh the likelihood of securing such documentation against simply letting the person go without intervention. Furthermore, a summary of the facts that support the allegations of the petition is also required. This requirement means that the attendant social worker or police officer may need to write a detailed report before the commitment proceedings can begin. The affidavit includes the results of the physical examination of the patient if an examination is relevant to the patient's psychiatric condition.

Although the proceedings are summarily considered by the court, the contents of the petition include a termination date of treatment. Under *Donaldson*, due process requirements must be met. The petition commonly seeks an order requiring the person to undergo a specific period of treatment. The judge also reviews the filed petition, which is based on a statement of opinion that a respondent with a grave disability may require **temporary guardianship** or **conservatorship**, or both, and the reasons why. The **petitioner**, or the person alleging there is a need of greater care for a person with mental disabilities, must request that the court appoint a temporary guardian or conservator, or both. This request is attached to the statement of the reasons why the person needs temporary guardianship or conservatorship, or both.

If requested by a petitioner, the court can order an independent investigation and report as to whether guardianship or conservatorship is needed, or whether both are required. In this manner, the appointment of a guardian of an adult person occurs. As in the standard commitment proceedings, after the **petition for guardianship** is filed, there is a hearing and a determination as to whether the mentally disabled person should lose his or her civil rights to control finances, enter into a contract, or be able to refuse mental health treatment.

Oregon. The commitment process may be initiated by a county health officer, a physician, a judge, or two interested persons. The petitioner files the appropriate forms with the court to seek an order for a person to be involuntarily committed to a hospital (Or. Rev. Stat. §426.070; Or. Rev. Stat. §§426.228-426.234). If there is a need for an emergency evaluation, a peace officer may take the individual into custody. Again, none of these situations involve an actual criminal offense. The officer involved needs to exercise special care to declare the contact as a mental health engagement or welfare intervention and not an arrest or detention. In fact, at this stage the person is free to leave the area. Once the papers are filed, an investigator from the community mental health program interviews the detainee, as well as acquaintances. This investigator will advise the judge whether a hearing should be held or whether further detainment is recommended.

New York. The complexity of New York laws reflects a recent change to its mental health proceeding (Title B, Article 9.01-9.63). Under Article 9.39, an involuntary emergency process is initiated in one of three ways:

1. Medical certification, which requires that two physicians or providers examine a person and certify that he or she needs involuntary care and treatment in a psychiatric facility. This process is known informally as a "two p.c." — shorthand for "two physicians certify." This certification must be accompanied by an application for admission, made by someone familiar with the individual (e.g., a legal guardian, custodian, next of kin, treating psychiatrist, or someone who lives with the person) or by one of a list of government officials. The person's judgment may be too impaired to understand the need for such care and treatment.

2. Emergency admission based on the claim that the person has a mental illness that is likely to result in serious harm to self or others and for which immediate observation, care, and treatment in a psychiatric center may occur when it is appropriate. A plan for care is required, which mandates scheduled reviews of the commitment. A director of community services of an outpatient treatment facility can also determine whether there is a likely risk of harm to self and others.

3. The person sought to be committed poses a substantial threat due to mental illness, which includes the inability to meet his needs for food, shelter, clothing, and health care; displaying dangerous conduct; and not being in compliance with mental health treatment programs (N.Y. Mental Hyg. Law §9-39).

North Carolina. Under North Carolina law (N.C. Gen. Stat. §122C-261), a civil commitment process for any person not needing hospitalization can be initiated by anyone who has knowledge of that individual and knows that the respondent is either dangerous to self or is dangerous to others, or is in need of treatment in order to prevent further disability or deterioration that would predictably result in dangerousness. These non-commitment proceedings may direct that there be mental health treatment and can be heard by an assistant or deputy clerk of a superior court or a magistrate judge. The order requires the petitioner to take the respondent into custody for examination by a physician or eligible psychologist before release to a community facility.

Analysis. Two key differences appear in the state-by-state reviews. First, some states focus more on who files the petition (i.e., New York, North Carolina, and Oregon).

Second, other states pay closer attention to what information is filed in the petition (i.e., Arizona).

The Hearings

Arizona. Before a hearing in Arizona (Ariz. Rev. Stat. §36-539), the evaluating agency's medical director issues instructions to the treating physician or the psychiatric and mental health nurse practitioners to take all **reasonable precautions** to ensure that the proposed patient is not under the influence or the effects of drugs, medication, or other treatment as to be hampered in preparing for or participating in the hearing. Likewise, if the individual is being treated as a patient, a record of all medication or other treatments is presented to the court. Arizona law requires that the patient and the patient's attorney be present at all hearings, and permits the patient's attorney to present evidence that exonerates or helps explain why a commitment is not necessary. If the patient, for medical or psychiatric reasons, is unable to be present at the hearing and cannot appear by other reasonably feasible means, the court requires clear and convincing evidence that the patient is unable to be present.

New York. The New York approach (N.Y. Mental Hyg. Law §9.31) is the most formulaic, as a hearing must occur prior to a 60-day time limit for all individuals held in a psychiatric center. If the hearing occurs after the 60-day time limit, the psychiatric center director must apply to a judge for authorization to retain the involuntary-status patient. The facility director seeking the detention will give notice in writing to the detainee of a hearing for involuntary care and treatment. Every detained person must be notified when such an application for an extension in time is made and has the right to object at the hearing to being further detained involuntarily. Under the New York process, the involuntary detainee is represented by the Mental Hygiene Legal Service or by an attorney.

When an individual is processed for commitment or any relative or friend or the Mental Hygiene Legal Service recommends commitment, the hearing is held in the designated county of the hospital or in the hospital in which the patient was first admitted, or near the patient's residence. The hearing must be scheduled no more than five days from the date the commitment notice is received by the court.

Oregon. Under the provision of Oregon Revised Statutes (2017 ORS 426.095(1)), a contested hearing may be scheduled at a hospital, the person's home, or other place convenient to the court and to the person alleged to have a mental illness. The hearing is scheduled within five days of a judge issuing a temporary commitment order.

Analysis. It is rare that a hearing can be conducted in the home of a mentally person. While this is unlikely to occur, it recognizes that the patient's vulnerability may outweigh the convenience to the court.

North Carolina. Under the laws of North Carolina (N.C. Gen. Stat. §122C-1-545, 1985) a staff member of the Attorney General's office represents North Carolina's interests at commitment hearings, rehearings, and supplemental hearings held for admitted respondents. The respondent (mentally ill detainee) is always represented by counsel. If the respondent is indigent or refuses to retain counsel, then the respondent is represented by counsel as though indigent, according to rules adopted by the Office of Indigent Defense Services. North Carolina law requires that a hearing be set within 50 days from the commitment date.

Analysis. New York law states that the patient may have either an attorney or a layperson-advocate from the Mental Hygiene Legal Service. In contrast, Oregon law states that an attorney *and* a mental health examiner must be present at the hearing. Depending on the state, a patient might have different types of legal representation present, but there must always be independent advocacy representation for the mentally disabled respondent.

There are two additional points of interest in Arizona. First, the patient cannot be under the influence of any drugs and all records of her medications must be given to the court prior to the hearing. Second, the law notes that patients may not be present at the hearing if there is clear and convincing evidence as to the reason for their absence, such as extreme combativeness or needed restraint to sustain judicial decorum.

North Carolina states that the respondent or patient may have the attorney waive her presence. The law also states that commitment can occur with the "consent of the court," which is a different standard than clear and convincing evidence. North Carolina state laws concur with Arizona procedures that the patient should be free from any external or medication influences.

Another point of interest is that North Carolina distinguishes itself by the process of automatically setting separate hearings following the original admission procedure commitment. These different processes illustrate that in different states, there are different court proceedings for hearings, different review processes, and different advocacy standards depending on the stage of the commitment process.

The Length of Stay

Reflect on the over 14 years of confinement in the *Donaldson* case. Under current law, at the onset of the commitment cases, all detainees must be given a specific period for the length of the stay or a review date. The length of stay varies state by state, but the times for review are an integral part of the court orders. If the commitment stay is extended beyond the appropriate time with a review date, then the mental health institution could face financial consequences such as fines or liquidated damages.

Arizona. Arizona statutes (Ariz. Rev. Stat. §36-540F) provide maximum periods of inpatient treatment that the court may order, subject to the following limitations: (1) 90 days for a person declared through the commitment proceedings to be a danger to self; (2) 180 days for a person found to be a danger to others; (3) 180 days for a person found to have a persistent or acute disability; and (4) 365 days for a person found by the court to have a grave disability. All of the treatment periods mandate periodic review to verify that inpatient treatment continues to be necessary.

New York. The length of stay pursuant to inpatient treatment orders in New York (N.Y. Mental Hyg. Law §9.27(b)) can be up to 60 days. Beyond that time frame, the patient has a right to a review hearing, and as previously mentioned, a review of the case can be demanded in court by the respondent prior to the expiration of the six-month holding period.

North Carolina. Under North Carolina law (N.C. Gen. Stat. Ch. 122C, 261), the length of stay for commitment depends on the reasons for admission, the respondent's response to treatment, and the respondent's progress toward treatment goals. The maximum period is six months and is, of course, subject to mandatory scheduled judicial review.

Oregon. As per Oregon's statutes (Or. Rev. Stat. §§426.130(1)(b)(C), 426.130(2)), if the respondent is ordered committed for treatment, it cannot be for more than 180 days.

Analysis. Overall length of stay depends greatly on the state in which the patient is living, but does not exceed a year. The patient's stay can be extended; however, the patient has a right to an immediate hearing should the attending physician request of a judge that there be an extension of the involuntary commitment beyond the maximum periods permitted by the statute.

VOLUNTARY COMMITMENT

There may be instances in which there is an opportunity during a street encounter with a person who is in a dangerous mental state to convince the person to voluntarily agree to seek mental health treatment and commitment. As we consider the voluntary commitment process, think back to the case of Larry R. in the prologue. As in the involuntary process, there are mandatory due process procedures to guarantee understandable admission procedures and to clearly delineate the discharge processes.

State Statutes

Arizona. In Arizona (Ariz. Rev. Stat. §36-518), any individual 18 and over may voluntarily agree to commitment if there is clear and unequivocal written **informed consent**. Informed consent is permission granted by a patient that reflects knowledge of the possible consequences for the treatment, with acknowledgment that there are risks and benefits to the treatment. The agency that conducts the admission process for people in need of treatment will indicate if there is a need for an evaluation or if there are indicia that the disabled person will benefit from care. Informed consent may be given through a mental health care power of attorney form completed after an initial evaluation. Again, this is a process that involves a dilemma because if the patient is cognizant enough to recognize that she needs intensive psychiatric treatment, she may not be acutely ill.

Oregon. Like Arizona, in Oregon (Or. Rev. Stat. §426.220) the superintendent of any state hospital that treats the mentally ill can admit and hospitalize a person over the age of 18 without an independent judicial court order, but with unequivocal release conditions and a mandatory review date. The patient may have a nervous disorder or a mental illness, but is able to make a written admission application. Upon receipt of a self-commitment petition, the applicant may be voluntarily admitted. The admission is at the discretion of the administrator. Minors can be admitted if a parent, adult next of kin, or legal guardian presents the application.

New York. New York (N.Y. Mental Hyg. Law §15.13) has broad rules for voluntary commitment: Any adult may complete an application to receive mental health treatment. The person seeking commitment and treatment sends the application to any mental health facility's director.

North Carolina. In North Carolina (N.C. Gen. Stat. § 122C-211), any individual who needs care for mental health or substance abuse may seek voluntary admission by presenting him- or herself for evaluation to the facility. No physician's statement is required, but a signed and written application for evaluation or admission is necessary. Information provided by family members regarding the individual's need for treatment is reviewed in a later evaluation.

Analysis. Again, each state has a somewhat different structure or institutional process for voluntary mental health treatment. The terms for voluntary commitment are often vague and often unique to each mental health treatment program. Having an open procedure gives more people access to voluntary admission to treatment facilities, but due to limited resources, the treatment facilities may have to decline admission in favor of involuntary admittees. Nevertheless, throughout the country, individuals who seek a voluntary admission to mental health institutions are admitted or denied based on an independent professional evaluation designed to avoid prolonged institutionalization. It is important for social service agents to know that if a minor wishes to initiate a voluntary admission to a mental health treatment facility, a parent/legal guardian/next-of-kin must fill out the application for the minor, which makes it similar to the involuntary commitment process. There is judicial review with mandatory review dates, and counsel is appointed to represent the minor.

Discharge from Voluntary Commitment

The constitutional concerns for voluntary commitments are not as urgent as in the involuntary cases. Nonetheless, state laws still impose mandatory reviews and a determination of the process for the discharge of all mental health patients placed in closed and locked facilities. Generally, the statutory elements of discharge are embedded into the original order. Local familiarity with the state's procedural statutes is essential to understanding the application and legal framework for such mental health services.

It is rare for a community provider to prepare discharges for voluntary commitments. Hence, a state-by-state review is not needed. Nevertheless, there are some differences that are important to note. For example, Oregon and New York have a 72-hour holding period before the case must be brought before a judge. In New York, the patient can only be held beyond any statutory limitation period if there are reasonable grounds for the individual to receive more treatment. The reasons must be stated in court, under oath, and be approved by a judge. Under Arizona law, due process specifies that the medical director has the authority to discharge patients if the director deems it appropriate. The discharge is permitted without a court hearing or review if it occurs prior to the review date or automatic discharge period. By comparison, in North Carolina, if the patient files for discharge, the patient is then released upon that request. In those circumstances, however, discharge conditions can change or morph into an involuntary commitment if an allegation of grave disability emerges prior to the review date.

OUTPATIENT COMMITMENTS

There are economic and legal circumstances in which a person may be a danger to himself or others, but his level of care or intervention does not warrant commitment into a closed and locked mental health treatment facility, such as the secured wing of a hospital or locked segment of a residential treatment facility. In this instance, a behavioral health provider and family members can agree or a judge can direct a person in need of mental health services to undergo treatment and receive medications at a community health clinic. If a person is living in a stable home or residential group home and has an episodic breakdown or temporarily refuses medication, hospitalization may not be necessary or feasible due to limited bedspace and the prohibitive cost of hospitalization. For example, in Massachusetts, mental health and substance abuse disorders can be provided in ambulatory care settings, hospital outpatient clinics, or in a practitioner's office.

The outpatient treatment programs rely on a structured environment, but enable the patient to continue to work, sustain family life, and remain in school. By offering intensive daily or evening programs for treatment and counseling, they provide supervisory care and some isolation from community factors that may have caused a breakdown. Outpatient treatment also enables participants to retain a semblance of privacy by not necessitating the explanations of absences that occur with inpatient care. There is often more family involvement, as the treatment depends on the sustainability and stability of the family home environment. Family members are encouraged to abstain from alcohol and drugs in order to encourage and support an abstinence treatment environment at home.

Unfortunately, the overall effectiveness of outpatient treatment is not well known and is viewed by some providers as an inferior alternative and as delivery of "treatment as usual," rather than proactive, interventional care (Van Dorn, Kosterman, and Hawkins, 2010: 2), leading one commentator to respond "[O]ne of the paradoxical problems with our mental health services is that they are not visibly harmful. Most the research shows that treatment as usual (TAU) is neither harmful nor effective." (Bickman, 2008: 1114). Nevertheless, less acute disorders such as mood, anxiety, or substance abuse forms of mental illness, with common comorbidity factors, are prevalent in outpatient commitment programs and may need purposeful interventions. The disorders can trigger violence, criminal justice involvement, and inpatient care. In order to prevent less acute disorders from gaining momentum and developing into acute, toxic disorders, it is better to gain preliminary understanding, and perhaps control, of the less complex behaviors and symptoms through the use of outpatient services (Van Dorn et al., 2010).

EPILOGUE

As with the prologue, this chapter's conclusion represents a fact-based retelling of an actual case, but certain elements were changed to protect the identities of the participants.

Andy was finishing his last semester of college at a large state university. He was a high-achieving student in the College of Engineering and Science, with an "A" average. After graduation, he planned to join a prestigious defense contractor in his home town. Andy lived in a small, all-brick house his parents bought for him during his sophomore year. Knowing he was responsible, they put the house in his name so that one day he could use it as a rental property. Andy lived with his best friends from high school, Robert and Adam. However, both moved out in the final semester of their senior year.

Throughout their friendship, Adam and Robert had often laughed at Andy when he referred to voices and sounds that the others did not hear. In high school, Andy often froze and stared and then asked them what they thought about what he heard. In college, although Andy still froze and stared, and now wrote odd things on his garage walls, he stopped asking for their reactions to the voices and visions that haloed his head.

At the beginning of his senior year, Andy began dating Andrea, his first serious relationship. His behavior toward her became increasingly obsessive. He demanded that they speak throughout the day, tracked her whereabouts through their mobile phones, and sent her constant text and e-mail messages. She began to notice him sitting in the alleyway behind her apartment late at night or early in the morning and became frightened. Right before finals week in May, Andrea told Andy that she did not want to have any contact with him. The day after Andrea deleted him from her Facebook™ account and blocked his calls, Andy went to the hardware store and purchased five large containers of lighter fluid, a bag of cotton cleaning cloths, six rolls of paper towels, and a box of wooden matches. He returned home and wrote incoherent messages on his garage walls, such as "dogs jump around," "angels hit with peanut butter," and "I dropped my toe and all fell down." Next, he put all the small gifts Andrea had given him, the notes for his final exam, every picture in the house, his expensive wrist watch, and a bag of underwear on his bed. He doused it all with lighter fluid. Humming the same tune his voices sang, he then splashed the kitchen walls with lighter fluid. Andy pulled up a chair, sat down, and threw lit matches onto the bed. When lit, he said later, "the whole mess got a little hot." He took the chair outside and watched the flames lap through the windows and roof until the fire department arrived. The house burned like a brick pizza oven.

Setting fire to one's home is the crime of arson. However, the county attorney agreed not to file immediate charges if Andy did not contest an involuntary commitment proceeding. His parents filed a petition for a civil commitment after Andy was taken to the residential, inpatient treatment hospital. They presented the petition for inpatient treatment as Andy was thought to be a danger to himself and to others. The petition described his spiraling depression, historic accounts of voices and paranoia, and his increasing obsession with Andrea and her fear for her personal safety. Although no one was hurt in the fire, it illustrated Andy's likely indifference to property and the safety of others and his immediate need for treatment.

After he was admitted, Andy's parents hired an attorney and an immediate hearing was scheduled to determine the length of his stay. Comatose, Andy refused to speak and held his hands over his ears, non-responsively shaking his head. The mental health court judge, the Honorable G., listened to Andy's parents' testimony and reviewed the reports from the psychiatrist, the fire fighters, and the first responders, as well as relevant medical records. Judge G. found there was clear and convincing evidence that Andy's condition was rapidly deteriorating and he was in need of treatment. The judge made a further ruling that inpatient hospitalization was the least restrictive form of care and set the case for review in 45 days, informing Andy that whether he improved or continued to resist treatment, he could not leave the locked ward of the mental hospital. Andy only rocked in his seat. Unlike competency proceedings for a criminal trial, it was not necessary for him to have a cognitive engagement in the legal process.

Andy's cognitive functions slowly returned. With medication, group therapy, and individual counseling, he gained an understanding of his mental illness, but he was not mentally healthy or healed. Judge G. reviewed Andy's status every six weeks until, after six months, he found that Andy's care could be stepped down to supervised outpatient treatment. Andy was released and criminal charges were deferred to the county mental health court given his efforts at self-improvement through mental health treatment. The prosecutor informed Andy that there was a two-year statute of limitation for prosecution for an arson. In the meantime, compliance with counseling, remaining on his medication, and continued therapy were required as part of his agreement for diversion from criminal prosecution. If, however, during the period of suspended prosecution, Andy engaged in any criminal activity, the felony charge for arson of an occupied dwelling would be filed against him.

Andy's case is an example of both an involuntary commitment and an enabled voluntary commitment. Andy was not committed against his will but voluntarily acknowledged that he was a danger to himself and was in need of psychiatric intervention. Essentially, his commitment plan engaged an incentive to sustain treatment as the criminal charges were held in abeyance as long as Andy participated in the treatment plan. There was also a deterrence from re-offending or avoiding treatment, as criminal charges could be refiled should Andy relapse, refuse to complete treatment, or re-engage in criminal behaviors.

SUMMARY

▸ Many variations in the commitment processes exist throughout the states, and there is not a uniform process to compel treatment when there has not been an accompanying criminal offense.
▸ Every state has a conditional standard for admission into a closed, locked mental facility that refers to "danger to self" or "danger to others."
▸ States use their own structure of mental health laws for the benefit of their citizens.
▸ It is complicated for disabled individuals to learn a state's laws, standards for commitment orders, and the circumstances that trigger involuntary care when moving from state to state or for families who relocate with a mentally ill person.
▸ The meaning of involuntary and voluntary commitment processes, the definitions of terms in the statutes, and the statutes themselves need to be known in order to provide the best services for a mentally distressed person.

KEY TERMS

Acute disability

Civil commitment proceeding

Danger to others

Danger to self

Grave disability

Involuntary commitment

Order of commitment

Petitioner

Respondent

Voluntary commitment

CHAPTER REVIEW QUESTIONS

1. Describe the basic differences between involuntary and voluntary commitments.
2. The differences in the laws between the states makes consistency for mental health commitments complicated. Looking at the differences, answer the following questions:
   a. Do you think that there are certain standards that are better in some states than others?
   b. Do you think there should be a national standard for determining if a person is a danger to herself or others?
   c. What universal policy would you apply to all states? Why?
3. Should there be more effort to use the voluntary or involuntary commitment process, even when there was an initial criminal offense?
4. In comparing the states and their procedures for voluntary commitment, is there a state statutory scheme that you think is better or superior? Why or why not? What else should be added to the laws? Are they sufficient?

5. The Donaldson case, in which the U.S. Supreme Court ruled that people could no longer be detained in a mental treatment facility indefinitely, changed the face of mental health proceedings. Now people are released within weeks or months of their initial detainment when they are no longer an immediate danger. Has the pendulum swung too far?
   a. What do you think the policy of "catch and release" achieved?
   b. Do you think that the homeless may have a higher incidence of mental illness?
6. When you read about the state standards for voluntary and involuntary commitments, do you consider the economic effect of the treatment programs on a state?
7. Overall, is it sound policy to have variations across states with respect to standards for mental health commitment?
   a. Should insurance be a concern when it comes to involuntary commitment?
   b. Who pays for indigent mental health care in your city?
8. After reading about the arson that Andy committed, do you think that the prosecutor was correct in deciding not to pursue criminal charges in light of the psychiatric treatment?
   a. Do you feel it was a good or poor use of community resources to use the inpatient hospital rather than jail with a requirement for counseling?
   b. Do you think that because Andy was a college student, he was given better treatment than a middle-aged man who, with the same circumstances, set his house on fire?
   c. Do you think that Andy's lack of a criminal record was a factor in the decision not to prosecute him?
9. If your current state of residence is not one of the four considered in this chapter, undertake a similar analysis as performed in this chapter for (1) definitions of danger to self, (2) laws and processes associated with involuntary commitments, and (3) laws and processes associated with voluntary commitments. How do your state's standards compare to the states included in this chapter?

REFERENCES

American Psychiatric Association (1999). *Issues in Community Treatment of Severe Mental Illness: A Compendium of Articles from Psychiatric Services*. Arlington, VA: American Psychiatric Association Publishing.

Bickman, L. (2008). "A measurement feedback system (MFS) is necessary to improve mental health outcomes." *Journal of the American Academy of Child and Adolescent Psychiatry* 47(1): 1114-1119.

Duval, S., and R.A. Wicklund (1972). *A Theory of Objective Self Awareness*. New York: Academic Press.

El-Mallakh R.S., R.J. Roberts, and R.L. El-Mallakh (2008). "Mood disorders." Pp. 86-92 in Robert I. Simon and Kenneth Tardiff (eds.), *Textbook of Violence Assessment and Management*. Arlington, VA: American Psychiatric Publishing, Inc.

Goleman, D. (1995). *Emotional Intelligence: Why It Can Matter More Than IQ*. New York: Bantam Books.

Gordon, S. (2016). "The danger zone: How the dangerousness standard in civil commitment proceedings harms people with serious mental illness." *Case Western Reserve Law Review* 66(3): 657-700.

Hartman, G.R., R.M. Mersky, and C.L. Tate (2014). *Landmark Supreme Court Cases: The Most Influential Decisions of the Supreme Court of the United States*. New York: Checkmark Books.

Harvard Law Review (1974). "Note: Developments in the law — Civil commitments of the mentally ill." *Harvard Law Review* 87(6): 1190-1406.

Harvard Law Review (2008). "Note: Developments in the law — The law of mental illness." *Harvard Law Review* 121(4): 1114-1191.

Hickey, P. (2014) "Involuntary mental health commitments." *Behaviorism and Mental Health* (20 March). Retrieved at behaviorismandmentalhealth.com/2014/03/20/involuntary-mental-health-commitments/ in May 2017.

LeFrancois, B.A. (2014). "Voluntary Commitment." Pp. 947-50 in Andrew Scull (ed.), *Cultural Sociology of Mental Illness: An A-to-Z Guide*. Thousand Oaks, CA: Sage Publications.

Melton, G.B., J. Petrila, N.G. Poythress, and C. Slobogin (2007). *Psychological Evaluations for the Courts: A Handbook for Mental Health Professionals and Lawyers*. 3rd ed. New York: Guilford Press.

Meyer, R.G., and C.M. Weaver (2013). *Law and Mental Health: A Case-Based Approach*. New York: Guilford Publications.

Neff, K.D., S.S. Rude, and K.L. Kirkpatrick (2007). "An examination of self-compassion in relation to positive psychological functioning and personality traits." *Journal of Research in Personality* 41: 908-16.

JRank.Org (n.d.) "O'Connor v. Donaldson — Significance." Retrieved at law.jrank.org/pages/24781/O-Connor-v-Donaldson-Significance.html on 17 May 2017.

Rogers, L. (May 19, 2012). "My voluntary commitment to a mental institution: Pt. 1." *HubPages*. Retrieved at hubpages.com/health/Voluntary-Commitment-to-a-Mental-Institution on 17 May 2017.

Van Dam, N.T., S.C. Sheppard, J.P. Forsyth, and M. Earleywine (2011). "Self-compassion is a better predictor than mindfulness of symptom severity and quality of life in mixed anxiety and depression." *Journal of Anxiety Disorders* 25: 123-30.

Van Dorn, R.A., R. Kosterman, and J.D. Hawkins (2010). "The relationship between outpatient mental health treatment and subsequent mental health symptoms and disorders in young adults." *Administrative Policy in Mental Health* 37(6): 484-486.

Ward, C.V. (2014). "Mental Illness and Danger to Self. " *Mental Health Law & Policy Journal* 3: 253-319. Retrieved at http://scholarship.law.wm.edu/facpubs/1701 on 4 August 2017.

Wexler, D.B. (2013). *Mental Health Law: Major Issues.* Springer Science & Business Media.

CASE

O'Connor v. Donaldson, 422 U.S. 563 (1975)

LEGISLATION

Ariz. Rev. Stat. §36-540 (A)

N.C. Gen. Stat. §§122C-268(j), 122C-3(11), 122C-267(h), 122C-263(d)(1), 122C-271(a)

N.Y. Mental Hyg. Law §§9.31(c), 9.01, 9.60(C)

Or. Rev. Stat. §426

CHAPTER 7

Legal Competency and the Criminal Trial

CHAPTER OUTLINE

LEARNING OBJECTIVES

After reading this chapter, you should be able to:

▶ Distinguish between insanity when a crime was committed and mental incompetency to understand legal proceedings.

▶ Understand the legal standards or issues that trigger inquiries into mental incompetency proceedings.

▶ Recognize the due process issues that emerge from the judicial process requirements when a question of incompetency arises and a judge has notice of whether a person can legally participate in the proceedings.

▶ Recognize the different ethical concerns that can emerge during incompetency proceedings, such as whether there is a question of confidential privilege and ex parte discussions.

PROLOGUE

One of the book's co-authors participated in a situation similar to the one described as it occurred in court. Some of the elements were changed to protect the identities of the participants.

Keith, a 20-year old male defendant, approaches the judge when his name is called. Pursuant to the judicial routine, the county attorney filed a criminal complaint with the magistrate court alleging that Keith was at a public park at 3:00 a.m., after the park closed. He issued Keith a ticket citation, which alleged a third-degree misdemeanor for trespass, and then watched as Keith sauntered away from the area.

As in most misdemeanor charges, as the formal court proceedings against him began, Keith received a formal copy of the charges and was advised of his constitutional rights. When the prosecutor gave Keith the charging document, she also told him the penalty: $150 fine or 15 hours of community service. Keith looked at the attorney while holding the paperwork upside down. While sitting in the courtroom public area, Keith began to pick invisible, large creatures from his shoulders and chest, tossing them forcefully onto the ground. People seated nearby scooted away.

The judge verified Keith's name and then after advising him of the charge, the possible penalties, and his constitutional rights, the following exchange occurred:

Judge: Do you understand your rights? How do you wish to plea? Do you want to plead not guilty and have a trial, or plead guilty and pay the fine or perform community service work?

Keith: I see bubbles coming out of your head. They have your thoughts in them and I can read your thoughts. And you don't like me. Tell me, why are you thinking about that?

Judge: Do you understand these proceedings? Do you understand what I just told you?
Keith: Your bubbles are coming out really fast. I find them really confusing. I find this whole place to be discriminating. You really should control those ideas you have and treat everyone equally. I am, after all, Abraham Lincoln.

At this point, the magistrate judge stopped the proceedings and appointed an attorney to represent the defendant. Attorneys are appointed if the defendant cannot afford one, especially if there is a question of the mental competency of the accused. Criminal proceedings, even ones as simple as this non-violent offense, are suspended until it can be determined if the defendant is capable of understanding the nature of the legal charges.

Responses such as those reflected in this story to the routine questions of the legal process trigger questions as to whether the defendant understands what is occurring; that is, whether the defendant is legally incompetent and if the court proceedings must be suspended to make a legal determination. It should be noted that any constitutional right to a speedy trial is also often suspended when there is an allegation of mental incompetency that impedes the criminal judicial process.

In this chapter, we answer an important question for any trial: Is the defendant competent or mentally able to understand the judicial process? What is meant legally by the term incompetency? In answering these questions, we delve into constitutional issues, procedural rules, and the competency evaluation process.

We also address an important issue for many defendants: the restoration of competency. In this section, we examine how and when this occurs. The epilogue examines an actual case that provides insights into the issues discussed in this chapter. We begin, logically enough, with key distinctions between legal competency and insanity.

Chapter Overview

The question of the ability of a person accused of a crime to understand the charges and assist in the defense, commonly known as **competency to stand trial**, raises very different issues than whether a person was insane at the time the crime was committed. **Mental incompetency** is a barrier to the prosecution of a criminal offense. If at the onset of the criminal case or any time after criminal charges are filed, the defendant does not have the mental acuity to understand the judicial proceedings or the ability to provide assistance to her attorney in the preparation of the case, then the criminal proceedings are suspended until the mental competency of the accused is regained or restored or the charges are dismissed in the interest of justice.

Once a question of incompetency to understand the proceedings is raised, then due process, equal protection, and right to counsel provide the accused with constitutional protection. Certain legal procedures are followed, beginning with the appointment of an attorney, followed by the judge ordering a mental health evaluation. The evaluation is then used to appraise the mental acuity of the accused. Legal hearings and review procedures are scheduled to determine if the mental competency of the defendant is restorable or actually restored. Ultimately, a **mental health court judge** (see Box 7.2) makes the final decision whether the defendant is able or unable to understand the criminal proceedings and whether criminal charges should be prosecuted, remain suspended or, in limited circumstances, be dismissed. Remember, though, the judge must be made aware of incompetency issues to trigger this review process.

The epilogue provides a detailed review of the attempted assassination of a U.S. Congresswoman and the murder of a federal judge. Using the court proceedings of the defendant, Jared Loughner, we review the process of how medication was ordered to restore Loughner's mental health competency by the involuntary administration of psychotropic drugs and medications.

FRAMING THE ISSUES

The first thing to understand is that the terms "insanity" and "incompetency" are *not* legally interchangeable, nor are "sanity" and "competency" (Bursztajn and Brodsky, 2016). The question of the ability of a person accused of a crime to understand the legal proceedings and assist his attorney is a matter of competency and due process of law. If there is an evident gap in the actual understanding or comprehension of the legal proceedings, then the issue of mental incompetency is raised.

A separate legal issue emerges when a person is accused of a crime and alleges that she is not guilty of committing a crime because she was legally insane at the time she committed the offense. Insanity is a defense to the crime, just as an alibi is a defense or mistaken identification is a defense. Insanity as a defense alleges that due to mental illness, disease, or impairment that existed at the time the crime was committed, the accused could not form the requisite element of mental intent to commit the particular crime.

INCOMPETENCY

The mental competency of a defendant raises completely different issues than does the defense of insanity. As the story contained in Box 7.1 suggests, a person may be incompetent to stand trial, but may have been cognizant or sane when the crime was committed. In the same instance, a person can be completely competent to stand trial, but can raise the defense of insanity at the time the crime was committed.

Constitutional Considerations

Under the U.S. Constitution, a person must be competent to stand trial. It is a violation of American constitutional protections under the Due Process Clause if the legal proceedings

BOX 7.1

The Law and Mental Health: Legal Standards for Incompetency

Andrea is an adult, but she has the intellectual capacity of a 12-year old child. She was arrested after she gave a letter to a policeman, saying that it contained poison, and asked the officer to deliver the letter to a local judge. Andrea was arrested, but her attorney quickly determined that she had organic brain damage and, while she was functional in that she cared for herself, she did not have the intellectual capacity to understand the judicial proceedings.

Andrea told her lawyer that she wanted to send the letter to the judge to scare her, but she really did not put anthrax into the envelope. She put in a concoction of corn starch, pepper, and some garden dirt. Apparently, finding the judge's address was too challenging and because Andrea knew that policemen were always helpful to her, she asked one to help her mail the letter. When her attorney asked her what the job of a judge was, Andrea told him that judges decided where people got to live, which is why she wanted to poison one.

In California, section 1367(a) of the criminal law penal code for competency requires that a person be able "to rationally participate in his or her defense." Essentially, the prosecution of a person cannot proceed if either of the following is true:

1. She is unable to understand the nature of the criminal proceedings (i.e., what is going on in the trial and why),

   or

2. She is unable to assist counsel in a rational manner. Rational manner means that the accused must have a rational as well as a factual understanding of the legal proceedings. For more on this standard, see *People v. Crosier* (1974) and *People v. Ramos* (2004).

For example, using this explanation of competency, Andrea may understand that it's wrong to send a letter containing poison and even admit that she wanted to do it, but she cannot explain or understand the criminal wrongdoing of her actions. Andrea does not have a rational understanding of the criminal proceedings.

In Mississippi, following *Goff v. State* (2009), if a trial judge receives information that, if objectively considered, reasonably suggests that a defendant "neither understands the proceedings, appreciates their significance nor rationally aids [the] attorney in his defense," then there must be a hearing to determine if a criminal case can proceed.

In considering the case of Andrea, a judge can accept information that she lives in the community, works or has worked, even part time, and can take care of basic needs. Remember, the question of competency triggers the judge's responsibility to determine if the defendant meets a threshold ability to understand the proceedings. It is not required that the accused have a sophisticated appreciation of the nuances of the criminal justice system.

The federal standards (18 U.S.C. §4241) state that at any time after the commencement of the prosecution for an offense prior to sentencing and prior to the completion of the sentence, the defendant, the prosecutor, or the defense attorney can file for a hearing to assure the competency of the accused to proceed. Under the statute, mental incompetency is defined as "a reasonable cause to believe that the defendant may be suffering from a mental disease or defect rendering him mentally incompetent to the extent that he is unable to understand the nature and consequences of the proceedings against him or to assist properly in his defense."

What if Andrea sent the letter to a federal officer? Under the federal standard, Andrea could be found by a judge to be incompetent, but with training and education, could be made competent to the level required for prosecution. Despite being permanently mentally disabled at the onset of the criminal proceedings, competency can be achieved, even temporarily, through counseling, repeated educational interventions, and medical treatment. In this instance, through educational courses and repeated instruction, Andrea could be brought to a level of understanding of the role of the judge, the judicial system, and her responsibility to obey the laws. Then, oddly, she could be prosecuted for her crime.

Sources: *Goff v. State* (2009); Grisso and Schwartz (2000); LaFortune (2016); *People v. Crosier* (1974); *People v. Ramos* (2004); 18 U.S.C. §4241 (2009).

continue without the accused fully understanding the nature of the charges pending against him due to mental defect or incapacity or if the accused cannot provide assistance in the defense of the case. An attorney is always appointed to represent a defendant when a question of the mental incompetency of the accused is raised, even if the charges are minor. The process to objectively determine if a person understands the legal proceeding is conducted at a **judicial competency hearing**.

Any party to the proceedings can request a competency evaluation. A defense attorney most commonly raises this issue, but notice can come through the judge's own observations or any other court officer, including court security, other court personnel, and even a prosecutor. If, as when Keith said he saw bubbles coming out of the judge's head, his statements or actions raise the question of his competency, then there is an affirmative, ethical duty to disclose in a public record concern about the defendant's inability to understand the proceedings. Defense attorneys may raise an issue of incompetency even if the accused does not want to have any delay in the proceedings while the psychiatric evaluation occurs.

In some cases, defendants will object to their attorney requesting a competency hearing because they do not believe they are mentally ill. Others will acknowledge that while they do not understand the proceedings, they do comprehend that a plea to the charges or a plea agreement will "get it over with" — even if they don't understand what "it" is. For an investigator or police officer, it may be part of the investigation to determine or acknowledge that an individual may have a mental illness. Police reports are an important source of information and insight into the possible issues that may emerge in the prosecution of a criminal case. If law enforcement personnel hide this information or fail to disclose it, it can build fundamental error into a criminal case and could result in the loss of a legitimate prosecution.

The allegation of a history of mental disease, disability, and defect alone is not sufficient to mandate a competency evaluation hearing. Even if a person has an ongoing psychiatric disorder, known organic mental deficiency, or is otherwise mentally disabled, the prosecution may proceed if the defense attorney does not raise a question of the competency of the accused. The attorney for the defendant may need to provide the judge with an **offer of proof** or an avowal that based on her conversations and interactions with the defendant she has a legal basis to believe the defendant is basically competent, relying on independent or corroborating evidence. If the charges are relatively simple, such as in the scenario in the prologue, the defense attorney may not wish to suspend the criminal proceedings and prolong the prosecution of the case, especially if her client is in custody. The attorney may feel that while there may only be a rudimentary understanding of the judicial process, the accused knew that sleeping in the park was illegal and that the judge is not a grapefruit.

Criminal Rules of Procedure

If, however, the charges are serious, as in Andrea's case, for example, it is important for the defendant to fully understand the consequences of a plea of guilty or the importance of a trial proceeding. In this situation, her defense attorney will notify the court that the competency of the defendant is a concern. For the process of determining a person's competency for a legal prosecution, it is not relevant that he or she was competent in the past, even the day before the hearing; competency only matters at the instant time of "right now" during the court's conducting of the competency evaluation hearing as to whether the individual defendant can be legally prosecuted. The judge's decision focuses only on whether the accused has a fundamental understanding of the legal process. Under most state laws, the judge cannot proceed unless the criminal defendant can effectively consult with and understand her attorney throughout all legal proceedings.

The standard for the determination of competency emerged in the 1960s with the U.S. Supreme Court decision of *Dusky v. United States*. Milton Dusky was accused of the kidnapping and rape of an underage female. In his trial proceedings, the record clearly showed that he was suffering from schizophrenia and was actively responding to voices and visions. In reviewing the facts that emerged during the proceedings, the Supreme Court ruled that there must be a competency evaluation before a case can proceed if the judge had reasonable cause to believe that the defendant fails to have a rational or factual understanding of the judicial process. (*Dusky*, 444). As the case of Keith in the prologue indicates, although the criminal charges may be minor and there is no evident victim or report of violence, once the judge has lawful or legal notice that the accused may not understand the proceedings, the criminal proceedings are suspended or **statutorily tolled** without a violation of the accused's constitutional right to a speedy trial (Roesch, Zapf, et al., 1999).

Now known as the *Dusky* three-prong test for competency, the following three questions are considered by the judge before the criminal case can lawfully proceed. A preliminary judicial determination that the defendant is legally competent or incompetent is based on the judge's **findings** in regard to the following inquiries:

1. Does the defendant effectively communicate with his attorney?
2. Does the defendant have a factual understanding of the proceedings?
3. Does the defendant have a rational understanding of the proceedings?

If any of the answers are no, then the defendant may be legally incompetent. If all the answers are yes, then the defendant is legally competent and the case can proceed.

Once an attorney is aware that the client may not understand the legal proceedings, she can engage in an independent investigation before launching a formal request for judicial intervention and suspension of the trial proceedings. This is especially important if the defendant is being held in jail in lieu of bail or speedy trial rights are affected. People providing legal assistance should consider the factors that indicate a competency hearing may be necessary:

▶ Does the accused have prior presentence reports that indicate there is a history of mental illness or declarations of incompetency?

▶ Are there hospital records or medical records that indicate the individual receives services from a mental health provider or has a classification of severely mentally ill (SMI)?

▶ Is there a payee for benefits that are received by the accused?

▶ Are there cases pending with child protective services that involve the accused?

▶ Is additional information available through family members that can assist with understanding the mental condition of the accused?

▶ Has the accused been hospitalized in the state mental hospital? The only way a person is sent to the state hospital is through a serious mental illness diagnosis.

▶ Is there a known history of head injuries, especially injuries to the frontal lobe?

▶ What is the defendant's work history and why is a person not working?

▶ Does the accused have special education records from school? This does not mean that the accused is incompetent, but having these records may trigger the responsibility of the attorney or police officer to ask more questions about whether the defendant understands the proceedings.

The decision as to whether a person is legally competent to proceed to trial is commonly decided by a different judge than the judge assigned to handle the criminal or civil litigation proceedings. In other words, the trial judge may receive the initial notice that the defendant is not legally competent. To protect the integrity of the proceedings and the defendant, the case is then transferred to a different judge, often known as a mental health court judge (Box 7.2).

Once the issue of the mental competency of the defendant is raised and the criminal charges are suspended, then the mental health court judge will appoint a mental health specialist, such as a psychiatrist or certified psychologist, to examine the defendant and set

BOX 7.2

Mental Health Court Judge

Frequently, one of the county judges is designated to be the mental health judge and handles all aspects of the civil and criminal cases that involve people with mental illnesses. This judge typically determines competency to stand trial for the county, as well as questions of civil commitment to a mental health facility. In this role, the mental health judge will not only supervise competency cases but may also decide if a legal guardian should be appointed for incompetent adults. The designated mental health judge will also conduct the hearings to determine if a person is a danger to herself or others and should be involuntarily committed to a mental hospital.

The mental health court judge supervises people referred to the community mental health court where the criminally accused person has mental disabilities that interfere with compliance with court orders in criminal cases. Again, this applies when the defendant is mentally competent, i.e., able to understand and participate in the criminal proceedings, but due to mental illness needs special programs and post-conviction supervision. In larger jurisdictions, there will be a lower court judge, such as a magistrate and/or municipal court judge, assigned to review the cases of mentally ill defendants in need of treatment in lieu of criminal prosecution of non-violent misdemeanor offenses. If it is a serious offense, such as a felony, then a judge of general jurisdiction, such as a district, superior, or county court judge, will be responsible for managing this specialty "problem-solving" court. In smaller jurisdictions, one judge will handle the felony and misdemeanor mental health court referrals.

The mental health court assignment judges receive special training and coaching to better understand the issues and concerns of mentally ill persons. In the course of the training, judges learn what characteristics emerge with the restoration of competency, as well as alternatives for sentencing options when a person has mental illnesses or disease. For example, suppose that in our opening scenario, although Keith saw bubbles coming out of the judge's head, he also could effectively communicate with his attorney and knew it was wrong to sleep in the park at night. Keith is essentially competent, but mentally ill. The defense attorney may ask the prosecutor to refer the final sentencing and disposition of Keith's case to a mental health court. Then, the mental health court judge assigned to Keith's case will keep the matter under her supervision as part of the case assignments of the judge's mental health court jurisdiction. In this judicial setting, given Keith's diagnosis of a mental illness, his homelessness and evident lack of financial resources to pay a fine, as well as his likely inability to qualify to perform community service, the misdemeanor mental health court judge can offer Keith more appropriate and effective supervision. This may include providing proof of continuing to take medication, attending counseling support sessions, looking for a permanent residence, and regularly reporting to the court's supervisory staff.

a hearing date. The defendant undergoes a battery of tests that includes a mental health evaluation, historical assessments, family reports, and other factors to help objectively and independently evaluate the defendant's competency to proceed with the criminal prosecution. This information is disclosed in a report to the judge during a special hearing about the mental status of the defendant. Remember, the information is not about the pending criminal charges, but is provided to help the judge assess whether the *Dusky* three-prong test is satisfied. The judge must know by a **preponderance of evidence** whether the defendant has the cognitive ability to understand the proceedings.

Ethical Obligations

All communications received by an attorney or originating from an attorney are "privileged." Under the rules of evidence, the term **privileged communications** refers to any exchange between the client and attorney and that such communications cannot be disclosed to any person without the express permission of the client. Disclosure could result in the information being excluded from judicial use. On the one hand, the law requires that a criminal defendant understand the legal proceedings and it can impose an affirmative duty on the defense attorney to disclose indicia of mental illness that affects the progress of the criminal law proceedings. On the other hand, the lawyer cannot disclose the contents of the attorney-client communications, which could include a triggering event that raises issues of mental incompetency.

For example, if the client tells the attorney that he cannot hear the proceedings because the same voices that told him to dismember his next-door neighbor are still shouting out orders, then the attorney must seek to suspend the proceedings and permit psychologists and psychiatrists to conduct independent evaluations to ascertain the defendant's ability to understand the criminal charges. This is not a question of insanity as a legal defense to the crime. The lawyer cannot, however, disclose his client's confession or knowledge of the details of the homicide. To comply with legal obligations, an attorney may simply state to the judge and prosecutor in an open court proceeding that there is "information and belief" that the defendant suffers from a mental or psychological disorder, but the attorney will not repeat the conversation or give the reasons for the his opinion.

Ex Parte Communications with the Judge

One ethical issue that non-court personnel, law enforcement, or jail staff must be aware of is that they cannot communicate directly with the judge about what was heard or what the defendant said to himself, including that little green men are following him. If anyone from security, prosecution, or even a defense witness speaks to the judge without all parties present or consenting to the independent disclosure, this is known as an ***ex parte* communication** with the judge. This type of communication means that the judge learned something about the case that is evidentiary in nature, but the information is presented to the judge outside of the due process procedures or without equal, simultaneous disclosure to all parties. If a judge learns anything about the defendant, the case, the evidence, or even the mental status of the defendant that is outside and/or is without the knowledge of the prosecutor and defense counsel, the judge must recuse or excuse herself from considering anything else about the case.

For example, a judge was advised that the defendant, accused of trespassing on a college campus, had been shouting, running around in the court corridors, and "acting crazy." Security officers for the court sent a note to the judge's secretary warning the judge, which was then kept in the defendant's court record. The judge was later reprimanded for an ethics violation for receiving the communication about the conduct of the accused independently and separately without notice to all parties, especially the defendant.

Legal Proceedings

Who then has the responsibility for reporting issues of mental competency and when should concerns be raised? Think about the scenario in Box 7.3 and determine what the best course of action would be.

If the judge dismisses the charges, the judge can also order that guardianship proceedings be initiated. If a family member volunteers to be a guardian, then the guardian can order the defendant committed for civil mental treatments. This process also means that

BOX 7.3

What Would You Do?

If the defendant is accused of a violent crime or if the defendant cannot or has not posted bail, then the defendant is housed at the jail, most commonly in a special detention acute mental health unit. There is frequently a heightened suicide watch or increased observation area because these individuals often demonstrate psychotic or dissociative behaviors and cannot be safely held in the same population with other jail inmates. In many jail units, due to understaffing and low budgets, the inmates are kept naked in windowed cells to enable one guard to monitor multiple people (Press, 2016).

Suppose you have arrested a well-dressed, articulate man for embezzlement and fraud. He has a wife and three children. During the transportation, he sighs, looks out the window, and says to himself, but loudly enough for you to hear him, "I think I will be better off dead to my family. My insurance will cover me until this hits the front page and then it's cancelled and I'm toast." You know that if you report him as being potential suicidal, he will be kept naked in a cell on a police watch. Do you report the incident? Do you question him more about it? What if he also says he had no idea you were taking him to the airport? He didn't order a taxi.

What if you are a court officer who is transporting a prisoner, and on the way, she starts explaining that on her home planet of Pluto, the legal processes are very different. Note that there is nothing on the transport notes or jail records that indicates that she has any sort of mental illness or disability. There is also nothing that indicates that she is dangerous to others or a danger to herself. How would you handle this situation? Who would you notify? Would you tell anyone? Why are the answers to these questions important to justice?

If there is a serious criminal accusation pending or uncertainty as to the nature or cause of the mental illness, then there may be different types of psychological evaluations requested by the defense attorney. The more serious the charges and the penalty, the greater the depth of the inquiry. Sometimes there will be a one-hour exam, while if there is a neuro-psychiatric exam, it will take hours and cost thousands of dollars. Each exam is performed with the duty to determine if the accused can proceed through the legal accusation process.

Confidentiality issues can also emerge with respect to statements the defendant makes to the psychiatrist hired by the defense attorney to prepare for the trial, or if the mental health specialist is to determine the competency of the defendant. Remember, the psychologist or mental health specialist appointed by the judge to evaluate the mental competency of the defendant may be considered to be an agent of the state and the same confidentiality rules may not apply. This varies according to different states and policies. Generally, however, the questions to evaluate competency do not raise issues pertinent to the prosecution or defense of the criminal case. There is a question as to whether a person who is thought to be mentally incompetent can waive his or her right to the privilege of non-disclosure by a medical provider.

To prepare for the hearing, the judge appoints a licensed or certified psychiatrist or psychologist, sometimes even two, to examine the defendant. In high profile cases, such as a homicide where the accused is facing the death penalty, the attorney for the defendant has the right to self-select an additional examiner. The examiners typically have 30 days, but usually no more than 45 days, to conduct tests, psychiatric or psychological evaluations, medical investigations, and mental analysis procedures. In some jurisdictions, a 15-day extension can be permitted. The results of the tests are compiled into separate reports and filed as sealed records into the court file. Each report details the person's history and present symptoms; a description of the psychiatric, psychological, and medical tests that were used; and the examiner's findings and the examiner's opinion as to the prognosis of the defendant to recover from his or her mental illness with treatment.

While the criminal charges may be suspended during a competency evaluation period, police continue to investigate the crime, interview witnesses, and gather evidence, although there is a suspension of the constitutional time demands required for the prosecution of a case. For example, in most instances, a criminal trial commences within 120 days of the offense. If a question of the competency of the defendant is raised, however, the time to bring the charges is tolled or stayed. This means that the accused may remain in jail or involuntarily committed to a state-run, locked mental facility while his mental competency is evaluated. If the question of competency is complicated by a comorbidity of mental illnesses, substance abuse, and a resistance to treatment, the holding period can last months.

Within 120 days of raising an issue of mental competency, the judge must hold an initial hearing or conduct a trial-type proceeding in which witnesses are sworn and evidence is accepted about the mental condition of the defendant. The judge must find by a preponderance of the evidence that the defendant is suffering from a mental disease or defect and is unable to understand the nature and consequences of the proceedings or assist properly in his or her defense. Alternatively, the judge can determine that the defendant is competent and that the criminal proceedings should be reinstated and continued.

The hearing is a formal proceeding. An attorney represents the defendant and the government is commonly represented by a government attorney. Both parties may subpoena witnesses and are entitled to cross-examine witnesses who testify at the competency hearing, and the defendant can testify. In essence, it is a civil law, not a criminal law proceeding, as the purpose of the hearing is for the judge to make a determination of competency, regardless of the defendant's opinion. Think about it: If a person is mentally incompetent, he cannot legally waive or assert a right to this hearing because technically the accused may not be competent to give up or accept the constitutional right of confrontation.

Under the U.S. federal code (18 U.S.C. §4241), determination of mental competency to stand trial can occur at any time after the prosecution of a case begins through to the sentencing hearing. Judicial review of the competency can even occur during the probation period or prior to the completion of a prison sentence. This also means that a person can go through competency evaluations multiple times. The application and consideration of the mental status of the accused depends on the moment, not the status of the proceedings. This means that if the defendant is competent when the plea is accepted, but then deteriorates into an incompetency status prior to sentencing, the judge cannot impose a sentence. Similarly, if the defendant is sentenced, but during the period of probation she violates probation and becomes incompetent, then the court hearing for the violation of probation cannot be conducted.

Following hearing and review of the evidence provided in the psychiatric report, there are four options for the judge:

1. The defendant is found to be competent to stand trial and the case proceeds accordingly. The accused understands the proceedings.
2. The judge accepts the doctor's finding that the person is not competent, but the accused may be responsive to a restoration of competency. The interventions include taking medications to restore balanced or cognitive mental health and requiring the defendant to complete remedial education courses to familiarize the defendant with the role of the judge and prosecution, as well as additional assessments. In all cases, the charges or disposition of the criminal matter are stayed and the status of the case is reviewed periodically by the judge.
3. If the evidence indicates that the individual cannot be restored to competency, such as when there is permanent brain injury, then the judge can require the accused to engage in educational programs, training, and review of basic judicial procedures in an effort to achieve competency. The case is set for review within 180 days. Sometimes restoration of competency is achieved by evidence that the accused has progressed to the point of having a better understanding of the proceedings.

4.   If the judge accepts evidence and finds that there is no substantial probability that the person can be restored to competency, then the case may be dismissed without prejudice after a statutory period of time. The case can be refiled against the individual if the prosecutor has reason to believe that competency is restored due to independent evidence or circumstances. This option is especially possible if there is a hint that the accused was malingering or faking illness.

due to an individual's mental, or in some cases physical, disabilities, the person can no longer be in control of personal finances or enter into contracts, such as leases or credit card agreements, or make many personal decisions. (There is more information about guardianships in Chapter 11.)

The judge is required to consider the least restrictive alternative during the pendency of a mental health evaluation. After considering the factors of the defendant's charges and behavior, the judge can release the accused, detain him in jail, or order him to be detained in a closed and locked mental health treatment facility. As in all cases, if an order to detain the defendant is made, then reviews of the judge's orders must be entered. The decision to detain or release involves consideration of the following factors: What is necessary for community safety? Did the defendant cooperate with the evaluation? Is he or she a threat to public safety? Is the accused willing to participate in a treatment program knowing that criminal charges are pending upon the restoration of competency?

Generally, psychologists, education specialists, and social workers who review the trial processes with the defendant also supervise these programs. They discuss the judicial due process proceedings with defendants, including concerns about the rights of the accused, the role of the judge and jury, and any sentencing options. They don't, of course, discuss the merits of the individual criminal charges with the defendant or infringe on the defendant's constitutional rights, as the attorney is not usually present.

Throughout the proceedings, there are periodic reports submitted to the judge. Over time, the reports will indicate whether the accused has gained understanding of the proceedings and is now competent or whether it appears that competency cannot be restored. In the decision of *Jackson v. Indiana* (1972), the Supreme Court ruled that a person could not be held indefinitely. If there is a delay, then the defendant's attorney can ask the judge for a hearing about the progress, or lack of progress, with the defendant's case. For example, if the accused is arrested and held in jail for trespassing, the criminal offense may have a 90-day jail maximum sentence. If the criminal process is suspended because of an incompetency proceeding and the accused remains in jail, it is likely that after four months, the defense attorney will bring a motion to release the defendant because the period in detention exceeded a possible jail sentence. This outcome often leads to a revolving door mental health syndrome. Consider, for example, the scenario presented in Box 7.4. How would you answer the questions posed at its conclusion, given what you understand about the legal demonstration of competency to this point?

COURT-ORDERED RESTORATION OF COMPETENCY

If the defendant is found to be incompetent due to mental illness and the medical examiners believe that the condition is treatable, then there a process that can be ordered known as compulsory **restoration of competency**. Some states will send the offender to the state mental hospital, but now, due to the high expense of hospital care and medications, most communities seek to first provide counseling treatment within the jail and monitor the administration of voluntary prescribed medications. Sometimes if the offense is not violent and the offender seems amenable to learning, the interventional treatment can also be directed with in an outpatient, out-of-custody setting, especially if the accused is already taking medications.

If the person is in custody, especially for a violent offense, and there is no evidence of progress toward competency, then the judge can order psychotropic medication and treatment, a restoration practice known as **synthetic competency**. The defendant can stipulate or agree to the use of this artificial form for the restoration of competency. Artificial

---

BOX 7.4

Thinking About the Issues

Legal proceedings concerning matters of competency are intended to protect the accused. There also may be a public safety issue. Protecting the rights of the accused while protecting society raises complex issues. For example, a neighbor's 911 call indicates that Jack is standing naked in his yard, eating the grass. When the police arrive, they start to arrest Jack for indecent exposure. Jack then starts flailing, biting, and kicking, and shouting that he is a government experiment and to move him will cause the ground to dislodge. Jack's misdemeanor indecent exposure offense has now morphed into a felony charge for resisting arrest.

1. What do you, as a law enforcement officer, include in the report?
2. What information should you obtain from family members or neighbors?
3. Does Jack need social services or jail? Does his behavior warrant removal from society through punishment, as indecent exposure and becoming violent is a disturbance? Should there be an effort to dismiss the criminal case and instead seek a mental health evaluation?

There are many steps in the process to protect the rights of a defendant when a question of competency arises. However, as the case of Ralph Tortorici (Box 7.5) suggests, competency may not be all that difficult a standard to attain.

BOX 7.5

Competency in Practice:
The Case of Ralph Tortorici

Ralph Tortorici, a psychology student at the State University of New York at Albany, entered an ancient Greek history class on December 14, 1994, the last day of classes for the term, secured the classroom doors with a firehose and took the class hostage with a large hunting knife and a high-powered rifle. He announced that he had a computer chip in his brain and needed to see the president.

After about two and a half hours of negotiations, Tortorici fired a round from his rifle to demonstrate his resolve, and hope for a peaceful surrender dimmed. At that point, one of the hostages, Jason McEhaney, wrestled with Tortorici for control of the rifle and the former was shot in the leg and groin. Tortorici was subsequently stabbed in a fight with another of the hostages for control of the hunting knife. Police quickly gained control of the room and Tortorici, who was subsequently charged with multiple counts of kidnapping, aggravated assault, and attempted murder. His lawyer entered a plea of not guilty by reason of insanity.

Ralph Tortorici had a long and well-documented history of mental illness. He was twice assessed by the Capital District Psychiatric Center, where he was evaluated as delusional and paranoid. He claimed to police and psychiatrists at the time, some two years prior to the incident at the University at Albany, that the government had planted a surveillance device in his penis. A court-ordered psychiatric evaluation concluded that Tortorici was suffering from a delusional disorder and was not competent to stand trial. A second evaluation found that he suffered from a very serious mental illness, including paranoia that was consistent with schizophrenic paranoid type.

After a brief commitment to Mid-Hudson Psychiatric Center, doctors found Tortorici competent. The question of his not-guilty-by-reason-of-insanity plea was then a matter for the jury to decide. In a trial that began in late 1995 and lasted until January 1996, Tortorici was tried, found guilty on 10 counts—4 of kidnapping, 4 of reckless endangerment, one of first-degree assault, and one of first-degree criminal use of a firearm—and sentenced to from 15 years and 8 months to 40 years in prison.

As to Tortorici's release from the Mid-Hudson Psychiatric Center and restoration to competency questions, one of the prosecutors in the case, Cheryl Coleman, offered the following observations: "Somebody once described 'competent' as knowing the difference between a judge and a grapefruit. I think [Tortorici] knew that. Was he competent to help his counsel? Of course he wasn't. So in the spirit of competence, was he competent? No. Did he fit the *legal definition* of competency? Yes, probably" (Frontline; emphasis in the original).

Tortorici lived 41 additional months while housed in one of New York's nine general male prison facilities that also provided the highest possible level of care by the state's Office of

Mental Health. On August 10, 1999, Tortorici died after hanging himself in his prison cell. This was his second attempt to take his own life. At the time, he was being seen daily by mental health staff and participated in weekly treatment. Tortorici was 31 years of age.

Sources: Dao (1994); Frontline (n.d.); Grondahl (1994); New York State (1999).

competency often occurs if the defendant was taking medications and issues of mental competency emerged during a lapse of treatment.

If, however, there is a refusal to take medication, then a court hearing is necessary. Under Supreme Court decision *Washington v. Harper* (1990), a judge can only order **involuntary medication** to restore a person to competency or retain a person in competency if the judge has a hearing that is separate from the issue of whether the individual is competent at the onset of the case or proceeding. This judicial position is re-emphasized in the 1992 decision of *Riggins v. Nevada*, where the Court found that medication treatment must specifically be the least restrictive alternative for the accused.

A second, distinct legal question for the judge to determine is whether medication is the most likely means by which the defendant will be restored to mental competency. In other words, if the defendant has an incurable brain disorder or permanent brain injury, medication will not likely restore competency and a court order for the defendant to take antipsychotic medication may not be appropriate. If, however, there is indication that medication can help the defendant understand the proceedings, then drugs can be ordered, even if the accused objects to treatment. The judge is often in a quandary because the medication is being ordered prospectively—that is, the medication can be ordered even without the defendant having previously been given the medication *if* the jail or mental hospital staff think that medication is necessary. The defendant cannot refuse, despite side effects, unless the defendant can establish there is no evidence of positive indicia of direct medical benefit given the accused's diagnosis of mental illness.

EPILOGUE

The information that forms the core of the epilogue was taken from the following sources: United States v. Jared Loughner (2011); Federal Bureau of Investigation (2012).

The case of *United States v. Jared Lee Loughner* illustrates the process of determining incompetency to stand trial. Loughner committed horrific crimes, including intentional homicide of a federal judge and a child and the attempted murder of a U.S. Congresswoman, but he could not be immediately criminally prosecuted because of his apparent mental incompetency to understand the nature of the charges and his inability to provide his defense attorney any credible assistance.

Remember, it is irrelevant whether Loughner was insane at the *time of his crime* — the issue is whether he was mentally competent and able to understand the nature of the criminal charges or provide competent assistance to his defense attorneys after his arrest. It was alleged that Loughner was sane when he committed his crimes, as the investigation revealed he knowingly and deliberately purchased guns and ammunition with the intended purpose to murder Congresswoman Giffords. Loughner was eventually restored to mental competency by the use of synthetic medications, but the process illustrates the time frame and legal procedures for a federal competency review.

Loughner, born in 1988, grew up in Tucson, Arizona. On January 8, 2011, he went to a Tucson neighborhood shopping center where U.S. Congresswoman Gabrielle Giffords was speaking in an open forum she called "Congress on Your Corner." Members of her staff, including Ron Barber and Gabe Zimmerman, accompanied her. In the crowd was 9-year old Christina Taylor Green and approximately 50 other people. Chief United States District Court Judge John Roll entered the parking lot to go to the grocery store. Judge Roll, as a private citizen in the neighborhood shopping center, walked up to Congresswoman Giffords to say hello while Giffords was engaged in the congressional business of meeting her constituents.

People stood in line to take pictures with Giffords, and her staff chatted with the crowd. None were armed. Prior to this occasion, when asked what security assistance she was provided to her during community visits, Representative Giffords said, "Someone carries my purse." Earlier, in November 2010, Giffords won re-election following a highly contentious campaign in which her opponent, Jesse Kelly, circulated campaign materials with assault rifles and with images of Giffords targeted in a bull's-eye. Loughner apparently fixated on Giffords during this election and perceived that shooting her would be hailed as a heroic effort.

Jared Loughner was known slightly to law enforcement and well to the administrators of Pima Community College. Labeled as "difficult," "unpredictable," and "subject to violent outbursts," faculty and staff at the school expressed concern regarding his mental stability. Loughner also posted rambling, slightly incoherent, but violent diatribes on Facebook™ and Myspace™. He lived with his parents, had little history of employment, and was a loner. He also never committed any actual acts of violence or harm prior to January 8, 2011.

In the busy parking lot of the centrally located store, Loughner positioned himself and began to fire with a pistol, shooting Giffords in the head at point-blank range before firing on the other bystanders. He immediately killed Giffords' aide, Gabe Zimmerman, Judge Roll, Christine Green, and others as they stood in the parking lot line. Within minutes of the initial fire, he stopped to reload his gun and was tackled and thrown to the ground by constituents, who sat on him until emergency crews arrived.

Loughner was then transported to the Pima County Jail and later the U.S. Detention Facility for processing and evaluation. He asserted his right to remain silent and demanded an attorney.

Think of your responsibilities if you were a first responder and charged with transporting Loughner to the jail. Suppose that he makes irrational statements. He also tells you that he watched Gabby Giffords die and repeatedly states how the Congresswoman died and how he watched her float away. As a responder, you are well aware that Representative Giffords is still alive, was responsive, and was transported for surgery. When he is not uttering nonsense or revenge comments, he is silent and catatonic, and stares at you as though you were a new form of creature that is unknown to him. Do you have a duty to report the comments? Why or why not? Are you aiding the defense or prosecution by documenting his comments? Now that you know about the complex issues regarding incompetency to stand trial, how would this information affect your opinion or attitude?

In Loughner's case, a defense attorney was appointed by the U.S. Magistrate Court judge within 24 hours of his arrest. Apparently, though, Loughner denied that Congresswoman Giffords was alive. He insisted that he watched her die and heard voices that confirmed his beliefs.

On March 7, 2011, the Assistant U.S. Attorney filed the motion to determine competency as the government received information that Loughner was unable to understand why he was charged with a criminal offense when he thought he was a hero, killing someone who was targeted as an enemy. The government alleged that there was evidence in the public domain suggesting the defendant may have mental issues.

The prosecutors agreed that there was some evidence of mental issues and it was necessary to have a psychiatric exam. Although the preliminary police reports disclosed Loughner's mental state and attitude from postings in social media, Loughner asserted his right to remain silent and the prosecutors did not know very much about his mental condition. Despite the anger and outrage of the Tucson community against Jared Loughner, the criminal proceedings for murder were suspended for psychiatric evaluations of his competency.

While detained in a U.S. Bureau of Prisons medical facility, the psychiatric staff concluded that Loughner was not competent and he was held to determine if he could be restored to competency. The judge ordered psychiatric evaluations and tests be conducted to determine if he could be restored to a state of mental competency. This order suspended the criminal prosecution of the case. Because Loughner had attempted to assassinate a federal employee while she was working in her capacity as a Congresswoman, he was prosecuted under federal homicide laws and was kept in a federal prison-like hospital until the competency mental health evaluations were completed.

Federal Circuit Court Judge Bybee conducted a hearing pursuant to 28 C.F.R. §549.46(a), referred to as a *Harper* hearing (see *Washington v. Harper*, 1990) to determine if Loughner should be involuntarily medicated on an emergency basis to help in the restoration of competency. In Loughner's case, the judge found, or made "findings of fact," that Loughner was incompetent to proceed with the criminal prosecution, and he was remanded to a federal detention facility and ordered to take medications to help him recover mental stability and comprehension. Remember, Loughner did not have a long history of mental disease and the reporting psychiatrists felt that current medications could stabilize him. The prison treating providers relied on the use of medications for synthetic competency and used drugs to stabilize Loughner, but not necessarily cure him of mental disease. Despite Loughner's objection to the use of medication, the judge issued a 117-page opinion ordering treatment for what was diagnosed as schizophrenia and debilitating mental incompetency. The judge found that Loughner would benefit from involuntary medication because he became enraged and was throwing objects, spitting, and having auditory hallucinations during the evaluation by government psychiatrists who were appointed to consider his incompetency status.

Throughout this process, the community and victims continued to heal. Their statements were recorded and examined. Every witness was interviewed and the evidence was catalogued. In the meantime, the court proceedings continued. Eventually, Loughner was found to be sufficiently competent after being compelled to take medications and by engaging in psychiatric treatment. The defendant was offered the plea of "guilty but insane," as he met the Arizona legal foundation that although he was delusional and paranoid when he murdered and injured so many, he was cognizant of his behavior and intended the consequences of his actions. On August 17, 2012, Jared Loughner, slumped in a chair at the federal courthouse, stated 19 times that he pleaded guilty to the crimes of the mass shooting at the Tucson grocery store parking lot. The plea to life sentences without parole was in exchange for the prosecutors agreeing not to seek the death penalty. Be aware, though, that despite Loughner's restoration to competency through involuntary medication, the prison has no duty to continue to administer psychotropic medications following his plea as a competent criminal. It is likely the defendant may regress into mental illness in the highly secure federal facility.

SUMMARY

▸ Having a complete understanding of the difference between insanity or incompetency at the onset or during the criminal proceeding is a critical learning responsibility for mental health support professionals.

▸ If a person accused of criminal charges does not have a minimal ability to understand the reasons for the prosecutor's accusation, assist legal counsel, or comprehend the sentencing mandates, the criminal charges are suspended.

▸ Under American jurisprudence laws, if a judge is informed that the accused is not mentally competent, an attorney is always appointed for the defendant while the competency of the defendant is tested.

▸ The judge relies on the report of a mental health specialist, such as a psychiatrist or certified psychologist, who examines the accused by using various evaluations tools to assess the mental competency of the defendant. Following the examination, the judge at a public hearing can make legal findings and declare that it is possible to restore competency through counseling, medicine (synthetic competency), or treatment

▸ The determination of competency to proceed with criminal law proceedings must be made within a time frame proscribed by law as the criminal prosecution is suspended during the evaluation period.

▸ The question of competency to proceed may raise ethical issues for judges, attorneys, and professional mental health support people. While the defendant may say things that imply there is a lack of comprehension, if the statements are made pursuant to a client-professional relationship, the disclosures could be prohibited or limited.

CHAPTER REVIEW QUESTIONS

1. Supposed the accused has a known mental equivalency of a 6-year old. What are some questions that could be asked to determine if the person is capable of proceeding with a charge of attempted murder?
2. Distinguish between sanity and competency. Why are these distinctions critical to the criminal justice process? Are there other issues involved?
3. The judge considers all relevant information to assess whether a person is competent to stand trial. What other issues should a judge consider? What should be investigated?
4. Many defendants claim to have amnesia about the events that surround the crime. Is this a case of incompetency due to the fact that the accused cannot assist in the defense of the case?
5. How can a judge determine that a defendant has been restored to competency after receiving education and training about the legal system?
6. Why is it prohibited for a judge to receive *ex parte* information about a case when considering the mental competency of a defendant?
7. What is the three-prong test in a *Dusky* inquiry for mental competency?
8. Why would a defense attorney not want to suspend a criminal case if he suspects his client is not competent?
9. Why would the fact that a person had a history of mental illness or disease not automatically trigger a competency review?
10. What type of evidence will a judge have for a competency hearing?
11. Consider the role and obligations of the defense attorney in this process. Reflecting on what you have read thus far, how would you answer each of the following questions?
    a. How might learning that one's client suffers from mental disease or disability impact the defense attorney's relationship with her client?
    b. What are some factors a lawyer might consider in deciding what to disclose or not to disclose to the prosecutor about her client's mental state?

KEY TERMS

Competency hearing
Competency to stand trial
Ex parte communications
Findings
Involuntary medication
Mental health court judge
Mental incompetence

Offer of proof
Preponderance of evidence
Privileged communications
Restoration of competency
Statutorily tolled
Synthetic competence

REFERENCES

Bursztajn, H., and A. Brodsky (2016). "Are competence and insanity purely medical concepts?" Retrieved at http://www.brown.edu/Courses/BI_278/Other/Clerkship/Didactics/Readings/COMPENCE%20AND%20INSANITY.pdf on 15 July 2016.

Federal Bureau of Investigation (2012). "Jared Lee Loughner Sentenced in Arizona on Federal Charges in Tucson Shooting." The FBI Report Phoenix Press Release. Retrieved at https://archives.fbi.gov/archives/phoenix/press-releases/2012/jared-lee-loughner-sentenced-in-arizona-on-federal-charges-in-tucson-shooting on 18 July 2017.

Grisso, T., and R.G. Schwartz (2000). *Youth on Trial: A Developmental Perspective on Juvenile Justice. Chicago*: The University of Chicago Press.

Kinney, B. (2007) "Comment: An Incompetent Jurisprudence: The Burden of Proof in Competency Hearings." *University of California, Davis Law Review* 43: 2.

Lacy, M. (2011). "Suspect in Shooting of Giffords Ruled Unfit for Trial." *The New York Times.* Retrieved at http://www.nytimes.com/2011/05/26/us/26loughner.html on 15 July 2017.

LaFortune, K. (2016). "Oklahoma Leads the Way on Juvenile Competency." *Monitor on Psychology* 47(1): 32.

Reisner, A., J. Piel, and M. Miller (2013). "Competency to stand trial and the defendants who lack insight into their mental illness." *Journal of the American Academy of Psychiatry and the Law* 13: 85-91.

Roesch, R., P.A. Zapf, S.L. Golding, and J.L. Skeem (1999). "Defining and assessing competency to stand trial." Pp. 327-349 in *The Handbook of Forensic Psychology*, A.K. Hess and I.B. Weiner (eds.). Hoboken, NJ: John Wiley.

Starr, D. (2012). "Can you fake mental illness? How forensic psychologists can tell whether someone is malingering." Retrieved at http://www.slate.com/articles/health_and_science/science/2012/08/faking_insanity_forensic_psychologists_detect_signs_of_malingering_.html on 15 July 2016.

CASES

Dusky v. United States, 362 U.S. 402 (1960)

Goff v. State, 14 So. 3d 625, 644 (Miss. 2009)

Jackson v. Indiana, 406 U.S. 715 (1972)

People v. Crosier, 41 Cal. App. 3d 712, 716 (1974)

People v. Ramos, 34 Cal. 4th 494, 507 (2004)

Riggins v. Nevada, 504 U.S. 127 (1992)

United States v. Jared Loughner, CR-11-0187-TUC-LAB (2011)

United States v. Loughner, 672 F.3d 731 (2012)
Washington v. Harper, 494 U.S. 210 (1990)
Wieter v. Settle, 193 F. Supp. 318 (W.D. Mo. 1961)

LEGISLATION

18 U.S.C. §4241 — Determination of Mental Competency to Stand Trial to Undergo Postrelease Proceedings (2009)
Utah Code Ann. §77-15-1

CHAPTER 8

Mentally Ill Defendants: Defenses, Pleas, and Verdicts

LEARNING OBJECTIVES

At the conclusion of this chapter, you should be able to:

▸ Compare the insanity defense with mental competence to stand trial.
▸ Ascertain the elements required for the different tests that apply to the insanity defense as well as how insanity is proven and rebutted in the course of a criminal trial.
▸ Explain when and how psychotic mental illness may be predicted through observation of the modus operandi of the offender.
▸ Explain the applicability of the temporary insanity defense, and the diminished capacity defenses, such as post-traumatic stress disorder, spousal abuse, and somnambulism, as they may exonerate or excuse criminal behavior.

PROLOGUE

This interpretation of the story of Andrea Yates was taken largely from the following sources: Adams and Adams (2016); CNN Library (2017a); Cohen (2012); CourtTVNews.com (2006); O'Malley (2004); Spencer (2002).

Thirty-six-year old Andrea Yates felt the despair settling into her mind. Clinically, she had been suffering from postpartum depression and postpartum psychosis since the birth of her fourth child, Luke, nearly two years earlier. Six months ago, she had her fifth child, conceived only weeks after Luke's birth. While she had suffered from various forms of mental disease since her teens, her most recent episode of depression started as a tiny black crack in the corner of her head, almost as though she could turn quickly and see it against the back wall of her brain. She felt the gradual split of her mind and brain, white to black to white with the black brackish division becoming deeper and thicker.

Andrea could hear a voice scolding her. The voice, joined by a chorus of singers, told her that pleasures and joy must be punished, destroyed. She asked the voice if she accepted her own destruction, could she spare her children? The booming voice condemned her. She must save them from harm. She must free her babies. She must end their bondage.

Listening carefully to the directions sung to her by the chorus, she filled the bathtub. She felt that what she was going to do next was kind. She first retrieved Paul, aged 3, and held the child close to her, sighing as he snuggled into her chest. The voices now were shouting their instructions through the crack in her mind as it splintered into mirror fragments. Andrea then held the child under the water in the tub. After he stopped moving, she placed her son neatly on her bed.

After a few minutes, listening to the voices, she deliberately, purposefully, and intentionally drowned three more children in succession: Luke, 2; John, 5; Mary, 6 months. They joined brother Paul on their mother's bed. The eldest, 8-year old Noah, was the most difficult as he thrashed and fought her restraining arms. Noah was left floating in the tub.

Andrea called 911 and told the police she murdered her five children. She then called her husband at work and told him to come home. Despite what she may have believed at the time, as the medical examiner explained during the trial, each of the five children suffered "slow death."

In this chapter, we explore what happens when the defendant is competent to stand trial, but she may not be criminally liable for the act of which she stands accused because she lacks the requisite mental capacity to intentionally commit the crime. While the question of insanity at the time of the criminal offense emerges as a legal defense in court to excuse an intentional criminal act, first responders, criminal investigators, and emergency personnel need to be aware of the issues that emerge when insanity—as opposed to incompetency—is alleged by the defense attorney in the course of a criminal prosecution. What the first responders, from emergency medical team members to police officers, observe and hear at the scene of the crime or upon apprehension of the chief suspect not only may have a bearing on the competency of the accused, but may also substantiate or raise doubt as to the defense of insanity or the likelihood of sanity of the accused.

The scene from the Yates house, as well as any scene of a horrific homicide, will be replayed and re-enacted before a jury if there is a trial and before the judge if there is a sentencing hearing. If sanity is an issue, it will be the observations of the first officers on the scene that will be initially reviewed by the triers of fact. Impartiality, detachment, and compassionate engagement with the defendant is as critical as the preservation of the crime scene. Inhumanity through homicide is always unexpected, but the investigators must be just as professional and composed on the witness stand, sometimes years later, as they were when they first encountered the aftermath of an event like the one in the Yates house.

Chapter Overview

As was described in Chapter 7, incompetency is very different from insanity, although both topics consider the state of mind of the criminally accused for a judicial proceeding. Incompetency means that a person cannot provide legal assistance to his or her attorney, or due to mental illness, disease, or defect cannot understand the nature of the criminal charges or contribute to the preparation of the defense prior to or during a legal proceeding.

Insanity is a defense, akin to self-defense, defense of others, entrapment, or consent, which are described as justification, excuse, or **affirmative defenses**. If the defendant offers an affirmative defense, then the jury or judge can find that although a crime was committed, the elements of the defense, for example, self-defense, negate the requisite specific mental intent necessary to prove the crime was committed. By illustration, in the prologue you learned that Andrea Yates intentionally and deliberately murdered her children. Later court proceedings indicated she was competent and could aid her attorney in the preparation of her defense in the criminal case against her. She understood the criminal accusations and the nature of the charges. She contended, as a criminal defense to the murders, that internal voices, hallucinations, and the diseases of her mind prompted and controlled her conduct and subjugated her free will. The jury accepted her defense to the homicides and found she was not guilty by reason of insanity. As we will learn throughout this chapter, there are different types of mental diseases or defects that constitute a legal defense and defeat the mental intent or *mens rea* to commit a specific intent crime, such as murder.

FRAMING THE ISSUES

We will examine the legal defenses of mental illness as they are presented in court, but we must be cognizant of the fact that there are many different perspectives on how and when the defense is presented in the course of a trial. Each of the defenses implies different aspects of the theory of why the defendant's judgment was affected by a mental disease or disability. Clearly, first responders and providers will not need to know the precise legal terms and courtroom procedures, but it is still important that they understand how and when matters of mental illness arise in the courtroom. The theories of the defense summarize in general categories and descriptions clusters of legal principles that are not necessarily mutually exclusive, but serve as a checklist of how, when, and why evidence of mental illness is presented in a trial.

According to an eight-state study, the insanity defense is used in less than 1 percent of all court cases and, when used, has only a 26 percent success rate. Of the cases where an insanity defense was successfully proved, fully 90 percent of the defendants had been previously diagnosed with a mental illness (Schouten, 2012). Proof of insanity is just one form of a criminal defense from the conviction of a crime. Evidence of other mental illnesses, such as organic mental disability, psychotic disruptions, and personality disorders, can also be presented to prove an individual's mental intent was interrupted by mental illness that actually directed the defendant's purposeful intent to commit a criminal act. Clearly, while a person may understand the wrongfulness of a criminal act or be able to distinguish between right and wrong, overpowering impulses, uncontrollable rages, and psychological impairments can cause a person to engage in criminal behavior. Successful proof that a person committed a crime due to a mental illness may exonerate a defendant or lessen the charges, for example, from first-degree murder to a lesser offense, which results in a lighter prison sentence.

So, why is insanity or mental illness an issue of importance to the first responder or police officer? First, the first person on a scene is the investigator. It will be his observations, recordation, and reports that are used to create and re-create the scene. Piecing together the puzzle of what occurred when a crime or crimes occurred frames how the crime was carried out and what was the motivation or intent of the offender. By understanding the crime scene, the prosecutor and defense attorney can frame their case. The presence of obvious clues, like a dismembered body, informs the legal issues of insanity or mental issues. The inclusion of subtle signs, such as signatures from a serial killer, are held to frame later investigations and tie in other offenses.

Second, in this chapter, we will learn about how the condition of insanity emerges in the course of a trial. By understanding the historical development of the insanity defense, we will trace how the definition that emerged in England in the 1800s is still in use today. As a defense, it is raised by the defense attorney to rebut an element of a crime, that of the *mens rea* or "evil intent," which may be negated by proof of mental illness. In the third section of the chapter, the elements associated with two forms of mental disorder are examined: temporary insanity and the circumstances of a diminished mental capacity. Again, the lack self-control against harming another person is proved in order to mitigate or reduce the criminality of powerful, purposeful, intentional, and irrational conduct. Throughout this chapter and into the epilogue, we will look at insanity through the lens of the first responders. While these issues emerge in the courtroom, the evidence that either proves or disproves the mental state of the defendant starts with the initial police encounter.

HISTORY OF THE INSANITY DEFENSE

The American legal system holds people answerable for engaging in crimes, but as our legal system is based on British common law, we accepted British legal theory that if a person committed a crime while affected by persistent psychiatric disease or intervening mental illness, he or she may not be guilty of the crime due to insanity.

Before 1800, criminal defendants in England who were found not guilty by reason of insanity were set free. Then an attempt was made on the life of King George III while he attended a play (Eigen, 1995). The jury found the attempted assassin, James Hadfield, a member of an extreme religious sect, to be insane; they acquitted him by reason of insanity and he was released. Four days after the jury's decision, Parliament passed the Criminal Lunatics Act of 1800, which required that a person found not guilty by reason of insanity be held in custody "until his Majesty's pleasure shall be known." This law changed the outright release of the defendant to require that although the accused was found not to be guilty of the crime, he was nevertheless to be held in an asylum until released by the monarchy.

Today, under British precedent, as well as American law, a defendant who is found not guilty by reason of insanity may be held by the judge in a closed and locked mental facility until there is sufficient evidence that the mental health of the defendant is, in fact, fully restored (see 18 U.S.C. §4243). A second aspect of insanity that emerges from our adoption of British common law principles that defined insanity emerged in the case of Daniel M'Naghten (Box 8.1).

CRIMINAL PROCEDURE: THE WHEN AND THE HOW OF A PLEA OF INSANITY

After the prosecuting attorney files criminal charges and the defendant appears for the initial court appearance, the defendant has the choice of entering a plea of not guilty or guilty. The defendant can qualify the plea of not guilty with notice of an assertion of a plea of not guilty by reason of insanity; or can qualify the plea of not guilty by asserting a defense of temporary insanity or diminished mental capacity. Disclosure of the use of an affirmative defense then triggers notice to the prosecutor that the mental state of the defendant is a legal issue in the defense of the criminal charge.

Affirmative defenses are a complex topic. Most people are familiar with the affirmative defense of self-defense to justify striking a person in response to a violent attack; mistaken identity as an affirmative defense for the identification of a perpetrator; or the affirmative defense of consent in response to an allegation of rape. The assertion of the affirmative defense of insanity, temporary insanity, or diminished capacity against *any* crime in which there is a necessary element of specific intent may be a new perspective. Technically, an affirmative defense is a set of facts that refute, dispute, or defeat the allegations of the prosecutor. The affirmative defense of mental illness, however, acknowledges the prosecutor's evidence is true, but all of the elements of the crime are not provable: The intent to commit the crime — an essential element — was guided or produced by mental illness and disease.

In the remainder of this chapter, we explore what occurs after the defendant enters this form of plea. We will also consider what happens if a defendant enters a plea of guilty but mentally ill.

BOX 8.1

The Law and Mental Health:
Regina v. Daniel M'Naghten

In 1843, Daniel M'Naghten was charged with the murder of Edward Drummond, secretary to the Prime Minister. At the time of his arrest, he told police that he came to London to murder the Prime Minister, Sir Robert Peel, because persecution by the Tories had destroyed his peace of mind. M'Naghten shot Peel's secretary by mistake. Asserting insanity as a legal defense, M'Naghten's lawyers successfully convinced the jury through expert witnesses that the defendant was delusional and insane and should be found not guilty. At the time, however, the jury was not provided a meaning of insanity.

Queen Victoria took considerable interest in the case. After the acquittal of M'Naghten, she wrote to the Prime Minister to ask for the imposition of a stricter rule for insanity, a highly unusual act for the sovereign. Her interest may have been due to two concerns. First, the avowed reason was that Peel was her prime minister and an attack on a member of government, even if it was unsuccessful, was an attack on the Crown. Second, Queen Victoria had herself been the target of assassination three times by 1842, the most recent one less than a year before M'Naghten fired his shots at Drummond. The Queen ordered a panel of 15 judges to thereafter write a standard to inform, define for, and instruct the jury as to when (or if) insanity was properly proven as a defense to the crime. The panel then wrote the following instruction to guide the trier of fact:

> In all cases that every man is presumed to be sane ... until the contrary be proved ... and that to establish a defense on the ground of insanity, it must be clearly proved *that, at the time of the committing of the act, the party accused was laboring under such a defect of reason, from disease of the mind, as not to know the nature and quality of the act he was doing, or if he did it, he did not know he was doing what was wrong* (Regina v. Daniel M'Naghten, [1843], 8 ER 781, Vol. 8 p. 722) (emphasis added).

This statement—but especially the italicized clause—is the basis of what is known as the **M'Naghten Rule**. In many states, this definition standard still guides judges and juries to determine if the accused successfully established that he or she is not guilty by reason of insanity.

The sentencing orders of M'Naghten are also still in practice today. Although M'Naghten was acquitted by reason of insanity, he spent the rest of his life in mental hospitals, dying in Broadmoor Asylum in 1865, having survived more than 20 years at the notorious Bethlem Hospital, also known as Bedlam.

Sources: Diamond (1956); Moran (1981).

Timing in the Investigation of a Not Guilty/Insanity Plea

The assertion of the insanity defense commonly occurs once formal proceedings against the defendant are filed in court or the accusation commences. It is unlikely that police officers or first responders need to know all the legal nuances of this defense at the onset of an impartial criminal investigation. If an investigation reveals the likelihood that the defendant will raise the issue of insanity, then the responsibility of the detectives and other police officials is to continue collecting evidence objectively and impartially. They know that it is up to them to testify only as to what was observed without comment on the appropriateness of any given defense.

Consider the case of John Wayne Gacy, a prolific serial killer. Between 1972 and 1978, it is alleged that he raped and murdered at least 33 young men and boys in the Chicago area. Despite these horrific crimes (i.e., Gacy slowly suffocated his victims while sexually assaulting them in his home), his allegation that he was insane during the murders was rejected by the jury. Law enforcement detectives testified to the extensive measures Gacy undertook to avoid detection. He was meticulous in his burial and disposal of his victims. His later claim of accidental erotic asphyxiation was discounted by the corner's reports demonstrating the strangulations took hours. Gacy was executed by lethal injection at the Statesville (IL) Correctional Center in 1994.

A side note to the Gacy case illustrates that obsessive voyeurs or watchers of serial murders often emerge during the intensive news coverage of ghastly cases. Author Jason Moss (1999) wrote a book about Gacy and became so enthralled by the serial killer that he frequently communicated with Gacy on death row and even disguised himself to gain access to the notorious murderer. Moss was dubbed a "serial-killer groupie" due to the intensity of his fascination with this class of offenders. Moss committed suicide in 2006 (Kalil, 2006).

The Verdict: Proving Insanity

At the onset of a trial, the prosecution has the burden of proof or responsibility to convince a jury or a judge that the elements of a criminal offense transpired and the defendant was the perpetrator of the crime or crimes. Evidence is presented through the testimony of witnesses, documents, and experts to convince the trier of fact, beyond a reasonable doubt, of the facts alleged in the criminal complaint against the defendant. Remember, the defendant has the right to remain silent during the trial and that silence cannot be considered by the jury or judge as an indicator of guilt. The right to remain silent remains intact throughout the criminal proceedings. The defendant is not required to present a defense.

The key to success in a criminal trial is meeting the burden of proof. The plea of insanity can shift the burden of proof as to whether the mental condition of the defendant excuses the criminality of his offense. The burden of proof is the responsibility of the prosecutor, who must prove the disputed charge(s), factual allegations, and identity of the accused with evidence that is convincing beyond a reasonable doubt. The burden of proof has two components: (1) the **burden of production** and (2) the **burden of persuasion**. The burden of production is the obligation to present evidence to the judge or jury. The burden of persuasion is the duty to convince the judge or jury that there is sufficient reliable and convincing information that satisfies a certain legal standard, such as beyond a reasonable doubt, that the facts as alleged took place. This means that the prosecutor must introduce enough compelling evidence to persuade the trier of fact of the truth of the allegations of the crime. A burden of persuasion in some circumstances is that there be clear and convincing evidence; in a civil case and for some criminal defenses, there need be only a preponderance of the evidence.

If the defendant chooses to do so and presents a defense or refutes and rebuts the evidence, he or she can do so through cross-examination of prosecution witnesses. The defendant can also rebut the evidence or present a defense to the accusation through independent evidence after the state finishes its presentation. This is accomplished through defense witnesses, documents, or expert testimony, or through the testimony of the accused, should she give up the right to remain silent. The defendant can present an alibi defense, a mistaken identity defense, or self-defense to raise doubt as to his or her criminal responsibility.

If insanity or diminished capacity is a defense, then the defendant can rebut the prosecutor's evidence and argue through cross-examining witnesses or in her case-in-chief that she could not control her conduct due to mental illness at the time the crime was committed. Therefore, the prosecution cannot satisfy one of the necessary elements of the crime—*mens rea* or specific intent to commit the crime. Remember, though, a criminal mental state is an essential crime element for the insanity defense to apply. Driving while impaired by alcohol, for example, cannot prompt an insanity defense because the elements of the crime do not include specific intent to drive while impaired. It is a general intent crime. In *United States v. Torniero*, the court rejected a theory of insanity that compulsive gambling led to the crime of interstate transportation of stolen jewelry because the defense failed to link the compulsive conduct of gambling and the crime of theft.

Each state and the federal government have statutory formulae that define appropriate or acceptable legal defenses to the commission of a crime, and the insanity defense is the most controversial of all criminal defenses. In some instances, the prosecutor will present evidence to establish that the defendant was sane at the time of the crime, but then the burden of establishing an insanity defense shifts to the defendant and he assumes the burden of proof. This is known as "shifting the burden of proof." Then it is the duty of the defendant to rebut or refute the state's evidence of sanity against his legal defense through cross-examination of the state's witnesses or in the defendant's case-in-chief.

Remember, however, the defendant is not required to testify and his silence cannot be used as indicia of guilt. In some states, the defense will prove the insanity defense by establishing that the defendant was insane by a **preponderance of the evidence**, or slightly less than a featherweight of 50 percent. Again, this means that mental disease or illness negated the mental intent or *mens rea* necessary for a criminal conviction. In other states, the proof of insanity must be convincing beyond a reasonable doubt.

The issue of who has the burden of proving insanity is a complicated state-by-state legal structure and is the source of much legal commentary and controversy. Unlike any other defense, shifting the burden of proving insanity sometimes is the responsibility of the defendant and sometimes falls to the prosecution (Jackson, 1994; see also 18 U.S.C. §17(b)). In Colorado, Florida, Massachusetts, New Jersey, North Dakota, Oklahoma, and Tennessee, the prosecutor, when faced with an insanity defense, presents evidence that the defendant was *not* insane. For example, in the John Gacy case, the prosecution proved that since he was so methodical in his preparation and cover-up of the murders, he acted knowingly and deliberately. Gacy's attorneys presented evidence of his psychosis and psychopathy in his brutal serial murders, but the jury rejected the defense theories.

Nevertheless, if insanity is a defense, then following the defense's presentation of evidence through expert witnesses, testimony, or documentary evidence, the prosecution presents evidence. This consists of refuting experts and testimony to rebut the defense of insanity by alleging there were other explanations for the murderous, inexplicable conduct other than mental disease. In all cases, the role of the police investigators, first responders, and detectives must be objective, thorough, and detailed as they provide the critical evidence with respect to the relevancy and reliability of sanity or an insanity defense.

For example, in South Carolina in 1995, Susan Smith strapped her two sons, ages 3 years and 14 months old, into their car seats and then let the car roll off the edge of a pier and into a lake (Eftimiades, 1995). She later claimed, as one defense, that she was mentally ill and her illness impaired her judgment when she committed the crimes. Police testimony disclosed that her true motivation was to have a relationship with a wealthy local man who opposed having a family. Her first reports that her children were taken in a carjacking while she was stopped for a red light were also quickly disproved by police investigators; this was improbable because the red light in the isolated intersection where she claimed the carjacking occurred would not have been triggered unless there was cross traffic. Thorough and objective police investigation provided evidence that her intent to kill was motivated by a desire to change her life and her decision that her children were in the way (Chuck, 2015).

The leading U.S. Supreme Court review of the national standards for insanity and the constitutionality of the burden of proof for an insanity plea is found in *Clark v. Arizona* (2006). Clark presented evidence that he shot and killed a police officer at a traffic stop because he believed his town in Arizona was controlled by space aliens. He was a diagnosed schizophrenic and pleaded the insanity defense in hopes that his mental disorder would excuse his criminal mentality. A psychiatrist testified on his behalf. The Supreme Court ruled that Arizona's law placing the responsibility to prove insanity on the defendant was constitutional. The Court also noted the irony of a situation in which a defendant claiming insanity must not be all that crazy if he mounted a defense based on insanity. Of course, this comment by Justice Souter seems to ignore the fact that the mental state he refers to addresses competency at the time of trial and not the defendant's sanity when the crime was committed.

Throughout this chapter, you will read many examples in which the state proved that the defendant was sane at the time of the offense. Similarly, the jury can find that the defendant was insane at the time of the offense and, therefore, is not guilty of the crime. The decision to accept insanity as an excuse or justification for the crime is the final judgment of the jury. An allegation that the state failed to meet this burden of proof is a common ground for appeal. The language for the jury to apply to reach a verdict or decision and accept insanity as a defense to the crime is contained within the "form of the verdict," a set of formal instructions typically given to the jury prior to their deliberations (see Box 8.2).

BOX 8.2

California's Verdict Form for Insanity Defense

You have found the defendant guilty of <insert crime[s]>. Now you must decide whether (he/she) was legally insane when (he/she) committed the crime[s].

The defendant must prove that it is more likely than not that (he/she) was legally insane when (he/she) committed the crime[s].

The defendant was legally insane if:

1. When (he/she) committed the crime[s], (he/she) had a mental disease or defect; AND

2. Because of that disease or defect, (he/she) did not know or understand the nature and quality of (his/her) act or did not know or understand that (his/her) act was morally or legally wrong.

None of the following qualify as a mental disease or defect for purposes of an insanity defense: personality disorder, adjustment disorder, seizure disorder, or an abnormality of personality or character made apparent only by a series of criminal or antisocial acts.

[Special rules apply to an insanity defense involving drugs or alcohol. Addiction to or abuse of drugs or intoxicants, by itself, does not qualify as legal insanity. This is true even if the intoxicants cause organic brain damage or a settled mental disease or defect that lasts after the immediate effects of the intoxicants have worn off. Likewise, a temporary mental condition caused by the recent use of drugs or intoxicants is not legal insanity.]

[If the defendant suffered from a settled mental disease or defect caused by the long-term use of drugs or intoxicants, that settled mental disease or defect combined with another mental disease or defect may qualify as legal insanity. A settled mental disease or defect is one that remains after the effect of the drugs or intoxicants has worn off.]

You may consider any evidence that the defendant had a mental disease or defect before the commission of the crime[s]. If you are satisfied that (he/she) had a mental disease or defect before (he/she) committed the crime[s], you may conclude that (he/she) suffered from that same condition when (he/she) committed the crime[s]. You must still decide whether that mental disease or defect constitutes legal insanity.

[If you find the defendant was legally insane at the time of (his/her) crime[s], (he/she) will not be released from custody until a court finds (he/she) qualifies for release under California law. Until that time (he/she) will remain in a mental hospital or outpatient treatment program, if appropriate. (He/She) may not, generally, be kept in a mental hospital or outpatient program longer than the maximum sentence available for (his/her) crime[s]. If the state requests additional confinement beyond the maximum sentence, the defendant will be entitled to a new sanity trial before a new jury. Your job is only to decide whether the defendant was legally sane or insane at the time of the crime[s]. You must not speculate as to whether (he/she) is currently sane or may be found sane in the future. You must not let any consideration about where the defendant may be confined, or for how long, affect your decision in any way.]

[If you conclude that at times the defendant was legally sane and at other times the defendant was legally insane, you must assume that (he/she) was legally sane when (he/she) committed the crime[s].]

[If you conclude that the defendant was legally sane at the time (he/she) committed the crime[s], then it is no defense that (he/she) committed the crime[s] as a result of an uncontrollable or irresistible impulse.]

If, after considering all the evidence, all twelve of you conclude the defendant has proved that it is more likely than not that (he/she) was legally insane when (he/she) committed the crime[s], you must return a verdict of not guilty by reason of insanity.

Source: California Penal Code §§25, 25.5.

Note: Information included within brackets refers to conditions that may not apply in all cases.

LEGAL TESTS FOR INSANITY

In an insanity defense, as we have learned, the accused admits to committing the crime, but claims innocence owing to a lack of mental capacity to understand that what he or she was doing was wrong. Courts throughout the nation rely on different tests or standards to determine if the accused meets the legal test for insanity when the crime was committed. In this section, we review elements of three primary tests (Hayes, 2017):

1. *M'Naghten Test* — This is based on the British case we reviewed earlier in the chapter. If the defendant has a disease of the mind such that he does not know the nature and quality of the act he was doing, or if he did commit a criminal act, but he did not know that what he was doing was wrong, then the insanity defense prevails.

2. *Irresistible Impulse Test* — A defendant may know that his or her actions are wrong but commits them due to a compulsion prompted by mental illness.

The focus is on the lack of volition or self-control of the accused. In many states, this test is coupled with the M'Naghten test to find that aspects of planning the crime may impede or negate the insanity defense.

3. *Model Penal Code Standard* — This test combines the M'Naghten and the irresistible impulse rules into a common standard that requires evidence of an established history of mental illness, organic brain damage, and uncontrolled volition. Under its definition, psychopaths and sociopaths are prohibited from claiming insanity as a defense.

A fourth standard, the **Durham Test**, is used only in New Hampshire and considers scientific psychological evaluations and diagnosis, rather than conduct. The jury must accept or reject the mental health specialists' expert opinions. Given the reach of the M'Naghten test and the Model Penal Code standard, we turn next to a detailed explanation of how those rules are applied.

Applying the M'Naghten Rule

The M'Naghten Rule focuses on whether the defendant knew or understood right from wrong at the time the offense was committed. States that follow the M'Naghten Rule are Alabama, Alaska (modified), Arizona, California (modified), Florida, Georgia (modified), Iowa, Louisiana, Minnesota, Mississippi, Nebraska, Nevada, New Jersey, New Mexico, North Carolina, Ohio, Oklahoma, Pennsylvania, South Carolina, South Dakota, Texas, Virginia, and Washington. These states accept the M'Naghten principle that requires there be proof that the defendant did not understand the moral wrongfulness of the conduct. Remember, the evidence must be convincing either beyond a reasonable doubt if the prosecution must prove sanity or by a preponderance of the evidence if the defense has the burden of proving the defendant was insane. The M'Naghten test is used as the definition of insanity for the jurors to decide whether to exonerate or excuse the defendant from the criminal consequences of his conduct due to mental illness. Therefore, to establish a defense of insanity, there must be convincing evidence presented to the trier of fact that the defendant, while committing the crime, failed to understand the legal wrongfulness of the conduct. In these cases, with evidence presented through expert psychiatrists, medical history, psychological testing, and information about the crime itself, the judge or jury can exonerate the defendant and excuse the criminality of the offense in light of the mental illness.

If the law requires the state to disprove insanity, then the prosecutor must prove that the defendant was sane, despite any macabre or bizarre conduct preceding the crime. For example, in Colorado, the prosecutor has the burden to prove the defendant understood right from wrong when committing the crime and, therefore, was sane. In this instance, the jury accepts the state's version of the intentional mental state of the accused and finds the defendant guilty as charged. The state's evidence, again through prosecution witnesses, experts, and documents, that the defendant's mental state was such that he comprehended that his behavior was morally wrong, despite *such a defect of reason, from disease of* the mind, as **know** the nature and quality of the act he was doing ... and **know** he was doing what was wrong (emphasis added, citing the M'Naghten Rule).

In this regard, consider the case of James Eagan Holmes. At midnight on July 20, 2012, Holmes, dressed in protective combat gear, walked into a movie theater in Aurora, Colorado (CNN Library, 2017b). He threw two tear gas canisters into the crowd and started to fire his shotguns and handguns, killing 12 people and injuring 70. He fired more than 200 bullets. Upon his capture, he confessed to booby-trapping his apartment with explosives and flammable liquids. While Holmes admitted that he committed the mass murder—at the time, one of the worst in U.S. history—his attorneys argued that he did not know what he was doing. His claims of insanity, however, were not based on his actions or that he was lacking thought and reasoning.

The jury found that Holmes was "sane enough" when he opened fire, despite testimony and evidence of what were clearly psychiatric issues. Police investigators retraced his actions and documented his planning as to the choice of time, location, weaponry, and execution. The detectives testified that Holmes was meticulous in his planning and actions. He told police he did not want his shootings to be confused with an act of terrorism, but only to send a message that "there was no message." He just wanted to be "The Joker," a character from the Batman movies. The jury found that while Holmes may have been delusional and fixated on a fantasy, and that his acts were unconscionable, he was not so psychotic as to be incapable of differentiating between right and wrong. He was found guilty of more than 160 counts of intentional homicide and attempted murder. In reviewing the decision, a reporter noted that

> while Holmes had severe mental illness and schizophrenia, this did not amount to legal insanity when he carried out his rampage. It is perhaps darkly fitting that the jury ruled Holmes, like his purported fictional counterpart, to be mentally disturbed and still guilty of murder (Lennard, 2015: 3).

Jeffery Dahmer and the Insanity Plea: How Insane Do You Have to Be?

Between 1978 and 1991, serial killer Jeffery Dahmer murdered at least 17 men and boys, storing their corpses in vats and saving "trophies" of human skulls and genitalia, sometimes eating the heart and biceps of his victims (*State v. Dahmer*, 1992). The jury ignored previous diagnoses of borderline personality disorder, schizotypal personality disorder, and a psychotic disorder. Dahmer was convicted of all murder charges. Dahmer was beaten to death by a fellow inmate in 1994.

Some commentators have contended that if the plea of insanity does not work with a psychologically damaged person like Dahmer, no other criminal could expect acquittal based on an insanity defense. Other scholars contend that serial killers such as Dahmer, Gacy, and Holmes can never expect to be exculpated by an insanity defense, owing largely but not exclusively to the degree of planning required to commit the crimes and their furtive actions in covering them up.

Applying the Model Penal Code

The **Model Penal Code** follows a different structure when applied in cases of defense of alleged insanity. It is used in Arkansas, Connecticut, Delaware (modified), the District of Columbia, Hawaii, Illinois, Indiana, Kentucky, Maine (modified), Maryland, Massachusetts, Michigan, New York, North Dakota, Oregon, Rhode Island, Tennessee, Vermont, West Virginia, Wisconsin, and Wyoming. Under this standard, also known as the substantial capacity test, the defendant may be found to be not guilty by reason of insanity if two essential components are satisfied. First, the defendant must be diagnosed with a mental disease or mental defect. This means that the defendant has severe intellectual deficiencies or was or is being treated for a profound mental illness, such as schizophrenia, paranoia, or a psychosis.

Second, the defendant must prove that at the time of the incident, he was unable to appreciate or did not possess the cognitive ability to understand the criminality or wrongfulness of the conduct, or lacked the ability to control an impulse that led to the crime. In other words, he did not have the essential mental capacity to commit the offense (Morse, 2011).

As this chapter has shown, it is clear that insanity is a difficult defense. While sadistic and cruel behavior may be inexplicable, a motive for the crime may be discernable. For example, the investigator may need to turn to experts to understand what motivates a killer. Understanding and profiling the behaviors of an aberrant personality may help identify the perpetrator, helping to discover who he is or why he kills. There are federal resources for community responders that can guide and inform them as to the behaviors of a mentally ill person, which could help resolve unthinkable crimes.

Another aspect of studying the insanity defense as a police officer, first responder, or investigator involves identifying a profile of who is a serial killer to help in cases of unsolved murders. Consider the importance of the development of the Federal Bureau of Investigation (FBI) Behavioral Analysis Unit (BAU) as, according to John Douglas, former chief of the FBI's serial killer crime unit, there are typically 25 to 50 active serial killers (Morton, Tillman, and Gaines, 2014; Moss, 2015; see also Gresham, 1993; Silva, 2002). An important part of the FBI's BAU is the National Center for the Analysis of Violent Crimes (see Box 8.3).

GUILTY BUT MENTALLY ILL: GUILTY BUT INSANE

The Insanity Defense Reform Act of 1984 altered the rules of evidence for jury consideration of the defense of mental illness of defendants in federal criminal proceedings, and state laws soon followed the federal standards. The new laws limited the legal relevancy of insanity defenses that were based on long histories of mental disorders, as opposed to evidence of the immediate mental condition of the defendant at the time of the crime. Equally important, federal and then state legislators enacted a legal plea or verdict known

BOX 8.3

Identifying Violent Criminals: National Center for Analysis of Violent Crimes

Identifying a person who is capable of committing inconceivable multiple and serial murders is challenging and yet achievable. Projective profiling is an opportunity to examine likely behaviors, signs of motivating factors, and the personality of a serial killer whose murders have trademarks or patterns. The intensive analysis combines psychology, neurology, and behavioral science to predict likely characteristics and preferences of a violent human predator. The FBI Academy investigatory team at Quantico, Virginia developed a collaborative investigative analysis that emerged from examinations of police investigations of unsolved murders. Known as the National Center for the Analysis of Violent Crimes (NCAVC), the training facility is located at the FBI Academy. Four analysis units are dedicated to establishing assessments in categories that range from counterterrorism, crimes against adults, to crimes against children that are incorporated into the Violent Criminal Apprehension Program, known as ViCAP.

In addition to psychopathy, a lethal combination of thinking disorders, periodic violence, and impulsivity that you read about in Chapter 2, there are also conduct disorders, antisocial behaviors, reactions, and deadly personality disorders. In the aftermath of murders, psychiatrists can testify that the offender met the profile of having an antisocial personality disorder that makes a person capable of indifference to human life. For the moment, however, we will consider how sophisticated analysis can actually describe central characteristics of a person likely to be linked to a particular series of homicides to help law enforcement narrow their search for a suspect. This is a behavioral analysis of the mannerisms, experiences, and psychological make-up of known criminals to correlate them to suspects' patterns, providing insights to solve cases and even to prevent future crimes.

Howard Teton was the founder of the FBI's then revolutionary concept of using theories of applied criminology to identify predictive behavior in order to capture killers. Teton started out as a California police officer in 1958 and received a degree in criminology at the University of California, Berkeley. During college, Teton saw parallels between his classes in forensics and abnormal and criminal psychology and the crime scenes he encountered on the job. After he became an FBI agent, he convinced the Bureau to recognize there was an "M.O." — *modus operandi* or method of operation — that typified psychotic or psychopathic murderers.

In 1977, Theodore "Ted" Bundy escaped from prison in Colorado. Bundy was one of the most prolific sadistic serial killers, having confessed to killing at least 30 young women. The

FBI published a synopsis of its psychological assessment of Bundy's M.O. to law enforcement agents: Bundy looked for victims at beaches and colleges and preferred young, attractive women with long hair parted in the middle. Bundy was eventually stopped for a traffic violation in Florida, where police were able to quickly link items found in his car to the published behaviors associated with Bundy's murders in three other states.

The Academy's training methodology relies on outlining the facts of a case and then examining how aspects of the criminal's personality are revealed in the crime scene. The ViCAP relies on computer analysis to identify and link signature aspects in violent serial crimes. In a thorough study to both debunk the myths about serial killers (e.g., they don't stop killing because they are in prison, college, or admitted to a mental facility) and supplement an enforcement data base, FBI agents Robert Morton, Jennifer Tillman, and Stephanie Gaines prepared a study of methodologies to assist in unsolved serial criminal investigations. In a meticulous data review, the agents provided greater scope to law enforcement investigators who work on active, unsolved murder cases.

According to Morton, Tillman, and Gaines of the FBI's Behavioral Science Unit, prior to arrest, 32.6 percent of the offenders were formally diagnosed by a mental health professional with a psychiatric disorder — 42.9 percent with a personality disorder, 19 percent with a psychotic disorder, 11.9 percent with developmental disorders, and 11.9 percent with mood disorders. To develop the profile of the serial killer, data analysis correlates the likely motivation of the killer with the type of body disposal; associated military service; psychiatric disorders; the lure ruse; the race, gender, and age of the victims; and the lack of any relationship with the victim. In most cases, the motivation is sexual, but DNA is infrequently found. While circumstantial motivation is difficult to determine, the serial murderer may have multiple purposes that evolve throughout the series of murders. The NCAVC has uniquely qualified experts who then provide insightful investigative and behavioral assistance.

The work at the academy is so predictively precise that when FBI agents were searching for the kidnappers of the president of ExxonMobil, Sidney Reso, in 1992 the government behaviorists correctly predicted that the people who captured Reso were not, as suspected, eco-terrorists. They were, as the FBI factually and precisely surmised, a local couple who liked expensive things, lived beyond their means, were familiar with Exxon security patterns, and owned a golden retriever.

Similarly, in the investigation of a horrific serial killer of young lovers in Italy, the FBI's analysis reported that the killer was of a type known in their data base: a lone, sexually impotent male with a pathological hatred of women who satisfied his sexual cravings through killing. As noted in the book *Monster of Florence* by Douglas Preston and Mario Spezi, the serial killer's profile clearly met the description of a likely suspect, but due to Italy's investigatory process, the likely offender was not questioned.

Sources: FBI News (2013); Morton et al. (2013); Preston and Spezi (2008).

as **guilty but mentally ill (GBMI)**. Alaska, Arizona, and Georgia permit some form of an insanity defense, but also authorize the jury to return a verdict or for the defendant to enter a plea of "guilty except insane" or "guilty but mentally ill." (The ironic contradiction in the term "guilty except insane" has produced many legal debates. See Stimpson 1994; Phillips and Woodman 2008; Stoll 2009.) Idaho, Montana, Kansas, and Utah rejected any insanity defense and permit only a plea or verdict of "guilty but mentally ill." These states do not recognize insanity as a defense to any crime.

The finding of "guilty, but mentally ill," (GBMI) acknowledges that while the defendant committed the crime and was mentally ill at the time of the event, the mental illness was not so severe as to relieve her of criminal responsibility. The defendant who receives a verdict of GBMI or enters a plea of GBMI to the criminal charge is sentenced as if she was found guilty. The court can determine whether the defendant should receive mental health treatment in jail or prison or as a condition of probation. This is essentially an advisory for mental health treatment. Then, if the defendant is declared to be "cured" of the mental illness, then she is required to serve the rest of the sentence in prison, jail, or on probation without further mental health interventions or conditions.

The outcome is different for a defendant acquitted with an insanity defense. If found not guilty by reason of insanity, then the defendant is committed to a mental hospital until there is a declaration of finding by a reviewing judge that the individual is no longer in need of mental health treatment (Kutys and Esterman, 2000. The defendant is not incarcerated in jail or prison.

In this regard, consider the following two cases. In the first case, Jared Lee Loughner attempted to murder Congresswoman Gabrielle Giffords and killed U.S. District Court Chief Judge John Roll, as well as other Tucson, Arizona citizens. Once restored to competency through medication and treatment, he pleaded "guilty except insane," pursuant to Ariz. Rev. Stat. §13-502(A) (2007). The plea was accepted in the U.S. federal court and avoided the possibility of the death sentence. He was sentenced to life, plus 140 years in prison.

In the second case, Andrea Curry-Demus killed Kia Johnson by enticing her to her home, paralyzing her with a drug, cutting Johnson's infant from her womb, and then wrapping the victim's head in plastic and duct tape until she died. In this instance, the Pennsylvania judge refused to enter a verdict of not guilty by reason of insanity, but instead directed that Curry-Demus be found guilty but insane. She was sentenced to life without the possibility of parole (Reed, 2010).

The cases involving persons who later employ an insanity defense are clearly complicated. Their defenses may seem simple at first glance, but the combinations of legal elements and medical diagnoses are far from simple. Moreover, as suggested in Box 8.4, the complexities of such cases begin at investigation.

BOX 8.4

What Would You Do?

Defense attorneys also hire private investigators to gather evidence and interview witnesses. What types of physical evidence, witness statements, and records would be relevant and/or admissible for jury consideration for a defense of insanity? What if, as a trained investigator, you disagreed with the theory of defense prepared by the defendant's attorney? Do you have any obligation to speak up, and what are your obligations regarding corroborating evidence?

TEMPORARY INSANITY AND DIMINISHED CAPACITY DEFENSES

The jury or finder of fact can also accept alternative defense reasoning to exonerate the accused based on the defense of **temporary insanity** or the defense of diminished capacity. In these circumstances, the accused may have a history of stability, mental acuity, long-term employment, and sometimes strong family relationships. However, owing to an external event or highly stressful repressed memory, the defendant "snaps" or breaks down and commits a violent crime. The defense attorney presents evidence of a personal psychological trauma, a history of undisclosed parallel psychiatric illnesses, or a medical condition that renders a person unable to know or control behavior at the time of the commission of the crime. It assumes that the person cannot choose between right and wrong or control the spontaneous wrongful actions at the moment of the crime due to extraneous circumstances. Impairment by drugs or alcohol is usually not admissible as evidence for the defense of temporary insanity because the offender intentionally consumed alcohol or substances and could reasonably have anticipated the resulting loss of mental control (Covey, 2009).

Historically referred to as the crime of passion defense, temporary insanity exonerations were historically linked to an impassioned spouse who found his or her mate *in flagrante delicto*, that is, committing the very act of wrongdoing. The most common instigator of responsive violence was finding a loved one in an act of sexual infidelity with another person. The first example of the defense plea for temporary insanity in the United States came in the 1859 trial of Daniel Edgar Sickles, a U.S. Congressman. In 1852, 33-year old Sickles married Teresa Bagioli, age 15 and pregnant with his child. Seven years later, he shot and killed his friend Philip Barton Key II for having an affair with Teresa, catching them *in flagrante delicto*. Sickles' lawyer, future Secretary of War Edwin Stanton, proposed a defense never tried before in the United States: not guilty due to temporary insanity. Stanton claimed Sickles was so enraged at his wife's faithlessness that he could not differentiate between right and wrong. Sickles was acquitted of murder as not guilty for reason of insanity; moreover, he was further acclaimed by his peers for ridding the District of Columbia of Key, a notorious adulterer. Of historical interest, the victim was the son of Francis Scott Key, who wrote "The Star-Spangled Banner." For his part, Sickles gained fame as the general whose unauthorized movement of Union troops at Gettysburg in 1863 may have helped win the battle (Arrington, 2015).

Today, the temporary insanity plea or defense to a crime is presented to mitigate the possibility of premeditation, although there may be evidence of planning, purchase, or deliberate conduct. The essence of defense for the factually guilty person is that honor, revenge, or tragic circumstances—not mental illness in its more traditional form—compelled the defendant to commit a criminal act. The facts in the case often reveal a conflict between the victim and the offender.

Diminished capacity is not the same defense as insanity, temporary or otherwise. As we will explore throughout the rest of the chapter, **diminished capacity** offers a psychological explanation by which the defendant admits that she broke the law but, due to long-term deteriorating circumstances, should not be held fully criminally responsible for doing so. Her mental state was impaired or "diminished." Essentially, as a result of mental illness, disease, or disability, the psychological ability to form a specific intent to commit a particular criminal offense, such as murder, is impeded or disrupted. In some instances, defense expert testimony will inform the jury that an unrelated condition triggered a hallucination or distortion that created an illusion and enabled criminal behavior in an otherwise law-abiding person. In this toxic combination of mental illness and harmful behavior, a different or unrelated rationale emerges in the mind of the offender to justify intentional criminal conduct.

The scenario presented in Box 8.5 provides a reflection on the complications that emerge with temporary insanity or, perhaps, applicable diminished capacity. This story, based on a true account, raises questions about when, why, or if criminal conduct should be prosecuted.

It is the defense's burden of proof to establish by a preponderance of the facts that the accused has, in the language of the law, had an episodic break from reality that interfered or affected moral judgment and committed the crime (Berger, McNeil, and Binder, 2012). For example, in 1994, national talk show host Jenny Jones produced a program about men who had secret crushes on other men. During the taping of the program, Scott Bernard Amedure admitted he had a crush on his buddy Jonathan Schmitz, who thought he was meeting his ex-girlfriend when he accepted the invitation to "meet someone with a secret crush on him" on the talk show.

Schmitz rebuffed Amedure's advances, which included a description of Amedure's sexual fantasy. Three days later, Schmitz purchased a 12-gauge shotgun, confronted his "admirer" at his home, and killed Amedure. The defense presented a "gay panic" defense,

BOX 8.5

Thinking About the Issues

A father witnesses his son, Jason, age 12, struck in the head by a fly ball at a professional baseball game. Unconscious, Jason is rushed to the hospital and after hours of surgery, his father is told that while Jason will live, he will remain in a vegetative state. All expenses are paid for by insurance and the baseball team. Six months later, the father goes to the hospital care unit, where he strikes and seriously injures a nurse who is caring for the boy. He then pulls the feeding tube and breathing support systems from his son. The father has a gun and threatens to shoot all who approach until his son dies. He then surrenders.

1. What defenses, if any, could be available to the father?
2. Should prosecution continue or is this a situation for a prosecutorial decision of nolle prosequi, a Latin phrase meaning "unwilling to prosecute," but which in the law means "do not prosecute."
3. What other options covered in this chapter may apply to this scenario?
4. Which defense do you think applies: temporary insanity or diminished capacity?
5. Did the father "snap" or mentally fall apart?

which was defined as a state caused by undesired homosexual advances. However, the jury did not believe the defense, finding Schmitz guilty of second-degree murder. He was sentenced in 1996 to 25-50 years in prison. His conviction was overturned, and a new trial ordered. The 1999 trial result was the same: Guilty and a prison sentence of 25-50 years. He was released from prison in 2017.

As a postscript to the Schmitz case, *The Jenny Jones Show* was later sued for negligence, the claim being that the show and its host had created a hostile scenario without considering the social consequences. A jury awarded $25 million to Amedure's family; however, upon review, the appellate court denied that *The Jenny Jones Show* had predictable liability and vacated the judgment. The Michigan Supreme Court declined to hear the case upon appeal (Swenson, 2017).

The "Twinkie" Defense

The **"Twinkie" Defense** is not a recognized legal defense, but is a catchall term coined by reporters during the trial of former San Francisco City Supervisor Dan White for the murder of San Francisco City Supervisor Harvey Milk and Mayor George Moscone. White had been a highly organized, clean-cut, nutritionally conscious athlete when he started to binge on junk food and began to emotionally unravel. White entered City Hall by climbing through a basement window to avoid metal detectors, evaded the mayor's body guard, shot and killed Moscone, reloaded the gun, and then walked across the building and murdered Harvey Milk.

At trial, the defense attorneys asserted that it was White's consumption of junk food that triggered homicidal tendencies. Moreover, the courtroom testimony referred to Ding Dongs® and Ho Hos®, not Twinkies®. A defense psychologist successfully convinced the jury that White's over-consumption of a junk food diet—by whatever name—was evidence of White's increasing psychotic disorders. The jury found White to be incapable of premediated murder, accepting the explanation that his conduct was due to his diminished capacity resulting from blasts of refined sugar and a sugared food diet that triggered depression. They returned a verdict of guilty of voluntary manslaughter, rather than first-degree homicide, for which White was sentenced to eight years in prison.

Post-Traumatic Stress Disorder

Post-traumatic stress disorder (PTSD) is a mental illness that often emerges as a psychiatric traumatic response to war or other violent confrontations. Essentially, PTSD presents through dissociative flashbacks, hyperarousal symptoms, survivor guilt, and sensation-seeking behaviors. As the basis of a criminal mental health defense, by offering expert witnesses, defense attorneys present the PTSD diagnosis to explain the defendant's actions and therefore exonerate him from criminal activity. Non-criminal behaviors associated with PTSD include, but are not limited to, the following: fatigue, muscle/joint pain, headache, difficulty concentrating, memory loss, sleep disturbance, and skin rash. In Box 8.6, we assess what may be considered as evidence in a PTSD case.

BOX 8.6

Evidence for PTSD

In 1979, James David Houston, an Army veteran, killed a man who Houston thought was reaching for a gun. Houston said they were in the restroom and the victim made a derogatory racial remark and then reached for something in his pocket. The defense attorney presented evidence that Houston had been in heavy combat situations, and put forth the theory that the accused was in a dissociative mental state at the time of the murder and furthermore that he had delusions that he was in combat or under attack when the crime occurred.

Houston was convicted of second-degree murder, but that conviction was successfully appealed on the basis of the state's failure to bifurcate the trial, as the defendant employed two affirmative defenses, self-defense and temporary insanity. The appellate court ruled that since there were two possible defenses, the judge should have determined which, if either, defense was relevant. At retrial, Houston pleaded nolo contendere (no contest) to manslaughter charges and was sentenced to 15 years, 3 years being suspended.

Sources: Berger et al. (2012); *Houston v. State* (1979).

Note that the PTSD form of diminished mental capacity, like other defenses, is not limited to homicides. Consider the following three cases. In the 1995 case of *United States v. Cartagena-Carrasquillo*, the defendants, charged with possession of cocaine–related offenses, attempted to argue that due to the stress of war and combat, they did not know the difference between right and wrongful conduct. Although the defense was rejected as having an insufficient basis to enable the jury to consider its relevancy, this same plea was accepted in the 1995 case of *United States v. Rezaq*, which arose from a charge of air-craft piracy. In contrast, in the case of *State v. Percy*, a Vietnam War veteran successfully mounted an insanity defense based on having a PTSD flashback that resulted in an accu-sation in 1986 of sexual assault and kidnapping. His claims raised appellate review issues, in which Percy's statement that he was not in control of his behavior during the crime was challenged, along with questions as to proper jury consideration of the expert testimony as to his sanity (Berger et al., 2012).

Battered Spouse Syndrome

A subset of PTSD is a form of temporary insanity called the **battered spouse syndrome**, also known as **battered wife** or **battered child syndrome** (Downs, 1996; Dutton and Painter, 1993; Kempe, Silverman, et al., 1962). Originally coined by psychologist Lenore Walker (1979), the condition of battered spouse syndrome is said to exist when a partner, or a child, has a documented developmental response of helplessness to mental and physical abuse insti-gated by a person with whom he or she has an intimate or familial relationship. After series of incidents or years of abuse, the victim turns on the domestic offender with rage and vio-lence that often ends in murder or mayhem. It is presented here as a theory of a legal, court-room-justified defense in the context of loss of criminal intent, but has social connotations as an outcome of domestic violence. Battered spouse syndrome is not mental illness per se, but the resulting violence against the abuser is defensible as a mental breakdown.

Domestic abuse follows an extremely predictable pattern. The abuser wins over the partner with lots of affection, grand gestures, and pressures for an exclusive, personal commitment. This "honeymoon" is quickly followed by episodes of emotional, physical, and psychological abuse that is pointed and quick, such as a slap, a public insult, or hit-ting the wall instead of the partner. The abusive acts are followed by a responsive period of excessive emotional reactions, romantic efforts, and a temporary lull from confronta-tion. The next confrontation escalates into more physical violence, with stronger isolating behaviors, greater psychological tension, and deeper undermining of the victim that is followed by even higher levels of romance, control, remorse, and demonstrative guilt with remonstration for forgiveness. As the violence becomes more profound, so do the levels of manipulation for responsive love and affection until the recipient partner believes that the triggering violence and abuse is the fault of the victim. The cycle continues until there is unrelenting co-dependence involving control through violence and forgiveness with unhealthy fears and terror. In rare instances, the victim will break and respond with vio-lence in a form of temporary insanity.

Three cases are instructive in this context. First, in a San Diego County prosecution, a jury acquitted a woman who killed her drunken husband. Tired of the ongoing physical abuse and following a harsh beating, she took the large pot of the family's hot breakfast oatmeal and slowly drenched her passed-out husband. Before dying, he told officers that he felt "a burning sensation," by way of explaining the extent of his injuries. The jury found the woman's evidence of scars, broken bones, and police calls for service exonerated her intentional, ultimately murderous action. [NOTE: Co-author Anne Segal worked as a law clerk on this case in 1980 and believes it was one of the first times this defense was successfully presented.]

Second, in a 1994 prosecution, Lorena Bobbitt claimed that in a violent confrontation, her husband of four years raped her and then passed out in an alcoholic stupor. She then found a knife and cut off his penis, tossing it into a field from the window of her car as she drove away after the incident. She was arrested; shortly thereafter the penis was recovered and re-attached following a ten-hour surgery. During the trial, the jury heard evidence of sexual selfishness, and expert witnesses for both sides painted a picture of ongoing abuse in which Lorena emotionally unraveled after her husband threatened her. His exact words, she claimed, were: "I will find you, whether we're divorced or separated. And wherever I find you, I'll have sex with you whenever I want to." Lorena's attorneys argued that this pattern of abuse and rape created an "irresistible impulse" to protect herself, which qualified as defensible insanity justified in light of the abuse. The jury accepted her defense and she was absolved of the crime.

By contrast, the third case involves a murder investigation in Adams County, Illinois (*People v. Fleming*, 1987). In 1986, Bessie Fleming, a wealthy farmer's wife, claimed that an intruder shot her husband, Tom. She then said she shot her husband as he attempted to shoot her. Finally, she claimed that she shot her husband after years of his physical abuse. Prosecutorial investigations disclosed that there was a history of reports of abuse. Defense and prosecutorial experts agreed that Ms. Fleming was a battered woman. However, the prosecution claimed that she was mentally stable at the time of the homicide. The fact that Ms. Fleming's account as to why she shot husband in the back through a blanket changed during her three separate taped versions of the incident weakened her defense. Moreover, forensic research by the law enforcement officers found that Ms. Fleming, the family book keeper, had drained accounts, failed to pay taxes, and failed to pay loans, and that she had embezzled a substantial amount of money from her husband's business accounts. Her defense requesting exoneration due to the history of abuse was rejected by the jury, and she was found guilty of murder.

Homicidal Somnambulism: The "Sleepwalking Defense"

Violent sleepwalking, known in its extreme form as homicidal somnambulism, is another example of a diminished capacity defense (Guy, 2015). In 1846, Albert Tirrell killed Maria Bickford, his mistress, by slitting her throat. The facts in the case were never in dispute. However, Tirrell's lawyer, Rufus Choate, a famed Boston litigator, offered a unique defense at trial. He stated that Tirrell, long known to suffer from sleepwalking, killed Bickford, if indeed he did kill her, when overcome by "the insanity of sleep." The defense convinced the jury that Tirrell should not be held accountable for Bickford's death. Not satisfied with one acquittal, Choate used the same defense when Tirrell was charged with setting several fires in a vain attempt to cover up the murder. Once again, Choate's new defense swayed the jury and Tirrell was acquitted.

Through 2005 the somnambulism defense had been employed 68 times with varying degrees of success (Guy, 2016). For example, consider the defendants' fates in two modern cases that employed this defense. First, Joseph Mitchell was acquitted of strangling his 4-year old son and attempting to murder his two other children, ages 13 and 10, who then fought him off (Williams, 2015). The defense expert witness testified in this Durham, North Carolina case that the defendant was effectively unconscious or in a deep sleep at the time of his attack. Stress and lack of sleep triggered a non-REM parasomnia, the modern technical definition of the insanity of sleep. In this instance, the prosecution unsuccessfully attempted to prove that financial difficulties compelled Mitchell's violent actions against his children. The investigators established Mitchell's financial difficulties and the absence of non-REM parasomnia history as their theory of his motives, but the jury accepted the defendant's version of events (*Chicago Tribune*, 2015).

Compare this result to the case described in *Arizona v. Falater*. In 1997, Scott Falater stabbed his wife Yarmila 44 times, dragged her into a backyard pool, and held her head underwater. He provided evidence of sleepwalking and claimed that he was sleep-deprived at the time of the crime. However, the police found that Falater tried to conceal evidence of the crime, hiding bloody objects in a Tupperware container in his car. A neighbor witnessed the actions by the pool, testifying that the defendant motioned to his dog to lie down, a possible sign of consciousness. Found guilty, he was sentenced to life in prison without the possibility of parole.

There are numerous other psychological behaviors that present as uncontrollable acts and therefore are relevant to a criminal defense to a specific intent crime. For example, **pyromania** is the uncontrollable desire to set fire to things for the psychological gratification derived from starting and observing the fire. This psychological behavior is used to negate the specific *mens rea* requirement for murder, enabling a conviction for a second-degree homicide (*Faulkenberry v. State*). With a **mutually amnesic relationship** defense, an unconscious personality commits a criminal offense of which the conscious personality may have no awareness; therefore the lack of cognition can be used to lessen criminality. Multiple personality or multiple identity disorders are characterized by the presence of two or more distinct identities that alternatively take control of behavior, masking the ability to recall personal information, and arguably enabling the offender to shift the mental culpability. These defenses are also used as a mitigation for criminal responsibility but are not outright exonerating defenses.

These are all unique pleas/verdicts that are instructive about the mental condition of a person when a crime is committed. The questions remain as to when the actual purpose and intent of the offender are affected by mental disorders and as to whether the loss of mental control, acuity, or cognitive reasoning should lessen the penalty for or excuse harm to another person. Investigation and documentation of behaviors that either substantiate or invalidate diminished capacity, temporary insanity, and psychological impairment point to the significant roles played by both first responders and police investigators in determining the status of the accused's mental state at the time of the crime and its relevance later at a trial or guilty plea proceeding.

EPILOGUE

This is a composite vignette, taken from several real cases and fictionalized to protect the identities of the people involved.

Sue and Bert were married for nearly 40 years, having met as preteens in middle school and having married right after high school graduation. John sold used cars, and Sue was a waitress. Quiet people, they had no close friends and never associated with a church or other community organizations. There had never been any children, but, as they often remarked to each other, they had each other.

Bert noticed that Sue had started to "drift off," unaware that she had just repeated a story or had answered a question with a non-responsive answer. Never good with names or directions, Sue started having confusion about both people and locations. They both laughed when she told him that she wandered through the local hardware store looking for milk and eggs. After a couple of months, her mental state became worse, and she accidentally set the kitchen on fire after she forgot that she was making a cheese sandwich and walked outdoors to work in the garden. Bert found the car keys in the freezer, the iron inside the washing machine, and food beneath the sofa pillow.

The local doctor was baffled as to the cause of her deteriorating mental condition. In her late 50s, she did not have the symptoms of Alzheimer's disease and had no personal or family history of mental illness. A specialist they consulted eliminated all the "usual suspects," as brain scans showed no tumors and a series of neurological tests all but eliminated all forms of dementia. Given her history and recent events, he suggested that Sue had a dissociative disorder. In this disease, sufferers exhibit severe disturbances or changes in memory, consciousness, identity, and general awareness of themselves and their surroundings. The specialist prescribed a regimen of drugs and other treatments, but he was not optimistic about a quick or complete recovery.

Bert hired 24-hour home health providers and their monthly bills skyrocketed, exceeding $6,000. They had health insurance, but it did not cover long-term care. Their savings being quickly depleted, Bert had to work longer hours at the car lot just to meet their daily expenses. After two months, he could no longer afford 24-hour care, and increasingly Bert resorted to locking Sue in their bedroom, which had an attached bathroom. He left her with adequate food and drink, but no access to the outside world beyond a television tuned to the same channel 24/7.

After a year of Sue's downward spiraling mental health and upward spiraling medical expenses, Bert was heartbroken. He adored Sue and had never loved another person more than he loved her. Ordinary medical expenses and the healthcare bills from Sue's mental illness diagnosis continued to eat into their savings. The vivacious, cheerful woman he had loved his entire life had morphed into a disheveled, foul-mouthed stranger who stared vacantly at him or the television. When she addressed him, she screamed obscenities and insults.

More than this, however, Bert was exhausted and mentally fragile. He knew that if he put her in long-term residential care, it would be the final financial straw. The only other option was indigent placement in a county mental hospital, under which they would have to declare bankruptcy, signing over literally all their assets to the county and leaving him penniless as a 58-year old man. He also knew that if she could comprehend her situation, she would not want to continue living. In fact, during a last moment of lucidity, Sue, in the presence of a home health nurse, begged Bert to help her die.

Two weeks later, Bert came home to find Sue had chopped up a prized ceramic animal collection. He stared at Sue as she played with the painted chips. He then filled the bathtub, emptying it because he thought the water was too cold. He refilled it with warmer water. Bert then dressed his wife in her wedding dress, sprayed her with his favorite perfume, and put lipstick on her. Moving her into the bathtub, he held Sue under the water and calmly watched as she struggled briefly and then stopped. He laid her on the bed and called 911. When the first responders arrived on the scene, Bert admitted them to the house, saying, "This is what Sue wanted, and I couldn't refuse her last conscious wish."

Upon reviewing Bert's case, the county prosecuting attorney is left in a quandary. Clearly, Bert intended to take Sue's life, which fit the state's definition of first-degree murder. However, this tragic case could elicit several different legal actions from the prosecuting attorney's office. Consider each one in turn.

1. A defense attorney could argue at trial that this was a case of temporary insanity, where Bert's aberrant and illegal conduct derives from a highly emotional and stressful situation that made him incapable of making a sane and informed decision about Sue's request to end her life. That is, at the time the crime was committed, Bert's judgment was so clouded by the events of the past six months that he was incapable of knowing the exact nature of his alleged criminal act. This defense hinges on states of sanity before the act and after the act; however, convincing the jury that the defendant was suffering from a time-specific case of diminished capacity is a tall order for any lawyer.

2. The prosecuting attorney could proceed with single counts of both first- and second-degree murder and let the jury decide the appropriate charge and verdict. Bert's acts were intended to make his life better and did not "put her out of her misery." She was not in pain, she was not suffering. He killed Sue knowingly, deliberately, and intentionally. The doctors said there was a possibility of recovery, but Bert wanted her out of the way quickly.

Which course of action do you think would be appropriate for the state to take in this case? Reflecting on the content of this chapter, what is the basis of your choice?

SUMMARY

▶ There is a clear distinction between incompetency to stand trial or proceed with the judicial process and the defense to a criminal charge of insanity: If a person is incompetent, the prosecution cannot proceed until competency is restored; if a person pleads not guilty by reason of insanity, then the defense of insanity is used to negate intentional mental culpability.

▶ The mental state of the defendant at the time the crime was committed is an element of proof when mens rea is in issue.

▶ The burden of proving insanity depends on the law in the state where the crime was committed, with some states requiring the prosecutor to prove the defendant was sane at the time of the crime and other states shifting the burden of proof of insanity to the defendant. In the latter case, the state rebuts the defense with expert witnesses, testimony, and documentary evidence.

▶ Three major theories or legal frameworks are used by the different states to prove whether a defendant is insane: the M'Naghten test, the irresistible impulse test, and the Model Penal Code standard. Essentially, each test requires proof of a substantial mental illness that accompanies the inability to distinguish right from wrong or the inability to control the criminal conduct.

▶ The FBI has developed anticipatory profiling of serial killers and offenders to help law enforcement narrow their search for offenders of unsolved serial crimes, such as murder and rape, by focusing on their mental motivations and criminal signatures.

▶ Some states have adopted an additional form of plea or verdict known as "guilty but mentally ill."

▶ In using the defense of temporary insanity, the defendant alleges that an episodic breakdown or "snap" caused her to commit an intentional criminal offense.

▶ Different legal theories of diminished capacity are presented as defenses to juries throughout the United States, including post-traumatic stress disorder, battered spouse syndrome, bingeing on junk foods, and sleepwalking.

▶ The defenses of temporary insanity and diminished capacity for the criminal offense mitigate or reduce the criminality of the offense and often reduce the criminal accusation to a lesser offense, enabling the defendant to serve less prison time or to be eligible for probation.

CHAPTER REVIEW QUESTIONS

1. Compare and contrast incompetency (Chapter 7) and insanity (this chapter). What is the significance of each term for the criminal justice process?

2. Provide an analysis of the historical evolution of the insanity defense, giving special attention to the M'Naghten Rule.

3. How is insanity proven or disproven? What type of witnesses are used? What type of experts are presented? What facts are relevant if an insanity defense is presented?

4. Compare and contrast the M'Naghten Rule and the Model Penal Code. Explain why you prefer one standard over the other.

5. What is a "form of the verdict" for the insanity defense? What is being used in your state? Where do you find the form of the verdict? Do these instructions provide enough structure to enable the jury to correctly apply the standards for insanity to the criminal offense?

6. Andrea Yates was sent to a low-security mental hospital in Texas and will likely remain there for the rest of her life. Do you think that her sentence is a just result given the finding of the jury?

7. The chapter reviewed four alternative defenses that would mitigate, diminish, or exculpate a person's guilt. What are they? Rank them from most credible to least credible, indicating the basis for your rankings.

8. "The burden of proof can shift from the defendant to the prosecution if the state law requires the government to prove the defendant was sane, rather than insane, when the crime was committed." What does this statement mean? How is it explained to the jury? Does the jury need to know that there must be proof beyond a reasonable doubt that the defendant was sane at the time of the crime?

KEY TERMS

Affirmative defenses
Battered spouse/wife/child syndrome
Burden of persuasion
Burden of production
Diminished capacity
Guilty but mentally ill
In flagrante delicto

M'Naghten Rule
Model Penal Code
Modus operandi
Mutually amnesic relationship
Post-Traumatic Stress Disorder (PTSD)
Pyromania

REFERENCES

Adams, C., and C. Adams (September 1, 2016). "Andrea Yates now: Hospitalized mom still 'grieves for her children' 15 years after drowning them." *People Crime*. Retrieved at http://people.com/crime/andrea-yates-now-she-grieves-for-her-children-15-years-after-drownings/ on 10 September 2017.

American Psychiatric Association (2012). "*DSM-IV* and *DSM-5* Criteria for the Personality Disorders." Arlington, VA: American Psychiatric Association. Retrieved at http://www.psi.uba.ar/academica/carrerasdegrado/psicologia/sitios_catedras/practicas_profesionales/820_clinica_tr_personalidad_psicosis/material/dsm.pdf on 28 July 2017.

American Psychiatric Association (2013). *Diagnostic and Statistical Manual of Mental Disorders*. 5th ed. Arlington, VA: American Psychiatric Association.

Arrington, B.T. (January 9, 2015). "The temporary insanity defense comes to America." *We're History*. Retrieved at http://werehistory.org/temporary-insanity/ on 20 July 2017.

Associated Press (June 7, 1999). "Sleepwalking given as a defense by man in killing of wife." *The New York Times*. Retrieved at http://www.nytimes.com/1999/06/07/us/sleepwalking-given-as-defense-by-man-in-killing-of-wife.html on 3 February 2018.

Banner, A. (June 1, 2015). "The James Holmes trial and the insanity defense." Huffington Post. Retrieved at http://www.huffingtonpost.com/adam-banner/the-james-holmes-trial-an_b_7418648.html on 22 June 2017.

Berger, O., D.E. McNiel, and R.L. Binder (2012). "PTSD as a criminal defense: A review of case law." *Journal of the American Academy of Psychiatry and the Law* 40(4): 509-521.

Chicago Tribune (March 12, 2015). "Violent sleepwalking defense works for boy's strangler." Retrieved at http://www.chicagotribune.com/news/nationworld/chi-violent-sleepwalking-defense-20150312-story.html on 11 September 2017.

Chuck, E. (June 23, 2016). "Susan Smith, Mother Who Killed Kids: Something Went Very Wrong that Night." *NBC News*. Retrieved at https://www.nbcnews.com/news/us-news/susan-smith-mother-who-killed-kids-something-went-very-wrong-n397051 on 9 June 2017.

CNN Library (June 22, 2017). "Andrea Yates facts." *CNN*. Retrieved at http://www.cnn.com/2013/03/25/us/andrea-yates-fast-facts/index.html on 23 August 2017.

CNN Library (July 2, 2017). "Colorado theater shooting fast facts." *CNN*. Retrieved at http://www.cnn.com/2013/07/19/us/colorado-theater-shooting-fast-facts/index.html on 11 August 2017.

Cohen, A. (March 11, 2012). "10 years later, the tragedy of Andrea Yates." *The Atlantic*. Retrieved at https://www.theatlantic.com/national/archive/2012/03/10-years-later-the-tragedy-of-andrea-yates/254290/ on 19 August 2017.

Covey, R.D. (2009). "Temporary insanity: The strange life and times of the perfect defense." *Boston University Law Review* 91: 1597-1688.

Diamond, B.L. (1956). "Isaac Ray and the trial of Daniel M'Naghten." *American Journal of Psychiatry* 112: 651-6.

Downs, D.A. (1996). *More Than Victims: Battered Women, the Syndrome Society, and the Law (Morality and Society Series)*. Chicago: University of Chicago Press.

Dutton, D.G., and S. Painter (1993). "The battered woman syndrome: effects of severity and intermittency of abuse." *American Journal of Psychiatry* 63: 614-622.

Eigen, J.P. (1995). *Witnessing Insanity: Madness and Mad-doctors in the English Court*. Princeton, NJ: Yale University Press.

Eftimiades, M. (1995). *Sins of the Mother: The Heartbreaking True Story Behind the Susan Smith Murder Story*. New York: St. Martin's Press.

Findlaw (2017). "Insanity defense among states, criminal procedure." Retrieved at http://criminal.findlaw.com/criminal-procedure/the-insanity-defense-among-the-states.html on 11 September 2017.

Garrison, A.H. (1998). "The history of the M'Naghten insanity defense and the use of posttraumatic stress disorder as a basis of insanity." *American Journal of Forensic Psychology* 16: 39-88.

Gresham, A.C. (1992). "The insanity plea: A futile defense for serial killers." *Law and Psychology Review* 17: 193.

Guy, F. (July 2, 2015). "Sleepwalking murders: To kill while asleep." *Crime Traveller.* Retrieved at https://www.crimetraveller.org/2015/07/sleepwalking-murders/ on 11 September 2017.

Jackson, R.L. (November 28, 1994). "LAW: Insanity as a Defense Faces Tougher Burden of Proof: The legal landscape has shifted since John Hinckley was found not guilty. New federal statutes ease the task for prosecutors." *Los Angeles Times.* Retrieved online at http://articles.latimes.com/1994-11-28/news/mn-2506_1_insanity-defense on 15 July 2017.

Kempe, C.H., F.N. Silverman, B.F. Steele, W. Droegemuller, and H.K. Silver (1962). "The battered child syndrome." *Journal of the American Medical Association* 181: 17-24.

Kutys, J., and J. Esterman (November 1, 2009). "Guilty but mentally ill (GBMI) vs. not guilty by reason of insanity (NGRI): An annotated bibliography." *The Jury Expert: The Art and Science of Litigation Advocacy; Bias, Voir Dire & Jury Selection.* Retrieved online at http://www.thejuryexpert.com/wp-content/uploads/KutysTJENov2009.pdf on 14 July 2017.

Hayes, C. (2017). "The four tests used for determining legal insanity." *Black's Law Dictionary, Free Online Legal Dictionary*, 2nd ed. Retrieved online at http://thelawdictionary.org/article/four-tests-used-determining-legal-insanity/ on 12 July 2017.

Healy, J. (August 3, 2015). "Jury rejects mental Illness argument for James Holmes in Aurora theater rampage." *The New York Times.* Retrieved online at https://www.nytimes.com/2015/08/04/us/jury-rejects-mental-illness-argument-for-james-holmes-in-aurora-theater-rampage.html on 27 July 2017.

Kalil, Mike (June 13, 2006). "Best-selling author of book on serial killer kills himself." *Las Vegas Review-Journal.* 1B.

Kang, H.K., B.H. Natelson, C.M. Mahan, K.Y. Lee, and F.M. Murphy (2003). "Post-traumatic stress disorder and chronic fatigue syndrome-like illness among Gulf War Veterans: A population-based survey of 30,000 veterans." *Journal of Epidemiology* 157: 141-148.

Lennard, N. (July 2015). "He is sane: James Holmes' trial showed that the insanity plea is a mess." *Splinter.* Retrieved at http://splinternews.com/he-is-sane-james-holmes-trial-showed-that-the-insan-1793849238 on 1 August 2017.

Linedecker, C.L. (1980). *The Man Who Killed Boys: The John Wayne Gacy Story.* New York: St. Martin's Press.

Maeder, T. (1985). *Crime and Madness: The Origins and Evolution of the Insanity Defense.* New York: Harper and Row Publishers.

Maudsley, H. (1874). "Law and insanity." *Popular Science Monthly* V: 77-88.

Moran, R. (1981). *Knowing Right From Wrong: The Insanity Defense of Daniel McNaughtan.* New York: The Free Press.

Morton, R.J., J.M. Tillman, and S.J. Gaines (2014). "Serial Murder Pathways for Investigations." Washington, DC: Federal Bureau of Investigation. Retrieved at https://www.fbi.gov/file-repository/serialmurder-pathwaysforinvestigations.pdf/viewZMoss, G. (2015). "How Many Active Serial Killers Are There Right Now?" Retrieved at https://www.bustle.com/articles/112070-how-many-active-serial-killers-are-there-right-now on 12 March 2018.

Moss, J. (1999). *The Last Victim: A True-Life Journey in the Mind of a Serial Killer.* New York: Grand Central Publishing.

O'Malley, S. (2004). *Are You There Alone? The Unspeakable Crimes of Andrea Yates.* New York: Simon and Schuster.

Phillips. J., and R.E. Woodman (2008). "The Insanity of the Mens Rea Model: Due Process and the Abolition of the Insanity Defense." *Pace Law Review* 28: 3/1.

Pogash, C. (November 23, 2003). "Myth of the 'Twinkie defense'/ The verdict in the Dan White case wasn't based on his ingestion of junk food." *SFGate.* Retrieved at http://www.sfgate.com/health/article/Myth-of-the-Twinkie-defense-The-verdict-in-2511152.php on 2 August 2017.

Preston, D., and M. Spezi (2008). *The Monster of Florence: A True Story.* New York. Grand Central Publishing.

Ray, I. (1838). *Treatise on the Medical Jurisprudence of Insanity.* New York: Charles C. Little and James Brown.

Reed, P. (January 26, 2010). "Woman Guilty but Mentally Ill in Baby Theft Case." *Pittsburgh Post-Gazette.* Retrieved at http://www.post-gazette.com/local/city/2010/01/25/Woman-guilty-but-mentally-ill-in-baby-theft-case/stories/201001250210 on 5 August 2017.

Robinson, D. (1996). *Wild Beasts and Idle Humors: The Insanity Defense from Antiquity to the Present.* Boston, MA: Harvard University Press.

Ross, M. (January 11, 1994). "Lorena Bobbitt's Trial for Cutting Penis Begins: Court: Defense will argue that abuse drove her to mutilate husband. His lawyers say it was jealousy. The media and T-shirt sellers mob Virginia town." *Los Angeles Times.* Retrieved at http://articles.latimes.com/1994-01-11/news/mn-10704_1_lorena-bobbitt on 14 July 2017.

Samour, Judge C.A. (2016). "Effectuating Colorado's capital sentencing scheme in the Aurora theater shooting trial." *Denver Law Review* 93: 577-93.

Schouten, R. (2012). "The Insanity Defense: An Intersection of Morality, Public Policy, and Science." *Psychology Today.* Retrieved at https://www.psychologytoday.com/blog/almost-psychopath/201208/the-insanity-defense 22 February 2018.

Silva, J.A, M.M. Ferrari, and G.B. Leong (2002). "The case of Jeffery Dahmer: Sexual serial homicide from a neuropsychiatric developmental perspective." *Journal of Forensic Sciences* 47: 1347-59.

Spencer, S. (2002). *Breaking Point*. New York: Diversion Books.

Stimpson, S. (1994). "State v. Cowan: The Consequences of Montana's Abolition of the Insanity Defense." *Montana Law Review* 55: 2/12.

Stoll, M. (2009). "Miles to Go Before We Sleep: Arizona's 'Guilty Except Insane' Approach to the Insanity Defense and Its Unrealized Promise." *Georgetown Law Review* 97: 1767.

Swensen, K. (August 23, 2017). "A 1995 TV show surprised him with his gay secret admirer. This week he leaves prison." *The Washington Post*. Retrieved at https://www.washingtonpost.com/news/morning-mix/wp/2017/08/23/a-1995-tv-show-surprised-him-with-his-gay-secret-admirer-this-week-he-leaves-prison/?utm_term=.9ae4d83147d7 on 11 September 2017.

Taylor, S. (July 27, 1981). "Issue and debate; The plea of insanity and its use in criminal cases." *The New York Times*. Retrieved at http://www.nytimes.com/1981/07/27/us/issue-debate-last-november-plea-insanity-its-use-criminal-cases.html?pagewanted=all&mcubz=3 on 22 August 2017.

University of Minnesota (2010). *Criminal Law*. Chapter 2.4. *Burden of Proof, Criminal Law Libraries*. Retrieved at http://open.lib.umn.edu/criminallaw/chapter/2-4-the-burden-of-proof/ on 12 June 2017.

Walker, L.E. (1979). *The Battered Woman*. New York: Harper and Row.

Williams, C. (March 5, 2015). "Psychiatrist backs up sleepwalking defense in Durham murder trial." *Spectrum News*. Retrieved at http://www.twcnews.com/nc/triangle-sandhills/news/2015/03/5/psychiatrist-backs-up-sleepwalking-defense-in-durham-murder-trial.html on 4 September 2017.

CASES

Clark v. Arizona, 548 U.S. 735 (2006)

Faulkenberry v. State, 649 P.2d 951 (Alaska 1982)

Ford v. Wainwright, 477 U.S. 399 (1986)

Houston v. State, 602 P.2d 784 (Alaska 1979)

People v. Fleming, 507 N.E.2d 954 (Ill. App. Ct. 1987)

Regina v. M'Naghten (1843) 8 E.R. 718; (1843) 10 Cl. & F. 200

Rex v. Arnold, 16 How St. Tr. 695 (1724)

State v. Dahmer, Milwaukee County Cir. Court, Wis. Case No. F-912542 (1992)

State v. Falater, No. CR1997-000928-A (Ariz. Super. Ct. Maricopa County), appeal docketed, No. CR1997-000928-A (Ariz. Ct. App.ful. 26, 2004

State v. Percy, 548 A.2d 408 (Vt. 1988)

State of Texas v. Eddie Ray Routh, No. 11-15-0036CR (2015)

United States v. Cartagena-Carrasquillo, 70 F.3d 706 (1st Cir. 1995)

United States v. Rezaq, 918 F. Supp. 463 (D.D.C. 1996)

United States v. Torniero, 735 F. Supp. 725 (1984)

LEGISLATION

California Penal Code §§25, 25.5; *People v. Skinner*, 39 Cal. 3d 765, 217 Cal. Rptr. 685, 704 P.2d 752 (1985)

18 U.S.C. Part III, Chapter 313, §4243. Hospitalization of a person found not guilty only by reason of insanity

Correctional Treatment of the Mentally Ill

LEARNING OBJECTIVES

After reading this chapter, you should be able to:

▶ Distinguish between the often-competing goals of treatment and custody.
▶ Compare and contrast the challenges confronting the mentally ill participating in community-based correctional services.
▶ Compare and contrast the challenges confronting the mentally ill housed in institutional corrections.
▶ Appreciate the complex issues related to mental illness and the application of the death penalty.

PROLOGUE

This prologue is based on the following accounts, as well as an interview conducted by Anne F. Segal with Slevin's attorney of record, Matthew Coyte: Broyles (2013); Gerber (2013). Stephen Slevin died at the age of 62 in 2017.

In August 2005, 49-year old Stephen Slevin decided to drive across country. He had struggled with depression and other mild forms of mental illness throughout his lifetime, but was otherwise physically healthy. He felt that the trip would help him cope with his never-resolved sense of helplessness. Unfortunately, Slevin was drinking alcohol while he drove. As he was passing through Doña Ana County, New Mexico on Friday, August 24, 2005, Slevin was pulled over for driving while intoxicated, a simple misdemeanor.

Booked into the 846-bed Doña Ana County Detention Facility (DACDF) in Las Cruces, Slevin was subsequently placed in a solitary, padded jail cell with a hole in the floor for a toilet. He remained in isolation until Monday, when he had a video arraignment on the misdemeanor criminal charges. Despite his mental vulnerability and fragility, Slevin remained in a solitary confinement cell. He was prescribed medication, although he was never actually seen by a medical professional. The tranquilizer medication made him even more vulnerable to isolation, and he continued to spiral into mental chaos. "He was placed in a situation that sounds 'pretty,'" said Matthew Coyte, Stephen's civil attorney in a phone interview with Anne Segal. "They called it 'medical observation,'" he continued. "What it really means that someone checks and makes sure that [the detainee] has not killed himself. There is no exercise, no contact with other people, no treatment. It is toxic for the mentally ill."

After nearly 20 months of having his food tray passed through a slot, and having no human contact and no physical exercise or fresh air, Slevin was transferred to the New Mexico Behavioral Health Institute (NMBHI) for a mental health competency evaluation.

At this point, he weighed 133 pounds, his hair was overgrown, his beard was at his navel, his toenails curled under his feet, he was not aware of his surroundings, and "he smelled so badly that the personnel remembered his stench years later," Coyte said. He suffered from bedsores and skin fungus.

Following two weeks of treatment at NMBHI, Slevin was discharged and returned to DACDF where he was again placed in solitary confinement. Back in jail, he pulled out his own tooth due to dental neglect. Having spent 22 months in jail accused of but not tried for an offense that does not require any mandatory jail time, Slevin was released and all charges against him dismissed.

Slevin's release is not the end of the story. In January 2012, after a federal civil trial held in Santa Fe, New Mexico, some 300 miles north of Las Cruces, the jury awarded Slevin a $22 million judgment against Doña Ana County. About a year later, in March 2013, the amount was lowered to $15.5 million, but Doña Ana County agreed not to dispute the judgment or the amount. The county's insurance covered $6 million, while the county's citizens were obligated to pay the rest. As Slevin told a reporter with Albuquerque's KOB television station, "It was never about the money. We made a statement about what happened to me. Prison officials were walking by me every day, watching me deteriorate. Day after day after day, they did nothing, nothing at all, to get me any help."

The topic of the treatment of persons with mental illness taken into custodial care is not only a legal issue, it also has moral and humanitarian elements. Under the best of conditions, when a detainee or inmate is healthy both physically and mentally, prisons and jails can be difficult living environments. Even community placement, with and without supervision, can prove troubling for the mentally ill, as such conditional release comes with rules whose violation often means incarceration.

Chapter Overview

The decisions and practices that led to Stephen Slevin's abhorrent detention are not all that rare, as we shall see in this chapter. The nation's correctional system, introduced in Chapter 1, was never designed to house large numbers of mentally ill defendants, convicted misdemeanants, or felons. The specific needs of such inmates often make them vulnerable to the predations of other inmates and, on occasion, to abusive and inattentive correctional staff. In this chapter, we first examine the distinctions between treatment and custody as goals of the nation's correctional system. Simply put, the extent to which a correctional facility is primarily oriented toward custody makes the treatment and care of all inmates, but especially inmates with serious mental illness or disease, a difficult proposition.

Second, we explore the nation's correctional system, which consists of two main arms: community-based corrections and institutional corrections. We examine the involvement of mentally ill defendants in community-based corrections, including sentencing alternatives, probation, and parole, as well as the various types of associated mental health programs. We also describe institutional corrections, which represents perhaps the greatest threat to the health and welfare of mentally ill convicted offenders. We review the extent to which the mentally ill find themselves in prisons and jails and what they face when incarcerated. Institutional mental health programming is also a central topic in this section.

The third section of this chapter addresses the execution of the mentally ill. Here, we examine the social, moral, and legal elements associated with the employment of society's ultimate sanction.

The chapter's epilogue provides a composite case of a kleptomaniac. The accused is offered the opportunity to participate in an alternative to traditional criminal justice processing, participation in a mental health court. In this case, we follow the accused from arrest to diversion from the criminal court.

To orient our discussion of corrections and the mentally ill, we start with the key distinctions between the goals of treatment and custody in correctional settings. We encourage the reader to recall the Slevin case in the consideration of these important topics.

FRAMING THE ISSUES

Two organizational goals drive the entire correctional system. One goal maintains that those supervised within the community or confined in the nation's jails and prisons should be offered therapeutic solutions intended to change the law-violating behavior that brought them to the attention of the criminal justice system, a position designated as the **treatment perspective**. The second goal suggests that the primary purpose of any correctional program is to provide for the maximum containment level necessary to control the movement and general conduct of its clients, a position called the **custody perspective**. For more than 40 years, these two perspectives and their associated goals have been at the center of a debate about the central objectives of the nation's correctional system generally, but especially institutional corrections (Craig, 2004). Both the treatment and custody perspectives have implications for mentally ill persons.

Custody is the legal or physical control of a person. Whenever an entity assumes this level of responsibility for a human being, it must provide certain comforts and needs for that person, generally defined in terms of shelter, healthcare, food, and clothing. Such obligations, however important, are often seen as secondary to the restriction of the person-under-custody's liberty and subsequent threat to the community. That is, custody involves varying levels of **security**, the latter being defined as the state of freedom from perceived or actual threats to individual and community health, welfare, and general well-being.

Should the inmates' current or prior behavior warrant additional custodial measures, they are assigned to institutions with higher security levels. A maximum security prison facility, as a correctional system response to high-risk offenders, maximizes all forms of inmate custodial restraints. Such facilities have in-depth protection at their perimeters, including several chain-link fences topped by barrier wire and, in some cases, high physical walls and external patrols. As inmate threat-level classifications decrease, prisoners are assigned to facilities with lower security classifications, the general categories, from highest to lowest security, being supermax, maximum, medium, and minimum security. Internal movement about the most secure facilities (i.e., maximum security and supermax prisons) is highly restricted. However, even medium security prisons maintain a fairly high level of internal and external security intended to meet the worst-case threat posed by incarcerated inmates. The security constraints found in minimum security facilities provide more symbolic than real physical constraints on inmates, as there are often no walls, fences, or guard towers.

Treatment refers to the application of a specific method of therapy based on a diagnosis. At its most basic level, specialized treatment staff view offenders as "sick persons" whose illnesses must be addressed using specific and focused therapeutic regimens. In the years following World War II, prison systems across the nation, including the Federal Bureau of Prisons, experimented with various types of prison-based treatment programs. Treatment was defined rather broadly during this "Golden Age" of treatment programming, and included such diverse approaches to offenders as psychoanalysis, anger management, Alcoholics Anonymous/Narcotics Anonymous, various forms of drug therapy, and behavior modification; other methodologies often found previously only in mental hospitals and similar clinical settings were offered in prisons (Street, Vinter, and Perrow, 1966; Zald and Street, 1964).

Treatment staff, whether the services are provided in a jail, prison, or the community, must establish a trust relationship with the "client" and the individual clinical provider or therapist, sometimes referred to by clinicians as the client-provider relationship. **Custody staff**, typically referred to as correctional officers or COs, rely on authority, regimentation, and prison architecture as their main tools. Custody staff employ largely coercive methods to achieve their goals related to inmate restraint and custody; treatment staff, who in the main have much higher levels of education, rely on persuasion and tact (Farmer, 1977; Hepburn and Albonetti, 1980; Lombardo, 1984). These different perspectives, skill sets, and educational attainment levels can create conflict between the two distinct sets of correctional staff (Hepburn and Albonetti, 1980). As Craig (2004: 968) notes: "The goal of controlling inmates subsumes all other goals. Even rehabilitative programming, which may involve time away from the prison routine or better quarters than can be had in the general population, is a privilege that may be granted or taken away."

For their part, community-based facilities and treatment centers generally operate at far lower security levels than any form of institutional corrections. Probation and parole services, as the largest purveyors of community corrections programming, rely on a legal contract, a probation or parole agreement for conditional release, to control client behavior. Probation or parole officers may be required, by state law, to be armed, or firearms may be authorized but not required. For their part, half-way houses and residential programs employ very few traditional security measures, preferring instead to rely on inmate-staff relationships to control behavior.

These two different sets of goals beg a central question for institutional corrections: Can treatment goals can be achieved in a custodial setting? Donald Clemmer (1940) was one of the first to observe the inherent conflict between the two goals sets represented by treatment and custody. The literature on the overlay of therapeutic programs onto a custodial environment reveals an important lesson: As custody assumes a greater emphasis, then treatment becomes deemphasized, and vice versa (Adams and Ferrandino, 2008; Faiver, 1998; Fellner, 2006). Practically, this means that maximum security prisons are poor clinical environments for treatment providers. On the other hand, community-based programming offers perhaps the best hope for establishing client-provider relations based on trust and mutual respect. However, even correctional programming offered outside of a prison setting must necessarily have some security elements.

COMMUNITY CORRECTIONS

Community-based services cover a range of specific programs. While some such programs may place restrictions on offender behavior, like residing in a semi-secure facility or following a strict set of rules for living free in the community, most allow offenders to live in their own homes, work at their jobs or attend school and training programs, and enjoy nearly the all freedoms and liberties accorded other community residents.

Extent of the Problem

A sentence of probation is perhaps the most common. However, we begin our review of community-based programming with sentencing alternatives other than probation. Indeed, judges may combine one of the following sentencing alternatives with probation or even incarceration. Next, we examine probation, which is the backbone of the community corrections system. Finally, parole is also an important form of community corrections, as the former inmate seeks to readapt to life outside of prison.

Sentencing Alternatives. Judges have many **sentencing alternatives** available. The range of practices may be restricted by local practice and state law. The most common alternatives, used in lieu of or, as previously suggested, in concert with either probation or institutional corrections, include the following (Families Against Mandatory Minimums, 2013):

▶ *Fines* — Also called "tariff fines," fines are tied to a specific type of crime.

▶ *Restitution* — This consists of payments by the convicted offender for all or some of the loss and expenses incurred by the victim of the crime.

▶ *Home Confinement/Electronic Monitoring* — The former, also known as **house arrest**, requires the offenders to stay home when not working, attending school, or participating in treatment, while the latter refers to the wearing of an electronic device that signals the physical location of the wearer and is often combined with home confinement.

▶ *Halfway Houses* — Halfway houses represent an intermediate housing option where offenders can be monitored and confined but work in the community; halfway houses are used to support prisoner reentry and as alternatives to incarceration.

▶ *Restorative Justice* — This holistic approach seeks to address the imbalance in society created by the criminal incident by employing discussion, dialogue, apologies and forgiveness, and direct and indirect reparations; it involves the victim or victims, perpetrator, community members, and representatives of criminal justice system.

The exact number of individuals given alternatives to incarceration, outside of probation services, is a gray area in criminal justice. For example, the Bureau of Justice Statistics counts persons placed in a diversion program or discharged from probation in favor of a mental health court in the same reporting category as those who failed to meet the conditions of probation (see Box 9.1) (Kaeble and Bonczar, 2016). Moreover, it is generally believed that the use of alternative sentences other than traditional probation is becoming a less common occurrence (Fuller, Sinclair, et al., 2017). This characterization is especially true of the federal system, where prison only is the sentenced imposed against 87 percent of the convicted offenders, largely due to mandatory minimum sentences; 7 percent receive a sentence of probation only, and the rest, about 6 percent, receive other alternative sentences (Saris, Breyer, et al., 2015).

The nationwide use of early diversion programs for the mentally ill, such as crisis intervention teams, or later diversion into mental health courts, is rather abysmal, earning the nation an overall C+ grade for the breadth of all such programs in the United States (Stettin, Frees, and Lamb, 2013). Instead, large numbers of mentally ill offenders find their way into probation, parole, and the nation's prison and jail system, as we reveal in the next sections.

Probation. Annually, most persons convicted of crimes in America are placed on probation, which is, as described in Chapter 1, both a sentence and a form of conditional release back into the community, this time authorized by the sentencing court. In 2015, that number stood at 3.8 million probationers. According to the National Survey on Drug Use and Mental Health, 33.6 percent of persons indicating that they had been on probation in the past year also reported suffering from any mental illness (AMI), while the mental illness rate for this condition among adults not on probation was 18.3 percent (Substance Abuse and Mental Health Services Administration [SAMHSA], 2013). Shifting to serious mental illness (SMI) reveals a slightly different picture: 10.8 percent of probationers indicated an SMI, while 3.9 percent of adults not on probation gave the same response (SAMHSA, 2013). Given nearly 4 million probationers, a reasonable estimate would be that at any given time in 2015, 1.2 million probationers indicated that they suffered from AMI, while SMIs afflicted 410,400 probationers.

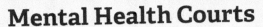

BOX 9.1

Mental Health Courts

One successful effort to diffuse the street-to-cell channel for the criminally mentally ill was implemented by the judges assigned to the criminal court dockets. Conceived as a specialty problem-solving court and a "one-stop-shopping" approach to the juncture of justice and mental health, akin to juvenile or family courts, judges developed protocols for judicial referrals to a docket known as **mental health courts (MHC)**. In the late 1990s, sentencing judges felt they were seeing seriously mentally ill defendants in disproportionately large numbers recycling through the judicial system, sometimes seeing the same people with the same reasons for arrest on multiple occasions: disorderly conduct, public intoxication, petty theft. A new court process was developed to divert individuals who had a documented diagnosis or verified mental illness, and who were charged as first-time or non-violent criminal offenders. The diversion court separated the mentally ill from adjudication in the criminal justice court into a non-conviction, therapeutic process.

Essentially, MHC participants have their criminal charges reduced or dismissed following the successful completion of a court-approved counseling or education program. Typically, if a person fails to complete the program, the charges are reinstated and the criminal prosecution ensues. If he or she completes the program successfully, the charges are dismissed and, if allowed by state law, there is no criminal record. In an ideal situation, the MHC candidate is identified at the first court appearance and is quickly referred to the specialty court to begin personal efforts for community-based treatments and interventions.

Starting in Anchorage, Alaska, Ft. Lauderdale, Florida, Seattle, Washington, and San Bernardino, California, mental health courts now operate in over 300 judicial jurisdictions. The structure of the mental health courts varies widely, including the target populations, the nature of the charges that may be eligible for MHC (e.g., felony versus misdemeanors), the plea arrangements, and the intensity by which the court supervises compliance. Some judges require the defendants to come to court for weekly check-in and progress reports, while other courts accept notice of termination or completion.

Sources: Council of State Governments (2008); Trawver and Rhoades (2013); Verhaaff and Scott (2015).

Parole. Parole, also described in Chapter 1, is the conditional release of felony prisoners after they have served a statutorily defined portion of their prison sentences. It is not automatic, as either a parole board or some other state-level authority reviews each case prior to granting parole. As with probation, estimates of parolees with some form of mental disease, whether it is a case of reporting any mental illness or a serious mental illness, vary widely (cf., Ditton, 1999; Feucht and Gfroerer, 2011; Osher, D'Amora, et al., 2012). Again, an examination by the National Survey on Drug Use and Mental Health reveals that 33.4 percent of all parolees reported a serious mental illness, while the same condition was reported by 18.5 percent of all persons not on parole during the past 12 months (SAMHSA, 2013). AMIs were reported by 12.1 percent of parolees and by 4 percent of all persons not on parole during the past year (SAMHSA, 2013). Extrapolating from the 2015 figure of 870,000 parolees nationwide, we can reasonably suggest that at least 105,270 parolees in the United States suffered from a serious mental illness, while 290,580 parolees reported the less serious AMI.

As described in Box 9.2, probation and parole are the workhorses of the U.S. penal system. The next topic in this section, however, reviews the mental health clients of community corrections, including several alternatives to either probation or incarceration, which in the latter case would also eliminate the parole entirely.

Mental Health Clients

The personal-biographical characteristics of community corrections mental health clients are instructive. One consistent research finding is that half of all women on probation and parole report experiencing some form of mental illness; moreover, their SMI rates are three to four times greater than reported in the general population (SAMHSA, 2012). Female probationers also exhibit higher levels of mental illness than do males (Ditton, 1999). Thus, community programming that targets female clients should be sensitive to the specialized needs of women, which can include gynecological issues, housing and family support matters, and partner/spousal abuse concerns (Mays and Winfree, 2014).

BOX 9.2

Thinking About the Issues

Probation and parole, but especially the former, are the backbone of the U.S. penal system. If people were not placed on probation or released on parole, the correctional system, as well as state and federal budgets, would quickly be overwhelmed. Consider, too, that at least 1.5 million parolees and probationers suffer from some form of mental illness, while over half a million report the far more serious and complicated SMI.

1. Given the large number of mentally ill people who are incarcerated, what do you think about using mental condition as a determining factor in who is granted either probation and parole? Should it be a mitigating factor (i.e., viewed positively when considering conditional release) or an aggravating factor (i.e., working against awarding conditional release)?

2. Do you think that this policy shift would create additional community-based problems that might prove as costly in terms of money and additional criminality?

3. Who do you think would benefit from such a policy shift? How?

Age, too, is a matter that community programs may need to consider, as middle-aged probationers—between the ages of 45-54—are the most likely to be identified as mentally ill, whereas probationers who were younger than 25 had a lower reported mental illness rate (Ditton, 1999). Older parolees and probationers, then, may face general health and mental health–related issues not among the challenges confronting younger ones.

Race also may be important for community corrections practitioners to consider: Black and Hispanic probationers were nearly half as likely to report a mental illness as were White probationers (Ditton, 1999). Older, White females may face challenges within community corrections deriving in part from their higher than average rates of mental illness. Given that these same patterns also existed among prison inmates, it is reasonable to assume that parolees would be similarly arrayed across these dimensions (Ditton, 1999).

Besides such personal-biographical concerns, legal, medical, and behavioral concerns give insights into why it is important to consider the mental health of community corrections clients. The following list, while not exhaustive, is suggestive of the breadth of the problem:

- ▸ *Instant Offense* — Mentally ill probationers are more likely to have their most serious offense be a violent crime than are other inmates (Ditton, 1999). The differences between mentally ill and other probationers for other offenses were not as striking.

- ▸ *Comorbidity* — Another issue is co-occurring substance abuse and mental illness among both probationers and parolees, also described in Chapter 4 as comorbidity (Osher, D'Amora, et al., 2012). By itself, mental illness can cause adjustment problems, but probationers and parolees with both conditions are more likely to fail on supervised release than those with one or the other (Baillargeon, Williams, et al., 2009; Louden and Skeem, 2013; Matejkowski and Ostermann, 2015).

- ▸ *Behavioral and Attitudinal Issues* — Mentally ill parolees and probationers exhibit a general inability to follow rules and procedures, ranging from key elements of their conditional release to "maintaining their hygiene, complying with rules and adhering to routines, and concentrating and learning" (Osher, D'Amora, et al., 2012: 15; see also Baillargeon et al., 2009; Manchak, Kinnealy, et al., 2014). Among parole-eligible inmates, mental illness is highly correlated with co-occurring substance abuse and antisocial personality disorders (Matejkowski, Draine, et al., 2011). Moreover, their scores on criminal thinking and criminal attitude measures are often higher than non–mentally ill inmates (Morgan, Fisher, et al., 2011). As a general observation, mental illness among inmates is also associated with antisocial attitudes (Wolff, Morgan, and Shi, 2012).

Mental Health Programs

The preceding body of research suggests that treating all mentally ill community corrections clients the same would be a mistake. Critical to any program's success is the clear, valid, and reliable identification of the extent and nature of the alleged mental illness. At least two screening devices have shown much promise in this regard (Louden, Skeem, and Blevins, 2013). First, the **Kessler Psychological Distress Scale (K6)** is a six-item self-report screening tool that discerns mental disorder (*DSM-IV* Axis I) from general distress (Kessler, Andrews, et al., 2002). It has been extensively tested in the general community in large-scale epidemiological studies and probationers (Kessler, Barker, et al., 2003; Louden et al., 2013). The second is the **Brief Jail Mental Health Screen (BJMHS)**, which is also intended to discern the far more serious *DSM-IV* Axis I mental disorder from general distress, this time employing an eight-item interview scale, all the items answerable as "yes" or "no" (Steadman, Scott, et al., 2005). Both the K6 and BJMHS, which take minutes to administer, have been shown to work equally well on men and women (Louden et al., 2013), although there is some disagreement as to whether the latter underreports mental issues for women (Steadman et al., 2005).

Probation and parole services have created several programs and practices specifically designed to work with mentally ill offenders, including offenders designated as dual diagnosed. The combination of mental illness and drug abuse may require the application of another layer of treatment specializations not readily available in these traditional sentencing alternatives. An increasingly common sentencing alternative that comes into play for mentally ill defendants is **jail diversion**. Diversion from the criminal justice system can occur as early as the first responder's initial contact with the mentally ill detainee or suspect. It can also occur during initial legal proceedings, such as through voluntary and involuntary commitments, and pretrial proceedings, and even removal to some form of diversion from traditional criminal justice processing (see Box 9.3).

Diverting the mentally ill from jail is generally effective, both in terms of outpatient success and cost. This observation is particularly the case in the event the "client" enters a **forensic assertive community treatment (FACT) program**, which combines treatment, rehabilitation, and support services in a self-contained clinical team drawn from various psychiatric, nursing, and addiction counseling disciplines; specifically, while initial costs may be high, these costs are offset by reduced numbers of lengthy jail and prison stays (Cusack, Morrisey, et al., 2010; De Matteo, LaDuke, et al., 2012; Lamberti, Weisman, and Faden, 2004).

Finally, the interaction and collaboration between the supervisory element (i.e., the probation/parole agent) and the treatment element (i.e., the mental health worker) is essential for the mentally ill offender's satisfactory reintegration into the community. As programs like FACT inform us, for community programming to work for mentally ill clients, there must be close coordination between the work of the criminal justice supervisory agent, whatever the specific title, and mental and physical health workers assigned to the client (Malik-Kane and Visher, 2008).

Probation officers and parole supervisors who express the belief that mental health issues alone are predictors of failure may have to be educated to include drug abuse or comorbidity with mental health in the mix (Louden and Skeem, 2013). In addition, when probation or parole officers closely interact with mental health staff, there is a tendency to rely on coercive measures to force compliance, which itself is not helpful to the therapeutic

BOX 9.3

The Sequential Intercept Model

Chapter 1 included an overview of the criminal justice system in Figure 1.2. In traditional criminal justice processing, people enter that system with arrest and exit at various points. The diversion model, first described in Chapter 1 and elaborated on in this chapter, suggests that there are additional ways to transfer individuals out of what is for many mentally ill persons a highly corrosive physical, social, and mental environment, thereby limiting their "penetration" into the formal system and additional criminalization. The Sequential Intercept Model, first described in detail by Mark Munetz and Patricia Griffin, focuses our attention on key intercept points in the criminal justice process where timely interventions can help those accused of crimes who also suffer from serious mental illness. Specifically, the **Sequential Intercept Model (SIM)** identifies five points at which timely intervention and removal of a mentally ill person from formal justice processing will help both the accused/convicted person and society. These points include:

1. Intercept 1: Law Enforcement and Emergency Services — This intercept addresses the issue of pre-arrest diversion from the criminal justice system. Given law enforcement's role in deciding who goes forward, diversion at this point has the great potential to impact the lives of mentally ill arrestees and detainees in positive ways. As shown in Chapter 5, for example, reliance on Crisis Intervention Teams can limit the mentally ill person's penetration into formal criminal justice processing.

2. Intercept 2: Initial Hearings and Initial Detention — In Chapter 1, we described these processes in detail. The ideal candidates for diversion at this point are those accused of low-level misdemeanors closely associated with their mental illness (e.g., public nuisance or panhandling). Such diversion programs are also highly dependent on the presence of mental health workers in the hearing courts and at the detention facilities.

3. Intercept 3: Jails and Court — One would hope that by the time a person enters jail or a trial setting, those defendants who are statutorily eligible for diversion would have been diverted. Perhaps the best hope for those mentally ill persons still in the system at this stage is the mental health court (Box 9.1), although judges generally have the power to, at a minimum, order a psychiatric hold and evaluation on a suspect or even a convicted offender.

4. Intercept 4: Reentry — This intercept involves multiple stakeholders, whether reentry into the community be from jails, prisons, or hospitals. As described in this chapter, the central focus is on having a reentry plan, one that provides continuity of care between corrections and community healthcare agencies that will assume a role in the reintegration of the mentally ill person. Any transition between institutional

corrections and the community should include assessing, planning, identifying, and coordinating transitional care.

5. Intercept 5: Community Corrections and Community Support Services — As described in Chapter 1 and elaborated on later in this chapter, probation is the workhorse of the U.S. correctional system. Along with parole, these approaches to community corrections process nearly all convicted offenders in the nation, and communications and cooperation between their agents and mental health specialists managing the mental healthcare aspects of probationers and parolees play crucial roles in this intercept.

The extent to which the SIM has been widely adopted or its impact on recidivism (i.e., the return to crime) and mental health relapse is unknown at this time. There is general agreement among mental health professionals, however, that the utilization of the SIM offers perhaps the best hope for reversing the criminalization of the mentally ill that began over 40 years ago.

Sources: DeMatteo, LaDuke, et al., (2012); Griffin, Heilbrun, et al. (2015); Lamb and Weinberger (2011); Munetz and Griffin (2006); Osher, Steadman, and Barr (2002); Redlich and Cusack (2010).

relationship between the client and the mental health provider (Draine and Solomon, 2001). Mental health service providers and community release supervisors should work together, but the former must not abandon their emphasis on establishing a trust relationship with the client, whereas the latter are primarily concerned with compliance. As the case described in Box 9.4 suggests to us, sometimes things do not go according to plan.

INSTITUTIONAL CORRECTIONS

Jail and prison inmates with severe mental disorders are very likely to face physical and mental jeopardy, along with the potential loss of civil rights and due process. Roughly 2 million individuals with serious mental illnesses are booked into the nation's jails each year (Sabol and Minton, 2008). As described in the Slevin case, jails represent a unique threat for at least four reasons. First, besides the nation's 3,000-plus jails, every police and sheriff's substation has a lockup, which is essentially a small cell or windowless room where people are confined for upwards of 24 hours while awaiting transfer to jail. Given that there are over 17,000 policing agencies in the United States, and that it is a safe bet each one operates at least one if not several lockups, their number must approach 20,000. Jails process over 13 million people each year, some staying a couple of hours, most staying about 2 to 3 months, but many residing in them up to a year (Irwin, 2013: xxiii; Sabol and Minton, 2008: 2). The large number of facilities and the huge volume of clients makes oversight for something like mentally ill inmates highly problematic for local jurisdictions (Hounmenou, 2012).

BOX 9.4

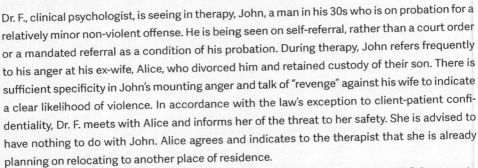

What Would You Do?

Dr. F., clinical psychologist, is seeing in therapy, John, a man in his 30s who is on probation for a relatively minor non-violent offense. He is being seen on self-referral, rather than a court order or a mandated referral as a condition of his probation. During therapy, John refers frequently to his anger at his ex-wife, Alice, who divorced him and retained custody of their son. There is sufficient specificity in John's mounting anger and talk of "revenge" against his wife to indicate a clear likelihood of violence. In accordance with the law's exception to client-patient confidentiality, Dr. F. meets with Alice and informs her of the threat to her safety. She is advised to have nothing to do with John. Alice agrees and indicates to the therapist that she is already planning on relocating to another place of residence.

Before Alice can relocate, John visits her and says he "just wants to talk." Contrary to what she was advised, Alice admits John to the apartment, whereupon he stabs her to death. He makes no attempt to abscond and is arrested and charged with premeditated murder. John's attorney pleads insanity, claiming that it was an unplanned, instantaneous reaction to an emotional state. Dr. F. testifies as to his therapy sessions with John and his discussion with Alice. Trial is by judge, and John is found not guilty by reason of mental disease or defect but remanded to a state psychiatric hospital for treatment.

Before being transported to the psychiatric hospital, while still housed in the county jail, John requests a meeting with his psychologist. John states emphatically and reassuringly during the meeting that Dr. F.'s testimony was correct.

As the facts in this actual case suggest, even when the professional staff in a community treatment setting do exactly what they are supposed to do, bad things happen. Do you see any alternative course of action for the clinical psychologist? How about for the judge in the original case? What about the probation officer on the original charge?

Second, while there are several methods for jails to demonstrate that they meet certain standards of care, small-town or small-county jail have little incentive to undergo this expensive and time-consuming process (Penn, 2015). Moreover, jail certification means that a given facility has the *minima* for all inmates. Moreover, few jails have medical facilities on-site or even 24-hour a day medical personnel. In short, jails can be dangerous places in which to house the mentally ill even temporarily.

Third, jail staff, largely consisting of correctional officers (COs), have historically shown an insensitivity to or little awareness of the special needs of mentally ill inmates (AbuDagga, Wolfe, et al., 2016). With adequate training, COs can contribute to the care and treatment of the mentally ill inmates (Appelbaum, Hickey, and Packer, 2001). The ratio of therapeutic or medical jail staff to total inmates is generally lower than in prisons, meaning fewer specialized staff to address the issues of mentally ill inmates (Bronson and Berzofsky, 2017).

Finally, as institutions designed for long-term incarceration, prisons tend to have on-site medical facilities, including psychiatric services with related mental health professionals on staff (Bronson and Berzofsky, 2017; Chari, Simon, et al., 2016). The absence of access to such services or the requisite staff can be taken as part of a larger governmental failure to provide prison inmates with basic human and civil rights. This failure has, in turn, led to much litigation. In response, some states and the federal government operate separate facilities whose mission it is to provide for the mental and physical well-being of prison inmates. The number of bedspaces at such institutions is relatively limited and small in comparison to the number of inmates incarcerated in all state and federal facilities.

A given prison or prison system may feel pressured to gain certification from an independent, national organization, such as the American Correctional Association. As with jails, this process examines whether a facility meets some minimal standard of care for its charges, including the provision of physical and mental healthcare services. Day-to-day prison life can erode anyone's mental well-being, let alone physical health. In other words, while the services may exist, those inmates defined as in need of help (see Box 9.5) may not have regular access to them (Bronson and Berzofsky, 2017; Wilper, Woolhandler, et al., 2009).

Extent of the Problem

By this point, the distinction between jails and prisons is a clear one. What is less clear, however, is the extent to which each one contains inmates with mental health problems or the severity of those problems.

Jails. While literally millions of individuals cycle through the nation's jails each year, some being admitted and released several times in those 12 months, the pulse of the nation's jail population is taken erratically, and insights to the state of the mentally ill in jail are even more rare. According to the most recent survey of jail inmates' mental health, roughly one in 4 jail inmates met the Kessler Psychological Distress (K6) scale threshold for serious psychological distress (SPD) in the 30 days prior to the survey, as contrasted with one in 20 for the standardized U.S. population; a mental health professional had told 44 percent of all jail inmates that they had a mental disorder (Bronson and Berzofsky, 2017: 1). Given an average daily population for the nation's jails of 721,300 inmates in 2015 (Minton and Zeng, 2016), this suggests to us that there were 187,538 mentally ill persons with a SPD jailed on any given day in 2015, while upwards of 320,000 had some form of mental disorder.

Prisons. On any given day in 2015, the nation's prisons held an estimated 1,526,800 prisoners under the jurisdiction of state and federal authorities (Carson and Anderson, 2016: 1). Of this number, 14 percent, or 213,752, met the K6 threshold for SPD in the prior 30 days, while 37 percent, or 564,916 prison inmates had been told at some point by a mental health professional that they had a mental disorder (Bronson and Berzofsky, 2016: 1). Again, the SPD rate is far above that for the standardized general population of the United States.

BOX 9.5

Mental Illness and Institutional Life

In Chapter 4, we dealt with the National Institute of Mental Health's legal definition of serious mental illness (SMI). We learned in Chapter 4 that in 2015 roughly 4 percent of the nation's population suffers from an SMI. This is an important figure to remember as we look at the experiences of the mentally ill within the correctional system.

The federal government, which provides most of our concrete insights into the mental health of prison and jail inmates, does not conform to the previously discussed standard legal definition of SMIs. Specifically, in its surveys of inmates, the federal government distinguishes between two types of mental issues, determined by two sets of questions. The first mental issue is called **serious psychological distress (SPD)**. Inmates were asked how often they have felt one of the following conditions in the previous 30 days, with those who said all the time given a score of 4 for that item and those who said none of the time accorded a value of 0 for that item (Bronson and Berzofsky, p. 2): (1) nervous, (2) hopeless, (3) restless or fidgety, (4) so depressed that nothing could cheer them up, (5) everything was an effort, and (6) worthless. For these 6 items, the range of summated scores was 0 to 24, and anyone with a score higher than 12 was assessed as an SPD.

A second issue is a history of mental health problems, which is more in line with the legal SMI definition and included the following (Bronson and Berzofsky, p. 2): "(1) manic depression; (2) depressive disorder; (3) schizophrenia and another psychotic disorder; (4) post-traumatic stress disorder; (5) another anxiety disorder, such as panic disorder or obsessive-compulsive disorder; (6) a personality disorder, such as antisocial or borderline personality; or (7) a mental or emotional condition other than those listed above." In most of these conditions, the inmate would have to be aware of a formal diagnosis to include it on his or her history of mental problems.

A crucial problem for mentally ill inmates is that, owing to their life challenges, they are less able to cope with life in prison or jail. This problem, in turn, leads to poorer adaptation to institutional rules and procedures than is the case for non-afflicted inmates. As an example, researchers have found that inmates with schizophrenia and intellectual disability (ID), the latter being neither an SPD or a SMI, commit rule infractions at a higher rate than other inmates. Moreover, they spend more time in disciplinary lockdown and are less likely to obtain parole than inmates not so afflicted. It is also highly likely that jail and prison surveys underestimate the percentage of mentally ill, especially those suffering from paranoid schizophrenia.

Sources: AbuDagga et al. (2016); Adams and Ferrandino (2008); Appelbaum, Hickey, and Parker (2001); Bronson and Berzofsky (2017); Fellner (2006); Hart, Moore, et al. (2016); Morgan, Edwards, and Faulkner (1993); Roesch et al. (1993); Steadman, Osher, et al. (2009); Toch and Adams (1987); Wilper et al. (2009).

Mental Health Clients

As with the review of the community correction system, a good starting point for institutional corrections is with the personal-biographical characteristics of its mentally ill clients. In terms of gender, several studies point to the overrepresentation of mental illness among women in both prison and jail. For the general U.S. population, we know that one in 10 persons aged 18 and over fits the current American Psychiatric Association (APA) criteria for symptoms of a mental disorder; that figure is slightly higher for women (12.4%) than men (8.7%) (James and Glaze, 2006). Roughly two-thirds of all female jail and prison inmates report a history of a mental health problem, compared to rates of 35 percent among male prison inmates and 41 percent for male jail inmates (Bronson and Berzofsky, 2017: 4). For SPDs, we find a similar pattern: one in five female prisoners and one-third of female jail inmates report SPDs, while 14 percent of male prisoners and one-quarter of male jail inmates have that level of mental distress (Bronson and Berzofsky, 2007: 4). Regardless of gender, the mentally ill are overrepresented in jails and prisons, when compared to the age-adjusted rates for the general population; however, women report even higher numbers than men.

Age plays less of a role in prisons than it did in community programming (Bronson and Berzofsky, 2017: 5). Specifically, there was little variation by age, as one in 6 persons aged 18 to 64 reportedly met the threshold for SPD, while those prison inmates in the oldest age category (65 or older) were *less likely* than those in the youngest age category (18 to 24) to pass the SPD threshold (10% versus 15%). A similar pattern was observed among prison inmates who had been told they had any mental illness. However, age produced a more ambiguous picture among jail inmates. For jail inmates aged 18 to 44 and aged 55 to 64, the prevalence rate for SPD was 26 percent; however, jail inmates aged 45 to 54 reported an SPD prevalence rate of 29 percent. There was some slight variability for being told about any mental illness by age groups as well. As a general observation, it appears that inmates 65 or older were less likely to report having any mental health problem than were the members of any other age group.

When compared to the prevalence rates for SPD among Black (12%) and Hispanic (12%) prison inmates, those reported for White and Other Race inmates—the latter made up of American Indian/Native Alaskans, Asians, Native Hawaiians, other Pacific Islanders, and persons of two or more races—were higher (17% and 20%, respectively) (Bronson and Berzofsky, 2017: 4). Whites and Other Race jail inmates had the highest rates of a history of SPD (31% and 32%, respectively), while the rates for Hispanics and Blacks hovered around 22 to 23 percent (Bronson and Berzofsky, 2017: 4).

These patterns were repeated for a history of mental health problems, although the prevalence rates were two to three times higher for each racial grouping. Specifically, over half of White prison inmates and six in ten White jail inmates reported a history of mental illness, a pattern that was replicated among other prison and jail inmates (48% and 56%, respectively). Roughly three in ten Black jail inmates reported this level of mental illness, while it was reported by between one-quarter and three in ten Hispanic prisoners and Hispanic jail inmates, respectively. In short, Whites and Other Race prison and jail inmates have higher prevalence rates for both a history of mental illness and SPD than is the case for Hispanics and Blacks.

In the review of community corrections clients, we found that legal, medical, and behavioral concerns distinguished the mentally ill inmates from those without such an illness. The same is true of inmates of prisons and jails, but there are differences as well as similarities. For example, consider the following:

▶ *Instant Offense* — Property and personal offenders in prison were significantly more likely to have SPD or a history of mental illness problems than were drug, DWI/DUI, or other public order offenders. Among jail inmates, only violent offenders had a significantly higher prevalence of SPD, while violent and property offenders in jail both had significantly higher prevalence rates than did jail inmates accused of drug, DWI-DUI, or other public order offenses (Bronson and Berzofsky, 2017: 7).

▶ *Number of Times Arrested* — The number of times arrested can be taken as a proxy indicator for "revolving-door corrections." The prevalence rate for SPD within the prison population increases as the number of times one has been arrested in his or her lifetime goes up. For example, the prevalence rate for prison inmates on their first arrest is 12 percent, but for those arrested 11 or more times, the rate is 18 percent (Bronson and Berzofsky, 2017: 7). Among jail inmates, the prevalence rate for SPD varies little with increases in the number of times arrested, but it is higher, averaging 23 percent (Bronson and Berzofsky, 2017: 7). With respect to the question of a history of mental health problems, the prevalence rates for both jail and prison inmates increases as the number of arrests goes up, starting at 27 percent for prisoners and 31 percent for jail inmates with no prior arrest, rising to 49 percent for prisoners and 56 percent for jail inmates arrested 11 or more times (Bronson and Berzofsky, 2017: 7). Overall, then, it appears that there is a "churning effect" on prison *and* jail inmates, so that the greater the number of arrests, the greater the likelihood of both SPDs and the development of a history of mental health problems (see also Fuller, Sinclair, and Snook, 2016).

▶ *Total Time in a Correctional Facility* — For more than 75 years, criminologists have studied the role of time in prison on mental and physical health (Clemmer, 1940). Recent prison-based surveys reveal that serious psychological distress shows little correlation with *total time served in all previous incarcerations*. Only for those prison inmates that have served 5 or more years does the prevalence rate go up significantly, and, in this case, SPD goes from an average of about 14 percent to 17 percent (Bronson and Berzofsky, 2017: 7). Among jail inmates, only those in the 1-4 years category have a rate that is different from the average of 24 percent, and, in this case, SPD drops to 22 percent. A history of mental health problems presents a starkly different picture. As the time served goes up, the prevalence rates for a history of mental health problems increase. For prison inmates, the rates go from

29 percent for those with no prior time in a correctional facility to 43 percent for those individuals with 5 or more years; for jail inmates, 35 percent report having been told that they have a mental health problem, while for those with 5 or more years inside, that figure rises to 54 percent (Bronson and Berzofsky, 2017: 7). The time one spends incarcerated is far more likely to be linked to a history of mental health problems than the incidence of SPDs.

▶ *Comorbidity* — Among inmates with mental illness and substance abuse problems, the presence of both is far more problematic than either one by itself (Scott, Dennis, and Lurigio, 2015; Walters and Magaletta, 2015; Wilson, Frakas, et al., 2014). The effects of substance abuse and mental illness on inmate adjustment to jail or prison life appear to be additive (Houser, Belenko, and Brennan, 2011). Jails are probably not the right place to engage inmates in therapeutic treatments for either mental disorders or drug dependence, given the relatively short jail stays. As one jail staff member succinctly observed: "Jails and jailers are not equipped to deal with these issues [caused by the seriously mentally ill inmates], we are not doctors and county jails can't afford to have one on staff" (AbuDagga et al., 2016: 12). Prison, which is likely to be "home" for far more than a single year, may be a more stable platform from which to treat both types of illness. Yet, the percentage of mental illness among inmates and the percentage receiving care for those illnesses are quite different (Chari et al., 2016). Also, several studies suggest that the problem may even worse for women than for men (Houser et al., 2011; Scott et al., 2015).

▶ *Behavioral and Attitudinal Issues:* — Generally, prison and jail inmates with mental illness are far more likely than other inmates to support a criminal lifestyle and criminogenic values and risk factors (Morgan et al., 2010; Wilson et al., 2014). Mentally ill persons adhering to antisocial attitudes and exhibiting antisocial behavior are likely to create more problems for correctional staff than other inmates (Torrey et al., 2014). From a purely inmate management perspective, then, mentally ill inmates can be a disproportionate drain on prison and jail resources (AbuDagga et al., 2016; Adams and Ferrandino, 2008; Fuller et al., 2017).

Mental Health Programs

As described earlier in this chapter, jails employ several different short and easily interpreted tests of inmate mental stability during the **inmate intake screening**, sometimes called **receiving screening**. We do not endorse either of the ones described earlier in this chapter, but rather offer them as examples of what is available. Prisons, too, have a vested interest in determining the mental stability of those individuals placed in their charge. However, they typically house inmates for far longer periods of time and their intake processing is far more intensive and lengthy as well. For example, the **Admission and Orientation Program** in a Federal Bureau of Prisons facility occurs over the first 30 days of commitment (Federal Bureau of Prisons, 2014). Prisons also tend to use more complex measures of prisoner intellect and mental stability. For example, since the 1960s, prisons have employed the Minnesota Multiphasic Personality Inventory (MMPI) in its various incarnations as a way of determining inmate suitability for rehabilitation or treatment (Edwards, 1963; Zager, 1988). The MMPI has also been used to classify inmate security risks, as the test can measure such things as depression, psychopathic deviate, and schizophrenia, among other things (Gover, 2011). This highly valid and reliable test takes time to administer, as the extended version consists of over 500 items and the shorter, restricted version has 338 items (Ben-Porath, 2012). There is also an expense associated with using and interpreting it.

The APA's fifth edition of the *Diagnostic and Statistical Manual of Mental Disorders*, also known as the *DSM-5*, is another widely used test (APA, 2013; Suris, Holiday, and North, 2016). The DSM methodology is particularly useful for highlighting an inmate's proclivities for drug abuse and dependence (Mumola and Karberg, 2006). Among the disorders it can reveal are neurodevelopmental disorders (e.g., ADHD, intellectual disability, autism, and motor disorders); schizophrenia spectrum and other psychotic disorders (e.g., catatonia); bipolar and related disorders; depressive disorders (e.g., persistent depressive disorder); anxiety disorders (e.g., panic attack and panic disorder); obsessive-compulsive disorder and related disorders (e.g., hoarding disorder); trauma and stressor-related disorders (e.g., PTSD); dissociative disorder (e.g., dissociative amnesia); disruptive, impulse control, and conduct disorders (e.g., oppositional defiant disorder and conduct disorder); substance-related and addictive disorders; neurocognitive disorders (e.g., dementia); personality disorders (e.g., antisocial personality disorder), and dozens of others (American Psychological Association, 2013). Some but not all the disorders included in the *DSM-5* have implications for the operation of a prison or jail. There is some disagreement as to whether the antisocial personality disorder subtest of the *DSM-5* can predict intra-institutional disruptive behavior (Edens, Kelley, et al., 2015).

Tests such as the MMPI-2 and the *DSM-5*, and the shorter K6 and BJMHS, are front-end screening methods for determining who is a risk to whom, including themselves and the institution. They may also be used as screening for inmate access to limited prison-based programming, including general education, drug treatment, sex-offender therapy, and the like. Tests such as the MMPI-2 and *DSM-5* also require trained personnel for their administration. Jails, if they screen incoming inmates, tend to use the short, abbreviated tests, in large measure because they do not have the breadth of medical services found in many prisons and the inmates are staying for far shorter periods.

Even with a thorough mental health screening, the mental health treatment options available to a jail or prison are limited (Adams and Ferrandino, 2008). In terms of policies and procedures, inmates on medication can be required to come daily to the medical unit to receive it, assuming such a unit exists. Otherwise, a guard may visit the inmate and watch him or her consume the medication in the CO's presence. Also, should the behavior of the inmate in the housing unit be problematic, the facility may move him or her to the medical unit or a special housing unit (SHU). The problem with SHUs is that they are home to a wide array of inmates, including ones in protective custody, such as sex offenders, who may be a bad choice of residential partner for a mentally impaired inmate.

Problematically, few small jails have either a medical unit or an SHU. The alternative to either one may be solitary confinement (see Box 9.6), which, as shown in the Slevin case, is fraught with problems as well. Movement of such jail inmates into an alternative to jail, such as a formalized jail diversion program for the mentally ill, may be a viable alternative.

BOX 9.6

Special Concern: Solitary Confinement

Stephen Slevin lived alone for nearly two years. **Solitary confinement**, which is defined as the isolation of an inmate from all human contact—sometimes including correctional officers—for 22 to 24 hours per day, is used by correctional personnel as a way of isolating troublesome inmates or as punishment or both. Sometimes inmates are placed in solitary confinement to protect them from the predation of other inmates. However, it is a dangerous and sometimes deadly practice, especially when taken to extremes, as was the case for Slevin.

Solitary confinement can precede suicide attempts or be the locus for suicide completions. Researchers have reported that prisoners confined in solitary are three times more likely to attempt or complete suicide than those who have never experienced it. Contacts with staff and other inmates have been shown to be important predictors of suicide prevention. As a general practice, even when suicidal ideation is not a foreseeable possibility, solitary can be detrimental to the mental health of a reasonably stable person or push a person suffering from a generalized mental illness into the SPD/SMI category. Recidivism among persons placed in solitary, irrespective of their mental condition, is higher, although this could be related to the reasons that they "earned" solitary in the first place.

While it is doubtful that the practice will be discontinued in its entirety, the length of solitary confinement, the context and purpose, the mental condition of the inmate being confined, and the potential for individual and collective liability not covered in the legal doctrine of respondeat superior should be considered by staff and supervisors employing or enforcing it. Some correctional facilities, such as supermax prisons, rely on **Administrative Segregation (AS)**, a 22-to-23-hour-a-day version of solitary confinement, as a means of prisoner control, suggesting that it is unlikely to be abandoned in those types of correctional institutions. Also, a meta-analysis by Morgan and associates suggests that the long-term detrimental effects of AS may not be as common as previously thought. However, the more extreme form represented by the Slevin case may not fit this characterization. Moreover, housing inmates with preexisting mental illness in AS may, suggest Hafemeister and George, constitute a violation of the Eighth Amendment's prohibition against cruel and unusual punishment.

Sources: Arrigo and Bullock (2006); Cochran, Toman, et al. (2017); Coid, Bebbington, et al. (2002); Daigle, Daniel, et al. (2007); Hafemeister and George (2013); Mears and Bales (2009); Morgan, Gendreau, et al. (2016); Snow and Biggar (2006); Torrey, Zdanowicz, et al. (2014).

Treatment Programs. Mentally ill inmates can be encouraged to participate in whatever treatment programs are available, such as career planning, stress management, diet/nutrition and exercise, conflict resolution, substance use/dependency problems, self-esteem enhancement, assertiveness training, medication adherence, problem-solving skills, and the like (Bewley and Morgan, 2011). There are specific alternatives available for mentally ill inmates housed in both prisons and jails that have shown promise. For example, **dialectical behavior therapy (DBT)** is an evidence-based intervention intended to enhance the self-control and impulsivity controls of inmates confined in prison (Van de Bosch, Koeter, et al., 2005) and jail (Moore, Folk, et al., 2016). In the jail-based abbreviated version, inmates participate in an eight-week DBT skills group, while the prison-based program lasts approximately one year.

The inmates may be their own worst enemies in a correctional setting. As observed by the Treatment Advocacy Center (2007: 4):

> Illogical thinking, delusions, auditory hallucinations, and severe mood swings often lead to bizarre behavior by individuals with severe brain disorders who are in jails and prisons. Such bizarre behavior is disquieting to other non-ill inmates who frequently react with violence against those with brain disorders, thereby making life in jail a brutal experience for them. A serious form of assault that sometimes occurs behind bars is attempted or actual rape. All inmates in jails or prisons are at risk for such attacks, but inmates who are confused by their illness and less able to defend themselves are more vulnerable.

In short, a prevailing opinion among treatment specialists is that prisons and jails should be the placement of last resort for persons diagnosed with SMI. The illness not only makes treatment difficult inside a prison or jail, but the behavior of mentally ill inmates can make them targets of abuse by other inmates and, on occasion, by staff as well (AbuDagga et al., 2016; Adams and Ferrandino, 2006; Torrey et al., 2014).

It is a well-established fact that the first few weeks following release from prison or jail are the highest risk time for re-offending, injury, or death (Binswanger, Stern, and Deyo, 2007; Cloud and Davis, 2013; De Matteo, LaDuke, et al., 2012). Coordinating services for the transition from prison or jail to the community, what is called **community reentry planning**, has been shown to reduce recidivism and increase the likelihood of a healthy outcome for participants (Draine and Herman, 2007; Wang, Hong, et al., 2012).

EXECUTING THE MENTALLY ILL

The United States stands alone among the Western industrialized nations when it comes to executing offenders for capital crimes (Death Penalty Information Center, 2017a). With respect to mental-capacity aspects of the death penalty, three questions drive our interest. First, what about executing persons with severe developmental disabilities not the result of an illness, what used to be called severe mental retardation? The practice of executing such an individual was allegedly put to rest in *Atkins v. Virginia* (2002). In *Atkins,* the Supreme Court ruled that if a person met the APA's definition of mental retardation, currently defined as intellectual developmental disorder, then he or she could not be executed. The agreed upon definition of this condition is significant sub-average intellectual functioning accompanied by significant limitations in adaptive functioning, all of which originated before the age of 18 (Blume, Johnson, and Seeds, 2009).

Second, what about a defendant's competency? Chapter 7 addressed the question of general competency to stand trial. To recap, if a person is incapable of participating in his or her own defense, then the trial cannot proceed. However, as suggested in Box 9.7, should a person found guilty and sentenced to die subsequently develop mental illness rendering them incapable of understanding the consequences of the death penalty, then that person cannot be executed.

Finally, is mental illness by itself a basis for denying the application of the death penalty? Between 1977 and 2006, roughly a thousand persons were executed in the United States. Of that number, it is estimated that 10 percent suffered from a serious mental illness either at the time of the crime's commission or at the point of execution (Amnesty International, 2006: 7). Through October 20, 2017, that figure has grown to 1,463 executions, suggesting that upwards of 146 individuals afflicted with a serious mental illness have been executed (Death Penalty Information Center, 2017b).

Numbers only tell part of the story. Consider four examples of persons with SMI executed since 1977 (American Civil Liberties Union, 2009; Death Penalty Information Center, 2017c):

- Texas executed Kelsey Patterson in 2004. He had a decades-long history of mental illness and had been diagnosed as a paranoid schizophrenic. He was found guilty of two murders in 1992. The Texas Board of Pardons and Paroles recommended that Patterson's sentence be commuted to life, but the governor signed the death warrant.
- Manny Babbitt, a Vietnam War veteran and victim of PTSD, was executed in California in 1999. The details of his crime—the murder of a 78-year old woman during a burglary—suggested a flashback episode to his time in the military. Babbitt participated in the Battle of Khe Sahn, one of that war's bloodiest and most violent military encounters. As a recipient of the Purple Heart and a war veteran, he received a funeral with all military honors.
- Andrew Brannon, a decorated two-tour-of-duty Vietnam War veteran who suffered from PTSD and bipolar disorder, was classified by the Veterans Administration as 100 percent disabled. He was pulled over by a Georgia sheriff's deputy for driving more than 100 miles per hour. Brannon subsequently lost his temper and engaged the deputy in a shoot-out. Brannon was hit once in the abdomen, and the deputy was hit nine times and killed. Brannon is shown on the unit's video shooting the severely wounded deputy at point-blank range after reloading his weapon. Brannon was executed by Georgia in 2015.
- Roger Berget was executed by Oklahoma in 2000. As a youth, he suffered a head injury and later was diagnosed with bipolar disorder. Berget and a partner carjacked a vehicle and Rick Patterson, its driver, ultimately killing Patterson with a shotgun. Berget also admitted to a second, unconnected murder.

BOX 9.7

Law and Mental Health: Executions and Competency

In 1986, the U.S. Supreme Court considered the issue of the imposition of the death penalty when a person has evidence of mental illness after conviction. This legal issue skirts the question of sanity at the time of the crime's commission, as the defendant's guilt has been determined by a court of law. Rather, it turns on whether the appellant is competent to be executed. In *Ford v. Wainwright*, Alvin Ford had demonstrable mental illness after he was convicted and sentenced to death for murder. In prison, Ford indicated that he was the Pope of Rome, and that he and prison officials worked with the Ku Klux Klan. He said that guards tortured his family, and he controlled his own execution.

The Supreme Court upheld the common law prohibition against executing the insane. Justice Thurgood Marshall, in writing the opinion, said that it was a "savage and inhumane" violation of the Eighth Amendment to execute a person deemed insane at the time of execution. In this opinion, the Court specified the procedures required to evaluate competency prior to execution, directing that even if a person is found to be competent to stand trial and is found to be sane at the time of the crime, he or she must also have appropriate mental capacity to be executed. In a concurring opinion, Justice Powell stated: "[T]he test for whether a prisoner is insane for Eighth Amendment purposes is whether the prisoner is aware of his impending execution and of the reason for it" (477 U.S. at 401).

In a postscript to Ford's case, Alvin Bernard Ford died in prison on February 26, 1991. He died of natural causes, described in his obituary as respiratory distress. Two years earlier, a federal court ruled that Ford was sane and could be executed. At the time of his death, this judgment was under appeal.

The Ford standard was reaffirmed by the U.S. Supreme Court in a 2007 case. *Panetti v. Quarterman* involved a former serviceman, Scott Panetti, who was convicted of murdering his in-laws in 1995. He was found guilty at trial, where he acted as his own attorney and offered a defense of not guilty by reason of insanity. Panetti's subsequent appeals went unanswered. When Texas set a date of execution, a panel of experts ruled that Panetti did understand the reason for his execution. Panetti appealed once more and won a stay of execution on the grounds that Texas had not followed the guidelines set forth by Ford. Specifically, once he had made a "substantial threshold showing of insanity," he ought to have been given an impartial hearing and afforded the opportunity to cross-examine the experts. In this case, however, Texas did not afford Panetti the opportunity to refute the opinions of the experts concerning his competency to be executed.

The State of Texas has not given up on executing Panetti, setting an execution date in 2014, which the U.S. Court of Appeals for the Fifth Circuit also stayed. Panetti claims that he has no money for a lawyer or experts to determine his competency. Texas resisted paying for either. By 2016, he was represented by lawyers from the Texas Defender Service, which provides counsel in death penalty cases. In 2017, a three-judge panel of the Fifth Circuit sent the case back to Texas to be heard in the district court. In July 2017, Panetti's attorneys expressed confidence that the district court in Texas will find that Panetti, after 40 years of documented schizophrenia and serious mental illness, is too incompetent to be executed.

Another issue remains largely unresolved with respect to mental illness, competency, and the death penalty. Specifically, can the state force a mentally ill person to take medication to restore competency? Forcing medication upon a mentally ill person to achieve a legal status of competency, called synthetic competency, is a practice about which there is no legal consensus, but in at least one case, Singleton v. Norris (2003), it was decided that the state could force the inmate, a paranoid schizophrenic, to take medication for issues related to health and safety in the prison; Singleton was subsequently executed.

Sources: Bonnie (2007); *Ford v. Wainwright* (1986); New York Times (March 9, 1991); *Panetti v. Quarterman* (2007); Singleton v. Norris (2003); Texas Tribune (October 15, 2015; July 11, 2017).

In 2006, the American Bar Association (ABA) passed a resolution calling for the exemption of those with SMI from the death penalty. According to a more recent (2016) ABA report, other professional psychological associations have issued similar statements, including the APA, the American Psychological Association, National Alliance on Mental Illness, and Mental Health America. The United Nations, the European Union, the Council of Europe, and the Inter-American Commission on Human Rights have all urged countries that use the death penalty not to impose it on persons with mental illness. Until 2012, only Connecticut exempted a defendant from execution due to serious mental illness that was not itself a defense to prosecution (Connecticut General Statutes, 2009); Connecticut removed the death penalty as a punishment in that year. The execution of the mentally ill could be the next major death penalty challenge facing the Supreme Court (Winick, 2009).

EPILOGUE

This epilogue, while true to the methods, procedures, law, and practices, is fictional. We can find cases like it in probably any mental health court, but this one represents an ideal situation. However, we have consulted several sources in preparing this epilogue, including APA (2013); Council of State Governments (2008); Grant, Kim, and Odlaug (2009); Grant, Odlaug, et al. (2013); Odlaug, Grant, and Kim (2012); Redlich, Hoover, et al. (2010); Sarteschi and Vaughn, (2013).

Had John's case gone to trial in district court, the jury would likely have found the 20-year old guilty of breaking and entering into a private residence. But this was not the case, as John was diverted from traditional processing and into an MHC. The facts in the case supported a conviction for B & E. After all, he had forced open a set of French doors (police had fingerprint evidence of this aspect of the crime), and gaining entrance to the home by the use of force is the legal definition of breaking and entering. At the time of his arrest at the crime scene, he had no "burglary tools" or containers with which to carry the stolen items, so the jury probably would not have found him guilty of the additional charge of attempted burglary. However, in John's mind, burglary was precisely his intent, though this was not something he shared with his attorney. He simply planned, like many of his ilk, to use a couple of pillow cases to carry away his ill-gotten gains.

Luckily for John, as burglary is a far more serious crime, a silent alarm quickly summoned a nearby police cruiser. John was apprehended as he was making his first reconnaissance of the house and its contents. He did not want just any old items from a house; he had a mental "shopping list." The arresting officers took John to the local jail for processing, after calling in a crime scene investigation team to process the house.

John and his family had learned five years previously that he suffered from kleptomania. According to the *DSM-5* diagnosis [302.32 (F63.3)], kleptomania is a condition whereby the afflicted person suffers from an impulse control disorder characterized by the inability to resist the impulse to steal. The objects of theft are often of little value and not needed by the thief, either for personal use or resale. The kleptomaniac simply must have them. In his case, John was diagnosed when, as a juvenile, he shoplifted some items from a second-hand store, items that individually were of little value but collectively had a value of nearly $100. He was quickly caught, and sentenced by a juvenile court judge to six months in the state reformatory, as this was not John's first scrape with the law. What John learned there was that if he really wanted to enjoy his thefts, he would have to enter a home when no one was there, so he could enjoy the entire enterprise to its maximum effect.

John also abused drugs, mainly "uppers," as he suffered from depressive disorders, a not uncommon condition for kleptomaniacs. The drugs were a kind of self-medication that allowed him to function normally most of the time. However, when he was planning a "heist," as he liked to characterize these house burglaries, he stopped taking them for a couple of days. This time he had not stopped in time, and his use of drugs had caused him to be careless, leading to tripping the alarm and his arrest. The only good news was that the police failed to find the cache of stolen items he had hidden at home.

At detainment, John was given the local jail's version of the Brief Jail Mental Health Screen (BJMHS). After this screening, John talked to his jailers about suicide. Expressions of suicidal ideation by kleptomaniacs is not all that unusual, as researchers report that many suicide attempts are directly related to kleptomania. The jailers, upon the recommendation of the treatment staff, immediately put John in a special anti-suicide cell and notified his counsel, the prosecutor, and the judge assigned to John's case. The judge ordered a psychiatric hold and examination for John.

The presiding judge, upon reading John's psychiatric report, had his case transferred to the county's mental health court, which was a special session of her own court. At a pre-adjudication hearing in front of the judge, the county prosecutor, defense counsel, and John agreed to a treatment plan created by the court's intervention staff. John would be placed on probation for three years, assuming he abided by the regular conditions of release and participated in court-mandated counseling; further, he would need to take antidepressant drugs. John also volunteered for a field experiment using memantine, an Alzheimer's drug that had shown promise for reducing impulsiveness in shoplifters. As the study was a double-blind, wherein neither John nor the researchers knew who received memantine or a placebo, John would also participate in the MHC's other targeted interventions, which included reporting to the court (and the MHC's treatment staff) bi-weekly, at which time he would be drug tested, looking for the presence of his medications and the absence of other drugs, and attending regular community-based group therapy sessions.

John's case represents an ideal situation. All parties communicated with each other. The policies and procedures, and, more importantly, the mental health court, were in place to respond quickly and appropriately to a situation such as John's. Given the growth of such courts, other mentally ill offenders may find themselves also being diverted from the criminal justice system into community treatment programs overseen by a MHC.

SUMMARY

▶ The treatment perspective implies that the correctional system must provide its "clients" with access to therapeutic solutions for the ills that brought them into the system or those they suffered because of their criminal sanction.

▶ The custody perspective is built on the idea that any correctional system must provide for the maximum containment level necessary to control the movement and general conduct of its clients.

▶ The higher the level of custody required to control an institution's clients, the lower the emphasis on and application of therapeutic programming.

▶ Besides probation, sentencing alternatives include fines, restitution, home confinement/electronic monitoring, house arrest, halfway houses, and restorative justice.

▶ There are several screening devices available for correctional personnel to use in determining which inmates have a serious mental illness, however it is defined.

▶ There are multiple non-APA definitions in use to describe mental illness problems within the correctional system, including serious mental illness (SMI), any mental illness (AMI), serious psychological distress (SPD), and a history of mental health problems.

▶ Jail diversion and forensic assertive community treatment programs have shown great promise for the successful reintegration of mentally ill offenders, especially if supported by a well-developed community reentry plan.

▶ Jails, more than prisons, are a problematic environment for mentally ill inmates.

▶ Persons with mental illness have been executed for capital crimes, which begs the question: How much mental illness is enough to avoid the death penalty?

CHAPTER REVIEW QUESTIONS

1. First, describe the roles of custody and security in operating a correctional institution. Next, define treatment. How can treatment conflict with custody and vice versa, as treatment and custody staff perform their respective duties and obligations?

2. Define alternative sentencing. List and define five forms of alternative sentencing. Are they stand-alone sentences? How are they expected to work?

3. Describe the key personal-biographical features of the community corrections mental health clients. Which of these features most surprised you and why?

4. Describe the key legal, medical, and behavioral concerns associated with mentally ill probationers and parolees. Which of these concerns most surprised you and why?

5. This chapter includes two screening devices that show much promise in helping to identify inmates with serious mental illness. What are they? Have they been shown to have general application to correctional settings?

6. Describe the key personal-biographical, legal, medical, and behavioral concerns associated with mentally ill jail and prison inmates. Which of these concerns most surprised you and why?

7. Define each of the following terms: serious psychological distress and history of mental health problems. How do they compare to serious mental illness and any mental illness, two other terms often used by correctional researchers?

8. Define solitary confinement. Discuss the issues associated with its use.

9. How do you feel about the execution of the mentally ill? Which arguments for banning its use resonate with you? Could you see a situation in which it was acceptable to execute a mentally ill person? Explain your answer.

10. How does the Sequential Intercept Model (SIM) relate to diversion? In preparing your answer to this question, be sure to review the chapter's epilogue.

KEY TERMS

Administrative segregation (AS)

Admission and Orientation
   Program

Brief Jail Mental Health Screen (BJMHS)

Community reentry planning

Custody

Custody perspective

Custody staff

Dialectical behavior therapy (DBT)

Dynamic security

Fines

Forensic assertive community treatment
   (FACT) program

Halfway house

Home confinement/electronic
   monitoring

House arrest

Inmate intake screening

REFERENCES

Abramson, M.F. (1972). "The criminalization of mentally disordered behavior: Possible side-effect of a new mental health law." *Hospital and Community Psychiatry*, 23: 101-105.

AbuDagga, A., S. Wolfe, M. Carome, A. Phatdouang, and E.F. Torrey (2016). "Individuals with serious mental illness in county jails: A survey of jail staff's perspectives." Washington, DC: Public Citizen.

Adams, K., and J. Ferrandino (2008). "Managing mentally ill inmates in prison." *Criminal Justice and Behavior* 35: 913-927.

American Bar Association (2016). *Severe Mental Illness and the Death Penalty*. Chicago, IL: American Bar Association.

American Civil Liberties Union (2009). "Death penalty and mental illness." New York City: American Civil Liberties Union. Retrieved at https://www.aclu.org/report/report-mental-illness-and-death-penalty on 3 November 2017.

American Psychiatric Association (2013). *Diagnostic and Statistical Manual of Mental Disorders* (5th ed.). Arlington, VA: American Psychiatric Publishing.

Amnesty International (2006). *USA: The Execution of Mentally Ill Offenders*. London, UK: Amnesty International.

Appelbaum, K.L., J.M. Hickey, and I. Packer (2001). "The role of correctional officers in multidisciplinary mental health care in prisons." *Psychiatric Services* 52: 1343-47.

Arrigo, B.A., and J.L. Bullock (2007). "The psychological effects of solitary confinement on prisoners in supermax units." *International Journal of Offender Therapy and Comparative Criminology* 52: 622-40.

Baillargeon, J., B.A. Williams, J. Mellow, M.J. Harzke, S.K. Hoge, G. Baillargeon, and R.B. Greifinger (2009). "Parole revocation among prison inmates with psychiatric and substance use disorders." *Psychiatric Services* 60: 1516-1521.

Ben-Porath, Y.S. (2012). *Interpreting the MMPI-2-RF*. Minneapolis: University of Minnesota Press.

Bewley, M.T., and R.D. Morgan (2011). "A national survey of mental health services available to offenders with mental illness: Who is doing what?" *Law and Human Behavior* 35: 351-63.

Binswanger, I.A., M.F. Stern, and R.A. Deyo, et al. (2007). "Release from prison — a high risk of death for former inmates." *The New England Journal of Medicine* 356: 157-165.

Blume, J.H., S.L. Johnson, and C. Sees (2009). "Of Atkins and men: Deviations from clinical definitions of mental retardation in death penalty cases." *Cornell Journal of Law and Public Policy* 18: 689-733.

Bonnie, R.J. (2007). "Panetti and Quarterman: Mental illness, the death penalty, and human dignity." *Ohio State Journal of Criminal Law* 5: 257-83.

Breyer, P.B., C.R. Breyer, D.L. Fredich, R.E. Barkow, W.H. Pryor, Jr., and J.J. Wroblewski (2015). *Alternative Sentencing in the Federal Criminal Justice System*. Washington, DC: U.S. Sentencing Commission.

Bronson, J., and M. Berzofsky (2017). "Indicators of mental health problems reported by prisoners and jail inmates, 2011-2012." *Special Report*. Washington, DC: Bureau of Justice Statistics, U.S. Department of Justice.

Carson, E.A., and E. Anderson (2016). *Prisoners in 2015*. NCJ 250229. Washington, DC: Bureau of Justice Statistics, U.S. Department of Justice.

Chari, K.A., A.E. Simon, C.J. DeFrances, and L. Maruschak (2016). "National survey of prison health care: Selected findings." *National Health Statistics Reports*. No. 96. Washington, DC: U.S. Department of Health and Human Services.

Clear, T.R. and N.A. Frost (2015). *The Punishment Imperative: The Rise and Fall of Mass Incarceration in America*. New York: New York University Press.

Clemmer, D. (1940). *The Prison Community*. Boston: Christopher.

Cloud, D., and C. Davis (2013). "Treatment alternatives to incarceration for people with mental health needs in criminal justice system: The cost-savings implications." New York: VERA Institute of Justice, Substance Use and Mental Health Program.

Cochran, J.C., E.L. Toman, D.P. Mears, and W.D. Bales (2018). "Solitary confinement as punishment: Examining in-prison sanctioning disparities." *Justice Quarterly* 35: 381-411.

Coid, J., P. Bebbington, R. Jenkins, T. Brugha, G. Lewis, M. Farrell, and M. Singleton (2002). "The national survey of psychiatric morbidity among prisoners and the future of prison healthcare." *Medicine, Science and the Law* 42: 245-50.

Council of State Governments (2008). *Mental health courts: A primer for policymakers and practitioners*. Washington, DC: U.S. Department of Justice.

Craig, S.C. (2004). "Rehabilitation versus Control: An Organizational Theory of Prison Management." *The Prison Journal* 84: 92S-114S.

Cusack, K.J., J.P. Morrisey, G.S. Cuddeback, A. Prins, and D.M. Williams (2010). "Criminal justice involvement, behavioral health service use, and costs of forensic assertive community treatment: A randomized trial." *Community Mental Health Journal* 46: 356-363.

Daigle, M.S., A.E. Daniel, G.E. Dear, P. Frottier, L.M. Hayes, A. Kerkhof, N. Konrad, A. Liebling, and M. Sarchiapone (2007). "Preventing suicide in prisons, Part II, International Comparisons of suicide prevention services in correctional facilities." *Crisis* 28: 122-130.

Death Penalty Information Center (2017a). "Executions and death sentences around the world." Washington, DC: Death Penalty Information Center. Retrieved at https://deathpenaltyinfo.org/death-penalty-international-perspective#interexec on 3 November 2017.

Death Penalty Information Center (2017b). "Facts about the death penalty." Washington, DC: Death Penalty Information Center. Retrieved at https://deathpenaltyinfo.org/documents/FactSheet.pdf on 3 November 2017.

Death Penalty Information Center (2017c). "Examples of mentally ill inmates who were executed." Washington, DC: Death Penalty Information Center. Retrieved at https://deathpenaltyinfo.org/mental-illness-and-death-penalty#executions on 3 November 2017.

DeMatteo, D., C. LaDuke, B.R. Locklair, and K. Heilbrun (2012). "Community-based alternatives for justice-involved individuals with severe mental illness: Diversion, problem-solving courts, and reentry." *Journal of Criminal Justice* 42: 64-71.

Ditton, P.M. (1999). *Mental Health and Treatment of Inmates and Probationers.* Washington, DC: U.S. Department of Justice, Bureau of Justice Statistics.

Draine, J., and D.B. Herman (2007). "Critical time intervention for reentry from prison for persons with mental illness." *Psychiatric Services* 58: 1577-1581.

Draine, J., and P. Solomon (2001). "Threats of incarceration in a psychiatric probation and parole service." *American Journal of Orthopsychiatry* 71: 262-67.

Edens, J.F., S.E. Kelley, J.L. Skeem, K.S. Douglas (2015). "DSM-5 antisocial personality disorder: Predictive validity in a prison sample." *Law and Human Behavior* 39: 123-29.

Edwards, John A. (1963). "Rehabilitation potential in prison inmates as measured by the MMPI." *Journal of Criminal Law and Criminology* 54: 181-5.

Eisenberg, L., and L. Guttmacher (2010). "Were We All Asleep at the Switch? A Personal Reminiscence of Psychiatry from 1940 to 2010." *Acta Psychiatrica Scandanavica* 122: 89-102.

Fellner, J. (2006). "A corrections quandary: Mental illness and prison rules." *Harvard Civil Rights–Civil Liberties Law Review* 41: 391-412.

Faiver, K.L. (1998). *Health Care Management Issues in Corrections.* Lanham, MD: American Correctional Association.

Families Against Mandatory Minimums (2013). "Alternatives to incarceration in a nutshell." Washington, DC: Families Against Mandatory Minimums. Retrieved at http://famm.org/wp-content/uploads/2013/08/FS-Alternatives-in-a-Nutshell-7.8.pdf on 3 November 2017.

Federal Bureau of Prisons (2014). Inmate Admission & Orientation Handbook. Greenville, Illinois: U.S. Department of Justice, Federal Bureau of Prisons.

Feucht, T.E., and J. Gfroerer (2011). *Mental and Substance Use Disorders among Adult Men on Probation or Parole: Some Success against a Persistent Challenge.* Rockville, MD: Substance Abuse and Mental Health Services Administration.

Fogel, D. (1975). "... *We are the Living Proof ...*" *The Justice Model for Corrections.* Cincinnati: Anderson.

Fuller, D.A., E. Sinclair, H.R. Lamb, Judge J.D. Cayce, and J. Snook (2017). *Emptying the "New Asylums": A Beds Capacity Model to Reduce Mental Illness Behind Bars*. Arlington, VA: Treatment Advocacy Center.

Fuller, D.A., E. Sinclair, and J. Snook (2017). "A crisis in search of data: The revolving door of serious mental illness in super utilization." Arlington, VA: Treatment Advocacy Center.

Gerber, M. (March 8, 2013). "After 2 years behind bars without trial, N.M. man to get $15.5 million." *Los Angeles Times*. Retrieved at http://articles.latimes.com/2013/mar/08/nation/la-na-nn-stephen-slevin-15-million-settlement-20130308 on 27 February 2018.

Gover, B.L. (2011). "The utility of MMPI-2 scores with a correctional population and convicted sex offenders." *Psychology* 6: 638-42.

Grant, J.E., S.W. Kim, and B.L. Odlaug (2009). "A double-blind, placebo-controlled study of the opiate antagonist, naltrexone, in the treatment of kleptomania." *Biological Psychiatry* 65: 600-606.

Grant, J.E., B.L. Odlaug, A.A. Davis, and S.W. Kim (2009). "Legal consequences of kleptomania." *Psychiatric Quarterly* 80: 251-9.

Grant, J.E., B.L. Odlaug, L.R.N. Schreiber, S.R. Chamberlain, and S.W. Kim (2013). "Memantine reduces stealing behavior and impulsivity in kleptomania: A pilot study." *International Clinical Psychopharmacology* 28: 106-11.

Griffin, P.A., K. Heilbrun, E.P. Mulvey, D. DeMatteo, and Carol A. Schubert (eds.) (2015). *Sequential Intercept Model and Criminal Justice: Promoting Community Alternatives for Individuals with Serious Mental Illness*. New York: Oxford University Press.

Hafemeister, T.L., and J. George (2013). "The ninth circle of hell: An eighth amendment analysis of imposing prolonged supermax solitary confinement on inmates with a mental illness." *Denver University Law Review* 90: 1-54.

Hart, S.D., R. Roesch, R.R. Corrado, and D.N. Cox (1993). "The referral decision scale: A validation study." *Law and Human Behavior* 17: 611-23.

Hepburn, J.R., and C. Albonetti (1980). "Role conflict in correctional institutions: An empirical examination of the treatment-custody dilemma among correctional staff." *Criminology* 17: 445-59.

Hounmenou, C. (2012). "Monitoring human rights of persons in police lockups: Potential role of community-based organizations." *Journal of Community Practice* 20: 274-92.

Houser, K.A., S. Belenko, and P.K. Brennan (2011). "The effects of mental health and substance abuse disorder on misconduct among female inmates." *Justice Quarterly* 29: 799-828.

Irwin, J. (2013). *The Jail: Managing the Underclass in American Society*. Berkeley, CA: The University of California Press.

Kaeble, D., and T.B. Bonczar (2016). *Probation and Parole in the United States, 2015*. Washington, DC: U.S. Department of Justice, Bureau of Justice Statistics.

Kessler, R.C., G. Andrews, L.J. Colpe, E. Hiripi, D.K. Mroczek, S.L. Normand, E.E. Walters, and A.M. Zaslavsky, (2002). "Short screening scales to monitor population prevalences and trends in non-specific psychological distress." *Psychological Medicine* 32: 959-976.

Kessler, R.C., P.R. Barker, L.J. Colpe, J.F. Epstein, J.C. Gfroerer, E. Hiripi, M.J. Howes, S.L. Normand, R.W. Manderscheid, E.E. Walters, and A.M. Zaslavsky (2003). "Screening for serious mental illness in the general population." *Archives of General Psychiatry* 60: 184-189.

Lamb, H.R., and L.E. Weinberger (2011). "Meeting the needs of those persons with serious mental illness who are most likely to become criminalized." *Journal of the American Academy of Psychiatry and the Law* 38: 549-54.

Lamberti, S., R. Weisman, and D.I. Faden (2004). "Forensic assertive community treatment: Preventing incarceration of adults with severe mental illness." *Psychiatric Services* 55(11): 1285-1293.

Louden, J.E., and J.L. Skeem (2013). "How do probation officers assess and manage recidivism and violence risk for probationers with mental disorders? An experimental investigation." *Law and Human Behavior* 37: 22-34.

Louden, J.E., J.L. Skeem, and A. Blevins (2013). "Comparing the predictive utility of two screening tools for mental disorder among probationers." *Psychological Assessments* 25: 405-415.

Malik-Kane, K., and C.A. Visher (2008). "Health and prisoner reentry: How physical, mental, and substance abuse conditions shape the process of reintegration." Washington, DC: Urban Institute.

Matejkowski, J., J. Draine, P. Solomon, and M.S. Salzer (2011). "Mental illness, criminal risk factors and parole release decisions." *Behavioral Sciences and the Law* 29: 528-553.

Matejkowski, J., and M. Ostermann (2015). "Serious mental illness, criminal risk, parole supervision, and recidivism: Testing of conditional effects." *Law and Human Behavior* 39: 75-86.

Mays, G.L., and L.T. Winfree, Jr. (2014). *Essentials of Corrections.* 5th ed. New York: Wiley-Blackwell.

Mears, D.P., and W.D. Bales (2009). "Supermax incarceration and recidivism." *Criminology* 47: 1131-1166.

Minton, T.D., and Z. Zeng (2016). "Jail inmates in 2015." Washington, DC: U.S. Department of Justice, Bureau of Justice Statistics.

Morgan, D.W., A.C. Edwards, and L.R. Faulkner (1993). "The adaptation to prison of individuals with schizophrenia." *Bulletin of the American Academy of Psychiatry and the Law* 21: 427-433.

Morgan, R.D., W.H. Fisher, N. Duan, J.T. Mandracchia, and D. Murray (2010). "Prevalence of criminal thinking among state prison inmates with serious mental illness." *Law and Human Behavior* 34: 324-336.

Moore, K.E., J.B. Folk, E.A. Boren, J.P. Tangney, S. Fischer, and S.W. Schrader (2016). "Pilot study of a brief dialectical behavior therapy skills group for jail inmates." *Psychological Services.* Retrieved at https://www.ncbi.nlm.nih.gov/pubmed/27617479 on 1 November 2017.

Morris, N. (1974). *The Future of Imprisonment.* Chicago: University of Chicago Press.

Mumola, C.J., and J.C. Karberg (2006). *Drug Use and Dependence, State and Federal Prisoners, 2004.* Washington, DC: U.S. Department of Justice, Office of Justice Programs.

Munetz, M.R., and P.A. Griffin (2006). "Use of the Sequential Intercept Model as an approach to decriminalization of people with serious mental illness." *Psychiatric Services* 57: 544-9.

New York Times (March 9, 1991). "Alvin Ford, 37, Dies; Stricken on Death Row." Retrieved at http://www.nytimes.com/1991/03/09/obituaries/alvin-ford-37-dies-stricken-on-death-row.html on 1 November 2017.

Osher, F., D.A. D'Amora, M. Plotkin, N. Jarrett, and A. Eggleston (2012). *Adults with Behavioral Health Needs Under Correctional Supervision: A Shared Framework for Reducing Recidivism and Promoting Recovery*. New York: Council of State Governments.

Penn, J.V. (2015). "Standards and accreditation for jails, prisons, and juvenile facilities." Chapter 63 in R.L. Trestman, K.L. Appelbaum, and J.L. Metzner (eds.), *Oxford Textbook of Correctional Psychiatry* (pp. 359-364). New York: Oxford University Press.

Pew Center on the States (2007). "When offenders break the rules: Smart responses to parole and probation violations." Washington, DC: The Pew Charitable Trusts.

Redlich, A.D., and K. Cusack (2010). "Mental health treatment in criminal justice settings." Pp. 421-440 in B.L. Levin, K.D. Hennessy, and J. Petrila (eds.), *Mental Health Services: A Public Health Perspective*. New York: Oxford University Press.

Redlich, A.D., S. Hoover, A. Summers, and H.J. Steadman (2010). "Enrollment in mental health courts: Voluntariness, knowingness, and adjudicative competence." *Law and Human Behavior* 34: 91-104.

Sabol, W.J., and T.D. Minton (2008). Jail inmates at midyear 2007. Washington, DC: Bureau of Justice Statistics, U.S. Department of Justice.

Sarteschi, C.M., and M.G. Vaughn (2013). "Recent developments in mental health courts: What have we learned?" *Journal of Forensic Social Work* 3: 34-55.

Scott, C.K., M.L. Dennis, and A.J. Lurigio (2015). "Comorbidity among female detainees in drug treatment: An exploration of internalizing and externalizing disorder." *Psychiatric Rehabilitation Journal* 38: 35-44.

Snow, L., and K. Biggar (2006). "The role of peer-support in reducing self-harm in prison." Pp. 153-166 in G.E. Dear (ed.), *Preventing Suicide and Other Self-harm in Prison*. Basingstoke, UK: Palgrave-Macmillan.

Steadman, H.J., F.C. Osher, P.C. Robbins, B. Case, and S. Samuels (2009). "Prevalence of serious mental illness among jail inmates." *Psychiatric Services* 60: 761-65.

Steadman, H.J., J.E. Scott, F. Osher, T.K. Agnese, and P.C. Robbins (2005). "Validation of the brief jail mental health screen." *Psychiatric Services* 56: 816-822.

Street, D., R.D. Vinter, and C. Perrow (1966). *Organization for Treatment*. New York: The Free Press.

Suris, A., R. Holliday, and C.S. North (2016). "The evolution of the classification of psychiatric disorders." *Behavioral Sciences*. Retrieved at https://www.ncbi.nlm.nih.gov/pmc/articles/PMC4810039/ on 1 November 2017.

The Texas Tribune (October 20, 2015). "Panetti case highlights cracks in execution law." Retrieved at https://www.texastribune.org/2015/10/20/panetti-case-highlights-possible-gap-execution-law/ on 1 November 2017.

The Texas Tribune (July 11, 2017). "The Texas death row inmate Scott Panetti to get further competency review." Retrieved at https://www.texastribune.org/2017/07/11/texas-death-row-inmate-scott-panetti-get-further-competency-review/ on 1 November 2017.

Toch, H., and K. Adams (1987). "The prison as dumping ground: Mainlining disturbed offenders." *Journal of Psychiatry and the Law* 15: 539-553.

Torrey, E.F., M.T. Zdanowicz, Sheriff A.D. Kennard, H.R. Lamb, D.F. Eslinger, M.C. Biasotti, and D.A. Fuller (2014). "The treatment of persons with mental illness in prisons and jails: A state survey." Arlington, VA: Treatment Advocacy Center.

Trawver, K.R., and S.L. Rhoades (2013). "Homestead a pioneer mental health court: A judicial perspective from the last frontier." *American Behavioral Scientist* 57: 174-88.

Van den Bosch, L.M.C., M.W.J. Koeter, T. Stijnen, R. Verheul, and W. van den Brink (2005). "Sustained efficacy of dialectical behaviour therapy for borderline personality disorder." *Behaviour Research and Therapy* 43: 1231-1241.

Verhaaff, A., and H. Scott (2015). "Individual factors predicting mental court diversion outcome." *Research on Social Work Practice* 25: 213-28.

Walters, G.D., and P.R. Magaletta (2015). "Comorbid antisocial and substance misuse proclivity and mental health service utilization by female inmates: Testing the worst of both worlds hypothesis with the PAI." *Psychological Services* 12: 1-28.

Wang, E.A., C.S. Hong, S. Shavit, R. Sanders, E. Kessell, and M.B. Kushel (2012). "Engaging individuals recently released from prison into primary care: A randomized trial." *American Journal of Public Health* 102(9): e22-9.

Wilper, A.P., S. Woolhandler, J.W. Boyd, K.E. Lasser, D. McCormick, D.H. Bor, and D.U. Himmselstein (2006). "The health and health care of U.S. Prisoners: A nationwide survey." *American Journal of Public Health* 99: 1-7.

Wilson, A.B., K. Farkas, K.J. Ishler, M. Gearhart, and R. Morgan (2014). "Criminal thinking styles among people with serious mental illness in jail." *Law and Human Behavior* 38: 592-601.

Winick, B.J. (2009). "The Supreme Court's evolving death penalty jurisprudence: Severe mental illness at the next frontier." *Boston College Law Review* 50: 785-858.

Wolff, N., R.D. Morgan, and J. Shi (2013). Comparative analysis of attitudes and emotions among inmates: Does mental illness matter? *Criminal Justice and Behavior* 40: 1092-1108.

Zager, L.D. (1988). "The MMPI-based criminal classification system: A review, current status, and future directions." *Criminal Justice and Behavior* 15: 39-57.

Zald, M., and D. Street (1964). "Custody and treatment in juvenile institutions: An organizational analysis." *Crime and Delinquency* 10: 249-56.

CASES

Atkins v. Virginia, 536 U.S. 304 (2002)
Ford v. Wainwright, 477 U.S. 399 (1986)
Panetti v. Quarterman, 551 U.S. 930 (2007)
Singleton v. Norris, 319 F.3d 1018 (8th Cir. 2003)

LEGISLATION

Conn. Gen. Stat. §53a-46a(h)(3) (2009)

Part III

Special Issues

This part of the book details three special issues related to mental healthcare and criminal justice: juveniles, harassing behaviors, and at-risk populations. The nation's children are the focus of Chapter 11. This chapter details how children are treated by four separate, but often overlapping, societal "stands": the juvenile justice system, the mental health system, the child protection service system, and the educational system. Chapter 11 makes us think in new ways about three forms of behavior that concern the mental healthcare system and, at times, also cause a response by the justice system: hoarding, homelessness, and stalking and other harassing behaviors. The sociological, legal, and mental aspects of these behaviors receive close inspection in this chapter. Finally, Chapter 12 reveals that much of the world views mental healthcare as a human right. When the rights of any individual or group are not acknowledged, then the person or group is considered at-risk of further depredations. The chapter explores how the intersection of healthcare and criminal justice impacts four such at-risk populations: the elderly; military veterans; gay, lesbian, bisexual, transgender, and queer communities; and racial and ethnic minorities.

CHAPTER 10

Juveniles and Mental Illness: Special Considerations

LEARNING OBJECTIVES

After reading this chapter, you should be able to:

▶ Understand the juvenile justice court system framework and the procedures and terminology applicable to juvenile courts.

▶ Understand the role of the juvenile justice system in the treatment of mentally ill youthful offenders.

▶ Appreciate how the mental healthcare system deals with mentally ill youthful offenders, including the identification of correlates of mental illness in early childhood and the connections between conduct disorders, drugs, and delinquency.

▶ Articulate how mental competency is important for the juvenile justice system, and the role of mental illness in suicidal ideation, murder, and prostitution.

▶ Understand the ways the educational system contributes to the school-to-prison pipeline for youth, especially mentally ill youth.

▶ Specify the mental illness factors associated with deadly violence by youth.

PROLOGUE

This is based on a true account, but the names and location were changed. Any similarity to known people and locations is coincidental.

She was such a waif. When Officer Berra Davis found her living in one of the carts from an abandoned carnival roller coaster ride on the edge of her assigned patrolling area, the child said she was 13, but looked like she was 8. She weighed about 70 pounds and had blond hair and sunken blue eyes.

Officer Davis took the girl, who said her name was Claire, to juvenile hall on charges of trespassing and possession of stolen property. The main reason, however, was that juvenile hall was the only safe place she knew to take the little girl at 1:30 in the morning.

During the ride to juvenile hall, Claire alternated between whispering to herself and singing to "Sam," who she said was seated next to her. She sometimes spoke in nonsensical or non-sequential sentences. Claire was grimy and her face was smudged. Her blond hair was a tangled mess. She smelled of feces and urine. Her clothes—dirty red stretch pants, a teddy bear tee shirt, and an oversized yellow hoodie with "Casual Friday" written on the back—were covered with grease, food spots, and other spots whose origins Officer Davis could only guess.

A few days after dropping her off at juvenile hall, Officer Davis stopped to check on Claire's placement. To her surprise, Claire was still in the detention facility. The intake officer said that Claire was a little hard to place because she had a history of running away from foster homes, and, while they were awaiting a visit and diagnosis from a licensed therapist, the nurse at the facility believed that Claire suffered from schizophrenia. The young girl was also clearly traumatized by her life on the streets.

Knowing it was not a police-approved practice when there is a pending prosecution case, Officer Davis nonetheless decided to check on Claire to see how she was doing. In the juvenile court visiting room, Claire said that her mother was always homeless, and that she had been born on the floor of the women's bathroom at a public park. Claire's mom had received and lost custody of her more times than she could remember.

As Officer Davis talked with Claire, she noted that the teenager still whispered to herself and her invisible friend Sam. Claire told Davis, without much emotional inflection, that she was diagnosed with various mental disorders, including depression, bipolar disorder, and post-traumatic stress disorder. Claire chuckled about that and then said, "It isn't post. It's now and tomorrow. I just have the 'heebeegeebees.'" Claire also revealed to Officer Davis that her mother suffered from schizophrenia with paranoia. She frequently burned her daughter with cigarettes or locked her in a closet all day. Davis noted to herself that Claire seemed quite comfortable chatting about her own and her mother's psychological diagnoses. It was as though she was talking about classes she liked in school. Claire had been to six of them so far through her years in the foster care programs.

Although Officer Davis knew it was against departmental policies and procedures, not to mention good common sense, she decided to bring Claire home to have Thanksgiving dinner with her own family. Her mom, a judge in Arizona, and her sister and her family were all coming to Davis's house. She felt that she could show Claire how families really live. She even bought Claire a new outfit and shoes in anticipation of the event.

On Thanksgiving morning, Officer Davis left her bustling house and fudged a little on the check-out documents at the juvenile hall, implying that she was taking Claire to "see family." It was not a complete lie; she just was not forthcoming about whose family Claire would see.

Claire loved her outfit. She said she had not had any new shoes for several years, always getting worn-out ones from thrift stores or special kid programs. She helped Officer Davis set the table, following the directions of "fork left the spoon and knife alright."

Just as Officer Davis, now called Miss Berra by Claire, was calling everyone to eat, she noticed the teenager had not returned from a trip to the bathroom. She had walked out the back door, leaving her old clothes. Claire was gone. Berra's mother comforted her, noting, "She's a child who was left alone in her crib, kept under hot water a little too long, physically abused by someone whom she loved, neglected by the system. She likely has a genetic predisposition to mental illness that, in the best situation, needs constant medical treatment. She doesn't trust anyone and can't. Oh," continued Berra's mother, "and you never should have given her those new shoes."

Officer Davis reported the incident to both juvenile hall authorities and her supervisor. Davis was disciplined by the police department and placed on a two-week suspension and given a one-year probation. She was told not to work with juveniles and had to call for back-up if there was a minor or a mental health case. As for Claire, she simply disappeared.

CHAPTER OVERVIEW

Juveniles receive special consideration in the American justice system. First, we examine just how the juvenile justice system favors legal intervention for children and adolescents. That is, rather than punishing a minor for violating the law, the juvenile justice system tries intervention, treatment, and non-punitive consequences for actions that, if committed by an adult, are criminal. Moreover, as we make clear, sometimes the juvenile justice system gets involved simply because of the age status of the youth. Under the **status offenses**, juvenile proceedings are initiated if an underage person drinks alcohol, smokes cigarettes, or is considered incorrigible. Ultimately, as in the adult justice system, the juvenile justice system is overwhelmed with high volume of cases and has low financial resources and few options.

Second, we explore the role of mental health issues in the juvenile justice system. Initially, we will explore the different types of common mental illnesses that emerge in early childhood. Researchers tell us that if a child with early symptoms of mental illness receives timely interventions and care, then there is a higher probability that he or she can avoid legal difficulties as an adult. Then we will also briefly explore marginalized behaviors known as social maladaptive interactions or characteristics of antisocial conduct disorder.

Finally, juvenile laws raise many aspects of personal behavior and consequences. It is critical for all of us to be aware of several special concerns that are found within the younger population all too often: suicide, sex trafficking, and aggressive conduct disorders. We will then consider how education and mental health could be a solution to keep the mentally ill out of prison, but here efforts are not highly successful. We end this chapter with an epilogue that focuses on when kids kill other kids.

FRAMING THE ISSUES

This chapter seeks to explain the links between juvenile justice and mental illness, and also promote the idea that juveniles who suffer from mental illness could be prevented from becoming adult offenders through proactive referral for treatment and care in community-based alternative settings. Although current resources are limited, through action and advocacy, such as we saw with students around the country in March 2018 following yet another mass shooting in a high school, changes in allocations for mental health services could occur.

The national goal for juvenile justice in the 1974 Juvenile Justice and Delinquency Prevention Act (JJDPA) was to divert youth from the traditional adult forms of punishment of custodial detention and incarceration to instead learn from their youthful mistakes through rehabilitation, treatment, and restorative justice. The ideals, however, quickly faded. As states experienced reductions in public mental health services for adults with mental illness, the availability of similar services for children also declined. Originally, like the adult programs that aimed for judicial intervention and treatment for the mentally ill, police and local communities also made proactive efforts to use the juvenile court and delinquency corrections programs to place children into mental health treatment. Now, rather than relying on family self-referrals, school and community management, and engagement of voluntary resources, courts are employed to direct and control juvenile misbehavior and delinquent conduct. Law enforcement, emergency medical personnel, and first responders — as well as second responders of probation officers, street social workers, and related service providers — all rely on juvenile detention and juvenile court services to engage and require compliance for services for mentally disturbed minors.

The Federal Advisory Committee on Juvenile Justice (2011) reported that the difficulties and limitations experienced by the juvenile justice system as it struggles to provide adequate services to its juvenile clients are the same difficulties and limitations facing the overtaxed adult services: insufficient resources, inadequate administrative capacity, lack of appropriate staffing, and lack of training for staff. Due to the lack of research, inadequate models of care, insufficient policy developments, and ineffective experience and training of staff, juvenile corrections personnel are deficient in providing adequate services to mentally ill juvenile offenders, especially in the community and out of the juvenile justice framework.

Furthermore, despite the interventional efforts of community workers, counselors, and juvenile social workers, the marked increase in violent crimes by juveniles in the 1980s caused formal processing of juveniles to spike upwards. The substantial number of violent crimes, prosecutorial policies toward aggressive delinquent behavior, and recidivism are overwhelming efforts to sustain the fundamental principles of juvenile justice that favor the rehabilitation/treatment model. In response to the increase in offenses such as robbery, arson, and assault and battery, prosecutors systematically refer charges against the juvenile offender to the adult criminal courts. In fact, by the early 1990s, adult prosecution of 15- to 18-year old juvenile offenders surpassed those who remained in juvenile proceedings, thereby skewing the number of juveniles who actually receive interventional and rehabilitation treatment rather than punishment (Skowyra and Cocozza, 2006).

The transition into adolescence is marked by growth spurts and the onset of puberty (i.e., sexual maturity). There are a variety of emotional and cognitive changes that emerge between 12 and 18 years of age, which are typical behavioral characteristics that help adolescents develop skills for independence, adjust to increased responsibilities, and navigate social interactions. Individual, but common, personal cognitive development focuses teenagers' awareness of change, increases the opportunity for risk taking, and affects impartial judgment. The transitions open and enable the influences of peers over parents (Spear 2000).

Psychologically, the growth that occurs organically in the teenage brain emerges by alterations in the prefrontal cortex and limbic brain areas and through increased amounts of dopamine in all systems that are sensitive to modulation, stress, motivations, and external stimuli. The transformations in the developing brain cause adolescents to behave in particular, if not peculiar, ways. The rapid-fire development of brain activity is highly susceptible to external influences and alteration with the introduction of alcohol and other substances. Artificial elements and abuse of drugs may contribute to the onset of mental illnesses or disabilities. Regarding teens and technology, the full impact of immediate and instant intimacy through social media, simultaneous communications, and peer pressure from virtual friends has yet to be assessed, understood, and studied.

A recent multistate study of almost 10,000 youths engaged in the juvenile justice system is informative. Children and adolescents held in pre-trial detention or secure care were significantly more likely to have a psychiatric disorder than were those released to the community. Almost 65 percent of the youth referred to adult court and 60 percent of the juvenile justice–detained youth met criteria for one or more mental disorders. An additional 35 percent of the youth who are only processed through the juvenile court initial intake proceedings are reported to have a provisional mental health diagnosis (Hoeve, McReynolds, et al., 2013).

Juvenile policy experts describe four public systems, upon which we rely throughout this chapter (Grisso, 2008). These systems, or "strands," occur when adolescents have mental problems that affect their functioning in society and, consequently, become entangled with some aspect of law and the juvenile justice system. The four strands that we concentrate on are:

1. *Strand One: Juvenile Justice System* — This strand is an outline of the juvenile justice system with an introduction to the terminology that is used for juvenile court proceedings;
2. *Strand Two: Adolescents and the Mental Health System* — This strand is a review of some of the major mental illnesses that are commonly identified in early childhood or infancy and how the disorders affect juveniles' functionality;
3. *Strand Three: Specific Needs and Child Protection Systems* — This strand is a closer examination of how legally troublesome behaviors emerge in conjunction with some, but not all, mental illnesses; and
4. *Strand Four: Children, Mental Health, and Education* — This strand represents a very broad issue as it is the core of childhood social functionality, but we are only going to consider the limited view about the effect of mental illness on students while they are in school, and how the "school to prison" pipeline was created.

This organizational framework allows us to topically examine the essential issues in the juncture between adolescent mental health and juvenile justice. There are many concerns about mental health and juveniles. We hope this chapter will inspire you to engage in more research that may one day resolve the problems we can only topically review.

STRAND ONE: JUVENILE JUSTICE SYSTEM

The underlying philosophy of juvenile legal proceedings is that a person under the age of 18 years of age deserves a second (and sometimes a third, fourth, or even fifth) chance to mature and "move on" if caught committing what for an adult would be a criminal offense. As such, rather than referring to the acts of stealing, consuming controlled substances, battery, and other offenses as "crimes," juvenile justice proceedings refer to such behavior as **"acts of delinquency."** A juvenile who is taken into custody by a law enforcement official is not technically arrested; rather, a juvenile is detained. Likewise, there is no juvenile jail or prison. There are either separate juvenile holding facilities or, if there is only a single county jail, then the juvenile must be isolated by sight and sound from adults (JJDPA, 1974, 2002). Such detention facilities are for intake processing or for short-term stays of juveniles suspected of committing an illegal act and are not used for post-adjudication long-term detentions. Juveniles can also be detained in a holding facility for a status offense — acts that are not legal because the offender is underage, such as smoking, violating curfew, or failure to attend school.

Thereafter, a juvenile can be "placed" in detention — home detention or residential care — following a hearing by a juvenile court hearing officer or judge. This is akin to an adult bail proceeding. Following the initial court hearing, minors are appointed counsel and then a petition for delinquency is either admitted or denied. The petition, like a criminal complaint, informs the juvenile, the family, the victim (if any), and the court of what actions the prosecutor alleges violated the law. The juvenile admits or denies the allegations. If the charges are denied, the juvenile court judge conducts a hearing that is similar to an adult trial and the prosecutor will be required to prove the allegations. The juvenile's defense attorney can present a defense or through cross-examination and witnesses raise issues as to the sufficiency of the evidence. If the judge decides the charges are true or proved or if the juvenile admits to the charges, then the juvenile is declared a delinquent and is made a **ward of the court**. Whether the juvenile has two loving parents or none at all, the juvenile court, through social workers, probation officers and, ultimately, the judge, will direct the treatment and placement of the juvenile.

If the juvenile is found to be delinquent, he may be detained at home, in a residential treatment facility or group home, or in a long-term prison-like corrections facility. The minor can be required to complete mental health evaluations, treatment, and, sometimes, a term of residential commitment for mental illness. The process requires regular court reviews and monitoring to evaluate improvement, response, and whether the placement is in the child's best interest. Delinquents can be ordered to be monitored through drug testing and medication screenings, and for compliance with counseling regimes.

The historical purpose for the special terminology of the juvenile justice system is to free youthful offenders from the associated criminal titles, burdens, and classifications that adults receive for the same actions (Mays and Winfree, 2012). Although juveniles are appointed legal counsel to represent them in delinquency proceedings, juveniles do not have the right to a jury trial. As discussed earlier, if the offense is violent or if the juvenile has had substantial contact with law enforcement, the prosecuting attorney has the discretion to ask the judge to refer or transfer the minor to adult court. The argument for the referral to the adult court is that the juvenile court philosophy of rehabilitation or restorative justice through community service is not effective or appropriate here. The juvenile judge commonly holds a hearing to ascertain whether the juvenile can be restored to youthful status and considers the nature of the crime, the violence associated with the offense, and any recidivism. The expression "throwaway children" gives us to understand that if a juvenile enters the adult system, he is not likely to leave it (Richette, 1969).

If a person is under the age of 18 and is not under the care of a parent or guardian, then the juvenile court can also assume legal authority or guardianship of the minor through a petition to the juvenile (or family) court. This process creates what is known as a **dependency status**. The classification of dependency indicates that the minor did not commit a criminal act, but needs to be under the supervision of the juvenile court system. The finding of dependency enables the juvenile court judge to also act as the parent for the minor as a ward of the court. The juvenile judge then can order that the dependent minor live in a residential group home, take medication, and attend school and counseling, as the judge acts *in loco parentis* for the minor. In the example of Claire, the runaway described in the prologue, there is dual agency. Her trespass and runaway offenses led to her legal classification as a delinquent; her mother's abandonment led the court to classify her as a court dependent or a "ward of the court."

Not all juveniles are so fortunate as to be kept in the juvenile system that favors mental health treatment and interventions rather than punishment. While the national presumption is in favor of juvenile rehabilitation, if the offense is violent in its nature, the accused is an older teenager, and the community does not have adequate resources to treat mental illness, then adult court may be the only viable alternative. Or should it be? In that vein, consider the fate of Benjamin in Box 10.1.

STRAND TWO: ADOLESCENTS AND THE MENTAL HEALTH SYSTEM

Youth who are detained or processed through the juvenile justice system have a higher incidence of diagnosed mental illness than the general population of people of the same age. It is estimated that two-thirds of juveniles who are held in closed and locked detention facilities have the criteria for one or more diagnosed or diagnosable form of mental illness, disease, or handicap (Gottsman and Schwarz, 2011). One in five suffer from a mental illness so severe that their mental impairment will likely impede their ability to function in society and develop the skills to become a responsible adult (Skowyra and Cocozza, 2006). Mental disorders in emerging juveniles are complicated because the child-to-adolescent spectrum is a highly volatile. It is a unique period of physical, emotional, and developmental change that is characterized by rapid and simultaneous growth, involving personal and intellectual stages that include intense peer and personal scrutiny. Box 10.2 contains several shorthand lists of warning signs about youth mental illness.

BOX 10.1

What Would You Do?

Benjamin was a gentle, shy, and socially awkward 16-year old high school sophomore who played the violin, took Advanced Placement courses in school, excelled at mathematics, and built intricate Lego models. An only child, his parents sheltered him because he had a learning disability, did not make friends easily, and felt he did not fit in. He was a well-regarded Boy Scout who came close to achieving the rank of Eagle Scout.

Benjamin also hid his considerable psychological distress from his parents, though there was a family history of severe mental illness. He heard voices that urged him to burn things. His parents had no idea that he was setting fire to crumpled pieces of paper on their home patio. Watching the flames somehow helped to quiet his often-troubled thoughts.

One day, the voices became unbearable. Benjamin filled a liter water bottle with gasoline, bicycled a half-mile to the home of a classmate, broke in through a window, stole credit cards, and poured gasoline around the rooms. He knew the homeowners were away on vacation. "None of it made any sense," his father later said. When Benjamin was found later, he was, in his father's words, "psychotic and hallucinating."

The home was nearly destroyed by fire, but fortunately no one was injured. One week later, Benjamin was arrested. The judge and prosecutors rejected attempts to grant him youthful offender status that would have permitted Benjamin to be treated through the juvenile court system. Benjamin's attorney dismissed the option of an insanity plea because confinement was long and open-ended. Benjamin pleaded guilty to felony third-degree arson as an adult and was sentenced to 4 to 12 years in the New York State Department of Corrections and Community Supervision. After the beatings, assaults, and evident worsening of severe mental health disease, Benjamin was placed in solitary confinement at Fishkill state prison, where he committed suicide.

Youths sent to adult prisons are 36 times more likely to commit suicide, 5 times more likely to be sexually assaulted, and have a high likelihood to recommit crimes and return to prison as an adult. Each year, almost 50,000 16- and 17-year olds are arrested and face the possibility of prosecution as adults for largely minor crimes. Do you think that there might have been a different result if Benjamin were detained in a juvenile corrections facility or a mental health treatment facility? Do you believe that Benjamin's offense — arson of a home —was so serious that despite his mental illness, society was safer having him in an adult facility? What are some of the other options the prosecutor, judge, and defense attorney could have used other than having Benjamin, the only child of a family with a history of serious mental illness, be sentenced to prison as an adult when he was still a juvenile?

Source: Grondahl (2014).

BOX 10.2

Warning Signs of Youth Mental Illness

The American Psychological Association provides the following list of general behavioral traits in children who may be experiencing mental health issues:

- Changes in school performance
- Poor grades despite strong efforts
- Excessive worry or anxiety
- Hyperactivity
- Persistent nightmares
- Persistent disobedience or aggression
- Frequent temper tantrums

In older children and pre-adolescents, the following are considered important:

- Substance abuse
- Inability to cope with problems and daily activities
- Changes in sleeping and/or eating habits
- Excessive complaints of physical ailments
- Defiance of authority, truancy, theft, and/or vandalism
- Intense fear of weight gain
- Prolonged negative mood, often accompanied by poor appetite or thoughts of death

Some additional behaviors include:

- Decrease in enjoyment and time spent with friends and family
- Significant decrease in school performance
- Strong resistance to attending school or absenteeism
- Problems with memory, attention, or concentration
- Big changes in energy levels or eating or sleeping patterns
- Physical symptoms (stomach aches, headaches, backaches)
- Expressed feelings of hopelessness, sadness, anxiety, or frequent crying
- Frequent aggression, disobedience, or lashing out verbally
- Excessive neglect of personal appearance or hygiene
- Substance abuse
- Dangerous or illegal thrill-seeking behavior
- Overly suspicious of others
- Seeing or hearing things that others do not

Sources: Bryne (n.d.); American Psychological Association (2017).

Triggers of Mental Illness in Early Childhood

There are more than 200 classified forms of mental illness. Characteristics related to youths' psychiatric diagnosis collapse into primary, but mutually exclusive, analytic categories: mood disorders, nervous disorders, conduct disorders, developmental disorders, and personality disorder. We will also consider a cluster of behaviors characterized as an antisocial personality. Remember too that there are many, many other mental health disorders that refer to or are caused by problematic social or living conditions as well as organic brain disorders, traumatic injuries, and reactions induced by medications or abuse of illicit drugs (Warner, 2006).

The Center for Mental Health Services estimates that one in every 33 children and one in 8 adolescents are affected by a mood disorder, most commonly **depression** (Hammond, 2007). As it pertains to youth offenders, depression is a form of mental disorder that generally refers to mental behaviors such as major depressive states, bipolar disorder, and manic episodes. Depression, as defined by the American Psychiatric Association's *DSM-5* (2013), is characterized by poor appetite or overeating, insomnia or hypersomnia, low energy and fatigue, low self-esteem, poor concentration, and feelings of hopelessness. Any behavior that persists more than a year in juveniles should be referred for treatment.

Within this context are mood disorders that present with anger, irritability, and hostility. The irritable mood that often accompanies depressive disorders increases youths' probability of inciting angry responses from others that then increase the risk of triggering more physically aggressive acts toward or by the depressed youth (Underwood and Washington, 2016). Within the mood disorder diagnosis, 3 to 7 percent of juveniles have bipolar disorder diagnoses. This cerebral illness is evidenced by dramatic mood swings. Children will be unusually happy and then become sad and inactive, with wildly extreme conduct swings that cause changes in sleep, energy level, and clarity of thinking. Someone not familiar with childhood-to-adult development may find this to be an unexpected progression since depressed adults frequently express sadness, not anger. Irritability and hostility among youth with depressive disorders is recognized as a psychiatric disorder because the internalized connection between anger and mood is the basis of self-harm, while adults commonly suppress internal hostility as a coping mechanism (Grisso, 2002: 145).

Sometimes bipolar disease can be a precursor to cutting, self-harm, or attempted suicide. Although the depressive mental disorder has some genetic basis, research indicates that bipolar disorder may be traced to brain structure or function. With treatment and medication, the illness can be controlled. Of youth involved with the juvenile justice system, it is estimated that approximately 15 to 30 percent have diagnoses of depression or dysthymia (i.e., pervasive depressive disorder) (Weiss and Garber, 2003).

Another cluster of mental illnesses that commonly has a childhood onset is described as **nervous disorders**, and includes anxiety disorders or behaviors associated with panic, separation anxiety, generalized anxiety, and the obsessive-compulsive disorder. The obsessive-compulsive disorder (OCD) is debilitating to a minor who does not have the mental tools of cognition to balance brain commands (APA, 2013). In other words, the adolescent experiences repetitive, impulsive, and persistent thoughts and images that cause anxiety. There may be rituals or stereotyped behaviors that are not enjoyable, but are repeated over and over and are perceived to prevent an unlikely, irrelevant event from occurring. For example, a person will jiggle a doorknob three times to stop an earthquake or constantly wash her hands in fear of contamination from money, despite the fact that neither is likely to occur (Abramowitz and Jacoby, 2014).

Another common form of childhood mental illness is known as post-traumatic stress disorder (PTSD). Between 11 and 32 percent of children who are victims of or witnesses to crime or are delinquent receive diagnoses of PTSD (Abram, Teplin, et al., 2004). Its appearance is unpredictable because PTSD emerges from unexpected events, such as when the child is the victim of a crime or a witness to a highly emotional event, such as a sexual assault or a criminal act of violence. Sensitive reactions to school bullying or ostracizing by peers also can trigger this mental health disorder.

Symptoms include flashbacks, nightmares, severe anxiety, and uncontrollable obsessive thoughts about the event. If left untreated, post-traumatic stress disorder may result in difficulties with interpersonal relationships, unresolved cognitive functioning, and eating disorders. It can also cause other mental health problems, such as depression, substance abuse, and suicidal thoughts. The responsibility for recommending treatment for the victims of and witnesses to criminal offenses is paramount. Knowing and recognizing that a child, even as young as 4 or 5, could be traumatized by observing and absorbing criminal acts and years later develop serious mental illness should motivate any public service provider to encourage families to get psychological help to lessen the likelihood of future struggles with PTSD. Research shows that a traumatized child will lose focus on learning following exposure to loss such as homelessness, death, or imprisonment of a parent or loss of a trusted caregiver (De Bellis and Zisk, 2014).

Conduct Disorders, Drugs, and Delinquency

Disruptive behavior disorders, including conduct disorders, oppositional defiant disorder, and attention deficit hyperactivity disorders (ADHD), represent another problematic class of childhood mental illness. These disorders are characterized by poor self-control, limited regulation of personal behaviors, inability to sustain attention, and lack of impulse control (Purdie, Hattie, and Carroll, 2002). Specifically, ADHD affects approximately 9 percent of school-age children. In approximately 80 percent of ADHD cases, there appears to be a genetic origin (Stern, 2001). ADHD in a preschooler or elementary school child is linked to disarray within the neuropsychological function of the brain's prefrontal lobes that affects the child's ability to hold mental events and re-engage after disruption (working memories); ability to self-reflect (internalization of speech); ability to identify personal goals (self-regulation of motivation and arousal); and ability to analyze and synthesize the effect of one's own behavior on others (Stern, 2001).

Behavioral mental illnesses affect approximately 9.5 percent of children aged 4-17 years, or 5.4 million children (Heston, 2013). Boys are affected by conduct behavioral disorders at a rate that is two to three times higher than girls (Grisso, 2008). Females, however, have higher rates than males of mood disorders, such as major depressive episodes and anxiety disorders as well as substance abuse disorders (Teplin, Abram, et al., 2002).

Conduct behavioral disorders are known to be disturbing, invasive, or distracting, and the risk of aggression increases if the disease goes untreated. Conduct disorders in juveniles can increase the risk of engaging in aggressive behaviors. Emotional symptoms such as anger, failure to engage in self-regulatory conduct, and impulsivity increase the risk of delinquency. Hence, responses and behaviors that would be ordinary in a non-ADHD youth can spiral out of control in an adolescent with a conduct disorder. Children with ADHD and conduct disorders are more likely to commit crimes as adults. While only one-third of adolescents with conduct disorders such as ADHD eventually develop antisocial personality disorder in adulthood, about two-thirds have non-violent or violent offense records as adults (Grisso, 2008).

Moreover, a 14-year study found that ADHD and antisocial behavior in a child, as described below, was among the most important predictor of later offending behavior at age 32 (Foley, Carlton, and Howell, 1996). This study of adult inmates concluded that 25.5 percent had ADHD symptoms as children and still had them as adults. The researchers maintain that unresolved or untreated ADHD plays a role in delinquency, and moreover, that individuals with the risk factors for ADHD or other conduct disorders are more likely to engage in antisocial or criminal behavior. Additionally, many offenders with ADHD were either not diagnosed as children, or if diagnosed, never received treatment to control the AHDH or treatment was discontinued after puberty. Researchers further report that youth with disruptive behavior disorders (conduct disorders, oppositional defiant disorder (ODD)) will display more physically aggressive behavior; when comorbid with AHDH, ODD is linked to chronic delinquencies and repeat offenses during adolescence (Grisso, 2008).

ADHD is generally treatable with medication, behavioral training, and intervention counseling. Early intervention is key, as a young child is more capable of learning coping and self-regulation skills to challenge the onset of hyperactivity and impulsivity than an older person (Purdie et al., 2002). However, as with other aspects of childhood development, engaging in effective and purposeful treatment and assessment is fraught with complications and problems, as the child or young adult often cannot succeed due to the same factors that lead to delinquent misbehavior: lack of commitment, inconsistency in treatment, and limited family engagement.

As revealed in Chapter 4, antisocial personality disorder is a serious mental illness by which juveniles can also harbor profound mental disorders and engage in serious behavioral, if not violent, propensities. Juveniles with antisocial personality disorder (APD) are known to manipulate and hurt others in what is regarded as unethical, immoral, and irresponsible behavior in violation of social norms and expectations; this behavior begins at a young age (APA, 2013). Childhood APD is more complex because adults are willing to think that a child will grow out of an aberrant personality even though the behaviors, linked together, demonstrate a possible path to highly abusive, unconscionable behavior or rage and social dysfunction.

According to the *DSM-5* (APA, 2013), there are distinctive criteria that emerge:

1. Beginning at the age of 15 years, there is a failure to obey laws and norms by engaging in behavior that results in criminal arrest or would warrant juvenile detention. The inability to conform one's conduct includes lying, deception, and manipulation. Further evidence of impulsive behavior, irritability, aggression, blatant disregard for the safety of others, irresponsibility, and lack of remorse emerges throughout adolescent development.

2. There is evidence of comorbidity with other forms of conduct disorders, such as ADHD or ODD, before the age of 15.

3. The antisocial behaviors do not commonly occur in conjunction with schizophrenia or bipolar disorder (APA, 2013). There is also an indication that APD involves a neuro-anatomical or biological genetic predisposition; as shown through MRI scanning there is evidence of uncoupled connections between the frontal and parietal lobes, which are associated with attention, self-regulation, and the ability to resolve internal conflict (Barbour, 2013).

Children may also evidence abuse of siblings, peers, and pets, as well as late age bed wetting. They may engage in killing, torturing, or dissecting animals and deriving pleasure from the acts. They are sometimes members of a gang where the child is rewarded for brutality, criminal behavior, and aggression (Mayo Clinic, 2017). The scenario in Box 10.3 concerns a child with APD and is based on a true account.

There is substantial evidence for a relationship between substance abuse and delinquency, as well as continued aggression into adulthood for substance-abusing youth. In a survey of 1,100 youth detained at Cook County juvenile detention facility, nearly 60 percent of the males and over two-thirds of the females had one or more psychiatric disorders; one-half of the males and almost one-half of the females had a substance use disorder (Teplin et al., 2010). Substance use disorders were found in 40 to 50 percent of the delinquent youth, but only in 15 percent of the non-delinquent youth (Grisso, 2008). Conduct disorder and substance use disorders are quite prevalent in youth in juvenile courts. Substance use disorder has deeper implications for the protection of children in juvenile justice custody because youth entering juvenile detention facilities from the street may engage in aggressive or self-injurious behaviors due to withdrawal from drugs or due to the harmful effects of untreated mental illness that is masked by substance abuse (Grisso, 2008).

There are no absolutes with respect to childhood mental illness and delinquency. A child may be extremely quiet or withdrawn, burst into tears, or have great expressions of irrational anxiety or outbursts of anger, and these behaviors may just be acting out or could be symptomatic of episodes of mental illness. The first and best response should be to encourage support from friends and family or self-help support groups if there are

BOX 10.3

Thinking About the Issues

Consider the case of Brent, an adorable 11-year old with brown hair flopping above wide brown eyes. He was detained at juvenile hall for stealing his grandfather's BB gun and shooting at the windows of passing cars from a freeway overpass. When asked about his living situation, his mother said that he started living with his father because she kept finding dead cats in his laundry basket. He also set the cats on fire. His mother felt that she couldn't communicate with him as he was apathetic to her concerns. Brent demonstrated some classic symptoms of antisocial personality disorder: torturing animals, fire-setting, and difficulty with authority.

Here the question is that of intervention and treatment. The prefrontal cortex of the brain appears to be different as to the mental wiring and brain function of an individual with antisocial personality disorder and may likely be genetic (Aggarwal, 2013; Raine, 2000). While children with an antisocial conduct disorder may be charming and engaging, their internalized behavior can also be unconscionable and they can be indifferent to the pain and harm their conduct causes to others. Brent is young and looks just like a normal kid.

1. What should be done for interventions?
2. Should his parents be informed of the possible diagnosis of antisocial personality disorder?
3. Should Brent be told?

Sources: Gregory, ffytche, and Simmons (2012); Aggarwal (2013); Tucker (2013); Raine (2008); Spear (2000).

reasons to be concerned. Therapy for all family members in the household is critical to learning how to cope with challenges and changes. Most importantly, seeking help and support should never be associated with any stigma or shame.

STRAND THREE: SPECIFIC NEEDS AND CHILD PROTECTION SYSTEMS

In this section, we focus on specific juvenile conduct that may occur because of mental or organic illnesses. First responders often encounter someone who acts a little differently. Is dying one's hair six different colors an expression of freedom or a cry for attention? What if the person is 8 years old? What if a child says that because everyone calls her a bully, she does not want to "stick around"? Learning about cues to recognize a mentally disturbed person might help lead to a life-saving intervention.

Mental Competency for a Juvenile

Children may also have cognitive disorders due to organic reasons or birth defects. For example, Down syndrome is a chromosomal deficiency that can be identified during pregnancy; it causes a person to be born with low or moderate intellectual function. Birth injuries, such as hypoxia (i.e., the deprivation of adequate oxygen at birth) or anoxia (i.e., total deprivation of oxygen), can lead to the medical disorder known as cerebral palsy and sometimes to severe brain damage and cognitive dysfunction. Juvenile Huntington's disease is an inherited genetic disease that causes progressive degeneration of the nerves inside the brain that impairs cognitive function and causes movement disorders. It is evidenced by involuntary writhing, slow eye movement, and slow processing. Fetal alcohol spectrum disorder, long known simply as fetal alcohol syndrome or FAS, or drug addiction–related disorders are caused by maternal neglect or the mother's use of alcohol or controlled substances during pregnancy. These parental abuses can lead to mental and physical disorders in infancy that last through adolescence and into adulthood.

Brain damage that triggers mental illness is not uncommon. Blows to the head (what we now call traumatic brain injury or TBI), physical trauma, infections, and high, unresolved infant fevers can impact a developing person's intellectual reasoning, impulsivity, and anger management and impair cognitive function. There is also low correlation between juvenile delinquency and infant-onset intellectual developmental disability. The rate of juvenile misconduct by teenagers who have permanent cognitive loss is in the same ratio as misconduct by juveniles who have adolescent-onset mental illness.

Mental handicaps can affect the ability of a person to understand the nature of the charges against them in a competency proceeding. Even juvenile offenders must have a basic understanding of the legal proceedings before the allegations of delinquency can proceed. Similarly, a juvenile can be found to be mentally incompetent at the time the offense was committed, the juvenile equivalent of not guilty by reason of insanity. The juvenile court trial judge can accept a defense that a youth is not responsible for his or her acts of delinquency due to being mentally ill at the time the offense occurred. In Oklahoma, the state revamped its juvenile incompetency standards by directing that judges determine whether an accused has "developmental immaturity" and therefore can be found to be incompetent for prosecution (LaFortune, 2016).

Even if there is concern about the juvenile's overall comprehension, the accused must have the immediate or **present ability** to understand the legal proceedings at the time the proceedings commence for the proceedings to ensue. For example, in the Wisconsin case of *In re Jacob* M.W. (2004), the juvenile suffered from head trauma, Tourette syndrome, attention deficit disorder, and mild intellectual disability, but nevertheless was able to understand the role of the court and explain to his attorney the reason he was in trouble. A fourteen-year old from Delaware had the academic skills of a second grader and was classified as mildly intellectually deficient with the low ability to care from himself but was found competent because the defense attorney could coach him (State v. J.S. No.0312013339, 2005).

Consider, in this regard, the case of Adam, which is summarized in Box 10.4. While he clearly has the ability to care for himself, he may not have the ability to understand right and wrong behavior.

BOX 10.4

Thinking About the Issues

Adam, age 15, is diagnosed with Down syndrome and has the functional intellectual capacity of an 8-year old. The police were called after he pulled off the dress and underwear of his 3-year old sister Jillian in the front yard because he wanted to see what her private parts looked and felt like. He did not have the intent to assault her nor could he likely formulate malevolent purposeful conduct.

The police officers terrified him, but he did like the rotating lights of the police car. Adam's functional incompetency probably precluded prosecution for the delinquent act of sexual assault. The juvenile court judge could, however, decide that Adam should be declared a ward of the state in a dependency proceeding, even if his parents were loving and caring, if only to assure the community that he received educational interventions and his little sister Jillian would be protected. The prosecutor's office may decline to pursue a delinquency case because its attorneys probably could not prove Adam had either the necessary mental capacity or the intent to harm; moreover, it is unlikely that he is mentally competent to stand trial. If, however, a judge was convinced that Adam could distinguish right from wrong and understood the concept of a judge and had mental competency to stand trial, then an admission of delinquency by the juvenile to the court is possible.

Adam would not be made a dependent ward of the state unless juvenile court intervention was necessary and direct court supervision is in his or his sister's best interest, though he would not necessarily be removed from his home. His removal from the home could occur if his family did not follow through with counseling. Therefore, despite Adam's act of sexual misconduct, because of his mental deficiency or even mental disease, the juvenile justice process may not necessarily punish him if there are available juvenile services dedicated to treating and monitoring his behavior without placement in an institutional correctional facility.

Note that when Adam turns 18 years old, should he have a similar encounter with the criminal justice system, he will be seen as a fully functioning and capable adult, even though he has a child's mental capacity. In that instance, it is likely that Adam would be sentenced as an adult.

1. Do you think that Adam should always be treated as a child by the justice system?
2. Should the status of juvenile depend on the mental or chronological age of the accused?
3. It's clear that Adam will never "get better" with medication or treatment. What are the best interventions the police and courts can offer to educate Adam about his conduct in the future?

Source: Sanborn (2008)

Source:// Sanborn, J. B. (2008)

In addition to questions regarding the competency of a juvenile offender who may be functioning below his or her chronological age, questions arise as to the competency of young witnesses, as discussed in Box 10.5.

Suicidal Ideation

Another behavior that accompanies many different forms of mental illness—not just depression or conduct disorder—is **suicidal ideation**, or suicidal thoughts that may or may not result in an attempted or completed suicide. The deliberate taking of one's life is not a mental disorder per se, but mental illness is often the proximate cause of a suicide. The effects of youth suicide go well beyond the act of killing oneself, impacting those who survive the death—parents, friends, peers, and others in the community. More than 90 percent of people who die by a completed suicide have a history of depression or other mental disorders and substance abuse issues; the mental state that prompts suicide is

---

BOX 10.5

Law and Mental Health

The age of a child determines if he or she is competent to be a witness in a case. A young child or one who is mentally disabled and is a witness in a case must be able to understand the testimonial oath to tell the truth when questioned. Either the attorney (defense or prosecuting) or the judge can request a **witness competency** hearing. The trial judge will make a judicial ruling as to whether a child is competent after asking questions during this preliminary proceeding. If a child only knows that he will get spanked if he doesn't tell the truth, then the child may not be a competent witness. If the child can correctly distinguish between what is the truth — a pen is not an ice cream cone — and what is a lie — the chair is a potted plant — the child may be found competent to testify. The judge asks different questions to elicit information to assess the ability of the child to give a competent account of the facts. As the decision rests primarily with the trial judge, she will decide if the proposed witness is legally competent by assessing his manner and his apparent level of intelligence, and may resort to an examination that will tend to disclose the child's capacity and intelligence as well as his understanding of the obligations of an oath. There is no precise age that determines competency as "it depends on the capacity and intelligence of the child" (United States v. Wheeler, 159 U.S. 523, 524). Many states have presumptive age thresholds. In New York, a child is presumed to be competent at age 9. If the child is less than 9, the hearing is the mandated process to assess the competency of a young witness.

Source: N.Y. Crim. Proc. Law §60.20(2); Wheeler v. United States (1895).

often in combination with external circumstances such as age, gender, ethnicity, family dynamics, and stressful life events (Moskos, Achilles, and Gray, 2004).

Although the correlation between criminal justice and suicide may not be immediately evident, contact of a first responder with a young person contemplating taking his or her own life requires specialized knowledge and intervention skills to engage, help, and dissuade that individual. Suicide is the third-leading cause of death for people between 15 and 24 (Centers for Disease Control and Prevention, 2000), surpassed only by accidents and homicides. The rising trend in youthful suicide is attributed to the increase in the rates of clinical depression, increased firearm availability, diminished influences of the family, increased personal freedoms, and increased exposure to drugs and alcohol. In one recent study, the glorification of the deceased through the media and the social dynamics that surround the reporting of tragic deaths is also thought to influence other suicides, triggering cluster suicides (Mueller, 2017). "The media crafted a story about why youth die by suicide that emphasized academic pressure over other plausible causes. In so doing, the media may have broadened ideas about when suicide is seen as an option" (Mueller, 2017: 154).

Between 1991 and 2005, about 8 percent of ninth and tenth graders reported suicide attempts (Centers for Disease Control and Prevention, 2007). An analysis of more than 500,000 U.S. teens found that while the suicide rate was going up for males, the rate for girls aged 13 to 18 increased by 65 percent between 2010 and 2015, and the number of girls who expressed suicidal thoughts increased by 12 percent (Twenge, Joiner, et al., 2017). The researchers also found that 48 percent of teens who spent 5 or more hours per day on electronic devices reported one suicide-related ideation or expressed an interest in death , compared to 28 percent who spent less than an hour a day.

Given this body of research on youth suicide, first responders should be aware of possible warning signs (Gould and Kramer, 2001; Segen, 2011; Winfree and Jiang, 2010):

- ▶ Recent Loss — through death, divorce, separation, broken relationship, self-confidence, self-esteem, loss of interest in friends, hobbies, or activities previously enjoyed.
- ▶ Change in Personality — sad, withdrawn, irritable, anxious, tired, indecisive, apathetic.
- ▶ Change in Behavior — can't concentrate on school, work, or routine tasks.
- ▶ Change in Sleep Patterns — insomnia, often with early waking or oversleeping, or nightmares.
- ▶ Change in Eating Habits — loss of appetite and weight, or overeating.
- ▶ Fear of Losing Control — acting erratically, harming self or others.
- ▶ Low Self-Esteem — feelings of worthlessness, shame, overwhelming guilt, or self-hatred: "everyone would be better off without me."
- ▶ No Hope for the Future — believing things will never get better, or that nothing will ever change.

- *Self-Harm* — Any mention of dying, disappearing, jumping, shooting oneself, or other types of self-harm.
- Substance Abuse — Drug use and abuse brings the child into closer contact with at-risk groups, which may promote social estrangement, isolation, and desire for self-harm.

The rate of youth suicide is decreasing where there are publicized suicide prevention programs, as well as parental restriction of access to handguns and increased use of anti-depressant drugs. Community health specialists can provide immediate grief counseling and work with media outlets to lessen dramatic depictions of self-importance or glorification when a self-inflicted death occurs within a school or neighborhood.

In communities with decreased rates of substance abuse as well as lower rates of community violence, the impulse to self-inflicted death was also impacted. With greater community service efforts directed toward intervention and prevention, as well as funding for crisis center hotlines, publication of media guidelines (prevention strategies to educate journalists about the prevalence of copycat suicides among adolescents), and aggressive efforts for referrals to treatment when signs are observed, the rate of suicide may slow.

Moreover, strong support environments, socializing individuals into groups, and consistent emphasis on social supports all help to either re-direct suicidal ideation or displace it. High levels of community support as well as a positive presence of school in the adolescents' community network are also important factors. School protections as well as parental expectations, parental supervision, and increased parental involvement in their children's lives may decrease suicidal ideation and attempts (Winfree and Jiang, 2010).

Recent work by criminologists reinvigorated interest in how other adolescents or non-parental adults can influence juveniles. That is, the influence of peers is consistently found to be the most robust predictor of delinquency, including gang behavior. Another theory, however, adds a different spin on the problem. Differential social support and coercion theory of crime suggests that social interactions, both supportive and coercive, figure into youthful development of self-control, attitude toward delinquent behavior, and mental health. Using data drawn from the 1995 National Survey of Adolescents (NSA), Kurtz and associates (2014) examined the connection between coercion and delinquent behavior. They found that juveniles who are the recipients of constant, overbearing coercive tactics eventually developed strong self-directed anger, high-externalized control, and weak social bonds. These individuals have non-violent legal difficulties but are likely to have persistent mental health problems. This form of coercive control is evident in prisons or closed mental hospitals. On the other hand, juveniles who suffer coercive controls that are erratic or conditional and receive unpredictable disciplinary consequences for disobedience from a dominate force, tend to develop strong anger toward other people, have low self-control, and suffer weak, alienated social bonds. Victims of erratic control by a secondary person may fail to develop their own forms of personal self-control that mediates criminal impulses, especially if there is no parental reprimand against deviant behavior. While far from conclusive, research of this nature does add grist to the scientific basis of coercive control as a precursor of delinquency. See Brown (2004); Colvin, Cullen, and Vander Ven (2002); Hunter (1951); Kurtz, Linnemann, and Green (2014); Orwell (1948); Pratt, Cullen, et al. (2010); Richardson (2016); Truesdell (March 25, 2017); Wareham and Boots (2012).

Sex Trafficking and Minors

When you think about whether mental illness or mental coercion is a driving force for juvenile misconduct, consider the plight of youth sex workers, particularly those in their early teens. It is unlikely that a child would seek sexual relations with numerous strangers without the undue dominance and control of another person. **Domestic minor sex trafficking (DMST)** is rising, with an estimate of between 15,000 and 50,000 child victims per year who traded for sexual favors in exchange for financial remuneration (Jordon, Patel, and Rapp, 2013). In 2003, the FBI and the Justice Department launched the Innocence Lost National Initiative. Their goal was to address child prostitution in the United States. The average age of girls engaged in this behavior is between 12 and 14, and for boys and transgender youths it is between 11 and 13 years old. To social workers, community workers, and counselors, victims of trafficking appear as clients in multiple settings, including the child welfare system, hospital emergency rooms, health departments, domestic violence shelters, mental health facilities, youth shelters, and the criminal justice system (Jones, Engstrom, et al., 2007).

One of the biggest challenges in rescuing sex-trafficked victims is that law enforcement does not consistently identify child prostitutes as victims, but as delinquents. Youthful prostitutes also often do not self-identify as victims, but instead as consensual participants; therefore, they will often not seek help. Statistics following local enforcement and their treatment of prostituted minors reinforces this inherent conflict: 60 percent of the juveniles detained used for sex trafficking were ultimately treated as victims and handled as dependent children in the juvenile courts, but 40 percent of underage sex workers were treated as offenders or essentially as consensual prostitutes (Halter, 2010). The treatment (or mistreatment) was based on the juvenile's level of cooperation, whether there was an identified trafficker of the child, prior record of the juvenile, as well as how the involvement in prostitution was discovered (Halter, 2010). In all circumstances, although there may be a question of correlation between sex trafficking of minors and issues of mental health, the long-term mental health of any victim of sexual assault, especially of minors, should be considered and addressed by street responders.

Runaways are the largest source of underage sex workers in the United States. Some researchers suggest that a large percentage of children leave home due to physical, sexual, or psychological abuse (National Incidence Studies of Missing, Abducted, Runaway and Throwaway Children [NISMARTC], 2002). Many have low self-esteem and are extremely vulnerable. Other researchers suggest that the younger a girl is when she first becomes a victim of sex trafficking, the greater likelihood that she was as a victim of sexual abuse with resulting mental disorders (Cole, Sprang, et al., 2016). This history of chronic abuse includes other forms of mistreatment, such as physical abuse, emotional abuse, and/or sexual abuse by several perpetrators. Other forms of family dysfunction may also increase the victim's vulnerability, such as addiction and domestic violence.

The cycle of abuse worsens once youth enter the world of DMST. They are already vulnerable and can be lured into the industry with false promises and overstated monetary rewards. Once they are in a trafficking network, they are usually severely abused and neglected. The sex workers are threatened by their traffickers and, through psychological coercion, or brainwashing, feel that they are unable to leave the dominating pimp or madam. The child prostitutes are often charged for their room and board and are told they need to work off the debts before they can leave (Cole et al., 2016). Young girls are usually presented along with adult females and often are found to be closely associated with escort and massage services; private dancing, drinking, and photographic clubs; major sporting and recreational events; major sporting and cultural events; and conventions and selected tourist destinations.

A 2017 study commissioned by Covenant House Field Center for Children's Policy, Practice and Research indicated that the key to ending trafficking of young people is to eradicate youth homelessness (Covenant House, n.d.). In interviews with 911 homeless youth across 13 U.S. cities, nearly one-fifth of them indicated that they were or had been victims of human trafficking, being used for sex or labor. Sex trafficking is defined as the recruitment, harboring, transportation, provision, obtaining, patronizing, and soliciting a person for a commercial sex act and further that the act was inducted by force, fraud, or coercion, or that the person induced to perform the act is a minor (Mzezewa, 2017).

With limited access to persons with whom they can form normal relationships, juvenile sex workers are commonly instructed by dominate adults to fear authorities, fear arrest, and fear deportation. Many times, victims, even when isolated from their capturers, will not disclose their involvement in prostitution, especially to law enforcement, due to shame, fear of being arrested, and personal trauma. Researchers indicated that a majority of youth sex workers have lower educational levels when compared to the general population and tend to come from lower socioeconomic backgrounds. The youth sex workers are often medically and nutritionally deprived and, upon discovery or arrest (depending on the state's laws), describe their circumstances of captivity as including brutalization, beatings, rapes, torture, psychological abuse, and isolation (Jordon et al., 2013). While the responsibility of the first responder regarding victims of sex trafficking may arise in a criminal context, there may also be a duty to also consider mental health and juvenile intervention alternatives.

STRAND FOUR: CHILDREN, MENTAL HEALTH, AND EDUCATION

Juvenile offenders face an all too common circumstance: the school-to-prison pipeline. Data from the U.S. Department of Education's Civil Rights Data Collection (CRDC) disclosed the laws, policies, and practices that pushed young, male students—particularly

African Americans with disabilities—out of school, into the criminal justice system, and especially into prison (Langberg and Fedders, 2013). We turn next to an examination of how schools view their role in this pipeline and the mental health issues related to recidivism. In this context, our societal **second responders**, such as teachers, resource officers, juvenile probation officers, and social workers, can intervene and interrupt the flow of the pipeline.

Schools and Misbehavior

In the 1990s and early part of the 21st century, when a student violated school policies with respect to safety, the solution was expulsion. By using school security officers (SROs) and zero tolerance practices for drugs and violence, policymakers enacted out-of-school suspension for infractions. By 2005, two-thirds of American students were supervised by security officers in their schools. More officers in schools had the effect of leading to more official interventions. For example, 43 percent of all delinquency complaints in North Carolina were school-based and the fourth most common complaint was "disorderly conduct at school" (Langberg and Fedders, 2013: 657). The age range for expulsions ranged from high schoolers to children as young as 6 years old. In fact, in 2006, over 3.3 million students were suspended and 100,000 were expelled from the nation's schools (U.S. Department of Education, 2006).

The presence of law enforcement became intertwined with the everyday administration of a school, which then resulted in higher rates of arrest and expulsion for minor incidents. Misbehaviors that were tolerated as "teachable moments" from which students could learn, grow, and develop now resulted in the long-term consequences of expulsion (Langberg and Fedders, 2013). The Office of Civil Rights (2012) reported that students with disabilities who needed special education services were twice as likely as their non-disabled peers to receive one or more out-of-school suspension directives. As we have learned throughout this chapter, students with mild forms of mental illness, such as hyperactivity, depression, or cognitive dysfunction, have the greatest challenges to reach maturity, especially in a structured school environment. Expelling troubled (and troubling) students resulted in a culture of juveniles with unmet educational needs, direct involvement with juvenile court, and, as we read, a likely referral or waiver to adult court for not being amendable to rehabilitation. The cycle created stigmatization, lack of motivation, and academic failure. In essence, the process of suspension of youth facilitated a pipeline from school to prison.

Those who worked in law-related fields advocated for appropriate educational services, standards, and opportunities. In some courts with innovative policies, juvenile social workers now come to the school hearings and juvenile proceedings with the actual educational histories, mental health challenges, and personal history struggles of the expelled student to try to get the student back into school (Kahn, O'Donnell, et al., 2007). The underlying belief is that by obtaining strong educational services for those who struggle with mental health challenges, we will also see a reduction in juvenile involvement in the criminal justice system. For example, students in one law school created a special education advocacy program. In creating legal arguments against expulsion as a matter of school policy, the law students found that when young students received psychological, social worker, and parental counseling through the schools, this academic intervention is far more beneficial to the students than a court finding of delinquency. The advocacy program convinced the juvenile court judges that educational services in the community were not available in locked, adult facilities and that there was greater hope with intervention by education than with correctional detention.

In the discussion of appropriate educational services, it is easy to argue that treatment through the schools and academic services may be the best way to change the flow of arrest and jail for the mentally ill. When a juvenile court uses the leverage of consequences to reinforce requirements for treatment, medication, and counseling, juveniles receive the benefits of treatment and gain the advantage of not being removed from society and nondelinquent peers (Kahn et al., 2007).

Recidivism

Sometimes the best efforts of the educational innovators to keep kids in school and out of institutions are not successful. As with all resources for mental health, opportunity depends on the state's budget. Juveniles with mental health externalizing problems, such as oppositional defiant disorder (ODD) or attention deficit hyperactivity disorder (ADHD), have high statistical associations with repetitive acts of delinquency. ODD is marked by consistent defiant, hostile, and disobedient behavior toward authority figures and is shown to be a precursor to youth violence and adult deviance (Wareham and Boots, 2012). The antisocial conduct cluster of ODD also reveals patterns of school failure, peer rejection, and inability to respond to academic interventions to intercede when there is failure to achieve academically. While the behaviors are treatable, the high expense and low opportunity and motivation for change mean that treatment is not always practical. One teacher indicated that there were so few mental health resources in the school that she felt she was just preparing her inner-city third graders to read prison menus.

A study of 915 youths serving juvenile probation in Texas assessed the youths' mental health issues and the correlation between mental health and recidivism (McReynolds, Schwalbe, and Wasserman, 2010). The sample was 79 percent male with an average age of 14 to 15 years old. In their educational history, the youths had completed the eighth grade with a significant history of grade retention. Nearly a third had two or more prior offenses, and, of those, a third of the population had a pending or prior felony. Of all the youths, 43 percent reoffended within one year of their first detention. Within this sample, almost half of the youths also had descriptive criteria of one psychiatric disorder, with the most common being substance abuse. Thirty-four percent had comorbidity with a second mental disorder. The overall recidivism rate for youths with any disorder was higher than youths with no disorder (49.5% versus 38.3%) (McReynolds et al., 2010).

A meta-analysis of 23 recidivism risk studies confirms that mental health conditions elevate the risk for recidivism (McReynolds et al., 2010). Interestingly, severe psychopathology conditions, such as suicide or a psychosis, did not reveal a correlation to recidivism, whereas PTSD and those conduct problems involving less severe psychopathology, such as stress, anxiety, and substance abuse, indicated a propensity to reoffend. Delinquent children with conduct problems demonstrated by acts of impulsivity, substance abuse, and an inability to sustain treatment had higher odds of failing to complete their post-delinquency release conditions. Juveniles with disruptive conduct disorders, such as oppositional defiant disorder and ADHD, also had failure odds that were double that of other delinquent children (McReynolds et al., 2010).

Admittedly, the forms of mental illness that are not identified at birth or in infancy are harder to anticipate or distinguish, but they are equally critical to identify. Knowing that behavioral outbursts or misconduct can occur due to a biologically based conduct disorder, first responders and community providers should encourage counseling, treatment, or other interventions when a child first demonstrates a mental breakdown to avoid or prevent teenage difficulties. Correctional officers, probation officers, and juvenile social workers should learn to identify and distinguish mental illnesses in juveniles from "growing pains" and acting out. Although this book is not a guide to psychological or psychiatric diagnosis and treatments, we suggest that having a basis to recognize when or how mental illnesses are likely to emerge in juveniles can help street providers to make positive decisions about when to intervene with troubled youth.

We framed this chapter around four strands. Consider the descriptions of each strand found above and then consider the following questions:

1. Why should we consider juveniles apart from adults? What distinguishes one group from the other?

2. Regardless of what is happening to juveniles in the nation's justice system, what should be, in your opinion, the primary goal when addressing issues of delinquency, treatment, and punishment?

3. Given what you have learned through the preceding nine chapters about mental illness and the criminal justice system, which strand do you think could provide the most hope for those mentally ill juveniles caught up in the justice system? Explain your choice.

In the epilogue below, we review the harsh facts that surround the unknown cause of the most horrific form of violence we know: kids who, with no provocation, kill or attempt to kill unarmed, innocent students. Each offender described below planned and executed deliberate acts of unspeakable violence. The number of incidents will likely have increased by the publication of this book and will remain without resolution or solutions. One scholar suggested that if teachers, who often spend more time with children than parents, are vested with the authority to identify mentally ill young children, then some early childhood interventions could avoid this form of teenage tragedy.

EPILOGUE

The following sources provided much of this epilogue's content: Brown (2004); Bryne (n.d.); Ehrenfreund and Lu (2017); Grisso (2008); Karch, Dahlberg, et al. (2006); Langman (2009); Langman (2018); Moreno (2017); Rice and Hoffman (2015); Schuppe (2018).

Children who kill, with their targets often being either their parents or other children, are a highly controversial topic in contemporary society. Adolescent mass shootings are a special subset of mass killings. Of the 129 shooting events that resulted in the death of 4 or more people, one in 7 took place at a school. For example, two child mass shooters, Andrew Golden, age 11, and Michael Johnson, age 13, pulled a fire alarm to flush students and teachers out of their Jonesboro, Arkansas middle school on March 24, 1998, killing 4 girls and a teacher and wounding 10 others. On April 20, 1999, two disgruntled high school seniors, 17-year old Dylan Klebold and 18-year old Eric Harris, opened fire at their school, Columbine High School in Littleton, Colorado. During their hour-long rampage, one teacher and 12 students were murdered. In the incident's aftermath, U.S. law enforcement agencies changed officer training to create protocols for stopping an active shooter and promoted academic awareness of mentally ill juveniles and young adults.

On Valentine's Day, February 14, 2018, Nikolas Cruz, 19, carried a black duffle bag and backpack loaded with magazines and an AR-15 semiautomatic rifle into Marjory Stoneman Douglas High School in Parkland, Florida. He had been expelled earlier for disruptive and violent conduct. He activated the fire alarm and shot people inside classrooms, killing 17 people — 14 students and 3 faculty members whose ages ranged from 14 to 49 years old. He wounded 14 more. At this point, Cruz discarded the rifle, vest, and ammunition in a stairway and blended in with the students fleeing the building, sauntering away. He then went to a local store and bought a soda, and was eventually stopped by police as he walked down the street, seemingly untroubled by his murders. Although he was described by his attorney as being a "broken human being," he was also "fully aware of what was going on" and is likely to be considered competent to participate in the proceedings. Students later expressed that they were not surprised that he shot unarmed students and that they had feared and shunned him. Prosecutors are seeking the death penalty. On May 18, 2018 at Santa Fe High School in Texas, yet another mass shooting occurred on the school's campus.

The mass teenage or young adult killers have all had some documented history of mental illness. Sandy Hook shooter Adam Lanza had mental disorders and was known to suffer from depression, anxiety, and obsessive-compulsive disorders. He was also known to have an atypical preoccupation with violence. Columbine killer Eric Harris was documented retrospectively as rage-filled, having antisocial personality disorder, and lacking a conscience; his partner Dylan Klebold was psychotic, paranoid, and delusional. Reports revealed that Nikolas Cruz had a significant history of mental illness as well as likely antisocial behavioral disorders (he was known to torture animals; was sadistic; had a significant history of angry, abrasive, and belligerent behavior; and lacked empathy).

Consider further the case of Morgan Geyser and Anissa Weier, lifelong friends in Waukesha, Wisconsin. As 12-year old sixth graders in May 2014, they shared their secrets, their homework, and, apparently, their psychotic delusions. Together the girls methodically planned the murder of their 12-year old classmate, Payton "Bella" Leutner. They wrote out a supply chart. In a photographic depiction, akin to a "to do" list, the girls listed "pepper spray, map of forest, camera, cheesecake" and adding "the will to live" before listing "kitchen knife."

Both girls later separately told law enforcement officers that they planned the murder to pay homage to an online horror character called Slender Man. The girls were convinced that the cartoon creature was real and could kill their families unless appeased by their commitment to homicidal activity. Slender Man is a fictional, faceless monster who lurks on websites throughout the internet. He is often portrayed in a dark suit with octopus-like tentacle hands. The girls thought his subliminal message was directed to them and if they did not kill, he would kill. They believed they had to kill their friend to become "proxies" or servants to Slender Man and their role was necessary to protect their families from him. Each told friends of the plan. Slender Man was regarded by devotees alternately as a sinister force and an avenging angel. The friends agreed, though, that to become a servant, you had to kill a friend. In describing the non-existent creature, Morgan detailed how Slender Man had sharp tendrils that were real in life as well as in her dreams. In Morgan's bedroom, police found dozens of crude drawings of Slender Man, as well as disfigured Barbie dolls branded with Slender Man's figure. Morgan also believed that she could communicate telepathically with Slender Man and could see and hear other fictional characters, including unicorns, characters from Harry Potter books, and the Teenage Mutant Ninja Turtles. She believed that she had Vulcan mind control, as depicted in the *Star Trek* series.

After luring their friend to a secluded part of a park, the girls stabbed her 19 times. Under careful and dispassionate professional interrogation, Anissa described how Morgan stabbed Payton first and then she, Anissa, followed, stabbing their friend numerous times. One of the strikes was within one millimeter of Payton's heart, which would have been immediately fatal. In released video tapes of the confession, Anissa matter-of-factly stated, "We told her that we were going to get help, but we really weren't. . . . We were going to run and let her pass away. So, we ran." Anissa later told police that while they were walking into the woods with their victim, they saw Slender Man and saw him again during the stabbings. In response to questioning about how she got the knife from Anissa, Morgan, with almost a singsong voice, answered, "She shoved it into my hands. There it was." In describing the grisly scene, Morgan said that she didn't know what she did: "It didn't feel like anything. It was like air."

Despite suffering repeated stab wounds and being left for dead, Payton crawled out of the wooded park and was found by a passing bicyclist. She was taken to the hospital and survived. Anissa and Morgan, although 12 years old, were charged as adults for attempted homicide. Under Wisconsin's criminal law procedures, a jury makes the decision if an accused was mentally ill at the time of the crime. Morgan's lawyers established that she suffered from schizophrenia and is on the psychotic spectrum, making her prone to delusions and paranoia.

Anissa's legal and medical experts stated that "Anissa's broken mind caused her to lose touch with reality." Anissa was under the control and command of a delusional disorder. Medical professionals said that she had a diminished capacity to separate reality from fantasy. Described as a loner who struggled to fit in, she found a friend in Morgan. After her parents' divorce, teachers noticed symptoms of depression, but her father testified he thought she was just a normal kid. Together, Anissa and Morgan developed an integrated delusional belief system and partnership and together made calculated plans to kill their friend Payton. Pursuant to a plea of guilty and to avoid a prison sentence, the judge directed that both girls be committed to state mental hospitals. Morgan Geyser will remain in the state mental hospital for 40 years, and Anissa Weier will be in a locked mental facility for 25 years.

Whether acting individually or with others, children who kill, especially those who kill other children, challenge both the mental health system and the criminal justice system. Society at large also wrestles with the broader implications of such acts, whether committed with firearms or other weapons, with claims often made that the perpetrator, alleged or otherwise, was mentally ill. As we have seen in this chapter, however, such acts rarely occur without warning. Sensitizing first responders and family members to those warning signs remains a monumental but essential goal.

SUMMARY

- The juvenile courts use special procedures and terminology for the legal process of adjudicating juveniles to help prevent stigmatization of criminal conduct, favoring treatment, counseling, and non-punitive consequences for youth.
- As in the adult justice system, the resources for counseling and treatment in the juvenile justice system are overextended and undersupplied in most communities. Also as in the adult systems, communities are using the judicial process to compel resolution of mental health problems for juveniles.
- Disruptive conduct disorders, such as hyperactivity or ADHD, affect children's ability to focus and concentrate in school and when these disorders are untreated, children have high failure rates in juvenile intervention programs and school, resulting in recidivism, as the diseases are found in a high percentage of people in prison.
- Suicide is a progression of mental illness that may result from depression or glorification of a way out of school and peer pressures. Education programs, media awareness, and antidepressant medications help decrease juvenile suicides.
- Education is a key intervention to juvenile delinquency and mental illnesses. When expulsion became heavily utilized, it created a pipeline from school to prison that overincluded the mentally ill. Greater emphasis on diverting students from school terminations to treatment programs in schools creates viable alternatives from prison.
- Kids who kill have a range of motivations for their actions, but mental illness is an underlying factor.

KEY TERMS

Acts of delinquency
Disruptive behavior disorders
Depression
Dependency status
Domestic minor sex trafficking (DMST)

Nervous disorders
Present ability
Status offense
Suicidal ideation
Ward of the court

CHAPTER REVIEW QUESTIONS

1. What are some of the behaviors associated with ADHD?
2. Why would cases involving domestic minor sex trafficking be considered a mental health issue?
3. What is the philosophy of rehabilitation or therapeutic intervention for juveniles who violate the laws?
4. Should there be more or less emphasis on the philosophy that juveniles and adults be treated the same?
5. Describe mental illnesses, such as depression, anxiety, and conduct disorders.
6. What is suicidal ideation? Why is it an important issue with juveniles?
7. Are there any commonalities with teenage homicidal shooters ?
8. How does education interrupt the cycle of mental illness and criminalization of the mentally ill with respect to juvenile offenders?
9. How can a person with Down syndrome or other organic brain illness be found to be competent to stand trial?
10. Discuss the differences between the adult criminal justice system and the juvenile justice system.
11. Why is there a difference between delinquency and dependency juvenile cases?
12. If a young child is the victim of a sexual assault, how can the charges be proven if she is not a mentally competent witness? What different ways could a child's reliability to testify be tested or presented?

REFERENCES

Abram K., L. Teplin, D. Charles, S. Longworth, G. McClelland, and M. Dulcan (2004). "Posttraumatic stress disorder and trauma in youth in juvenile detention." *Archives of General Psychiatry* 61: 403-410.

Abramowitz, J.S., and R. Jacoby (2014). "Obsessive-Compulsive Disorder in the DSM-5." Clinical Psychology, University of North Carolina at Chapel Hill. *American Psychological Association*, V21:N2: September 2014, 221.

Aggarwal, I. (2013). "The role of antisocial personality disorder and antisocial behavior in crime." *Inquiries Neuroscience*. 5:09: 1-21.

American Psychiatric Association (2013). *Diagnostic and Statistical Manual for Mental Disorders*. 5th ed. Washington, DC: American Psychiatric Association.

American Psychological Association (2017). "Teen suicide is preventable." Retrieved at http://www.apa.org/research/action/suicide.aspx on 5 November 2017.

Barbour, P. (2013). "Criminal thinking: a cognitive-behavioral approach." Retrieved at https://vdocuments.mx/documents/antisocial-personality-disorder-568c1a1113ea7.html on 22 February 2018.

Berg, N., O. Kiviruusu, S. Karvonen, O. Rahkonen, and T. Huurre (2016). "Pathways from problems in adolescent family relationships to midlife mental health via early adulthood disadvantages — a 26-year longitudinal study." *PLoS ONE* 12(5): e0178136. Retrieved at https://doi.org/10.1371/journal.pone.0178136 on 22 February 2018.

Brown, R. (2004), "The 'American Taliban' versus the Junior 'Beltway Sniper': Toward understanding death, 'brainwashing,' 'terror,' and race in the court of public opinion." *DePaul Law Review* 53: 1663-74.

Bryne, J. (n.d.) "Normal teenage behavior vs. early warning signs of mental illness." Retrieved at http://www.asmfmh.org/resources/publications/normal-teenage-behaviour-vs-early-warning-signs-of-mental-illness/ on 5 November 2017.

Centers for Disease Control and Prevention (2017). "Suicide fact sheet." Retrieved at https://www.cdc.gov/injury/index.html on 3 November 2017.

Cole, J., G. Sprang, R. Lee, and J. Cohen (2016). "The trauma of commercial sexual exploitation of youth: A comparison of CSE victims to sexual abuse victims in a clinical sample." *Journal of Interpersonal Violence* 31: 122-146.

Colvin, M., F.T. Cullen, and T. Vander Ven (2002). "Coercion, social support, and crime: An emerging theoretical consensus." *Criminology* 40: 19-42.

Covenant House. (n.d.) "Labor and sex trafficking among homeless youth." Loyola University, New Orleans, University of Pennsylvania. Retrieved at https://covenanthousestudy.org/landing/trafficking/ on 23 February 2018.

Daniel, S., D. Goldston, A. Harris, A. Kelley, and G. Palmes (2004). "Review of literature on aftercare services among children and adolescents." *Psychiatric Services* 55: 901-912.

DeBellis, M., and A. Zisk (2014). "The biological effects of childhood trauma." *Child Adolescent Psychiatric Clinician of North America* 23: 185-222.

Ehrenfreund, M., and D. Lu (January 27, 2016). "More people were killed last year than in 2014 and no one's sure why." *The Washington Post*. Retrieved at https://www.washingtonpost.com/graphics/national/2015-homicides/ on 15 November 2017.

Federal Advisory Committee on Juvenile Justice (2011). "Summary of organizing meeting." Retrieved at https://facjj.ojp.gov/ojpsddry/Documents/facjj_minutes_october_2011_final.pdf on 21 November 2017.

Foley. H.A., C. Carlton, and R.J. Howell (1996). "The relationship of attention deficit hyperactivity disorder and conduct disorder to juvenile delinquency: legal implications." *Bulletin of the American Academy of Psychiatry and the Law* 24: 333-345.

Foster, E.M., A. Qaseem, and T. Connor (2004). "Can better mental health services reduce the risk of juvenile justice system involvement?" *American Journal of Public Health* 94: 859-65.

Gould, M.S., and R.A. Kramer (2001). "Youth suicide prevention." *Suicide and Life-Threatening Behavior* 31: 6-31.

Grondahl, P. (November 5, 2014). "Selkirk man, 21, takes his own life in prison cell. Family ties mental illness, abuse in prison to hanging." *Times Union.* Retrieved at http://www.timesunion.com/local/article/21-year-old-state-prisoner-from-Selkirk-hangs-5870531.php on 6 November 2017.

Greenberg, G., D. Velting, and D. Shaffer (2003). "Youth suicide risk and preventive interventions: A review of the past 10 years." *Journal of the American Academy of Child and Adolescent Psychiatry* 42: 386-405.

Gregory, S., D. Ffytche, A. Simmons, V. Kumari, M. Howard, S. Hodgins, and N. Blackwood (2012). "The antisocial brain: Psychopathy matters. A Structural Mri investigation of antisocial male violent offenders." *Architecture of General Psychiatry.* 69: 962-972.

Grisso T. (2008) "Adolescent offenders with mental disorders." *Future of Children* 18: 143-164.

Halter, S. (2010). "Factors that influence police conceptualizations of girls involved in prostitution in six U.S. cities: child sexual exploitation victims or delinquents?" *Child Maltreatment* 15: 152-160.

Hammond, S. (2007). *Mental Health Needs of Juvenile Offenders.* Washington, DC: National Conference of State Legislatures.

Heston, J., A. Olson, A. Waterfield, S. Presgrove, M. Hughes, M. Hoffman, and V. Arnold (2013). "Attention Deficit Hyperactivity disorder in children and adolescents." echappellTDMHSASResearchTeam (February 22): 101-116. Retrieved at https://tn.gov/assets/entities/behavioral-health/attachments/Pages_from_CY_BPGs_101-116.pdf on 23 November 2017.

Hoeve M., L. McReynolds, G. Wasserman, and C. McMillan (2013). "Health disorders on severity of reoffending juveniles." *Criminal Justice and Behavior* 40: 289-301.

Jones, L., D.W. Engstrom, T. Hilliard, and M. Diaz (2007). "Globalization and human trafficking." *Journal of Sociology and Social Welfare* XXXIV: 107-22.

Jordon, J., B. Patel, and L. Rapp (2013). "Domestic minor sex trafficking: A social work perspective on misidentification, victims, buyers, traffickers, treatment, and reform of current practice." *Journal of Human Behavior in the Social Environment* 23: 356-369.

Kahn B., P. O'Donnell, J. Wernsman, L. Bushell, and A. Kavanaugh (2007). "Making the connection: Legal advocacy and mental health services." *Family Court Review* 245: 486-400.

Kamenstein, J. (1997). "The inner-morality of justice: The case for consistency and legality." *Cardozo Law Review* 18: 2105-151.

Karch, D., L. Dahlberg, N. Patel, T. Davis, E. Logan, H. Hill, and L. Ortega (2006). "Surveillance for violent deaths — National Violent Death Reporting System, 16 States." *Surveillance Summaries*. 58/SS-1: 1-43.

Kurtz D., T. Linnemann, and E. Green (2014). "Support, coercion, and delinquency: Testing aspects of an emerging theory." *Journal of Crime and Justice* 37: 309-326.

LaFortune, K. (2016) "Oklahoma leads the way on juvenile competency." *American Psychological Association Judicial Notebook* 47-1: 32.

Langberg, J., and B. Fedders (2013). "How juvenile defenders can help dismantle the school-to-prison pipeline: A primer on educational advocacy and incorporating clients' education histories and records into delinquency representation." *Journal of Law and Education* 42: 653-690.

Langman, P. (2009). *Why Kids Kill: Inside the Minds of School Shooters*. New York: St. Martin's Press.

Langman, P. (2018). "Resources on school shootings, perpetrators and prevention." Retrieved at https://schoolshooters.info on 22 February 2018.

LeCloux, M., P. Maramaldi, K. Thomas, and E. Wharff (2016). "Family support and mental health service use among suicidal adolescents." *Journal of Child and Family Studies* 25: 2597-2606.

Mayo Clinic (n.d.). "Post-traumatic stress disorder (PTSD) Patient Care and Information." Retrieved at https://www.mayoclinic.org/diseases-conditions/post-traumatic-stress-disorder/symptoms-causes/syc-20355967 on 4 November 2017.

Mayo Clinic (2017). "Antisocial Personality Disorder." Retrieved at https://www.mayoclinic.org/diseases-conditions/antisocial-personality-disorder/symptoms-causes/syc-20353928 on 22 February 2018.

Mays, L., and L.T. Winfree (2012). *Juvenile Justice*. 3rd ed. New York: Wolters Kluwer.

McReynolds L., C. Schwalbe, and C. Wasserman (2010). "The contribution of psychiatric disorder to juvenile recidivism." *Criminal Justice and Behavior* 37: 204-16.

Mental Health America (2017). "Mental illness and the family: Recognizing warning signs and how to cope." Retrieved at http://www.mentalhealthamerica.net/recognizing-warning-signs on 4 November 2017.

Moreno, I. (November 2, 2017). "Wisconsin girl reaches plea deal in slender man case." Retrieved at https://www.usnews.com/news/best-states/wisconsin/articles/2017-09-28/wisconsin-teen-in-slender-man-stabbing-case-due-in-court on 22 November 2017.

Moskos, M., J. Achilles, and D. Gray (2004). "Adolescent suicide myths in the United States." *Crisis: The Journal of Crisis Intervention and Suicide Prevention* 25: 176-182.

Mueller, A. (2017). "Does the media matter to suicide? Examining the social dynamics surrounding media reporting on suicide in a suicide-prone community." *Social Science and Medicine* 180: 152-159.

Mulvey E., C. Schubert, and A. Piquero (2010). *Pathways to Desistance: Final Technical Report*. Retrieved at https://www.ncjrs.gov/pdffiles1/nij/grants/244689.pdf on 22 October 2017.

Mzezewa, T. (April 17, 2017). "Homeless youth at high risk of human trafficking." *The New York Times*. Retrieved at https://kristof.blogs.nytimes.com/2017/04/17/homeless-youth-at-high-risk-of-human-trafficking/ on 23 February 2018.

National Institute of Mental Health (2017). "Bipolar disorder in children and teens." Retrieved at https://www.medicinenet.com/bipolar_disorder_in_children_and_teens/article.htm#what_is_bipolar_disorder on 4 November 2017.

National Incidence Studies of Missing, Abducted, Runaway and Throwaway Children (2002). "Runaway/throwaway children: National estimates and characteristics." Retrieved from https://www.ncjrs.gov/html/ojjdp/nismart/04/index.html on 20 November 2017.

Office for Civil Rights (2012). "Expansive survey of America's public schools reveals troubling racial disparities." Retrieved at https://www.ed.gov/news/press-releases/expansive-survey-americas-public-schools-reveals-troubling-racial-disparities on 22 November 2017.

Patel A., S. Flisher, and P. McGarry (2007). "Mental health of young people: a global public-health challenge." *Lancet* 369: 1302-1313.

Purdie, N., J. Hattie, and A. Carroll (2002). "A review of the research on interventions for attention deficit hyperactivity disorder: What works best?" *Review of Educational Research* 72: 61-99.

Raine, A., T. Lencz, S. Birhrle, L. LaCasse, P. Colletti (Feb. 2000). "Reduced prefrontal gray matter volume and reduced autonomic activity in antisocial personality disorder." *Architecture of General Psychiatry* 57: 119-127.

Raine, A. (2008). "From genes to brain to antisocial behavior. Current directions in psychological science." *Sage Journals* 17: 5.

Rice, T.R., and L. Hoffman (2015). "Adolescent mass shootings: developmental considerations in light of the Sandy Hook shootings." *International Journal of Adolescent Medicine and Health* 27: 183-7.

Richardson, J.T. (2016). "Brainwashing and mental health." Pp. 210-215 in H.S. Friedman (ed.), *Encyclopedia of Mental Health*. 2nd ed. Boston: Elsevier.

Richette, L.A. (1969). *The Throwaway Children*. J.R. Lippincott, Philadelphia.

Sanborn, J. B. (2008). "Juveniles' Competency to Stand Trial: Wading through the Rhetoric and the Evidence." 99 J. Crim. L. & Criminology 135 (2008-2009).

Schuppe, J. (2018) "Who is Nikolas Cruz? School shooting suspect joked about guns, worrying classmates." *NBC News* February 15, 2018. Retrieved at https://www.nbcnews.com/news/us-news/who-nikolas-cruz-florida-school-shooter-joked-about-guns-worried-n848266 23 February 2018.

Segen, J.C. (2011). *The Doctor's Dictionary*. Amazon Digital Services.

Shanks, L. (2010). "Evaluating children's competency to testify: Developing a rational method to assess a young child's capacity to offer reliable testimony in cases alleging child sex abuse." *Cleveland State Law Review* 58: 575-602.

Skowyra, K., and J. Cocozza (2006). "Blueprint for change: A comprehensive model for the identification and treatment of youth with mental health needs in contact with the juvenile justice system." Delmar, NY: Policy Research Associates.

Spear, L.P. (2000) "Neurobehavioral changes in adolescence." American Psychological Society. Retrieved at http://faculty.weber.edu/eamsel/Classes/Child%203000/Adolescent%20Risk%20taking/Lectures/3-4%20Biological/Biology%20II/Spear%20SV%20(2000).pdf on 10 December 2017.

Stepanuan, S., S. Sidhu, and E. Bath (2016). "Juvenile competency to stand trial." Child and Adolescent Psychiatric Clinics 25: 49-59. Retrieved at http://www.childpsych.theclinics.com/article/S1056-4993(15)00087-5/pdf on 2 November 2017.

Stern, K.R. (2001). "A treatment study of children with attention deficit hyperactivity disorder." Fact Sheet 20. Washington, DC: Office of Juvenile Justice and Delinquency Prevention.

Truesdell, J. (March 25, 2017). Dynasty Star Catherine Oxenberg's Fight to Save Daughter from Group That Allegedly Brands Women." People: Human Interest. Retrieved at http://people.com/human-interest/dynasty-star-catherine-oxenbergs-fight-to-save-daughter-nxivm/ on 25 October 2017.

Turkewitz, J., P. Mazzei, and A. Burch (2018). "Suspect confessed to the police that he began shooting students 'in the hallways.'" The New York Times. Retrieved at https://www.nytimes.com/2018/02/15/us/florida-shooting.html on 22 February 2018.

Tucker, A. (2013). "Are babies born good? New research offers surprising answers to the age-old question of where morality comes from." Smithsonian Magazine. Retrieved at https://www.smithsonianmag.com/science-nature/are-babies-born-good-165443013/?no-ist=&src=longreads&page=8 on 1 November 2017.

Underwood, L., and A. Washington (2016). "Mental illness and juvenile offenders." International Journal of Environmental and Residential Public Health 13: 228. Retrieved at http://www.mdpi.com/1660-4601/13/2/228/htm on 23 November 2017.

U.S. Department of Education (2006). "Office for Civil Rights, Civil Rights Data Collection, 2006, National and State Estimators." Washington, DC: U.S. Department of Education.

Wareham, J., and D. Boots (2012). "The link between mental health problems and youth violence in adolescence: A multilevel test of DSM-oriented problems." Criminal Justice and Behavior 39: 1003-24.

Weiss B., and J. Garber (2003). "Developmental differences in the phenomenology of depression." Developmental Psychopathology 15: 403-430.

Winfree, L.T., and S. Jiang (2010). "Youthful suicide and social support: Exploring the social dynamics of suicide-related behavior and attitudes within a national sample of US Adolescents." Youth Violence and Juvenile Justice 8: 19-37.

Wolpaw, J., and J.T. Ford (2004). "Assessing exposure to psychological trauma and post-traumatic stress in the juvenile justice population." Los Angeles, CA: National Child Traumatic Stress Network.

Yurgelun-Todd, D. (2007). "Emotional and cognitive changes during adolescence." Current Opinions in Neurology 17: 251-257.

CASES

In re Jacob M.W., 690 N.W.2d 886 (2004)(Wisconsin)
State v. J.S. No.0312013339, Del. Fam. Ct. LEXIS 75, at *3 (Fam. Ct. Aug 2 2005)
Wheeler v. United States, 159 U.S. 523 (1895)

LEGISLATION

Juvenile Justice and Delinquency Prevention Act (1974), Pub. L. No. 93-415, 42 U.S.C.
    §5601 *et seq.*)
Juvenile Justice and Delinquency Prevention Act (2002), reauthorized by the 21st
    Century Department of Justice Appropriations Authorization Act, Pub. L. No. 107-273,
    116 Stat. 1758)
N.Y. Crim. Proc. Law §60.20(2)

CHAPTER 11

Mental Illness Issues in the Community

CHAPTER OUTLINE

LEARNING OBJECTIVES

After reading this chapter, you should be able to:

▶ Recognize when a community member is spiraling from collecting objects to accumulating so many household items or pets that it may be evidence of self-neglect or deteriorating mental illness signaling hoarding.

▶ Understand the profiles of the homeless population and identify the circumstances of and solutions for the chronically homeless.

▶ Identify behaviors and obsessions that are associated with various types of stalking and cyber-bullying.

▶ Understand the terminology and application of "stay away" orders of protection as they are used to proactively prevent criminal behavior.

▶ Understand issues that affect the mentally infirm who may need guardianships.

PROLOGUE

The following is a compilation of different accounts to illustrate an example of hoarding behavior. Any similarity to an actual person, location, or incident is a coincidence.

Ohio resident Barbara was a multi-millionaire. Through careful investments and living frugally, she and her husband, Howard, amassed a fortune. After her husband died in 1985, Barbara, then 65 years old, decided to move. She purchased a home that overlooked the city, paying a million dollars for the luxury dwelling.

Childless and with no one to help her, Barbara packed up her belongings herself. The problem she had was that she could not bear the thought of leaving any item she owned behind in her old home, whether it was a bit of paper, an item of furniture, or a random piece of clothing. She had collections of magazines, newspapers, plastic containers, and paper towel tubes. She had thousands of kitchen gadgets and small appliances. They would all have to make the trip with her.

Barbara decided to purchase a moving van when all the movers who came to survey her home belongings refused to pack or move them, citing the health hazards associated with the large quantity of mouse and rat droppings around her household goods. She did find four men from a day-labor shelter who were willing to pack the van, but she watched them vigilantly to make sure nothing was stolen or left behind.

Barbara drove the 18-wheeler, parking it in front of her new home. Exhausted by the thought of unpacking the truck, she spent six months shopping at the local thrift stores for beds, furniture, and kitchen items. Every time she went into a thrift store, she became overwhelmed by the need to liberate all the couches and chairs. She could hear voices of past conversations emanating from the various pieces of furniture, and she knew it was her responsibility to save them from certain destruction or further abandonment.

After six months of the neighbors complaining about the 18-wheeler parked in front of her house, Barbara arranged for everything to be moved from the van into the main house, as well as a guest house. After she was "settled in" with her possessions, she marked a path from her favorite chair to the refrigerator and had the boxes stacked along each side. She continued to forage in the neighborhood for abandoned items, following a rigid mental checklist for the items that had to be "rescued." The police ordered her to stop rummaging through garbage cans in the common alleyway behind her house. She bought a motorcycle and parked it in the dining room and then, worried it might get stolen, bought 15 mattresses to hide it. She found comfort in the sounds of the mice and rats running through the garbage that she could not bear to throw away.

When the health department came to her home with a court order issued after numerous anonymous complaints, the workers found her sitting in a chair with only a track to the toilet and the cabinet of canned foods. She was filthy, her hair matted. Any items of value were taken by the crews hired to clean the house as their perceived "reward" for the dirty work, despite their high hourly wage. It took months to empty the house, which ultimately was torn down due to infestation of insects, rats, and other vermin.

Barbara did not violate any criminal laws, only administrative health and safety ordinances. She did not harm anyone. She never spoke to her neighbors. She was just mentally ill.

This situation of hoarding exemplifies the situations described in this chapter whereby a person who is highly functional and may have a strong and positive life declines into a mental state we do not fully understand. Barbara's conduct, like the other forms of behaviors presented throughout this chapter, is not definitively criminal behavior. While most people would find her lifestyle unnatural and unsafe, they would also agree that Barbara doesn't need punitive consequences, only mental health care and treatment.

CHAPTER OVERVIEW

Those who work in the criminal justice profession will experience many incidents in which people who are mentally ill engage in non-criminal, but socially disruptive, conduct. This chapter explores foundational issues that emerge when addressing community apprehensions about people who are mentally ill and live in our communities.

First, we will consider the facts and the law as we weave our knowledge of the mind and brain into the complexity of what happens when a person's accumulation of items and/or pets becomes so tangled in their persona that it raises questions about their physical well-being and mental health. While the problem may be evident, the solutions are challenging to the families of the hoarders and to first responder investigators.

In the second section of the chapter, on the opposite end of the spectrum, we will explore the problem of homelessness and the behaviors of people who reduce their worldly possessions to what can fit in a garbage bag.

In the next sections of the chapter, we will explore the volatile situations involving stalkers, feuding neighbors, and fighting family members. We will learn about legal intervention available before wrongful activity transpires that may fend off a possible criminal act.

We conclude this chapter's pragmatic approach to considering issues of mental illness by looking at circumstances for the use of a guardianship where there is a concern for a person's mental acuity to handle financial and personal affairs. The appointment of a guardian is not commonly the responsibility of a first responder or the work of law enforcement. Nevertheless, when working with people affected by the topics that we cover in this chapter, as well as in other chapters, a foundational knowledge of the process that are useful as a referral suggestion if first responders encounters a vulnerable person who is struggling with mental health issues.

The range of issues in this chapter is broad, but they all focus on how mental health issues in the community can become increasingly problematic, and potentially involve the criminal justice system, if not addressed swiftly and directly by the community. Even without a report of criminal behavior, first responders, law enforcement officers, and street providers may be engaged to investigate and resolve situations to avoid criminal consequences. Our goal is to help identify and develop the tools, resources, and ideas to guide law enforcement to the alternative solutions that do not necessarily depend on the criminal justice system. This section starts with an issue that recurs throughout this chapter: How should providers respond when there is a non-criminal individual behavioral disorder—a social disorder such as the over-accumulation of garbage, perceived harassment within a community, or the evident vulnerability of a homeless person? Or, more simply, what should be done when a person is just mentally ill?

FRAMING THE ISSUES

As we have explored throughout the book, the deinstitutionalization of the mentally ill and integration of the disabled into the community can cause tensions if the need for tolerance lags behind the personal experiences of the community. Although you may be sensitive to and compassionate about the differences in people due to your education, age, or professional interests, many community members may become fearful or have negative reactions when people act differently or exhibit unexpected public behavior. For example, the psychological syndrome of hoarding things or animals has a lengthy history associated with mental health issues, but overall, hoarders are not criminal; nor are they highly visible. In contrast, some of the homeless population keep their worldly possessions in a shopping cart. The visibility of mentally ill homeless people generates fears for safety and security, even though the only issue may be that they may be mentally ill. Homelessness produces many problems for which there is a dearth of solutions. Although we may not understand the reason for homelessness, we can examine some solutions that work for people with mental illness.

Our personal lives are bounded by electronic devices and reality television. For some who are lonely or isolated, imaginary relationships become real and then transform into obsessive hunting, haunting, and hounding. The mental illness that morphs into obsession may not be noticeable to the offender but it is terrifying to the target. Also, as our communities grow larger with resulting seclusion, tensions can arise if a dispute erupts in a neighborhood. Homeowners who normally are rational, sane members of a community can spiral into mental instability over the disposal of grass clippings. Families and neighbors use "stay away" orders to prohibit personal contact and communications. Again, even if no criminal event occurs, there is a fear that a crime could be committed by someone who is perceived to be mentally ill or unstable. This is a sampling of problems that are not necessarily in the context of criminal law violations, but instead within the parameters of mental illness and a healthy society.

HOARDING

Hoarding disorder (HD) is a cognitive, chronic neuropsychiatric disorder that is associated with substantial distress, functional impairment, and social disruption and isolation that is manifested through inappropriate accumulation of object clutter. The APA's *DSM-5* now classifies HD as a distinct disorder under the category of obsessive-compulsive and related disorders. It is also known as in-home object hoarding disorder. The psychiatric impairment associated with an obsessive need to collect, keep, retrieve, and save material items engulfs the individual and causes health risks, health code violations, evictions, and other problems that may be ultimately indicative of personal abuse and self-neglect. Again, this behavior is not, per se, criminal, but can affect the families of hoarders and, in some instances, the community. HD affects roughly 6 percent of the nation's population (American Psychiatric Association, n.d.). It is characterized by the acquisition of physical items or personal articles, coupled with a failure to discard large volumes of possessions that results in the substantial accumulation numbers of personal objects, knick-knacks, clutter, periodicals, books and other items in such quantities that the functionality of the living areas of the home of the resident(s) is impeded and impaired.

A compulsive hoarder is defined as an individual who has a collection of possessions so large that it encroaches on the amount of usable living space within the residence of the hoarder. The consequences of compulsive hoarding become severe when there is a corresponding inability to maintain basic living activities, such as gaining access to the bathroom or the kitchen to maintain personal hygiene and sanitary living conditions, and when the ability to move throughout the home or residence is impeded or blocked by the depth of the accumulation of the personal articles. Hoarding also increases the risk of illness from unsanitary conditions as well as injury and death from falls and fires.

The remarkable growth in the psychological behaviors associated with excessive hoarding prompted the American Psychiatric Association (2013) to include it as a new disorder in the *DSM-5*, as noted above. Overall, hoarding things is associated with high levels of stress, social disruption, functional impairment, and personal and societal costs. Excessively cluttered homes coupled with the inability to care for, clean, or discard any items due this mental behavior disorder is associated with safety hazards, financial challenges, and familial consequences.

There are interesting etiological factors in the hoarding disorder. It is most common among older adults ages 55 to 94 years. The disorder may emerge from a crisis around emotional attachment. Although the cause of hoarding disorder has yet to be found, hoarding is described an aspect of an obsessive-compulsive disorder that may emerge following the loss of a loved one, or an aspect of post-traumatic stress following a highly disruptive event or a period of high emotional anxiety. During the grieving period, the collection of items helps to alleviate emotional disorder, or there is emerging difficulty in making decisions. It has been noted that hoarders are no more likely than non-hoarders to report having experienced a lack of money, food, clothing, or shelter during their lifetime. However, in a study of 81 hoarders or persons with an obsessive-compulsive disorder, nearly one in 5 of the participants reported a period of homelessness in their lives.

Hoarding negatively affects family dynamics: People who hoard also report high levels of distress and exhibit high levels of experience with rejection. Family rejection of a loved one with a hoarding disorder is higher than family rejection for obsessive-compulsive disorder and is comparable to levels of rejection of a family member with schizophrenia. There is almost a uniform rejection of a family member who has severe hoarding tendencies, as well as demonstrable low insight, tolerance, and willingness by family members to encourage treatment to resolve the mental disorder. In Tolin and associates' (2007a) study of 665 family members reported by a spouse, parents, children, or grandparents as suffering from hoarding behaviors, reporters described great stress, strain, and personal embarrassment about the condition of the home. A subset of children of identified hoarders showed significant rejection of compulsive hoarders by the children while also reporting elevated childhood distress, less happiness, more difficulty making friends, reduced social contact in the home, and increased intra-familial strain (Tolin, Frost, et al., 2007b).

Treatments for Object Hoarding

Successful cognitive behavioral therapies for HD exist. Although fewer than 45 percent of the individuals who self-identified with HD sought mental health treatment, more than four-fifths of these same subjects acknowledged that treatment is beneficial (Mathews, Uhm, Chan, and Gause, 2015). Frost and associates (2012) found that the refusal to engage in treatment exacerbated the discord with family members and the ambivalence toward helpful intervention seemed to further alienate and frustrate family members. Even with the successful programs, however, family members, hoarders, and community support members must all work together to address and resolve the compulsion to acquire and save; otherwise, recidivism is 95 percent (Frost et al., 2015).

While the resolution (or lack of it) of hoarding may be addressed with attentive family members and support systems, older isolated adults with multiple deficits in social, functional, and physical domains can result in self-neglect and living in squalor. Severe self-neglect often occurs with older adults who have cognitive and affective disorders that impact their personal safety and well-being. Considering the cruel nature of physical or psychological outcomes from neglect and vulnerability of the elderly, there needs to be greater community emphasis on victim services to prevent the spiral into physical and mental chaos.

Animal Hoarding

Compulsive hoarding has an associated psychological disorder that is not well understood: **animal hoarding**. There is substantial literature about how people and companion animals form positive, nurturing and appropriate human/animal relationships enhance quality of life and mental acuity. Yet, within this bond, highly dysfunctional human relationships with animals may emerge that require law enforcement or government administrative attention and intervention. One of the most perplexing and problematic forms is an excessive ratio of animals to humans in a household. Eventually, this condition can become a deleterious situation of comorbidity of animal neglect and human self-neglect.

Characteristics of Animal Hoarding

Animal hoarding is a special manifestation of compulsive hoarding and is defined as a person who (1) accumulates a large number of animals or has more than a typical number of companion animals; (2) fails to provide minimal standards of nutrition, sanitation, and veterinary care; (3) fails to acknowledge the deteriorating condition of the animals (including disease, starvation, or death) within the environment (severe overcrowding, extremely unsanitary conditions); and (4) the human is essentially oblivious or unaware of the negative effect of the collection of animals on his or her own health and well-being or that of other family or community members.

Animal hoarding is found to result in significantly more unsanitary conditions than object hoarding and poses significantly more threat to the health of the humans. Community service investigators reported a lack of sanitation coupled with large numbers of animals, often sick, dying, or dead, which increases the likelihood of zoonotic diseases for the occupants and the community. Characteristically, the living conditions were heavily cluttered, unsafe, and unsanitary through the accumulation of animal excrement in human living areas, and included a nonfunctioning bathroom and the presence of dead animal carcasses in the house. Animal hoarders often have limited home functionality, as evidenced by non-working showers or stopped-up or unusable kitchen sinks. The humans in the relationship may have poor personal hygiene, including a failure to maintain a sanitary bedroom, kitchen, dining room, or living room. Essentially, animal hoarders commonly do not have the ability to safely remain in or leave their home.

We need not provide the diagnostic psychological tools used to classify hoarders, but the following categorical descriptions offer insights into the types of people with this disorder. The methods of classifying types of such hoarders are based on information that is usually available to local law enforcement, animal welfare officers, or mental health specialists involved in the investigations. A study by the Tufts University Hoarding of Animals Research Consortium (HARC) was designed to provide information on the understanding and classifying of animal hoarders (Patronek, Loar, and Nathanson, 2006). The study divides animal hoarders into three basic sub-categories: (1) the overwhelmed caregiver, (2) the rescue hoarder, and (3) the exploiter hoarder. First responders should have an understanding of what evidence or information is admissible for a trial or hearing as well as an understanding of the etiology, the diagnostic criteria described in this chapter, and the associated features of the disorder if called upon as a prosecution witness.

Overwhelmed Hoarder. The overwhelmed hoarder once had the capability to provide appropriate care to animals, but due to an unanticipated incident—such as a death in the family or a personal change of circumstances — becomes overwhelmed by the responsibility of caring for one or two pets. Rather than divesting him- or herself of the pets in the household, the overwhelmed hoarder acquires more animals. While the hoarder has strong emotional attachment to the animals, he or she—the disorder is typically associated with a person who lives alone—continues to acquire more animals as though this will fill the void or relieve the experience of being overwhelmed.

The overwhelmed hoarder tends to withdraw from the community and will acknowledge there is a problem, but will minimize the situation rather than deny it. The hoarder will initially work cooperatively with an investigator and will make an attempt to comply with recommendations, while annoucing that all these actions are the result of unnecessary interference by neighbors or family members.

Rescue Hoarder. This hoarder is difficult to define and react to appropriately since the behavior emerges because in the context of "rescuing" animals from other hoarders. As the name implies, the rescue hoarder has a desire to help animals. However, this desire morphs into an obsession and leads the rescue hoarder to seek out more animals than is healthy. Again, the person begins with a clear ability to care for animals appropriately. However, as the desire to rescue animals increases, eventually the person's capacity to provide minimal care is exceeded. At that point, the individual will not admit to being a subjugated hoarder. A rescue hoarder does not want to meet with assistance agencies because the hoarder feels that he or she is the only person who really cares or can care for the animals, despite their numbers. These people are not isolated from their communities and, in fact, usually are part of a network that accepts dropped-off animals that are in need of care (Reinish, 2009).

Consider the case of Kimi Peck, a person who was found with 60 dogs in her camping trailer in Cheyenne, Wyoming. Peck claimed to be a "rescue operation" before she was prosecuted for animal abuse. While most animal shelter rescuers spend thousands of hours finding "forever homes" for abandoned pets, they also recognize that some animals simply cannot be saved. Peck, however, felt it was her duty to save and keep all animals, sometimes accumulating as many as 100 rescue dogs. Unfortunately, although she established a Chihuahua rescue, Peck did not permit many adoptions of her dogs. Her neglect, despite her self-perceived heroic intentions, resulted in criminal prosecution for animal cruelty.

Exploiter Hoarder. The exploiter hoarder—a phenomenon that can exist as a couple or extended family situation—will actively acquire animals to fulfill financial or status needs, but is unable to develop empathy for or emotional relationships with the animals as their numbers increase and their suffering becomes evident. The animals are used (or intended to be used) for commercial sales or monetary gain, sometimes in dog or rabbit breeding centers, called puppy or rabbit mills. This type of hoarder believes that his superior knowledge and abilities for the business of breeding exceeds anyone else's, but cannot admit that his business plan or dream for riches is failing.

Interventions with Animal Hoarding

The conflict between the hoarder and the animal welfare authorities can trigger a spiral into mental decline and greater dysfunction in the absence of sensitive collaboration. The animal hoarder has a profound emotional dependence on the animals. The abrupt removal of the animals or the client from the animals can cause suicidal ideation or threats of homicide. There can also be an ethical dilemma if a caseworker realizes that disclosure of the harmful environment will result in a complete disruption of the home and psychological safety of the hoarder. At the point of surrendering the animals, animal welfare and public health authorities must collaborate to avoid further damaging the hoarder's sense of identity, self-esteem, self-control, and, often, their purpose for living. It is critical that animal protection caseworkers intervene in a manner that minimizes the hoarder's potential losses and further identifies available resources for counseling and treatment.

In the following scenario, we examine how an innocent intention can become an obsessive, even destructive behavior. Consider how the problems started and then think about the solutions as we continue to learn about different social solutions for people who are not criminal, but may be mentally ill.

Law enforcement officers, social workers, health care workers, and animal care workers may find themselves inadvertently investigating a hoarding case and ultimately testifying in an administrative hearing or even a trial about the case (see Box 11.2). In such situations, the description of the physical environment of the house and animals' health, shelter, and available food and water, as well as any statements by the owner, must be carefully documented or recorded. Due to the sensitive nature of the issues and the public concern for the well-being of animals, if there is a criminal prosecution or an administrative hearing for animal cruelty, it is essential that there are detailed examinations, unambiguous records, photographic documentation, and specific examination of each animal for potential court proceedings. Video recordings may prove useful, especially if the pets are exotic, are not properly socialized, or are highly diseased or in ill health. Being prepared to be a witness in any proceeding is as critical as taking the oath to tell only the truth and the whole truth.

BOX 11.1

What Would You Do?

Nancy was devastated when her husband of 52 years died. Now a childless widow of 78, she had been the primary caretaker of her husband for over 10 years. Shy by nature, she had little contact with her neighbors.

Nancy first noticed the three baby javelinas soon after her husband died. She saw them early one morning with the mother. These wild boars, which have large, heavy, and thick bodies, resemble huge pig-like rats and are remotely related to the hippopotamus. They are smelly, hairy, ugly creatures, and Nancy knew they needed her, desperately. They would die without her. She loved them. She put out bowls of water and lettuce and carrots and watched them gobble up the vegetables.

Within weeks, Nancy's herd grew to 10 animals, then to 15, and then she lost count. They ate her flowers and plants and destroyed her irrigation system. She noticed her neighbor photographing her as she scattered their food. Within a few days, she received a petition signed by her surrounding neighbors asking her to stop feeding the javelinas as they were destroying community plants and irrigation systems, tipping garbage cans, and terrorizing pets and children. She ripped the petition into pieces and fed it to her precious javelinas.

A wildlife animal protection officer came to her home and advised her that it was illegal to feed wildlife. Nancy insisted that her bird feeder must have overflowed. She was shown videos of her feeding the javelinas taped by the neighbors. That night, she put more food outside. The officer came by the next day, again with photos and videos, and issued her a criminal citation for violation of the law that prohibited unlawful feeding of wildlife by intentionally, knowingly, or recklessly attracting or otherwise enticing wildlife into an area. During the ensuing trial, her neighbors testified to seeing her outside at all hours of the night, scattering food. The prosecution also provided evidence through an expert witness that her psychological dependence on the herd of wild animals was akin to hoarding. In arguing that Nancy be found guilty, the prosecutor also said she needed counseling.

Do you think that feeding wild animals is a form of hoarding animals? Why or why not? What were some alternatives that the animal control officer, the neighbors, or the community could have utilized in lieu of prosecuting this shy and isolated woman? If Nancy is found guilty, should she be ordered to undergo counseling? Why or why not? As noted above, untreated hoarding has a 95 percent recidivism rate (Frost et al., 2015). Do you think that she may reoffend? If so, what would make her stop? What if the officer found, in addition to the proclivity to feeding wild animals, that Nancy's house was cluttered to the point of being impassable? Should the officer, who is a representative of wildlife enforcement, do anything?

HOMELESSNESS

Alfred Postell, a bearded homeless man who carried his belongings in a white plastic bag, was charged with criminal trespass after he was found by police sleeping in an entryway. When summoned to the D.C. Superior Court, Postell stood before Judge Thomas Motley. Motley asked the defendant if he had a lawyer. "I am a lawyer," Postell answered. It turned out that Postell had graduated Harvard Law School in 1979 and also held degrees in economics and accounting. In fact, Postell graduated with the same Harvard Law School class as Judge Motley and Supreme Court Chief Justice John Roberts. Of course, that all happened before Postell developed and failed to treat schizophrenia and thereafter became homeless.

As described in Chapter 5, the homeless sleep on sidewalks, use libraries and bus stations for bathing, and rely on 24-hour fast-food restaurants for respite from the weather. Many walk the streets, communicate with the unseen, and live in abandoned buildings, public parks, bus shelters, and under bridges. It is reported that homeless shelters are so populated by mentally ill wanderers that they have the appearance of psychiatric wards (Advocacy Treatment Center). In the opposite extreme from home object hoarding, the homeless live with all the worldly possessions they have at the moment in carts, bags, and coat pockets. However, different community health and safety issues emerge when the homeless, the mentally ill, and, on occasion, the criminal justice system collide.

Nationally, section 330(h)(4)(A) of the United States Public Health Service Act defines a homeless person as "an individual who lacks housing (without regard as to whether the individual is a member of a family), including an individual whose primary residence during the night is a supervised public or private facility (e.g., shelters) that provides temporary living accommodations or the individual is in transitional housing" (Jarvis, 2015). A 2016 U.S. Housing and Urban Development survey indicated that, based on a one-night count of people sleeping on the streets, an estimated 549,928 people were homeless (Henry, Watt, et al., 2016). The researchers found that a majority (68%) were staying in emergency shelters, transitional housing, or safe havens and 32 percent were in unsheltered locations. Approximately 355,212 of those counted were individuals, and 194,716 were families with children, of which 60 percent were under 18 years of age. Among the homeless, 169,000 people were identified as being severely mentally ill (U.S. Housing and Urban Development, 2015).

Nationwide Issues and Concerns

The trend of homelessness affects smaller cities as well. For example, in Roanoke, Virginia, population of approximately 950,000 people, the homeless population increased 363 percent between 1987 and 2007, and 70 percent were receiving mental health treatment or had in the past (Hammack, 2007). In Albany, Georgia, it was reported that the closure of the Thomasville Southwestern State Mental Hospital contributed to a dramatic increase

BOX 11.2

Preparing to Testify in Court

Preparing to testify in any legal proceeding can be the most complicated, emotionally draining, and humiliating process a first responder may experience as a professional. While investigators and detectives are seasoned witnesses, most cases don't result in a trial or hearing and are settled with a plea agreement. Therefore, for the street officer, it may be months or years between an investigation and appearing in court to testify. Despite the personal horror or disgust a responder may experience in cataloguing the dead animals in the home of a hoarder, each sentence and word of the written report is subject to dissection and review. Personal knowledge of what was observed or witnessed by the officer is the mainstay requirement of admissible, reliable evidence. If the officer doesn't remember if there were ten dead dogs and three sick horses, the questioning prosecution attorney can **rehabilitate** the witness by handing her the police report and asking that she read and refresh her memory; or the questioning defense attorney can **impeach** the witness by showing the jury that the witness does not have independent recollection of the facts and is therefore not an appropriate eye-witness to the events.

It will not matter to the judge or jury that the law enforcement officer just worked an all-night shift, that the events happened a year earlier, or that the scene was so horrific that the officer may have psychologically blocked it from memory. The on-scene professionals must be able to describe, in detail and with perfect recollection, the misery first observed and later entered into a police record.

The officer will not know if a particular case will ever be set for a trial. Therefore, to prepare for possible trial, she must write all of the details that will either prompt recollection or give the information to make it appear as though the officer has personal recollection. Consider that there were 1,553,980 arrests for property crimes in the United States in 2014 (Federal Bureau of Investigation, 2015). If the accused is incompetent, restored to competency, disappears, reappears on an arrest warrant, and then requests a trial, the arresting officer will still need to have the same picture-perfect recollection of the scene two years later as on the day of the offense. By cataloguing the detail, the officer can help the prosecuting attorney charge the offenses correctly, enable the defendant to enter a plea to offenses actually described in the complaint, and then accurately recollect during cross-examination.

Officers will receive notice of the proceeding by way of a subpoena or summons to appear in court on a particular date and time. In most offices, the prosecuting attorney will meet with the officer to review the reports and testimony. Defense attorneys also have the right to interview witnesses before they testify. The failure to cooperate can be used to discredit a recalcitrant witness by implying she has something to hide or isn't truthful. The interviews can be recorded to make sure there are no inconsistencies between the first and second round of recollections. It never fails to amaze an attorney, judge, or jury when a professional witness, such as a police officer, is observed waiting hours before coming into the courtroom and then does not recall anything about the incident. Time spent memorizing and remembering the contents of the report only assures the jury hears the truth as it was recorded. Witnesses, even fellow police officers or members of patrol teams, are not permitted to listen to other testimony unless the witness is the designated primary investigator and remains in the courtroom for the duration of the trial.

Sources: Federal Bureau of Investigation (2015); American Bar Association (n.d.).

in people seeking help at the homeless shelter. In 2017, San Diego, California reported outbreaks of Hepatitis C when more than 400 people encountered infected human feces on the sidewalks. Homeless people and injecting drug users are more vulnerable to the disease due to lack of consistent access to bathrooms and hand washing areas.

People become homeless for a variety of reasons and self-report that economic problems, such as a loss of a job, relationship discord, loss of a home, and alcohol and other health problems, caused their current homeless status. Ten percent state that they choose to be homeless. On an individual level, the population is primarily male and middle aged (National Law Center on Homelessness and Poverty, 2014). In a sample of 330 homeless individuals in Minneapolis, the duration of homelessness is related to inconsistent work history, a low level of education, and participation in the foster care system as a youth (Jarvis, 2015).

It is a mistake to ignore the factor of homelessness when considering mental illness and drug and alcohol abuse. Not all homeless people have mental illness and not all the mentally ill are homeless. As we reported in earlier chapters, nearly one in 5 adults in the United States (18.5%), or 43.8 million people, experience mental illness in a year. Within this population, 26 percent of the homeless adults who stay in shelters live with serious mental illness and 46 percent have severe mental illness and/or substance abuse disorders (National Alliance on Mental Illness, 2017). Within this population, 15 percent are categorized as being chronically homeless (U.S. Interagency Council on Homelessness, 2017).

Chronic homelessness is defined as an unaccompanied adult with a disabling condition—most commonly a serious mental illness, substance-related disorder, developmental disability, or chronic physical disability—who experiences homelessness for a year or longer or experienced at least 4 episodes of homelessness within the last 3 years for a cumulative 12 months (Pearson, Montgomery, and Locke, 2009). While people experiencing chronic homelessness make up a small number of the overall homeless population, they are among the most vulnerable. They tend to have high rates of behavioral health problems, including severe mental illness and substance abuse disorders, conditions that may be exacerbated by physical illness, injury, or trauma. Furthermore, they are the least likely to get mental health treatment.

While the reasons for homelessness and the statistics about it are readily available, when it comes to community concerns and conflicts about the solutions, answers are not immediately evident. It is clear that law enforcement officers find themselves not only acting as law enforcers, but also as psychiatric social workers with the added responsibility to recognize that they may need to respond differently to a seriously mentally ill person who also lives without a stable home shelter. For the minor criminal offenders, rather than providing housing through the jails, the New Orleans Municipal Court holds final disposition hearings at the shelters because many of the 34,000 outstanding arrest warrants are attributable to the homeless and mentally ill and the paperwork for arrest, release, and re-warrant for a chronic petty offender is overwhelming the courts. One public defender has a chronically mentally ill homeless client who has been arrested 186 times (Abrams, 2016). In St. Petersburg, Florida, and Santa Cruz, California, there are municipal ordinances that criminalize sleeping on the street, but prosecution of the offenders is almost impossible as assuring due process and notice of the court hearings has become unmanageable. Researchers for the Project on Policing Neighborhoods found that although officers did not arrest the homeless mentally ill for minor offenses, the cost for personnel and police resources to provide alternatives to arrest in order to satisfy constitutional equal protection mandates makes the alternatives difficult to endorse. Disparate treatment comes into play when, for example, police cannot ignore a homeless man urinating on the sidewalk, but then arrest a college student for engaging in the same act.

Criminality and Homelessness

Through bans on camping in public areas, loitering, panhandling, and the implementation of exclusionary zoning that limits land use for accommodating shelters, temporary housing, or low-income developments, cities and counties have, in effect, criminalized homelessness. The National Law Center on Homelessness and Poverty estimates that 53 percent of cities prohibit sitting or lying down in particular public places, such as parks, and 43 percent prohibit sleeping in vehicles (National Law Center on Homelessness and Poverty, 2014). Although peaceful panhandling is a form of protected free speech (*Reed v. Town of Gilbert*, 2015), business owners usually have government prosecution on their side. Small storefronts rely on foot traffic that can be deterred by someone lying across the threshold with the attendant smells of urine and unwashed body odor, and the owners are quick to call the police for arrests. The added security cost is fuel to lobby for further prohibitory ordinances. On the balance, however, the cost of providing legal defense for those arrested for violations then also falls upon the municipalities.

In a shift in national consciousness, some cities are moving from managing homelessness through arrests, disbursement, or outright ignoring of the homeless population to trying to engage in affirmative efforts to end homelessness by utilizing proactive federal, state, and local policies. The strategic focus is to embed programs with new ideas that will help end homelessness. Although it is impossible to resolve all structural causes of homelessness—for example, lack of affordable housing, wage stagnation, the wealth gap, and inadequate health and social services for people on the brink of poverty, law enforcement and street providers can promote programs that are sustainable.

In this regard, consider the following examples. A coalition of churches in Costa Mesa, California, uses an intervention called "Check-in Center," where homeless individuals "check in" their belongings during the day to enable them to be productive instead of spending hours guarding their possessions (Jarvis, 2015). "**Housing is healthcare**" places a premium on finding a stable residence, which is the linchpin to resolving problems of treatment for medical and mental conditions within the homeless population (Lozier, n.d.: 1; see also Doran, Misa, and Shah, 2013). Chronically homeless persons require substantial social services to help stabilize a psychiatric problem. There is mounting evidence that the combination of housing and treatment is most effective in facilitating both housing stability and treatment success.

For programs to succeed, it is important to recognize that chronically homeless individuals are generally unable to meet or commit to many preconditions for housing. The goal, then, becomes providing an affordable home without the demands for sobriety, demonstration of basic living skills and personal hygiene, or commitment to treatment engagement, all of which are typically required by most housing programs. Operating as "Housing First" or "Pathways to Housing," the programs set access to a home for the chronically homeless as the first goal. Severely mentally ill persons seem more inclined to voluntarily seek therapy subsequently, rather than first respond to a treatment-linked mandate, so putting treatment and its often-rigorous conditions secondary to being in a home is more effective. In a study of almost 3,000 homeless people with serious mental illness, the subjects remained in stable housing for up to 5 years, provided there were safe and affordable supportive services that were eventually utilized after housing was provided (Lipton, Siegel, et al., 2000).

Given such programs, law enforcement can refer the chronically homeless to housing within the community rather than within the correctional system. However, there is a dearth of affordable housing units. In 1970, there were 6.5 million low-income units and 6.2 million renters. By 1985, demand grew to 8.9 million low-income households, but the affordable units funded through United States Code (see 42 U.S.C. §1457f) had dropped to 5.6 million units due to budget cuts and lack of federal funds (Doran, Misa, and Shah, 2013; Joint Center for Housing Studies at Harvard University, 2016).

These policy decisions increased the landscape of homelessness throughout the United States. Another path appears to be the funding of a voucher program to permit the chronically homeless person to stabilize through qualified housing of his or her choice, followed by case management treatment of any underlying mental issues or drug addiction, or both. While integrating housing and clinical services improves outcomes for resolving mental illness for the homeless, the costs can be considerable.

A simple survey of national programs dedicated to fighting homelessness lists 150 administrative entities that pay salaries, have officers, make statistical computations, and host excellent websites, but probably have no on-site space for residential use, which illustrates limited direct services for homeless people. In the meantime, street providers and law enforcement officials will continue to grapple with reconciling the position of community members, that they have the right to walk safely on the city sidewalks, with the position of homeless persons, that they have the right to sleep on them.

While homelessness and hoarding appear to result from untreated courses of mental illness, we also need to consider factors that enable or perpetuate mental illness. In Box 11.3, consider how government programs may encourage mental health treatment, but then creates financial dependency on the continued diagnosis and treatment of mental illness.

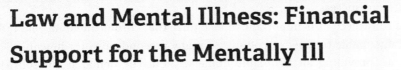

BOX 11.3

Law and Mental Illness: Financial Support for the Mentally Ill

The Social Security and Supplemental Security Income (SSI) programs are the largest of several federal financial assistance programs, and provides monetary supplements to low-income citizens with disabilities to pay for food, clothing, and shelter. Individuals under 18 years old can be declared disabled if there is a physical or mental impairment, including an emotional disability or learning loss that results in marked or severe functional limitation and can be expected to result in death or has lasted more than 12 months. For adults 18 years and over, a financial supplement is awarded when there is a certified, medically approved, reviewed determination of a physical or mental impairment that results in an inability to do any substantial gainful activity. Alcoholism and addiction are prohibited impairments for eligibility, although one form of substance abuse when coupled with a psychiatric diagnosis is allowable. The disability must be expected to result in death or to last for 12 or more months. If there is a determination of eligibility for SSI payments, funding may be decreased upon evidence of ownership of land, a car, personal property, bank accounts, or assets usable for goods or shelter.

Mental health diagnoses are the major category for recipient financial aid and benefits and are virtually the only avenue available for access to government-supported financial payouts without evidence of a physical impairment, such as evidence of chronic and debilitating pain. Unfortunately, as low-income families experience growing economic hardship, many find that applying for mental health SSI payments is the only way to survive.

The need for financial supplements that depend on a psychiatric diagnosis thereafter essentially shapes personal identity and capacity and has accompanied the significant rise in the number of Americans who are prescribed psychotropic medications. Medication use rose from 13 percent of the national population in 1997 to 19 percent in 2007. In 2007, antipsychotic medications were the third-highest-selling pharmaceutical, at $13.1 billion. Antidepressant use increased 400 percent between 2005 and 2008. Proof of use and consumption of the antipsychotic drugs is a frequent requirement for continued receipt of SSI benefits, despite their side effects and the likelihood of diversion into the illicit, after-distribution black market.

In a sample case study reviewed by Hanson and associates, a male who was slashed in the stomach with a kitchen knife by his live-in female friend subsequently had her "over-the-top" violent behavior recognized as a qualifier for SSI disability. Instead of pressing criminal charges, he called for a psychiatric evaluation and accompanied her through a diagnosis of permanent disability for bipolar manic depression, PTSD, and agoraphobia (fear of crowded places) for which she was thereafter declared mentally disabled and provided medication and financial subsidies. The girlfriend then channeled her two children into SSI qualifications and obtained Section 8 subsidized housing. The use of medications that justify economic subsidies may reduce overt psychiatric behaviors, but it also cultivates dependency on opiates. The SSI-based survival strategies generate income for the mentally ill, but the medicalization of subsidized support may also diminish the future of the mentally ill and their functionality in the work place.

Sources: Hansen, Bourgois, and Drucker (2014); Social Security Administration (n.d.).

TARGET VICTIMS AND THE MENTALLY ILL: STALKING

As we have read throughout this chapter, frequently there are mental health concerns that arise when people act differently from the norm. With hoarders and the homeless, there is not necessarily a violation of the law, but there could be one if the behaviors become unreasonable or cause fear in other people. In this section, we are going to highlight some personal behaviors or conduct issues that could be criminal or invoke a fear of criminal conduct if carried out. We will then consider what can be recommended by way of an injunction or a protective order against actually experiencing the threatened criminal misconduct. We will also examine situations in which the people may not be mentally ill, but spiraling conditions can evoke instability and more problems if not addressed and resolved.

Scary Strangers, Fighting Neighbors, and Violent Families

In this context, we will review three separate areas of behaviors that often have a mental health component. In the context of each type of non-criminal behavior, we will review what, if any, first responder responses may be available to try to prevent a crime from occurring in the future (American Bar Association, n.d.).

(1) **Stalking** behaviors:
   a. There is a series of acts or threats or repetitive behaviors that are directed to a specific person (a target);
   b. There is no known or only a momentary personal or physical relationship between the parties; and

    c. The actions of the stranger are frightening, alarming, annoying, or harassing to the target. The actions can be physical or take place through an electronic medium, such as the internet.

  (2) Neighbors and mentally disordered behaviors:

    a. There are elevated tensions, threats or harassment, and disputes between or among members of a neighborhood or community;

    b. There is a series of actions by a neighbor that have become annoying and harassing; and

    c. The harassments appear to be capable of resolution only with a court directive for parties to "stay away" from each other to prevent an escalation of violence or harm.

  (3) Domestic violence issues:

    a. There is a police response to a domestic altercation with an allegation or evidence of violence, physical harm, or property damage that occurs between or among people in a domestic relationship or people in the same household. In this situation, there can also be a report of a fear that a domestic violence altercation could occur, even without an overt act of violence.

    b. There may or may not be an overt mental health issue, but underlying fear, paranoia, behavioral disorders, and aberrant conduct can trigger judicial or police interventions and treatment requirements.

    c. The domestic relationships are commonly defined as spouses, children, grandparents, siblings, intimate partners (i.e., sexually active), or people residing in a common residence.

Scary Stranger Issues of Stalking and Responsive Remedies

Stalking is a complex form of mental illness that is classified as a delusional disorder. This obsessional disorder occurs when there is a perception of interaction or mistreatment or a misinterpreted sign that is mistaken as an actual positive response from the unaware target or acquaintance. The stalker misconstrues the presence of the target, contact by the target, or unintended interaction with the target as an affirmation of their purported relationship, no matter how innocent or accidental is the conduct of the victim (Edwards, 1992). In this regard, consider each of the following types of stalkers.

    Erotomania Stalkers. This type of stalker expresses the delusional belief that he or she is passionately loved by the victim, as part of a delusional disorder. According to the *DSM-5* (APA, 2013), a person with delusional disorder holds a belief that is not based in reality and is not mollified or does not modify his behavior when presented with evidence contradictory to his belief. Ten percent of erotomania stalkers with a delusional disorder focus on a theoretical spiritual union rather than a sexual attraction (Corwin, 2008). If they become violent, however, they may direct the violence toward a third party perceived to be interfering with their relationship. The stalkers come from all walks of life and intelligence levels and often do not have a criminal history. They do, however, have other diagnosable mental illnesses, such as paranoia and obsessive-compulsive conduct with socially maladaptive behaviors. Of concern to law enforcement is the stalker who is triggered into anger and whose obsession becomes violent. Sometimes stalkers in these categorical descriptions formerly had a friendship relationship with the target, but cannot accept it when their love interest is no longer interested in them.

A Threat Management Unit with the Los Angeles Police Department described the obsessive stalker as interpreting perceived symbols or signs that makes them the most important person in the victim's life, which then results in terrorizing the victim. Control of a nuanced form of this obsession may be resolved by restraining orders, described later in this chapter, but often requires more subtle responses as an aggressive intervention could have devastating consequences if the stalker is publicly embarrassed. Remember, in this form of stalking, the actions of the stalker could be impliedly innocent by the claim that all the interactions are reciprocal and reciprocated. Law enforcement may instead need to encourage the victim to explore options for additional security, relocate to a new, undisclosed residence, and change phone numbers and online presence.

Love Obsessional Stalker. Love obsessional stalkers choose victims they encounter, no matter how fleeting the acquaintance, or the victims are co-workers with whom the stalker has superficial interactions, but with whom he or she has had no definable personal relationship. The victims are generally known by the stalker, perhaps as a friend of a friend, a bank teller or grocery store clerk, or even a person who makes copies for the office. The communication efforts of the stalker are creative yet unintelligible from the perception of the victim. Often the stalkers are affluent, well-educated professionals with no real personal life other than the obsession target. The profile may be that of a **sociopath**, but with the mental illness characteristics of schizophrenia hallucinations or bizarre obsessive-compulsive disorders. The *DSM-5* (2013) notes that while a sociopath has behaviors relating to the antisocial personality disorder, the sociopath is often nervous, easily agitated, volatile, and prone to emotional outbursts. A striking behavior of the sociopath is that she will form an attachment to a particular group of individuals, but not have regard for societal rules. Often, however, the stalker's life from all outward appearances is seemingly normal. This stalking behavior type manifests as an orchestrated, calculated, relentless harassment campaign intended to make the victim aware of the stalker's existence through suggestions, symbolic gestures, and complex irrational behavior that is only understood by the stalker (Bonn, 2018).

Celebrity Stalkers. Most threats and attacks on public figures start as fan mail — celebrities can receive up to 20,000 letters a week. "If presumably stable people will hand a maitre'd several hundred dollars to sit close to a celebrity during dinner, it should not surprise us that mentally disordered people have a preoccupation with these affairs," said Park Dietz and his associates (1991). In a study for the National Institute for Justice, they reviewed 2,000 variables to develop a prediction profile of the type most likely to cause physical harm to a high-profile public figure. An examination of more than 140,000 pieces of "nut mail" sent to celebrities—some of which contained blood, hair, or dead animal parts—showed that celebrity stalkers often shared a common delusion that they telepathically communicate with their victims (Dietz et al., 1991).

Furthermore, people with celebrity stalking disorder have difficulty understanding that the television personalities are performing a job. They mistake the friendly, engaging manner of the television personality as an invitation to enter into a personal relationship. The television becomes the conduit, as it creates an illusion of intimacy. Mentally disordered people are set on a different channel when forming attachments, which can be dangerous, even fatal, for those who inspire them.

Media attention to violence based on star obsession was first directed to John Bardon, who killed the star of the hit show *My Sister Sam*, Rebecca Shaffer, who was at the height of her television career. John Hinckley's obsession with movie star Jodie Foster inspired him to attempt to assassinate then-President Ronald Reagan. Less than two hours after his assault on the President, Hinckley wrote a letter to Foster stating, "As you well know by now I love you very much. Over the past seven months I've left you dozens of poems, letters and love messages . . ." (Pinals, 2007).

Mark Chapman, the killer of Beatle John Lennon in 1980, felt that the homicide was helpful to save Lennon, as well as himself, from harm or a miserable fate (Dietz et al., 1991). Chapman, with a long history of clinical depression, substance abuse, and delusional obsessions, became incensed that Lennon's luxurious lifestyle contradicted the Beatle's musical themes of simplicity and peace and felt that he needed to help the world and Lennon by killing him.

Consider Margaret Ray, suffering from schizophrenia and erotomania, who was caught stealing talk show host David Letterman's Porsche and claimed that Letterman was her husband. After trespassing on his property numerous times she was sentenced to prison. Ray finally gave up on Letterman and started to stalk astronaut Story Musgrave. In another case, Justin Bieber was followed by an obsessive man named Dana Martin who not only tattooed the pop star's face on his leg, but was discovered with plans to murder and disembowel the singer.

Celebrity stalking behavior is broad in scope, but must be evaluated as to potential threat as well as charted with some degree of gradient variations of common mental disorders. First responders may not work with superstars, but every community has local celebrities, and first responders may need to be aware of unnatural obsessions and the need for directional intervention for the stalker as well as proactive security for the unaware recipient (Dietz et al., 1991). The purpose of describing these personality associations is to familiarize the responder with unusual but problematic conduct that may, with appropriate intervention, be addressed before any actual or harmful criminal conduct occurs.

CYBER-STALKING AND CYBER-BULLYING

The number of issues that emerge with cyber-stalking and cyber-bullying are enormous and result in an extremely complex form of police investigation. This section is intended only to acquaint first responders with informational sources and referral suggestions as well as provide them an opportunity to recognize on a basic level the issues that accompany a report of cyber-stalking.

People throughout the world now communicate instantly through electronic media, such as phones, tablets, and computers. A photo, text, video, or e-mail sent to one person can "go viral" and spread to hundreds of thousands of people within minutes. It has been reported that 40 percent of college students have been the victim of cyber-stalking at some time in their lives (Reyns, Henson, and Fisher, 2012). The instant interaction that allows strangers to connect also has become a medium of misconduct in that communications are used to threaten, harass, intimidate, or even cause psychological harm. Cyber-harassment and cyber-bullying create different forms of victimizations. **Cyber-harassment** typically involves acts that torment, annoy, terrorize, offend or threaten an individual through repeated, if not chronic, e-mails, instant messages, or other electronic communications that are made with the intent of psychologically pursuing or distressing the targeted recipient. **Cyber-bullying** is defined as actions by a person, commonly under the age of 18, that include tormenting, threatening, harassing, or embarrassing another young person, or instigating such behavior, using the internet or another electronic medium such as a cell phone.

Although there are over 100 state and federal laws regulating cyber/psychological behaviors, there is still little legal precedent as to what constitutes a cyber stalker and little prediction as to who will engage in prohibited conduct and how it affects the person receiving the communications. One of the first reported cases is that of 13-year old Megan Meier, who completed suicide after being harassed on the internet. According to the reports, Megan had an online crush on someone she thought was a male peer, but she was actually corresponding with the mother of neighborhood teenage girl. After the "boy" lulled Megan into a cyber relationship, the imposter sent negative messages to the young teenager, such as "the world would be a better place without you" (Steinhauer, 2008). After the trial and conviction of the author of the messages, an appellate court judge set aside the misdemeanor conviction of the woman after noting that her behavior, however heinous, was not a violation of existing laws.

In this context, it is not necessarily the mental health of the stalker that is the issue, but how the unwanted electronic communications create fear, intimidation, stress, or anxiety in the target victim. The repetitive nature of the cyber-stalking may cause the victim to lose a sense of control over his or her life, never knowing when the stalker may appear. The fact that the stalker can access the victim at any time from any distance undermines the victim's sense of security and mental stability.

While the stalker may have a myriad of reasons for posting material through the internet, the reaction of the victim is definitively alarm, stress, and fear. The emotions may result from a threat or from concern for a family member, or the distribution of a communication may generate helplessness and self-derogation, depression, and, as we saw in the Meier case, suicide. The possibility of threat, alarm, distress, and danger can also be a basis for a request for proactive protection by a court order if there are incidents of stalking, cyber-bullying, or cyber-stalking. In Box 11.4, the standard procedure for obtaining a court-ordered injunction against harassment or violence is examined. Although there are differences in the states, all jurisdictions recognize the authority of the court to direct that threatened conduct not become a real harm.

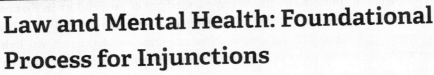

BOX 11.4

Law and Mental Health: Foundational Process for Injunctions

Personal protection orders or injunctions are mechanisms by which a person, known as the "petitioner," proactively obtains a directive or order from a judge against another person, a "respondent." The petition gives notice to the respondent of a requested protective order through details contained in the document that describe the course of conduct that makes the petitioner feel threatened, harassed, fearful, or degraded. The petition is a declaration under oath that is written by or for the petitioner and is then served or sent by legal process to the respondent. The respondent must know that a protective order was requested. Then the judge may issue a temporary order that prohibits direct or indirect contact, communication, or visual vicinity between the parties, or she may deny the order and set the matter for a hearing.

The court orders are variously known as orders of protection, restraining orders or civil protection orders, stay-away orders, protection from abuse orders, civil harassment restraining orders, no-contact orders, and anti-harassment orders. The restraining orders are **injunctions** because the court orders prohibit an action or conduct to forestall a possible violent encounter before a crime occurs. Under some protective orders, if any contact occurs, even an e-mail, an arrest may result. In other words, the contact, however slight and otherwise lawful, is the basis of a separate criminal offense. For example, sending a text message or taking a photo is not per se a crime, but the violation of the judge's injunctive order not to contact the person named in the protective order may be a criminal law violation.

For the due process procedures, if a judge issues a protective order *ex parte* (only one party is present before the judge), then a hearing must be scheduled by the petitioner, or person who feels in danger by the threatened presence of the other. The hearing enables the respondent to either appear and contest the issuance of a protective order or admit the allegations and agree to the injunction. At the court hearing, the petitioner will testify as to what he experienced due to the conduct of the respondent. As stated above, a violation of the personal protection order can result in a violation of the law, even if the contact or conduct, per se, is not criminal. Consequences for violation of protective orders range from civil contempt or financial penalties to misdemeanor or felony charges.

The judge will listen to both sides and decide whether to continue the no-contact order, modify it, or dismiss the order. After the hearing, even if the respondent does not appear in court, the judge may issue an order prohibiting any contact by the respondent to the petitioner or members of the petitioner's family, and can direct the respondent to remain a certain distance from the petitioner. The specifics of the procedures vary throughout the country. The orders can be issued by the criminal courts in conjunction with a bail review; in family courts in the context of a divorce proceeding; or in a civil court when the petitioner presents allegations of violence, stalking, or harassment, or by an initiative prompted by the target/victim as a stand-alone civil action prior to any criminal conduct actually occurring.

The injunction can be issued by a judge if the target testifies that perceived behaviors that were instigated by an individual cause or create fear, threat, victimization, invasion of privacy, as well as a myriad of other personal emotional reactions that arise from previous personal interactions between the parties. The injunction can be ordered even if the respondent denies any threatening contact occurred. The judge is asked to direct a cease and desist directive against future contact. Remember, the judge can face public condemnation if she does not issue the injunction and harm later occurs.

Injunctions for stalking and cyber-bullying or celebrity injunction/protective orders can be requested by threat assessment specialists or mental health clinicians when the threatened individual or target is genuinely afraid of a future attack even if there is no preexisting relationship between the parties. This form of "stranger danger" injunction is issued when a victim seeks legal protection from contact, harassment, or stalking from a relatively unknown person who is abnormally obsessed or mentally unbalanced and fixated on the target acquaintance, celebrity, or virtual stranger. The behaviors involve elements of control, manipulation, fear, and a belief of psychological power over the victim, and the injunction is used to interrupt or redirect the focus into mental health treatment or care. Unfortunately, sometimes the stalker misconstrues every interaction, real, imaginary, or even televised, as an affirmation of the purported relationship, including a court order not to contact the victim again.

The protective order can be issued to expressly prohibit contact by an individual, but it may not be a sufficient deterrent. The criminal justice system provides a more severe sanction to ensure the offender desists from future contact as 53 percent of the state laws increase penalties when there is evidence of a violation of an existing protective order. For example, South Carolina Code section 16-3-1710 provides that if "at the time of the harassment an injunction . . . was in effect prohibiting the harassment, the corresponding criminal charge will be increased."

Source: DeJong and Burgess-Proctor (2006).

NEIGHBORHOOD FIGHTS, FITS, AND RUN-INS

Knowing who and what constitutes a neighborhood is an important responsibility of law enforcement, and using strategies for keeping the peace throughout a community is foundational to the functionality of a locality. As we have seen throughout this chapter, while there is a clear responsibility to respond when a law is broken, there may be an opportunity to inquire about a situation, resolve it, or placate people before the law is violated, even if there is no reasonable fear or a low probability of harm. When a person acts differently than what is expected as normal, there is a question as to whether law enforcement should become involved, investigate, or just referee. While not domestic violence or a threat from a stranger, a dispute between neighbors can erupt into the most violent and hostile confrontations, sometimes causing backyards to morph into battlefields. The modern happenstance of how or why people live next door to each other is inexplicable. While most next-door neighbors are content to chat with each other as they take out the trash, some people have to balance the decision to stay in their most expensive life investment against the mental health of the person who chose to buy the house next door.

Consider the allegations regarding a physical assault on a United States Senator that involved a dispute about yard waste. In 2017, U.S. Senator and physician Rand Paul was tackled and had six ribs broken after his neighbor, a retired anesthesiologist, threw Senator Paul to the ground for carelessly disposing of grass clippings. Neighbors of both men stated that their quibbling had turned to a feud between these two well-educated and economically successful men, one that had been brewing for years.

In another circumstance, one neighbor sat on his roof constantly watching his lonely female neighbor. At the hearing to cease his constant surveillance, he said he was trying to prove she sunbathed in the nude. Tragically, the victim of his obsession ultimately completed suicide. In another neighbor dispute, a man who was distraught over his neighbor constantly videotaping him lowered his pants and "mooned" his bare bottom at the camera. He was then charged with the sexual offense of indecent exposure. The jury found him not guilty.

The problems that exacerbate the poor relationship are as individual as the houses they live in. In examining responses to conduct before it becomes criminal, one option is the use of litigation, known as alternative dispute resolution (ADR) or mediation. ADR can be used in lieu of court-ordered restraining orders or injunctions by neighbors who are not able to reach an amicable resolution of their conflicts.

Serious verbal attacks, such as hate slogans, ethnic slurs, or religious or racially derogatory chants, may arguably justify civil litigation if it appears there is a pattern of harassment that interferes with any person's quiet enjoyment of his home. There may be a violation of the **laws of nuisance**, prompting a civil action alleging that the neighbor's actions unreasonably interfere with the enjoyment of one's property, which can also include an allegation of illegal activities. For example, posting Nazi slogans or flying a

Confederate flag next to Jewish or African-American neighbors could be the basis of a nuisance lawsuit. This litigation, however, is balanced against the First Amendment rights of the offending neighbor as well as the obligation to prove a pattern of harassment that implies harm to or discrimination against the target neighbor. The offending conduct must be behavior that far exceeds a personal opinion. Nuisance lawsuits arise under the state and federal civil rights acts and are complicated, costly, and very difficult to sustain.

For the first responder, approaching neighbors who are feuding over the location of trash cans or having blue flower pots in an earth-tone neighborhood presents a complicated role as a negotiator, mediator, and agent for law enforcement. The officer is in the middle of a situation that has been deteriorating for years. While the neighbor may think it is perfectly appropriate for the police to haul off the offender for not being color-coordinated, it's not likely to be a violation of the law or even grounds for an injunction. Clearly, stranger stalking is a situation that absolutely justifies stay-away orders, but neighborhood disputes usually develop over time through communication failures and inappropriate expectations of the adjacent homeowner. It is almost impossible for law enforcement to keep people who live next door to each other from having contact with each other, and a court order injunction may not be necessary or enforceable. For example, one neighbor harassed an adjacent neighbor who parked in the alley by putting trash around her car, writing words on her windshield, and placing garbage cans close to her bumper. After an intermediary pointed out that the discord was due to the neighbor's new security light shining into complainant's bedroom window, the target neighbor changed the direction of the bulb. However, in another instance, two neighbors squabbled over walking dogs on a community walking path. After a judge issued an order prohibiting one neighbor from being within 100 feet of the other, the complaining neighbor stood on the track and then called 911 when the offending neighbor walked past.

Whatever the situation, a judge makes the decision of whether an injunction is necessary after a contested hearing. The due process procedure is the same as for a stalker injunction. In one instance, after a deputy sheriff indicated there must be proof of neighborly misconduct, the petitioner wanted a judge to view 250 hours he recorded to demonstrate the annoying behavior of the respondent neighbor. In denying the injunction against harassment, the judge instead issued a restraining order against the petitioner and directed him to stop constantly videotaping the neighbor.

Other solutions an officer may suggest include a referral to the county or city civil ordinance compliance officer or a homeowners association. **Mediation** is gaining popularity in many jurisdictions. This intervention refers warring neighbors to a neutral source to work on an amicable solution after airing their mutual aggravations against the other. In one successful program, neighbors signed a **contract for civility** that listed their grievances, their solutions, and their methods for future resolution should matters again deteriorate, in lieu of court-issued restraining orders.

Sadly, a harassment injunction may be erroneously issued as a vendetta, for revenge, or to disgrace one neighbor in front of the community. There may not be enough time to make an objective investigation of the legitimacy of the complaint, and the judge may issue the order to avoid the risk of responsibility if harm does occur in the absence of an order of protection. In Arizona, for example, an injunction may be issued based on false, misleading, or exaggerated allegations as the judge hears only one side of the accusation before issuing an injunction. In one instance, a neighbor fabricated harassment behaviors to gain a political advantage during a contested election. Furthermore, a restraining order can result in a negative credit report, affect standing in a licensing procedure, or interfere with a security clearance.

DOMESTIC VIOLENCE AND PROTECTIVE ORDERS

An altercation between persons in a domestic relationship is commonly known as **domestic violence**, and if reported will usually result in an investigation and likely arrest for criminal offenses such as assault, battery, disorderly conduct, and criminal damage to property. "Domestic relationship" commonly refers to spouses or intimate (sexual) relationships; however, under Illinois law, for example, and that of most other jurisdictions, domestic relationship also includes former spouses, children, siblings, parents, grandparents, individuals related by blood through a common child, roommates in a shared dwelling, and disabled or elderly adults and their caregivers.

In this instance, the incidents of violence are not indicative of mental illness or disease, but may indicate emotional instability and volatility. Awareness of domestic violence as a crime that is committed predominately against women first occurred in the 1970s. Prior to this time, family violence was limited to the context of divorce and questions of violence against children. Through research inquiry it was found that when children were abused or witnessed abuse, family violence was perpetuated and a systematic demand for reform emerged.

Societal awareness of the need for effective law enforcement interventions following domestic violence altercations between family members created a byproduct of secondary supervision of the family, namely judicial protective orders. In a domestic situation, recognizing that judicial supervision of non-criminal contact in the aftermath of an episode of family violence is often necessary, the courts developed anticipatory procedures to prohibit physical or verbal contact between hostile family members, even if the subsequent contact is initiated as a good faith gesture of reconciliation. The restraining orders were developed to permit a cooling down period, an opportunity for a sense of safety, as well as an effort to interrupt the revolving door of domestic violence by which the offender could immediately pressure the victim into dismissing the charges without repercussions or consequences. Every state has different procedures to try to reduce the incidence of domestic abuse by limiting contact between family members or intimate partners when there is any expressed fear of future harm. Law enforcement officers are often confronted with situations in which a restraining order may be issued against a son by a mother, a nephew by an aunt, or a grandchild by an elderly grandparent due to a threat of violence.

For law enforcement officers, investigating and arresting someone for violation of a domestic-based protective order can be challenging. The public policy protections favor judicial intervention before harm occurs, but the evidence is often based on "he said/she said" statements of contact or allegations of harm. Emotions are high and people are quarreling, threatening physical acts of violence, or complaining about the mental stability of the person with whom there was once a loving relationship.

After the injunctions are issued and arrests occur, family members often put pressure on the complainant to drop charges if there is reconciliation with the intimate partner. The officer faces a dilemma when addressing disputes regarding possible liability if an injunction is not enforced. Restraining orders and injunctions do not, of course, provide a bullet-proof vest. Again, while domestic violence episodes are not indicative of mental illness, there is often an undercurrent of unpredictable behavior and response that may require proactive legal intervention. The injunctions are utilized with other risk management strategies to guide decisions of the people affected by the injunctions. They are one aspect of threat management and should be effective when used in conjunction with counseling, treatment, and other mental health services.

Assessment of literature on the topic of the effectiveness of protection orders is limited, as there is inconsistency throughout the states as to when and if protective orders are to be issued. A 2010 psychiatric-based analysis concluded that restraining orders can be effective in threat management, but the study also indicated that the orders are violated 40 percent of the time and may erupt into greater risks or tension. Consider the questions in Box 11.5 to help assess when or if law enforcement should be involved before there is a broken law.

GUARDIANSHIPS

In this final section, we will review another issue that emerges with non-criminal mental health conduct: a protective order that directs that one person is fully and legally responsible for the care of someone who is unable to manage his or her financial or personal affairs. This is known as a guardianship. Law enforcement personnel need a foundational understanding of the legal issues that emerge with guardianships, as they are frequently associated with the care of a person who is mentally ill, diseased, or disabled.

The duty of a guardian is to protect a person who is unable to care for him- or herself. Guardianship is a legal relationship whereby the decision-making powers of one person — known as the "ward" or the "respondent" — are transferred to another person. The paperwork is filed by a petitioner and the court grants the authority to the "guardian." Guardianship was designed to protect those who have been determined not to be mentally and, on occasion, physically competent to make their own decisions. For example, even if a person is mentally alert, but is paralyzed due to an accident, then a guardian may be appointed.

The United States is one of the few places that does not have a national system of guardianship. Instead, we use a loosely monitored court system to track guardians—sometimes

BOX 11.5

Thinking About the Issues

The right of a judge to direct behavior of a person, especially before there is a disputed or contested court hearing to air both sides, is controversial. Nevertheless, law enforcement is committed to keeping the peace and not to making a determination if a person is mentally ill or not. Having interventional strategies can help resolve conflicts without court orders or interference. What follows is a fictionalized account, but is similar to many filed requests for injunctions:

Two neighbors were good friends and vacationed together, had meals together, and even attended each other's children's weddings. One day, one of the neighbors decided to block the other from social media in response to a critical comment posted about her dietary habits. Then a fence was built, and then a 12-foot secondary fence was built next to it. Now there are over 25 security cameras, pictures of pigs painted on the wall, a stuffed pig, a flag with pig in a sex act, a painting of a donut, and audio of pig noises. Battles over the placement of garbage cans have generated hundreds of police calls.

1. What do you think could be done to help these neighbors work out their grievances without suggesting they go to court for a restraining order? Will a restraining order work or just cause more police calls to enforce the restraining orders?

2. What do you see as the primary problems in your suggested approach? What are the advantages? Disadvantages?

3. Do you think the police should encourage a community-based resolution system, such as a neighborhood association, contracts for civility, or a police mediation program?

4. What if you felt a person was exaggerating his problems with a neighbor or was "baiting" the neighbor in an effort to try to cause problems? What are some solutions?

family members, sometimes guardianship companies—to account for the financial and physical well-being of their charges. In most states, guardianship is the substitute entity with the capacity to make all personal decisions about health, home, and personal matters. In comparison, there is a less intrusive type of personal management called a conservatorship. The appointed conservator primarily makes decisions about financial management and can be the payee for government or trust benefits. Both guardianships and conservatorships are legal interventions by the state through a court-appointed representative.

A guardianship as a legal process is initiated by a **petition to seek guardianship** on behalf of an individual. The request for guardianship is commonly predicated on a request to evaluate a vulnerable adult by a physician when there is a question of the adult's capacity to live independently and manage his or her finances. The question of the need for a guardian emerges with dementia; degenerative illnesses; and neurological, psychiatric, or other medical conditions that impair decision making and make an individual vulnerable to fraud, embezzlement, or scamming.

The definition of an incapacitated person in the Uniform Guardianship and Protective Proceedings Act (UGPPA) is that an individual is unable to receive and evaluate information or make or communicate decisions to such an extent that the individual lacks the ability to meet essential requirements for physical health, safety, or self-care.

There are six elements reviewed by a physician about which a judge must be informed to justify the appointment of the guardianship (Moye and Naik, 2011):

1. *Medical Condition* — The judge must be informed of the specific disorder that is causing diminished capacity and whether it is a neurological or psychiatric condition.

2. *Impairment of Cognition* — The judge will be advised by an examining physician if the impairment of cognition is temporary and reversible or if it is permanent and degenerative. Also considered is how the medical condition affects alertness, decision making, judgment, insight, and memory.

3. *Loss of Everyday Functioning* — The judge will be informed about the individual's ability to manage everyday events, particularly the basic activities of daily living, such as finances, health, and functioning in the home and community.

4. *Loss of Values* — The physician's report will also describe a person's risk taking and problem solving. For example, if a person was always financially meticulous, but then started wasting money on internet scams, there may need to be an intervention. This consideration requires a balance of autonomy against protection.

5. *Indication of a Risk of Harm to the Intended Ward* — The judge will also consider if the appointment of a guardian has been balanced against the individual's sense of independence. For example, there may be a conservator with limited authority to manage investments, but not the ward's day-to-day spending.

6. *Lack of Capacity* —The ward must appear not to have the means or ability to ensure his or her future capacity. If the problem is just a matter of improving hearing or taking medications, a guardianship may not be merited and will be reviewed.

The role of the judge varies from state to state. In some jurisdictions, the judge is the mental health court judge, while in other states, it is the probate judge who resolves petitions for guardianship or conservatorship. A judge appoints an attorney for the person against whom the petition for guardianship is filed. Under due process procedures, the judge accepts evidence by testimony and exhibits that the subject of the guardianship is, in fact, cognitively disabled to make a finding that legal incapacity is warranted. The judge can accept or reject the stated need for a surrogate to assume decisional control for the individual. In rejecting a petition for conservatorship, the judge may determine that while a person may be quirky, she has the capacity for independent decisions and lifestyle. Remember Barbara from the prologue? While she was negotiating the purchase of her new home, driving a moving van, and acquiring numerous items, she was likely cognizant and able to address her financial and living needs. However, when the responders later discovered that she had declined into a situation where she saw no need for personal hygiene or to address the infestation of vermin, and was likely unable to properly account for her financial well-being, referral for a conservator, if not a guardian, was warranted by law enforcement. Again, she is not a criminal, only mentally ill.

Following the hearing or court petition, if the judge makes a finding of incompetency, she will appoint a third-party conservator, trustee, or guardian to act on behalf of the mentally disabled person. If a person needs a guardianship, a family member, close friend, or even a public official, known as a public fiduciary, undertakes the responsibility of paying bills or even directing residential placement for the mentally ill, handicapped, or cognitively deficient person.

The primary purpose of this section is to enable people to be aware of the guardianship standards and procedures for substitute authority, as well as be sensitive to the issues should there be an inquiry, as you will read in the next chapter, about fraud or loss of the mentally disabled individual's funds. The issue has criminal law connotations when a disabled person has been scammed or it appears there is financial loss under suspicious or fraudulent circumstances.

EPILOGUE

In the epilogue, we deal with the following question: When should or must mental health professionals inform a possible victim or authorities about a threat to the health and well-being of the victim? The question is answered to a great extent by the summation and review of the facts and law that emerged from two California cases and which are now, essentially, national policy.

There is a significant difference in patterns of behavior between stalking and harassment. Stalking is significantly associated with intimacy-seeking motivation while harassment involves resentful motivation. Both may be instigated by virtual strangers to the intended victim, but with increasingly aggressive and intrusive behaviors. Both stalking and harassment are one-sided, uninitiated and unwanted by the target.

We examine here two instances of insanity and obsession through two court cases: *Tarasoff v. Regents of the University of California* (1976) and *Thompson v. County of Alameda* (1980). The *Tarasoff* case involved a graduate student, Tatiana Tarasoff, who was stabbed to death by a man who had fixated on her and had confessed his murderous intent to a school psychologist prior to killing her. The *Thompson* case involved a known juvenile sex offender who was released without warning by the police into a community and, within 24 hours, murdered a neighborhood child.

These two decisions by the California Supreme Court initiated the national directive that, essentially, if a patient tells a mental health professional that he or she intends to harm another person or if the patient is known to have an extraordinary propensity for violence, the professional, albeit a therapist or police officer, must take reasonable steps to protect the potential victim(s). The responsibility includes directly warning the victim or warning the community most closely affected by the possible offender, such as publication of the residency of known sex offenders. This position has been endorsed by most states.

The responsibility of law enforcement to warn a person about impending peril first emerged in the case of *Tarasoff v. Regents of the University of California*. In 1969, Prosenjit Poddar killed Tatiana Tarasoff. Poddar was born in India in the "untouchable" caste. He came to the University of California, Berkeley, as a graduate student in 1967 and in 1968 he met Tatiana. They saw each other regularly and on New Year's Eve of 1969, she kissed him. He interpreted the act as a serious commitment to their relationship, but she, in response, said she was not interested in him.

As a result of the rejection, Poddar fell into a depressed emotional crisis, neglecting his appearance, his studies, and his health. He spoke disjointedly and often wept. He accosted Tatiana two or three times to ascertain why she did not love him and recorded their conversations. By October, he sought psychological help. The psychologist, Dr. Lawrence Moore, wrote to the University of California campus police alerting them that, in his opinion, the defendant was suffering from paranoia and acute and severe schizophrenia. Poddar confided in Dr. Moore that he intended to kill Tatiana. Moore recommended that Poddar be civilly committed as a danger to himself and others. He was briefly detained and then released when he appeared to be rational.

Dr. Moore's supervisor at UCB advised the treating psychologist that there would be no further action with respect to Poddar. On October 27, 1969, Poddar went to the Tarasoff home and shot Tatiana and stabbed her. No one warned the Tarasoffs or Tatiana of her peril. The family sued the therapists and the campus police for failing to warn them of the impending danger. Ultimately, Poddar's conviction was reversed for erroneous jury instructions for manslaughter. Eventually, he was released from prison, returned to India, and married an attorney.

In the civil lawsuit against the university for therapist failure to warn a third party, the court returned a finding that a therapist must exercise the reasonable degree of skill, knowledge, and care ordinarily possessed and exercised by members of the profession. Although confidentiality is an essential privilege, the court summarized by noting: "The protective privilege ends where the public peril begins" (*Tarasoff*, 56).

The court concluded that the therapists could not escape liability even though Tatiana herself was not their patient. The court ruled:

> When a therapist determines, or pursuant to the standards of his profession, should determine, that his patient presents a serious danger of violence to another, he incurs an obligation to use reasonable care to protect the intended victim against such danger. The discharge of this

duty may require the therapist to take one or more of various steps, depending upon the nature of the case. Thus, it may call for him to warn the intended victim or others likely to apprise the victim of the danger, to notify the police or to take whatever other steps are reasonably necessary under the circumstances. (*Tarasoff*, 57)

The California decision imposed a duty on therapists, and arguably police officers, to be proactive and take precautions for the safety of a person who is directly threatened by a patient. There is now a requirement that a therapist assumes responsibility for the safety of the patient, but also any third person whom the therapist knows to be threatened by the patient. Prior to this decision, the responsibility of law enforcement involved detaining an individual who is a danger to himself or others, but the *Tarasoff* decision also mandated responsibility to a third person by a psychiatric treatment provider if a danger becomes known to the provider.

By contrast, in *Thompson v. County of Alameda*, the Thompsons, a husband and wife and their minor son, lived in Piedmont, California. A few houses away, James F., a juvenile offender, lived with his mother. James had been in the custody of Alameda County and was confined to a juvenile correctional county institution. He was described as having "latent, extremely dangerous and violent propensities regarding young children and that sexual assaults upon young children and violence connected . . . were a likely result upon releasing him into the community" (*Thompson*, 749).

The juvenile detention center knew that James had indicated that he would, if released, take the life of a young child residing in the neighborhood, although he did not specify which child he intended to be his victim. He was released on temporary leave to his mother's custody at her home. The county detention facility did not warn James's mother, the local police, or the parents of any young children within the immediate vicinity of James's home of the facts. Within 24 hours of his release from the juvenile facility, James murdered the Thompsons' son in the garage of James's home.

The California Supreme Court eventually found that although there is an obligation to warn all citizens of foreseeable harm, there is no duty to warn people of specific dangers unless the victim was identifiable. A requirement that local police warn people was not found to be realistic, as it necessitated officers to knock on every door in the community and give warning or 24-hour police escort to all possible victims with every released offender.

The obligation to disclose the whereabouts of sex crime offenders is limited to record keeping, but does not mandate warning potential victims of possible violence. The standard is that when a potentially dangerous offender is released, if there is a predictable harm to a named or readily identifiable victim or group of victims, who can be effectively warned, then there can be liability for failure to warn. However, if the victim is not known to the assailant, but is a member of a public group of potential targets, there is no obligation to warn the community.

SUMMARY

▶ In-home object hoarding is a neuropsychiatric disorder that is symptomized by the acquisition of physical things coupled with the failure to discard, in which the substantial accumulation of items causes the living areas to be impeded and personal safety is put at risk.

▶ Animal hoarding is the accumulation of animals in an excessive ratio to the humans to the extent that the animals are neglected or abused. The three types of animal hoarders are the overwhelmed hoarder, the rescue hoarder, and the exploiter hoarder.

▶ Investigation into animal and object hoarding requires sensitivity and caution as the hoarder may not perceive him- or herself as being in violation of the law or societal rules.

▶ A chronically homeless person is characterized as a person who, over a period of years, does not have intact housing and also suffers from mental illness. The current move to resolve homelessness is to find appropriate low-income housing that is not preconditioned on requirements for treatment or social care.

▶ Under current law, if a person is declared eligible for income disability payments due to mental disease, the recipient must sustain the mental illness to continue to receive government financial assistance, a situation that leads to dependency on mental illness and psychotropic drugs, rather than achievement of mental health.

▶ Restraining orders are court orders that prevent a family member, loved one, stranger, or neighbor from contacting a target; restraining orders are intended to prevent violent confrontations or contacts from occurring.

▶ The mentally disabled, declining, or organically impaired adult may be subject to a guardianship proceeding if it appears that there is an inability to manage one's finances or person; the guardianship helps to protect the individual from becoming a victim of harm by others through fraudulent financial transfers, neglect, or abuse.

KEY TERMS

Animal hoarding
Civil protection orders
Chronically homeless people
Conservatorship
Contract for civility
Domestic violence
"Housing is healthcare"

Injunctions
Laws of nuisance
Mediation
Orders of protection
Petition to seek guardianship
Severely Mentally Ill (SMI)
Sociopath

CHAPTER REVIEW QUESTIONS

1. What are the characteristics of an object hoarder? What are some of the solutions to object hoarding?
2. Define and distinguish between the three types of animal hoarding disorders. Why are they different? What treatments, if any, are appropriate for hoarding animals?
3. What are some of the perils that you, as a law enforcement investigator, face when removing property or animals from the possession of a hoarder?
4. What rules, laws, and regulations permit or prohibit people from building temporary shelters in parks and public places? Should there be a prohibition against or in favor of temporary shelters? Explain your reasoning.
5. What is the legal purpose of restraining orders?
6. When are restraining orders effective and when are they not effective? Are they useful in giving the respondent notice or warning that a person perceives herself to be in danger, even if it's not realistic?
7. Consider the different behaviors that are presented in this chapter. Which ones do you believe are actually criminal and should be prosecuted? Which ones do you believe are not criminal, although they could be harmful to social peace? Which behaviors do you believe should never involve law enforcement?
8. Explain why hoarding property or animals should be a public health concern. What are the best practices for enforcement of public health laws?
9. Preparing to testify in court is challenging. Why does an officer need to keep careful records and notes even when the case is a misdemeanor charge, such as unlawful feeding of wildlife?
10. Why should or should not law enforcement or the community itself have an affirmative duty to warn people that there may be a dangerous person now living in the neighborhood?

REFERENCES

Abrams, E. (2016). "With so many homeless caught up in the criminal justice system, N. O. holds night court at a shelter." New Orleans Public Radio. Retrieved at http://wwno.org/post/so-many-homeless-caught-criminal-justice-system-no-holds-court-shelter-3 on 1 December 2017.

American Bar Association (n.d.). "Orders of Protection." Retrieved at https://www.americanbar.org/portals/public_resources/aba_home_front/information_center/family_law/domestic_violence/orders_of_protection.html on 12 December 2017.

American Bar Association (n.d.). "Love your neighbor? How to keep petty annoyances from turning into major headaches." Retrieved at https://www.americanbar.org/

content/dam/aba/migrated/publiced/practical/books/home_ownership/chapter_7.authcheckdam.pdf on 16 December 2017.

American Psychiatric Association (2013). *Diagnostic and Statistical Manual of Mental Disorders*. 5th ed. Washington, DC: American Psychiatric Association.

American Psychiatric Association (n.d.). "What is hoarding disorder?" Retrieved at https://www.psychiatry.org/patients-families/hoarding-disorder/what-is-hoarding-disorder on 25 March 2018.

Baer, M. (2010). "Cyber stalking and the internet landscape we have constructed." *Virginia Journal of Law and Technology* 15: 153-172.

Benitez, C.T., D.E. McNiel, and R.L. Binder (2010). "Do protection orders protect?" *Journal of the American Academy of Psychiatry and the Law* 38: 376-85.

Bonn, S.A. (2018) "Can you tell a psychopath from a sociopath?" *Psychology Today*. Retrieved at https://www.psychologytoday.com/us/blog/wicked-deeds/201801/can-you-tell-psychopath-sociopath on 22 February 2018.

Buckner, F., and M. Firestone (2000). "'Where the public peril begins.' 25 years after Tarasoff." *Journal of Legal Medicine* 21: 187-222.

Chasson, G., A. Carpenter, J. Ewing, B. Gibby, and N. Lee (2014). "Empowering families to help a loved one with Hoarding Disorder: Pilot study Family-As-Motivators training." *Behavior Research and Therapy* 63: 9-16.

Cherniack, E., and A. Cherniack (2014). "The benefits of pets and animal-assisted therapy to the health of older individuals." *Current Gerontology and Geriatrics Research*. Retrieved at https://www.hindawi.com/journals/cggr/2014/623203/ on 27 December 2017.

Choi, N., J. Kim, and J. Asseff (2009). "Self-neglect and neglect of vulnerable older adults: Reexamination of etiology." *Journal of Gerontological Social Work* 52: 171-187.

Corwin, M. (November 3, 2008). "Inside the LAPD's Threat Management Unit." PoliceOne.com. Retrieved at https://www.policeone.com/communications/articles/1752120-Inside-the-LAPDs-Threat-Management-Unit/ on 22 December 2017.

Cyberbullying Research Center (n.d.). "Cyberbullying facts." Retrieved at https://cyberbullying.org/facts on 30 December 2017.

Davis, J. (2016). "Stalking and restraining orders: Stalkers and other obsessional types: A psychological Typology of those who stalk ..." *Psychology Today*. Retrieved from https://www.psychologytoday.com/blog/crimes-and-misdemeanors/201606/stalking-crimes-and-victim-protection on 23 December 2017.

DeJong, C., and A. Burgess-Proctor (2006). "A summary of personal protection order statutes in the United States." *Violence Against Women* 12: 68-88.

Dietz, P., D. Matthews, C. Van Duyne, D. Martell, C. Parry, T. Stewart, J. Warren, and J. Crowder, (1991). "Threatening and otherwise inappropriate letters to Hollywood celebrities." *Journal of Forensic Sciences* 36: 185-209.

Doran, K.M., E.J. Misa, and N.R. Shah (2013). "Housing as health care — New York's boundary-crossing experiment." *New England Journal of Medicine* 369: 2374-77.

Edwards, L. (December 1992). "Trespassers of the heart." *Eyewitness*, pp. 34-40.

Federal Bureau of Investigation (2015). Crime in the United States, 2014. Washington, DC: U.S. Department of Justice.

Frost, R. (2000). "People who hoard animals." *Psychiatric Times*. Retrieved at http://www.psychiatrictimes.com/obsessive-compulsive-disorder/people-who-hoard-animals on 14 December 2017.

Frost R., G. Patronek, A. Arluke, and G. Steketee (2015). "Hoarding of animals: An update. *Psychiatric Times*. Retrieved at http://www.psychiatrictimes.com/addiction/hoarding-animals-update on 14 December 2017.

Frost, R., D. Ruby, and L. Shuer (2012). "The buried in treasures workshop: Waitlist control trial of facilitated support for hoarding." *Behavior Research and Therapy* 50: 661-667.

Fukuchi, A. (2011). "A balance of convenience: The use of burden-shifting devices in criminal cyber harassment law." *Boston College Law Review* 52: 289-338.

Hays, S. (October 17, 1990). "Inside celebrity obsessions: Threat: Most letter writers are just blowing off steam, according to a Newport Beach study of 'nut mail' and other fixated behavior." *Los Angeles Times*. Retrieved at http://articles.latimes.com/1990-10-17/news/vw-2495_1_newport-beach on 22 December 2017.

Hazelwood, S., and S. Koon-Magnin (2013). "Cyber stalking and cyber harassment legislation in the United States: A qualitative analysis." *International Journal of Cyber Criminology* 7: 155-68.

Jarvis, J. (2014). "Individual determinants of homelessness: A descriptive approach." *Journal of Housing Economics* 50: 23-32.

Joint Center for Housing Studies at Harvard University (2016). "Housing challenges." Chapter 6 (pp. 31-36) in *The State of the Nation's Housing 2016*. Boston, MA: Joint Center for Housing Studies at Harvard University. Retrieved at http://www.jchs.harvard.edu/sites/jchs.harvard.edu/files/son_2016_200dpi_ch6.pdf on 3 December 2017.

Hammack, L., and M. Adams (December 15, 2007). "Roanoke turns its focus on homeless." *Roanoke Times*. Retrieved at http://www.roanoke.com/webmin/news/roanoke-turns-its-focus-on-homeless/article_0449a5e8-f769-50cb-ba4f-cebbf4db6c49.html on 9 November 2017.

Hansen, H., P. Bourgois, and E. Drucker (2014). "Pathologizing poverty: New forms of diagnosis, disability, and structural stigma under welfare reform." *Social Science and Medicine* 103: 76-83.

Henry M., R. Watt, L. Rosenthal, and A. Shivji (2016). "The 2016 annual homeless assessment report (AHAR) to Congress." U.S. Department of Housing and Urban Development, Office of Community Planning and Development. Retrieved at https://www.hudexchange.info/resources/documents/2016-AHAR-Part-1.pdf on 15 December 2017.

Huber, M., R. Balon, L. Labbate, S. Brandt-Youtz, J. Hammer, and R. Mufti (2000). "A survey of police officers' experience with *Tarasoff* warnings in two states." *Psychiatric Services* 51: 807-9.

Jarvis, J. (2015). "Individual determinants of homelessness: A descriptive approach." *Journal of Housing Economics* 30: 23-32.

Kerr, A., M. Morabito, and A. Watson (2010). "Police encounters, mental illness and injury: An exploratory investigation." *Journal of Police Crisis Negotiations* 10: 116-32.

Landau, D., A.C. Iervolino, A. Pertusa, S. Santo, S. Singh, and D. Mataix-Colis (2011). "Stressful life events and material deprivation in hoarding disorder." *Journal of Anxiety Disorders* 25: 192-202.

Lipton, F., C. Siegel, A. Hannigan, J. Samuels, and S. Baker (2000). "Tenure in supportive housing for homeless persons with severe mental illness." *Psychiatric Service* 51: 479-86.

Logan, T., L. Shannon, R. Walker, and T. Faragher (2006). "Protective orders questions and conundrums." *Trauma, Violence and Abuse* 7: 175-205.

Lozier, J. (2017). "Housing is health care." Nashville, TN: National Health Care for the Homeless Council. Retrieved at https://www.nhchc.org/wp-content/uploads/2011/10/Housing-is-Health-Care.pdf on 22 December 2017.

Mathews, C., S. Uhm, J. Chan, and M. Gause (2015). "Treating hoarding disorder in a real-world setting: Results from the Mental Health Association of San Francisco." *Psychiatry Research* 237: 331-338.

Melamed, Y., I. Doron, and D. Shnitt (2007). "Guardianships of people with mental disorders." *Social Science and Medicine* 65: 118-123.

Mithers, C. (July 20, 2015). "When is a rescuer a hoarder?" *Los Angeles Times*. Retrieved at http://www.lamag.com/longform/when-is-a-rescuer-a-hoarder/2/ on 14 December 2017.

McCoy, T. (July 13, 2015). "The homeless man who went to Harvard Law with John Roberts." *The Washington Post*. Retrieved from https://www.washingtonpost.com/local/social-issues/the-homeless-man-who-graduated-from-harvard-law-school-with-chief-justice-john-roberts/2015/07/13/63257b5c-20ca-11e5-bf41-c23f5d3face1_story.html?utm_term=.bb1f2a0ff560 on 10 December 2017.

McPhate, M. (September 8, 2017). "California today: A deadly outbreak stalks San Diego." *The New York Times*. Retrieved at https://www.nytimes.com/2017/09/08/us/california-today-a-deadly-outbreak-stalks-san-diego.html on 23 October 2017.

Moye, J., and A. Naik (2011). "Preserving rights for individuals facing guardianship." *Journal of the American Medical Association* V305(9): 936-937.

Nathanson, J. (2009). "Animal hoarding: Slipping into the darkness of comorbid animal and self-neglect." *Journal of Elder Abuse and Neglect* 21: 307-324.

National Alliance to End Homelessness (2016). "Chronically homeless." Retrieved at https://endhomelessness.org/homelessness-in-america/who-experiences-homelessness/chronically-homeless/ on 16 December 2017.

National Alliance on Mental Illness (2017). "Mental health by the numbers." Washington, DC: National Alliance on Mental Illness. Retrieved at https://www.nami.org/Learn-More/Mental-Health-By-the-Numbers on 22 December 2017.

National Health Care for the Homeless Council (2006). "Housing is health care." Nashville, TN: National Health Care for the Homeless Council. Retrieved at https://www.nhchc.org/wp-content/uploads/2011/10/Housing-is-Health-Care.pdf on 4 December 2017.

National Law Center on Homelessness and Poverty (2014). "No safe place: The criminalization of homelessness in U.S. cities (July 16, 2014). Retrieved at https://www.nlchp.org/Home%20Page on 28 December 2017.

Padgett, D., V. Stanhope, B. Henwood, and A. Stefancic (2011). "Substance use outcomes among homeless clients with serious mental illness: Comparing House First with Treatment First programs." *Community Mental Health Journal* 47: 227-32.

Padgett, D., L. Gulcur, and S. Tsemberis (2006). "Co-occurring serious mental illness and substance abuse." *Research on Social Work Practice* 16: 74-83.

Parekh, R. (2017). "What is hoarding disorder?" Washington, DC: American Psychiatric Association. Retrieved at https://www.psychiatry.org/patients-families/hoarding-disorder/what-is-hoarding-disorder on 8 December 2017.

Pasquale, D. (April 11, 2008). "Responding to civil disputes." *Police: The Law Enforcement Magazine*. Retrieved from http://www.policemag.com/blog/patrol-tactics/story/2008/04/duty-tips-responding-to-civil-disputes.aspx on 16 December 2017.

Patronek G., L. Loar, and J. Nathanson (2006). *Animal Hoarding: Structuring Interdisciplinary Responses to Help People, Animals and Communities at Risk.* Medford, MA: Hoarding of Animals Research Consortium. Retrieved from http://vet.tufts.edu/wp-content/uploads/AngellReport.pdf on 1 December 2017.

Pearson, C., A. Montgomery, and G. Locke (2009). "Housing stability among homeless individuals with serious mental illness participating in housing first programs." *Journal of Community Psychology* 37: 404-17.

Pepper, C. (1989). "Guardianship: Friend or foe of America's frail and elderly?" *Journal of Elder Abuse and Neglect* 1: 65-74.

Pinals, D. (2007). *Stalking: Psychiatric Perspectives and Practical Approaches.* New York: Oxford University Press.

Reinish, A. (2009). "Characteristics of six recent animal hoarding cases in Manitoba." *Canadian Veterinary Journal* 50: 1069-73.

Reyns, B.W., B. Henson, and B. Fisher (2012). "Stalking in the twilight zone: Extent of cyberstalking victimization and offending among college students." *Deviant Behavior* 33: 1-25.

Rosenheck R., W. Kasprow, W. Frisman, and W. Liu-Mares (2003). "Cost-effectiveness of supported housing for homeless persons with mental illness." *Archives of General Psychiatry* 60: 940-51.

Salter, M., and C. Bryden (2009). "I can see you: Harassment and stalking on the internet." *Information and Communications Technology Law* 18: 2 99-122.

San Francisco Task Force on Compulsive Hoarding (2017). "San Francisco task force on compulsive hoarding." San Francisco: Mental Health Association of San Francisco.

Retrieved at http://mentalhealthsf.org/san-francisco-task-force-on-compulsive-hoarding/ on 6 December 2017.

Schwemm, R.G. (2011). "Neighbor-on-neighbor harassment: Does the fair housing act make a federal case out of it?" *Case Western Reserve Law Review* 61: 865-931.

Sloane, D. (December 8, 2015). "Inside the mind of John Lennon's killer." CNN. Retrieved at http://www.cnn.com/2015/12/08/us/mark-david-chapman-lennon-interviews/index.html on 23 December 2017.

Social Security Administration (n.d.). "Benefits for people with disabilities." Retrieved at https://www.ssa.gov/disability/index.htm on 12 December 2017.

Steinhauer, J. (November 24, 2008). "Closing arguments in trial of mother in cyberbullying that ended in girl's suicide." *The New York Times*. Retrieved at http://www.nytimes.com/2008/11/25/us/25myspace.html on December 24, 2017.

Sullivan, T., N. Weiss, C. Price, and N. Pugh (2017). "Criminal protection orders for women victims of domestic violence: Explicating predictors of level of restrictions among orders issued." *Journal of Interpersonal Violence*. Retrieved at http://journals.sagepub.com/doi/10.1177/0886260517736274 on 10 December 2017.

Tatum, S. (November 7, 2017). "Attorney calls attack on Sen. Rand Paul 'regrettable dispute between two neighbors.'" CNN. Retrieved at http://www.cnn.com/2017/11/06/politics/senator-rand-paul-suspect-attorney/index.html on 14 December 2017.

Tolin, D., R. Frost, G. Steketee, and K. Fitch (2007a). "Family burden of compulsive hoarding: Results of an internet survey." *Behavior Research and Therapy* 46: 334-344.

Tolin, D., R. Frost, G. Steketee, and K. Fitch (2007b). *Buried Treasures: Help for Compulsive Acquiring, Saving and Hoarding.* New York: Oxford University Press.

Treatment Advocacy Center (2016). "Serious mental illness and homelessness." Arlington, VA: Treatment Advocacy Center. Retrieved at http://www.treatmentadvocacycenter.org/storage/documents/backgrounders/smi-and-homelessness.pdf on 26 December 2017.

Tompkins, M.A., and T. Hart (2009). *Digging Out: Helping Your Loved One Manage Clutter, Hoarding and—Compulsive Acquiring.* Oakland, CA: New Harbinger Publication.

U.S. Department of Housing and Urban Development (2016). *The 2016 Annual Homeless Assessment Report (AHAR) to Congress.* Washington, DC: U.S. Department of Housing and Urban Development. Retrieved at https://www.hudexchange.info/resources/documents/2016-AHAR-Part-1.pdf on 15 December 2015.

U.S. Interagency Council on Homelessness (2017). "Ending chronic homelessness." Washington, DC: U.S. Interagency Council on Homelessness. Retrieved at https://www.usich.gov/goals/chronic on 22 December 2017.

U.S. Department of Justice (1999). *Cyberstalking: A New Challenge for Law Enforcement and Industry.* Washington, DC: U.S. Department of Justice. Retrieved at http://www.justice.gov/crimina l/cybercrime/CS.htm on 22 December 2017.

Watson, A., V. Ottati, M. Morabito, J. Draine, and A. Kerr (2010). "Outcomes of police contacts with persons with mental illness: The impact of CIT." *Administration and Police in Mental Health and Mental Health Service Research* 37: 302-17.

Wooster, L., D. James, and F. Farnham (2015). "Stalking, harassment and aggressive/ intrusive behaviors towards general practitioners: (2) associated factors, motivation, mental illness and the effects on GPs." *The Journals of Forensic Psychiatry and Psychology* 27: 1-20.

LEGISLATION

Ariz. Rev. Stat. §12-1809.
Illinois Domestic Violence Act of 1986, 720 Ill. Comp. Stat. Ann. 5/12-3.2 *et seq.*
S.C. Code Ann. §16-3-1710
Uniform Guardianship and Protective Proceedings Act (n.d.). Retrieved at http://www. uniformlaws.org/ActSummary.aspx?title=Adult%20Guardianship%20and%20 Protective%20Proceedings%20Jurisdiction%20Act on 24 December 2017.
42 U.S.C. §1437f — "Low-income housing assistance." Retrieved at https://www.law. cornell.edu/uscode/text/42/1437f# on 16 December 2017.
U.S. Public Health Act §330A(e), as amended from 42 U.S.C. §254(e) and §317(k)(2) of the Public Health Service Act, as amended (42 U.S.C. §247b(k)(2)). Retrieved at https:// www.federalregister.gov/documents/2009/07/17/E9-16959/section-330ae-of-the- public-health-service-act-as-amended-42-usc-254ce-and-section-317k2-of-the on 15 December 2017.

CASES

People v. Poddar, 10 Cal. 3d 750, 518 P.2d 342 (1974)
Reed v. Town of Gilbert, 135 S. Ct. 2218 (2015)
Tarasoff v. Regents of the University of California, 17 Cal. 3d 425, 551 P.2d 334 (1976)
Thompson v. County of Alameda, 614 P.2d 728 (Cal. 1980)

CHAPTER 12

Justice for the Mentally Ill: Human Rights and At-Risk Groups

CHAPTER OUTLINE

LEARNING OBJECTIVES

After reading this chapter, you should be able to:

▶ Discuss the concept of mental health as a basic human right, especially as it relates to the development of U.S. public policies and practices on the issue.

▶ Specify the nature and extent of elder abuse, along with the various responses to this problem.

▶ Express how military veterans' issues can also concern the criminal justice and healthcare systems.

▶ Understand that personal identification as a member of one of the various gay, lesbian, bisexual, and transgender communities can result in minor and major victimizations that have the potential to erode that person's mental and physical well-being.

▶ Describe how race and ethnicity play a role in mental health–criminal justice interface.

PROLOGUE

This vignette is a composite of several incidents known to the authors.]

The ambulance took four minutes to arrive at 703 Carbondale Street. When Margaret and Ray purchased this house in the Havenhearst retirement community, they had asked the real estate agent for a place close to a fire station or ambulance service because Margaret had a heart condition. Ray wanted to make sure emergency response time was fast. A stroke killed Margaret less than a year after they moved in, but Ray continued to reside in the home alone for the next two decades, until his daughter, Sarah, moved in to care for her father two years ago.

Two emergency medical technicians (EMTs) approached the house and rang the doorbell, which was set into a metal frame next to a steel security gate. They did not receive an answer, although the 911 operator assured them the caller was alive. As the EMTs rang the bell again, a rescue truck from the same fire station arrived, as was standard operating procedure, and three fire fighters joined the EMTs; they quickly wielded their gas-powered saw and cut the security door off its hinges.

When the EMTs and fire fighters gained entry to Ray's home, they found him on the floor in the living room, feet from an old-fashioned telephone, on which he was still talking to the 911 operator. The fire fighters returned to their unit, while the EMTs went to work. They had stabilized Ray and placed him on a gurney when a sheriff's deputy arrived. This, too, was SOP when a call involved a possible injury, especially to an elderly person.

The deputy, a practiced hand at responding to calls for service in Havenhearst, noticed that Ray, clad only in underpants and a t-shirt, had extensive bruising on his upper arms and neck. He had several facial scratches, but the EMTs had staunched any bleeding and started him on an IV drip, concerned that he might go into shock. The officer turned first to the EMTs and asked the patient's name. Turning next to the man on the gurney, the deputy asked, "Who did this to you, Ray?" Ray did not reply at once, but only turned his head away from the officer. Then he slowly turned back to face the deputy and said, "It was Sarah."

Thirty minutes later, sheriff's deputies found Sarah drinking her third beer with a bourbon chaser at a bar two blocks from her father's home. As she was arrested, handcuffed, and placed in one of the deputy's vehicles, she said loudly to no one in particular, "He was so demanding. I couldn't leave him for a minute. I just needed a break, dammit, a couple of hours to myself."

Ray's story is reflective of the fates that befall many older Americans, from dementia and wandering away to other non-criminal actions, such as hoarding and homelessness, to, in this case, being the victim of abuse by a caregiver. Moreover, Sarah's actions are consistent with research on caregivers, as female caregivers more than males tend to express symptoms of "caregiver stress" and depression (Amirkhanyan and Wolf, 2006). As the nation's population ages, incidents such as this one will no doubt become far more common. But seniors are only part of the problem of systemic interface. This chapter explores a range of current issues that will likely challenge mental health service providers and the justice system into the foreseeable future. We also consider several avenues of relief for each specific issue. It remains to be seen whether politicians at all levels of government, from our local communities to the nation's capital, have the political will and financial resources to address all or any of them.

Chapter Overview

This chapter consists of five topics arranged into two interrelated themes: mental healthcare as a human rights issue and four at-risk groups that have a high potential for the loss of these rights. Thus, we begin this chapter with a global policy theme, global in terms of the world and global in terms of its potential impact on certain segments of any nation's population: mental healthcare as a basic human right. This section includes a brief look at how the United States and other nations view the mentally ill. This section includes the rights of mentally ill offenders, but especially those in prisons and jails.

The remainder of the chapter details the challenges in healthcare access often experienced by four at-risk groups. The first at-risk group is the nation's elderly, irrespective of mental health. While not a new phenomenon, the increase in the number of senior citizens means that the potential for elder abuse and victimizations is higher today than just 20 years ago. In this section, we explore the nature and extent of the concerns about our aging citizens, as well as possible solutions.

The second persons-at-risk group consists of military veterans with mental health problems. After examining various veterans' issues, we review programs, treatment options, and reintegration alternatives. Like the elderly, the number of veterans is significant, even as their absolute numbers decline with the deaths of World War II and Vietnam veterans. The relatively small number of service personnel fighting the nation's recent conflicts around the world means that those in combat situations tend to experience higher levels of combat-related stressors and injuries than in previous wars.

The members of the third at-risk group have gender identities that may be different from their biological sex. These differences can generate significant animosity originating not only within certain oppositional segments of society, but also within the healthcare and criminal justice systems. Once again, we review the extent and nature of the risks involved, as well as possible ways to reduce this enmity.

Finally, we examine the ties between race and ethnicity and the mental health–criminal justice interface. In recent years, the nation has witnessed many police-citizen conflictual interactions with a race- or ethnicity-based component; adding mental health to the mix creates even greater concerns for justice. As with the previous three at-risk groups, we examine how and where race or ethnicity influences the overlay of the mental healthcare and criminal justice systems, as well as possible conflict resolutions.

The book's final epilogue merges several previous themes. *State of Texas v. Eddie Ray Routh* involves a military veteran who experienced major mental health and social issues adjusting to civilian life, including diagnoses of PTSD and other mental disorders, and two other veterans who tried to make a difference in his life. For their efforts, the two men were shot and killed by Routh. Military veterans. PTSD. Homicides. And a criminal trial. This epilogue clearly touches many "hot button" issues.

This final chapter examines several current points of controversy for the intersection of criminal justice and mental health. The topics included in this chapter are no less important because we examine them last. Without the preceding 11 chapters, much of what is discussed in this one would make little sense.

FRAMING THE ISSUES

It can be argued that how a nation or global community treats its mentally ill residents reflects its basic values. The rights of the mentally ill are fundamental human rights. The United Nations' *Universal Declaration of Human Rights* (1948) identified 30 basic human rights. Article 1 declared: "All human beings are born free and equal in dignity and rights. They are endowed with reason and conscience and should act towards one another in a spirit of brotherhood." Article 25, section 1 notes the following:

> Everyone has the right to a standard of living adequate for the health and well-being of himself and of his family, including food, clothing, housing and medical care and necessary social services, and the right to security in the event of unemployment, sickness, disability, widowhood, old age or other lack of livelihood in circumstances beyond his control.

The United States also has similar pronouncements about life, liberty, and the pursuit of happiness, including specific mental health rights, ones we discuss later in this chapter.

These statements logically lead to an additional question: To what extent has the global community or the United States worked to achieve these goals, especially in terms of the mentally ill and their contacts with the criminal justice system? Answering this question should provide insights into our present condition and what the future may hold for mentally ill persons both in this nation and around the world.

The second framing concept found in this chapter centers on the identification of risk groups. An **at-risk group** is one whose members, owing to some unique and common characteristics or qualities, including but not limited to mental illness, find themselves in precarious or dangerous situations. They might be fraud or abuse victims; they could lack basic needs, including food, shelter, and clothing; their physical health could be fragile, owing to injury, disease, or age. Moreover, given this book's overarching theme, they have come to the attention of the criminal justice system, whether as a crime perpetrator, victim, or witness.

There are at least three reasons to consider the groups identified in this chapter as at-risk, but we suspect that other reasons exist as well. First, individuals may be viewed as at-risk because of *special vulnerabilities*, which can be economic, social, political, psychological, or medical in origin. For instance, we have described several situations involving senior citizens who, in addition to the usual health issues associated with growing old, may present with symptoms of mental illness, including but not limited to Alzheimer's disease (AD). Memory facilities designed specifically for the care and comfort of AD victims are expensive or, when subsidized, have few bedspaces. AD-victim caregivers may see no option but to care for them at home, abandon them to local indigent-care facilities or, worse yet, to the streets. Whichever fate befalls them, their special vulnerabilities can lead to criminal victimizations.

Second, *victims of indifference* are a group considered at-risk because society has failed to provide adequate care for them when their own resources—and often those of their immediate families—become exhausted. Victims of indifference are easily forgotten people who blend into society at large, or they can form groups that live in aggregations that effectively isolate them from the social mainstream. For example, we may not see at-risk military veterans among us, because, outside of a few street venders and panhandlers, they do not all wear signs that say "disabled veteran" or "unemployed vet." There are millions of military veterans. Some, a minority, live on the streets, vets of wars ranging from Vietnam to the two Gulf Wars to the current global conflicts. When they return to civilian life, most simply try to blend in with the rest of us, until they do not.

The third reason is complex and controversial. Certain groups, but especially members of various gay, lesbian, bisexual, transgender, and questioning or queer communities (GLBTQ) have had what can best be described as difficult relationships with both the mental health and criminal justice systems. That is, rather than being indifferent toward these groups, some members of society view them with varying degrees of *intolerance*. GLBTQ individuals with mental health problems who have contacts with the criminal justice system have been described as bereft populations, their special needs neglected, left unaddressed, or largely forgotten (Alarid, 2000; Robinson, 2011; White and Kurpius, 2002). In their interactions with society and the mental health system, they are often the victims of additional prejudice and discrimination, which can lead to self-stigma (Dworkin and Li, 2011; Eliason and Chinn, 2014; Herek and Garnett, 2006).

Racial and ethnic minorities, too, have long been the victims of intolerance, discrimination, and bias within both the mental health and the criminal justice systems. Persons of color who are also mentally ill are more vulnerable to systemic predations than similarly afflicted Caucasians. They are at-risk in many of the same ways as are the elderly, military veterans, and GLBTQ persons, but with the added risk factor of intolerance based on race or ethnicity, what has been described as "the blight of dual discrimination" (O'Hara, 2014; see also Bhui, 2016).

The shape of the future is unknowable. Factors outside the control of politicians and other policy makers could make other issues far more urgent. For example, the nation may have to address an unknown set of public health or criminal justice issues related to a specific drug-abuse epidemic, threat of war, economic recession or depression, or world-wide sociopolitical unrest. What we propose is that you consider the topics included in this chapter, look around your community, your nation, and the world, and think about what else might pose serious threats to the thinly stretched resources of both the mental healthcare and criminal justice systems. The information contained in this chapter is not meant to answer all questions, but, rather, to engage the reader in discussions about what needs to change and how, starting with the questions contained in Box 12.1.

Thinking About the Issues

In the preceding section, we described two main themes. One was the claim that mental healthcare services are a basic human right. Consider each of the following questions with respect to any linkage between human rights and mental healthcare.

1. We label the shortcomings of the U.S. mental healthcare system in addressing certain at-risk groups as a possible human rights issue. What do you think about this claim?

2. "The United States should not be concerned with what the rest of the world says about human rights." Argue for or against this statement.

Second, we asserted that members of certain groups, owing to shared characteristics that define them, are at-risk of experiencing difficulties with the criminal justice system that other people not in those groups, but similarly afflicted with mental diseases or disorders, may not experience. Think back through previous chapters about the risks faced by the identified populations or groups not included in this chapter and answer the following questions.

3. What did you see as the greatest risks faced by each? Explain how you reached your conclusions.

4. What should be the singular principle that underlies any discussion of an at-risk group's right to access mental healthcare services? Explain your reasoning.

HUMAN RIGHTS ISSUES

Human rights are the unrestricted access to dignity, equality, and mutual respect, which should have no regard to nationality, religion, or personal beliefs. Such rights are viewed as universal (i.e., belonging to everybody in the world), inalienable (i.e., they cannot be taken away), and indivisible and interdependent (i.e., no one, including governments, can select which to grant and which to withhold).

The United Nations, along with its affiliated World Health Organization, include access to medical and mental care as a fundamental and basic human right. The pre-eminent source on this issue is the **International Bill of Rights**, which is composed of the United Nation's Declaration of Human Rights (1948), the International Covenant on Civil and Political Rights (1966), and the International Covenant on Economic, Social and Cultural Rights (1966).

Most nation states also recognize the rights of special subpopulations, including the mentally ill, although this recognition has only occurred since the early 1990s (Perlin, 2009). In 2008, the **Convention on the Rights of Persons with Disabilities**, a United

Nations international human rights treaty, came into force. Article 1 of the Convention defines its purpose as seeking "to promote, protect and ensure the full and equal enjoyment of all human rights and fundamental freedoms by all persons with disabilities, and to promote respect for their inherent dignity" (United Nations, 2008). As of 2017, 172 nations and the European Union had adopted the Convention (United Nation, 2017). The U.S. Senate has yet to ratify the treaty, and it failed on the one occasion it was brought up for a vote (Helderman, 2012).

The question becomes, is this all sound and fury and no resolution or action? To answer this question, we turn first to world views on mental health rights, followed by an examination of these issues within the United States.

Global Views on Mental Health Rights

The United Nations provides a glimpse into the conundrum of mental healthcare access through its *Mental Health Atlas* (World Health Organization [WHO], 2015). This document suggests that worldwide, the member states are far from full compliance, although improvements are expected by 2020. The extent to which actions have been taken—for example, to provide comprehensive, integrated, and responsive mental health and social care services in community-based settings—is linked to the nation's wealth, as mental healthcare is assigned a lower priority than other even more basic needs, such as reliable food sources, adequate shelter, clothing, and clean water (WHO, 2015).

One measure of services rendered is the **treatment gap (TG)**, which is the number of people needing a specific service but who do not get it, expressed as a percentage (Kale, 2002). A high TG of 98 percent would mean that nearly everyone needing a particular service is not getting it, while a TG of 15 percent would mean that very few people are not getting it. The TG for people with mental disorders in all nations around the world approaches 50 percent. In nations with few resources, the TG exceeds 90 percent (Patel, Maj, et al., 2010), again suggesting that access is highly correlated with a nation's finances.

Putting aside the costs of mental health, we must consider at least three other factors when looking globally at mental health. First, there is a lack of qualified psychiatric and psychological professionals around the world (Ngui, Khasakhala, et al., 2010). Half of the world's population lives in a nation where there is less than one psychiatrist for every 100,000 citizens, while there is one per 1,000 population in high-income nations (WHO, 2015). Second, there is an inherent distrust in many nations of Western approaches to mental illness that rely on psychotropic drugs. These approaches have been characterized as both "neo-colonialist" and "neo-missionary" in nature (Mills, 2014; Suman, 2010, 2014; Watters, 2011). The leaders and citizens of developing nations are leery of becoming the dumping ground for U.S. and European pharmaceutical companies looking for new markets for their wares. Related to this issue, many cultures view mental illness quite differently from the orientations expressed by Western medicine (Suman, 2010), a perspective also addressed in Chapter 2. Third, regional wars, ethnic conflicts, and the like make the business of mental healthcare not only needed, but also difficult and dangerous (Spiegel, Checchi, et al., 2010). As refugee populations grow into the millions, as we have witnessed over the past decade, their mental health needs have grown accordingly.

The world community recognizes the importance of health care for the mentally ill. However, compliance with emerging standards is somewhat behind recognition of the problem. We turn next to a similar analysis of what is happening in the United States with regard to the same set of issues and concerns.

Mental Health Rights and Issues in the United States

Earlier chapters addressed the deinstitutionalization of the mentally ill and the criminalization of mental illness. These reviews suggest that the United States has a mixed history in its dealings with the mentally ill. The first attempt to pass national legislation to benefit the mentally ill occurred in 1854. Social activist Dorothea Dix (b.1802-d.1887) lobbied Congress to pass the **Bill for the Benefit of the Indigent Insane**. This legislation would have put aside 10 million acres whose sale would have benefitted the mentally ill. The bill passed both houses of Congress, but was vetoed by President Franklin Pierce.

The next major piece of federal legislation was the **National Mental Health Act** (1946), as Congress recognized the problems associated with veterans returning from World War II (Herman, 1995). Prior to this Act and the interest it provoked in psychiatry and mental illness, the nation suffered a dearth of qualified medical professionals, a fact that concerned Congress, as millions of combat-exposed veterans returned stateside. Recall, too, that this was decades before the medical profession recognized PTSD, although the diagnosis of "battle fatigue" or "combat stress reaction" was well established by World War II, and an even earlier diagnosis, "shell shock," which was likely caused by a traumatic brain injury (TBI), was in use as far back as World War I (Department of the Army, 2009; Shepard, 2000). The Act also authorized the creation of the National Institute of Mental Health (NIMH), an organization mentioned many times in this book, although the NIMH was not formally established until 1949.

The deinstitutionalization of the mentally ill had unintended consequences, ones addressed in several previous chapters. Several other pieces of federal legislation exacerbated this problem. In 1963, as part of President John F. Kennedy's "New Frontier," Congress passed the **Community Mental Health Act**, which, through grants overseen by the NIMH, provided federal monies for community mental health centers and research. The Act sought to fund 1,500 centers that would have provided community-based services for nearly 250,000 individuals, which is about half of all mentally ill persons institutionalized at the time (Smith, 2013). Congress, however, did not provide funding for the centers' long-term support and the states failed to fund adequately the community treatment center initiative (Mechanic and Rochefort, 1990). Only about half of the projected centers needed for national coverage were opened and even these facilities underserved the needs of the chronically mentally ill (Dowell and Ciarlo, 1983). Finally, the Social Security Amendments of 1965 created **Medicaid**, which accelerated the pace of deinstitutionalization and subsequent criminalization of the mentally ill. States saw Medicaid as a chance to empty their mental hospitals and shift the financial burden of mental health treatment to the federal government. This latter goal, owing in part to congressional underfunding of the community mental health initiative, did not happen.

In 1980, the Congress passed **Mental Health Systems Act**, signed into law by President Jimmy Carter, which was intended to make up the community health centers' underfunding. Most provisions of the law, however, were repealed by Congress during President Ronald Reagan's administration. In 1981, Congress authorized the **Mental Patients' Bill of Rights** (42 U.S.C. §9501). Key rights, some of which are subject to modification, include the following:

1. The right to appropriate treatment and related services in a setting and under conditions that—
   a. are the most supportive of such person's personal liberty; and
   b. restrict such liberty only to the extent necessary consistent with such person's treatment needs, applicable requirements of law, and applicable judicial orders.
2. The right to an individualized, written, treatment or service plan (such plan to be developed promptly after admission of such person).
3. The right not to receive a mode or course of treatment, established pursuant to the treatment plan, in the absence of such person's informed, voluntary, written consent to such mode or course of treatment (may be modified in an emergency or when lawful under a commitment order).
4. The right to informed consent prior to treatment or participation in experimentation.
5. The right to freedom from restraint or seclusion, other than as a mode or course of treatment or restraint or seclusion during an emergency.
6. The right to confidentiality of such person's records.
7. The right to privacy.

This Act was in part a response to *Wyatt v. Stickney*, which established minimum standards for the care and treatment of the mentally ill (see Box 12.2).

One might question the current state of mental healthcare across the nation. As we described in Chapter 1, the United States spends more per capita on healthcare than any other industrialized Western nation and ranks at the bottom in terms of service delivery. Great disparities in healthcare access exist across the nation (Davis, Stremikis, et al., 2014). Mental Health America [MHA] (2017a) ranked the 50 states and the District of Columbia in terms of the prevalence of mental health problems and access to mental health care. The top five states in this assessment were (1) Massachusetts, (2) South Dakota, (3) Minnesota, (4) Vermont, and (5) Connecticut. The five lowest ranked states were (47) Idaho, (48) Indiana, (49) Arizona, (50) Mississippi, and (51) Nevada. As summarized by MHA (2017b), "to meet their mental health needs, providers in the lowest ranked states would have to

BOX 12.2

Law and Mental Health:
Wyatt v. Stickney (1971)

In 1970, the State of Alabama cut its cigarette tax. This tax largely supported Alabama's state-wide mental health services, including the Bryce State Mental Hospital in Tuscaloosa, which housed 5,200 patients. At Bryce and across the state, staffing positions disappeared and fewer staff had to work with the same number of patients. Seeing these cuts as intolerable, faculty at the University of Alabama's Department of Psychology instituted a lawsuit against the state calling for the reinstatement of all staff. However, conditions at Bryce before the layoffs were so bad, a local reporter compared them to those he had witnessed at Nazi concentration camps at the end of World War II. Thus, simply reinstating staff would have done little to alleviate the already abysmal conditions at Bryce.

The original lawsuit was assigned to U.S. District Court Judge Frank M. Johnson in Montgomery. He ruled that while a federal issue might be found in the operation of Bryce, it was not simply that staff had been fired. Rather, a federal suit would have to address violations of the minimum standards required for persons involuntarily held by the state in an institution such as Bryce. The suit, it was determined, would go forward in the name of 15-year old Ricky Wyatt, an inmate at Bryce and the nephew of one of its laid-off employees. As the Alabama Disabilities Advocacy Program (2004: 3) notes, the goals of plaintiff's litigation were to: "(1) establish a constitutional right to treatment on behalf of people with mental illness, (2) establish a constitutional right to habilitation on behalf of people with intellectual disability (ID), and (3) set minimum standards regarding safety, education, training, medication, nutrition, physical accommodations, staff/patient ratios, individualized treatment and aftercare."

The case was merged with ones brought by patients at Alabama's two other inpatient mental health facilities. Court-ordered agreements that emerged from this litigation formed the basis of federal standards for the care of people with mental illness or what was known at the time as mental retardation but which is now called intellectual disability. The resulting "Wyatt" standards include: (1) humane psychological and physical environment, (2) qualified and sufficient staff for administration of treatment, (3) individualized treatment plans, and (4) minimum restriction of patient freedom.

Wyatt was an open case for 33 years, being finally resolved in 2003 when U.S. District Court Judge Myron Herbert Thompson found Alabama in compliance with the agreement. Interestingly, a 268-bed hospital is scheduled to replace the 5,200-bed Bryce facility in 2020.

Sources: Alabama Disabilities Advocacy Program (2004); APA (2013); *Wyatt v. Stickney* (1972).

treat six times as many people than providers in the highest ranked states." For example, in Massachusetts there is one mental healthcare worker for every 200 residents, whereas in Alabama the ratio is 1:1,200 (MHA, 2017b: 33). About half of all Americans with mental health problems receive no treatment, a treatment gap of 50 percent, the worldwide average. By any standard, America's mental health system requires state and federal legislative action, particularly with respect to public funds and full attention to existing legal mandates.

In closing, the relationship between healthcare access and incarceration is instructive. Six of the 10 states with lowest access to mental healthcare also have the highest incarceration rates, which includes the states of Alabama (48), Arkansas (47), Mississippi (46), Texas (44), Georgia (41), and Florida (40); six of the 10 states with the most access to mental health also have the lowest incarceration rates, which includes the states of Maine (1), Rhode Island (2), Massachusetts (3), Minnesota (4), New Hampshire (6), and Vermont (7) (incarceration rankings low (1) to high (51) in parentheses; MHA, 2017a: 16). Given the rates of mental illness for jail and prison inmates reported in Chapter 9, investments in a state's mental healthcare delivery system would seem to bear fruit beyond simply providing services to more people in need. Besides having the opportunity to divert some offenders into expanded community healthcare centers, providing proactive healthcare for those individuals with mental health issues who are in the community could reduce society's reliance on jails and prisons as "the new asylums."

Access to mental healthcare services has come to be defined globally as a human right. This nation's record when it comes to meeting its mental healthcare needs is troubling. We suggest an understanding of the following four at-risk groups demonstrates not only the breadth and depth of their problems, but also possible ways to change this characterization of at-risk. We begin with some of the nation's most vulnerable citizens, the elderly.

ELDER MISTREATMENT

Defining who qualifies as elderly is a daunting task. In most industrialized nations, the age of 65 is the point of both retirement and the onset of old age (Jugdutt, 2016), although many in the field of geriatrics, the medical sub-discipline that deals with the health issues of the elderly, find this definition somewhat arbitrary (Singh and Bajorek, 2014). Another convention refers to those between 65-74 years of age as "early elderly" and those persons aged 75 and over as "late elderly" (Orimo, Suzuki, et al., 2006). Geriatric oncologists typically use the age of 70 as a beginning point for defining the elderly (Kristjansson and Wyller, 2010). Surgical risks also start to climb for persons 70 and older (Turrentine, Wang, et al., 2006). Still, modern social conventions hold strong at the 65-years-of-age benchmark as the point at which humans in modern industrialized nations become elderly and, where practicable, we use it as well.

Mistreatment also has several meanings. It can refer to a failure to show someone respect. Pushing past a person in line who is obviously ill or infirm is a form of mistreatment, although even the "victim" may simply shrug it off. Mistreatment can refer to the failure to act to help another person or a specific act taken against another person. In such cases, no laws may be broken, but social conventions are flaunted or ignored. Consider a son or daughter who fails to check up regularly on a parent living alone and far away; there may be no law that requires it, but social convention would suggest that such failures to act constitute neglectful mistreatment.

Action taken directly or indirectly by one person against the interests of another and the failure to act in accord with a legally mandated requirement may constitute *law-violating* mistreatment. For example, a licensed caregiver contractually agrees to care for a dependent person, but his or her failure to provide the agreed-upon services in a timely fashion causes injury or death. In another case, a person in a similar position of trust empties the dependent person's bank account and takes off for points unknown, financially ruining the "client."

In cases of **elder mistreatment** someone acts against an elderly person or fails to act on that person's behalf, and the latter is victimized. Many of these incidents are clear violations of criminal law; in other cases, the actions or failures to act may be litigated as torts in civil court.

Understanding the Issues

Based on 2016 U.S. Census Bureau (2017a) projections, the number of citizens aged 65 or older exceeded 50 million. This population segment grew from 9 percent in 1960 to 15 percent in 2016 (World Bank, 2017a). The future will be even grayer. Mather and associates (2015) calculated that by 2060, there will be more than 98 million senior citizens in the United States, representing 24 percent of the population. These changes will strain the nation's infrastructure and resources. For example, as Baby Boomers age, they will cause a 75 percent increase in nursing home care needs by 2030. AD victims will nearly treble by 2050, up from 5 million in 2013 to 15 million. Social Security and Medicare expenses will increase by 50 percent in 2050.

Medical researchers and social scientists reveal a darker side to growing old in America. In a nationally representative study of persons aged 60 and older, Acierno and associates (2010) reported the following one-year prevalence rates for elder abuse: 4.6 percent for emotional abuse, 1.6 percent for physical abuse, and 0.6 percent for sexual abuse. However, the lifetime prevalence rates for each form of abuse were 4 to 5 times higher. The researchers also found a 5 percent potential for neglect or financial abuse *by a family member*. Just over one in 10 elderly persons participating in the survey reported abuse or potential for neglect other than for financial exploitation. Low social support within their communities significantly increased the risk of nearly every form of mistreatment. Other studies generally reinforce the value of social support as a bulwark against elder abuse (Amstadter, Moreland Begle, et al., 2010; Comijs, Penninx, et al., 1999).

A two-wave panel study of victimized and non-victimized seniors, where information was collected from each group at two points in time, revealed that a prior victimization experience increased second-wave reports of negative outcomes by 200 to 700 percent (Acierno, Hernandez-Tejada, et al., 2017). Measures of negative outcomes included *DSM-5*'s major depressive disorder, generalized anxiety disorder, and posttraumatic stress disorder. Social support between the two waves of data collection functioned as a protection against all negative outcomes except PTSD, which, along with depression, was the mental health disorder most impacted by prior victimizations.

The unexpected death of a senior citizen under the care of another individual is a worst-case elder-care mistreatment scenario. Abuse or neglect may not be the immediate cause of death. Rather, death can occur later, due to a history of neglect or abuse. For example, Lachs and associates (1998) studied a New Haven, Connecticut, cohort of seniors over at least nine years. In their analyses, the researchers statistically removed the influences of the subjects' demographic characteristics, chronic diseases, functional status, social networks, cognitive status, and depressive symptomology. They found that the risk of death was higher for cohort members who were either mistreatment victims or suffered from self-neglect when compared to those who reported no such mistreatment or self-neglect (Lachs, Williams, et al., 1998).

Working Toward Solutions

Negative outcomes for seniors, ranging from depression to death, are linked to prior neglect and abuse. Supportive communities, including social engagement by the elderly with others in their immediate social environment, show promise as prophylactic and healing forces. Law enforcement **wellness checks** for those living alone or with caregivers can enhance senior well-being. Geriatric social workers specializing in the signs of abuse and neglect, including self-neglect, can also reduce the incidence of both negative mental conditions and deaths (McInnis-Dittrich, 2014). Similarly, educating members of the criminal justice system across the board could reduce subsequent mental and physical health problems of the elderly offenders, victims, and witnesses. There are also far more general community-wide efforts to help seniors, such as the Silver Alert program (Box 12.3).

Medical professionals responding to the needs of the elderly are another part of this society-wide problem. Elder mistreatment is a medical diagnosis: "Elder abuse and neglect includes any act of commission or omission that results in harm or threatened harm to the health and welfare of an older adult" (American Medical Association, 1994: 4-24). The elderly, on average, see their physicians five times a year; however, physicians initiate only about 2 percent of the reported cases of abuse and neglect. A study of Ohio-based family physicians and internists revealed that 72 percent had no exposure or minimal exposure to the physical, emotional, or sexual abuse of senior citizens (Kennedy, 2005). The study's doctors estimated the prevalence of such abuse and neglect at 25 percent lower than is typically reported in the medical literature. In the early 2000s, only about 10 percent of U.S. medical schools required course work or a specific rotation in geriatric medicine; where such courses are offered as electives, only about 3 percent of medical school graduates take them (Alliance for Aging Research, 2003).

BOX 12.3

Silver Alert

In 2005, Oklahoma state representative Fred Perry created an Amber Alert system for senior citizens called **Silver Alert**. Currently, 26 states use the Silver Alert program, which is limited to providing services for missing persons 65 years of age and older who have AD, dementia, or some form of mental illness. Nine other states employ a program like Silver Alert, but that operates under a different name, such as Golden Alert or Senior Citizen Alert. An additional eight states include alerts for missing senior citizens under existing endangered person or missing person advisories. Essentially, Silver Alerts function like Amber Alerts, putting up descriptions of missing seniors on electronic bulletin boards and telephone alerts.

The gerontological research community, however, views programs such as Silver Alerts as a mixed blessing. There is an abiding concern that such programs can further isolate and stigmatize the elderly, but especially those with mental disorders and dementia. They generally recommend that local law enforcement consult with geriatric social workers and others who specialize in the problems of the elderly before implementing such programs.

Sources: Alzheimer's Association (2008); American Association of Retired Persons (2014); Carr, Muschert, et al. (2009); Gergerich and Davis (2017).

The need for geriatric education for health professionals remains high (Bardach and Rowles, 2012). Medical association guidelines and some state laws require physicians and other healthcare professionals to inquire into their patients' living conditions at the time they are seen. Such inquiries may reduce the incidence of some negative outcomes, but the compliance rates are unknown. Moreover, it is possible that in some instances welfare checks are perfunctory in nature, as doctors may view eldercare as "frustrating" and "boring" (Higashi, Tillack, et al., 2012). Physicians, and perhaps other medical and social work professionals, need ongoing education and training about elder abuse (Dong, 2005; Higashi et al., 2012).

VETERANS

A military veteran is any individual who has served in the armed forces. The United States' treatment of its military veterans has been uneven at best. According to the Veterans Administration (VA, n.d.), the Continental Congress promised to give veterans of the Revolutionary War pensions, although it was primarily the states and local communities that provided medical and healthcare. Prior to the War of 1812, the U.S. Congress authorized the first residential and medical facility for veterans, followed in the late 19th century by additional benefits and pensions for veterans and their widows and dependents. After the Civil War, all states, including those that seceded from the Union, created residences and medical care facilities for disabled veterans. Over the next 50 years, veterans of the Civil War, Indian Wars, Spanish-American War, and Mexican Border period received care in these state-run facilities.

The 20th century saw changes to local- and state-run assistance for military veterans as demands increased. Congress established a system of veterans benefits at the start of World War I. However, this system was disjointed and distributed benefits and services through three different federal agencies. Congress created a Veterans Bureau in 1921, which brought together under one umbrella agency a wide array of federally operated programs, including residential homes, public health services, and hospitals. In 1930, President Herbert Hoover signed an executive order creating the Veterans Administration (VA) to coordinate and consolidate all governmental activities taken on behalf of veterans.

Congressional passage of the **Servicemen's Readjustment Act of 1944**, known as **the G.I. Bill**, helped shape veterans' services for several generations. The bill's intent was to help millions of returning veterans at the close of World War II with a range of benefits that included financial support to facilitate attending high school, college, or vocational/technical school; low-cost home mortgages; and low-interest business loans. It is estimated that by 1956, nearly 8 million veterans had accessed the G.I. Bill (Bennett, 2000; Bond and Turner, 2002; Olson, 1974).

The **Veterans Health Administration (VHA)**, the largest of the three elements that makes up the VA, currently operates the world's largest healthcare system. The majority of America's medical, nursing, and allied health professionals receive training through the VA. The VHA operates 152 hospitals, 800 community-based outpatient clinics, 126 nursing home care units, and 35 domiciliary facilities, the latter used largely for homeless veterans. The domiciliary programs, which offer clinical and rehabilitation programs for veterans, are part of the VA's Mental Health Residential Rehabilitation and Treatment Programs (VA, n.d.).

Understanding the Issues

As of 2017, there were nearly 18.5 million veterans in the United States (U.S. Census Bureau, 2017b), one-half aged 65 or older. The next largest single group is between 35 to 54 years of age, meaning the likelihood is high that many of them fought in the nation's most recent wars in Iraq, Afghanistan, and the worldwide war on terror. Nine in ten veterans are men.

During the Vietnam War, just under 3 million U.S. military personnel served "in country." Of this number, it is estimated that 800,000, or roughly one in 2.5 veterans, suffered from PTSD (Dieter, 2015). In the nation's more recent military conflicts, over 300,000 veterans from the Afghanistan and Iraq conflicts received a diagnosis of PTSD (Dieter, 2015). The exact number of individual troops that served in one or more of the recent theaters of war has not been made public since 2013 for unspecified security reasons. The best estimate is 2.5 million (Ruiz, 2013). However, at least 40,000 individuals served 5 or more tours of duty in combat zones and 400,000 service men and women returned for 3 or more tours (Adams, 2013).

There are other long-term medical concerns besides PTSD associated with military service. Nearly 40,000 Vietnam veterans made claims to the VA about the side effects of a toxic substance known as Agent Orange; however, as of 1993, the VA had substantiated less than 500 such claims for disabilities (Fleischer and Zames, 2001). Many scientists believe that there are several neurobehavioral disorders linked to Agent Orange exposure (Committee to Review the Health Effects of Vietnam Veterans Exposure to Herbicides, 1994). Similarly, after the 1991 war against Saddam Hussein, a chronic, multi-symptomatic illness called "Gulf War Syndrome" affected at least 175,000 veterans (Dieter, 2015).

A traumatic brain injury (TBI) is also a concern for some veterans. While TBIs accounted for about 12 percent of the Vietnam War's casualties, the rate for more recent conflicts is estimated at 22 percent (VA, 2017a). Between 60 and 80 percent of military personnel diagnosed with a blast injury may also have suffered a TBI. A random sample of 1,965 soldiers sent into combat revealed a probable PTSD prevalence rate of 14 percent, while the prevalence rate for a TBI was 19 percent (Schell and Marshall, 2008). The researchers reported that TBIs, PTSD, and depression tend to co-occur.

There is clear evidence that Vietnam and the Iraq-Afghanistan wars have cost the nation more than their multi-trillion-dollar price tag; tens of thousands of dead soldiers, marines, sailors, and airmen; and over 1,150,000 American service men and women injured (Blasco, 2014; DeBruyne, 2017; Dieter, 2015; Ruiz, 2013; Thompson, 2015). The human and economic costs will continue to be calculated for decades to come. In terms of the latter, long-term mental and general healthcare and treatment costs of the nation's recent wars are estimated at between $2.4 and $4 trillion (Stiglitz and Bilmes, 2008; Trotta, 2013).

Another important issue is the incarcerated veteran, but especially the mentally ill veteran. Between 1980 and 2004, the percentage of jail and prison inmates that had served in the U.S. armed forces increased to account for 24 percent of all inmates (Bureau of Justice Statistics [BJS], 2015). Since 2005, however, the percentage of jail and prison inmates who were veterans declined to 8 percent of all inmates. Most (77%) jail and prison inmates who served in the U.S. military received an honorable or general discharge under honorable conditions; only 5 percent of prison inmates and 6 percent of jail inmates received a less than honorable or bad conduct discharge (BJS, 2015). One-quarter served five or more years.

In 2010-2011, veterans in the nation's jails had reported mental health issues at a higher rate than was the case for non-veterans (55% versus 43%, respectively) in jail (Bronson, Carson, et al., 2015). With respect to prison inmates, the reports were somewhat lower for both groups: Veterans-as-prison-inmates were still more likely to indicate that they had been told about a mental health issue than was the case for non-veteran prisoners (48% versus 36%, respectively). Among jailed veterans, the rate of diagnosed PTSD was twice that of non-veteran jail inmates (23% versus 11%, respectively). For veterans in prison, the same differential was noted, although the base rates for each group were higher (31% versus 15%, respectively). Relatedly, more combat veterans in jail (60%) or prison (67%) had been told they had a mental problem when compared to non-veteran jail (44%) or prison

(49%) inmates (Bronson et al., 2015). Given that these figures represent tens of thousands of veterans, they add another layer to the questions surrounding the nation's treatment of its veterans, especially with the high rate of honorable service. This fact means that, in most cases, incarcerated mentally ill veterans remain eligible for VA benefits (VA, 2015).

Working Toward Solutions

Part of the problem would appear to be a failure by American society to recognize fully the impact of combat on returning veterans. This statement includes the various military services. The U.S. Government Accountability Office [GAO] (2017) reported nearly two-thirds of all service personnel separating from the military for misconduct between 2011 and 2015 had been diagnosed with PTSD, a TBI, adjustment problems, or alcohol-related issues in the two years prior to their discharge. One in four received a less-than-honorable discharge, meaning they were not eligible for the full array of VA benefits. The GAO found that the Army and Marine Corps may not have adhered to their own training, screening, and counseling policies in these instances. The GAO also reported that the policies of the Air Force and Navy on these matters are inconsistent with those directed by the Department of Defense (DOD), an observation disputed by the DOD.

In 2017, the GAO (2017: 31) recommended that all U.S. armed forces should:

1. screen certain servicemembers for PTSD and TBI prior to separation for misconduct;
2. train servicemembers, including officers, on how to identify mild TBI symptoms in the deployed setting; and
3. counsel dischargees about VA benefits and services during the process of separating certain servicemembers for misconduct.

While it is too soon to know whether these recommendations have been followed, it is interesting to note that, when offered the opportunity prior to the report's publication, the VA did not respond to any of the GAO's specific claims. For its part, the Department of Defense (DOD) took exception with several GAO recommendations, suggesting that the GAO was attempting to create new DOD policy. Given the somewhat combative response of the DOD to the GAO report, it may take congressional action for full compliance. In the meantime, we need only look at the prison and jail statistics to understand the significance of the GAO report.

A recent development may help to address the needs of some mentally ill veterans. Effective June 2017, the VA, recognizing the problems faced by persons with other than honorable discharges (OTH), notified the public that it was prepared to offer stabilization care for former servicemembers presenting themselves at any of its facilities with an emergency mental health need (VA, 2017b). The VA estimates that there are about half a million individuals in the OTH category. As the VA (2017a) states in its public notification about this policy: "VA views the decision to provide immediate care to these former servicemembers as a moral and humanitarian obligation. The focus is on saving lives."

However, this policy only allows for a maximum 90 days of treatment and the condition must be service-connected.

Besides its expansive medical care system, which treats a range of mental conditions, the VA operates the **National Center for Posttraumatic Stress Disorder**. The National Center consists of seven VA centers of excellence arrayed on each coast and Hawaii. The mission of the National Center is "to advance clinical care and social welfare of America's Veterans and others who have experienced trauma, or who suffer from PTSD, through research, education, and training in the science, diagnosis, and treatment of PTSD and stress-related disorders" (VA, n.d.). The National Center supports clinical trials and biological studies intended to reduce or alleviate the symptoms of PTSD sufferers (VA, 2017c: 12-13). The VA has begun to explore treatment variations to meet the unique needs of women veterans with PTSD (VA, 2017c). The National Center is also conducting research into TBI treatment, as well as the comorbidity of all three. In this regard, the VA has initiated the Polytrauma System of Care at 4 of its rehabilitation centers and 21 Polytrauma Network Sites located throughout the nation.

The **veterans treatment courts (VTC)** are specialty courts, like drug courts and mental health courts. The VTCs have proven an effective method of diverting veterans out of the criminal justice system where allowed by law and legal custom (Knudsen and Wingenfeld, 2015), especially when paired with the Sequential Intercept Model (Chapter 9) through the more general Veterans Justice Programs (Blue-Howells, Clark, et al., 2013). In this case, the Veterans Justice Programs employ Veterans Justice Outreach to divert eligible veterans to VTCs (Intercept 2) or coordinate services for incarcerated veterans (Intercept 3). A second VA program, Health Care for Reentry Veterans, prepares incarcerated jail and prison inmates (Intercept 4) for reentry into the community. HTCs, which operate early in the SIM, are essential to keeping justice-involved veterans from penetrating more deeply into the criminal justice system.

The VA indicates the number of VTCs has grown from fewer than 100 in 2011 to 461 in 2016 (Flatley, Clark, et al., 2017; Hartwell, James, et al., 2013). In fact, between 2015 and 2016, the nation added 116 such courts. Three-fourths of these courts operate as separately designated VTCs, while the remainder function as a veterans' docket of an existing drug, mental health, hybrid drug/mental health, or criminal court (Clark et al., 2017). Most (71.3%) accept cases involving both veterans and active duty personnel; fully two-thirds also allow VA healthcare ineligible veterans to appear.

The VTCs divert the military veteran from traditional criminal justice processing as the prosecution is suspended while the suspected offender receives and completes treatment. The average time of contact is 14 months for misdemeanors and 18 months for felonies. While it is too early to declare the programs a success, preliminary findings suggest positive outcomes (Hartwell et al., 2013; Knudsen and Wingenfeld, 2015).

Researchers report that veterans' rates of traumatic experiences, as expected, are much higher than for the general population (VA, 2017a). However, most of these experiences occurred prior to enlistment. Such a finding suggests that the military services need to review their enlistment screening (Hartwell et al., 2013). This finding, however, should not be seen as mitigating the debt owed by the United States to its military veterans.

BOX 12.4

What Would You Do?

A member of your family recently returned to his parents' home after eight years in the Marine Corps. He is a decorated combat veteran. You know something about what he did overseas, but he has never really shared many details, preferring to say, "I did my duty. Nothing more and nothing less." He lives at home with his parents, who are your relatives too, but he is not actively seeking a job. While he does not appear to suffer from any specific physical injuries or psychological distress, you have noticed a distinct change in how he interacts with friends and family. He just is not himself since he left the military, but especially since his last tour of duty in Southwest Asia.

What if you accidentally discovered that your veteran-relative had accessed websites associated with race-based hate groups, especially ones that direct viewers to engage in violence against specific racial groups? What would you do?

Consider what you would do if your veteran-relative made specific threats against another family member, but then said, "Oh, I'm just kidding. You know I wouldn't harm anyone." You know that for members of the infantry, killing others was part of the job description. What actions would you take?

What if your veteran-relative disappeared one morning? He never showed up for breakfast and his room is empty. You know that he has little cash, not enough to start a new life or even support himself for more than a couple of days. What would you do?

As suggested in Box 12.4, the veteran's family can often serve as a first line of assistance. However, the family members need to know about the range of government-funded resources available to their veteran-kin, which is often not the case. As you read the vignette summarized in this box, you should not lose sight of the fact that only about 3 percent of all veterans—3 in 100—are justice-system-involved (Blue-Howells, Clark, et al., 2013).

GENDER IDENTITY

Gender refers to culturally defined and socially agreed upon conduct norms governing behaviors deemed appropriate for men and women. There need be no biological basis for a person's **gender identity**, meaning this self-conception is independent of the sex assigned at birth. Gender identity should be considered when talking about the impact of one's gender on the intersection of mental health and criminal justice. **Sexual orientation** refers to an individual's attraction to or preference in sexual partners, and can include persons with the same gender identity, a different one, or both. As previously noted, GLBT is an acronym that stands for gay, lesbian, bisexual, and transgender.

Over the past decade, a Q has been added to this acronym, signifying queer or questioning and reflects the GLBT communities' (1) effort to reclaim the term queer and change it from a pejorative to a positive one, (2) view of queer as an umbrella term that captures the nuances of all the other states of being, or (3) perspective on queer as a term that captures the intersection of race and culture in one's sexual orientation or gender identity (Grisham, 2015). Questioning refers to those persons who exist between the heterosexual and GLBT worlds. The preferred term today, then, is **GLBTQ**.

Understanding the Issues

The U.S. Census Bureau has never asked nor will it ask in the 2020 census any questions about the gender identity of U.S. citizens (U.S. Census Bureau, 2017c; Wang, 2017). According to the most recent survey of American adults, based on a nationally representative sample, 10 million adults identified as gay, lesbian, bisexual, or transgender (GLBT) persons in 2016, which represented 4.1 percent of the adult population in the United States (Gates, 2017). In addition, women outnumbered men when it comes to identifying as GLBTQ (Gates, 2017).

In mental health terms, the American Psychiatric Association [APA] (1974) removed homosexuality from the sixth printing of the *DSM-II* in 1974. Partial remnants of that diagnosis remained until 1987, when they were completely removed from the *DSM-III-R* (APA, 1987). The *DSM-III-R* continued to recognize Sexual Disorders Not Otherwise Specified, which referred to persons with persistent and marked distress over their sexual orientation. The *DSM-5* (APA, 2013) includes several disorders related to one's sexual and gender orientation, but the states of being gay, bisexual, transgendered, queer, or questioning are not considered to be mental disorders. Members of the various GLBTQ communities, like heterosexuals, can have sexual- and gender-related mental issues, but their sexual or gender orientations are not among them, a position endorsed by the American Psychological Association (1987) over 30 years ago.

Largely owing to discrimination, prejudice, and violence directed at them, members of GLBTQ communities are overrepresented as clients of the mental health system. That is, some of the disorders stem from aggressive acts specifically committed against them because of their gender identities. The term **microaggressions** is sometimes used to characterize subtle forms of discrimination directed at oppressed groups, which, in the current situation, can degrade GLBTQ persons' mental health (Nadal, Issa, et al., 2011).

Much aggression directed at GLBTQ communities is far from micro in nature and far from subtle (Gonzales, Davidoff, et al., 2015). The major-crime victimization rates of GLBTQ persons are far higher than those who do not share this designation (Cramer, McNiel, et al., 2011; Pilkington and D'Augelli, 1995). **Hate crimes**, criminal offenses owing to a person's special status, are more violent than non-hate-motivated crimes (Hein and Scharer, 2012). They also have far more deleterious mental health consequences: Not only do the victims blame themselves for being victimized, such people may feel doubly at fault for being a GLBTQ victim. Overlay GLBTQ identity with the status of being a minor, and the victims may feel an even greater sense of abandonment, as suggested in Box 12.5.

BOX 12.5

GLBTQ Youth as an At-Risk Group

Chapter 10 identified juveniles as a special subpopulation. Add membership in a GLBTQ community to status as a minor, and the potential for additional vulnerabilities in an already vulnerable population increases. While researchers question the idea that GLBTQ youth complete suicide at higher rates than other children, they do appear to report more attempts. They also express higher levels of stress and depression than non-GLBTQ youth. Their reported levels are very similar to those experienced by representative samples of urban, racial/ethnic minority youths, a finding that supports the idea that **minority stress** is a potentially debilitating force that confronts both youthful subpopulations.

Research on GLBTQ youth exhibits several shortcomings, including concerns about the clinical validity of the non-DSM-5 measures of stress and depression employed by the researchers and the questionable representativeness of the youths sampled. In its totality, however, the researchers have detailed the overall at-risk status of GLBTQ youth, particularly their susceptibility to microaggressions and outright victimization, including abuse at the hands of their caregivers. These generalizations are especially important for homeless GLBTQ children, an additional status, which, as suggested in Chapter 11, can add another layer of risk in the lives of the homeless, adults or children, old or young.

Sources: Choi, Wilson, et al. (2015); Coker, Austin, and Schuster (2010); Haas, Eliason, et al. (2011); Mustanski, Garofalo, and Emerson (2010); Russell and Fish (2016); Whitbeck, Chen, et al. (2004).

As criminal perpetrators, GLBTQ persons with mental disorders often face prejudice and discrimination emanating from their criminal peers, criminal justice officials, and prison or jail mental health personnel (Alarid, 2000; Robinson, 2011; White and Robinson Kurpius, 2002). At the point of arrest or investigation, they may be confronted by police who are doubly hostile, first to the suspects' status as possible offenders and second to their identities as GLBTQ (Wolff and Cokley, 2007). Researchers have found that juries express homophobic biases against GLBTQ defendants (Hill, 2000; Shane and Ragatz, 2011). Legal aid societies provide attorneys with special instructions on how to select juries in cases involving GLBTQ defendants (Greater Hartford Legal Aid, 2015). In prisons and jails, GLBTQ inmates often find themselves subjected to high levels of victimization or stigmatizing segregation (Alarid, 2000; Robinson, 2011).

Working Toward Solutions

The health-justice concerns of GLBTQ persons reflect larger problems with U.S. culture and social practices. Discriminatory and prejudicial actions directed at gay, lesbian, bisexual, transgendered, questioning and queer individuals do not occur in a political or social vacuum (Dworkin and Li, 2003). Solutions to this multi-layered problem, however, have proved elusive. Creating safe zones, where members of GLBTQ communities need not be concerned about facing discrimination and prejudicial treatment, is a remedial and short-term solution. A more permanent solution would be to change the cultural bias that generates intolerance, discrimination, prejudicial actions, and violence directed at the GLBTQ communities, which by anyone's standards represents a monumental task.

Relatedly, the education and training of all criminal justice personnel likely to encounter members of GLBTQ communities would do much to alleviate the intolerance, prejudice, and outright bias experienced by individuals in various GLBTQ communities. As noted above, some legal aid societies have begun to educate their members about the special circumstances and needs encountered when a GLBTQ person is involved in a matter being contested, whether in a civil or criminal court. The victimizations suffered by mentally ill members of GLBTQ communities that encounter the justice system reflect overarching matters of inequality within society. One set of issues cannot be remedied without addressing the other.

RACE AND ETHNICITY

Race and ethnicity can be difficult to measure. For example, a trend among Americans is to identify as multi-racial or multi-ethnic or both. For its part, **race** refers to distinct groups based on hereditary characteristics. Physical characteristics such as skin color, hair texture, facial features, and stature provided the early basis for the anthropological classifications of race, which included Caucasoid, Mongoloid, Negroid, and Australoid.

Such racial distinctiveness depends on physical, geographical, national, and cultural isolation. In the 21st century, race is of little biological or anthropological significance (American Anthropological Association, 1998). Nowhere is that more clearly demonstrated than in America, where racial distinctions have blurred even further in the children of multi-mixed-race parents. Human variation is simply too great to support the idea of race used throughout most of the 20th century (Keita, Kittles, et al., 2004: 519). These scientific statements aside, the contentiousness of the social and legal uses of race in American society remains a constant feature of contemporary life.

Ethnicity refers to a group's common social or cultural traits. Ethnic groups may have their own language, religion, and customs. An important element of ethnicity is the sense that as a group they are distinct from the larger society. **Ethnic identity**, like gender identity, refers to how people see themselves, and may not have anything to do with how others see them.

Based on these definitions, African Americans are a racial group, whereas Hispanics are an ethnic group. However, several racial groups claim the cultural modifier of Hispanic or Latin, further complicating matters. For example, there are Hispanics of European descent, while many Afro-Caribbean people descend from African and Spanish origins; there are also Hispanics descended from both Spanish colonialists and various American indigenous groups.

Understanding the Issues

Currently, the federal Office of Management and Budget (OMB, 1997), the agency that standardizes such information for national counts, requires five minimum categories: American Indian or Alaska Native, Asian, Native Hawaiian or Other Pacific Islander, Black or African American, and White; it also recognizes two ethnic designations: Hispanic or Latino and Not Hispanic or Latino. Moreover, the OMB allows people to identify with two or more races, but the ethnicity choice is still limited to either Hispanic/Latino or not Hispanic/Latino.

In the most recent U.S. Census (2010), Whites accounted for 72.4 percent of the national population. Blacks or African Americans added 12.6 percent, while the percentage of Asians was 4.8 percent. Persons who self-identified as Native Americans and Alaska Natives were 0.9 percent of the national population; Native Hawaiians and Other Pacific Islanders added another 0.2 percent. About 9 percent of all persons included in the 2010 Census claimed either two or more races (2.9%) or some other race (6.2%). Hispanic and Latino Americans, all of whom were also counted in some other unincluded racial category, accounted for 16.3 percent of the population.

The impact of perceived race-based discrimination on mental health is well established: Discrimination is highly correlated with poor mental and physical health (Kessler, Mickelson, and Williams, 1999; Pascoe and Richman, 2009). The microaggressions that devalue members of various GLBTQ communities similarly impact racial and ethnic minorities. Moreover, treatment providers are often among the sources of such microaggressions, which can lead to further stigmatization and negatively impact depressive disorders (Gonzales et al., 2015). Racism can also negatively influence mental health practitioners' decisions (Bhurga and Ayonrinde, 2001; Clark, 2009; Hoberman, 2012; Phelan, Dovidio, et al., 2014). For example, one study found that African Americans are more likely than Whites to be diagnosed with highly stigmatizing psychotic spectrum disorders. Not unexpectedly, then, African Americans were also more likely than Whites to be found not criminally responsible by a court-appointed mental health professional, even controlling for sociodemographic characteristics, the number of criminal charges, and other possibly confounding variables (Perry, Neltner, and Allen, 2013).

Racial and ethnic minorities face discriminatory practices within the operation of the criminal justice system at many different junctures, from being observed on the streets by police to supervision on probation or parole (Walker, Spohn, and DeLone, 2018). In fact, simply having contact with the criminal justice system has serious consequences for the mental health of minority individuals who lived in disadvantaged areas during their adolescence (Sugie and Turney, 2017). Once again, the potential for bias is high when the two systems overlap in their responses to mentally ill minority-group offenders.

Working Toward Solutions

Solutions to discriminatory practices based on race and ethnicity have also proven elusive. Until the United States addresses this problem in its totality, including all social, political, economic, and healthcare aspects, interim measures may alleviate some of the treatment insensitivities and outright discrimination experienced by racial and ethnic minorities. At the practitioner level, education and training should emphasize culturally sensitive assessment and treatment models, ones that can be used both in the broader community and within correctional psychiatric facilities (Perry et al., 2013). African-American patients/prisoners, owing to previous contacts, often mistrust White clinical practitioners, which the latter may take as symptoms of paranoia, possibly leading to their higher rates of diagnosis along the psychotic spectrum of disorders (King, 1992; see also Perry et al., 2013). Efforts by clinicians to establish a strong therapeutic alliance with African-American clients have been shown to reduce racial disparities in psychiatric treatment (Davis, Deen, et al., 2011).

Appropriate responses by clinicians can only do so much. Mental health service disparities by race, first observed nearly 20 years ago by the Office of the Surgeon General (2001), have improved somewhat. However, significant barriers still restrict African-American, Hispanic, Latino, Asian-American, and Native American access to high quality mental health services (Smith and Trimble, 2016). Ways to respond systematically to both the needs and barriers do exist, as suggested in Box 12.6.

In summary, it would be naïve to assume that without resources for new programs or meaningful penalties for failing to comply with existing or new laws, the nation will see changes in attitudes and practices solely by following a simple prescription. The experiences of the elderly and veterans largely represent indifference; galvanizing the public to work on their behalf is a far easier task than is the case for victims of intolerance. Intolerance of others, whether it is a person whose gender identity many view as problematic or a member of a different racial or ethnic group, cannot be eradicated overnight. And, given the "hidden nature" of many of its operations, this task may be even more difficult to achieve within the criminal justice system.

EPILOGUE

This epilogue tells the story of the case State of Texas v. Eddie Ray Routh and is based on several key sources. The first is the legal response to the shooter's appeal to Texas's Eleventh District Court of Appeals (Eddie Ray Routh v. State of Texas, 2017). Additional insights come from Lamothe (2015); Shapiro (2015); and Spies (2015a, b).

Three men drive onto a shooting range. Two of the men, Christopher Scott Kyle and Chad Hutson Littlefield, saw the trip as a therapeutic experience for the third individual, Eddie Ray Routh. Kyle was a former Navy SEAL sniper, one of the most celebrated in U.S.

BOX 12.6

Working to Remediate Inequities Based on At-Risk Group Membership

Elena Schatell maintains that the nation can remediate this problem, at least in terms of providing mental health services, by following several straightforward guidelines. These guidelines would be the same for services in the general society or within the criminal justice system. They include:

1. Follow National Standards — The U.S. government has established a series of standards for culturally appropriate services, such as providing equitable, understandable, and respectful care and services in a way that respects the cultural health beliefs and practices of patients drawn from different racial and ethnic groups; offering free language assistance; and encouraging the recruitment and retention of staff with the requisite cultural background and language skills.

2. Educate and Train Mental Health Staff to Be Culturally Competent — This requirement is especially important if the service provider is from a different racial or ethnic background from the service population.

3. Develop Culture-Specific Mental Health Education Tools — Educational materials that cover the symptoms, treatment options, and local resources should be easily accessible and, once again, available in the languages of the populations served.

4. Establish and Engage Community Partners — Community partnerships have been described at several points in this book. As such partnerships are established, every effort should be expended to make certain that the behavioral health providers, educators, community leaders, families, and government agencies are aware of the emphasis on culturally competent services.

5. Continue Conversations and Research — There is a lack of information about the impact of race- or culture-based attitudes, beliefs, and trends on the convergence of mental health and criminal justice. However, open communications and conversations between stakeholders, which should include virtually every member of the community, are central to making an agenda such as this one work.

Source: Schatell (2017).

military history, and the author of a best-selling book, *American Sniper* (2012), which Clint Eastwood would later make into a blockbuster movie. Kyle was committed to improving the lives of returning veterans. Littlefield was Kyle's friend who was also devoted to veterans' causes. In early January 2013, Routh's mother, who knew of Kyle's mission to help veterans, asked him to intercede on behalf of her son, who was experiencing major problems adjusting to civilian life. The answer was the trip to a shooting range. Only one of the three would leave it alive.

A seven-year veteran of the Marine Corps, Routh had served six months near Baghdad in 2007-2008 as a prison guard and a weapons specialist, along with a brief 2010 humanitarian mission to Haiti. An honorably discharged veteran, he was not simply having trouble adjusting to civilian life. In fact, he was diagnosed by Department of Veterans Affairs clinicians as suffering from PTSD; he was also prescribed a regimen of antipsychotics and antidepressants. Routh subsequently claimed to experience auditory hallucinations and suffered from paranoia merged with schizophrenia. At some point in his treatment, he expressed suicidal ideation on several occasions, including one where he threatened to kill himself with a handgun. VA doctors, believing that Routh suffered from alcohol abuse, suggested that he commit himself for inpatient treatment, which he declined, and he stopped taking his medication as well. His most recent VA hospitalization was in January of 2013, about a month prior to the homicides.

It was at this point that Kyle and Littlefield entered Routh's life. Kyle had access to a shooting range at an 11,000-acre resort. He had previously brought troubled veterans to the range, where they bonded over shooting experiences. On the afternoon of February 2, 2013, as the three were making their way to the resort and its shooting range, Kyle and Littlefield texted each other several times. First, Kyle texted Littlefield, noting about Routh, "this dude is straight-up nuts." Littlefield replied: "sitting behind me, watch my 6," meaning watch my back. To this request, Kyle replied: "Got it." After the three arrived at the range, the timeline of events is unclear. Sometime between 3:15 and 5:00 P.M., Kyle was shot six times, while Littlefield received five or six bullet wounds, depending on whether one bullet exited and re-entered his body. Both men were dead at the scene, having been shot by two different weapons.

A firearms expert would later opine that Kyle's shooting was an ambush, as he apparently did not see the shooter; his wounds to the upper portion and right side of his body were incapacitating and certainly terminal. Littlefield was shot twice in the back; he was on his knees and unable to move when a third shot to the head spun him around. In the most likely scenario, Littlefield was on his back when the final shots hit him in the top of the head and face. The physical evidence at the scene suggested that all shots had been fired from close range. Routh fled the scene in Kyle's pickup and was later apprehended by local police, after a ten-minute chase, with one of the murder weapons in his possession. In an interview with a Texas Ranger, Routh admitted the shootings. These elements of the crime were essential as the state had to prove that Routh, as the shooter, was capable of knowing the difference between right and wrong, and planning and executing an ambush is an important element in this scenario.

The trial began two years after the shootings occurred. It would become a battle of the experts, as psychiatrists on each side made diametrically different claims as to the mental state of the defendant at the time of the crimes. First, the state, as the party with the burden of proof in this legal action, presented its case-in-chief, which was basically that Routh, with malice of intent and in complete control of his mental faculties, did shoot and kill two human beings, namely Christopher Scott Kyle and Chad Hutson Littlefield. They presented as a "star witness" the Texas Ranger to whom Routh confessed, although, under cross-examination, the Ranger's description of the defendant sounded a bit odd or at least some of Routh's behavior and comments were odd, if not "crazy" sounding. The prosecution also showed the jury a video of Routh during his custodial interview with police investigators, in which Routh described "taking a couple of souls," and claiming he had more to take.

Next, the defense presented a series of character witnesses consisting of family members and friends, who described not only the Routh they knew, but also their impressions of his mental state in February 2013. In addition, a defense psychiatrist explained that Routh had serious mental health issues, including schizophrenia, prior to the homicides. The defense psychiatrist also described how Routh believed that his co-workers were cannibals and had plans to eat him, Routh. The defense's psychiatrist indicated that the defendant was not capable of knowing right from wrong at the time he killed Kyle and Littlefield owing to a severe mental disease or defect.

The state called rebuttal witnesses, its own psychiatrists. The first, who had spent several months observing and communicating with Routh, believed that the defendant's psychotic "symptoms" stemmed from marijuana and alcohol abuse, both of which he ingested on the morning of the crimes. This psychiatrist believed that Routh was faking schizophrenia and was, in fact, suffering paranoid personality disorder (PPD), a non-psychotic disorder that does not qualify as insanity under Texas law. Persons with PPD rarely confide in others, and tend to misinterpret harmless comments and behavior as malicious (Paranoid Personality Disorder [*DSM-5*, 2013]). Moreover, PPD should not be diagnosed with persons suffering from schizophrenia (Schizophrenia Spectrum and Other Psychotic Disorders [*DSM-5*, 2013]), which is why it was important for the prosecution psychiatrist to discount the claim of schizophrenia spectrum disorder with paranoia. This witness, in contrast to the defense psychiatrist, maintained that Routh may have been paranoid, but he was not legally insane under Texas law when he committed the two murders. A second forensic psychiatrist gave a similar opinion, indicating that it was likely the defendant's use of drugs, including alcohol, marijuana laced with formaldehyde, and PCP, helped trigger events. Interestingly, all three psychiatrists agreed that Routh likely did not suffer from PTSD, which was the initial finding of the VA doctors.

After deliberating less than two hours, the jury returned to the courtroom with a verdict. They found the defendant guilty of two counts of capital murder. Routh was sentenced to life in prison without the possibility of parole. Shortly after being committed to the Texas Department of Criminal Justice (TDCJ), Routh was transferred to a prison mental unit for evaluation. He remains in TDCJ custody.

Routh appealed his conviction through Texas's appellate process. He claimed three reversible errors at trial. First, he claimed that the jury's verdict was incorrect because the appellant did not know at the time that he committed the crimes that his actions were wrong. Second, Routh maintained that the trial court acted inappropriately by not granting the defendant's motion to suppress statements made to the Texas Ranger. Finally, Routh claimed the trial court abused its discretion by overruling his request for a mistrial. In 2017, a three-judge panel of Texas's Eleventh District Court of Appeals, after reviewing the claims made by Routh in light of the testimony and evidence, rejected Routh's claims.

It is probably a bad idea, and in some cases even illegal, to put a loaded weapon in the hands of a mentally ill person, especially someone who is clearly suffering from a severe mental disease. In hindsight, these homicides were probably preventable. Indeed, Kyle's and Littlefield's inexperience dealing with profoundly disturbed persons, veterans or otherwise, should play no role in any legal assessment of the events leading up to their deaths. Such observations, no matter how valid, do not clear Routh of culpability in this case. But questions about his mental state at the time he committed the homicides remain unanswered. In seems reasonable, nonetheless, to suggest that the justice system, including its courts, educate itself more fully on a wider range of mental disorders that can impact a person's ability to formulate intent or even competency to stand trial. Experts in varying professional fields have, over the ensuing years, commented on the Routh case. We may yet see more legal machinations concerning military veterans and the definition of debilitating mental disease.

SUMMARY

- The rights of the mentally ill are fundamental human rights.
- There are many international conventions and treaties that address the rights of the mentally ill, but demands tend to outstrip service availability owing to economic reasons.
- An at-risk group is one that, owing to some unique and common characteristics or qualities, which can include mental illness, finds itself subjected to prejudice, discrimination, and violence.
- The history of the United States' treatment of its mentally ill citizens is one of fits and starts to remedy the problem, resulting in healthcare responses that vary widely by state.
- The federal response to mental health concerns has largely been one of creating laws but failing to provide the funding to implement the programs inherent in them.
- Investing in community mental health, for all citizens but especially for vulnerable populations, could reduce our nation's reliance on its prisons and jails as an alternative to mental hospitals.
- Elder mistreatment consists of acts against a person aged 65 or older or the failure to act on behalf of such a person who in some way suffers an injury, loss, or death.
- Elderly persons are victimized by strangers and relatives alike, but the presence of a social support network and educated medical, mental health, and social work professionals can do much to alleviate these problems.

▸ Expanding benefits to offender-veterans and supporting issue-sensitive responses to offender-veterans, such as Veterans Treatment Courts, may help reduce the level of incarceration among the nation's military veterans.

▸ Member of GLBTQ communities are overrepresented as clients of the mental health system, largely owing to the high levels of discrimination, prejudice, and violence directed at them, not just by some members of the public, but also by criminal justice and health care professionals.

▸ Solutions to the victimizations experienced by members of GLBTQ communities lie in expressions of greater tolerance toward those with a different gender identity from one's own, communities that include legal minors as well.

▸ Intolerance also permeates societal responses to the nation's various racial and ethnic minorities, including those by mental health and criminal justice professionals.

▸ Solutions to problems associated with race and ethnicity are elusive; however, full enforcement of existing laws, along with mandatory training and education for criminal justice professionals, would help to reduce discriminatory practices.

KEY TERMS

At-risk groups
Bill for the Benefit of the Indigent Insane
Community Mental Health Act
Convention on the Rights of Persons with
Disabilities
Elder mistreatment
Ethnicity
Ethnic identity
Gender
Gender identity
G.I. Bill
GLBTQ
Hate crimes
Human rights
International Bill of Rights

Medicaid
Mental Health Systems Act
Mental Patients' Bill of Rights
Microaggressions
National Center for Posttraumatic Stress
Disorder
National Mental Health Act
Race
Servicemen's Readjustment Act of 1944
Sexual orientation
Silver Alert
Treatment gap (TG)
Veterans Health Administration (VHA)
Veterans Treatment Courts (VTC)
Wellness checks

CHAPTER REVIEW QUESTIONS

1. What is a human rights issue? How can access to adequate mental healthcare be considered a human rights issue?

2. How have other nations responded to the needs of the mentally ill? How well has the United States responded to these same needs?

3. This chapter is framed in terms of two ideas: human rights and at-risk groups. Define each term and explain how they can help us understand both present and future concerns of the mental health–criminal justice systems intersection.

4. Provide three answers to the following question: Why are certain groups within society described as at-risk? Which answer do you find most compelling and why? Which one is least compelling and why?

5. What is elder mistreatment? How prevalent is this problem? What are some ways it can be addressed and remediated?

6. Military veterans as a group pose few problems for society. A relatively small percentage, however, do encounter both the nation's criminal justice and mental health systems. What is the extent of this problem? What are some ways this problem can be addressed and remediated?

7. Gender identity is a term that some people find controversial. What is the basis for this controversy?

8. Women with mental illnesses can find themselves being treated differently by the mental health system than similarly afflicted men, especially when the criminal justice system is also involved. What is the extent of this problem? What are some ways this problem can be addressed and remediated?

9. Race and ethnicity have long been at the center of a debate in this nation, one that often starts with questions about bias and discrimination in the criminal justice system. Add mental health issues into the mix and to what extent do we see this debate manifesting itself in the nexus between the criminal justice and mental health systems? What are some of the ways this problem can be addressed and remediated?

10. What are the lessons of *State of Texas v. Eddie Ray Rough*? Hindsight is always perfect, but what could have been done differently in this case to avoid such a tragedy?

REFERENCES

Acierno, R., M.A. Hernandez-Tejada, G.J. Anetzberger, D. Loew, and W. Muzzy (2017). "The national elder mistreatment study: An eight-year longitudinal study of outcomes." *Journal of Elder Abuse and Neglect* 29: 254-69.

Acoca, L. (1998). "Defusing the time bomb: Understanding and meeting the growing health care needs of incarcerated women in America." *Crime and Delinquency* 44: 49-69.

Alabama Disabilities Advocacy Program (2004). "*Wyatt v. Stickney*: A landmark decision." Tuscaloosa, AL: Alabama Disabilities Advocacy Program. Retrieved at http://neurosciencecme.com/email/2006/120406landmark.pdf on 29 December 2017.

Alarid, L.F. (2000). "Sexual orientation perspectives of incarcerated bisexual and gay men: The county jail protective custody experience." *The Prison Journal* 80: 80-95.

Alliance on Aging (2003). *Ageism: How Healthcare Fails the Elderly*. Salinas, CA: Alliance on Aging.

Alzheimer's Association (2008). "Alzheimer's Association statement on Silver Alert." Chicago: Alzheimer' Association. Retrieved at https://www.alz.org/news_and_events_14004.asp on 29 December 2017.

American Anthropological Association (1998). "AAA statement on race." Washington, DC: American Anthropological Association. Retrieved at http://www.americananthro.org/ConnectWithAAA/Content.aspx?ItemNumber=2583 on 16 December 2017.

American Association of Retired Persons (2014). "Keeping wanderers safe: Silver Alert." AARP Oregon. Retrieved at https://states.aarp.org/or-wanderers/ on 29 December 2017.

American Medical Association (1994). *Diagnostic and Treatment Guidelines on Elder Abuse and Neglect*. Chicago, IL: American Medical Association.

American Psychiatric Association (1974). *DSM-II*, Sixth Printing. Washington, DC: American Psychiatric Association.

American Psychiatric Association (1987). *DSM-III-R*. Washington, DC: American Psychiatric Association.

American Psychiatric Association (2013). *DSM-5*. Washington, DC: American Psychiatric Association.

American Psychological Association (1987). *Policy Statements on Lesbian and Gay Issues*. Washington, DC: American Psychological Association.

Amirkhanyan, A.A., and D.A. Wolf (2006). "Parent care and the stress process: Findings from panel data." *Journal of Gerontology* 61B: S248-S255.

Amstadter, A.B., A. Moreland Begle, J.M. Cisler, M.A. Hernandez, W. Muzzy, and R. Acierno (2010). "Prevalence and correlates of poor self-related health in the United States: The National Elder Mistreatment Study." *American Journal of Geriatric Psychiatry* 18: 615-23.

Bardach, S.H., and G.D. Rowles (2012). "Geriatric education in the health professions: Are we making progress?" *The Gerontologist* 52: 607-18.

Bennett, M.J. (2000). *When Dreams Came True: The G.I. Bill and the Making of Modern America*. New York: Brassey's Inc.

Bhui, K. (2016). "Discrimination, poor mental health, and mental illness." *International Review of Psychiatry* 28: 411-4.

Bhurga, D., and O. Ayonrinde (2001). "Racism, racial life events and mental ill health." *Advances in Psychiatric Treatment* 7: 343-9.

Blasco, A. (2014). *The Costs of the Iraq, Afghanistan, and Other Global War on Terror Operations since 9/11*. Washington, DC: Congressional Research Service.

Bloom, B.E., and S.S. Covington (2008). "Addressing the mental health needs of women offenders." Pp. 160-176 in R. Gido and L. Dalley (eds.), *Women's Mental Health Issues Across the Criminal Justice System*. Upper Saddle River, NJ: Pearson/Prentice-Hall.

Blue-Howells, J.H., S.C. Clark, C. Van den Berk-Clark, and J.F. McGuire (2013). "The U.S. Department of Veterans Affairs Veterans Justice Programs and Sequential Intercept Model: Case examples in national dissemination of intervention for justice-involved veterans." *Psychological Services* 10: 48-53.

Bond, J., and S. Turner (2002). "Going to war and going to college: Did World War II and the G.I. Bill increase educational attainment for returning veterans?" *Journal of Labor Economics* 20: 784-815.

Bronson, J., E.A. Carson, M. Noonan, and M. Berzofsky (2015). "Veterans in prison and jail, 2011-12." Washington, DC: U.S. Department of Justice.

Carr, D., G.W. Muschert, J. Kinney, E. Robbins, G. Petonito, L. Manning, and J.S. Brown (2009). "Silver alerts and the problem of missing adults with dementia." *The Gerontologist* 50: 149-57.

Choi, S.K., B.D.M. Wilson, J. Shelton, and G. Gates (2015). *Serving Our Youth 2015: The Needs and Experiences of Lesbian, Gay, Bisexual, Transgender, and Questioning Youth Experiencing Homelessness*. Los Angeles: The Williams Institute with True Colors Fund.

Clark, P.A. (2009). "Prejudice and the medical profession: A five-year update." *Journal of Law, Medicine and Ethics* 37: 118-33.

Coker, T.R., S.B. Austin, and M.A. Schuster (2010). "The health and health care of lesbian, gay, and bisexual adolescents." *Annual Review of Public Health* 31: 457-77.

Comijs, H.C., B.W.J.H. Penninx, K.P.M. Kniperscheer, and W. van Tilburg (1999). "Psychological distress in victims of elder mistreatment: The effects of social support and coping." *Journal of Gerontology* 54B: P240-P245.

Committee to Review the Health Effects in Vietnam Veterans of Exposure to Herbicides (1994). *Veterans and Agent Orange: Health Effects of Herbicides Used in Vietnam*. Washington, DC: National Academy Press.

Covington, S.S., and B. Bloom (2007). "Gender responsiveness treatment and services in correctional settings." *Women and Therapy* 29: 9-33.

Cramer, R.J., D.E. McNiel, S.R. Holley, M. Shumway, and A. Boccellari (2011). "Mental health in violent crime victims: Does sexual orientation matter?" *Law and Human Behavior* 36: 87-95.

Davis, K., K. Stremikis, D. Squires, and C. Schoen (2014). "Mirror, mirror on the wall: How the performance of the U.S. health care system compares internationally." New York: The Commonwealth Fund. Retrieved at http://www.commonwealthfund.org/publications/fund-reports/2014/jun/mirror-mirror on 30 December 2017.

Davis, T.D., T. Deen, K. Bryant-Bedell, V. Tate, and J. Fortney (2011). "Does minority racial-ethnic status moderate outcomes of collaborative care for depression?" *Psychiatric Services* 62: 1292-8.

Department of the Army (2009). *Field Manual No. 6-22.5. Combat and Operational Stress Control Manual for Leaders and Soldiers*. Washington, DC: Department of the Army.

Dieter, R.C. (2015). *Battle Scars: Military Veterans and the Death Penalty*. Washington, DC: Death Penalty Information Center.

Dong, X. (2005). "Medical implications of elder abuse and neglect." *Clinics in Geriatric Medicine* 21: 293-313.

Dowell, D.A., and J.A. Ciarlo (1983). "Overview of the Community Mental Health Centers Program from an Evaluation Perspective." *Community Mental Health Journal* 19: 95-128.

Dworkin, S.H., and H. Yi (2003). "LGBT identity, violence, and social justice: The psychological is political." *International Journal for the Advancement of Counseling* 24: 269-79.

Eliason, M.J., and P.L. Chinn (2015). *LGBTQ Cultures: What Health Care Professionals Need to Know About Sexual Identity and Gender Diversity*. Philadelphia, PA: Wolters Kluwer.

Flatley, B., S. Clark, J. Rosenthal, and J. Blue-Howells (2017). "Veterans court inventory 2016 update: Characteristics of and VA involvement in Veterans Treatment Courts and other veterans-focused court programs from the Veterans Justice Outreach Specialist Perspective." Washington, DC: U.S. Department of Veterans Affairs, Veterans Health Administration.

Fleischer, D., and F. Zames (2001). *The Disability Rights Movement: From Charity to Confrontation*. Philadelphia: Temple University Press.

Gates, G.J. (2017). "In the U.S., more adults identifying as GLBT." Washington, DC: Gallup Management Consultation Co. Retrieved at http://news.gallup.com/poll/201731/lgbt-identification-rises.aspx on 16 December 2017.

Gergerich, E., and L. Davis (2017). "Silver alerts: A notification system for communities with missing adults." *Journal of Gerontological Social Work* 60: 232-44.

Gonzales, L., K.C. Davidoff, K.L. Nadal, and P.T. Yanos (2015). "Microaggression experienced by persons with mental illness." *Psychiatric Rehabilitation Journal* 38: 234-41.

Greater Hartford Legal Aid (2015). "Jury selection and anti-LGBT bias: Best practices in LGBT-related Voir Dire and jury matters. Hartford, CT: Greater Hartford Legal Aid. Retrieved at http://www.lambdalegal.org/sites/default/files/jury-selection-dec2015_final.pdf on 14 December 2017.

Grisham, L. (June 1, 2015). "What does the Q in GLBTQ stand for?" *USA Today News Network*. Retrieved at https://www.usatoday.com/story/news/nation-now/2015/06/01/lgbtq-questioning-queer-meaning/26925563/ on 14 December 2017.

Hartwell, S.W., A. James, J. Chen, D.A. Pinals, M.C. Marin, and D. Smelson (2013). "Trauma among justice-involved veterans." *Professional Psychology: Research and Practice* 45: 435-32.

Haas, A.P., M. Eliason, V.M. Mays, et al. (2011). "Suicide and suicide risk in lesbian, gay, bisexual, and transgender populations: Review and recommendations." *Journal of Homosexuality* 58: 10-51.

Hein, L.C., and K.M. Scharer (2012). "Who cares if it is a hate crime? Lesbian, gay, bisexual, and transgender hate crimes—Mental health implications and intervention." *Perspectives in Psychiatric Care* 49: 84-93.

Helderman, R.S. (December 13, 2012). "Senate rejects treaty to protect disabled around the world." *The Washington Post*. Retrieved at https://web.archive.org/web/20130921055440/https://articles.washingtonpost.com/2012-12-04/

politics/35624605_1_treaty-disabled-children-americans-with-disabilities-act on 30 December 2017.

Herek, G.M., and L.D. Garnets (2006). "Sexual orientation and mental health." *Annual Review of Clinical Psychology* 3: 335-75.

Herman, E. (1995). *The National Mental Health Act of 1946*. Berkeley, CA: University of California Press.

Higashi, R.T., A.A. Tillack, M. Steinman, H. Harper, and C.B. Johnston (2012). "Elder care as 'frustrating' and 'boring': Understanding the persistence of negative attitudes toward older patients among physicians-in-training." *Journal of Aging Studies* 26: 476-83.

Hill, J.M. (2000). "The effects of sexual orientation in the courtroom: A double standard." *Journal of Homosexuality* 39: 93-111.

Hoberman, J. (2012). *Black and Blue: The Origins and Consequences of Medical Racism*. Berkeley, CA: University of California Press.

Hohmann, A.A. (1989). "Gender bias in psychotropic drug prescribing in primary care." *Medical Care* 27: 478-90.

Jugdutt, B.I. (2016). "Changing demographics of the aging population with heart failure and implications for therapy." Chapter 1 in B.I. Jugdutt (ed.), *Aging and Heart Failure: Mechanisms and Management*. New York: Springer.

Kale, R. (2002). "The treatment gap." *Epilepsia* 43(Suppl.): 31-33.

Keita, S.O.Y., R.A. Kittles, C.D.M. Royal, G.E. Bonney, P. Furbert-Harris, G.M. Dunston, and C.N. Rotimi. (2004). "Conceptualizing human variation." *Nature Genetics Supplement* 36: S17-S20.

Kennedy, R.D. (2005). "Elder abuse and neglect: The experience, knowledge, and attitudes of primary care physicians." *Family Medicine* 37: 481-5.

Kessler, R.C., K.D. Mickelson, and D.R. Williams (1999). "The prevalence, distribution, and mental health correlates of perceived discrimination in the United States." *Journal of Health and Social Behavior* 40: 208-30.

King, P.A. (1992). "The dangers of indifference." *The Hastings Center Report* 22: 35.8.

Knudsen, K.J., and S. Wingenfeld (2015). "A specialized treatment court for veterans with trauma exposure: Implications for the field." *Community Mental Health Journal* 52: 127-35.

Kristjansson, S.R., and T.B. Wyler (2010). "Introduction." Chapter 1 in D. Schrijvers, M. Aapro, B. Zabotnik, R. Audisio, H. van Halteren, and A. Hurria (eds.), *Handbook of Cancer in Senior Patients*. Boca Raton, FL: CRC Press.

Kyle, C., and J. De Felice (2012). *American Sniper: The Autobiography of the Most Lethal Sniper in U.S. Military History*. New York, NY: William Morrow and Co.

Lachs, M.S., C.S. Williams, S. O'Brien, K.A. Pillemer, and M.E. Charlson (1998). "The mortality of elder mistreatment." *Journal of the American Medical Association* 280: 428-32.

Lamothe, D. (February 12, 2015). "The fatal intersection of Navy SEAL Chris Kyle and the Marine veteran who killed him." *The Washington Post*. Retrieved at https://www.washingtonpost.com/news/checkpoint/wp/2015/02/13/first-days-of-american-sniper-murder-trial-leave-questions-unanswered/?utm_term=.82b9e08ed775 on 12 December 2017.

Mather, M., L.A. Jacobsen, and K.M. Pollard (2015). *Aging in the United States*. Volume 70, No. 2. Washington, DC: Population Reference Bureau.

Mental Health America (2017a). "The State of Mental Health in America." Mental Health America. Arlington, VA: Mental Health America. Retrieved at http://www.mentalhealthamerica.net/issues/state-mental-health-america#Key on 30 December 2017.

Mental Health America (2017b). *The State of Mental Health in America 2017*. Alexandria, VA: Mental Health America.

McInnis-Dittrich, K. (2014). *Social Work with Older Adults: A Biopsychological Approach to Assessment and Intervention*. 4th ed. London: Pearson.

Mechanic, D., and D.A. Rochefort (1990). "Deinstitutionalization: An appraisal of reform." *Annual Review of Sociology* 16: 301-27.

Mills, C. (2013). *Decolonizing Global Mental Health: The Psychiatrization of the Major World*. Abingdon, UK: Routledge.

Mustanski, B.S., R. Garofalo, E.M. Emerson (2010). "Suicidality in a diverse sample of lesbian, gay, bisexual, and transgender youths." *American Journal of Public Health* 100: 2426-32.

Nadal, K.L., M-A Issa, J. Leon, V. Meterko, M. Wideman, and Y. Wong (2011). "Sexual orientation microaggressions: 'Death by a thousand cuts' for lesbian, gay, and bisexual youth." *Journal of LGBT Youth* 8: 234-59.

Ngui, E.M., L. Khasakhala, D. Nhetei, and L.W. Roberts (2010). "Mental disorders, health inequalities and ethnics: A global perspective." *International Review of Psychiatry* 22: 235-44.

Office of Management and Budget (1997). *Recommendations from the Interagency Committee for the Review of the Racial and Ethnic Standards to the Office of Management and Budget Concerning Changes to the Standards for the Classification of Federal Data on Race and Ethnicity*. Washington, DC: Federal Register. Retrieved at https://www.whitehouse.gov/sites/whitehouse.gov/files/omb/federal_register/FR199/ombdir15.pdf on 20 December 2017.

Office of the Surgeon General (2001). *Mental health: Culture, Race, and Ethnicity*. Washington, DC: Office of the Surgeon General.

O'Hara, M. (2014). "Mental health and race — the blight of dual discrimination." *The Guardian*. Retrieved at https://www.theguardian.com/society/2014/mar/26/black-minority-ethnic-mental-health-dual-discrimination on 20 December 2017.

Olson, K. (1974). *The G.I. Bill, the Veterans, and the Colleges*. Lexington, KY: University of Kentucky Press.

Orimo, H., J. Ito, T. Suzuki, A. Araki, T. Hosoi, and M. Sawabe (2006). "Reviewing the definition of 'elderly.'" *Geriatrics and Gerontology International* 6: 149-158.

Pascoe, E.A., and L. Smart Richman (2009). "Perceived discrimination and health: A meta-analytic review. *Psychological Bulletin* 135: 531-54.

Patel, V., M. Maj, A.J. Flisher, M.J. De Silva, M. Koschorke, M. Prince, and WPA Zonal and Member Society Representatives (2010). "Reducing the treatment gap for mental disorders: A WPA survey." *Word Psychiatry* 9: 169-76.

Perlin, M.L. (2009). "'A change is gonna come': The implications of the United Nations Convention on the Rights of Persons with Disabilities for domestic practice of constitutional mental disability law." *Northern Illinois University Law Review* 29: 483-98.

Perry, B.L., M. Neltner, and T. Allen (2013). "A paradox of bias: Racial differences in forensic psychiatric diagnosis and determinations of criminal responsibility." *Race and Social Problems* 5: 239-49.

Phelan, S.M., J.F. Dovidio, P.M. Puhl, D.J. Burgess, D.B. Nelson, M.W. Yeazel, R. Hardeman, S. Perry, and M. van Ryn (2014). "Implicit and explicit weight bias in a national sample of 4,732 medical students: The medical student CHANGES study." *Obesity: A Research Journal* 22: 1201-1208.

Pilkington, N.W., and A.R. D'Auguelli (1995). "Victimization of lesbian, gay, and bisexual youth in community settings." *Journal of Community Health* 23: 34-56.

Robinson, R.K. (2011). "Masculinity as prison: sexual identity, race, and incarceration." *California Law Review* 99: 1309-1409.

Ruiz, R. (2013). "Report: A million veterans injured in Iraq, Afghanistan wars." Forbes (November 4). Retrieved at https://www.forbes.com/sites/rebeccaruiz/2013/11/04/report-a-million-veterans-injured-in-iraq-afghanistan-wars/#17d7a6d06810 on 18 December 2017.

Rüsch, N., K. Lieb, M. Bohus, and P.W. Corrigan (2006). "Self-stigma, empowerment, and perceived legitimacy of discrimination among women with mental illness." *Psychiatric Services* 57: 399-402.

Russell, S.T., and J.N. Fish (2016). "Mental health in lesbian, gays, bisexual, and transgender (LGBT) youth." *Annual Review of Clinical Psychology* 12: 465-87.

Schatell, E. (2017). "Challenging multicultural disparities in mental health." Arlington, VA: National Alliance on Mental Illness. Retrieved at https://www.nami.org/Blogs/NAMI-Blog/July-2017/Challenging-Multicultural-Disparities-in-Mental-He on 29 December 2017.

Kraus, S.W., and L.L. Ragatz (2011). "Gender, jury instructions, and homophobia: What influence do these factors have on legal decision making in a homicide case where the defendant utilized the homosexual panic defense?" *Criminal Law Bulletin* 47: 237-56.

Shapiro, E. (February 20, 2015). "'American Sniper' trial: Eddie Ray Routh knew his actions were wrong, psychologist says." *ABC News*. Retrieved at http://abcnews.go.com/US/american-sniper-trial-eddie-ray-routh-knew-actions/story?id=29100358 on 12 December 2017.

Shephard, B. (2000). *A War of Nerves: Soldiers and Psychiatrists, 1914-1994*. London: Jonathan Cape.

Singh, S., and B. Bajorek (2014). "Defining 'elderly' in clinical practice guidelines for pharmacotherapy." *Pharmacy Practice* 12: 489. Retrieved at https://www.ncbi.nlm.nih.gov/pmc/articles/PMC4282767/pdf/pharmpract-12-489.pdf on 7 December 2017.

Smith, M. (October 20, 2013). "50 years later, Kennedy's vision for mental health not realized." *The Seattle Times*. Retrieved at https://web.archive.org/

web/20131023010233/http://seattletimes.com/html/nationworld/2022091710_
mentalhealthxml.html on 30 December 2017.

Smith, T.B., and J.E. Trimble (2016). *Foundations of Multicultural Psychology: Research to Inform Effective Practice*. Washington, DC: American Psychological Association.

Spiegel, P.B., F. Checchi, S. Colombo, and E. Paik (2010). "Health-care needs of people affected by conflict: Future trends and changing frameworks." *Lancet* 375: 341-5.

Spies, M. (November 23, 2015a). "Inside the tortured mind of Eddie Ray Routh, the man who killed American sniper Chris Kyle." *Newsweek*. Retrieved at http://www.newsweek.com/2016/01/08/inside-tortured-mind-man-who-killed-american-sniper-chris-kyle-397299.html on 12 December 2017.

Spies, M. (November 23, 2015b). "The undoing of Eddie Ray Routh." *The Trace*. Retrieved at https://www.thetrace.org/2015/11/chris-kyle-american-sniper-murder-eddie-routh-mental-records/ on 12 December 2017.

Stiglitz, J.E., and L.J. Bilmes (2008). *The Three Trillion Dollar War*. New York: W.W. Norton.

Sugie, N.F., and K. Turney (2017). "Beyond incarceration: Criminal justice contact and mental health." *American Sociological Review* 82: 719-43.

Suman, F. (2010). *Mental Health, Race and Culture*. 3rd ed. Basingstoke, Hampshire, UK: Palgrave-MacMillan.

Suman, F. (January 8, 2010). "The Americanization of mental illness." *New York Times Magazine*. Retrieved at http://www.nytimes.com/2010/01/10/magazine/10psyche-t.html on 3 December 2017.

Suman, F. (2014). *Mental Health Worldwide: Culture, Globalization and Development*. Basingstoke, Hampshire, UK: Palgrave MacMillan.

Trotta, D. (March 14, 2013). "Iraq war costs U.S. More than $2 trillion: Study." Reuters. Retrieved at https://www.reuters.com/article/us-iraq-war-anniversary/iraq-war-costs-u-s-more-than-2-trillion-study-idUSBRE92D0PG20130314 on 18 December 2017.

Turrentine, F.E., H. Wang, V.B. Simpson, and R.S. Jones (2006). "Surgical risk factors, morbidity, and mortality in elderly patients." *Journal of the American College of Surgeons* 203: 865-77.

United Nations (n.d.). "Human Rights." New York: United Nations. Retrieved at http://www.un.org/en/sections/issues-depth/human-rights/ on 12 December 2017.

United Nations (1948). *Universal Declaration of Human Rights*. Paris, FR: United Nations. Retrieved at http://www.un.org/en/universal-declaration-human-rights/index.html onn 16 December 2017.

United Nations (2008). *Convention on the Rights of Persons with Disabilities and Optional Protocol*. New York: United Nations.

United Nations (2017). "Chapter IV. Human Rights." New York: United Nations. Retrieved at https://treaties.un.org/Pages/ViewDetails.aspx?src=TREATY&mtdsg_no=IV-15&chapter=4&clang=_en on 30 December 2017.

U.S. Census Bureau (2017a). "Facts and figures: Older Americans month." Washington, DC: U.S. Census Bureau.

U.S. Census Bureau (2017b). "Sex by age by veteran status for the civilian population 18 years and over." Washington, DC: U.S. Census Bureau. Retrieved at https://factfinder.census.gov/faces/tableservices/jsf/pages/productview.xhtml?pid=ACS_15_1YR_B21001 on 18 December 2017.

U.S. Census Bureau (2017c). *Subjects Planned for the 2020 Census and American Community Survey*. Washington, DC: U.S. Census Bureau.

U.S. Government Accountability Office (2017). DOD Health: Actions Needs to Ensure Post-Traumatic Stress Disorder and Traumatic Brain Injury Are Considered in Misconduct Separations. Washington, DC: U.S. Government Accountability Office.

Veterans Administration (n.d.). "About the VA." Washington, DC: U.S. Department of Veterans Affairs. Retrieved at https://www.va.gov/about_va/vahistory.asp on 27 December 2017.

Veterans Administration (2015). "Benefits Assistance Service (BAS): Incarcerated veterans." Washington, DC: U.S. Department of Veterans Affairs. Retrieved at https://www.benefits.va.gov/BENEFITS/factsheets/misc/incarcerated.pdf on 31 December 2017.

Veterans Administration (2017a). "Traumatic brain injury and PTSD: Focus on veterans." Washington, DC: U.S. Department of Veterans Affairs. Retrieved at https://www.ptsd.va.gov/professional/co-occurring/traumatic-brain-injury-ptsd.asp on 29 December 2017.

Veterans Administration (2017b). "Emergent mental health care for former service members." Fact Sheets. Washington, DC: U.S. Department of Veterans Affairs. Retrieved at https://www.mentalhealth.va.gov/docs/Fact_Sheet-Emergent_Mental_Health_Care_Former_Service_Members.pdf on 27 December 2017.

Veterans Administration (2017c). *Women's Mental Health. National Center for PTSD: Fiscal Year 2016 Annual Report*. Washington, DC: U.S. Department of Veterans Affairs, National Center for PTSD.

Walker, S., C. Spohn, and M. DeLone (2018). *The Color of Justice: Race, Ethnicity, and Crime in America*. Boston, MA: Cengage Learning.

Watters, E. (2011). *Crazy Like Us: The Globalization of the Western Mind*. London: Robinson.

Whitbeck, L.B., X. Chen, D.R. Hoyt, K. Tyler, and K.D. Johnson (2004). "Mental disorder, subsistence strategies, and victimization among gay, lesbian, and bisexual homeless and runaway adolescents." *Journal of Sex Research* 41: 329-42.

White, B.H., and S.E. Robinson Kurpius (2002). "Effects of victim sex and sexual orientation on perceptions of rape." *Sex Roles* 46: 191-200.

Wolff, K.B., and C.L. Cokely (2007). "'To Protect and to Serve?': An exploration of police conduct in relation to the gay, lesbian, bisexual, and transgender community." *Sexuality and Culture* 11: 1-23.

Wang, H.L. (2017). "U.S. Census to leave sexual orientation, gender identity questions off new surveys." National Public Radio. Retrieved at https://www.npr.org/sections/

thetwo-way/2017/03/29/521921287/u-s-census-to-leave-sexual-orientation-gender-identity-questions-off-new-surveys on 16 December 2017.

World Bank (2017a). "Population, ages 65 and over (% of total)." Washington, DC: The World Bank. Retrieved at https://data.worldbank.org/indicator/SP.POP.65UP.TO.ZS on 17 December 2017.

World Bank (2017b). "Population, female (% of total)" Washington, DC: The World Bank. Retrieved at https://data.worldbank.org/indicator/SP.POP.TOTL.FE.ZS on 15 December 2017.

World Health Organization (2002). "Gender and mental health." Geneva, CH: World Health Organization. Retrieved at http://apps.who.int/iris/bitstream/10665/68884/1/a85573.pdf on 17 December.

World Health Organization (2015). *World Health Atlas*. New York: United Nations.

CASES

Eddie Ray Routh v. State of Texas, No. 11-15-00036-CR (2017)

Wyatt v. Stickney, 325 F. Supp. 761 (M.D. Ala. 1971)

LEGISLATION

42 U.S.C. §9501 — Bill of Rights (Pub. L. No. 96-398, title V, §501, Oct. 7, 1980, 94 Stat. 1598)

Public Law 79-487 (National Mental Health Act, 1946)

Public Law 88-164 (Community Mental Health Act, 1963)

Public Law 96-398 (Mental Health Systems Act, 1980)

Public Law 346-268 (Servicemen's Readjustment Act, 1944)

Afterword

Throughout this book we have given you numerous examples of problems, people, and perceptions in the context of criminal justice and mental health treatment. We have asked you to learn and then apply knowledge, experience, and your imagination to try and understand, if not resolve, issues for people who have mental illness. Clearly, each situation is as unique as the person who has the mental health disability or disease. We know now that mental illness is not new to our society, and that the public's reaction — be it compassion or resentment — to those with mental illness is a constant, unpredictable force.

Now that you have an awareness of the possible solutions for and unintended consequences that can emerge from encounters with a person with a mental illness, disease, or disability, what happens next? Any training program or treatment is only as effective as the person receiving it. What is expected of you now? We know that police will be expected to continue to detain and arrest people in mental crisis because there are few feasible community alternatives. We know that jails and juvenile detention facilities are unable to provide mental health care or treatment, nor should they be used as holding facilities for a mentally disturbed person. We know that people with mental illness will likely be mistreated or abused unless segregated from the general prison population and that segregation usually means isolation, solitary confinement, degrading protective nudity, and dehumanizing custodial observations. We know that most "cures" for mental health illnesses are temporary and last only as long as the medication, treatment, or counseling are effectively used. We know these things because the research conducted for this book did not indicate any realistic options other than criminalization for aberrant behavior or release with little or no restraint into the community. There are a few exceptional programs for counseling and treatment, but institutionalization is, was, and remains the norm for the mentally ill.

In addition, you learned in this book that the onset of a mental health episode is never predictable and that this reality presents specific challenges for police officers and other first responders. What may seem like an innocent, offhand, or even everyday occurrence can trigger a bizarre or even a violent response in a stranger or even a familiar person in your assignment region. Mental illness doesn't follow a pattern like a viral illness, such as a cold. A cold starts with a sneeze, and then maybe a fever develops, or aches and pains emerge, but the symptoms eventually will subside. Regardless of who the person with the cold is, the virus follows a common, recognizable pattern. In contrast, there is no predictable pattern for mental denigration or disintegration. Your responsibility as a skilled professional is to respond to the behavior using the tools you learned to anticipate conduct and exercise compassion, rather than fall back on a reaction that may be flawed or indicative of prejudice towards mental health. It is our hope that by learning about different types of conduct, diseases, and community solutions, you can become a proponent of compassionate and responsible services. Although you cannot predict the course of the disease, you can help treat it. Maybe one day, when we find a cure for the cold, there will also be a cure for mental illnesses.

Using the criminal justice system as the door to mental health treatment places a great burden on state and local resources, especially on budgets and personnel. Given the aberrant behavior of a mentally ill person, private insurance through employment or family care coverage is often unavailable or exhausted. While there are local, state, and federal allocations for treatment, this book has informed you of the imbalance between the demand for and the availability of services.

Today, the criminal justice system is like the locks and dams of a canal waterway: It passes its cargo — the offenders — through the penal system, into the community, and back again directed by little more than gravitational flow. As with the current of the canal waters, the release at the end of the criminal justice system does little more than transfer people, like cargo containers, from one end to the other. The sad reality is that while a mentally ill person is detained in a jail without medication or treatment, recovery is unlikely, if not impossible.

There are hopeful programs out there, like the CIT interventional education and training program, that instill the use of patience and compassion instead of weapons and deadly force. Greater training will eventually be the standard for all law enforcement officers, rather than the exception. Higher educational requirements, competitive salaries, and more internal personality aptitudes for professionals seeking police work will eventually pay off. The community investment in having qualified people, such as yourself, who are directed by a willingness to learn about the issues affecting the mentally ill and not by the use of legal force will help communities reach realistic goals for the reduction of violent confrontations. The more training that is provided and available to predict better responses, the more likely it is that an officer and an accused can avoid and prevent trigger-quick reactions in an emergency. In an escalating, deadly confrontation, knowledge and thoughtful reactions can turn a tragic and public loss into a publically acceptable and plausible solution.

Understanding the different forms of mental disease is only the first step in your preparation. You also need to anticipate the best practices to handle particular types of behavior. As a result of reading and applying the material in this book, we hope that your ability to recognize the uniqueness of mental illness will enable you to react proactively in these situations.

The authors of this book and other researchers in criminal justice have the responsibility to continue to focus on solutions. Throughout the book, we have reviewed programs and projects that may be available in a community. This is a call for action: Find out what future plans are available for law enforcement officers who become engaged with the mentally ill in your town or school. Although there are many projects and programs throughout this book and throughout the country, it is hoped that you will develop new ones or improve existing services. The following section lists a few suggestions for future development.

A FEW IDEAS

First, there is the increased use of TASERs, an electronic control device (ECD) that uses disabling jolts of electricity to temporarily stun the target involved in a violent confrontation. The use of ECDs is rapidly replacing soft, empty-hand tactics or pushing on a resistant person, and has been shown to reduce injuries by 60 percent in more than 24,000 cases (Wihbey 2015). ECDs may eventually replace deadly weapons in situations in which an officer recognizes that the suspect may be mentally ill. The rate of injury from ECDs suggests a need for balance between using TASERs, voice, and physical control, but ECDs are, nevertheless, preferable over the death of the target or officer.

By enabling families and responders to immediately reverse the death grip of the drugs, the drug addict/survivor may be able to get treatment and eventually recover. This proactive intervention is certainly another tactic that should be considered by future responders. This second, separate, solution for you to consider was raised in an advisory issued by the United States Surgeon General Jerome Adams in April, 2018. Due to high incidents of illegal opioids, such as heroin and fentanyl, Adams directed health care practitioners, family members, and first responders to have Naloxone, an overdose-reversing medication, available for immediate injection. The Surgeon General declared that a standard issue of naloxone should be readily available to manage a person dying from an opiate overdose. This proactive intervention for law enforcement and responders may save a life. The number of overdose deaths from illicit opioids and prescription medications doubled from 21,089 in 2010 to 42,249 in 2016. (U.S. Department of Health and Human Services 2018). Illegal substances exacerbate mental health disorders and personal chaos. (Scutti and Jimison 2018).

A third solution that emerges is the need for education and treatment as early as possible. Recognizing that mental health interventions can interrupt familial and individual cycles of mental illness is a critical responsibility of a community. Teachers have the ability to recognize problems and articulate concern when a child is exhibiting unusual behaviors associated with mental illness. With proactive changes in current regulations, teachers, with the assistance of first and second responders, should be able to engage in proactive referral, recommendations, and requests for mental health counseling without being stymied by regulations or parental indifference or obstacles.

Finally, legal responsibility to compensate for physical loss, damages, and injuries currently falls to local cities and towns. As we learned, the losses are often paid as a civil wrong after the deadly shooting by the police officer against an unarmed individual. The expansion of shared financial responsibility to drug companies and to weapons manufacturers is likely in the future. Also, as officers engage in more thorough, proactive, and intervention-based training, the imposition of liability could lessen. By providing evidence of using a high standard of care, the accusation of carelessness or indifference can be negated.

We have told you many stories that illustrate our message throughout this book. The passages are intended as a source of dimensional learning, demonstrating how facts can apply to legal theories and principles. Let's consider a final parable, a retelling of the Hans Christian Anderson story, "The Emperor's New Clothes."

> Long ago, a wealthy, vain emperor stated that he must be dressed in only the finest clothes in all of the land. Although his people were hungry and wore rags, he insisted that his clothes be made of gold and silk. One day two thieves came to the royal court and convinced the emperor that they were the finest weavers and tailors in a distant country. The held up clothes and garments, so they said, but there was actually nothing in their arms or hands but air and buffoonery. The emperor, afraid of seeming like a fool because he could not see their fine wares, loudly admired their invisible handiwork. The thieves insisted he pay them thousands of gold coins for their work. The emperor then insisted there be a parade for him to wear his finery. He walked through the streets completely naked, convinced that the clothes he wore were the finest that everyone, but him, could see. No one in the village dared contradict the emperor; they just averted their eyes. Finally one child said, "Why the emperor is not wearing any clothes? He's naked." The crowd drew in their breaths, expecting the emperor to punish her. Instead, he knelt next to her and said embarrassment, "You alone tell the truth. You are right. I am a fool."

Today, we may try to pretend that our mental health system treats everyone well and fairly. The naked truth is that our systems are failing and people are without adequate services. It is your job to see this and to say that the "emperor is not wearing clothes...": that our criminal justice system, together with our mental health services, need attention and coverage.

None of us know what future solutions may emerge, but we urge you to follow the words of Mahatma Gandhi and "be the change that you wish to see in the world." The power for change lies within each of you.

Anne Segal, Tom Winfree, Stan Friedman

REFERENCES

Scutti, S., and R. Jimison (2018). "Surgeon general urges more Americans to carry opioid antidote naloxone," CNN April 5, 2018. Retrieved at https://www.cnn.com/2018/04/05/health/surgeon-general-naloxone/index.html 5 April 2018.

United States Department of Health and Human Services (2018). "Surgeon General's Advisory on Naloxone and Opioid Overdose." Friday, April 6, 2018. Retrieved at https://www.surgeongeneral.gov/priorities/opioid-overdose-prevention/naloxone-advisory.html 6 April 2018.

Wihbey, J. (2018). "U. S. Department of Justice: Police use of force, Tasers and other weapons," Journalist's Resource. Retrieved at https://journalistsresource.org/studies/government/criminal-justice/u-s-department-of-justice-police-use-of-force-tasers-and-other-less-lethal-weapons 6 April 2018.

Glossary

Acts of delinquency: Juvenile terminology that refers to the acts of a person under the age of 18 years of age observed committing what for an adult would be a criminal offense, such as acts of stealing, consuming controlled substances, battery, and other violations of criminal laws.

Acute disability: A chronic, long-term mental illness, disease, or disorder that causes a such a constant state of personal chaos and loss that an individual is unable to care for himself or poses a danger to others.

Administrative segregation: A 22- to 23-hour-a-day version of solitary confinement; a means of prisoner control.

Admission and Orientation Program: A technique employed by the Federal Bureau of Prisons and other state prison systems that allows new inmates to learn the rules of prison life before being placed in the institution's general population.

Age of Reason: An 18th century movement that emphasized the pursuit of knowledge, especially about the ways that "man" viewed his place in the universe; includes the shorter historical period known as the Age of Enlightenment, which emphasized scientific thought and exploration.

Alzheimer's disease: A progressive form of dementia associated with the aging process, but which also can result from various forms of brain injury; associated with loss of memory, personality changes, and impaired reasoning.

Amnestic disorder: A memory disorder, characterized by the inability to create new memories, often associated with chronic alcohol dependence.

Animal Hoarding: The accumulation of an inappropriate ratio of animals to humans in a household by a person who (1) accumulates a large number of deteriorating animals or has more than a typical number of companion animals, and (2) fails to provide minimal standards of care within the environment. The human is essentially oblivious of the negative effect on personal health.

Antisocial personality disorder: A diagnosis for individuals who antagonize, manipulate, or behave harshly or with callous indifference towards others; shows no remorse. See, psychopathy and sociopathy.

Asylums: A formal institution, used extensively beginning in the Age of Reason, that provided shelter and support for the mentally ill, but often under conditions of neglect and abuse.

At-risk population: An identifiable group of individuals whose members, owing to some unique and common characteristics or qualities, including but not limited to mental illness, find themselves in precarious or dangerous situations.

Attention Deficit/Hyperactivity Disorder (ADHD): A neurodevelopmental mental disorder; characteristics include difficulty paying attention, excessive activity, and poor impulse control; symptoms occur prior to the age of 12 years.

Autism spectrum disorder: A name for a cluster of developmental disorders characterized by difficulties communicating and interacting with others but with a wide range of symptoms, skills, and levels of disability; begins in early childhood and is lifelong.

Availability samples: Also called convenience samples, these are groups of individuals that constitute readily accessible and willing participants in a research project and from whom data are collected.

Bedlam: Refers to the Bethlem Royal Hospital in London, which was an early psychiatric hospital and is now a modern psychiatric facility; its nickname became a term used to refer to a place of chaos and madness.

Bill for the Benefit of the Indigent Insane: An act of the U.S. Congress in 1854 that would have put aside 10 million acres, whose sale would benefit the mentally ill; the bill never became law. The first such legislative attempt to aid the mentally ill.

Biocriminology: A cross-over subdiscipline in criminology that looks at crime through the amalgamated lenses of biology, genetics, and biochemistry.

Bipolar disorder: A complicated cluster of mental diseases existing in several forms, all of which have radical shifts in mood, ranging from "up" or energized periods (i.e., manic episodes) to "down" or hopeless periods (depressive episodes).

Brain: The organ, psychologically separate from the human mind, that physiologically controls the function of the human body and regulates how and when the body responds to voluntary and involuntary cognitive directions.

Brief Jail Mental Health Screen (BJMHS): An eight-item, paper-and-pencil test given to new jail inmates that is intended to distinguish DSM-IV, Axis I mental disorder (i.e., serious mental illness) from general distress.

Canon Law: Ecclesiastical, or church, law but especially the law laid down in the Roman Catholic Church in the name of the pope.

Carbohydrates: Chemical compounds consisting of carbon, oxygen, and hydrogen; includes sugars, starches, and cellulose.

Case study: An in-depth examination of individuals or events that reveals important findings about the object of study.

Cause: A specific term in logic and science that describes something that produces an outcome or effect.

Census: A data collection method that takes the required information from everyone living in a specific and defined geopolitical area.

Childhood psychopathy scale: A technique created to measure the PCL-R in childhood and adolescence; see Psychopathy Checklist-Revised (PCL-R).

Chromosomes: High-density genetic storage devices; an ordinary body cell consists of 23 pairs of chromosomes, each with thousands of genes.

Chronically homeless: Unaccompanied adult with a serious mental illness, substance-related disorder, developmental disability, or chronic physical disability who is homelessness for a year or longer or experiences at least four episodes of homelessness within the last three years for a cumulative 12 months.

Civil commitment proceeding: The legal proceedings by which a person suffering from a mental disease, illness, or disorder is detained in a closed and locked treatment facility for a specified period of time for treatment and mental health interventions pursuant to an order of the court and periodic reviews.

Civil law: A system of laws that deals with private relations between members of a community, contrasted with criminal law or canon law; also, the predominant system of laws found in continental Europe and other nations of the world.

Civil protection orders: The order of a judge that directs, based on submitted evidence, that a person have no direct or indirect contact, communications, or be in the presence of another due to a fear or actual threat of physical harm.

Clinical trial/experiment: A type of experiment that takes place in a real-world setting; it is assumed that control and experimental groups receive the same or similar environmental influences and any changes in the experimental subjects is due to the stimulus or study factor.

Cognitive reasoning: Intelligence that distinguishes humans from most biological creatures demonstrated through the ability to navigate, assesses, and evaluate persona differences and behavior.

Cognition: The accumulation of information, intelligence, and cybernetic knowledge that informs the mind to process experiences and then translate the experiences into language and intellectual action.

Cohort study: A type of research design in which the identical group or groups are studied over time; does not provide individual subject information for each interval.

Color of law: The application of legal statutes or case law standards to factual circumstances to explain, define, or justify the interpretation of the law.

Community Mental Health Act: An act of the U.S. Congress in 1963 that provided federal monies for community mental health centers and research across the nation; see Mental Health Systems Act.

Community Reentry Planning: A coordinated services approach to prisoner reentry that allows for the transition from prison or jail back into the community.

Community service officers (CSOs): Officers that provide crisis intervention and follow up assistance as civilian police employees with professional training in social work or related fields through social service calls, transportation, shelter options. They do not carry weapons or have the authority to arrest, but they do complete police academy training programs.

Comorbidity: The presence of one or more additional disorders, diseases, or otherwise diagnosable conditions in addition to a primary disease or disorder diagnosis.

Competency hearing: The contested legal proceeding to objectively determine if a person has the mental capacity to understand the judicial process.

Competency to stand trial: The ability of a person accused of a crime to understand the reason for the criminal charges against her and to be able to assist in the defense of the case.

Compound: A substance made up of two or more molecules, a molecule being the smallest physical unit of an element or a compound and itself consisting of two or more atoms.

Concept: Mental representations of a thing, object, or idea.

Conscious mind: A human being's immediate thoughts, such as "I am cold," "I am hungry," or "I am anxious," that is reflected in topographical responses demonstrating connections between the mind and the brain.

Contract for civility: A mediation process in lieu of court-issued restraining orders by which aggrieved neighbors resolve grievances, engage in solutions, and determine methods for future resolution should matters again deteriorate.

Control: Refers the modification or alteration of the alleged cause, followed by a concomitant change in the effect.

Control group: A group of test subjects in an experiment that receives a placebo, whose effects are assumed to be negligible.

Convention on the Rights of Persons with Disabilities: A 2008 United Nations international human rights treaty to aid persons with disabilities, including mental illness.

Criminal justice system: Includes police, courts, and correctional agencies operating at the local, state, and federal levels, all of which work to treat all fairly, punish those guilty of criminal offenses, serve the public, and maintain social order.

Criminalization of the mentally ill: The statement reflects a change in legal and societal practice of committing people to jails and prisons rather than mental asylums for criminal offenses, as defendants undergo a transition from being insane to being a criminal because their behavior did not conform to societal norms and economic resources for mental health treatment.

Crisis intervention team (CIT): Specific training for law enforcement personnel that instructs first responders how to best engage with a mentally ill person who is spiraling out of predictable behavior, as well as instruction on public conduct without resorting to a lethal or violent confrontation.

Custody: The legal or physical control of a person.

Custody perspective: The idea that the primary purpose of any correctional program is to provide for the maximum containment level necessary to control the movement and general conduct of its clients.

Custody staff: Personnel in a jail or prison setting who are typically referred to as Correctional Officers or COs and who rely on authority, regimentation, and architecture as their main tools; they employ largely coercive methods to achieve their custody goals.

Danger to others: Cluster of threatened or actual behaviors attributable to mental illness or disease that indicates that without intervention or commitment an individual could harm other people, even if the harm is not actually manifested into criminal acts.

Danger to self: Cluster of threatened or actual behaviors attributable to mental illness or disease that indicates that without interventions or commitment to a closed and locked treatment facility, an individual could engage in self-harm such as suicide, personal neglect, or cutting.

Data: Information collected during research.

De-escalation training: The training by which law enforcement personnel learns that when there is no immediate danger to the mentally ill person or an immediate danger to others, to assess; listen in an unrushed manner; and to respond with words, body language, and tone to bring stability to a confrontation.

Demonic possession: A term, originating in Medieval times or even earlier, for a form of spirit possession, but in this case the "victim" is in the control of a devil or some other malevolent spirit; see divine madness.

Deoxyribonucleic acid (DNA): The building blocks of genetic material; the carrier of all genetic information.

Dependency status: Juveniles who are unable to live with parents or guardians and are placed under juvenile court supervision, even if they have not committed any wrongful act.

Depression: Behaviors that are characterized by poor appetite or overeating, insomnia or hypersomnia, low energy and fatigue, low self-esteem, poor concentration, and feelings of hopelessness.

Description: The first goal of theories; tells us what it is we are studying and provides a visual representation of the objects of study or the focus of the theory.

Dialectical behavior therapy (DBT): An evidence-based intervention intended to enhance the self-control and impulsivity controls of inmates confined in prison.

Disability: An impairment in one or more important areas of functioning.

Disciplinary orientation: The academic or theoretical orientation to which one looks for an understanding of the phenomenon under study.

Disruptive behavior disorders: Clustered behaviors characterized as conduct disorders that include oppositional defiance and attention deficit, which are characterized by poor self-control, limited regulation of personal behaviors, inability to sustain attention, and inappropriate impulse control.

Distress: A painful symptom associated with a mental disorder or disease.

Divine madness: A term, originating in Medieval times or even earlier, for a form of spirit possession, but in this case the "victim" is blessed by God or some other favorable spirit; see demonic possession.

Domestic minor sex trafficking (DMST): Juvenile victims who are or were traded for sexual favors in exchange for financial remuneration.

Domestic violence: An altercation between members engaged in a domestic relationship; usually results in an investigation and likely arrest for criminal offenses such as assault, battery, disorderly conduct, and criminal damage to property

Double-blind experiment: A research situation in which neither the subjects nor the researchers know who is in which group; however, their identities are known to those monitoring the study.

Drug abuse: A situation in which chemicals, whether they are legal or illegal, are being consumed on a too-regular basis, or their consumption has morphed into compulsive use.

Drug use: Experimentation or low use patterns of illicit drugs or diverted legal drugs.

Dynamic security: The personnel-related aspects of the internal means of maintaining control over prison or jail inmates.

Ego: The internal mechanisms that encompasses the psychological mind and brain functions, or inner personality traits, including subconscious, intellect, and human motive forces and thinking.

Elder mistreatment: Acts against an elderly person or a failure to act on that person's behalf that results in the elder person's victimization.

Electroconvulsive therapy: ECT, or "electro-shock" therapy, is a treatment modality used from the early 1930 to 1980s. Done under general anesthesia, ECT consists of an electric current passing through the brain that causes a seizure in the patient.

Entropy: A measure of disorder or randomness in a closed system.

Ethnic identity: Refers to how people sharing unique social or cultural traits see themselves and may not have anything to do with how others see them; see race.

Ethnicity: Refers to a group's common social or cultural traits, including language, religion, and customs; see race.

Etiology: Study of the origins or the causes of diseases or other conditions.

***Ex parte* communications:** Communication(s) by a party to a lawsuit with the assigned judge without the knowledge, presence, or consent of the other party to the lawsuit.

Exorcism: A highly ritualized spiritual ceremony intended to rid a victim of demonic possession.

Experiment: A research method undertaken to test a hypothesis.

Experimental group: The individuals in an experiment that receive the alleged cause of something called a stimulus or treatment variable.

Extroverted: Personality behaviors by which an individual prefers verbalization, gains energy from being with groups of people, and exhibits characteristics of charm, charisma, and persuasion.

4-Ps factor model: Provides understanding and prediction in the absence of a causal theory; suggests that behavior derives from three risk factors and one protective factors; see predisposing, precipitating risk, perpetuating risk, and protective factors.

Federal Gun Control Act of 1968: An act of Congress that limits who may legally possess a firearm or ammunition.

Fetal Alcohol Spectrum Disorder: A broad range of physical characteristics, symptoms, and behaviors associated with a developmental disorder diagnosed in an individual whose mother ingested alcohol during pregnancy.

Fetal Alcohol Syndrome: See Fetal Alcohol Spectrum Disorder.

Field trial/experiment: See clinical trial/experiment.

Findings: Judicial determination issued by a judge considering evidentiary facts in the case. In the case of mental illness that emerges prior to or during judicial proceedings, the determination is made that the defendant is legally competent or incompetent to proceed with the trial.

Fines: Monetary sanctions ordered by a court of law or other authority in lieu of or in addition to other sanctions, including incarceration.

Forensic Assertive Community Treatment (FACT) program: Alternative to incarceration that combines treatment, rehabilitation, and support services in a self-contained clinical team drawn from various psychiatric, nursing, and addiction counseling disciplines.

Free will: The ability to shape one's own fate, choosing between alternative courses of action without external constraints on the choices made.

Functional magnetic resonance imaging (fMRI): A technical-based technique to study the interactions and interrelationship between the mind and brain through computer imagery and known response to stimuli.

Functionalism: The function of the brain and the byproduct of its physical activity.

Furiosus: A medieval European term for a raving madman.

G.I. Bill: An act of the U.S. Congress, also known as the Servicemen's Readjustment Act of 1944, provided various types of financial support for returning W.W. II veterans.

Gender: Culturally defined and socially agreed upon conduct norms governing behaviors deemed appropriate for men and women.

Gender identity: A self-conception based on personal experiences that is independent of an individual's biological sex.

Generalizability: The notion that a study's findings can have implications beyond the specific situation from which they were derived; allows the researcher to drawn inferences and general conclusions from their work.

Genetics: The study of the heritability of a wide range of characteristics.

GLBTQ: An acronym meaning gay, lesbian, bisexual, transsexual, and queer/questioning; identifies at least six different communities organized in various ways and levels of structure around gender identity.

Great Confinement, the: A period that commenced in the late 17th and early 18th century characterized by placing the mentally ill and other socially undesirables into prisons and asylums; the age ended in 19th century but many contend that it continues to the present time in the form of jail and prison populations.

Halfway house: An intermediate housing option where offenders can be monitored and confined but work in the community.

Hate crimes: Criminal offenses that derive to the victim's special status; tend to be more violent than similar non-hate-motivated crimes.

History of mental health problems: One of two types of mental health problems recognized by the federal government in surveys of prison/jail inmates; like serious mental illness.

Hoarding disorder (HD): A cogitative, chronic neuropsychiatric disorder that is associated with substantial distress, social disruption, functional impairment, and social isolation that is manifested through inappropriate accumulation of object clutter.

Home confinement/electronic monitoring: An alternative to incarceration whereby the individual is subject to house arrest and wears a device that can detect or trace physical movement.

House arrest: An alternative to incarceration whereby the individual stays in his or her home when not working, attending school, or participating in treatment.

Housing is healthcare: An approach by which finding a stable residence is the linchpin to resolving problems of treatment for medical and mental conditions within the homeless population without requiring compliance and pre-conditional treatment programs.

Human rights: The unrestricted access to dignity, equality, and mutual respect, which should have no regard to nationality, religion, or personal beliefs.

Humoral balance: The idea that the various bodily humors must work in concert with each other in a form of stasis; historically, this balance was achieved by actions such as bloodletting.

Hysteria: A controversial and discounted mental disorder dating to Classical Greece that suggests mental illness in women is related to displacement of their genitalia and manifests itself as volatile emotions and overdramatic attention-seeking actions.

Injunctions/Restraining Orders/orders of protection: Protective orders issued by a judge against another person (respondent) to direct that there be no contact between the parties.

Inmate intake screening: Physical and mental review of an incoming jail or prison inmate; sometimes called receiving screening.

Insane asylums: Also known as a lunatic asylum, this was a facility intended to house people deemed a threat to society and themselves in a place of confinement; largely functioned as warehouses for the mentally ill, who often lived under degrading conditions, and eventually morphed into the modern psychiatric hospital.

Instantiated: How the mind and information is processed by the nervous system into commands, thoughts, and ideas.

Instinctual: Baseline and primitive awareness, which are the reflexive behaviors and the framework for neuro-information for the control guide for natural actions, such as pleasure and pain.

Insulin-coma therapy: A form of convulsive therapy practiced in the 1940s and 1950s; schizophrenics were injected with enough insulin to induce a coma, which, it was claimed, cured their disorders.

International Bill of Rights: A composite perspective on human rights, made up of the United Nation's Declaration of Human Rights, the International Covenant on Civil and Political Rights, and the International Covenant on Economic, Social, and Cultural Rights.

Introverted: Personality behaviors by which an individual is described to be quiet, more energized when alone, exhibits creativity when able to work alone, and is commonly described as thoughtful and a better listener.

Involuntary commitment: The contested judicial process by which a person, due to acute mental illness, disease, or disability poses a danger to self or to others and is directed by a court order to remain in a closed, locked mental treatment facility for a specified period of time.

Involuntary medication: A judicial process in which a judge decides if medication not previously used by the defendant is necessary and should be ordered to restore the defendant's mental competency to proceed with a criminal prosecution.

Judicial competency hearing: The judicial process by which it is determined if a person understands the legal proceeding and is able to assist in his legal defense.

Kessler Psychological Distress Scale (K6): A six-item self-report screening tool that discerns mental disorder (DSM-IV Axis I) from general distress.

Laws of nuisance: Civil action by which a neighbor's actions unreasonably interferes with the enjoyment of one's property, which can also include an allegation of illegal activities.

Leucotomy: A type of lobotomy intended to treat mental illness, surgically severing brain fibers; see transorbital lobotomy.

Lipids: Compounds constructed from fatty acids; they cannot be dissolved in water, but do become soluble in organic solvents.

Longitudinal studies: Research that includes several data collections at different points in time.

Lunatics: A nonmedical and currently offensive term used to describe mentally ill persons; derived from the belief dating back to Ancient Greece that mentally illness is associated with the phases of the moon.

Mediation: A legal process by which disputing parties use a neutral third party, often a judge or lawyer, to listen to the crux of the dispute to resolve the differences into a mutually satisfactory agreement without resorting to an adversarial proceeding.

Medicaid: A joint federal and state program intended to provide persons in need with support for medical costs; originally passed as part of a 1965 addition by the U.S. Congress to the Social Security Act.

Mental health care system: Structured around public and private agencies, organizations and institutions that employ a wide range of health care providers.

Mental health court judge: A judge with special training and subject assignment who handles all of the proceedings in a particular city, state, or regional court that pertains to mental health issues, such as competency to proceed to a trial, diversion from criminal prosecution for mental health treatment, or for guardianships.

Mental health courts (MHC): Specialized problem-solving courts the function as stand-alone courts or special sessions of other types of courts that deal with the legal problems of the mentally ill.

Mental Health Systems Act: A 1980 act of the U.S. Congress intended to make up the community health centers' underfunding; see Community Mental Health Act.

Mental incompetency: A barrier to the prosecution of a criminal offense as the defendant does not have the mental acuity to understand the judicial proceedings or the ability to provide assistance to counsel.

Mental Patients' Bill of Rights: A 1981 act of the U.S. Congress detailing a litany of rights afforded mental patients.

Mesmerism: The idea espoused by Swabian physician Franz Mesmer that the moon's gravitational pull is responsible for mental illness; early cures included wearing of magnets, while later treatment included individual and group hypnosis.

Metrazol Therapy: An early 1930s convulsive treatment for mental illness that consisted of giving the patient large doses of a chemical compound, metrazol, that caused seizures.

Mind: The structural organization within the organ of the brain that controls emotions, personalities, behaviors, and thought processes.

Minnesota Multiphasic Personality Inventory (MMPI): A standardized psychometric test of adult personality and psychopathology.

Moral insanity: A 19th century term for psychopathic behavior, referring to abnormal emotions and behavior that occur without any associated intellectual impairments or delusional conduct.

Moral treatment: An approach to mental disorders, originally associated with the Quakers in the 18th and 19th centuries, that emphasized a combination of early psychological and religious-based moral interventions in the treatment of the mentally ill.

National Center for Posttraumatic Stress Disorder: Consists of seven Veterans Administration centers of excellence arrayed on each coast and Hawaii specifically intended to assist U.S. military veterans suffering from post-traumatic stress disorders.

National Mental Health Act: A 1946 act of the U.S. Congress that recognized the mental health problems associated with U.S. military veterans returning from WW II.

Nervous disorders: Behaviors associated with panic, separation anxiety, generalized anxiety, the obsessive-compulsive disorders that inhibit balanced brain commands.

Neurocognitive disorders: Forms of dementia, including but not limited to Alzheimer's disease.

Neurotoxicity: A state that occurs when a biological, chemical, or physical agent produces an adverse effect on the central or peripheral nervous system.

Neurotoxin: Substances that change, generally for the worse, a part of the nervous system, generally by destroying nerve tissues.

Normative: The collective characteristics of the average or predictable patterns of responsive behavior in humans are fortunately indicia of a typical mind.

Nucleic acids: Complex forms of biochemical compounds; they include the same elements as proteins but tend to have phosphorous rather than sulfur.

Offer of proof: An avowal by an attorney that by relying on independent or corroborating information, certain facts are indisputable and there is no need to present actual evidence to sustain allegation. In the matter of a mental health concern, based on interactions with the defendant, there is a legal basis to believe the defendant is legally competent.

Operationalization process: A series of mental steps taken by a researcher to transform an abstract concept into something that is empirically measurable, or a variable.

Order of Commitment: The judicial directive specifying why a person is detained in a mental health treatment facility for a specified period of time to undergo medication regime, counseling, and interventions.

Panel study: A type of research design that employs multiple measures of the same group or groups of individuals—and they could be experimental or control subjects—over an extended period.

Perpetuating risk factor: An event or other force, whose presence continues the specific mental disorder and inhibits the patient's recovery, perhaps even causing a further decline; see 4-Ps factor model.

Personality: Characteristics that shape individual conduct that suggest that, for example, while all humans cry, the how and why of crying varies according to the individual's psychological mentality.

Petition to seek guardianship: A court-filed document that seeks protective orders to direct that the petitioner be fully and legally responsible for the care of someone who is unable to manage his or her financial or personal affairs.

Petitioner: This is the party who initiates a civil action against another or the filing entity.

Placebo: Something that has no therapeutic value that is given to the control group in an experiment, field study, or clinical study so that no one knows who received the stimulus.

Precipitating risk factor: An event or other force present in a person's immediate physical environment that increases the likelihood of a specific mental disorder; see 4-Ps factor model.

Preconscious mind: The alternative or second state, suggested by Freud, that remains readily accessible to the conscious mind as immediate memories are retrieved from it. It is the basis for humans to collect thoughts, tell stories, and share knowledge based on what they store in their mind; the brain later sorts through this information, effectively organizing the mind.

Prediction: The specification of when and under what circumstances something, including mental illness, is likely to occur.

Predisposing risk factor: A factor or identifiable element that increases a person's susceptibility to a specific mental disorder; see 4-Ps factor model.

Preponderance of evidence: The burden of proof needed to persuade a judge that a person is competent to stand trial. The proof required is just more than 50% that a person is legally able understand the proceedings.

Present ability (for mental competency): The ability of an adult or juvenile to have an understanding of the legal proceedings at the time legal proceedings commence, even if there was or is a history of mental illness, impairment, or organic disability.

Privileged communications: Communications received by an attorney or originating from an attorney, including any exchange between the client and attorney, which cannot be disclosed to any person without the express permission of the client.

Protective risk factor: An event or other force that functions as a personal or environmental influence to assist victims of mental illness in dealing with their sickness; see 4-Ps factor model.

Proteins: Large biomolecules, also called macromolecules, of carbon, oxygen, hydrogen, nitrogen, and sulfur, arrayed in single or multiple chains of amino acids, the latter being the building blocks of life; examples include hormones and enzymes.

Psyche: Freud's theories of the mind's conscience awareness and mental unconsciousness that addresses several basic sets of skills and procedures to understand the human nature.

Psychiatry: A medical subdiscipline dedicated to the study and treatment of brain diseases.

Psychology: The study of the human mind and its functions.

Psychometric tests: Standardized questions that measure certain aspects of personality and intelligence or cognition.

Psychopathic inferiority: A late 19th century term used to describe persons who suffered from emotional and moral aberrations owed to congenital conditions.

Psychopathy: See antisocial personality disorder.

Psychopathy Checklist-Revised (PCL-R): A 20-item rating scale created by psychologist Robert Hare for the express purpose of identifying individuals likely to be psychopaths.

Psychotic depression: Said to exist when an individual has severe depression plus some form of psychosis, including delusions or hallucinations.

Psychotropic drugs: Medicines intended to control that part of the mind associated with the disease symptomology.

Race: Refers to distinct groups based on hereditary characteristics.

Random sample: In research, a group or cluster of study units whereby each individual member of the group or cluster has the same probability of selection as any other unit.

Receiving screening: See inmate intake screening.

Relationship: In statistics, a measurable degree of association between a putative or assumed cause and its effect.

Rescue Hoarder: A desire to help abandoned or surrendered animals that becomes an obsession and leads to the acquisition of a number of animals that exceeds the person's capacity to provide minimal care. (See animal hoarding.)

Respondent: The party or entity that is the named party against whom a legal action is initiated in a civil proceedings.

Restitution: Payments by the convicted offender for all or some of the loss and expenses incurred by the victim of the crime.

Restoration of competency: The methodology by which a person who was found to be mentally incompetent to understand the nature of the judicial proceedings against them gains the ability to understand and participate in the criminal defense through education, medication, or psychological treatments. Despite the restoration of competency, a defendant may use the legal defense of insanity to exonerate or excuse his criminal conduct at the time the crime was committed.

Restorative justice: An approach to justice and fairness that seeks to address the imbalance in society created by the criminal incident by employing discussion, dialogue, apologies and forgiveness, and direct and indirect reparations; involves all stakeholders in the crime.

Schizophrenia: A chronic, severe, and disabling mental disorder effecting how a person thinks, feels, and behaves; victims feel as if they have lost touch with reality.

Second responders: Public service workers such as teachers, resource officers, probation officers, social workers, and other advocates who follow up with resources for the mentally ill and recommend, provide, or enable mental health interventions, treatment, and care.

Security: Freedom from perceived or actual threats to individual and community health, welfare, and general well-being.

Sentencing alternatives: Sanctions in lieu of incarceration, whether for felonies or misdemeanors.

Serious psychological distress (SPD): Mental health problems of a nature severe enough to cause moderate to severe impairment of a person's functioning in social, occupational, or educational areas of life.

Servicemen's Readjustment Act of 1944: See G.I. Bill.

Serious Mental Illness (SMI): A governmental classification of individuals that states that due to mental disorders, disease or brain damage, an individual is unable to seek or retain employment and is therefore eligible to receive economic and medical care subsidies from the government.

Silver alert: A type of public notice, like an Amber Alert, but focused on missing persons 65 years and older who have Alzheimer's disease, another type of dementia, or other forms of mental illness.

Sociopath: The mental health characteristics with schizophrenia hallucinations or bizarre obsessive conduct disorders that according to the Diagnostic and Statistical Manual of Mental Disorders (DSM-5) has behaviors relating to the antisocial personality disorder, but is often nervous, easily agitated, more volatile, and prone to emotional outbursts.

Sociopathy: Describes psychopathic behavior that has sociological origins (e.g., an individual who is poorly socialized into appropriate ways to interacting with others) or differentiates between persons with antisocial personality disorder (APD) who do appear to have a conscience (sociopaths) and those who have no conscience (psychopaths).

Solitary confinement: The isolation of an inmate from all human contact—sometimes including correctional officers—for 22 to 24 hours per day; see administrative segregations.

Spirit possession: The belief that gods, spirits, demons and the like can control the human body and mind, found in many religions around the world; see demonic possession and divine madness.

Spurious interpretation: When a relationship between two entities is said to be causal, when, in fact, that relationship is due to the interaction of both entities with a third force, variable, or factor.

Stasis: A state of equilibrium capable of sustaining a healthy individual, including a healthy brain.

Static security: The physical elements of both external security and internal security constraints of a prison or jail, including, for example, locked doors, sally ports, and internal gates.

Status offense: Juvenile proceedings that are initiated if an underage person drinks alcohol, smokes cigarettes, or is incorrigible and the delinquency of the offender is based on their age or status as a juvenile.

Statutorily tolled: The criminal proceedings are suspended without a violation of the accused's constitutional right to a speedy trial if a question or issue arises regarding the competency of the accused to understand the proceedings and the criminal prosecution cannot proceed.

Stimulus: The treatment variable—an alleged cause of something in an experiment, field study, or clinical study—that is received by only members of the experimental group; see placebo.

Suicidal ideation: Suicidal thoughts that may or may not result in an attempted or completed suicide. The deliberate taking of one's life is not a mental disorder *per se*, but mental illness is often the proximate cause of a suicide.

Suicide-by-cop: Generally recognized as an actual medical diagnosis and not simply a cultural designation, although the preferred medical term is law enforcement-forced-assisted suicide when there deadly force is required by police to compel compliance by an unwilling subject.

Synapses: Nerve cells connected by chemical gaps that move information into a central cortex, where it is then simultaneously re-distributed into a reaction before moving into the mind's storage facilities to a become long-term or short-term memory.

Synthetic competency: A process by which a person who is in custody and is alleged to be mentally incompetent with no evidence of progress towards competency, is ordered by a judge to undergo psychotropic medication and treatment. Artificial competency often occurs if the defendant was taking medications and issues of mental competency emerged during a lapse of treatment.

Systemic interface: The interconnectivity between two or more public-serving entities, or, in this case, between the criminal justice system and the mental health care system.

Tactical repositioning: A de-escalation technique by which officers move to another location that lessens the level of danger or threat to a person spiraling in a mental health crisis.

Taxonomical scheme: A method of classifying things or concepts into distinct groups, as well as the basis upon which decisions are made to place things or concepts into those groups.

Taxonomies: Resultant summaries or clusters of information that place available interpretations and understandings about a phenomenon into gross categorizations that are not necessarily mutually exclusive, but intended to further the search for answers.

Theory: A highly organized statement based on systematic observations concerning the phenomenon or class of phenomena under study.

Therapeutic interventions: A term referring to any healing or curative method that can be applied to a problem, in this case mental illness.

Time-order sequence: The requirement for causation that states an alleged or putative cause must precede the outcome in time.

Transorbital lobotomy: A medical procedure that employs an icepick-like device thrust through the top of each eye socket that effectively destroys the area of the brain in the frontal lobes responsible for emotionality. It is still performed in highly limited cases today; see leucotomy or lobotomy.

Traumatic brain injury (TBI): A neurocognitive disorder like dementia and amnestic disorder resulting from a head injury.

Treatment: The application of a specific method of therapy based on a diagnosis.

Treatment gap (TG): The number of people needing a specific service that do not get it, expressed as a percentage.

Treatment perspective: The idea that prison and jail inmates should be offered therapeutic solutions intended to change the law-violating behavior that brought them to the attention of the criminal justice system in the first place.

Treatment staff: Those professionals in a prison or jail responsible for implementing therapeutic treatment programs.

Trend study: A research method that looks at what is happening to similar groups through time.

Trepanning/Trephination: Two terms used to refer to an 8,000-year-old practice that involved drilling holes in a victim's head to allow evil spirits trapped within to escape.

Unconscious mind: Thoughts that are the hidden, bottom-of-the-iceberg base of mentality and the crux of psychological and psychiatric analyses, and, according to Freud's theories, are the true cause of most of human beings' predictable and unpredictable behaviors.

Understanding: Provides comprehension about the object or objects under study; answers the question, why does something happen?

Variable: In research, something that is measurable. Typically, a single concept yields one or more variables that can be measured by the researcher.

Veterans Health Administration (VHA): The largest of the three elements that makes up the VA, currently operates the world's largest healthcare system.

Veterans Treatment Court (VTC): A specialty diversionary court, like drug courts and mental health courts, that specializes in the legal problems of veterans.

Voluntary commitment: This is a legal process by which an individual who poses a danger to himself or to others engages in self-determination and initiates the process by which she is placed in a closed and locked facility for a specified period of time to obtain mental health treatment or interventions. Said holds can only occur for a specified period of time.

Ward of the court: The status given to juveniles who are found to be responsible for acts of delinquency and are then placed under the jurisdictional control of the juvenile court with respect to their home placement, treatment requirements, and behavioral responsibilities. Juveniles who also are unable to live with parents or guardians are under the juvenile court direction, even if they have not committed any wrongful act.

Welfare check: When there is no evidence of criminal conduct or activity, but the officer has a duty to inquire as to the well-being of a person, balancing the safety of a person against the right to be left alone.

Wellness checks: Visits by local law enforcement to the residences of persons identified as vulnerable or otherwise at-risk individuals.

Workhouses: Places of confinement and employment, established first in the 14th century, that eventually evolved into institutions intended to teach residents the proper work, moral, and personal values of a productive member of the community, largely through the application of order and discipline.

Case Index

Name Index

Subject Index

New York, 188

North Carolina, 188

Oregon, 187-188

commitments,

outpatient, 193-194

community mental health centers, 26, 27, 381

Community Mental Health Services Block Grant
(MHBG), 25

community reentry planning, 280

community service officers (CSOs), 156-157, 163, 164

community treatment, 148, 151, 178

community treatment center, 381

community-based programming, 9, 32, 264

comorbidity, 104, 114, 122-123, 130, 193, 212, 268, 269,
277, 310, 320, 329, 391

competency, 5, 8, 119, 128, 139, 195, 203-204, 205,
206-210, 212-213, 214, 215, 216, 217, 218, 219,
220, 227, 234, 242, 252, 260, 281, 282-283, 298,
312-314, 344, 401

evaluation process, 203, 206-207, 212, 213

restoration of, 213, 215-217

synthetic, 215, 218, 220

to stand trial, 8, 203, 209, 213

competency hearing

factors, 208

judicial options, 208-210, 213

concept, 4, 108, 109

conditional release, 261, 263, 265, 266, 267, 268

definition of, 31

general conditions, 31-32

special conditions, 32

conduct disorders, 113, 240, 278, 298, 300, 307,
308-311, 314, 321, 324, 351

conflict resolution, 146, 280

conscious mind, 81, 83

conservatorship, 187, 360, 361

contract for civility, 257

control, 110

control group, 111, 120

convenience samples, 112

correctional officers (COs), 263, 272, 279, 321

courts of general jurisdiction

definition of, 30

courts of limited jurisdiction

definition of, 30

criminal justice system

definition of, 21

criminalization of the mentally ill, 7, 50, 63, 65, 68,
142, 144, 146, 151, 271, 382, 413

criminologists, 126, 276, 316

crisis intervention team (CIT), 152-155, 166

cruel and unusual punishment, 279

custodial arraignment, 37

custodial encounter, 166

custody, 145, 150, 261, 262, 263, 264, 285

custody perspective, 262

custody staff, 263

cyber harassment, 353

cyber-bullying, 334, 352-355

cyber-stalking, 352-355

D

danger to others, 8, 157, 177, 178-184, 185, 190

analysis, 183

Arizona definition, 181

New York definition, 183

North Carolina definition, 182-183

Oregon definition, 183

danger to self, 147, 177, 178-183

analysis, 183

Arizona definition, 181-182

New York definition, 183

North Carolina definition, 182-183

Oregon definition, 184

dangerousness

analysis, 181, 186

death penalty

mentally ill, 280-283,

de-escalation, 142, 143, 144, 147, 149, 153, 154, 158

skills, 146, 149, 151, 159

verbal, 146, 152

training, 157

Thematic Apperception Test, 90

theory, 106, 108-112, 114, 125, 126, 130
 criminological, 126

therapeutic interventions, 62, 63

therapeutic relationship, 269, 271

therapy, 32, 63, 93, 110, 124, 195, 263, 272, 278, 280,
 285
 behavioral, 124
 behavoir modification, 124
 cognitive, 123
 electroconvulsive, 63
 insulin-coma, 63
 metrazol, 63
 non-medical, 93
 sex offender, 278

time-order-sequence, 107

tort, 165

tortious liability, 181-182

totality of the circumstances, 36

Tourette syndrome, 312

transorbital lobotomy, 62

trauma, 92, 96, 97, 125, 149, 243, 278, 488, 312, 318,
 391

traumatic brain injury (TBI), 107, 108, 109, 119, 120,
 312, 381, 389, 390, 391, 616

treatment, 22, 24, 25, 26, 27, 32, 33, 40, 41, 109, 110, 111,
 115, 120, 123, 125, 126, 129, 130, 131, 261, 262, 263,
 264, 265, 266, 269, 272, 277, 278, 280, 284, 285
 case management, 347
 community, 269, 272, 285
 correctional, 9
 drug, 25, 278, 415
 goals of, 263
 humane, 61, 142, 153
 inhuman, 49, 56
 inpatient, 177, 185, 190, 191, 195
 medical, 150, 161, 206
 mental health, 11, 63, 92, 145, 148, 152, 163, 174,
  175, 177, 186, 187, 188, 191, 192, 193, 195, 214, 242,
  278, 301, 304, 305, 338, 343, 345, 348, 355, 382

 mental illness, 49
 moral, 60-61
 outpatient, 185, 188, 193, 236
 prejudicial, 395
 programs, 64, 65
 psychiatric, 62,, 191
 residential, 26, 27, 63, 177, 193, 303
 right to, 383
 substance abuse, 22
 therapeutic, 50

treatment centers, 145

treatment facility, 145, 154, 163, 164

treatment gap (TG), 380

treatment group, 110-111

treatment personnel, 146, 151

treatment perspective, 262

treatment professionals, other, 123

treatment staff, 123, 263, 284, 285

trend study, 111

trepanning, 56, 62

trephination, 53, 54, 62

trespassing, 30, 33, 146, 159, 202, 211, 214, 298, 304,
 343, 352

trial de novo
 definition of, 30

true bill, 38

"Twinkie" defense, the, 345-346

U

U.S. Bureau of the Census, 111

U.S. Court of Appeals, 30

U.S. Department of Health and Human Services, 25

unconscious mind, 82, 83

Uniform Guardianship and Protective Proceedings
 Act (UGPPA), 361

United Nations, 283, 377, 379, 380

use of force continuum, 162, 166
 chemical force, 162
 electronic force, 162
 firearm (lethal) force, 162